Founded upon the Seas

Watercolour of a crocodile, or cayman, by the French naturalist Jean Théodore Descourtilz, 1824, from crocodiles observed in the Western Caribbean. It combines the features of the freshwater crocodile (Crocodylus rhombifer) *and the saltwater crocodile* (Crocodylus acutus). *Remains of both species have been found in the Cayman Islands.*

Founded upon the Seas

A History of the Cayman Islands and Their People

Michael Craton

and the New History Committee

Ian Randle Publishers

Kingston • Miami

First published in Jamaica, 2003 by
Ian Randle Publishers
11 Cunningham Avenue
Box 686
Kingston 6
www.ianrandlepublishers.com

National Library of Jamaica Cataloguing in Publication Data

Craton, Michael
Founded upon the seas : a history of the Cayman Islands and their people / Michael Craton

p. : ill. ; cm

Bibliography : p. . – Includes index

ISBN 976-637-118-0 Hardback
ISBN 976-637-117-2 Paperback

1. Cayman Islands – History
I. Title

972.921 dc 21

Published in the USA, 2003 by
Ian Randle Publishers Inc

ISBN 0-9729358-3-5 Hardback
ISBN 0-9729358-2-7 Paperback

Cover and book design by Robert Harris (Jamaica)
Set in Sabon 10.5/15x29
Printed in Hong Kong, China by Book Art Inc. Toronto

Contents

Foreword / *vii*

Preface / *ix*

1 Overture / *1*

2 First Comers: The Period before Permanent Settlement / *11*

3 Pioneer Settlers in Peace and War, 1700–1800 / *33*

4 Caymanian Slave Society and Emancipation / *63*

5 Early Government and the Sociopolitical Revolution of the 1830s / *89*

6 Slavery's Aftermath and The First Caymanian Migrations / *123*

7 Isolation, Neglect, and Self-Reliance, 1845–1898 / *145*

8 Change and Resistance: The First Commissioners, 1898–1914 / *173*

9 A Growing Society: Population Trends and Social Change, 1860–1914 / *191*

10 Making a World of Their Own: Caymanian Livelihoods and Lifestyles before World War One / *205*

11 Caymanian Churches and Schooling, 1846–1920 / *227*

12 Caymanians on the Move: Early Decades of the Twentieth Century / *253*

13 Rhythms of Change in Peace and War / *279*

14 Declining Dependency: Constitutional, Political, and Administrative Changes, 1944–2000 / *305*

15 The Engineered Miracle: Economic Development, 1950–2000 / *331*

16 Change and Adjustment: Population Changes and Immigration, 1950–2000 / *363*

17 Social Development: Health, Education, the Churches, and the Media, 1950–2000 / *377*

18 A Caymanian Nation: Out of the Past and into the Future / *401*

Notes / *421*

Bibliography / *489*

List of Illustrations and Acknowledgements / *503*

Index / *517*

Foreword

It is a great honour and pleasure for me to welcome this publication and to commend it to as wide a readership as possible, both here and overseas. This is truly a national history, one of which Caymanians and all those who call these islands "home" can be proud. It is most fitting that it should be published during the year of our Qunicentennial celebrations.

No country can understand its own character or fully appreciate its unique identity without an accurate knowledge of its past. It was in this spirit that the Honourable McKeeva Bush brought to the Legislative Assembly in 1988 a motion urging government to prepare a new history of the Cayman Islands. It has taken the commitment of successive governments to realise the vision expressed in that motion. Over the same time, the Cayman Islands has developed at an accelerating pace, making the need for an in-depth, readable account of our history more important with every passing year.

Though not intended as a textbook, this book will prove a treasure trove for teachers of history, social studies, and other subjects in the national curriculum. I commend it to educators, parents, and students with the earnest wish that it will have a significant effect on the next generation of Caymanians. Its broad and detailed coverage of our past should inform and entertain, but it should also excite discussion on many subjects, leading to further research and writing about our heritage.

I wish to extend my heartfelt thanks, on behalf of my ministry and the Cayman Islands Government, to all who have contributed to the preparation of this book. This was an unusual project, requiring the sustained efforts of the author and the members of the New History Committee working together over a six year period. We are indebted to the chairman of the committee, Dr. Pedley, for his meticulous guidance, and to the capable staff of the National Archive for their constant support behind the scenes. The dedication and hard work of all those involved has resulted in a publication that will, I believe, be read and enjoyed for many years to come.

Honourable Roy Bodden, MLA, JP

Minister for Education, Human Resources and Culture

March 2003

Preface

Founded upon the Seas: A History of the Cayman Islands and Their People has been long awaited. A generation has passed since the appearance of Neville Williams's book, *A History of the Cayman Islands*, which was commissioned to coincide with the Tercentenary of the Treaty of Madrid, 1670. Williams's overview of Cayman's history has served its purpose well. Nevertheless, its author looked forward to the day when "a much more detailed work" would be written, echoing a desire expressed many years ago by G.S.S. Hirst in his *Notes on the History of the Cayman Islands* (1910) that a full history would one day be "written afresh".

In November 1994 the Honourable McKeeva Bush, then Minister with responsibility for Culture, set in motion what would become known as "the new history" project. This brought to fruition a motion put forward by him as a back-bench MLA in 1988, which the Legislative Assembly accepted unanimously. In time, the New History Committee was formed, comprising Caymanians with training in various aspects of historical or cultural studies, many of whom had taught or otherwise worked in these areas. The committee's first brief was to interview candidates and recommend a suitably qualified historian. Its main responsibility, once research and writing were under way, was to give advice on the local and overseas sources to be consulted and to provide guidance on the shape of a work that had to meet the needs of the general public as well as the requirements of scholars.

Dr. Michael Craton, a distinguished specialist on the Caribbean who had written extensively on the history of the Bahamas, Jamaica, and West Indian slavery, was invited to undertake the project. Research and writing began in earnest in mid-1997. Most of the work took place at the Cayman Islands National Archive, using local archives as well as copies of archives from repositories overseas obtained through the Archive's extensive copying programme. Research also involved travel to the Sister Islands, Jamaica, and the United Kingdom. Through these means Dr. Craton was able to consult numerous sources that were unknown to Hirst and Williams, as well as to examine in much greater detail others that they were barely able to consult because of their circumstances.

The first complete draft of the text proved to be long and detailed, partly because of the quantity of new information available and the desire to include as much of it as possible. Consideration was given to the idea of publishing a multi-volume work. While this approach might have satisfied some in the academic community, the New History Committee did not feel it was appropriate. Their first obligation was to place in the hands of the public a single-volume history that would be readable and inviting, as well as being comprehensive, accurate, and scholarly.

Two courses of action were therefore adopted. One was to place in the collections of the National Archive the final version of the text delivered by Dr. Craton so that it would be available for researchers. The second was to undertake a major editing process designed to shorten the text and to make its style more accessible and readable. A professional editor, Claudette Upton, was invited to assist in this process. Between May 2001 and October 2002 the text was reduced by a third as it passed through various changes from the macro to the micro level. The majority of this work was done jointly by Dr. Philip Pedley, Director of the Cayman Islands National Archive, and Ms. Upton, with the committee and the author reviewing the results, providing feedback, and approving the final text. This lengthy process was essential in order to preserve the accuracy and argument of each chapter, to retain the authentic voice of the author, and to make the style and form of the work as inviting as possible. Readers who wish to may compare the published work with the original draft at the National Archive.

This book therefore springs from the combined efforts of Dr. Craton and the New History Committee. Researched, written, edited, and designed over a six-year period, it is in several respects a national history. Its genesis was a motion in the Legislative Assembly that sought to celebrate and promote a sense of national identity. The text and illustrations encompass the most important subjects, facts, and events in Cayman's history. And its analysis of the main currents in Cayman's past is addressed to the reader from a standpoint that is simultaneously modern, scholarly, and Caymanian.

This project could not have been undertaken without the assistance of many people and institutions, here and abroad. Dr. Craton and the New History Committee would like to express their sincere thanks to each of them. The New History Committee, which was entrusted with oversight of the project in 1996, has carried out its role with exemplary independence, conscious throughout of its responsibility to the public and grateful for the commitment of successive ministries and governments. The members who have served on this committee are:

Joy Basdeo
Leonard Bodden
Roy Bodden
Philip Pedley (Chairman)
Susan Barnes Pereira
Deborah McLaughlin

George Boldeau
Herbert Crawford
Leonard Dilbert
Patrice Donalds
Anita Ebanks
Carson Ebanks
Frank McField
Leonora Mendoza-Hydes
Julianna O'Connor-Connolly
Mary-Elizabeth Ebanks Rodrigues
Lucille Seymour
Richard Tressider
Claudette Upton (Editor)
Amy Wolliston

Various parts of the text were read by Patricia Bradley, Fred Burton, and Peggy Leshikar-Denton, who generously provided comments from their areas of expertise. Finally, I would like to thank my colleagues at the Cayman Islands National Archive. They have supported this challenging project to an extent that goes well beyond the usual responsibilities of an Archive staff, giving professional advice, technical assistance, and administrative support in myriad ways over the last six years.

PHILIP PEDLEY
Director, Cayman Islands National Archive
March 2003

CHAPTER 1

Overture

WITHIN THE BROAD SWEEP OF human history, the five-hundred-year span that makes up the history of the Cayman Islands may seem brief indeed. Yet any place that knows the stamp of human habitation over time will develop its own characteristics and rhythms, and Cayman is no exception. In fact, its character is the more striking because it emerged over a comparatively short time and within a community that was always small. Although five hundred years have passed since the first recorded sighting of the islands, it was only about three hundred years ago that people began to settle permanently on them. For much of their history, the Cayman Islands were among the most isolated, unknown, and unchanging countries in the British Empire. In the second half of the twentieth century, however, they became a major tourist destination and the fifth-largest banking centre in the world. During the same period, their resident population multiplied five times, swelled by people from many other nations. The story of how this remarkable transition took place is the subject of this book.[1]

Since pre-Columbian Amerindians are not known to have visited the Cayman Islands, the history of the islands and their people effectively began on 10 May 1503, when Christopher Columbus and his men were the first Europeans to sight and describe Cayman Brac and Little Cayman. This sighting gave Spain a claim to the islands by right of discovery.

Over the next century and a half, the Cayman Islands were given their permanent name and became better known. But they were mapped with limited accuracy, and wise navigators avoided them if they could, while the less wary sometimes went aground on their fringing reefs. The first people known to have stopped at the islands for more than a few hours were sailors from Sir

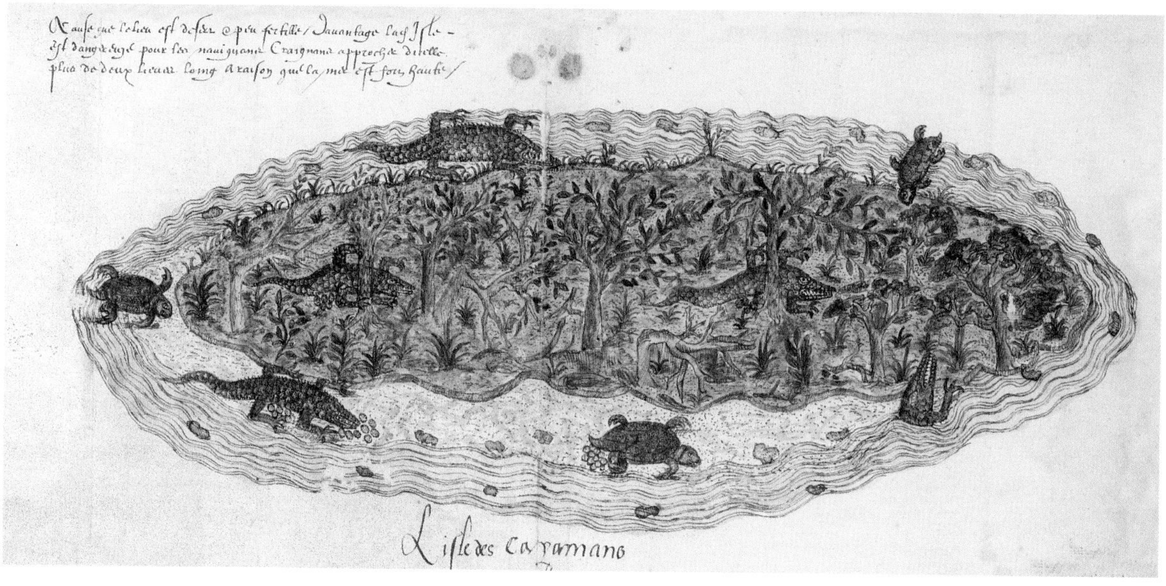

The earliest known sketch or "map" of any of the Cayman Islands: "Lisle des Cayamans" (The Island of the Caymans) from the Peck manuscript, ca. 1590. The manuscript reads: This is an island "on which nobody lives because there is no fresh water and also because the soil does not produce any goods except a great number of caymans and turtles which live in the sea as well as on land. . . . The meat of the cayman is not valued as food, being dull and flavourless. On the other hand, the meat of the turtle is good eating." (The island is either Cayman Brac or possibly a composite image of Cayman Brac and Little Cayman.)

Francis Drake's 1585–6 expedition to the West Indies. The first people recorded as having stayed more than a few days were a Dutch crew shipwrecked for sixteen weeks on Grand Cayman in 1630.

What first drew purposeful visitors – French and Spanish as well as Dutch and English – to the Cayman Islands was the abundance of turtles. Green turtles provided invaluable food for naval and military forces, ordinary mariners, and early settlers in other Caribbean islands. The Dutch and French showed little interest in claiming the Cayman Islands, but after the English captured Jamaica from the Spanish in 1655, they were seen as a useful adjunct to the new colony. England's claim to the Cayman Islands, asserted as early as 1662, was finally acknowledged by Spain in the Treaty of Madrid in September 1670.

Permanent settlement in the Cayman Islands began on Grand Cayman sometime between 1670 and 1730. Legend has it that early settlements were formed by runaway white soldiers and servants from Jamaica, shipwrecked sailors, and buccaneers seeking a quieter life ashore. In truth, the first permanent inhabitants were probably poor but respectable turtlers and logcutters, who settled down with their families and a few slaves to a lifestyle that was more congenial, though no richer, than they could have enjoyed in planter-dominated Jamaica. These pathfinder families – with surnames such as Bodden and Watler – were the nucleus of a small population that gradually evolved a distinctive Caymanian way of life.

The early settlers, who included women, were a scattering of subsistence farmers, mariners, and woodcutters. The men soon gained a reputation for being expert and hardy seamen. Of necessity, they roamed as far as they could in their sturdy, small schooners in search of turtle, logwood, and

A cayman, from the Peck manuscript (ca. 1590), which states: "This fish is terrestrial and aquatic", and is found on "Cayman Island where there is no human settlement only a great number of these fishes with large turtles".

wrecks, which they combed for building supplies and provisions. Far from deserving the label of pirates sometimes given them by the neighbouring Spanish, they were themselves subject to attacks by the Spanish. Contrary to popular legend, authentic English pirates such as Blackbeard and Rackham found little to attract them in the Cayman Islands, in the way of either booty or recreation.

The population grew at first by slow natural increase, and through the arrival of small-scale planters from Jamaica with their Negro slaves, English settlers expelled by the Spanish from the Miskito Coast in the 1780s, and the occasional runaway debtor or shipwrecked sailor. With little external help or governance, they managed their own affairs, led by those men of most substance or repute, with or without Magistrates' commissions from Jamaica. By 1800, the most important of these was locally known as "Governor" Bodden. Besides acting as the Chief Magistrate, he organised a militia, presided at the occasional public meeting, and may have performed marriages – though these usually took place in Jamaica.

Though remote from Jamaican affairs, the embryonic Caymanian community should not be viewed as lawless, godless, or illiterate. The 1830s saw significant local advances, representing the outermost ripples of changes in the British Empire. In 1831, as emancipation of the slaves approached throughout the empire, the first elected legislature in Cayman was set up, consisting of the appointed Magistrates and (in a separate body) Vestrymen chosen by free adult males. From that time, too, date the first formal churches and schools, established by Anglican and Methodist ministers and by the church-oriented Mico Charity. These pioneer missionaries were succeeded in the 1840s by the Presbyterians, who within a decade had won over much of Grand Cayman's population, and who had a major influence on religion and education well into the twentieth century.

A turtle, from the Peck manuscript (ca. 1590), which states: "This fish is four feet long and two and a half feet wide. According to the reports of sailors it can live up to 150 years. It is found on Cayman Island and lives in the sea as well as on land. It lays a large number of eggs and is good to eat".

The Cayman Islands experienced the traumas of slavery, and to some extent the race and class conflicts that followed the emancipation of the slaves in 1835. But in the absence of large plantations, and with half the population considered white, social divisions were much more subtle, and far less discordant, than anywhere else in the British Caribbean. Regardless of colour, people shared rel-

The Nova May *under construction, Cayman Brac, 1949.*

atively simple material circumstances, as well as common ways of life and work, faithful church attendance, and close-knit extended families, in which the women played a prominent role and the men were often away at sea.

Many ex-slaves sought the life of independent subsistence farmers and fishermen, filling in the unpopulated fertile spaces in the east and north of Grand Cayman. Over the same period, whites who had not been substantial slaveowners began the first permanent settlements in Cayman Brac and Little Cayman. There they developed a lifestyle and culture somewhat distinct from those of Grand Cayman. Almost totally dependent on the sea, "Brackers" were by the 1890s as ardently Baptists as were the people of Grand Cayman Presbyterians.

In the decade after emancipation, Caymanians began a tradition of migrating farther afield with their families in search of an easier life – though they always regarded the Cayman Islands as their true home and aimed to return if and when they could. So many settled in the Bay Islands of Honduras that Britain was briefly persuaded to declare those islands a formal colony (1852–9). Thereafter, Caymanians moved to Belize, the Miskito Coast of Nicaragua, and the relatively fertile islands of San Andrés, Old Providence, Corn Island, and the Isle of Pines. By the end of the century a migration had also begun to the southern port cities of the United States, particularly Tampa, Mobile, and Port Arthur.

Catboats off the Seven Mile Beach, ca. 1950.

Before 1900, change came extremely slowly in Cayman. In part this was due to an innate conservatism, based on Christian values. But it also reflected a lack of local resources and an indifference or unwillingness on the part of authorities in Jamaica and Britain to encourage change. In the long era of imperial *laissez-faire*, a small dependency that cost almost nothing, caused little trouble, and seemed to work on its own terms was thought best left alone. An imperial Act passed by the Westminster Parliament in June 1863 formally declared the Cayman Islands a dependency of Jamaica. But this important political development had little effect on people's economic and social circumstances for the next thirty years. Material improvements became more noticeable with the appointment by Jamaica of the first expatriate commissioner in 1898. Three of the most dedicated and long-serving of the early commissioners, George Hirst, Hugh Hutchings, and Allen Cardinall, did much to improve the economy, increase revenue, and bring the islands into the

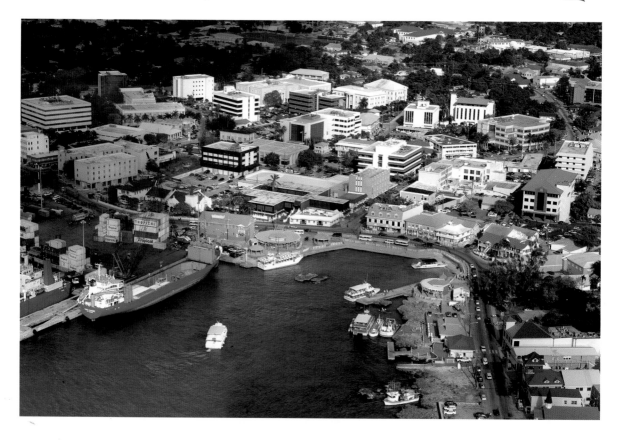

Aerial view of George Town, Grand Cayman, 2001.

twentieth century, though they sometimes faced opposition in the local legislature.

In some respects, the 54-member Caymanian Assembly of Magistrates and Vestry was the most democratic legislature in the Caribbean – with one representative for every one hundred islanders, and all districts, classes, and complexions represented. Yet the Assembly was sometimes dominated by merchants or shipowners, who could resist change if it posed a threat to their power. They particularly opposed increases in the level of import duties, even for such vital purposes as improving communications and public education. Until the 1920s the Cayman Islands were served only by sailing vessels, more than eighty years after a steamship service was established between England and Jamaica.

World War One did not greatly affect the Cayman Islands, and social and economic change thereafter continued to be slow. Unlike the Bahamas and Bermuda, the Cayman Islands did not profit from rum-running during Prohibition in the United States (1920–33). The terrible hurricane of 1932 had a devastating effect on all three islands, especially Cayman Brac, and these difficulties were intensified by those of the Great Depression during the 1930s. Gradually over the next fifteen years the greater movement of Caymanians to and from the United States, the enlistment of able-bodied Caymanian men in the Allied armed forces and merchant marine during

World War Two, and the establishment of a U.S. Navy and Coast Guard base on Grand Cayman between 1942 and 1945 combined to align Cayman more with the modern world.

With the end of World War Two (1945), the pace of change began to increase. It quickened still further after the achievement of Jamaican independence in 1962. The severing of political links with Jamaica at that time coincided with the final decline of the traditional industries of turtling, shipbuilding, and ropemaking. Caymanians were already looking for alternative incomes and ways of life. In particular, the men took employment as expert seamen in the hugely expanded postwar network of international shipping. The interaction with the short-lived West Indies Federation, which collapsed in 1962, and the break with Jamaica encouraged Caymanians to become more politically aware and to confront the need for a more modern administration, legal system, and civil service. At the same time, health and education services increasingly demanded modernisation.

Between the 1950s and 1970s, revolutions in communications opened up new vistas of development, first in tourism and then in banking. At the same time, with Britain's encouragement, Caymanians were taking increasing control of their own economy. Mariners began to give up the sea and migrants to return from the United States and Central America, drawn by the burgeoning opportunities in their Caymanian homeland. A rising tide of expatriates promoted and profited from the boom. Within half a lifetime, the gross national product of the Cayman Islands increased a thousandfold, and the surge brought major changes to the lifestyles and prospects of the Caymanian people.

Change brought with it problems as well as rising aspirations. Material improvements often seemed to outrun the infrastructure's capacity to accommodate them. Congestion, pollution, and crime, hitherto almost unknown, showed worrying increases. A growing dependence upon expatriates generated tensions on both sides. The frenetic pace of modernisation, the pressure of external influences, and materialism threatened to submerge traditional values and Cayman's distinctive culture.

As the twenty-first century approached, Caymanians undertook development of a ten-year plan, entitled Vision 2008. It was an opportunity to take stock, a truly communal effort initiated in 1998 that involved no fewer than two thousand participants. In their vision for the future, Caymanians acknowledged that making a nation means recognising their distinct cultural identity. Caymanians know themselves to be unique. But exactly what is it about the nature of their island homeland and their history that has made them what they are and given them their special place in the world? The following chapters will enable readers to decide the answer to this question for themselves.

This history of Cayman and its people is organised on broadly chronological lines, with each chapter looking at important events and trends. We begin with the islands in their uninhabited, pre-Columbian state, and with the recognition that all peoples are shaped by their environment as much as by historical occurrences. The natural setting of Cayman greatly influenced who settled here and when. The isolated and sometimes harsh physical environment tested the settlers' powers of adaptation and shaped their way of life and character – a process that continued over many decades. We might say that in recent times this equation has been gradually reversed. As they edged from the status of dependent territory to nationhood, the Caymanian people have increasingly sought new ways to shape their environment – physical, economic, and social – and to meet the challenges and responsibilities which the process of development brings.

Preparing for sea: the schooner Banks.

CHAPTER 2

First Comers

The Period before Permanent Settlement

THE AMERINDIANS WHO FIRST COLONISED MOST of the islands in the Caribbean probably did not settle or stop at the Cayman Islands. Christopher Columbus was the first European to record a sighting of the islands, in 1503. But he chose not to linger and explore them further. In the following century and a half, as Holland, France, and England challenged Spain's primacy in the Caribbean, the islands became better known – as shown by the growing accuracy of the maps made by the Spaniards and their rivals. The Cayman Islands came to be regarded as useful landmarks and as places to rendezvous, hide, or provision with turtles. But the islands were short of fresh water, surrounded by dangerous reefs, and inhabited by fearsome crocodiles. It was not until England conquered Jamaica in 1655 that the Cayman Islands were deemed worthy of claiming. Permanent settlement came even later, as Jamaica became more secure and its population grew.

Beginning about eight thousand years ago, three successive waves of Amerindians had settled almost the entire Caribbean long before the arrival of Columbus. Archaeological traces of all three peoples have been found in Jamaica, the Isle of Pines, and the southern cays of Cuba. But searches for Amerindian sites and artefacts in the Cayman Islands have proved unsuccessful. In the 1920s the first visiting archaeologist, Jesse Fewkes, was shown axeheads in Grand Cayman, but he concluded that they had been brought by modern mariners. Likewise, other experts believe that very old pottery shards are in fact imported items of post-Columbian date, while what appear to be fragments of shell tools were actually shaped by wave action.[1]

In 1994, the Florida archaeologist William Keegan, discoverer and explorer of dozens of Amerindian sites throughout the Bahamas, carried out an official search around the shores and in the caves of Grand Cayman but found nothing. Since the Cayman Islands are similar to many islands that were colonised by Amerindians, Keegan argued that the absence of Amerindian settlements showed that they were entirely unaware of them. Other archaeological surveys of all three islands in 1992 and 1995 "revealed no evidence of human occupation in the prehistoric period".[2]

Given the maritime skills and travel distances of the Amerindian migrants, however, it is almost inconceivable that none of them ever sighted the Cayman Islands. It is more likely that the islands were known to the Amerindians but did not particularly interest them. The islands had nothing that migrants or traders sought; they were at least a hundred miles from the nearest land; and they were deficient in fresh water and green provisions. Their beaches, lagoons, and swamps were guarded by fierce crocodiles. Caymanian waters abounded with turtles, but so did the more accessible islands closer to the Cuban coast.[3] Whatever the pre-Columbian peoples knew of Cayman, they did not linger or settle. This was also true of the first waves of European newcomers.

EUROPEAN DISCOVERY

Whether or not they were the first humans to encounter the Cayman Islands, Christopher Columbus and his men became the first Europeans known to have sighted the islands when they sailed past Little Cayman and Cayman Brac on 10 May 1503, on Columbus's fourth and final West Indian voyage. This event is clearly of great significance for Caymanians. For Columbus himself, though, it was a minor incident in his primary enterprise: the search for gold and other riches, and for a new and easier route to Asia.[4]

Cayman Brac seen from the northeast.

The fourth voyage of Christopher Columbus, 1502–04.

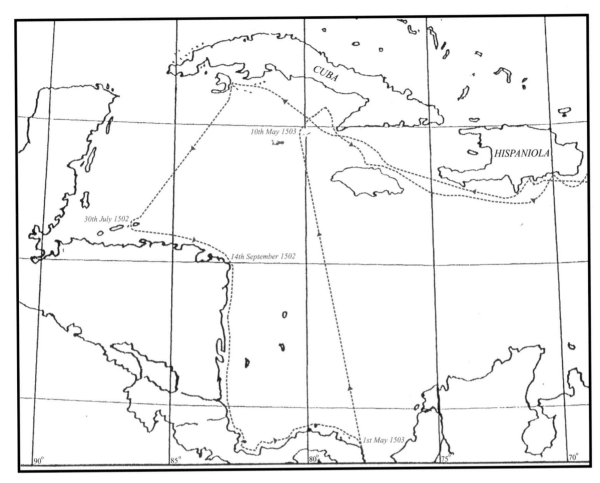

Columbus reached the mainland of present-day Honduras in August 1502. During the remaining months of that year and into the early months of the next, his expedition made its way slowly southward along the coasts of Central America, searching fruitlessly for the route to Asia, before finally abandoning its mission near present-day Panama. Battered by storms and eaten by shipworm, his four vessels were leaky and fragile. Before the expedition sought to return to Hispaniola, two of them were abandoned. The remaining two vessels, the *Capitana* and the *Santiago de Palos*, made as much headway eastward as they could against westerly winds and currents. But they grossly miscalculated the distance east they needed to travel. When they turned north, on 1 May 1503, they were still many miles to the west of Jamaica and Hispaniola, heading on a course that would take them towards the Sister Islands.

On the morning of Wednesday, 10 May, the Admiral and his remaining 120 crew – in the words of Columbus's son Ferdinand – "sighted two very small low islands full of turtles (as was all the sea thereabout, so that it seemed to be full of little rocks); that is why these islands are called *Las Tortugas*."[5] These two islets were, of course, Cayman Brac and Little Cayman.

Christopher Columbus

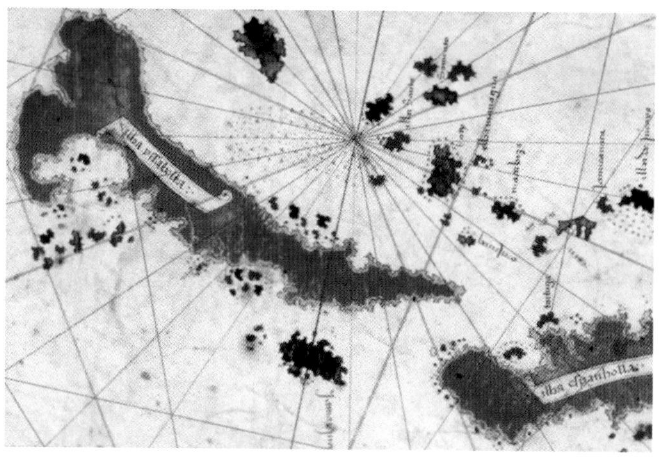

Detail from the Cantino Planisphere of 1502, suggesting possible European knowledge of the Cayman Islands before 1503.

Columbus's men were not in need of water and provisions, and the ships required constant pumping. So instead of landing they pressed on towards the north, arriving two days later at the Jardines de la Reina, off Cuba's southern shore. Columbus's sighting eventually placed two of the Cayman Islands on the map and identified them as a plentiful source of turtle. It also gave them their first name, which was based on the numerous, seasonal turtles that were visible rather than on the native caimáns, or crocodiles, which must have been out of sight.

In the explorer's subsequent troubles, the Cayman Islands were soon forgotten, and it was Jamaica that Columbus and his crewmen came to know – far better, perhaps, than they wished. Pumping day and night and praying that the timbers would hold, the expedition barely reached northern Jamaica, where they beached the ships at St. Ann's Bay. Columbus and his disgruntled crew were marooned there for almost nine months until, with the help of Taino Indians, they returned to the Spanish base in Hispaniola.[6]

Over the next century and a half the Cayman Islands became progressively better known, as the Protestant nations of western Europe challenged Catholic Spain's claim to the entire Caribbean by right of discovery and papal grant. This story can be told almost entirely through a study of the maps of the region, made in increasing numbers by the Spaniards themselves and their Italian allies, and by the Protestant French Huguenots, Dutch, and English who competed against them.

Detail from the world map by Vesconte de Maggiolo, 1511, with Jamaica (in blue) and two of the Cayman Islands.

Curiously, a map produced the year before Columbus sighted the Cayman Islands, the Cantino Planisphere (1502), shows a cluster of islets in roughly the right location. This may have been guesswork, or it may offer evidence that European cartographers knew of the Cayman Islands before Columbus sighted them. Probably based on Columbus's information, the 1511 map by Vesconte de Maggiolo shows just two islands but does not name them. The Turin Map of 1523 is the first to show three islands (in a triangular grouping), naming them not Las Tortugas after their turtles, but "Lagartos". *Lagarto* strictly

means lizard. In parts of Spanish America, however, it was used interchangeably with *caimán* – a word used by both Africans and Carib Indians to mean crocodile.[7]

Perhaps the first really convincing map to show the Cayman Islands was made by Juan Vespucci. Dated 1526, it shows the entire Caribbean and Gulf of Mexico with considerable accuracy of detail and scale. The three Cayman Islands were still depicted as a triangular group, but were correctly placed in relation to Jamaica, Cape Cruz, and southern Cuba, and for the first time were given a form of their present name: *Caymanos*.[8]

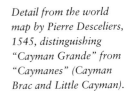

Detail from the world map by Juan Vespucci, 1526, showing all three Cayman Islands and the name "Caymanos".

The Vespucci map gives an accurate impression of what the Cayman Islands amounted to while the Spanish dominated the Caribbean. For the Spaniards, they were certainly not worth settling compared with the Greater Antilles, let alone the fabulously rich and extensive Mexico and Peru. Their dangerous reefs and uncertain currents probably made them too risky to land at for wood, water, or provisions. Nevertheless, they were vital landmarks for ships on the dangerous route home from Cartagena, Nombre de Dios, Santo Domingo, or Santiago. This route became more attractive in the 1560s, after the Spanish organised a system of annual convoys, called *los galeones*, in response to the threat of Protestant corsairs.[9]

The first maps of the western Caribbean to improve on Vespucci's were those used by the French Huguenot adventurers who, with Dutch and English allies, challenged Spanish control of the region from the 1530s. In 1545, Pierre Desceliers of Dieppe distinguished between "Cayman Grande" and the two smaller "Caymanes", though he was somewhat vague about their shape and placement. More impressive was the 1556 map of the northern Caribbean by Guillaume Le Testu of Le Havre. He gave them the single name "Caimannes" and drew them more correctly than any previous cartographer. The relative sizes of the islands, the distances between them, and their alignment relative to Cape Cruz and Point Negril were almost exactly to

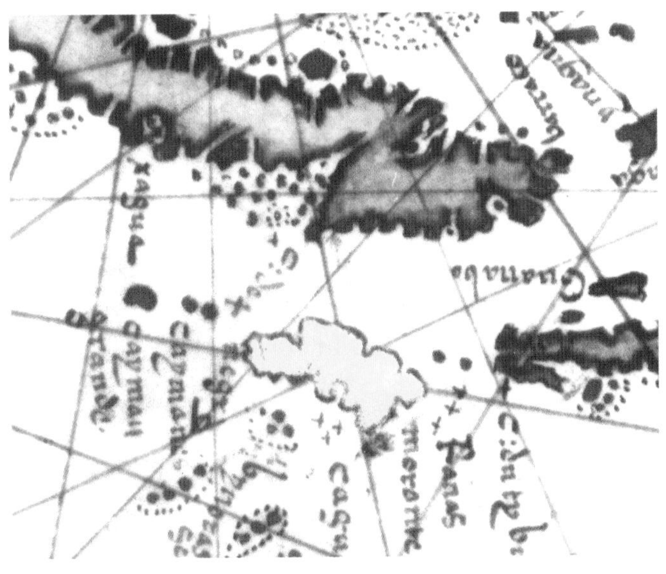

Detail from the world map by Pierre Desceliers, 1545, distinguishing "Cayman Grande" from "Caymanes" (Cayman Brac and Little Cayman).

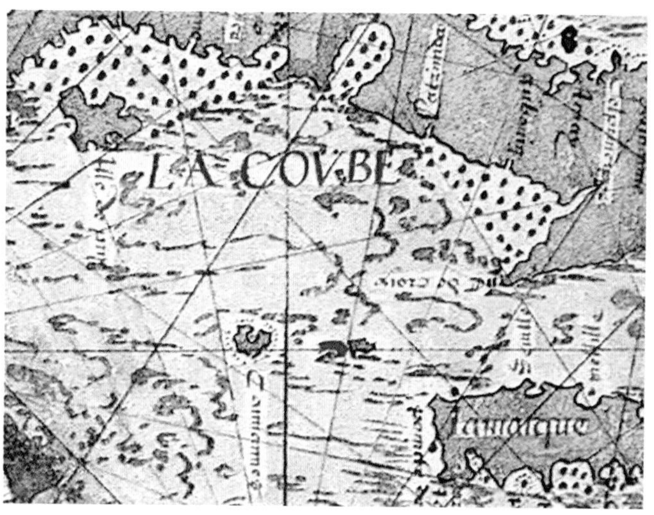

Detail from Cosmographie Universelle by Guillaume Le Testu, 1556, suggesting knowledge of the North Sound, Grand Cayman.

scale. The North Sound on Grand Cayman was shown for the first time. All this was evidence that the islands were becoming better known.[10]

It is not certain who were the first Europeans actually to land on the Cayman Islands, but an English commander and his men were the first about whom we have definite information. The date was 22 April 1586, and the leader was Sir Francis Drake, nicknamed *El Draco* (the Dragon) by the Spaniards, travelling in a convoy of twenty-three ships on his Great West Indian expedition of 1585–6. The story is told in several of the participants' journals, and illustrated in a commemorative map by Baptista Boazio.[11]

Drake's expedition was a pre-emptive strike. It ended two decades of unofficial conflict between England and Spain and began an equal period of formal war. The Cayman Islands were a natural rendezvous for the battered fleet and its sickly crews, where the commander hoped to replenish supplies of wood and water and stock up with much-needed fresh meat. The fullest account of the brief visit was kept by a sailor on board the *Primrose*, commanded by another Elizabethan hero, Martin Frobisher.

> The 18 of Aprill wee set saile the seconde time from *Carthagina* & the xxij of Aprill we fell with an Ile that had no people in hit. There wee fownde strawnge kindes of beastes & killed more than xx[ti] *Alligatos*. Those bee such serpentes as have bin in London to be seene. There weare *Crocadiles* which did Incounter & fight with vs, they live bothe in the sea & on lande. Wee tooke divers & made verie good meate of them, some of the same weare ten foote in lenghte.
>
> Also wee killed other little beastes like cattes & other little serpentes abowte 2 foote longe called *Guanos*, with a greate number of Turtles of huge bignes which served vs for verie good meate;
>
> This Ilande is a verie Deserte & wildernesse & so full of woodes as hit can growe. Wee thought to have watered there but could finde none. Wee staid there ij Daies & set the woodes on fire & soe departed.[12]

Sir Francis Drake

Another English privateer visited the Cayman Islands shortly after Drake – William King in 1592.[13] But until the middle of the seventeenth century, it was not the English or French but the Dutch who came to know the islands best. During the last three decades of Holland's eighty-year war with Spain (1621–48), Dutch captains used the islands systematically as a source of turtle meat, and they provided some detailed accounts of them. Stranded Dutch

mariners were also the first people whom we know to have spent more than a few days in the islands.[14]

One notable example was the Dutch fleet commanded by Admiral Pieter Adriaensz. On its way from southern Hispaniola in the summer of 1630, the crew first caught sight of Cayman Brac at a distance of four leagues (about ten miles), on the afternoon of 2 June. The warships were ordered to stand off till the next day "because it was not advisable to arrive there with the entire fleet at night". But three small "yachts" were sent ahead during the night to turn turtles, and the catch was taken aboard when the fleet came to anchor in the morning. Adriaensz's fleet then set sail for the Isle of Pines and Cape Antonio, but not before recording the earliest surviving detailed description of the Sister Islands:

Detail of Drake's voyage of 1585–6, showing the fleet stopping at Grand Cayman, 22–24 April 1586, by Boazio, 1589.

> These Caymans are two uninhabited low islands that cannot be spied from more than four or five leagues' distance. The easternmost one is very steep on the eastern end, with a cliff-like tip, and that side is very beautiful and clean-cut. The island extends WSW about three leagues. The western end is an empty point, behind which one can lay at anchor in six, seven and ten fathoms, but where one can easily lose an anchor and cable. The second island is about two leagues NNW from there, and is shaped like a triangle. One wishing to sail to the eastern end of that island encounters a reef that lies only a stone's throw from the corner. Having passed that you run to the northwest corner, which sits next to a sandy beach, where very tasty turtles come and lay their eggs in the sand from May to October, which due to the heat hatch in ten days. These turtles are most numerous on this western island, so that in one night one could obtain one or two thousand, some large enough to feed twenty or thirty men; they taste like veal. Here a lot of caimans (crocodiles) show themselves, after which the islands were named. There are also many sea birds which are good to eat. Otherwise the islands are very dry, rocky and sandy, without fresh water or fruits.[15]

Detail of a ship by Baptista Boazio, 1589.

Adriaensz's fleet did not sight Grand Cayman. But in the same year, the Dutch warship *Dolphijn*, a straggler from an attack on the Spanish Main, crashed into the reefs of Grand Cayman. The *Dolphijn* was an almost total wreck, but its crew was saved, along with much of its tackle and provisions. The enterprising Dutchmen set about constructing a yacht from the *Dolphijn's* broken timbers. After sixteen weeks they succeeded, naming the new boat *Cayman*. Shipping four of the *Dolphijn's* bronze guns and two iron pieces and burying the rest, the 122 survivors crammed aboard with their remaining

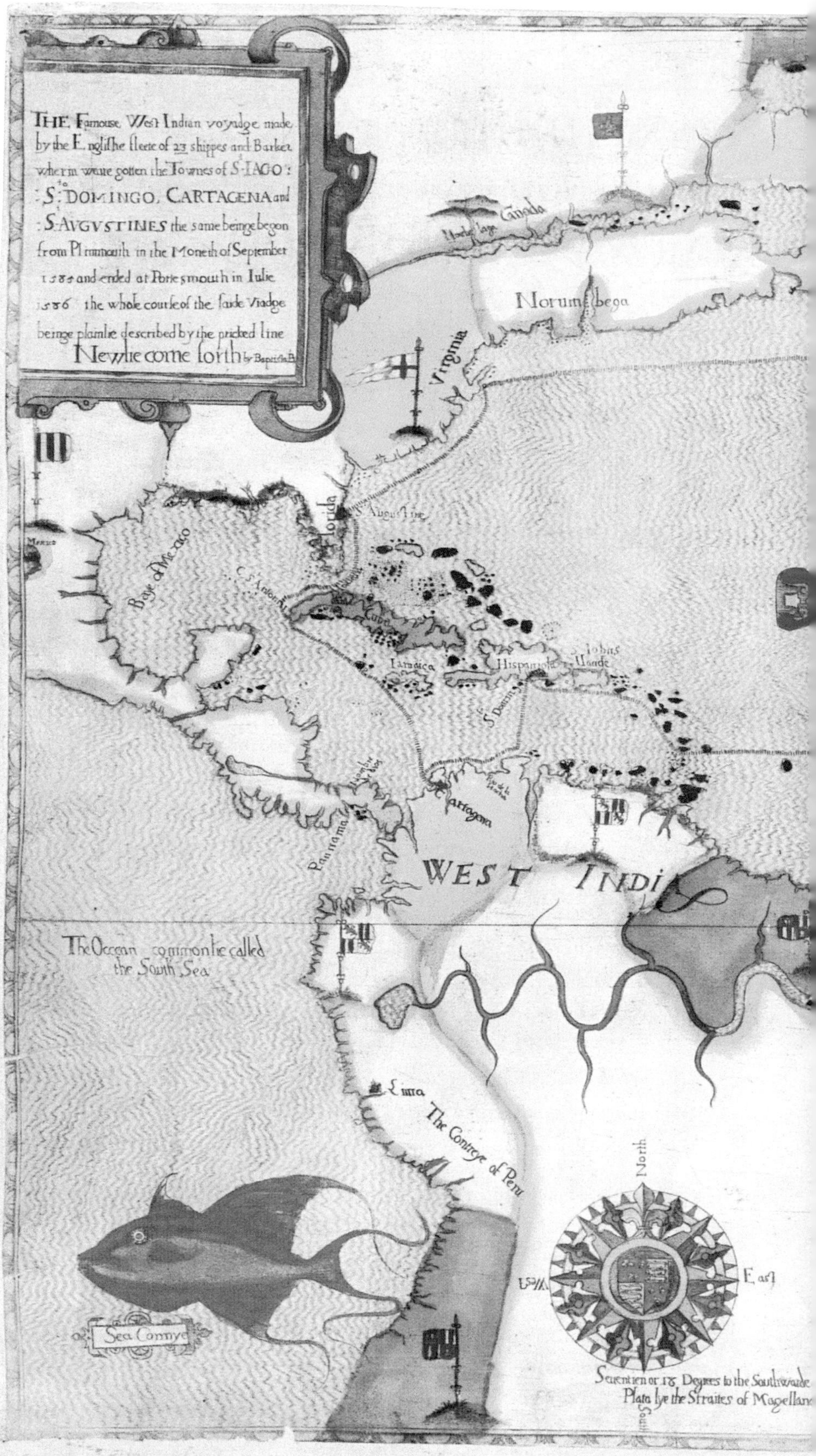

"The Famouse West Indian Voyadge made by the Englishe Fleet of 23 Ships and Barkes . . ." under Sir Francis Drake (leaving Plymouth on 14 September 1585 and returning to Portsmouth on 27 July 1586), by Boazio, 1589.

Norway
Sweden
Scotland
Irelande
England
Denmarck
Lowe Contries
France
Spaigne
Bayone
The waye Homewarde
Ilandes of Acores
Barbarie
Ilandes of Canaria
AFRICA
C. Blanck
Ilandes of Capo Verde
The waye Outwarde
Guinea
Equinoctiall Lyne
Brasill

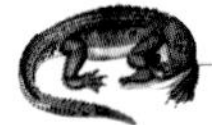

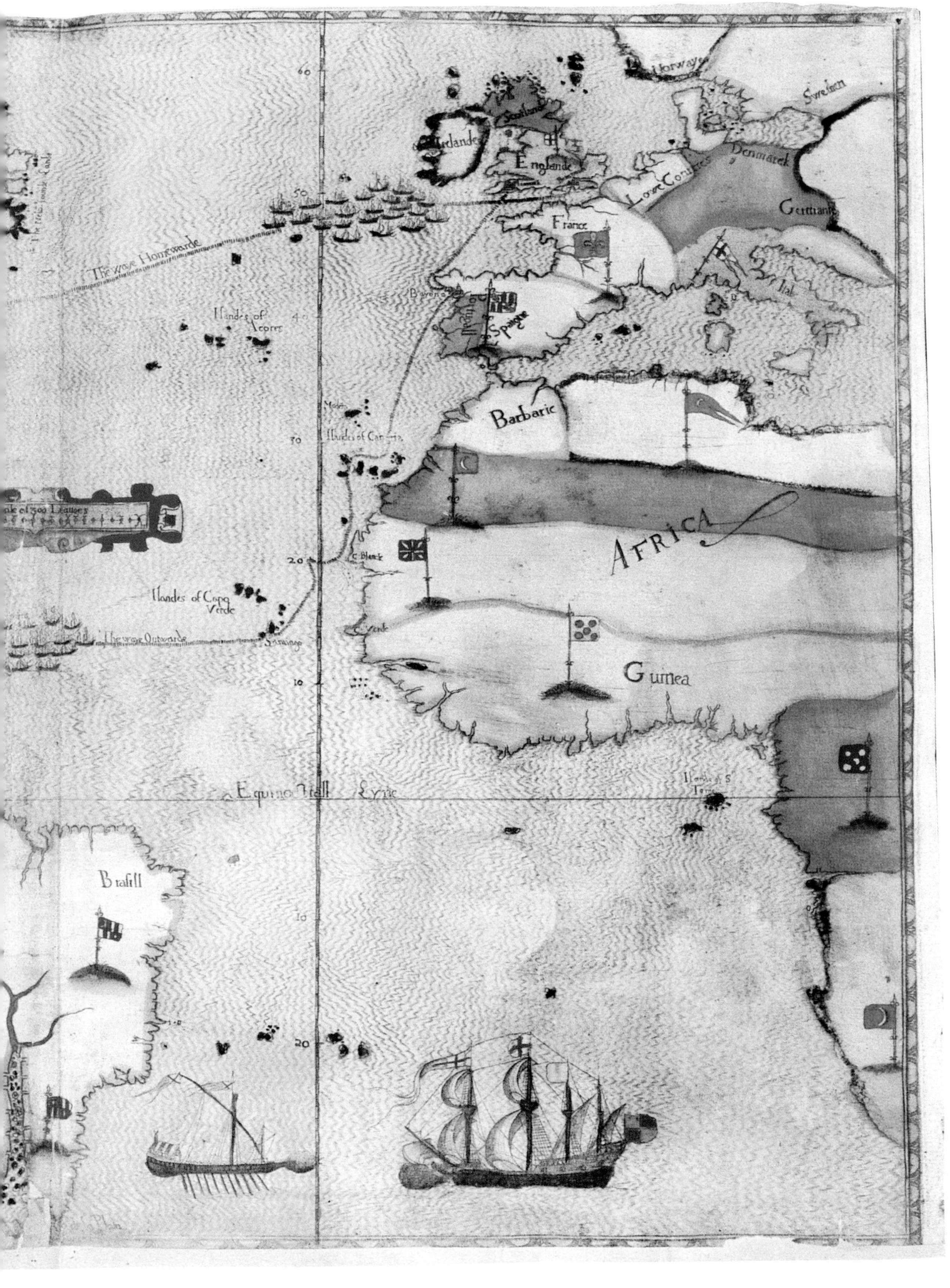

provisions and set sail for English Virginia or Dutch New Amsterdam (modern New York). Luckily, they encountered another Dutch fleet around the western end of Cuba. The crew was taken aboard other ships, and the *Cayman* was abandoned.[16]

Detail of a cayman by Boazio, 1589.

Holland officially made peace with Spain in 1648.But "beyond the lines" in the Caribbean, the unofficial war for supremacy against Spain continued. It was led by privateers with more or less shaky commissions, who came to be known as buccaneers. They were named for their custom of smoke-drying the meat of wild cattle over open fires called "boucans". They were a polyglot, mixed-race, fairly disreputable brotherhood, led at different times by Dutchmen, Frenchmen, and Englishmen. At first Spain's rival powers turned a blind eye to them and even encouraged them. But by the end of the seventeenth century, as those powers again became rivals, the buccaneers had either separated into their distinct nationalities or degenerated altogether into out-and-out pirates.[17]

Detail of a turtle by Boazio, 1589.

A key event in the process that led to the British acquisition of Jamaica and the Cayman Islands was the Spanish recapture, in May 1641, of the island of Old Providence (Providencia) off the coast of Nicaragua, which English Puritans had colonised ten years earlier. In retaliation, the English Captain William Jackson was furnished with three warships and "letters of marque and reprisal" and set out on a three-year rampage. His most significant success was the ease with which he took the island of Jamaica in March 1643. He subsequently made use of the Cayman Islands as a rendezvous.

Because he was more concerned with taking booty, Jackson did not attempt to hold onto Jamaica. Indeed, he planned to attack the Spanish Main, but his fleet was dispersed by storms. It regrouped at Grand Cayman between May and June 1643. During that time, Jackson set his men to killing and salting turtles, repairing his ships, and deciding on the next stage of the expedition. A third of the men were allowed to take a ship back to Barbados, while a second vessel deserted. But on 18 June Jackson and his most bellicose supporters set out for Roatán and Cape Gracias a Dios and a further eighteen months of campaigning.[18]

Turtle bones, harpoon head, and pottery from the probable site of the Dolphijn.

The results of William Jackson's exploits were generally disappointing. They were remembered in 1655, however, when Oliver Cromwell developed his great Western Design to overthrow the Spanish-American empire, including Jamaica. His forces under Admiral William Penn and General Robert Venables made as easy an inroad into Jamaica as Jackson had in 1643. But the mountainous island was not under English control until 1660, thanks to guerrilla tactics by pro-Spanish Maroons and reinforcements of Spanish soldiers from Cuba. From the conquest of Jamaica onwards, the Cayman Islands were to prove useful to English naval and merchant ships as stopping-off points, and especially as a ready source of turtle meat.[19]

THE COLONISATION OF JAMAICA

After the Spanish had been expelled from Jamaica, the Cayman Islands also proved a valuable source of turtle for the disbanded English soldiers and other settlers. Indeed, their reputation as a source of turtle made them a magnet for vessels of all kinds in the West Indies. One official writer, describing the varieties of fish around Jamaica in about 1662, makes special note of the Cayman Islands:

> The principall sort [of fish] is tortoise [turtle] which they take plentifully on this Coast [Jamaica], and 20 or 30 leagues to leeward lyes the Camana, whither resort in Maye, June and July all the Men of warr and merchants shipps from the Carribbee islands to victuall and loade with this fish, it being reputed the wholsomest and best meat in the Indies.[20]

It was probably to guarantee the supply of turtle, as well as to promote the security of Jamaica, that the Cayman Islands were included under the jurisdiction of recently conquered Jamaica. The Commission of the first royal Governor of Jamaica, sent by King Charles II in 1662, read in part:

> And forasmuch as there are severall little Islands adjacent to . . . Jamaica, and belonging to the Territories thereof, as the Camaines Islands, Salt Island, Pidgeon Island, and diverse others . . . which by Planting and raising Fortifications upon may be of great concerne and Advantage towards the security and well setling of our Island of Jamaica, these [Instructions] are therefore to authorize you to passe and consigne the Lands belonging to those other Isles . . . to any person or persons by graunt under our publique Seals of Jamaica, according to the tenure and Custome of the rest of our Plantations in Jamaica, and also to raise forts therein, as to your selfe by advise of the Councill shall seem necessary, and expedient, for the carrying on of our Interest and affaires in those parts.[21]

This document, declaring that the Cayman Islands were an integral part of English Jamaica in almost all respects, was to be of lasting significance for the islands. But for the time being, the English hold on Jamaica and its outlying islands was shaky. It did not

names if remembered the principall
sort is tortoise Wch they take plentifully
on this Coast and 20 or 30 leagues to
Leeward Lyes the Camana Whether
resort in Maye, June and July all the
men of Warr and merchants, Shipps
from the Carribbee Islands to Victuall
and Loade Wth this fish it being reputed
the Wholsomest and best meat in the
Indies

"The wholsomest and best meat in the Indies": turtle from Cayman, ca. 1662.

View of Port Royal and Kingston Harbours in the 1700s.

prove easy to attract settlers to Jamaica. Progress to establish plantations was slow, partly because the rough terrain made it easy for slaves to run away to join the ever-resistant Maroons, and partly because much of the coastline was vulnerable to attack. During the second half of the seventeenth century, Jamaica was much more of a maritime base than a plantation colony, centred on the mushrooming town of Port Royal.

Initially, Port Royal welcomed the international brotherhood that lived by preying on Spanish ships and vulnerable Spanish towns and plantations. From the middle 1660s to the 1680s, Port Royal was also a base for respectable merchants and a stopping place for many of the English trading ships passing from the Lesser Antilles back to Europe. In addition, dozens of small local vessels brought in provisions from other parts of Jamaica and nearby islands – including turtles from the Cayman Islands. By the end of the 1680s Port Royal was the most active seaport in the Americas.[22]

Between the catastrophic earthquake of 7 June 1692 and the town-wide fire of January 1703, however, Port Royal declined rapidly. The subsequent selection of Spanish Town as the Jamaican capital and Kingston as the colony's chief port symbolised a key change. It marked the vital transition of Jamaica from semi-piratical maritime base to settled plantation colony and hub of legitimate commerce. The central figures in this transitional period were Governor Sir Thomas Modyford (1664–70), his notorious associate, Captain (later Sir) Henry Morgan, and Modyford's successor, Sir Thomas Lynch (1671–84).[23]

Coppy of a Commission of Warre, by the Spaniard against the English in the West Indies, being the Translation of the Originall in Spanish

The Maestra De Campo Don Piedro Bayona y Villa Nueba Capt Generall of the Province of Paraguay, & Governor of the Citty of St Iago, of Cuba, and its Jurisdiction for his Maties &c

Whereas the Queen Governesse our Lady whom God preserve, by her Royall order dated in Madrid the 20 of Aprill 1669, and signed by her Royall hand and Subscribed by Don Gabriell Bernardo de Guiras her Secretary was pleased to informe me that Relation

Commission of War by the Spanish against the English, issued in Cuba, 1670.

BUCCANEERS AND PIRATES

During most of this period, England was supposedly at peace with its European rivals. The English government had signed non-aggression agreements with the French and Spanish at the same time that peace was concluded with the Dutch at Breda in 1667.[24] But in the Caribbean such treaties had minimal effect, especially in regard to the Spanish. Buccaneers under Henry Morgan soon resumed their unofficial war against the Spaniards, with the endorsement of Thomas Modyford. At the same time, the French became increasingly interested in the Western Caribbean, and competition with them intensified. In the midst of this activity, it is not surprising to find the Cayman Islands regularly mentioned in contemporary accounts from several nations.

In 1667, five Jamaica-based vessels worth £40,000 were seized by Spanish warships at the Cayman Islands. This was one of the pretexts used by Governor Modyford for issuing letters of marque against the Spanish to the Port Royal privateers.[25] Henry Morgan knew the Cayman Islands well and used them as a staging post for his bold inland strike against Sancti Spíritus, Cuba, in January 1668. They were a rendezvous for Morgan's much larger expeditions against Porto Bello and Maracaibo in 1668 and 1669 and his climactic attack on Panama in 1670–1.[26] In retaliation, the Cayman Islands became the target of a Spanish attack in the summer of 1669, led by the colourful privateer Manuel Rivero Pardal.

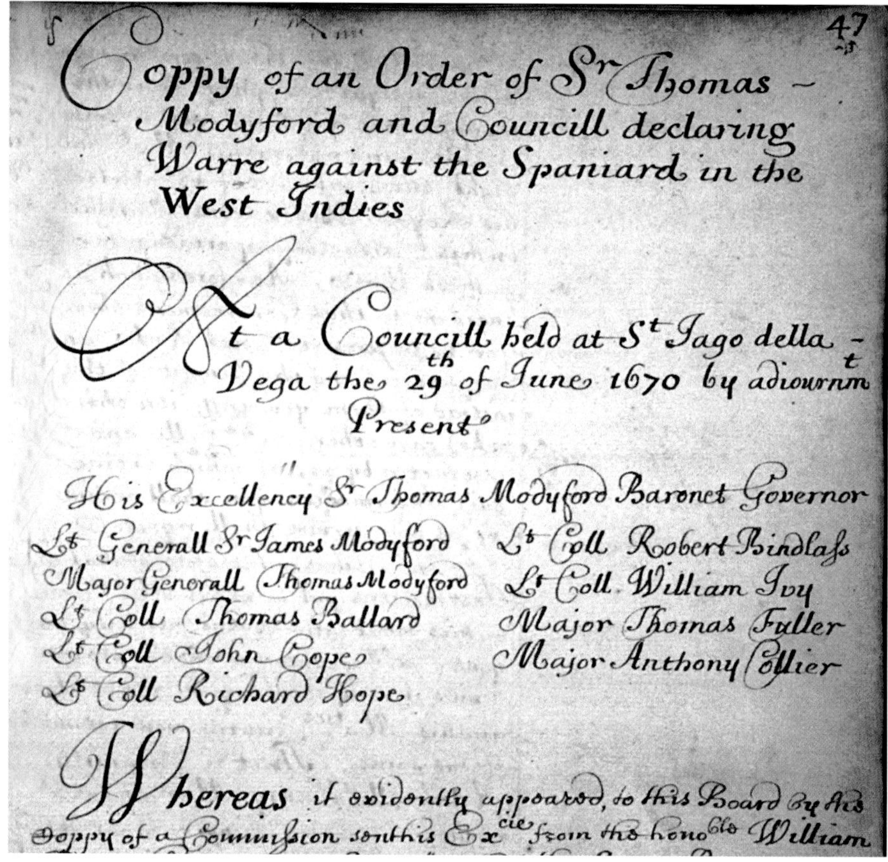

47

Coppy of an Order of Sr Thomas Modyford and Councill declaring Warre against the Spaniard in the West Indies

At a Councill held at St Jago della Vega the 29th of June 1670 by adiournmt

Present

His Excellency Sr Thomas Modyford Baronet Governor

Lt Generall Sr James Modyford — Lt Coll Robert Bindlass
Major Generall Thomas Modyford — Lt Coll William Ivy
Lt Coll Thomas Ballard — Major Thomas Fuller
Lt Coll John Cope — Major Anthony Collier
Lt Coll Richard Hope

Whereas it evidently appeared to this Board by the Coppy of a Commission sent his Excie from the honoble William

Order of Sir Thomas Modyford, Governor of Jamaica, declaring war against the Spanish, 1670.

In response to Morgan's actions, the Spanish Queen Regent issued a general decree authorising reprisals early in 1669. Following the attack on Maracaibo, the Governor of Cartagena gave Manuel Rivero Pardal letters of marque valid for five years. Armed with this commission, Rivero Pardal assembled a flotilla of five ships, led by the *San Pedro y Fama*, a frigate manned by ninety-six men and armed with "eight good guns, six petareos [culverins] and a good store of ammunition with granadoes [grenades] and stinck pots". With this small force he arrived off the southwestern shore of Little Cayman around 4 p.m. on 14 April 1669.[27]

Several turtling vessels were anchored at Hudson's Hole, Little Cayman, the largest being the Jamaican ship *Hopewell*, captained by Samuel Hutchinson. At the time of the Spanish attack Hutchinson was entertaining several other captains, including a Captain Ary, whom he called "Governor of the Caymans". The Spanish vessels – said to be "all great Shipps except one Tartan [galley]" – appeared, flying English colours. Coming within musket range, they suddenly lowered the English flags and raised Spanish colours, opened fire on the *Hopewell*, manned the tartan and several small boats, and prepared to board. Only one man on the *Hopewell* was killed. But the yard was shot away and the mainmast splintered, and several rounds of shot

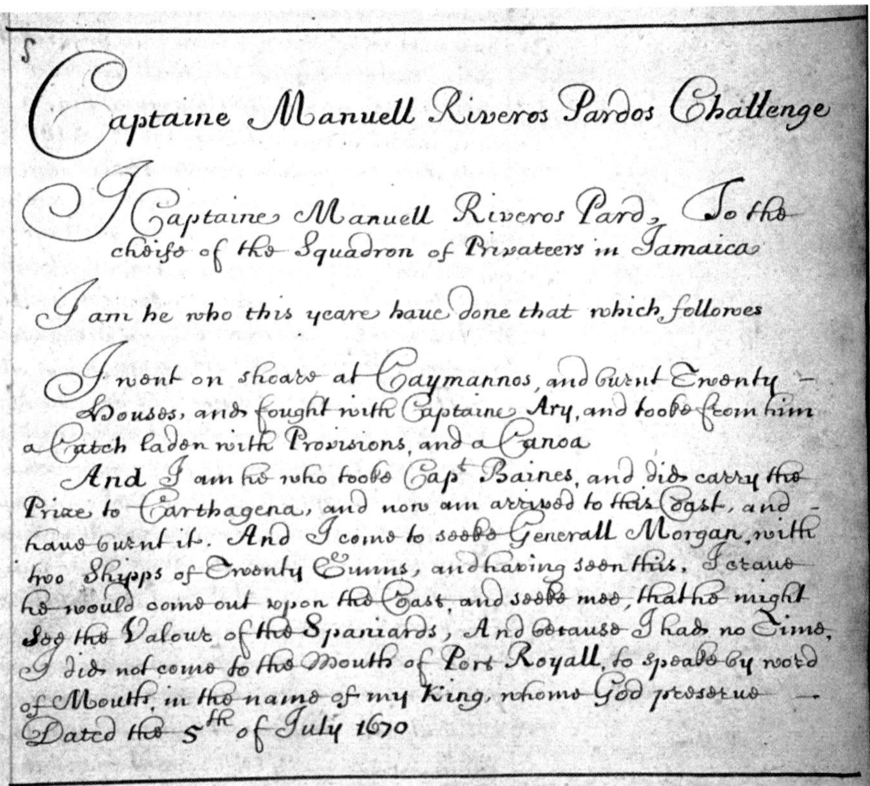

Captaine Manuell Riveros Pardos Challenge

I Captaine Manuell Riveros Pard, To the chiefe of the Squadron of Privateers in Jamaica

I am he who this yeare have done that which followes

I went on shoare at Caymannos, and burnt Twenty Houses, and fought with Captaine Ary, and tooke from him a Catch laden with Provisions, and a Canoa

And I am he who tooke Capt Baines, and did carry the Prize to Carthagena, and now am arrived to this Coast, and have burnt it. And I come to seeke Generall Morgan, with two Shipps of Twenty Gunns, and having seen this, I crave he would come out upon the Coast, and seeke mee, that he might see the Valour of the Spaniards, And because I had no Time, I did not come to the Mouth of Port Royall, to speake by word of Mouth, in the name of my King, whome God preserve

Dated the 5th of July 1670

Captain Manuel Rivero Pardal's challenge, boasting of his attack on Little Cayman, 1670.

went though the hull. The other Jamaican captains fled to their own ships, but were prevented from setting sail by a curtain of Spanish fire.

Hutchinson claimed to have stayed with his ship as long as any of his men would stand by him. He then ran the *Hopewell* on the rocks, went ashore with "Governor" Ary, and hid in the woods to avoid capture. Having sunk several small English ships and secured the rest, the Spaniards sent about two hundred armed men ashore at Little Cayman's eastern end (at a point still called Muddy Foots, presumably after Governor Modyford). These men marched the length of the island before ransacking and setting fire to the twenty or so turtlers' houses and huts. At one stage, Hutchinson and Ary came down to the edge of the woods and shouted out to the Spaniards, "demanding of them their Admiralls name and the reasons why they should come to destroy merchantmen and fishermen". They received no answer. After refloating the *Hopewell* by throwing overboard its cargo of salt (used for preserving turtle meat), Rivero Pardal sailed away with this boat as his chief prize, along with three turtling sloops and a ketch.[28]

Shortly afterwards, Rivero Pardal sailed back to Jamaica where he seized several more vessels and sacked some plantations on the north coast. In July 1670 he left a famous message pinned to a tree at Point Negril. It bragged of his exploit in the Caymans and issued a challenge for a head-to-head fight with Henry Morgan, "the chiefe of the Squadron of Privateers in Jamaica".

Henry Morgan as a young man.

The duel never occurred, for (as Rivero Pardal may have known) Morgan had already left with thirty-six ships and 1,850 men on his expedition against Panama. Shortly afterwards, Rivero Pardal was killed and his ship captured off Guantanamo Bay, Cuba. His vessel was taken to join Morgan's offensive.[29] Lurid accounts of Rivero Pardal's attack on the Cayman Islands (including an accusation that the Spaniards had burnt one crew alive with their ship) were sent by Governor Modyford to London. These served to justify his support for Morgan's attack on Panama.[30]

Far more important events, however, were already occurring on the diplomatic stage. King Charles II's ministers wanted a more effective treaty with Spain than that of 1667. Sir William Godolphin had therefore been sent to Madrid in the autumn of 1669 to carry out the delicate negotiations. After nine months the Treaty of Madrid was signed, and was ratified by England on 28 September 1670. The seventh article made a major concession to England:

> It is agreed that the most Serene King of great Brittaine and his Heirs and Successors shall have hold keepe and enjoy for ever with plenary Right of Soveraignty Dominion Possession and Propriety, all those lands, Regions Islands Colonies and Places whatsoever being or scituated in the West Indies or any other part of America which the said King of great Brittaine and his Subjects doo at present hold and possess.[31]

For the first time the Spanish were accepting the principle that effective occupation gave the right of possession in the Caribbean. By this they tacitly acknowledged (though no territories were specifically named) the English possession of Jamaica, along with Barbados and the various Leeward Islands settled and held since 1624. Concerning the Cayman Islands, the situation was more tenuous. But as far as the English were concerned (and had claimed at least since 1662), the Caymans were sovereign extensions of Jamaica. Nor could anyone claim that the islands were effectively occupied by any other power.

The French had no serious designs on the Cayman Islands and were prepared to accept England's primacy there. In fact, a French privateer was at Little Cayman at the time of the Spanish attack, but raised its national colours and stayed clear of the skirmish. An official French report on various Caribbean islands, drawn up in 1670, corroborated the details of Rivero Pardal's attack. It also set out the French position that the Cayman Islands were not valuable enough for France to claim or to fight over, when there were "other more important goals to seek and actions to take".[32]

Henry Morgan's savage but successful attack on Panama with the connivance of Governor Modyford jeopardised the Treaty of Madrid. Thomas Modyford was sacked as governor and replaced by the more diplomatic Sir

Thomas Lynch. Modyford and Morgan were shipped back to England and subsequently re-employed. To Lynch fell the difficult tasks of curbing the privateers and promoting peaceful planting and legitimate trade. He first offered a general amnesty but, when this had little effect, followed it with a fairly vigorous policy of suppression.[33]

A few days before Lynch's arrival, the Jamaican Council called for a year's amnesty for the "divers Soldiers, Planters, Privateers and other late Inhabitants of this Island who are now at Caimanos, Musphitos Keyes, and other remote places from this Island, who make scruple of returning hither, either fearing his Majesty's displeasure, or punishment for their past irregular Actions, or [expecting] being prosecuted by their Creditors".[34] Lynch's own instructions were even more generous, though limited to privateers. Those privateers who came in within a reasonable time and joined the Royal Navy or turned to legitimate trade or planting would be free from prosecution for any actions that had occurred between the restoration of King Charles II (1660) and the official promulgation in Jamaica of the Treaty of Madrid. They would also be allowed "quiet possession" of all goods acquired during that period – subject only to the King's and Governor's shares of tenths and fifteenths.[35]

Lynch gave the privateers further leeway by not proclaiming the treaty until November 1671, sixteen months after its original signing. But the results were disappointing: few of Morgan's followers came in to submit to government, and most had dispersed. Lynch and most of his successors did what they could to uphold the spirit and letter of the Treaty of Madrid. It remained to be seen over the succeeding decades whether England could sustain its claim to the Cayman Islands by the principle of effective occupation, while at the same time denying their use to the pirates who increasingly plagued the region.

The sixty or seventy years after the signing of the Treaty of Madrid (1670) are popularly held to have been the heyday of piracy in the Caribbean. The Cayman Islands are commonly believed to have been a pirates' haven, much like the Bahamas. Both ideas are greatly exaggerated, and require qualification. True pirates are no more or less than indiscriminate sea robbers. Their "heyday" in the Caribbean was during the twenty-six years of peace between the Treaty of Utrecht, in 1713, and 1739. During this period, unemployed fighting men turned to piracy while Britain and the other imperial powers were trying desperately to eradicate pirates in the interests of developing formal colonies and legitimate trade.[36] As part of that process, from as early as 1700, the Cayman Islands were gradually settled permanently and planted.

Until the 1730s, the Cayman Islands were used primarily as temporary settlements, although a few families had almost certainly settled before then.[37] They were bases for a seasonal turtle fishery that extended into the cays of southern Cuba, and for a trade in logwood from Campeche, Belize, and the

Bay Islands, which was hotly resisted by the Spanish. They were also becoming an intermediate stop for trading connections with the anti-Spanish Indians of the Miskito Coast. Those who spent time in the Cayman Islands were a raffish crew, almost exclusively male, consisting of turtlers, logwood cutters, would-be legitimate traders, and combers of wrecks. The Spanish regarded Cayman-based mariners as predators, and often called them pirates. For their part, the Spanish acted in ways that the English regarded as piratical. The region saw pirates of all kinds, most of whom knew of the Cayman Islands. But at no time were the Cayman Islands a true nest of pirates.

During the period 1670–1730, privateers, buccaneers, and even authentic pirates did occasionally visit the Cayman Islands. They stopped there to rendezvous, to obtain turtle, wood, and water, to careen their vessels, to share their loot, or to plan their next voyage. As a nominal dependency of Jamaica, the islands were a safe and proper location for legitimate privateers. But they were less attractive and more dangerous for pirates. There was little worth plundering except other visiting ships. And, unlike the Bahamas, they had no town where pirates could purchase provisions and supplies, spend their ill-gotten gains in riotous living, or transfer them into a more legal form of wealth. They offered even less than the Bahamas to attract successful pirates to settle down as respectable planters or merchants. Compared with the seven hundred islands of the Bahamas, the three Cayman Islands were too small, and too close to Jamaica, to offer easy hiding places, either for pirate ships or for ex-pirates seeking a life on the shore. During the main pirate era the Cayman Islands had few if any permanent inhabitants, so modern Caymanians have no authentic pirate legacies, either in their genes or in their cultural heritage.

A "boucan" or "bucan" (a frame for smoking meat), which gave rise to the term "buccaneer".

The most notable pirate tale involving the Cayman Islands in Daniel Defoe's best-selling *General History of the Pyrates* (published in 1724 under the pseudonym Captain Charles Johnson) was the story of a Welshman named John Evans. Formerly master of a Nevisian sloop and mate on a Jamaican privateer, Evans found himself, along with many others, unemployed and penniless after the Treaty of Utrecht. "Wages not being so good as formerly, and Births [berths] scarce because of the great Number of Seamen," Evans and a dozen others "agreed to go abroad in search of Adventures".

Leaving Port Royal in a canoe in September 1722, Evans and his associates robbed houses on Jamaica's north shore and took a Bermudian sloop off Ocho Rios. In this vessel, aptly renamed the *Scourer*, they prowled around Hispaniola and Puerto Rico. They plundered Spanish, Dutch, New England, and Jamaican vessels. Seizing the richest of their captures, the Dutch ship *Lucretia*, Evans and his fellows went to Grand Cayman early in 1723 with the intention of careening their vessel, sharing the spoils, and planning further "adventures".

In typical pirate fashion, captain and crew fell out over the division of the loot and future plans. The argument grew hottest between Evans and his boatswain, who refused the offer of a duel and was beaten, then shot the captain dead. At a loss for leadership, the pirates offered the captaincy to the former mate of the *Lucretia*, the only man among them capable of navigation. When he refused, they allowed him to sail off to Puerto Rico with the *Lucretia*, taking a few of the less hardened pirates with him. "Accordingly," as Defoe tantalisingly concluded, the remaining pirates "went ashore at the *Caimanes*, carrying with them about nine thousand Pounds among thirty Persons" – thus providing a basis, however flimsy, for the legends that pirates were among the Cayman Islands' earliest settlers and that pirate loot was buried in the islands.[38]

By 1730 the Cayman Islands offered the dwindling number of Caribbean pirates no more than a temporary refuge or an occasional rich wreck site. This is borne out by the story of the last British pirate we know to have used the Cayman Islands, Captain Neal Walker. In September 1730, Jamaican Governor Robert Hunter reported that the Spanish 54-gun warship *Genoesa* had been wrecked at the Pedro shoals, south of Jamaica, while carrying the Governor of Panama and a "great Treasure". Three vessels were immediately sent to the rescue. One of them brought in 240 survivors, but not the Governor of Panama (who was presumed lost), and no treasure whatsoever. Other survivors, under the second-in-command of the *Genoesa*, came ashore at Black River, Jamaica. From there a Captain Ware was sent to help at the wreck, but Ware instead spent three days profitably fishing for silver with the other sloops drawn to the scene.[39]

HMS *Experiment* was sent out to guard the wreck, causing Ware and the other plunderers to flee "to leeward" – towards the Cayman Islands. The *Experiment*, being leaky, soon returned to Port Royal and was replaced by HMS *Tryall*. Governor Hunter feared that the wreck had already been well pillaged. The *Tryall* did bring in 31,695 gold and silver coins, 8 bars of gold, and 105 silver ingots, but this was thought to be a mere fraction of what was

salvaged. Governor Hunter was forced to issue a proclamation against two of the captains he had originally sent to rescue the Governor of Panama and the others, but who had fished up treasure and disappeared. Chief among these was Neal Walker, commander of a three-masted snow (similar to a square-rigged brigantine) belonging to the Asiento Company.

On Christmas Eve, 1730, Hunter reported that in the same series of storms that had wrecked the *Genoesa* another Spanish vessel loaded with wine, brandy, and dry goods had gone ashore "upon one of the little Islands to the Leeward of this call'd the Camanas". Seven of the forty-six men aboard had been brought into Jamaica by a turtling vessel, along with the crew of Captain Ware's sloop, who claimed to have been wrecked at the Caymans after carrying Spanish survivors to the Cuban port of Trinidad. The men reported that Neal Walker had been busily plundering the Spanish merchantman. "It seems he takes refuge in one of the aforementioned Islands," wrote Hunter. "I shall do what I can to have him secured. In the mean time the Naval Officer has by my Order seized such Wines and Brandy as were brought off that Wreck by the Turtlers or the others, for the King, that it may be restored to the just Claimants."[40]

Governor Hunter ordered naval vessels to scour the Cayman Islands, but their searches were fruitless. The record is silent about what happened to Neal Walker, to the bulk of the treasure lifted from the wreck of the *Genoesa*, and to the rest of the wine and brandy plundered from the Spanish merchantman.

By the time of Neal Walker's escapade, any direct involvement in piracy by the Cayman Islands had become virtually impossible. In such small islands, so close to Jamaica, it would have been extremely difficult for any ex-pirate to conceal his disreputable past and permanently escape the retribution of the Jamaican courts. After 1730 the only pirates visiting the Cayman Islands were Spanish and French freebooters competing with the locals for wrecks, or drawn by the rather meagre opportunities of plundering the inhabitants or the ships temporarily anchored offshore. Thus, from being an occasional and temporary pirate base, the Cayman Islands became an occasional target of piratical outsiders, mainly Spanish. This was confirmation that the era of permanent settlement had already begun.

Surveying the land: the spirit of the early settlers.

CHAPTER 3

Pioneer Settlers in Peace and War, 1700–1800

PEOPLE DID NOT SETTLE PERMANENTLY on any of the Cayman Islands before about 1700, though, as we have seen, some temporary settlements existed before then. To be truly permanent, settlements require the presence of women and families, and it is only after 1700 that we have certain record of these. The allocation of land is another key indicator. The first formal land grants took place in the 1730s and 1740s. Records of these land grants, together with other records found in England, Jamaica, and Spain, enable us to address with a fair degree of certainty the important questions of when people first settled in Cayman and what kind of community they developed.

It is clear that a group of people from Jamaica were living in huts on Little Cayman in April 1670 and that they recognised the leadership of a Captain Ary, who may have had a home on Cayman Brac. That the huts already existed in April, before the turtle season was under way, suggests that they may have been more than temporary turtlers' shelters. There is no record that Rivero Pardal's men found crops to plunder or burn when they pillaged the huts. But according to one Spanish captive, four children were captured on Little Cayman, which would seem to indicate the presence of at least one family.[1] This cluster of huts might have become a permanent settlement if the soil had proved more fertile, the water supplies more reliable, and the island more secure from attack.

In these circumstances, it was natural that the centre of interest for permanent settlement should move from the Sister Islands to Grand Cayman. Though farther from Jamaica, Grand Cayman was closer to the main east-

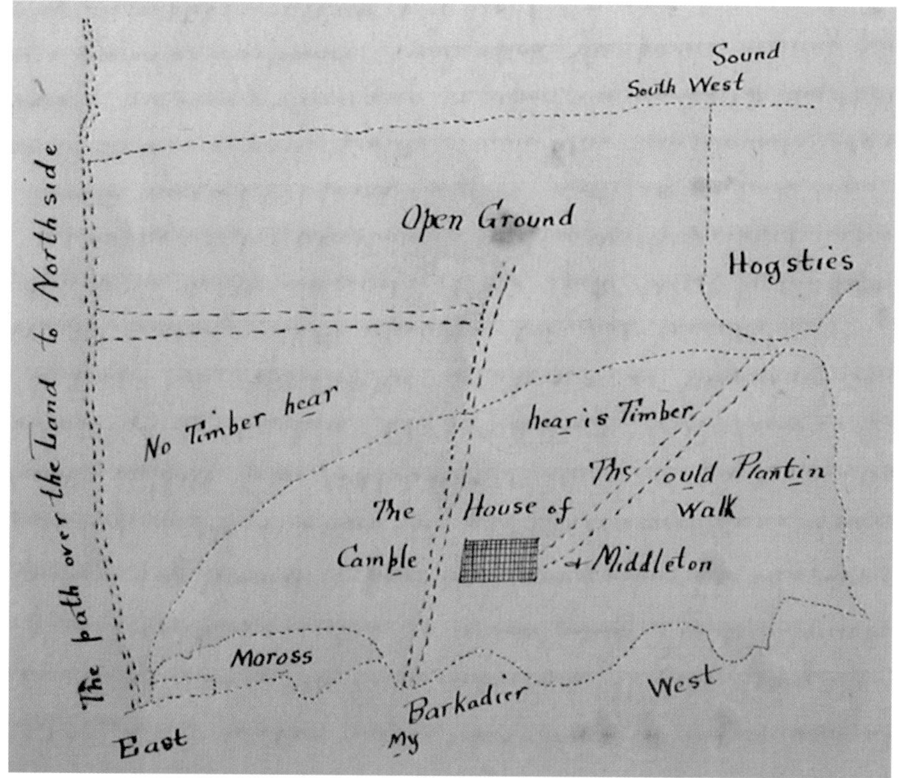

The first land grant in Grand Cayman, made to Daniel Campbell, John Middleton, and Mary Campbell in 1735.

Aerial view of the airport, industrial park, and Red Bay (1999), which includes the land granted to the Campbells and Middleton.

west shipping lanes and the shores of Central America. It was much larger, with better anchorages and a magnificent, if shallow, interior harbour. It was more fertile and better supplied with water, and had many more stands of valuable timber. It was also far less vulnerable to attack than the Sister Islands.

The East End of Grand Cayman may well have been the site of the first settlement on the island. It was the home of the first recorded inhabitant of Grand Cayman, Isaac Bodden, who was apparently born on Cayman around 1700 and is known to have married another Caymanian, Sarah Lamar, in 1735. The district of East End, formerly called Old Isaac's, was named after him. According to George Gauld, the official navy hydrographer whose 1773 map is one of the best surviving eighteenth-century documents about Cayman, Isaac Bodden was the grandson of the original Bodden, who was "one of Oliver Cromwell's soldiers . . . at the taking of Jamaica" in 1655. The original Bodden, "the Patriarch", as Gauld calls him, evidently came to Cayman sometime after this event.[2]

Oral tradition in Cayman has hallowed a slightly different account which was first set down by Nathaniel Glover and has often been accepted as fact. Nathaniel Glover was an American who settled in Cayman in 1831. A decade later he made this confident assertion to a newly arrived Wesleyan missionary:

> It is a well established fact that the first settlers were two soldiers from the disbanded army of Cromwell who came here about the year 1658 from Jamaica, whose names were Walter and Bowden, which plainly accounts for the numerous families of Watlers and Boddens throughout the Islands, the difference of the names only arising from some ignorant persons crossing the L in Walter instead of the T and spelling Bodden with 2 D's instead of one. Be that as it may, Walter and Bowden came here for the purpose of catching turtle.[3]

Glover was writing some 180 years after the events he describes and without the benefit of any records like Gauld's map. There is more evidence to support the "Bodden" in this account than the "Watler". Walters can indeed be found in the Jamaican lists of settlers from the earliest years, as are sundry Bowdens, Bawdens, Bourdons, and other possible variants of the surname Bodden. It seems likely that an original pair of Caymanian settlers may have been from these families, and that they first arrived in the late 1650s or 1660s, not as deserters or refugees but (as Glover himself stated) as "soldiers from the disbanded army of Cromwell" who came "for the purpose of catching turtle". We can speculate further that they and their families spent whole years, or several years at a time, on Grand Cayman, alternating between there and Jamaica until, in the second or third generation, they established permanent residence in Grand Cayman. It is probable, then, that the first resident Caymanian Bodden of whom we have notice was the grandson of the original Bodden to visit Cayman. The same may be true, though it can be said with less certainty, of the first resident Watler.[4]

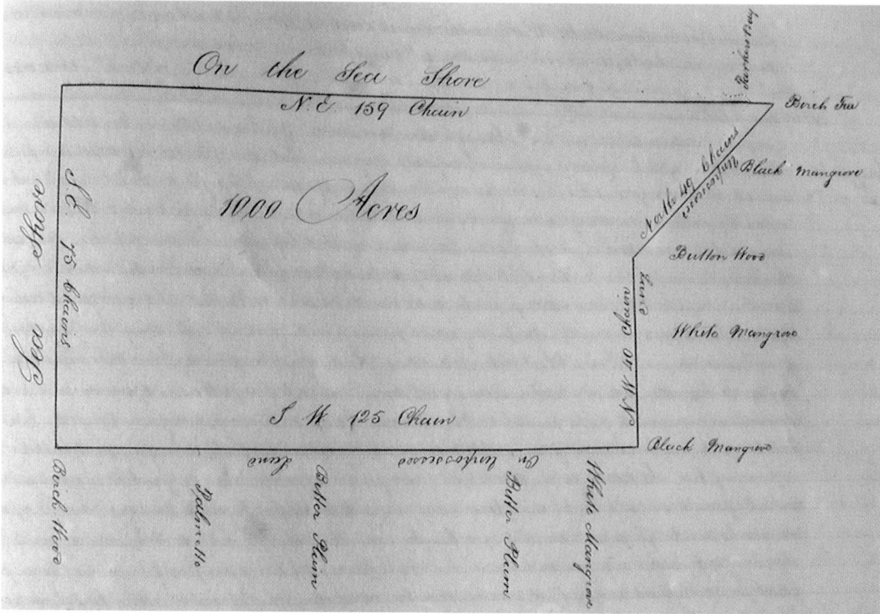

Land grant made to Samuel Spofforth in 1741.

The first documentary evidence of the early settlement of Grand Cayman consists of five large grants of land recorded by the Jamaican authorities in 1735 and 1741–2. The deeds, or "patents", for these grants were drawn up in the standard form prescribed in Jamaican laws for the allocation of all land in the colony. They are valuable for determining what land was first patented, and where logging and settlement began.

The first Cayman Island grant, recorded in 1735, may have reflected a desire by the Jamaican authorities to make land grants in undeveloped areas. This

Aerial view of northern West Bay (1999), which includes the land granted to Samuel Spofforth.

desire may have been made more urgent by the war with the Maroons (1730–39), who, it was feared, had a line of communication with potential allies in Cuba. The four land grants of 1741–2 were probably the result of a subtly different motivation. The ending of the Maroon threat signaled the beginning of a new phase of colonial expansion that spilled over into the Cayman Islands. Meanwhile, the outbreak of England's war with Spain and France (1739–48) increased the strategic importance of the islands.[5]

The 1741–2 patents included two significant conditions absent from the patent of 1735. People found to be already established in the granted lands were to be allowed to keep them, as long as they registered their claim within two years, and all grantees were to bring ten white servants into their plantation, regardless of how many slaves they owned.[6] These provisions seem to support other evidence that there was considerable informal settlement of Grand Cayman between 1735 and 1741, or even earlier. They also suggest how later smallholdings might have developed when enterprises failed or when white servants had completed their terms of service.

The 1735 patent and its accompanying plat or map are detailed and revealing.[7] The patent was enrolled at Spanish Town on 28 February 1735 for a huge grant of three thousand acres of land at Grand Cayman, made to three persons: Daniel Campbell, John Middleton, and Mary Campbell. Daniel and John were presumably partners, and Mary was probably Daniel's widowed mother rather than his wife, since at that time a wife could not hold property separately from her husband. It appears that all three lived together in Grand Cayman.

The Campbells and Middleton seem to have owned the entire stretch of land on the North Sound between what is now Red Bay Estates and the government's sewage plant and landfill, extending to North Sound Way, enclosing the entire industrial park and airport, and including on the south all the built-up areas along Crewe Road between Half Way Pond and Tropical Gardens.

In the original patent, the Campbell-Middleton holding was described as "A certain parcel of land containing by estimation Three thousand Acres more or less situate and being at the Grand Camanas being part of the Territories in America belonging to and depending on this our Island." The boundaries of the land are described, in the dense, unpunctuated language of such documents, as follows: "North upon the Sea and the Grand Sound East on the path leading from the Water Key to the South Settlements at the Spitt west Southerly on the Hog Styes and West on wast lands the west of Abrahams Plantain Walk so called and South on wast lands as by the Platt hereunto annexed".

The land was apparently not properly surveyed, and the accompanying plat or sketch was provided by the patentees, perhaps from memory. It shows a

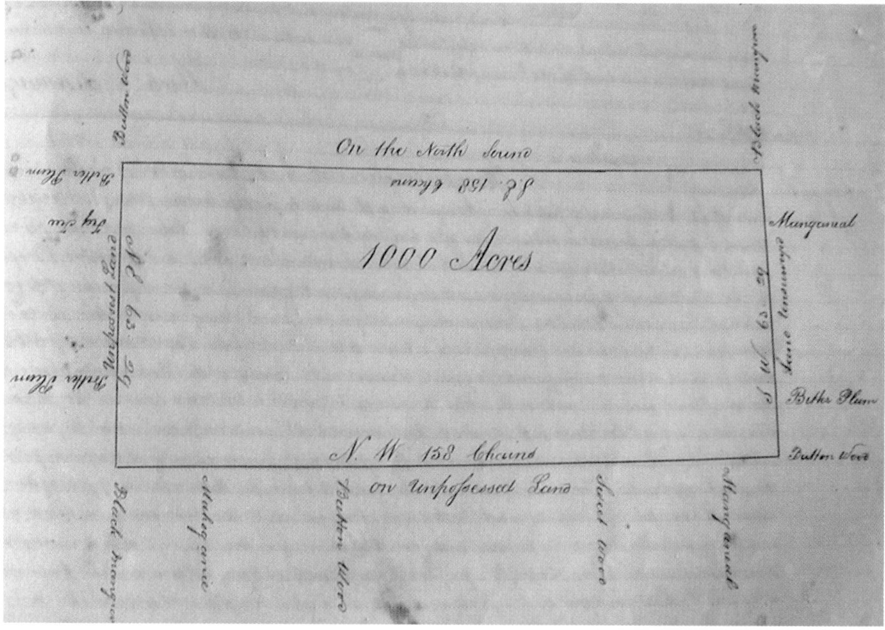

Land grant made to Murray Crymble in 1741.

diamond-shaped property enclosed within a dotted line. It is bounded on the north by the coastline of the North Sound, on the east by "The path over the Land to Northside", on the south by a stretch of "Open Ground" leading to the "South West Sound", and on the southwest by a large enclosed area labelled "Hogsties". "The ould Plantin Walk" is on the western half of the property, with a blank area beyond – presumably the "wast lands" noted in the plat.

Aerial view of land between George Town and West Bay (1999), which includes the land granted to Murray Crymble.

About a fifth of the land is still wooded (marked: "hear is Timber"), but at the centre of the property is a small sketched grid suggesting cultivation. Next to this is written the legend "The House of Cample & Middleton". Two paths cross the property: one from the house southwest towards the Hogsties, the other due south from "My Barkadier" to South West Sound, with a branch leading east towards a path that crosses the island.

The Campbell-Middleton land grant provides hints of other early settlements on Grand Cayman. The patent specifically mentioned "the South Settlements at the Spitt" at the southern end of the cross-island path. This was probably the tip of Prospect Point where recent building excavations have uncovered some of the oldest domestic artefacts found on Grand Cayman.[8] Prospect Point would have had advantages as an early maritime settlement. Protected from the sea by the reef, turtlers could have safely anchored their shallow-draft sloops and crawled their catch along its curving shore, known today as Crawl Bay.

The land grant patents and plats of 1741–2 are somewhat less revealing. But they show how the patentees attempted to select the best available land in Grand Cayman.[9] Three of the four seem to be one batch, authorised by Governor Edward Trelawny on the same day (20 August 1741). Officially surveyed by the same surveyor, Richard Jennings, between 20 and 31 October, the patents were all signed, sealed, and enrolled within the next five weeks. Two of the patentees, Murray Crymble and Samuel Spofforth, were wealthy absentee merchants who may have been more or less speculating in Caymanian land. The third, William Foster, a Kingston merchant like Crymble, is known to have been directly involved in the Cayman Islands. He may well have been the key figure in all three transactions, as well as the recipient of the most valuable stretch of land.

The clearest grant is the one made to Samuel Spofforth. Spofforth was a prominent Bermudian shipowner with good mercantile connections in Jamaica. He was mainly engaged in the trade of logwood from the Central American coast, but he also obtained mahogany from the Cayman Islands. He was granted a thousand acres at West Bay, extending from what is now the West Bay boat launch around North West Point as far as Spanish Bay Reef. Boatswain's Bay was eventually to develop in this area, but it was uninhabited in 1741.[10]

The thousand-acre plot patented to the prominent Jamaican merchant Murray Crymble was depicted as a simple rectangle, roughly two miles wide by eight-tenths of a mile long. The alignment of the plat (almost north to south, with the North Sound on its eastern side) shows it was on the neck of land between George Town and West Bay, north of the Campbell-Middleton grant, and behind Seven Mile Beach. Murray Crymble was an extremely wealthy man, listing in his will in 1746 trade goods, slaves, and outstanding debts owed

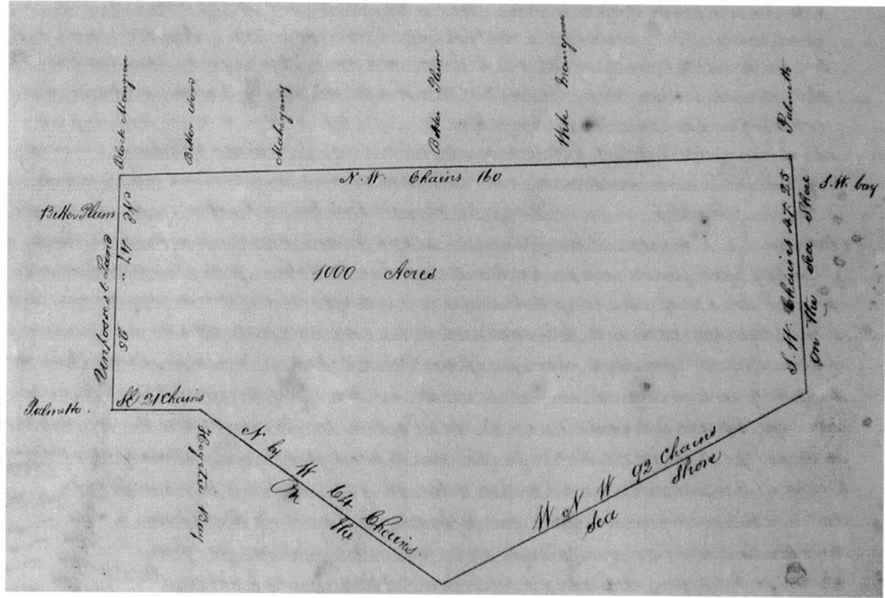

Land grant made to William Foster in 1741.

to him worth £52,619. He seems to have had mercantile dealings with Central America, including Roatán. But there is no evidence that he did anything to develop his Caymanian land, which today is some of the most valuable real estate in Cayman.[11]

Of the 1741 grantees, William Foster had the closest known connection to the Cayman Islands. His land grant appears to cover the entire area from the present centre of George Town south to Pull-and-Be-Damned Point off South Sound. Because of its location, William Foster's land might have been

Aerial view of George Town–South Sound (1999), which includes the land granted to William Foster.

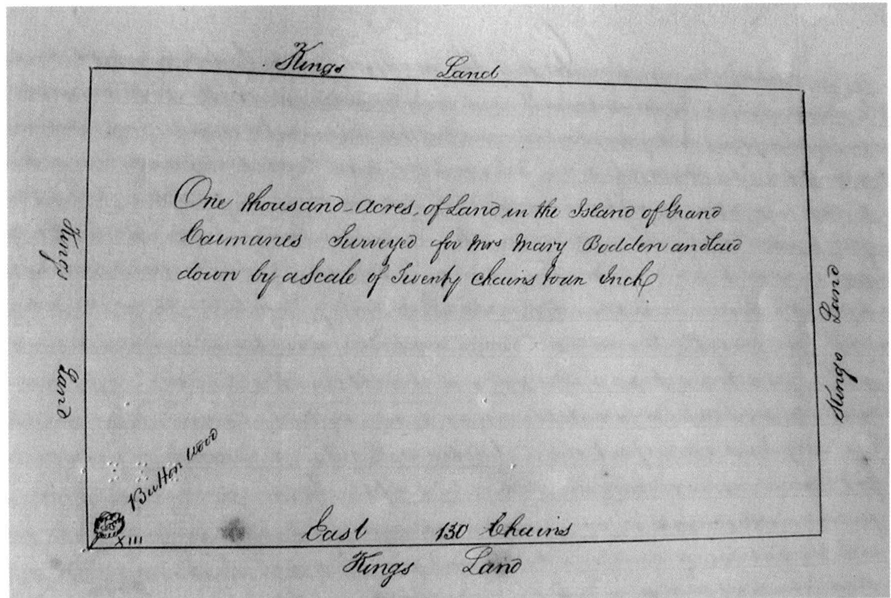

Land grant made to Mary Bodden in 1742.

more subject than the other 1641–2 grants to the limiting codicil included in each of them. This codicil stipulated that those who could prove, with two witnesses before a Magistrate, that they had occupied, planted, or felled trees within the granted land, could retain possession of that land, with thirty acres of adjacent woodland, provided that they took out a patent within two years.

As we shall see, William Foster was well acquainted with this part of Grand Cayman during the 1730s. But there is no evidence that he settled there

Aerial view of Newlands (1999), which includes the land granted to Mary Bodden.

or even stayed long. For that matter, there is no record of Fosters in Grand Cayman in the later eighteenth century, and there were no Fosters listed on Corbet's census of Grand Cayman in 1802. The Foster clan, which certainly existed in Cayman Brac from 1833 and later branched back to Grand Cayman, probably had connections in Jamaica as well as Grand Cayman. William Foster, the 1741 patentee, seems to have been one of several people involved in the Cayman Islands in the early days who had a more secure base in Jamaica. Almost certainly he was the same William Foster, described as a merchant of Kingston, Jamaica, whose inventory in 1756 was assessed at more than £65,000.[12]

The last of the eighteenth-century patentees, Mary Bodden, was the one with the strongest claim to a permanent Cayman Islands connection. Exactly how she fitted into the Bodden clan, however, and precisely where her grant (recorded on 15 January 1742) of a thousand acres was located remain uncertain. The plat on her patent shows a simple rectangle 1.6 miles long by a mile wide, aligned east and west, surrounded on all four sides by unpatented "King's land". According to the affidavit, the surveyor was a Thomas Newland. For this reason, and because her grant did not include land next to the coast, it is thought to have been in the area today called Newlands.[13]

THE BATTERSBY-FOSTER CASE

William Foster featured in a 1739 Jamaican court case that provides a clear picture of the early settlement of Grand Cayman. Brought against Foster by a fellow Jamaican, Benjamin Battersby, the case concerned the cutting, shipping, and sale of mahogany. The importance of mahogany was soaring at the time, as the British and European furniture industry developed. For a while mahogany surpassed turtle as Grand Cayman's most valuable product.[14]

The case was brought in the Jamaican Chancery Court at Spanish Town because "the Grand Caymans" was considered "a place within the jurisdiction of this court". The bill of indictment made by Battersby was based on a written agreement allegedly made on 11 December 1734 between Battersby and Foster, on one side, and "John Bodden of Grand Caymans" on the other. The purpose of the agreement was to "send or cause to be sent under the care of the said John Bodden eight negro men slaves to be marked on the left shoulder F:B:, the property of the said William Foster to the Grand Caymans in order to cut mahogany plank and to be under the immediate direction of the said John Bodden". Bodden was to receive either a quarter of the cut wood or a quarter of the proceeds of its sale. He agreed to set the Negroes to felling and cutting the mahogany and not to employ them otherwise "than for the equal benefit and advantage" of Foster and Battersby.

According to Battersby's account, John Bodden went to Grand Cayman in January 1735 with the eight slaves, "furnished and supplied . . . with all suitable necessaries and provisions for the said undertaking, to the amount of five hundred pounds and upwards". On arrival, he "applied to John Middleton and others who were persons residing and living upon the aforesaid Grand Caymanas for their advice in the choice of a place the most fit and convenient to employ the said slaves for the purpose aforesaid . . . according to the custom and usage of the residents there". Middleton recommended a wooded location just to the west of his own land – which he and the Campbells were in the process of patenting – on the very tract that Foster was to patent for himself in 1741. Here the slaves were put to work. They felled mahogany trees, cut them into planks, made a provision ground, and erected houses "on some part of the land at the equal and joint charge, cost and expense" to Battersby and Foster of another £500. This settlement and saw-yard was probably close to what is now the present Smith Road in George Town.

In November 1736, William Foster was said to have gone in person "at very great charge and expense" to Grand Cayman to check up on the joint operation and to see whether the enterprise could be expanded. Foster found the original area more or less worked out. John Bodden had made an agreement to cut timber on John Middleton's land on the North Sound "as far as a fixed line to the eastwards". Here the slaves were busy felling and sawing mahogany at a place that the locals already called Bodden's Works. William Foster prospected other likely areas and found one "at the South Side of the said place" – probably on the shore of Crawl Bay in the South Sound. John Bodden looked at and approved this site, particularly since the timber "could very conveniently be brought to the waterside".

William Foster then returned to Jamaica with a sketch map of the timbered areas around Bodden's Works and the South Side. He and Benjamin Battersby arranged to send twenty more slaves to Grand Cayman, along with a skilled sawyer called William Proser. Proser's job was "to assist and direct and instruct the said Slaves in the felling, sawing and squareing the said timber". Foster and Battersby also agreed to charter a ship in England to initiate a direct trade in mahogany between Grand Cayman and the mother country, in addition to trading through Jamaica.

At this point in the bill of indictment, Battersby provided a valuable description of how land was acquired in Grand Cayman at that time:

> . . . when ever a person intending to settle there with a Gang of Negroes to Cutt Mahogany the person so intending to Settle Chooses out a run of Land in which he puts his Slaves – and from thence the said Land belongs to and is deemed to be the property of the owner of the Slaves putt and Employed thereupon and the same is look't upon and Esteemed as the Sole and absolute property of the owner

> of such slaves and it is the Constant Agreement amongst all those who Live on the said place not to Encroach or run in upon Each others run nor to remove or put out any persons Slaves who have so settled and the person so offending is look't and deemed upon as a great Trespasser and is made Liable to make satisfaction to the other person and the aforesaid usage and Custom is well known and Observed by all who live at the Grand Caymanas aforesaid and is particularly well known to the said Wm. Foster tho he now denies that there is any such usage or Custom.

For a time, the partnership went very well. Up to October 1736, while Battersby had charge of the accounts, he reckoned that shipments of mahogany worth £3,000 were made by John Bodden and that "great profits and gains were made thereby". Relations then soured, apparently over an alleged debt of £1,000 owed to Foster by Battersby. According to Battersby, Foster took over the accounts and kept them secret, misappropriating shipments of both timber and supplies. Sometime in 1737, he allegedly entered into a clandestine new partnership with John Bodden, William Proser, and certain other local inhabitants. From that time on, the wood was shipped and sold for the sole benefit of the new partners, probably beginning with a shipment sent to Jamaica in the *Ann & Elizabeth* in May 1738.

Battersby's chief concerns were to establish his rights to the slaves, equipment, and land that he had formerly shared, to find out what had happened to them, and to recover his share of the timber cut in partnership with Foster. He asserted that the original slaves – referred to as "the old gang" – had first been turned out from the "plantation and land" they had settled and forbidden to cut any more timber. They had then been privately employed by Bodden and Proser on land and with equipment properly belonging in part to Battersby. Finally, they had been sold by Bodden – all this with the connivance of William Foster. Battersby also charged that the new partners had contravened both slave regulations and the rules governing the disposal of salvaged goods. He claimed that Foster and Proser had allowed the slaves to cut timber on their own account on Saturday afternoons, and that with the help of the slaves they had misappropriated three thousand pounds of cocoa from a Spanish wreck.

Battersby believed that he had been deprived of what he regarded as his share of the slaves, equipment, supplies, and timber – not to mention a proportion of the Spanish wreck goods. In addition, he had missed the chance to patent the land – as William Foster was to do for himself in 1741. Unfortunately the outcome of the case is not known, but it seems that Foster was the winner and Battersby the loser.[15] Besides providing an important description of what life was like on the Caymanian frontier in the 1730s, the case shows how Cayman's earliest settlers depended on Jamaica for the legal essentials necessary to civilised society.

Sketch of Port Royal, ca. 1830.

MARRIAGE RITES

Throughout the eighteenth century, those Caymanians who wished to have their marriages and baptisms formally endorsed had to go to Jamaica to have them solemnized. Twenty-eight marriages and some baptisms of Caymanians between 1733 and 1808 have so far been traced in the surviving parochial registers of Kingston, Black River, Savanna-la-Mar, Lucea, and Montego Bay. These are an invaluable resource for family historians. They also illustrate the pattern of intermarriage that was inevitable in such a small and isolated community, as well as hinting at the gradual development of a local ruling class.[16]

The first Caymanian marriage recorded in Jamaica was probably that of Isac and Sarah Bass, both "of the Grand Comanis", who were wed on 29 October 1732, probably in Port Royal parish church. Probably in the same parish three years later, on 9 November 1735, Isaac Bawden, mariner, and Sarah Lamar, widow, "both of Caymanas", were married. Who Sarah Lamar and her former husband were is unknown, but Isaac Bawden [or Bodden] was almost certainly the "Old Isaac" living at East End whom George Gauld met as a man "upwards of 70 years of age" in 1773 and described as "a native of the Island" and a grandson of the first Bodden.[17]

On the same day as Isaac and Sarah Bodden's church marriage, the baptism of two of their sons was recorded in a separate entry in the register. These were "Benjamin Lock Bawden son of Isaac Bawden & Sarah Lamar, born 17th day of December 1730" and "William Price Bawden, Son of Isaac Bawden & Sarah Lamar born 11th day of Novr. 1732". The second son may have been the William Bodden Sr. who was to be a Caymanian Chief

18 Francis Scrivan, bricklayer & Hannah Fountain widow of this Parish
Henry Potter, Carpenter, & Mary Singer widow both of this Parish
Novm 9 Isaac Bawden mariner & Sarah Lamar, widow, both of Caymanas
30 Robert Shergell, gentleman, & Rachel Combabatch widow both of this Parish
Thomas Smith Schoolmaster & Mary Fleming widow, both of this Parish

One of the earliest known marriages of Cayman settlers, Isaac Bawden and Sarah Lamar, recorded in 1735.

ht 21 Joseph Barton the Son of Joseph & Sarah Barton born 30th August last
do 4 John Michael, was born 27th August 1726 & baptized this day.
ov 9 Benjn. Lock Bawden son of Isaac Bawden & Sarah Lamar, born 17th day of December 1730
William Price Bawden, Son of Isaac Bawden & Sarah Lamar born 11th day of Novr 1732
True Copy Thomas Alves Rector

Two of the earliest known baptisms of Cayman settlers, Benjamin and William Bawden, recorded in 1735.

Magistrate until 1789 and the father of "Governor Bodden", his namesake who served as Chief Magistrate until 1823.[18]

A generation after these first marriages, two more unions were recorded, though the exact parish is not known. They seem to have been between two brothers and two sisters and were performed on the same day, 1 June 1765, between Waide Walter [sic], mariner, and Rachel Bawden, spinster, and between Stephen Walter, mariner, and Sarah Bawden, spinster. The first of these men was probably the Waide Watler Sr. who was a major slaveholder at Bodden Town in 1802.[19]

At Savanna-la-Mar, the site of the parish church of Westmoreland, at least eleven Caymanian marriages took place between 1762 and 1772. Eight of the twenty-two people involved were Boddens and six were Tathams; the remaining eight had seven different surnames. The pattern of close family alliances is shown by the first three entries. On a single day, 13 February 1762, James Tatham was married to Mary Boden and Benjamin Tatham to Rebecca Boden (all said to be "of the Island Camanoes"), and Mary, "daughter of James Tatham & Mary his Wife born in the Island of Camanoes Jany. 30th 1761", was baptised. Less than a year later, on 3 March 1763, John Tatham married another Rebecca Boden in the same church. Both James and John Tatham (spelled Tatum by then) were prominent slaveholders at Bodden Town in 1802, as were several others who were married at Savanna-la-Mar between 1762 and 1772.[20]

Several Boddens and Watlers from the Cayman Islands were married in the Hanover parish church at Lucea between 1776 and 1784. After that, the preferred location for Caymanian marriages seems to have been Montego Bay,

DEATHS.

March 29. AT Norfolk in Virginia, Capt. Jas. Murray, of the late Queen's American Rangers.

April 23. At the Grand Camaynas, aged 67, Wm. Bodden, esq. chief magiſtrate of that iſland.

The first known death notice of a Cayman settler, published in the Gentleman's Magazine, *London, 1789.*

Sketch of Savanna-la-Mar, ca. 1830.

by then the most important port in western Jamaica. Among these was William Bodden, widower, married to the former Mary Eden, widow, on 18 May 1788. This was probably "Governor" Bodden Jr., who in 1802 owned fifty-one slaves at Bodden Town. Another was Waide Watler, bachelor, who married Elizabeth Hughes, spinster, on 16 December 1791. He was almost certainly the Waide Watler Jr. of Prospect, who with his father, Waide Walter [Watler] Sr., owned almost as many slaves in 1802 as "Governor" Bodden.[21]

All in all, of those fifty-six or so Caymanians who we know were married in Jamaica between 1733 and 1808, no fewer than eighteen were Boddens (with various spellings), seven were Tathams (Tatums or Tatoms), seven were Watlers (including the two Walters), three were Coniors, two were Ebankses, and two were Edens. Many of these families were among the most substantial landowners and slaveholders listed in Corbet's 1802 census.

WAR AND PEACE

The development of the Cayman Islands was affected by the alternating pattern of peace and war that characterised the history of the Caribbean during what is sometimes called "the long eighteenth century" (1689–1815). Grand Cayman was being settled during a period that saw Britain frequently engaged in wars – nearly always with France, sometimes with Spain, and twice with her own former colonies on the mainland of North America.[22]

Except during the last French wars (1793–1815), trade slowed almost to a standstill during wartime, leaving the Cayman Islands more isolated than ever. Unlike other British colonies, Cayman did not develop as a base for privateering with its own Vice Admiralty Court to adjudicate prizes. Jamaica was preoccupied with the threat to its own safety from the French and Spanish colonies and from prowling enemy fleets. Roaming the Caribbean in wartime was dangerous for Caymanian vessels, but the islands themselves were generally safe from attack. They were too poor to constitute a worthwhile prize, and the nearby waters had since the 1740s been constantly patrolled by

British naval vessels looking to intercept enemy traders.[23] Only during the Maritime War (1778–83) – when Britain was fighting France, Spain, and Holland as well as her own rebellious colonies – was the balance of naval power seriously tilted against the British. It was during this time, in fact, that Grand Cayman suffered its only serious assaults. Even then, the Grand Cayman settlements survived, along with Jamaica, when Admiral Rodney's victory at the Battle of the Saintes in April 1782 restored naval control of the Caribbean to Britain.[24]

Grand Cayman experienced progress during intervals of peace. Besides turtling, Caymanians were involved in the trade in mahogany, logwood, and fustic between Jamaica, Central America, and Grand Cayman. Some of this trade was in ships that they owned themselves. This traffic reflected the settled state of Belize, and the extension of British protection to the Miskito Coast.[25] The Spanish conceded the right to cut mahogany and logwood on the Miskito Coast by the treaties of 1713, 1748, and 1763, but not the right to settle permanently. However, by the 1770s it was reckoned that there were

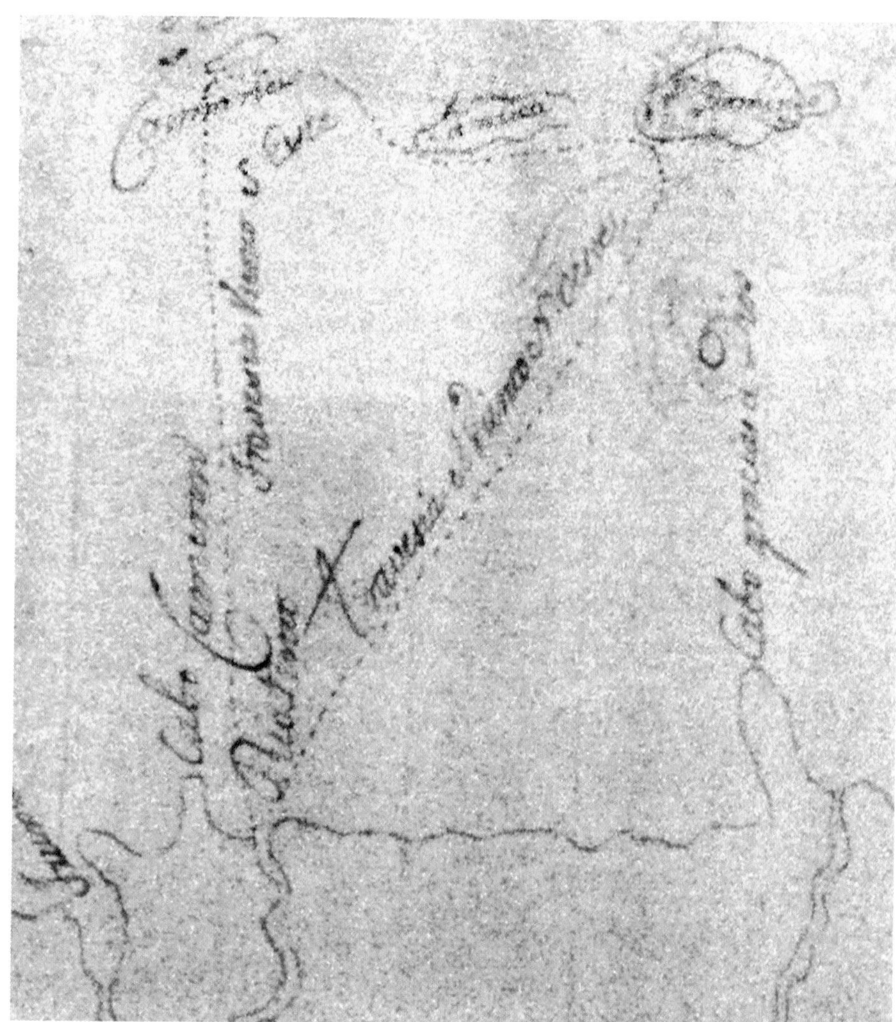

Sketch-map by Robert Hodgson, 1783, suggesting a trade route between Jamaica, Grand Cayman, and Central America.

at least three thousand British logcutters, traders, and planters with their slaves established on the Miskito Coast alone.

While this area was considered more important than Cayman, the role of the Cayman Islands is suggested by a fascinating memorandum and sketch-map sent to the Spanish authorities in 1783 by the turncoat Robert Hodgson Jr. Hodgson had succeeded his father as British Superintendent of the Miskito Coast, and he performed the same role for Spain after his capture during the Maritime War. His memo recommended the continuation of reciprocal trade between British and Spanish colonies and argued that Black River should become a free port for the coast of Central America.[26]

Hodgson's accompanying sketch-map shows a triangular trade route between Jamaica, Cayman, and Black River. Such a route would have allowed Central American produce sent via Cayman to enter Jamaica ostensibly from a British colonial source, and British goods intended for Spanish Central America to be cleared from Jamaica to a British destination where they would not be subject to customs inspection. This arrangement circumvented both the British navigation laws prohibiting export to foreign colonies and the Spanish laws forbidding direct trade with the British.

The extent to which this arrangement actually took effect or brought much prosperity either to the Cayman Islands or to the British settlers in Central America is not clear. In any case, it was fairly short-lived. During the Maritime War against Spain (1778–83), Governor Dalling of Jamaica and others had a far more grandiose plan: the takeover, with the help of their Miskito and Sambo Indian allies, of the entire territory of Nicaragua from the Caribbean to the Pacific. The catastrophic failure of this enterprise led to Britain's surrender of its settlements on the Miskito Coast in the Treaty of Versailles in 1783. The majority of British settlers were shipped off in 1786–7. Most went to Belize, Jamaica, and various offshore islands. But about three hundred, including slaves, settled in Grand Cayman.[27]

A decade of peace and the influx of new settlers facilitated change, but it was driven by a surge in cotton production. Grand Cayman's dwindling stands of mahogany were increasingly less attractive commercially. Raw-cotton prices, however, were soaring in response to the rapid expansion of the textile industry and the exclusion of the newly independent Americans from British trade. At the same time, the British trade in slaves was reaching its peak. In these circumstances, the more affluent and enterprising Caymanians, along with the settlers evicted from Central America in 1787, sought to establish new cotton plantations. This led to a brief economic upswing that was at its peak when Edward Corbet made his report on Cayman in 1802.

Whatever records were kept by eighteenth-century Caymanians appear to have been lost. But their economic history – and, therefore, clues to social

A page from the Shipping Registers for Jamaica, showing the export of "81 pieces of mahogany" from "Caymanoes" on the sloop Experiment, *owned by Samuel Spofforth, in December 1744.*

conditions in Cayman – can be traced in the detailed Jamaican shipping registers that have survived. In addition, Royal Navy ships frequently passed and sometimes stopped at the Cayman Islands. Their "Remark Books" provide rich information about the evolving society in Grand Cayman. Probably the most valuable early account is the one provided by the naval hydrographer George Gauld, who made the first accurate map of Grand Cayman and recorded a detailed description of it in 1773.[28]

In the shipping registers, the first vessel recorded as trading between Jamaica and the Cayman Islands was a 25-ton Bermuda sloop named the *Experiment.* It carried two guns and a crew of six, and was owned by the Bermudian merchant Samuel Spofforth. It left Kingston for the "Camanoes" in ballast on 21 September 1744 and returned twelve weeks later with eighty-one "pieces" of mahogany – presumably cut from Spofforth's land at West Bay. Another vessel engaged in this trade, the 30-ton sloop *Sarah*, is recorded as making a similar trip in 1745.[29]

None of the surviving shipping records for the later 1740s and early 1750s mentions Grand Cayman. But at the end of the Seven Years' War in 1763, there was a flurry of two-way trade between Grand Cayman and Jamaica. At the end of February 1764, a convoy of mahogany carriers came into Kingston from "Grand Caymanoes". They included the *Success* and the 30-

ton sloop *Eagle*, carrying eighty tons of timber between them. These two ships sailed under the protection of a 40-ton sloop also called *Eagle*, carrying another thirty tons of mahogany. In the next three months all three vessels were recorded as leaving Kingston for Grand Cayman with "dry goods".[30]

A mortar from the 1700s.

The first recorded Caymanian captain was William Bodden, in charge of the 10-ton schooner *Susanna*, owned by Robert Mitchell & Co. and probably built in Jamaica, which left Savanna-la-Mar for Grand Cayman in ballast on 28 December 1765. It has been speculated that this was the very voyage on which William Bodden carried his recently married son-in-law William Eden – the builder of "Pedro Castle" – to settle in Grand Cayman.[31]

THE CAYMANIANS OF THE EIGHTEENTH CENTURY

The Royal Navy officers whose vessels stopped at the Cayman Islands were concerned with finding and describing safe anchorages and obtaining water, wood, and food. Their Remark Books, however, provide valuable information about the inhabitants and their way of life and allow us to form an impression of how conditions in Cayman slowly changed. Two of the earliest Remark Book entries, made by the masters of HMS *Ferret* and HMS *Active* in 1765, offer glimpses of the two principal settlements in Grand Cayman soon after the end of the Seven Years' War. "The Island Lay ENE and WSW about 8 Leagues, and about 3 Leagues Broad . . . all near full of Low Trees," wrote James Smith of the sloop *Ferret*. "About 2/3 of the Island from the Eastward is a Village of about 30 Houses and may be known by a Large Parcell of Cokenutt Trees" – the first description of what was soon to be known as Bodden Town. "If you are willing to call at ye Hoggstyes which is the west part of the island as you past the SW Point," wrote Robert Christian of the ship *Active* a few months later, "Hall [haul] close to the Island & as soon as you open the West part of ye Island you see the Houses, & Boats will come of[f] to you."[32]

"Wood in great plenty [and] water may be gott by Carrying your Casks about 2 Miles from the Road," added Christian, "where you sink Casks in the Sand full of holes, and keep [a] man there to Dip and fill your water cask as it flows into those Casks . . . it makes very tedious without you sink a numr. Of Casks." Salt provisions were not to be had, but there was plenty of fish and turtle. At the right seasons of the year there were "some few refreshments" to be had in the way of "Yames, Plantons, Lymes fowles & Hoggs." Christian conservatively reckoned that there were no more than twenty families – perhaps a hundred free people and between fifty and a hundred slaves – living on the island. They engaged in little trade. "Most of there Employment," he wrote, "is cutting of Mahogany, Fustick &c. which they send to Jamacia

Description of Grand Cayman from the Remark Book of HMS Alarm *in 1764.*

His Maj.s Ship Alarm

Of Wooding and Watering	Provisions and Refreshments	Fortifications & Landing Place	Further Remarks in regard to Trade Shipping &c.
	Turtle in abundance	no Fortifications	Here is 16 Familys in different Parts that Subsists in Fishing & Cutting Mahogany. Small Vessels from Jamaica brings them necessarys & Carry off their Produce, they have no Military or Civil officer among them nor does there appear to have any occasion for any, all living at Peace with one another.

[*sic*]. There is 3 or 4 small scooners which belong to the Island which Employment is Turtelling & Sometimes to carry Mahogany up to Jamacia."[33]

Twenty-two years later, in August 1787, Captain John Hull of HMS *Camilla* provided a somewhat different view of Grand Cayman. He praised North Sound as a harbour sheltered from all winds and storms. "Off the entrance is a Bar with only Nine feet Water on it," he reported, "but the Turtlers having no larger Vessels than Turtlers, this place answers every purpose of the deepest Harbour, for heaving down, refitting &c. and during the Hurricane Months all their Craft are laid up there." A majority of the male inhabitants were turtlers or fishermen, all of them expert pilots for the island. Turtling was still the main industry. Apart from those shipped to Jamaica in the local "shallops", between 1,200 and 1,400 turtles were sold to "homeward bound Jamaica Ships as they pass to go through the Gulf of Florida".

Many turtles were still caught in the Cayman Islands, but an even greater number "in the Keys & Shoals on the South side of Cuba". Apparently Caymanian turtlers did not yet have to venture as far as the Miskito Coast for their catch, and direct Caymanian involvement in the logwood and mahogany trade there seems to have ended. The most recent traffic, in fact, had been in the opposite direction. Captain Hull noted: "About 300 people are lately on this Island from the Mosquito Shore, and adjacent Islands, who are making large Plantations for Cotton."[34]

While the shipping registers are unfortunately incomplete, there is plentiful evidence from the 1780s of a flourishing two-way traffic with Jamaican ports, including increasing export of cotton and import of slaves to work the cotton fields. Some of the ships cleared from Jamaica ostensibly for Grand Cayman may have been clandestinely destined for some foreign port. For example, the brig *Jenny*, cleared from Kingston for Grand Cayman in July 1784 with "35 pipes, 28 hogsheads, 382 casks" of madeira wine, was probably bound for Mexico, Louisiana, or the United States.[35] Some ships arriving in Jamaica from Grand Cayman may also have come indirectly from Central America, stopping at Grand Cayman en route.

The outgoing traffic in slaves and the incoming traffic in cotton will be examined in more detail in the next chapter, when we consider the short-lived Caymanian slave plantation economy. But the majority of ships cleared from Jamaica for Grand Cayman carried mainly provisions, so the registers give us an idea of Caymanian needs and lifestyle in the later 1780s. One example was the 25-ton schooner *Mary*, which cleared Kingston in August 1787 carrying "1-1/2 trunks of Rice, 1 trunk dry goods, 17 Packs twine, 2 kegs nails, 1 barrel of tar, 8 firkins Butter". Another was the schooner *Rover*, which left Kingston in March 1788 with "15 casks of sugar, 11 casks of rum, 1 Marble Slab, 4 Negroes, 11 Barrels of provisions, 2 Boxes of dry goods plus Coffee".[36]

George Gauld, who spent ten days on and around the island while making his hydrographic survey in 1773, was able to add valuable details about Grand Cayman and its inhabitants, as well as some of their own oral history. Unusually for a surveyor, Gauld offered some comments about their way of life, apparently struck by this unique island community. "The inhabitants may truly be said to live in a state of nature," he wrote.

> Whatever differences arise among them are generally submitted to the arbitration of neighbours; but if the Parties do not choose to stand by the Award, as there is no legal method of compelling them, they finally determine the matter by coming to blows and the victor gains the cause.[37] Accident and necessity have contributed much to encrease the number of the inhabitants. When a vessel has the misfortune to be wrecked on this Island, some of the survivors generally choose to remain in a place where the necessaries of life are so easily acquired: besides several people from Jamaica and other places, who are involved in debt resort to this Asylum where it is no easy matter to find them out, and bring them to justice. These accidental visitors frequently enter into matrimonial engagements, and so become Settlers. The women are numerous and those who are natives of the Island have a modesty in their looks, and a decency in their behaviour, not always to be met with between the Tropicks. There are few or no families on the Island but what are connected with the Boddens, either by the male or female side. They are very desirous of having a Clergyman and a Surgeon to reside among them. Though they are, in general, poor, or rather content with what nature requires, yet Capt. Bodden himself, and a few others are people of considerable property. They have about half a dozen Sloops and Schooners belonging to the Island, which they employ in Turtling and trafficking to Jamaica.

Trade Shipping &c

The Inhabitants always raised a little Cotton, which was sent to Jamaica for Sale but Turtling is the chief employment of the Men: many are caught round their own Island, but many more on the Keys & Shoals on the South side of Cuba: they are supposed to sell annually from 12, to 1400 Turtle to the homeward bound Jamaica Ships, as they pass to go through the Gulf of Florida a number are also sent to Jamaica in their Turtling Shallops, which are all the Vessels they employ. About 300 people are lately settled on this Island from the Mosquito Shore, and adjacent Islands who are making large Plantations for Cotton.

Description of Grand Cayman from the Remark Book of HMS Camilla *in 1787.*

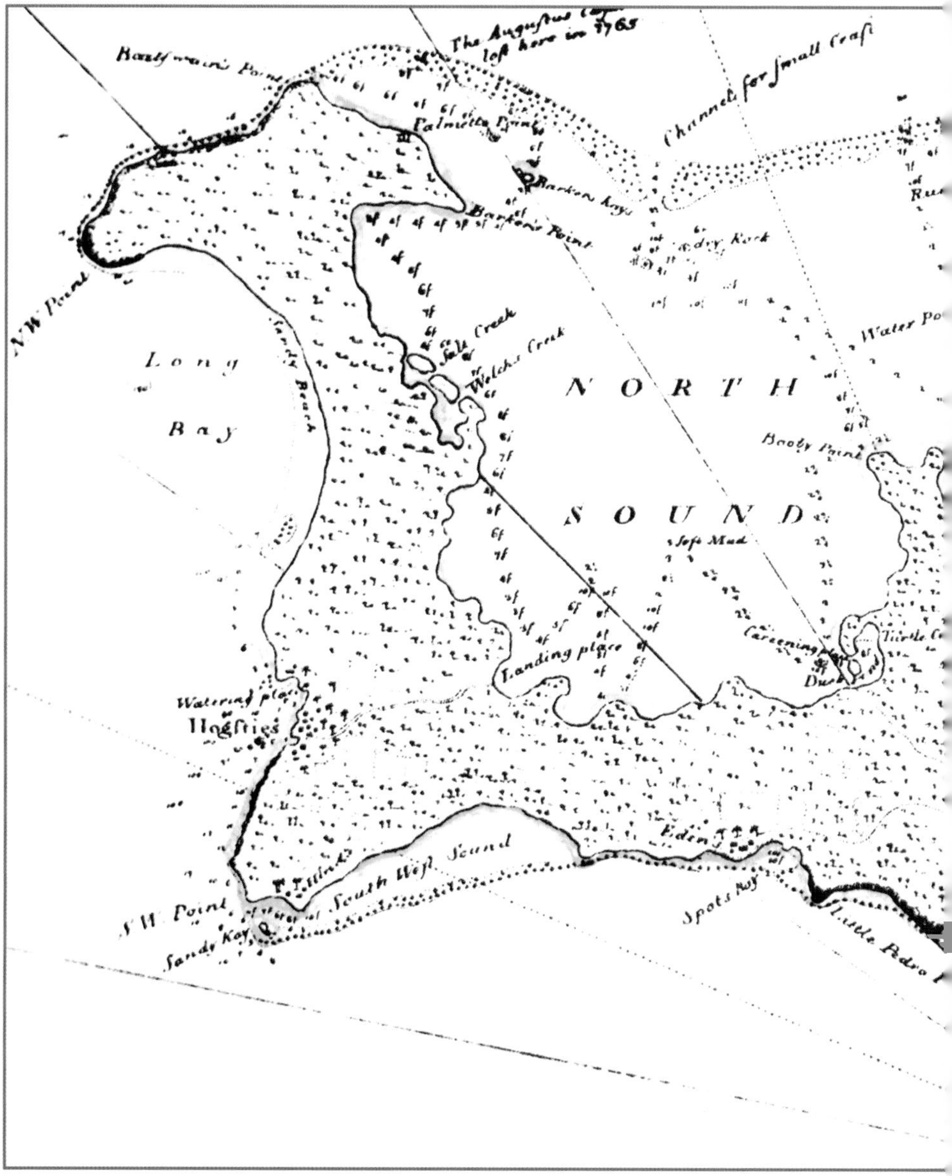

The first survey of Grand Cayman, made by George Gauld in 1773.

George Gauld recorded that "a great quantity" of cotton was grown for export along with turtles. He did not mention mahogany. Some sugar was produced for local consumption, but local resources of land, labour, and capital were insufficient to establish sugar plantations like those in Jamaica. The island did produce "Indian Corn, yams, sweet potatoes, pompions [pumpkins], plantains, melons, besides Limes, Oranges and most kind of the fruits and vegetables that are to be found in Jamaica". But though there were plenty of goats, there were "neither sheep nor black Cattle, and only two horses, which were lately brought there from Jamaica by accident".

Gauld also provided his own estimate of the population and where it was located, using as his unit the family, which would almost certainly have included black slaves as well as white or near-white kin. "Old Isaac Bodden,"

he wrote, "remembers when there were only 5 families; but at this time there are 21 at the South Side, which we have called Bodden Town, 13 at the West End commonly called the Hogsties, 3 at the East End, and 2 at Spot's Bay; in all 39 families, consisting of at least 200 white people, and above [the] same number of Negroes and Mulattoes."[38] Gauld's figures suggest that there were about 450 people living on Grand Cayman in 1773.

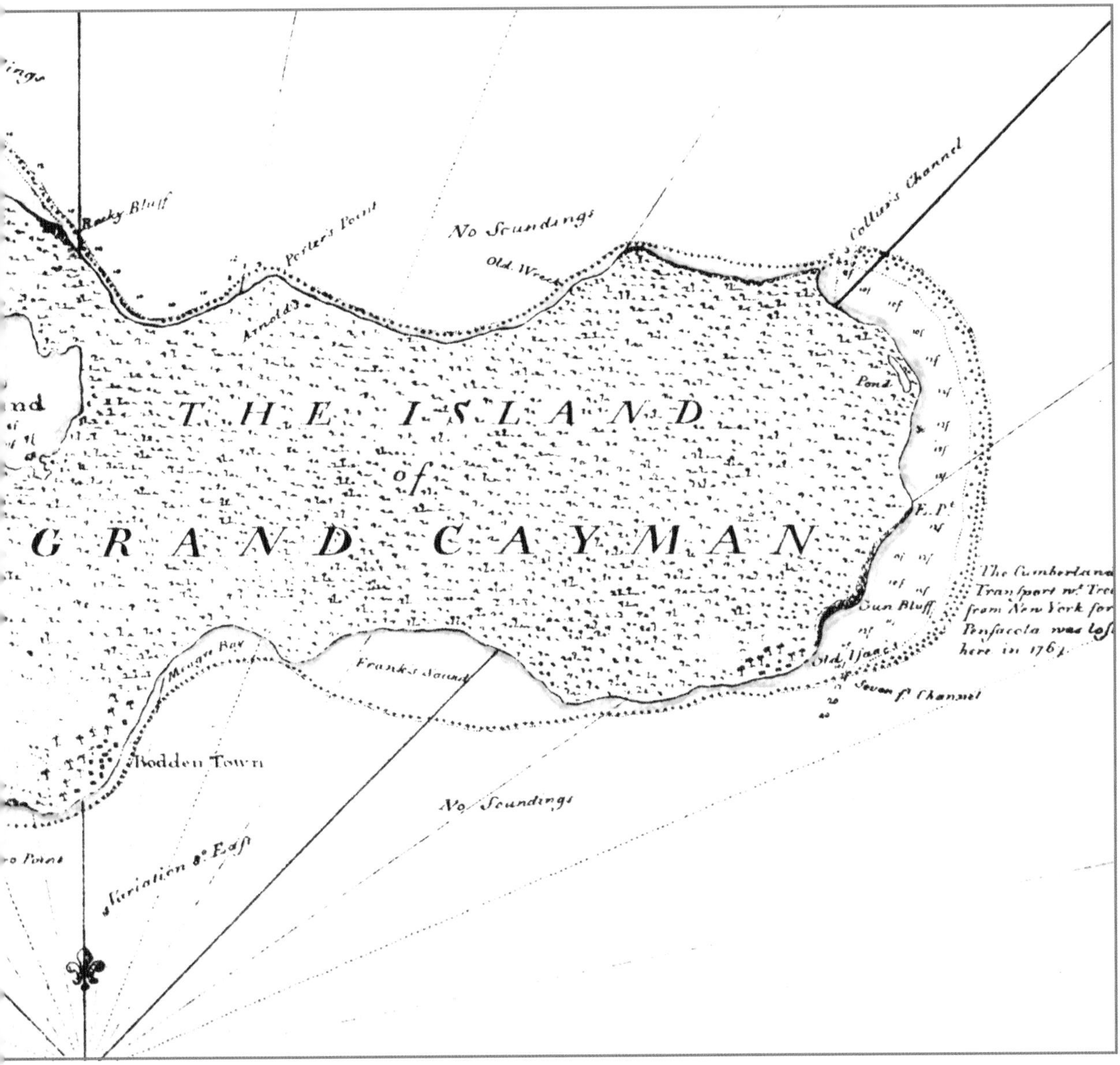

A generation later, at the time of Edward Corbet's more precise census in 1802, the population had doubled, totalling 933. Its distribution throughout the island, however, was similar. Bodden Town was still the largest settlement, with twenty-four white and eight free coloured families, totalling, with their slaves, 374 people. At "George Town formerly called the Hog Styes" were seventeen white and five free coloured families, making with their slaves 211

The first record of shipbuilding in the Cayman Islands: the Susan and Kitty, *built in 1783 and owned by William Bodden.*

people in all, including two free Negroes. Three white families lived at Spotts, with another eleven at nearby South West Sound, Prospect, and Little Pedro, totalling, with their slaves, 212 people. Since 1773, seven white families had settled at West Bay and three free coloured families at Boatswain's Bay, as well as three families of free Negroes, totalling 85 people in that district. At East End there were still only three families, one white and two free coloured, totalling twelve people including the slaves. The remaining two white and four free coloured families, totalling forty people including slaves, were settled at "Franks" Sound and North Side.[39]

SHIPWRECKS

By the end of the eighteenth century, turtling, logging, planting, and raising provisions for passing ships were the recognised and respectable occupations of the people of Grand Cayman. Less reputable, but almost equally important, was the pursuit called wrecking – that is, the salvage of vessels cast upon local and nearby Cuban reefs. Like the people of the Bahamas and the British Virgin Islands, Caymanians gained an undeserved notoriety for their avid pursuit of this chancy and dangerous trade.[40]

Most of the wrecked ships that the Caymanians combed came from Jamaica and other points to windward. As many Royal Navy captains noted, the islands were not precisely located on charts of the Caribbean for at least fifty years after George Gauld drew his accurate map of Grand Cayman.[41] Some writers pointed out that, for Caymanians, wrecking was an economic necessity and an almost providential opportunity. Local mariners were often prepared to risk their own lives not just to salvage ships, ships' stores, and cargoes, but to save the unfortunate people aboard shipwrecked vessels. Wrecks on the Cayman Islands were pretty well monitored from Jamaica and were subject to the strict salvage laws administered by the Vice Admiralty Court, as well as being policed by the Royal Navy ships on the Jamaican station.

A List of the Inhabitants of the Island of the Grand Cayman distinguishing their place of residence, number in each family and the slaves they possess &c.

White Families	Free people of Colour	Number in each family	Number of Slaves
At the East End			
John Thomas		3	
	Charles McLean	3	1
	Charles [illegible]	4	1
At North Side			
Stephen Bodden		10	3
	Jn Tatum Sen	4	1
	Jn Tatum Jun	8	1
At Bodden Town			
[illegible]		6	[illegible]

The first census of Grand Cayman, made by Edward Corbet in 1802.

In at least two cases, the wrecks were so large and the survivors so numerous that local resources were overwhelmed. In November 1767, the transport *Cumberland*, carrying 180 troops of the 31st Regiment from New York to reinforce the garrison of Pensacola in West Florida, was ripped open by Grand Cayman's East End reef. The encamped survivors almost starved before being saved by HMS *Adventure* three weeks later. Even more difficult problems were posed by the most momentous of all Caymanian maritime disasters, the Wreck of the Ten Sail, which occurred in the early hours of Saturday, 8 February 1794.[42]

The tragedy came at an especially bad time for the local inhabitants. The war against the revolutionary French had been under way for nearly a year, and Grand Cayman was still reeling from the devastating hurricane of October 1793.[43] The ten "sail" involved were the recently captured French frigate *l'Inconstante*, renamed HMS *Convert* and under the command of Captain John Lawford, and nine of the fifty-eight merchantmen that the *Convert* was convoying from Jamaica back to Great Britain. The story of their fate has been reconstructed from official correspondence, Jamaican newspapers, a remark-

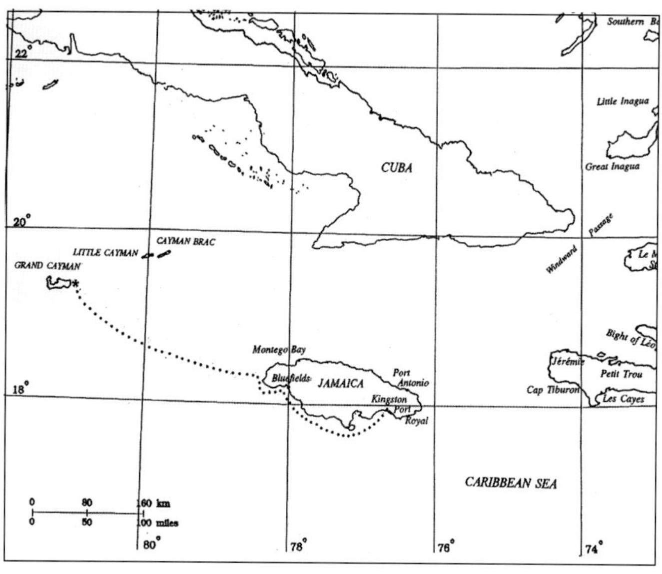

The route of the convoy under HMS Convert *from Jamaica to Grand Cayman, February 1794.*

able account by a surviving passenger, and the evidence brought forward in Captain Lawford's court martial.

As was typical of such a huge wartime convoy, Captain Lawford's charges were not easy to manage. After having some difficulty making up its complement of 220 men, HMS *Convert* left Port Royal on 28 January 1794 for Bluefields Bay, the usual rendezvous for ships from the southern parts of Jamaica. After a week, Captain Lawford led the thirty-two gathered merchantmen to Long Bay (Negril), where they joined twenty-six vessels from Jamaica's northern outports. This unwieldy fleet set out with a strong easterly breeze on Thursday, 6 February, expecting to pass well to the south of Grand Cayman within twenty-four hours. Despite some delays, Lawford still believed that he had passed Grand Cayman (which he thought was too far to the north to be visible) by nightfall on the following day. Before going to bed, he gave permission for a change of course several points to the north, to head directly for the western end of Cuba and the Florida Channel.

Around midnight, while most of the convoy were to the rear, or south, some six or seven merchantmen, against orders, moved ahead of the leading ship without being noticed by the watch on the *Convert*. At 3 a.m. a distress gun was heard. Captain Lawford was called on deck, and almost immediately a watchman aloft yelled "Breakers ahead. Close to us." This was the heavy sea breaking on the reef one mile off Gun Bay, on Grand Cayman's eastern end. Several merchantmen had already struck, but Captain Lawford, having given orders for the rest of the fleet to disperse, might have clawed the *Convert* clear had a panicky merchantman not twice fouled the frigate while on the opposite tack. In Lawford's own words,

> . . . (as the Breakers appeared in every direction and I could not tell from the Darkness of the Night to what extent they might run,) [I] deemed it most expedient to make the Signal for the Convoy to disperse and do the best for their own Safety that their own judgement could suggest, and as the Topsails were now sheeted home, the *Convert* would have certainly cleared the Breakers, if a Ship ahead had not unfortunately fallen on Board us, and before it was possible to extricate ourselves we got so near the Reefs, that all hopes of Clearing them vanished and she in a few moments struck, and very soon after Bilged.[44]

Admiral Sir John Lawford, K.C.B.

The morning revealed a horrific sight – a naval captain's worst nightmare. In Lawford's own words:

Aerial view of the East End coast (ca.1993), including the site of the Wreck of the Ten Sail.

> The dawning of the Day presented a most Melancholy scene, seven Ships and two Brigs on the same Reef with the *Convert*, a very heavy sea running and the Wind blowing directly on the Shore; from the bad appearance of the Weather the Merchant Ships would not venture near enough to us to give any effectual assistance, and the Ships on Shore could not assist each other; I immediately ordered out the Boats to provide as far as possible for the safety of the Ships Company, the Masts were Cut away, and by unremitting exertions untill Night, the whole of the Ships Company (excepting about Twenty who, as the Weather seemed to moderate, preferr'd staying on Board to the risque of getting on Shore) were put on Board two or three Vessels that appeared at a great Distance in the offing, or were put on the reef by means of rafts, &c. and taken up by Canoes.[45]

Miraculously, only eight people were drowned, including the master of the *Britannia*, who went down with his ship. But the plight of those marooned on shore was still grim. "Our situation, on arriving at the miserable hovels of the few inhabitants was only one degree better than that we had escaped from," wrote an army officer passenger; "no dry clothes, no meat, drink, or bedding were held out to us; what they had not they could not bestow." Having sent an order to those vessels still within reach to anchor at or lay off the Hogsties and take on as many people as they could accommodate, Captain Lawford set out on foot for George Town three days after the wreck, with two companions and a guide. Their 31-hour journey was "over the most execrable road imaginable; for three miles were hot burning sands, and sharp-pointed coral rocks, that would have foiled the attempts of the most dexterous animal to pass them without injury."[46]

At George Town, Captain Lawford sent off a flurry of distress messages: to Jamaica for help; to the Governor of Havana (England being at peace with Spain), asking for assistance to the now unescorted remnants of the

convoy; to his commander-in-chief, Commodore John Ford; and to the Admiralty in London. Only three days after the wreck, eight of the principal inhabitants of Grand Cayman had explained that the island was unable to feed or house so many unexpected visitors, so Lawford shipped off all he could in the ten merchantmen that had not already sailed on. The first to leave included Lady Emilia Cooke, the most well-connected passenger, and the naval and military officers travelling home.[47]

Within three weeks, several schooners and sloops had come from Jamaica with provisions and offers of help. Captain Lawford and his skeleton crew camped in tents on the beach at Gun Bay for almost six weeks, rescuing what they could and keeping a vigilant eye on their Caymanian and Jamaican helpers. None of the guns was fished up, but the mail carried in the *Convert* was saved, as was a large proportion of the cargoes of rum, wood, and cotton carried on the merchantmen's upper tiers. Most of the sugar, carried deeper in the vessels' holds, was spoiled and lost.[48]

As soon as he heard of the disaster, Commodore Ford sent HMS *Success* to Grand Cayman to rescue Captain Lawford and his men. The *Success* arrived in mid-March 1794 and stayed a short while before carrying Captain Lawford back to Port Royal and his court martial aboard the same ship. The court acquitted Lawford.[49] He went on to serve with distinction at sea until 1811, and was promoted to Admiral and knighted before his death in 1838 at the age of eighty-six.[50] It is not known what happened to the salvaged cargoes or what else of value was rescued from the Wreck of the Ten Sail. But it is pretty certain that the people of Grand Cayman did not go unrewarded for their efforts. "Governor" Bodden, for example, and his partner, Robert Clarke, were appointed as official salvors.

The full story of this dramatic episode has recently been unearthed by modern research, which dispels many of the legends that have grown up in the last 200 years. Contrary to popular myth, for instance, there was no "prince" aboard the *Convert*, nor were Caymanians granted perpetual freedom from taxation for rescuing him. The accounts of the wreck and the recovery efforts reveal an island society living under conditions somewhat less harsh than those faced by the first permanent settlers a hundred years before. Yet it was a growing community with its own complexities and challenges. The most important of these was the evolving relationship between slaves and slaveowners. As Corbet's report revealed, slaves and their owners were roughly equal in number in a community of fewer than 1,000 people. The character of this "Slave Society" calls for closer examination.

Cannon from HMS Convert *undergoing conservation treatment in 2001.*

An anchor off East End from a wreck in the 1700s.

CHAPTER 4

Caymanian Slave Society and Emancipation

THE ORIGINS, NATURE, AND LEGACIES of slavery are fascinating – and occasionally uncomfortable – aspects of Caymanian history. While we will never know the precise identity of the first slaves in the Cayman Islands,[1] we can be fairly certain that by the 1730s a few slaves had been brought by some of the early settlers, and that their numbers steadily increased as the colony grew. For about a century, from the 1730s to the early 1830s, slaves were essential to the Caymanian economy, especially for logging and cotton plantations. They also contributed to Caymanian society in other, unacknowledged ways. Before the complete emancipation of the slaves in 1835, Caymanian society was truly a Slave Society, though very different from the sugar-plantation colonies like Jamaica, where 90 per cent of the population were slaves. Recognition of this period of Caymanian history as a Slave Society is essential for a full understanding of the subtleties of present-day attitudes toward class and race.[2]

The first slaves in Cayman of whom we have certain knowledge were much like those in Jamaica at the time. They were a caste apart. Most would have been purchased, according to the need for labour and their owners' ability to pay for them. A few were probably acquired by chance: saved from wrecks or captured and re-enslaved after running away from Jamaica.

The earliest slaves were probably small gangs of adult males, acquired to cut mahogany. But as female slaves were brought to the islands, the gangs became more settled and formed their own family units. Ideally, all members of a slave family lived within the same household. But Caymanian slave-

Slaves logging in Grand Cayman in the 1730s.

holdings were generally small, so some slave families may have been divided among several households.

A settled slave community probably developed as the land was increasingly worked by logging between 1730 and 1780. As this community expanded to include equal numbers of females and males, as well as younger and older members, those slaves no longer needed in the fields probably became domestic bondservants. A handful of the most enterprising and capable male slaves may have become craftsmen or mariners.

Because there are so few written records about Cayman at this time, we must look elsewhere in the British Caribbean for descriptions of what slave life must have been like on Grand Cayman. Conditions were probably much like those in Jamaica before large-scale plantations were established, or like those in the English settlements at Belize or the Miskito Coast. Grand Cayman never developed large slave plantations like Jamaica's. But for thirty years or so from the 1780s onwards, it developed a Slave Society and a system of production similar to those in the Bahamas.

While Jamaica was being cleared of its virgin forest, Grand Cayman and the shores of Central America were also being tapped to supply the new market for mahogany and other woods. It was during this period that entrepreneurs like Battersby and Foster purchased small gangs of slaves. Branded like cattle and supervised by white overseers, the slaves were set to the backbreaking toil of clearing trails, felling trees, sawing valuable timber, and dragging it to the shore for loading aboard ships.

The slaves were set up in camps and outfitted with tools. But unlike slaves on sugar plantations who were provided with at least some food, they were expected to sustain themselves. A good proportion of the slaves' time was therefore given to working their own provision grounds close to the base camp. Despite this, they would have roved more and more widely to log the best stands of timber. The slaves in Cayman were not so abused as slave gangs on Jamaican plantations, but they were probably subject to a similar level of supervision. Caymanian masters were apparently reluctant to entrust slaves with jobs as craftsmen or to allow them the relative freedom of working at sea.

In 1773, George Gauld estimated that besides thirty-nine families totalling some two hundred whites, there were "above the same number of Negroes and Mulattoes" living in the Cayman Islands. These 250 or so slaves constituted the bulk of the workforce. They cut timber and raised cotton, as well as producing provisions for local consumption and for sale to passing ships.[3]

In the early years most of the slaves would have been African-born. Hans Sloane, an eighteenth-century writer on slavery, stressed both the cultural influences of Africa and the pattern of slave families. The Jamaican male slaves he describes may well have had their counterparts in Cayman:

> They have every one his Wife, and are very much concern'd if they prove adulterous, but in some measure satisfied if their Masters punish the Man who does them the supposed injury, in any of his Hogs, or other small Wealth. The care of the Masters and Overseers about their Wives, is what keeps their Plantations chiefly in good order, whence they every [ever] buy Wives in proportion to their Men, lest the Men should wander to neighbouring Plantations, and neglect to serve them.[4]

SETTLERS FROM THE MISKITO COAST

Slavery in Jamaica was eventually dominated by the rise of large sugar plantations. The Slave Society of the Cayman Islands, however, developed more along the lines of the frontier settlements of the Miskito Coast. It was from there that the largest single influx of new masters and slaves was to come, following the evacuation of the Miskito Coast by the British in the 1780s.[5]

At least three boatloads of migrants from the Miskito Coast arrived in Grand Cayman between February and May 1787. On 21 February, the schooner *Nancy* departed Black River for the "Great Caymanes" with twenty-six people aboard, twenty-four of whom were slaves. A month later, the schooner *Phoenix* sailed from Cape Gracias a Dios with seven free people and another twenty-four slaves. Finally, an unnamed vessel owned by Joseph Wood left from Pearl Lagoon and Bluefields on 30 May with eighty people aboard, consisting of Mr. Wood's entire family and all his slaves. Joseph Wood was probably the father of the three brothers who still owned seventy-six slaves among them at Bodden Town in 1834.[6]

About three hundred people from the Miskito Coast apparently settled in Grand Cayman in the late 1780s – some fifty free people (mainly white settlers and their families) and the rest slaves.[7] The newcomers increased the island's population by as much as 60 per cent, perhaps doubling the number of slaves. This sudden migration spurred efforts to establish new cotton plantations.

THE COTTON BOOM

Beginning in the 1770s, the British textile industry underwent rapid mechanization, which increased the demand for raw cotton. For about a generation from the 1780s onward, cotton prices rose.[8] As a result, cotton promised prosperity for all areas of the British West Indies where it could be grown. Climatically, the Cayman Islands seemed a good prospect, and a number of optimistic planters sought to fill the demand. They may have been ignorant of the threats posed by insects and soil depletion, as well as the possibility of a drop in raw-cotton prices. Nevertheless, they witnessed a short-lived cotton boom that had important effects on Cayman for some time.

The course of this boom can be traced in the shipping registers kept by Jamaica.[9] These records give details of the cargoes carried between Grand Cayman and various Jamaican ports, including exports of cotton and imports of slaves. The records are particularly rich for the years 1802–4 (mainly years of peace), when Caymanian cotton plantations were probably approaching a peak. Later entries suggest that the heyday of Caymanian cotton was already passing by 1810.

When we examine the shipping registers for the thirty months between January 1802 and July 1804, we find that some twenty-five small vessels were engaged in sailing between Grand Cayman and the Jamaican ports of Kingston and Montego Bay. Each made between one and nine round trips apiece. They ranged in size from 14 to 85 tons, with an average of 42 tons, and carried between three and seven crewmen each. Most were Jamaican-built, and more than half were owned, captained, and crewed by Jamaicans. At least eight schooners and a sloop, however, were owned, captained, and crewed by Caymanians. Two of these vessels were built in Grand Cayman. The

31.000
...Hundred & fifty Bags of Cotton & a Keg Turtle Shell
5718 55 .. 100 7 502 .. 10.000 Thirty Casks of Hams, & 200 Kegs Bread ..
...ty Boxes of Soap, Twelve Barr.s Prime Wine 5 & four Cases of Furniture
572 ... 13 .. 7 = 48 Kegs of Bread, 26 Hams, 7 Cwt fish
...lbs of Bacon ... 40 260 21356 ... 300
434 75 55 Sixty Six Kegs Bread, 5 Bags of ...

Shipping register, showing export of cotton and turtle from Grand Cayman to Jamaica (highlighted) on the schooner Industry, *1804.*

155

between the Twenty-ninth Day of June and the Twenty-ninth Day of September following, being the Quarter ending at latter period

GENERAL CARGO.

Hogsheads of Sugar.	Tierces of Sugar.	Barrels of Sugar.	Puncheons of Rum.	Hogsheads of Rum.	Bags of Ginger.	Casks of Ginger.	Bags of Pimento.	Casks of Pimento.	Bags of Cotton.	Tons of Logwood and Fustick.	Planks of Mahogany.	Casks of Coffee.	Casks of Melasses.	Bags of Cocoa.	Casks of Cocoa.	Casks of Indigo.	Tons of Nicoragua Wood.	Tons of Lignum Vitæ.	Negroes.	Barrels of Provisions.	Casks of Copper.	Barrels of Fruit.	Where bound.	Where and when Bond given.
												Do												
Ballast																							Norfolk	
Ballast																							Charleston	
			300																			40	Philadelphia	
Ninety Barr^s Flour,			32	Dry Goods & Ironmongery															6	20			Caymanas	
Ballast																							Charleston	
			2	& Sundry Dry Goods																			Indian Coast	
Ballast																							Alexandria	

Shipping register, showing import of slaves ("6 negroes") to Grand Cayman from Jamaica (highlighted) on the schooner Industry, 1804.

earliest was the *Polly & Betsy*, a 36-ton schooner, owned and captained by John Drayton and built at "Grand Caymanas" in 1785.[10]

The vessels bringing goods from Jamaica to Grand Cayman during this period carried many more slaves, and larger and more varied cargoes, than earlier trading vessels. These increases reflected both an expanding population and a flourishing plantation economy. They also reveal the buying power of cotton and other products from the Cayman Islands.

The shipping registers tell us a good deal about exports of slaves to Grand Cayman, though unfortunately they do not provide information about the names, ages, sex, or condition of the slaves. Between January 1802 and July 1804, for example, 153 slaves were conveyed from Kingston to Grand Cayman in fourteen voyages by six different ships. We do not know where slaves were sold on Grand Cayman, but the likely places include George Town Barcadere, Hogsties (George Town harbour), and Bodden Town. Newly arrived slaves may have been sold at auction. It seems equally likely, though, that they were already spoken for by Caymanian owners, perhaps in exchange for produce or obtained on credit, since the records do not show any slaves being returned to Jamaica. Assuming that most of them were adults recently brought from Africa, their average price would have been about £100 Jamaican currency. This represents a substantial capital investment: £15,300 for 153 slaves. Clearly, Caymanians purchasing slaves were optimistic about their economic future and were considered credit-worthy.

Cotton formed the largest and most valuable cargo between 1802 and 1804. In all, eighteen vessels made thirty voyages carrying 200,000 pounds in bags and bales. This quantity was worth a total of perhaps £15,000 to the shippers.[11] The figures suggest an annual Caymanian production of about forty tons a year, rising to perhaps sixty tons at its peak, once the plantations were fully developed. Comparing Cayman with the Bahamas, we can estimate that cotton producers in Grand Cayman may have employed as many as

three hundred able-bodied slaves on plantations extending over at least twelve hundred acres.[12]

Cotton production was less arduous than the year-round gang labour required for producing sugar, which was never a plantation crop in the Cayman Islands. Cotton was planted as seeds in lightly hoed land, and both planting and harvesting could be distributed throughout the year—with peaks for Anguilla cotton in January and June. Weeding the fields and plucking and cleaning the cotton bolls were tedious but not strenuous tasks. Nonetheless, it was always hard work. It was toughest in the first phase, when the land had to be cleared of trees, bush, and rocks, and in the years of decline, when exhausted soils and falling prices led masters to drive their slaves harder. The most efficient plantations in the Bahamas, for example, were between 150 and 225 acres, and were worked by anywhere from fifty to seventy-five slaves. The planter's aim was to produce five hundred pounds of cotton per acre with each slave producing fifteen hundred pounds per year. The average production was probably about half this, however, even in the best of years.[13]

In June 1802, according to Edward Corbet, thirty tons of cotton was being exported from Grand Cayman. Corbet reported that there were 545 slaves in Grand Cayman in 1802. They were divided among eighty-eight owner families, of whom sixty-six were white and twenty-two "people of colour". The majority of slaves (322) were owned by eleven white owner families, an average of 29.3 slaves per holding. These families were situated on the most arable land between George Town and Bodden Town, in an area measuring eight by two miles. The owners in this area (with their respective slave numbers) were Senior Magistrate William Bodden (51), John Bodden Sr. (51), Joseph Bodden (37), Waide Watler Sr. (31), and Samuel Morton (9), all at Bodden Town; William Eden (9) and another William Bodden (21) at Spotts; Thomas Thompson (56) and Waide Watler Jr. (17) at Prospect; and John Drayton (23) and Rachael Rivers (17) at George Town. The only persons listed as "free people of colour" who possessed enough slaves to make up small working gangs were John and James Tatum Sr. of Bodden Town (15), William, James, and Chloe Parsons of George Town (13), and Henry and Augustus Ebanks of Boatswains Bay (13).[14]

The data on slave imports and ownership clarify the picture of Caymanian Slave Society during the cotton boom. At the peak of production, there were fewer than a dozen cotton plantations, all situated in south central Grand Cayman and averaging about a hundred acres. They were owned by a closely interrelated and predominantly white elite, and worked by between twenty-five and fifty slaves apiece. Some two-thirds of Caymanian slaves lived and worked on these cotton plantations. The rest worked in far smaller groups as provision cultivators, stockmen, or domestics, with a tiny minority of craftsmen and turtle fishermen.

Most cotton-plantation slaves lived on their owners' land. Their dwellings were simple huts made of wattle (with or without) daub and thatch, clustered closer to each other than to their owner's house, and distinct from the dwellings of other groups of slaves. The more prominent slaveowners lived with their immediate families in the few substantial houses on the island. These buildings were far more modest in style than the typical Jamaican "great house". Except for William Eden's house at Great Pedro, built around 1780, they were usually one-storey dwellings. Framed in local hardwood, with wattle and plaster walls, they may have had verandas in front and perhaps all the way around. The roof was probably thatch rather than shingle, and the windows would have had shutters or louvres, rather than glass.[15]

THE DECLINE OF THE COTTON TRADE

The Caymanian cotton plantations seem to have declined even more rapidly than they developed. This change required many adjustments in the slave-labour economy in the twenty years before emancipation in 1834. During this period the British textile industry continued to expand. Its voracious demands, however, were increasingly supplied by the southern United States. In fact, cotton production in the U.S. was on such a large scale that raw-cotton prices dropped dramatically. As a result, West Indian cotton could no longer compete.

Less cotton to export meant that fewer ships were needed for trade between Cayman and Jamaica. Despite this, a higher proportion of these vessels were built, owned, and crewed by Caymanians. As in the Bahamas, the catastrophic drop in cotton exports made it essential to find alternative products to pay for imported goods. This change was reflected in the nature of out-

Pedro St. James, built by slave labour, ca. 1780.

bound and inbound cargoes.[16] A typically mixed cargo from Grand Cayman to Kingston, for instance, was carried by William Bodden's *Susan & Kitty* in November 1811. Its cargo consisted of nineteen bags of cotton; twelve barrels, ten baskets, and six baskets of corn; two barrels of tortoiseshell; one mahogany log; six hundredweight of corned fish; an anchor; twelve hundredweight of old copper; and eighteen puncheons of rum (wreck goods). The incoming cargoes were at least as varied as before, but generally in much smaller quantities – the supplies for a single household, perhaps, or a few months' stock for a single shop. William Bodden's *Charming Kitty*, for example, arriving from Kingston in November 1809, brought a variety of items: two barrels of sugar; six trunks, six boxes, one basket, and a small quantity of loose dry goods; one basket and five tubs "crockeryware"; one barrel of flour; three firkins of butter; three barrels each of beef and pork; one box each of raisins and currants; one small box of tobacco; one small box of bottled liquor; a cask of rum; and six barrels of bread.[17]

During the decade 1808–18 only Caymanian vessels were regularly involved in the trade between Grand Cayman and Kingston or Montego Bay, and their trade was much less frequent. They were all owned by prominent slave-owners. The vessels (and their owners) included the Cayman-built schooners *Susan & Kitty* and *Nelly* (William Bodden), *Eliza* (Waide Watler), *Favourite* (Thomas Thomson), *Three Brothers* (James Bodden), *Speedwell* (William Page), *William & James* (James Watler). There was also the schooner *Pelican* (a prize) and the curiously named *Smash Pipes*, both owned by William Parsons.[18]

By about 1810 slaves were no longer part of the cargoes carried by Caymanian shippers. This change did not spring from the outlawing of the British slave trade with Africa in 1807, for the inter-colonial trade remained legal until 1826. The fact is that fresh slaves were no longer needed because the cotton plantations were in decline and because for the first time the Caymanian slave population was growing by natural increase. The shift in the slave population, together with the changes in master-slave relations and in the way slave labour was organised as the plantations declined, made for increasing restlessness even before rumours of emancipation became reality.

THE SLAVE POPULATION

The profile of the Caymanian slave population deserves close study. As we have seen, life and work for slaves on cotton plantations was healthier than on sugar plantations. But the health of Caymanian slaves, measured by fertility and mortality figures, improved further as the cultivation of cotton declined. By 1826, the number of slaves in Grand Cayman had risen to 889, an increase of 63 per cent over the total of 545 counted by Corbet in 1802.

Slave dwellings with the slave owner's house in the distance.

The number of whites and other free persons had increased even faster, by 78 per cent (from 388 to 689). The rate of slave increase in Cayman contrasted sharply with Jamaica and other sugar-plantation colonies, where the slave population decreased during the same period. In just over five years, between 1 January 1821 and 1 April 1826, there were 133 births among the slaves of Grand Cayman and only 56 deaths: a rate of natural increase of about 17 per thousand per year.19 This was a comparatively high rate, exceeded only in the colonies of Barbuda, Anguilla, and the Bahamas.[20]

The concern of British abolitionists had earlier led to the systematic registration of British West Indian slaves. Accordingly, regular censuses of individual slaves in their ownership units began in 1813. By 1827 these censuses were required of all colonies except the Cayman Islands, British Honduras, and Anguilla. Slave registration in Cayman was overlooked until the final year of slavery in 1834 – and as a result Cayman was almost excluded from in the compensation offered by the British government.

There was only one slave census in the Cayman Islands, in April 1834. This was carried out somewhat hastily in anticipation of the Emancipation Act that came into force on 1 August 1834. Undertaken by James Minot Jr., it provides a snapshot of the slave population, rather than a moving picture. It was motivated mainly by the Caymanian slaveowners' concern for compensation, and as a result it provides valuable additional information about slave sales and prices. It shows what value was placed on slaves and the actual amounts each owner received in the compensation payout.[21]

The 1834 census reveals that the total population of slaves had risen from 889 in 1826 to 985 eight years later. At first glance this healthy rate of growth

in the slave population appears to be a decline from the earlier rate of 17 per thousand to something like 13 per thousand. The decline is due to the number of slaves being given their freedom during the last decade of slavery. Local records from 1810 show a small but increasing number of slaves buying or being given their freedom. But the list is almost certainly incomplete.

The 1834 census identified each slave by age and name (and thus sex), although it did not distinguish between African-born and Creole slaves. From these data we can develop a profile of the slave population according to age and gender and make a more subtle assessment of its demographic health. Any well-balanced community has a healthy proportion of different age groups among both men and women. But we would expect a slave population, especially in the earliest stage of plantation development, to be dominated by members in the middle age range, recently imported from Africa. We would also expect men to outnumber women by a ratio of about 3:2 and there to be very few old people, newborns, and children.

The Caymanian slave population in 1834 in fact had a healthy birth rate, a healthy proportion of young people, and very few persons over seventy years of age. There was a relatively high proportion of slaves in the middle age range, probably because many slaves were imported between 1783 and 1807 to work on cotton plantations. With such recent slave imports, many slaves at emancipation would have been African-born rather than Creole. Indeed, the proportion of African-born slaves as opposed to Creole slaves in Cayman at the end of slavery would probably have been higher than in many other colonies. This is a factor with important cultural implications.

One way to assess whether an African cultural identity was still valued is to look at slave names. Whether these names were African or non-African, and whether surnames were used, may indicate how slaves viewed their African heritage. The use of surnames, for example, suggests a more European identification.[22] In the 1834 census, some 680 of the 985 slaves (or 68 per cent) were recorded by just a single name. This suggests that an African outlook remained surprisingly late in the slavery era in Cayman.

Thirty-two per cent of Caymanian slaves had surnames in 1834. It is not exactly clear, though, how this figure should be interpreted. Taking the owner's surname was a frequent practice in the Cayman Islands, as elsewhere. But it was more popular with some common Caymanian surnames, such as Watler, than with others, such as Bodden. In several cases there seems to have been a positive disinclination to choose the owner's surname, or at least careful consideration about adopting it. For example, of the thirty slaves owned by the Magistrate James Coe Sr., six had single names only, six bore the surname Coe, and the remaining eighteen each had a different surname. Of the sixteen slaves owned by George Edward Bodden, only one male bore the owner's surname. Nine others had nine different surnames, and five of the

females bore second names that were Christian names rather than traditional surnames.

The choice of surname often seems to have been arbitrary, but it probably indicates a desire for respectability. In many cases a surname may have been chosen after a respected person. It may also have been a way to identify with the slave group that lived in the owner's household, rather than with the owner's family. Only in some cases was the surname apparently a mark of descent in the male line. Rarely was it a sign of informal marriage. Unlike Jamaica in the last years of slavery, the acquisition of a surname was probably not associated with baptism into the established church.

The single names used by 68 per cent of the Caymanian slaves in 1834 reveal patterns distinct from those of Jamaica and other plantation colonies. Some were unusual (such as Cruikshank, Christopherson, Gibbon, Tippoo Saib, and William Onesimus), while some may have indicated certain characteristics (Behaviour, Trusty, Kinky). No degrading names are recorded similar to those applied to slaves elsewhere (for example, the names Monkey, Villain, Whore, and Strumpet, used at Worthy Park, Jamaica). Very few names were derived from Roman and Greek mythology or European history, though a few have a Jamaican origin (such as Trelawny and Port Royal).[23] African names were much more common. There were six Cuba(h)s, three Mimbas, three Quashees, three Benebas, at least two Statiras, and one each of Briana, Coffee, Corta, Cuffy, Elmina, Juba, and Zebrah, as well as a Congo Tom and a Congo George. Some names appeared to be English but were derived from African equivalents (such as Sam for Sambo, Jack for Quaco, Joe for Cudjoe, Abby for Abba, Bina for Cubbena, and Phoebe for Phibba). Most of the slaves with African names were over forty years of age. A dozen were under twenty-five and six under ten years of age – demonstrating a desire on the part of younger slaves to retain some African heritage.[24] The overwhelming majority of single names, however, were common English Christian names such as Mary, Elizabeth, Sarah, William, Edward, and George. The choice of these names suggest that the slaves in Cayman and their owners shared some awareness of their common humanity, even if the two cultures – slave and free – were still distinct.

The 1834 slave census also reveals that in all age brackets the numbers of males and females were more equally balanced than in most other colonies. This suggests that Caymanian slaveowners purchased new slaves in almost equal proportions. Whether this pattern was designed to boost the slave population or was purely economic (female slaves were cheaper than males but just as useful for cotton production) is not known. The net result, however, was a comparatively fertile slave population.

There is no direct evidence of any form of marriage or regular family formation among Caymanian slaves. But if Cayman was like other colonies,

lasting unions, some form of marriage, and a pattern of nuclear families were probably common by the end of slavery. As we have seen, formal marriages by a clergyman in Jamaica were important to Caymanian whites from the earliest days. Once Magistrates were appointed from the late 1700s, formal marriage seems to have become general for whites and extended down the social scale into the free coloured population.[25] But there is no evidence that formal marriages were ever performed for slaves in the Cayman Islands. The limited census of April 1826 noted that eighteen marriages had been performed on the island in the previous five and a half years. But these marriages were presumably between free persons, including some non-whites. Though the first Anglican minister arrived in Grand Cayman in 1831, there is no evidence that he included the marriage of slaves among his ministrations.

The earliest local archives record the marriage of one newly freed slave; this entry also suggests that formal marriage rarely, if ever, took place outside the free population. On 15 April 1816, it was recorded that one Henry Clarke, "gentleman" (a white property owner) sold to Rachel Ebanks (a free coloured from Boatswains Bay, who signed her name with an "X") a male quadroon slave named George, alias George Bodden, for the sum of £100 Jamaican currency. On the same day, Rachel Ebanks, "for divers good causes and considerations" (that is, without any monetary payment) freed the same George Bodden in a separate deed. What made this transaction unique was the third document bearing the same date: a certificate from the Magistrate John Drayton "that George Bodden and Rachel Ebanks were by me lawfully joined together in the Holy Estate of Matrimony at the Island of Grand

The Public Recorder's records: Rachel Ebanks purchases George Bodden, 15 April 1816.

Island of
Grand Caymanas ss.}
Know all Men by these presents,
That I Henry Clarke of the Island aforesaid Gentleman,
and Elizabeth Mary his Wife) for and in consideration of
the Sum of One hundred pounds current money of Jamaica
me in hand well and truly paid by Rachel Ebanks, at, or
immediately before the ensealing and delivery of these presents, the Receipt whereof I do hereby acknowledge, Have
bargained, Sold, Aliened, Conveyed, Confirmed and delivered, and by these presents, do bargain, Sell, Alien, Convey,
Confirm and deliver, unto the said Rachel Ebanks, One
Quadroon Man Slave named George, alias, George Bodden,
for her to have, hold, occupy, possess and enjoy, the said
Quadroon Man Slave named George, alias, George Bodden,
to her, her heirs, Executors, Administrators and Assigns,

Island of
Grand Caymanas ss. }

Know all Men, by these presents, That I Rachel Ebanks, for divers good causes and considerations me hereunto moving, have Manumized, Enfranchised and for ever set free, from all manner of Slavery, Servitude and Bondage whatsoever, A Quadroon Man Slave named George, alias, George Bodden, for him the said George, alias George Bodden, to have and to hold the said Enfranchisement and Freedom, without any let, molestation, or hindrance whatever, from me, my heirs, Executors, Administrators and Assigns from henceforth for ever. In Witness whereof I have hereunto set my hand and seal this fifteenth day of April in the Year of Our Lord One thousand Eight hundred and Sixteen.

Signed, Sealed and delivered in presence of — — } (Sign'd) Rachel her X mark Ebanks

(Sign'd) James Coe Sen.

The Public Recorder's records: Rachel Ebanks frees George Bodden, 15 April 1816.

Caymanas on the fifteenth day of April in the Year of Our Lord One thousand Eight hundred and Sixteen".[26]

These documents probably point to the fact that both partners had to be free persons before a Magistrate would marry them. They also suggest more complex social realities. While ethnic miscegenation undoubtedly existed, it probably occurred within the strict limits of custom and outside the bonds of wedlock. Originally, miscegenation took only one form: clandestine liaisons between free white males and black slave women. Gradually, the number of non-whites increased, both because of white and non-white unions and because of the increasing number of liaisons between non-whites, whether slaves or "free persons of colour".

As time went on, a small but slowly increasing number of Caymanian slaves (most of them coloureds) bought or were granted their freedom. This allowed them to be formally married and even to own slaves themselves. One example is Elizabeth Jane Trusty, whose experience illustrates the complexities sometimes involved. Listed as a black, she was freed for the minimal sum of £5 by Elizabeth Mary Thompson in March 1809. Once freed, she moved into George Town and apparently prospered, building up a household that consisted of both free coloureds and slaves.

These are to Certify, That George Bodden and Rachel Ebanks, were by me lawfully joined together in the Holy Estate of Matrimony at the Island of Grand Caymanas, on the fifteenth day of April in the Year of Our Lord One thousand Eight hundred and Sixteen.

Given under my hand the day and Year above written at said Island of Grand Caymanas.

(Sign'd) John Drayton

(A true Copy Jas. Coe Senr., Recorder,)

The Public Recorder's records: Rachel Ebanks marries George Bodden, 15 April 1816.

Of six transactions naming Elizabeth Jane Trusty in the Public Recorder's records, five involved freeing slaves. Twice she received from a fellow free coloured, William Hinds, the small sum of £5 for freeing a black slave child: Grace Trusty in 1818 and Edward William Dixon Trusty in 1821. In 1819 she charged the white magistrate and shipowner William Page £100 for the freedom of Lettice, also known as Elizabeth Wright. She also paid a Jamaican couple, Isaac and Rebecca Orobio, £160 to free a black slave named Adam. Finally, in 1820 she paid £100 for the freedom of a black slave named Diana.[27]

Though she encouraged manumission, however, Elizabeth Jane Trusty was no dedicated abolitionist. In 1826 she purchased a mixed-race slave girl called Sally from James Watler Sr., and in the census of 1834 she still owned seven slaves – more than any other Caymanian ex-slave. Grace and Edward Trusty were probably her own children, born in slavery, who could be manumitted only by a third person. Elizabeth Trusty's will, dated May 1835, left all her property, including the compensation money for her former slaves, to these two "adopted" children.[28]

Caymanian slaves may have been denied formal marriage, but that would not have kept them from observing their own informal marriage rites (some of which survived into post-slavery days) or from forming family units. Family patterns are difficult to trace in the 1834 lists because males were recorded separately from females. In the larger slaveholdings, it is impossible to discern family relationships between the slaves. In smaller slaveholdings, though, enough hints (such as surnames) exist to trace various family patterns.[29]

Some Caymanian slaveholdings seem to have consisted of a simple nuclear family of mother, father, and children. Others comprised a nuclear family along with one or two members of the previous generation. For example, Susannah Collins of South West Sound owned seven slaves: the field slave Lewis (aged 45), the domestic slave Cinda (35), and five young slaves, probably their children, all listed as domestics.[30] An example of a more extended family seems to be the six slaves owned by Mary Bodden of George Town. These consisted of the field slave Trelawny (28), the domestic Caroline (24), and three girls, aged 4, 6, and 7, along with the field slave Mocho (50), who may have been the father of either Trelawny or Caroline.[31]

A third family pattern, which is more common, is the mother listed singly with her children. In these circumstances, the woman may have had a regular partner from another slaveholding, who might even have been living with her. Larger groups of twenty-five to thirty slaves had a gender and age balance typical for the slave population. This suggests that these groups were more or less self-contained clusters of family households. Large slaveholdings typically had a balance of males and females over at least three generations, which suggests that stable family households existed within each ownership group.[32]

Between 1800 and 1834 Caymanian society underwent major changes. These changes, while enabling many Caymanian slaves to live more like subsistence farmers, also produced sociopolitical and racial tensions just before, during, and immediately after emancipation.

Slave ownership became more general among the free population between 1802 and 1834, yet with no increase in the number or size of the larger slaveholdings. In 1834, there were 985 Caymanian slaves and 121 owners, compared with 545 slaves and 88 owners in 1802. The average slaveholding increased from 6.3 to 8.1 slaves. But this increase was much smaller than the 63 per cent increase in the general slave population. There were still only a dozen owners who had more than twenty slaves, accounting for 387 slaves overall. Only three owners held more than forty slaves, and the largest holding was fifty slaves. At the other end of the scale, fifty-seven people owned five or fewer slaves, accounting for 142 slaves overall. This included twenty people who owned a single slave each.

The web of slave ownership grew wider, therefore, and the total number of slaves increased. But in all likelihood slave groupings were rarely split up or transferred out of the owner's family. Slave families may have been encouraged, in fact, on the principle that they made for more contented workers, especially in the case of domestic slaves. These factors were especially impor-

tant as cotton plantations began to decline and large labouring gangs were no longer needed, as landholdings were split between children, and as the proportion of domestic slaves increased.

The largest slaveholding in 1802, for example, was split up, but merely by bequest within the same owner family. In 1802, Thomas Thompson of Prospect, whose own family consisted of thirteen persons, owned fifty-six slaves. When he made his will on 9 May 1811, Thompson bequeathed his plantation in three equal shares to his wife and two sons. He divided his slaves, along with the rest of his estate, almost equally between his wife, his two sons, and his six daughters. They were bequeathed in male-and-female pairs, including any children of the women slaves. These bequests were probably designed to form the nucleus of separate slaveholdings. Altogether, the slaves named in the will amounted to thirty-seven of the fifty-six slaves owned by Thomas Thompson in 1802. The rest were presumably sold, with the income divided equally among the beneficiaries.[33]

The owners of the largest slaveholdings in 1834 were almost all men. The two exceptions were widows, Mary Bodden and Dorothy Hinds, with forty-three and twenty-five slaves, respectively. It is remarkable, though, that more than a quarter of the slaveowners (34 of 121) were listed as women. Though most owned only a few slaves, they accounted for more than a fifth of the slaves overall (207), with an average holding of 6.1 slaves – not much smaller than the overall average. Twenty-one other women signed the registration documents on behalf of husbands who were away on voyages at the time of the census.[34] Clearly, the ownership and management of slaves was extended to women much more in Cayman than it was in other colonies.

Owning slaves in the Cayman Islands was not necessarily an indication of learning. A fifth of the male owners and over three-quarters of the women signed the registration documents with a mark rather than a name. Yet slave ownership was definitely a sign of rank. Once the cotton plantations declined, slaves would have often been the main capital asset held by the slaveowners. In fact, for a generation or more before 1834, slave sales were almost stagnant. In that year James Minot examined the records of all slave sales between January 1826 and December 1830. He found that there had been only twenty-eight local transactions. All of them involved the sale of single slaves, except for three women each sold with an infant child. The prices (in Jamaican currency) varied considerably. For example, field workers went for between £56 and £110 (according to age, strength, and gender), while an exceptional female domestic cost £110 and a male carpenter £115.[35]

These prices suggest an average of no more than £50 sterling (or about £75 Jamaican) for ordinary field and domestic slaves. This was close to the average of £46 10s 8d sterling per slave that was eventually awarded by the compensation authorities. The grand total claimed by slaveowners in the Cayman

Islands was £44,764 10s 2d. Though the owners actually received less than half what they claimed (a total of £19,700 sterling), these figures show that slaves in Cayman were valuable out of all proportion to what they could bring in from their labour.

Indeed, the 1834 returns show that Caymanian slaves, far from being a plantation labour force, were more like unpaid domestic servants. In 1834, 51 per cent of adult slaves (414) were officially counted as field labourers, and another 41 per cent (338) were listed as domestics. In contrast, 74 per cent of working-age slaves in Jamaica were counted as field labourers in 1834, and only 13 per cent as domestics.[36]

The slaves in the 1834 registration were distinguished by district. The figures paint an interesting socio-economic map of the Cayman Islands at the time. The most concentrated area of slave habitation was Bodden Town itself, home to 44.2 per cent of all Caymanian slaves (425) and nine of the twelve largest slaveholdings. Although it is an oversimplification, West Bay and South West Sound seem to have been almost entirely poor white or near-white areas, closer perhaps to what have been called slaveowning communities than true Slave Societies. George Town was beginning to show the characteristics of a West Indian market town, and it may have contained much of the island's free coloured population. But the heart of Caymanian Slave Society was to be found in the districts of Prospect and Bodden Town, containing much of the cultivated land. Prospect seems to have been characterised by estate units focused around the owners' houses. Bodden Town consisted of a concentrated knot of ownership units in which the white masters lived among a black slave majority.

Both Bodden Town and Prospect shared a complex set of interrelationships which were marked by conflicting desires, now that plantations had faded and slavery was winding down. On one side were the white owners, eager to hold on to the tenuous strands of control in a declining economy, and still dependent on their slaves. On the other side were the slaves, presumably wishing to make a life of their own once freedom finally came, anticipating a fuller life as self-sufficient subsistence farmers, and retaining the remnants of their traditional African culture.

The social climate in the years before emancipation was summed up from one perspective in 1841 by Nathaniel Glover. He was a slaveowning American who settled in Bodden Town in 1831. As an American, he undoubtedly had his own views about slavery (which continued in the United States for another generation). Recalling the last years of slavery in Cayman, he wrote:

> Slavery only existed here by name. The owners generally were over indulgent and the children of slaves were usually brought up in the houses of their masters and were often playmates to their children. They were much better provided for then than they are now since they became free. When I first came to the island

> in 1831 it was a second Eden and I thought it was impossible to have found a happier set of people. It was a delightful ride from Bodden Town to George Town. The negroes' provision grounds lined each side of the road and the trees were bending with their ripe and yellow fruits. An instance of thieving from each other was scarcely ever heard of.[37]

Despite the nostalgia expressed by Glover, Caymanian Slave Society, even in the years leading up to freedom, was probably characterised by suppressed conflict as well as cohesion. The desire of slaves to be free was in tension with the will of slaveowners to retain their dominance. This tension probably heightened rather than lessened as the end of slavery approached. It did not cease with the formal freeing of the slaves on 1 August 1834. Emancipation itself was supposed to be followed by a period of apprenticeship, during which the "apprentices" would be paid by their former owners to work for a further six years. This system was supposed to ease the transition from slavery to "full freedom". In Cayman, however, emancipation took a highly unusual course, as the apprenticeship system came to an abrupt end after only ten months.

Sam Sharpe, leader of the Jamaican slave rebellion in 1831 (above); an interpretive sign in northern Jamaica describing the outbreak of the rebellion (below).

There is no evidence in the years leading up to emancipation that a slave uprising was ever contemplated in Cayman. If such thoughts were entertained, they would have been checked by the bloody suppression of Sam Sharpe's slave rebellion in Jamaica in May 1832. News of this rebellion and its suppression may well have increased tension between the races in Cayman, in addition to feeding the slaveowners' fears that emancipation might soon be imposed by Britain. By this time the majority of the British public had already become abolitionists, and they were further stirred by descriptions of the slave rebellion given by missionaries expelled from Jamaica. Debates in the Westminster Parliament made it clear that emancipation was imminent. The only questions remaining were how to persuade freed slaves to continue to work for their former owners, and how much compensation to pay slaveholders for the loss of their human property.

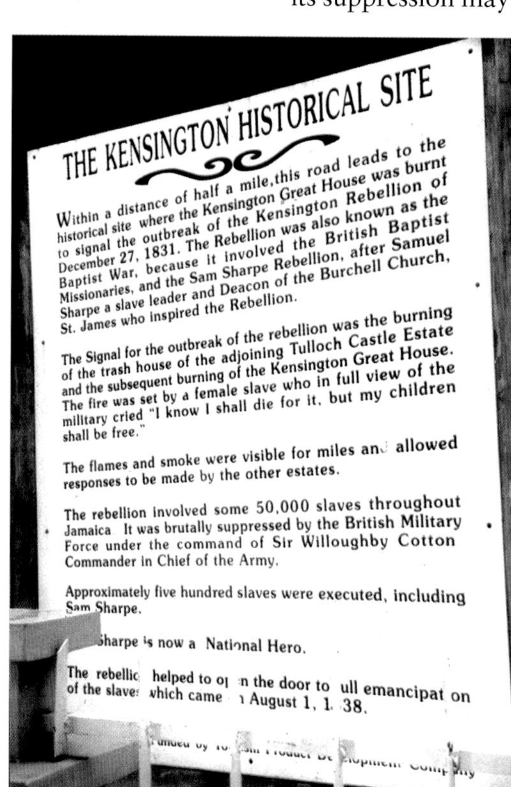

The Emancipation Bill was finally passed on 31 July 1833. But the compensation money it set aside (£20 million for the whole British Empire) was to be paid only for officially registered slaves. Up to this point, as we have seen, the slaves in Cayman had never been registered. Within a matter of months, therefore, the Caymanian slaveowners sent an urgent petition through Lord Mulgrave, the Governor of Jamaica, requesting slave registration and owner compensation.

The petitioners explained that they had not registered their slaves because of the imperfect connections between Jamaica and Cayman. They understood the importance of emancipation and sought the same compensation as Jamaican slaveowners. They described the current state of the slaves in Cayman as quiet, but indicated that this situation might not last. "Not having the benefit of a company of regulars, [the slaveowners] must consequently rely on the Island Militia," wrote the petitioners, "and if that be not furnished with the means of protection, they, their wives and their little children, must be at the mercy of men, who are suddenly to receive a boon of so extraordinary a nature, that their capability of duly appreciating it is a matter of considerable doubt." The petitioners asked for at least a hundred muskets for the militia. They also requested the first-ever official visit to the islands of a Jamaican governor. The petition was signed by John Drayton and the other six Magistrates, by James Coe Sr. ("the late Custos"), nine militia officers, and fifty-eight other slaveowners.[38]

William Wilberforce, Member of Parliament, who led the movement in Britain to abolish slavery throughout the British Empire.

No immediate reply was forthcoming from Lord Mulgrave. In November 1833, however, the Secretary of State in Westminster authorised the belated slave registration for the Cayman Islands, which was carried out the following year by James Minot. Then in February 1834 the Secretary of State decreed that the slaveowners in Cayman would receive compensation. This was welcome news. Emancipation itself occurred, in accordance with the Emancipation Act, at midnight on 31 July 1834. There is unfortunately no first-hand description of this momentous event in Cayman. But a few days prior to it, Lord Sligo, who had succeeded Mulgrave as Governor, had sent a "Private & Confidential" despatch to Westminister addressing the situation in Cayman. He stated that it was his intention to send a detachment of thirty men of the 2nd West India Regiment to keep the peace. He would also appoint a Stipendiary Magistrate to protect the interests of the Caymanian apprentices and commission the resident Anglican clergyman, Rev. Thomas Sharpe, as an additional Magistrate to deal with apprenticeship cases.[39]

Lord Sligo fulfilled these intentions and simultaneously answered the islanders' plea for a visit from the Jamaican Governor. In September 1834 he accompanied the West India Regiment detachment and the newly appointed Stipendiary Magistrate, Dr. Hulme, to Grand Cayman. Though he stayed only a few hours, the Governor swore in two local J.P.s as valuators for the slave compensation, learned of recently passed local laws, and drew up a pithy account of Grand Cayman and its people.

Sligo described Grand Cayman as rich and fertile, "covered with the most luxuriant Herbage". It was self-sufficient in provisions, including maize. It grew some cotton and tobacco, and it produced excellent horses, mules, and

cattle. The mosquitoes he described as "quite a national misfortune". The population of "almost 1000 white persons and almost 900 Apprentices" impressed him. "In point of stature and make," he wrote, "I hardly ever saw a finer race of men, their average height certainly very much exceeds that of any other country I have seen."[40]

Lord Sligo was optimistic about the course that apprenticeship would take in Cayman. But it was not long before problems surfaced, despite the newly appointed Magistrates and a detachment of soldiers to guarantee civil peace. Hulme, in fact, stayed only a few months, and Sharpe, who had arrived in 1831, not much longer. Both were discouraged by lack of financial support and by the difficulties of mediating between former slaveowners and former slaves.[41] In particular, the presence of black soldiers in the British West India Regiment angered some of Grand Cayman's prominent inhabitants. Their lawless behaviour both towards the soldiers and towards their own former slaves constituted a major challenge to public order.

By the spring of 1835, Sligo was facing a serious dilemma, despite the arrival of a new Stipendiary Magistrate. Conflicts in Grand Cayman between former masters and apprentices and between local inhabitants and the soldiers were creating questions in London about how due governance should be exercised in the Cayman Islands. It was in this context, prompted partly by the fact that the slaves had never been duly registered before 1834, that Sligo decided to free the apprentices in the Cayman Islands immediately. Well aware of the opposition this could bring from former slaveowners, he decided to issue the proclamation in person and to enforce it with a detachment of white British regular troops. Though a garrison remained necessary for the time being, he would withdraw the black troops of the British West India Regiment as soon as he could. He would rely on the new Magistrate, Dr. Thompson, and the other Magistrates, as well as the calming influence of the Anglican Church, to keep the peace in Grand Cayman.

The events that followed were dramatic. Lord Sligo sailed from Port Royal on 30 April 1835, in the largest warship on the Jamaica station, HMS *Forte*. He was accompanied by the sloop HMS *Serpent*, carrying Captain Anthony Pack and twenty-five men of the 84th Regiment, then part of the Jamaica garrison. The *Serpent* was sent ahead to alert the Magistrates and chief inhabitants, and to request them to attend the Governor on his arrival. HMS *Forte* anchored off George Town at 3 p.m. on Saturday, 2 May, and Custos Drayton, Dr. Thompson, and "25 of the Principal Inhabitants" came aboard. They were received formally in the ship's great cabin. Governor Sligo then announced that he had come to free the apprentices immediately. As expected, the hearers were thunderstruck at the news. One of the Boddens remarked that he had come aboard "a wealthy man possessing all I desired, and I am at this moment a beggar, without knowing where to turn for a crust of bread".[42]

Governor Sligo, addressing slaveowners in his cabin aboard HMS Forte *on 2 May 1835, announces that slaves in the Cayman Islands will be freed immediately.*

Some of the former slaveowners asked if the action could be delayed so they could draw up a petition against the "threatened evil". Sligo told them that that was impossible: his decision was final. In response to their obvious distress, the Governor recommended that they petition the King and Parliament, requesting recompense for the loss of apprentice labour. These efforts he pledged to support. Unfortunately, the Governor did not know that a despatch was already on its way from London, stating that the owners could expect no more than the slave compensation had already decreed.[43]

Lord Sligo explained that the proclamation would be made in the presence of the troops, accompanied by the local militia. The detachment of the 84th Regiment and HMS *Serpent* would then remain at Grand Cayman for at least a month. Following his address, the calm but downcast principal inhabitants returned to shore. The next morning, Sunday, 3 May, they were on hand when the Governor landed, to a salute from Fort George, at 7 a.m. Captain Pack of the 84th Regiment then read the proclamation, after which Lord Sligo gave a prepared speech to the masters and apprentices. To the masters he repeated the gist of his remarks of the previous day. His message to the apprentices, while paternalistic in the colonial mode, expressed a sensitivity to this unique situation.

> You who have been slaves and lately acting as apprentices, are by this decision made absolutely and unconditionally free; I trust you will show your gratitude to that nation which has made such great personal and pecuniary sacrifices to ensure your freedom, by your loyalty to your common Monarch, and by the

Captain Pack reads the Emancipation Proclamation in George Town on 3 May 1835.

willing and anxious obedience you will pay to the laws of the land. New duties devolve upon you with the new position which you now occupy; and I hope that by the steadiness of your conduct, and your peaceable demeanour, you will prove that this greatest of all earthly boons has not been unworthily bestowed upon you; you must now entirely depend upon your own industry for your support. You must recollect that you have now no person to feed you, no person to clothe you, no person to give you medical assistance if you are ill. You must depend upon your own exertions for all these things; you have no houses or grounds of your own; those that you have heretofore occupied must now be given up to their owners, your former masters, whose property they are; all belong to him excepting your furniture, clothes and the crops you have now in the ground; these you have a right to remove to where you please to go, if you mean to do so; but I trust that a sense of what is so decidedly your own interests will induce him to leave you in the quiet occupation of your grounds and homes. Though he who was your master is no longer so, recollect of what service he may be to you. Do not imagine that because you are now free you are independent of one another; no class of the community can be independent of the other. Those of you who have been well treated, recollect that it is now in your power to show your gratitude for past kindnesses; those who think that your masters have occasionally felt harshly towards you, recollect that probably you gave great provocation, and show that if they have been in the wrong, that will not now justify your acting improperly. I trust that on my next visit to this Island, I shall hear that your improved habits of industry, your quiet demeanour, and

270 PAPERS RELATIVE TO THE ABOLITION OF

GRAND CAYMANAS.

Enclosures in No. 388.

Enclosures in No. 388.

Jamaica, ss. A PROCLAMATION.

By his Excellency the Most Noble *Howe Peter*, Marquess of *Sligo*, Knight of the most illustrious Order of Saint Patrick, and member of His Majesty's most Honourable Privy Councils in England and Ireland, Captain-general and Governor in Chief of His Majesty's Island of Jamaica, and the Territories thereon depending in America, Chancellor and Vice-Admiral of the same.

Whereas the situation of the inhabitants of the Grand Caymanas having engaged the particular attention of His Majesty's Government, more especially as to the effect the recent changes under the laws of the Imperial Parliament have upon the structure of society in those Islands belonging to Great Britain, were slavery formerly existed; and the opinion of the law officers of the Crown having been obtained; I have received His Majesty's commands forthwith to communicate the decision at which they have arrived upon the question.

The Slavery Abolition Act having declared that all persons of the age of six or upwards, who, on or before the first of August one thousand eight hundred and thirty-four, had been duly registered as slaves, should become and be apprenticed labourers, and such registration not having been adopted as respects the Islands of the Caymanas, previous to the passing thereof, such unregistered slaves have in consequence become entitled to the unqualified enjoyment of their personal freedom: And whereas it is incumbent on His Majesty's Government to see the letter of the Slavery Abolition Act carried into full effect, I do hereby, under the directions of His Majesty's Government, declare and make known, that all such unregistered slaves at the Islands of the Caymanas, have become absolutely manumitted, and can no longer be lawfully treated as apprenticed labourers.

Fully alive, however, to the inconvenience which the course I am commanded to pursue must entail upon the private interests or those of the community of this Island, and the apparent injustice inflicted on the proprietors of negroes by this construction of the law, owing to the injury which they will sustain in being deprived of the services of their apprentices, still His Majesty's Government have no power to interpose, and it will be for Parliament itself to provide a remedy, and to decide how far those affected by the omission may be entitled to compensation for the loss unintentionally inflicted upon them. On this subject a most earnest representation will be made to the King. And I have the satisfaction in the mean time to make known that the Commissioners for Compensation in England consider the Caymanas as an appendage to Jamaica, and entitled to share in the compensation fund, according to the interests of the respective owners in those Islands.

Given under my hand and seal at arms, at Saint Jago de la Vega, the day of in the fifth year of His Majesty's reign, annoque Domini 1835.

By His Excellency's command.

The Emancipation Proclamation that ended slavery in the Cayman Islands on 3 May 1835.

your increased and increasing wealth will show your obedience to the laws, and that you deserve this great benefit which you now receive.[44]

Lord Sligo was extremely gratified when one apprentice stepped forward and assured him that "the change would be no change to him, as he would remain all his life with his Master who had always behaved so well to him". The rest of the apprentices, the Governor admitted, were much less certain, and "did not seem to have any feeling on the occasion or to know the extent of the blessing they were receiving".

A century of slavery in the Cayman Islands thus ended abruptly, with the transitional six years of apprenticeship cut short after less than a year. Slave Society in Cayman, though less divided than other Slave Societies in the Caribbean, and less cruel and bitter in its effects, was nonetheless fraught with

its own tensions. Attempts to address these tensions can be seen in the legislature of the 1830s, which was itself the outcome of earlier forms of government influenced by a Slave Society. In the generation between the official visits by Edward Corbet in 1802 and Governor Sligo in 1834, the population had doubled, the cotton-based economy had flourished and declined, and the system of slavery had slowly waned and suddenly ended. It was hardly surprising that the decade of the 1830s turned out to be one of unprecedented upheaval and change.

Custos James Goodchild Coe: lawmaker and leader in the 1800s.

CHAPTER 5

Early Government and the Sociopolitical Revolution of the 1830s

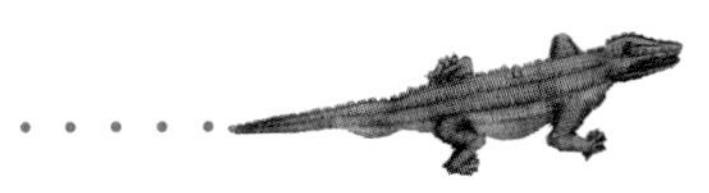

THE CAYMAN ISLANDS WERE SPARED the slave rebellions that erupted in Barbados in 1816, in Demerara in 1823, and, most notably, in western Jamaica in 1831–2. Yet they were well aware of such disturbances. The local population, both slave and free, was steadily increasing, and from at least 1823, the Magistrates and "principal inhabitants" of Cayman sought to fashion local laws to govern this community. In 1831, as western Jamaica was on the point of conflagration, this body was actually in the process of forming a new, elected legislature in order to ensure stability. This legislature proved partially successful. Emancipation in August 1834 and the unexpected end to apprenticeship in May 1835 plunged the Cayman Islands into social, economic, and political turmoil. To the credit of all sides, events stopped short of open conflict. Nonetheless, the crisis of adjustment from a slave to a free society was the sharpest upheaval in Caymanian history up to that time.

Sixty years before emancipation, an unusual episode had highlighted the imperfect control that Jamaica exercised over the Cayman Islands. The episode was one of wrongful enslavement. In September 1776, Captain Joseph Davis of the Jamaican schooner *Dove* sold seven "Sambos" (descendants of Nicaraguan Indians and Africans) as slaves to planters in Grand Cayman. Within weeks, a delegation of Sambos had arrived in Jamaica from the Miskito Coast, angrily demanding their release. They pointed out that treaties forbade the enslavement of their people, and they threatened fire and blood-

shed to the English settlements on the Miskito Coast if nothing was done. The Governor of Jamaica, Sir Basil Keith, took immediate action. He sent an aide with a Senior Magistrate's commission, and a small detachment of soldiers, to Grand Cayman on HMS *Porcupine*. Their orders were to return the captives to their home territory. The slave buyers were to be offered their money back, but if they refused to release the captives, they were to be compelled by force.[1]

The Caymanian planters offered no resistance, and the seven captives were carried back to Black River.[2] But the episode brought home to Governor Keith the indeterminate status of the Cayman Islands. He was surprised to learn from his law officers that the Cayman Islands had never been formally declared a dependency of Jamaica. No one knew to what extent Jamaican laws applied in the islands, or even "to what jurisdiction" they were "amenable". Keith strongly recommended that the Cayman Islands "be expressly declared a dependency of Jamaica and not left for the future to uncertain conjectures and experiments". This action could not possibly offend rival powers in the region, he said, "the English subjects thereon settled having enjoyed their property of it for such a series of years".[3] The American War of Independence intervened, however, and nothing was done. The question of Cayman's formal relationship to Jamaica remained unresolved for almost another century, until 1863.

Despite this continuing ambiguity, local affairs in the Cayman Islands were managed in the first instance by a number of Magistrates, one of whom usually served as Chief Magistrate. This system worked in the early years, at least to the satisfaction of the Magistrates and the property owners from whom they were drawn. But its flaws were exposed in a report prepared in June 1802 by Edward Corbet for the benefit of the Governor of Jamaica, George Nugent.

As a professional soldier, Nugent was concerned with matters of defence. Corbet therefore reported, amongst many other things, on the state of the militia and the unsatisfactory condition of the two local forts. The small fort at George Town was described as "not very well constructed" and, with just three light cannon, "by no means well equipped". The fort at Prospect Point was "intended to oppose the progress of an enemy landing in Sandy Bay". It was slightly stronger, boasting four small guns. The militia consisted of eighty men said to be fit to bear arms, though far fewer were actually armed. They were divided into four separate contingents: Bodden Town, George Town, South West Sound, and "Prospect, Spotts, & Little Pedro". They were under the command of four captains and three subordinate officers. The "officers" bore no official commissions but had been "chosen by the Inhabitants of the respective Quarters". Those at George Town were said to be "about to resign their situations in consequence of meeting with some opposition to their orders".[4]

Sir George Nugent

Corbet's assessment of government in Grand Cayman was less than reassuring. The Senior Magistrate, William Bodden, and four other Magistrates had been appointed in January 1798 by Lord Balcarres, the Jamaican Governor. Two of them had since died. This left the Magistracy entirely in the hands of William Bodden and his brothers James and Joseph, all of whom resided at Bodden Town (where they were respectively captain, lieutenant, and ensign of the local militia). Throughout Corbet's stay William Bodden was away visiting his son in Honduras, adding to the impression that no one was in charge.

"The only Laws or regulations in force they consider to be those of Jamaica as far as they are acquainted with them," reported Corbet. "They have no particular police. The Magistrates are understood to have the same power as those in this island [Jamaica], but when any new measure is to be adopted it is generally submitted by them to the consideration of the Inhabitants at large." The Magistrates faced a serious dilemma over a capital crime. One inhabitant who had killed another in a fight had been languishing in confinement for almost a year. Joseph Bodden doubted whether he or his brothers "or any one else in the island" possessed "sufficient knowledge to carry thro' a business of that nature". They were also concerned that they might not find "a proper and impartial Jury, almost the whole of the settlers being more or less connected by marriage". The Magistrates believed that the prisoner should probably be carried to Jamaica for trial, presumably to the assize court at Montego Bay. This was the port with which Caymanians had the closest connections and where they usually went to get married, as there was no clergyman on the island.[5]

Governor Nugent sent Edward Corbet's report to London in August 1802. In his covering letter Nugent expressed his desire to "establish a Judicature" in the Cayman Islands, "to give the Possessors a legal Title to the Lands which they occupy, to issue Commissions to the Officers of Militia, & to appoint some of the principal People Magistrates.[6] In later correspondence with William Bodden, the Governor refused a request to allow him and his brothers to resign as Magistrates because they were so often away on business in Honduras. "The principal Proprietors of a British settlement are bound to give up a portion of their time for the public benefit," Nugent cautioned the Senior Magistrate. "Should the Magistracy fall into improper hands, great mischief might result." Not long after this, however, war intervened, and despite his

Fort George, built in the 1780s and described in Corbet's Report.

continuing interest in Grand Cayman, more urgent matters prevented Nugent from following through on most of his plans for the island. In February 1806, he left Jamaica to take up a new appointment as Commander in Chief in India.[7]

After 1810, as the cotton plantations began to decline, control of the expanding but increasingly underworked slave population was a growing problem for the slaveowners. Like the plantocracy of Jamaica, they may have felt threatened by the revolutionary new black nation of Haiti. They would have learned with alarm about the explosive slave revolts of 1816, 1823, and 1831 in the British Caribbean. They may also have known of the growing demand in Britain to force West Indian planters to improve the condition of slaves – concerns that led eventually to the abolition of slavery.[8]

It was in this context, but responding to its own needs, that the judicial system in Grand Cayman slowly evolved. Successive Chief Magistrates William Bodden Sr., James Coe Sr., John Drayton, and James Coe Jr. established more or less the system of judicature that Governor Nugent had probably envisioned. The Magistrates acted in petty sessions to try minor criminal and civil disputes. On at least two occasions – both murder cases – they acted as an assize court.[9] The year 1810 saw the start of the oldest continuous administrative function in Cayman, that of the Public Recorder. This official recorded all marriages, wills, deeds, slave sales, and manumissions, as well as court transactions. These records are the earliest locally created archives in the Cayman Islands.

From at least 1816, the Magistrates constituted themselves as a Slave Court. Unlike Jamaica and other slave colonies, where slaves were tried before two or three Magistrates without a jury, the Cayman Islands Slave Court consisted of two or three Magistrates with a jury of twelve white men, all of them slaveholders.[10]

The most significant slave trial of which a record remains was that of the "Negro Wench" called Long Celia, owned by Thomas K. Eden. She was tried for inciting rebellion in October 1820. A witness named Sarah Harbourn testified that some days earlier Celia had come to her house and asked if she had heard the news that the slaves were soon to be freed. Sarah replied that she had not. Celia said that she had heard from a crewman on the Jamaican schooner *Mackerel* that in a few months the slaves would be free and "not be subject to the control of a Master". Papers about freedom were said to have come from England but to have been destroyed by the masters. On its next visit the Jamaica packet was expected to bring an emancipation decree.

According to Sarah Harbourn, Long Celia also claimed that the "Buchras" (white masters) well knew of the coming freedom, but whenever they were talking of it and a slave entered the room, the subject was dropped. Long Celia had asked Sarah, somewhat contemptuously, what was the point of the whites

The trial of Long Celia.

keeping the news to themselves, since once the decree came just "let two Negroes go to their houses with Machets they would run". When her turn came to address the court, Long Celia made what the record called "a slight and equivocating defence". The court found her guilty of "uttering seditious words, tending to stir up a revolution of the Negroes". The whipping of slave women was soon to be outlawed throughout the British West Indies, and the number of lashes for all slaves limited to thirty-nine. In this context, the penalty imposed by Magistrates John Drayton and William Page and the jury of twelve white slaveholders was especially harsh: "to receive fifty lashes on your bare body in some public place at Georgetown".[11]

THE BEGINNINGS OF SELF-GOVERNMENT

The first Magistrates ruled with some reference to Jamaican law. In 1802, as Edward Corbet had noted in his Report, "The Magistrates are understood to have the same power as those in this island [Jamaica], but when any new measure is to be adopted it is generally submitted by them to the consideration of the Inhabitants at large." But as the correspondence between Chief Magistrate William Bodden and Governor Nugent in 1804–5 discloses, this ad hoc system led to some confusion and conflict, particularly between William Bodden and the other landowners.[12] By at least 1823, the Chief Magistrate, James Coe Sr., and the other "Magistrates and principal inhabitants" of Grand Cayman apparently felt that they needed a more formal system of lawmaking and set of laws. Accordingly, they asked for and got commissions for several more Magistrates from Governor Lord Manchester.

The beginning of democracy in the Cayman Islands: the creation of the first elected legislature in December 1831.

1831.

Grand Cayman Ss. —

— At a Meeting held at Saint James's on the 5th December 1831: it was Resolved that Representatives should be elected for the different districts throughout the Island, for the purpose of framing Local Laws for its better government The Representatives for the different districts were accordingly elected on the 10th of same month, and met at George Town said Island, pursuant to advertisement, on the 31st December 1831. and on the 2nd January 1832. — The Magistrates also assembled but did not sit in the same room with the Representatives, forming as it were two Houses in imitation of the Council and Assembly of Jamaica. — And no law formed or passed by the Representatives to be deemed

valid

2

valid, until, it had received the assent of the Magistrates.——

——The names of the Magistrates and Representatives are as follow.——

——John Drayton Esqr. Senior Magistrate Robert Stephen Watler, Waide W. Bodden, John S. Jackson, James Coe Junr., Abraham O. Feurtado, Elin J. Parsons, and Nathl. Glover Esquires, Magistrates, and George W. Wood, James H. Wood, James Coe Senr., Wm. Eden, Junr., John Goodhew, James Parsons Senr., William James Bodden, Thomas Lindsay Thomson, Samuel Parsons, and William Bodden, Vestrymen.——

——An Act for the better Regulation of the Militia of Grand Cayman.——

——Be it Enacted, by the Authorities of this Island, and it is hereby

Enacted.

Then, on 13 December 1823, the Magistrates and "principal inhabitants" held a meeting at William Eden's residence at Pedro St. James. Their first decision was to lease the Pedro property from William Eden for £5 6s 8d a year. It would be used as an animal pound, court-house and jail, with a daily payment of 2s 11d authorised whenever there was a prisoner.[13]

The first laws passed were in the interests of property owners. One law decreed severe penalties for maiming or killing livestock that were found trespassing. Roaming livestock were to be brought to the pound at Pedro St. James, and their owners were to pay damages, fines, and upkeep costs when they claimed the animals. Another law levied a duty of 1.5 per cent on all "dry goods, provisions, liquors or any kind of merchandize whatever" sold by any non-inhabitant. A third law decreed "that from henceforth no slave shall retail any malt liquors, spirituous liquors or wines of any kind or quality". The penalty was a fine of twenty shillings and confiscation of the goods, with the proceeds divided between the treasury and the informer. These three laws were passed by eighteen persons, all of them prominent landowners and slaveowners, and a third of them Magistrates.[14]

In May 1824 the lawmakers passed another law to control the sale of liquor. It required that all retailers of liquor purchase a licence, costing £3 6s 8d a year, with a further enrolling fee of £5 paid to the Clerk of the Court. Licences had to be renewed each year. The names of licensees were to be officially published, and illicit retailers would be punished with fines and confiscation.[15]

The only other law from that session of which we have a record was aimed at preventing the importation of slaves who might have been transported from other islands to Cayman for acts of rebellion. The preamble to this law is significant because it points to earlier laws that do not appear to have survived. It refers to "a Law made in this Island some years ago" forbidding the import of transported slaves, which had been allowed to become dormant. The 1824 law itself demonstrated the Magistrates' zeal to turn away slaves thought to have been transported. Henceforward, any person bringing in a transported slave to work in Grand Cayman was to pay a fine of £50 Jamaican currency.[16]

TIGHTENING TENSIONS

There is an unfortunate shortage of documentation for the period between 1824 and 1830. From information recorded in 1831, though, it is clear that this was a period of steadily tightening tensions in Grand Cayman. On 26 October 1831, Custos John Drayton and Magistrates Robert Watler and Waide Bodden wrote a letter to Governor Belmore. The letter was taken in person to Jamaica by Waide Bodden, who, it was hoped, would bring a reply

The meeting at Pedro St. James on 5 December 1831, when the decision was taken to hold the first elections.

back from the Governor. The letter made several requests. The first was that the Governor appoint five new Magistrates, since there were only three Magistrates at the time, the fourth, William Hunter, having died recently. "There is in general too much opposition to the legal authorities," Drayton, Watler, and Bodden complained, so that as Magistrates they were sometimes "abused for want of authority to protect them". They asked the Governor to clarify if they had power to raise taxes, to build a jail, and to pursue legal redress to recover debts of any amount. Last, they requested that "some reprehension from His Excellency" might be expressed "to the Inhabitants of this Island respecting their opposition to the Authorities".

Governor Belmore immediately agreed to appoint the new Magistrates. Some months later, however, the Colonial Office disallowed the appointment of one of them, Nathaniel Glover, because he was an American rather than a British citizen. On all other matters raised by the Magistrates the Governor pointed out that he would have to seek advice from London because decisions about them were "far exceeding" his authority. He asked Magistrate Bodden for more detail on these subjects before communicating with London. He recommended that Bodden "supply the facts" in a suitable form with the assistance of a Mr. Beaumont, a member of the Jamaican Assembly who had introduced Bodden to the Governor. For reasons that are not clear, Bodden returned to Cayman without ever furnishing this information. It is probable that he arrived back in late November 1831. Within a month, any further action by Jamaica or London was forestalled by the outbreak of the tremendous slave revolt in western Jamaica known as Sam Sharpe's Rebellion.[17]

Before this rebellion and after Bodden's return, the principal inhabitants and Magistrates, including the five new appointees, began to reconstitute themselves into a more formal legislature. This action apparently took place without any approval from Jamaica or London. At a meeting at Pedro St. James on 5 December 1831, it was decided that the new legislature should consist of "representatives" and "Magistrates . . . forming as it were two Houses in imitation of the Council and Assembly of Jamaica". It was resolved that "Representatives should be appointed for the different districts throughout the Island for the purpose of forming Local Laws for its better Government." On 10 December two representatives each were "elected" for the districts of West Bay, George Town, South West Sound, Prospect, and Bodden Town. (The method of election is not known.) These ten representatives, later referred to as a Vestry, assembled for the first time on 31 December 1831 in George Town and met again on 2 January 1832. The eight Magistrates met at the same time but in a different room, carefully preserving the classic British form of a bicameral legislature. No law was "deemed valid" until it had received the assent of both houses.[18]

The first session of this legislature passed four laws. The most important of these was a law to regulate the militia. Each free male between sixteen and sixty capable of bearing arms was compelled to serve in the militia and to provide himself with a serviceable musket, bayonet, and ammunition pouch, unless he declared on oath that he could not afford them – in which case they would be provided "at the expense of the Island". Stiff fines were enacted for neglect of duty, ranging from 6s 8d for a private to £1 6s 8d for a major, to be enforced by a marshal within each company. There was no provision to enroll slaves, however, even in the event of foreign attack. This suggests that the militia was intended more as a police force than as a defence force against external threats.[19] The other Acts passed at this session dealt with licensing the sale of "spirituous liquors", regulating the meeting of the civil courts, and levying a tax "for the purpose of Building a Parsonage House and Jails, and other purposes required". In September 1832 the legislature passed two laws: one to create cattle pounds in four districts, and the other to arrange for all public roads to be cleared twice a year. Thereafter, the legislature appears to have met about twice a year for the next ten years, enacting laws and amendments on subjects as varied as a closer observance of the Sabbath to taxes on slaves, ships, houses, and livestock.[20]

The importance of law and order is evident from a warning notice about the police powers of Magistrates that was issued by the legislature in December 1833. "The Magistrates and Representatives assembled", it announced, expressed "their fixed determination strictly to abide by such local enactments as have been, or may be, from time to time passed, and punish all those who from obstinacy or other motives may set themselves in opposition to the

present system of Government". Three public officials had already been appointed by the new legislature – a clerk and treasurer in 1831, and a poundkeeper in 1832. Now, to reinforce the authority of the courts and legislature, an island constable was appointed in February 1835. Besides attending all court sessions, serving summonses, executing warrants, and committing criminals to jail, the constable was responsible for whipping convicted offenders and was put in charge of the jail and the "penal gang".[21]

KEEPING THE PEACE

Governor Sligo visited Grand Cayman in September 1834 during the early days of apprenticeship shortly after emancipation. Sligo was accompanied by black soldiers of the 2nd West India Regiment and by the first Stipendiary Magistrate, Dr. Hulme. On this visit he also commissioned the resident Anglican minister, Rev. Sharpe, as a Magistrate, giving him special authority to deal with cases involving apprentices. Unfortunately, neither Dr. Hulme nor Rev. Sharpe stayed long, while the presence of the West India Regiment caused more problems than it solved.

Some of the tumultuous events of the ten months of apprenticeship in Cayman can be followed from reports by Dr. Robert Thompson, the Stipendiary Magistrate appointed to succeed Dr. Hulme in February 1835. Custos John Drayton proved a useful and responsible ally, but Dr. Thompson found that his problems went much further than protecting the interests of the apprentices. They included controlling the lawless behaviour of some prominent inhabitants – including Magistrates and Vestrymen – towards blacks, whether former slaves or soldiers stationed to keep the peace.[22]

One case involved a trumped-up charge of assault and rape against two of the black soldiers. Several of the incidents between inhabitants and soldiers implicated the merchant and liquor retailer Richard Phelan. An Irish immigrant who had arrived from a wreck on the Cuban coast more than ten years before, Phelan had already risen to be Clerk of the Court and was to become a Magistrate. Several members of the near-white Parsons family were also involved. One was Samuel Parsons, Phelan's business partner and a Vestryman for West Bay. The others were James Parsons, a George Town Vestryman and formerly a major slaveowner, and his nephew, Ebin John Parsons, one of the eight Magistrates.[23]

Richard Phelan had got into a dispute with a Private Rafferty over his payment for a measure of cloth purchased at Phelan's store. Phelan sold the cloth on credit for ten shillings but then demanded fifteen, accusing Rafferty in front of Special Magistrate Robert Thompson of attempting to swindle him. When Rafferty, on Thompson's advice, offered ten shillings, Phelan took the

money but ordered the soldier out of his store, calling him a "Damned Affrican Negro Barbarian". Rafferty calmly responded that he was indeed an African but a better man than Phelan, being the son of an African king who, unlike Phelan, had never been in a Spanish prison. At this, Phelan rushed into the street and struck Rafferty several blows. The soldier, "a strong courageous man", responded so effectively that Phelan fled back into his house "and from an upper window offered two dollars to anyone who would beat Rafferty". An apprentice named Times, belonging to Samuel Parsons, took up the offer, but "Rafferty gave him three blows which were enough for him and then walked quietly home to his Barracks".[24]

That same morning, Ash Wednesday, Thompson had been informed by Samuel Parsons that a Private Hunter was drunk and interrupting church services. Thompson and the troops' commander, Lieutenant Williams, requested Magistrate Ebin Parsons to have Hunter placed in the public stocks. But shortly afterwards, Lieutenant Williams came to Thompson's house with several soldiers, dragging Private Hunter "all covered in blood and unable to stand". Hunter said that he had been beaten and abused by Richard Phelan while powerless to retaliate. James Parsons then burst on the scene and in a "bullying" manner said that he, not Phelan, had beaten Hunter, and asked what the Magistrate, the officer, and the soldiers intended to do about it. It was with difficulty that Thompson and Williams prevented the soldiers who were "ready to tear Parsons to pieces". The soldiers were ordered back to their barracks, and Parsons, still "speaking very violently of the soldiers", was told to go home and return the following day for a judicial investigation. Parsons went, but as he departed, Thompson heard him say "he cared not for Magistrate nor Officer nor King, he would lick them".[25]

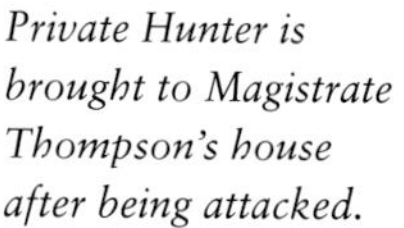

Private Hunter is brought to Magistrate Thompson's house after being attacked.

At this, a private soldier named Blunt, normally "a very quiet man" but a "very tiger" when provoked, who was sitting nearby with a musket by his side, got up and said that anyone who decried Dr. Thompson, his lieutenant, and the King deserved to be "beaten out of the yard". Parsons returned in an even greater fury, grabbed a club-sized piece of wood, and said "he would Kill the damned negro soldiers". Advancing with the musket in his hand, Blunt was ready to kill Parsons in self-defence; he was barely restrained by the Magistrate and persuaded to leave with the other soldiers. Parsons was escorted home by Thompson, still shouting abuse at the group of soldiers being "Marched or rather driven forward by Lieut Williams" towards their barracks. "He would fight them any one of them single handed, they were Affricans &c.", noted Thompson in his report.[26]

Another action involving Magistrate Ebin John Parsons was particularly provocative. A corporal and five men were marching along in single file when Parsons came galloping up behind them as if to run them down. At the last minute, he reined in his horse and demanded to know why they had not given way when a gentleman rode by. The corporal replied calmly that, since they were in single file, there was plenty of room for Parsons to pass. Parsons then asked him why the detachment did not salute him as a gentleman. The corporal responded that "it was customary to salute Kings Officers, of the Army or Navy, but they did not know him to be such". Angrily, Parsons whipped and spurred his horse and would have run the soldiers down, had not one seized the bridle. Parsons swung his whip at the soldier, missing him but causing him to let go, and passed on his way. The very next day, he proposed that the next session of the local Magistrates "draw up and sign a Petition to have these Affrican barbarians withdrawn from the Island, and a hundred white men sent in their place".[27]

In the following two court sessions, neither James Parsons nor Richard Phelan was found guilty of assault, largely because the Magistrates misconstrued the evidence of the soldiers, whose English was far from clear. However, concerned by the fact that Lieutenant Williams had forbidden his men to patronise Phelan's store, Phelan agreed not to press charges against Rafferty. Ebin Parsons was persuaded by Robert Thompson and the other Magistrates to withdraw his charge of disrespect against the soldiers. The petition to remove the soldiers was also deflected by Thompson. He argued that the British government had the right to place military detachments where it pleased. If a Magistrate behaved as badly as Ebin Parsons had towards the soldiers, the Governor of Jamaica was far more likely to withdraw the Magistrate's commission than to order the removal of the soldiers.[28]

When Thompson heard complaints about relations between masters and their apprentices, he (like most Stipendiary Magistrates elsewhere) was probably inclined to credit the masters' side, or to pass over cases "in silence so

as not to give unnecessary offence". But he appears to have been fair. In one dispute, for example, Hugh Collins, a master, complained that one of his female apprentices, Silos, had refused to do tasks assigned to her. Instead, it was found that Silos had served her master and farmed the provision grounds diligently, and that on one recent occasion she had refused to carry on her head a basket of provisions "part belonging to her master, part belonging to other negroes" a distance of eight miles.

Observing from Jamaica, Governor Lord Sligo found himself in an awkward position. Neither apprenticeship nor the use of the British West India Regiment as a police force was working. To complicate matters, he was receiving conflicting signals from London about how to bring the Cayman Islands more firmly under control. One memorandum from the Colonial Office declared that the local legislature was invalid and that Jamaican laws should be formally decreed valid for the Cayman Islands, while recommending that a Caymanian representative be allowed to sit in the Jamaican Assembly. Other advice ranged from the suggestion that Caymanians should be persuaded to submit voluntarily to the authority of Jamaica, to the opinion that the Cayman Islands needed a competent civil authority, not a garrison. In the end, the resolution of the situation was left entirely up to the Jamaican Governor.[29]

Sligo's decision, as we saw in Chapter Four, was to free the apprentices immediately, and he arrived in person in Grand Cayman on 2 May 1835 to announce their full emancipation. He was accompanied by Captain Anthony Pack and twenty-five men of the 84th Regiment from Jamaica. Feeling reasonably optimistic about the course that emancipation would take, Sligo left after a stay of less than twenty-four hours. Captain Pack and Dr. Thompson then turned their attention to their various responsibilities. They announced and explained the Emancipation Proclamation in each of the different settlements, arbitrated initial disputes, and confirmed that militia detachments were ready to face any possible trouble.

They rode first to Bodden Town on Tuesday, 5 May. There they found the masters discontented and angry and the apprentices sullen and uncertain. When Captain Pack, echoing Lord Sligo's address, alluded to "the Corrections and severity of some Proprietors to their Slaves", Thompson reported that "some Angry feelings were displayed by the Apprentices". But after much talking, Thompson and Pack left believing that the former apprentices were now aware of their new circumstances and that the masters were resigned if not satisfied. Pack was positively "astonished at the high state" in which he found the arms of the Bodden Town militia company.[30]

On their way back from Bodden Town, Pack and Thompson read the proclamation and inspected the militia at Pedro, Spotts, Prospect, and South West Sound. They found "some appearances of discontent" among the masters, "but not so strongly manifested as at Bodden Town". On 7 May, they held an "advice and explanation" session on Thompson's veranda. This was followed by a formal court, in which Custos Drayton joined Pack and Thompson on the bench to adjudicate a significant test case of relationships between former masters and former apprentices. In return for their use of house and land, Thomas Thompson, a former slaveowner, was demanding that two former apprentices continue to work four and a half days a week for him. But the apprentices were refusing to work for him at all, since Sligo's proclamation had freed everyone absolutely. "After some persuation", they agreed to work for Thompson two and a half days each week. This compromise was drawn up as a labour contract, signed by both parties, witnessed by Drayton, SM Thompson, and Pack, and lodged with the Custos.[31]

The following day, Friday, 8 May 1835, in front of Fort George, Captain Pack reviewed the entire military force at his disposal. It consisted of the twenty-five soldiers of his own 84th Regiment, a detachment of Royal Marines from HMS *Serpent*, the twenty men of the British West India Regiment garrison, and the eleven officers and seventy-six other ranks mustered from the local militia. "I was quite satisfied with the appearance of the troops," reported Pack, "and such evolutions as I put them through were tolerably well performed by the Militia. . . . their arms and uniforms being in excellent order & both officers and soldiers feeling proud of being incorporated with His Majesty's Troops."[32]

After this, Pack boarded HMS *Serpent*, accompanied by the white troops and marines, and sailed for the other Cayman Islands, where he read the proclamation to William Page and his handful of apprentices at Little Cayman. Being unable to land at Cayman Brac, he sent a message to a settler called Dealy, who was said to have recently settled there with his family and six apprentices. To Pack's surprise, Page's apprentices "did not receive the communication of their freedom with that joy which would be naturally expected". Except for one girl, who asked to be taken back to her mother in Grand Cayman, "they expressed their willingness to remain with their master and work as usual".

When Captain Pack arrived back at Grand Cayman on 17 May, the Magistrates reported no disturbances serious enough to delay his planned return to Jamaica at the beginning of June. One case, however, was significant. William Watler, an elderly landowner with a violent reputation, complained that his former apprentices refused either to work or to vacate the houses they had used as slaves. Accordingly, he had threatened to unroof the houses with a view to eject the occupants. Custos Drayton intervened, telling the ex-apprentices that they had to either work under agreed terms, pay rent, or find other accommodations. They were persuaded back to work for a time. But before Pack left the island, they were reported to be refusing to work for Watler once again.[33]

The Emancipation Proclamation is read in Little Cayman.

On Wednesday, 3 June 1835, Captain Pack and Captain Sweeny, along with the soldiers of the British West India Regiment and the men of the 84th Regiment, set sail in the *Serpent* for Jamaica. They were accompanied by SM Robert Thompson, who, despite his concerns about conditions in Grand Cayman, desperately needed to recuperate from recurrent bouts of fever.

In his report to Governor Sligo, written from Up Park Camp in Kingston, Captain Pack maintained that withdrawing both the British West India Regiment and the 84th Regiment was justified. But he noted that relations between former masters and former slaves in Grand Cayman were still far from stabilised. "Some negroes with whom I conversed said their masters would require too much work before many months for allowing them their houses and grounds," he wrote. One woman had told him that "the white inhabitants wished to incite the Negroes and work them up to a state of insurrection" but that "the Negroes were determined not to show any insubordination as they saw the woeful effects of it in Jamaica and that they would take warning from that". Captain Pack's belief (shared, he said, by SM Thompson and Custos Drayton) was that "the masters who were kind to their servants would not be disturbed by them, but that harsh masters would not get servants so readily". He predicted "that after a short time the Negroes would find it their interest to get into some honest employment, and that the proprietors would be glad to get them back in their service".[34]

SM Robert Thompson was considerably more nervous about the situation than Captain Pack. His diary entries and reports in 1835 and 1836 provide a convincing account of the complex social adjustments of this period. As early as 11 May 1835, Thompson noted that he had heard rumours that some ex-apprentices who had initially promised to continue to serve their former masters when needed had now refused to do so unless paid the "extravagant" wages of half a dollar (3s 4d Jamaican currency) a day. The behaviour of the ex-apprentices at Bodden Town also concerned him. After receiving the news of their emancipation with only "a sullen listlessness", they had become "very wild in their demonstrations of Joy. Shooting, Fiddling, Dancing, and drinking to excess".[35]

At the other end of the island, the situation was more promising. In West Bay, "peace and tranquillity" reigned. Masters and ex-apprentices were "entering into bargains, for work, and renting little properties. It is astonishing," wrote Thompson, "how peaceably the Great Change has been effected here." By the end of the week, he was more generally optimistic: "The proprietors are . . . setting about serving themselves, and it only requires a little money to enable them to get along equally as well, and perhaps as contentedly as before."[36]

The Sabbath, however, brought fresh alarms. Disturbed by a hubbub, Thompson was astonished to find the road outside his George Town house crowded with blacks on horseback,

> . . . galloping some with saddles some without, all driving like Jehu when he drove to Jezreel. I was obliged to go out and stop them, lest they would ride down foot people. . . . I have been informed that some proprietors whose Negroes principally left them, having more horses than they could take care of, having given their horses, and Mares with Colts, to favorite Negroes to take care of them, [the Negroes] ride them where they please and let the proper Owners have them only when [they] wish to ride them. And as their Masters had set the example of always Galloping, the Negroes in all the pride of imitation, mounted their horses and came from Windward in a body to Church, driving Mares with Colts and horses, as fast as they would go. I was never more wrathful, to see God's holy day and God's Creatures at the same time so horribly abused on so sacred an instance by these ignorant Wretches.[37]

It was with great relief that on the following Sunday, Thompson was able to note: "Today the Negroes have not come down as they did last Sabbath. Having been made to understand that I would cause to be arrested any one of them or more should act so disorderly on the Lord's Day."[38]

Bodden Town, with the densest concentration of ex-slaves, was the chief focus of social tension. The proprietors wanted to obtain as much labour for as few wages as possible, in return for the former apprentices' continued use of houses and grounds. The ex-slaves wanted to keep "their" houses and

Ex-slaves riding their horses to church on Sunday.

grounds without obligation if possible, and to work when and as they wished, for the highest possible pay. Even before the departure of HMS *Serpent*, Robert Thompson was noting with alarm how the lines were drawn. "Some of the Proprietors, having driven their Negroes from their houses, in consequence of their not complying with their wishes in working for them as formerly, without remuneration," he wrote on 25 May, "the Negroes have entered into a resolution . . . to go to the East end of the Island, where there is unoccupied land, and there clear for themselves Grounds and build a Cottage . . . away from the white people."[39]

The following day, Thompson wrote even more urgently. "An alarming dread has begun to be entertained by the Negroes, that when I go away their Masters will attempt to subjugate them again to Slavery. The alarm has been pretty general and seems to have risen from some foolish expressions of Women, who have said that they will either do so or drive them away out of the Island." Thompson reported that he had spoken to proprietors who had expressed "a Sullen wish that the Negroes would all go away, to the east end, or out of the Island". Some of the ex-apprentices had indeed gone to the east and north of Grand Cayman, well beyond lands claimed by their former masters, and begun clearing grounds, but this was not a quick fix. "They must have food of which there is now a scarcity," Thompson wrote. "Their Grounds do not afford them sustenance . . . and they will return and steal Provisions . . . and more difficulty will arise out of this than any other Circumstance." One man had already been caught taking provisions worth four dollars (i.e., £1 6s 8d Jamaican currency) from his former provision grounds and carrying them off into the woods. When he was brought to court, Thompson

allowed another Justice to try the case "to show them they would be punished whether I was there or not". Fined the value of the provisions he had taken, the man paid up rather than go to jail.[40]

Ten months after returning to Jamaica for recuperation, Robert Thompson was persuaded by Governor Lord Sligo to make a second, brief visit to Grand Cayman in 1836. The Governor wanted him to assess the results of emancipation in Cayman, so as to shed light on what might happen once the apprentices in Jamaica were freed in August 1840 (as was then planned). Thompson stayed less than a week. His investigations were remarkably thorough, and he made considerable efforts to be even-handed. But his observations did not augur well for economic success or social harmony.[41]

SM Thompson landed at George Town on Saturday, 19 March 1836, and immediately consulted with Custos Drayton about the best way to carry out his commission.[42] They decided to prepare an eight-point questionnaire, to be answered by "principal inhabitants" in public sessions held on successive days at George Town, Spotts, Bodden Town, and West Bay. At these meetings, all participants would have the opportunity to add comments or make complaints. Not surprisingly, the liveliest sessions were at George Town and Bodden Town. The meeting at Spotts, held at the home of Magistrate James Coe Sr., was attended almost exclusively by the "principal inhabitants" themselves. At West Bay no one appeared except those hoping for free medical services.

Those who responded formally were all former slaveowners, and it is not surprising that most of their answers were similar. They spoke with candour, even passion, and were obviously more comfortable in the formal court setting than their ex-slaves. However, some statements aroused murmurs from the ex-slaves present, and Thompson recorded some counter-testimony, both in court and privately outside. Dissension was most obvious over the first and fifth points of the questionnaire: "What has been the conduct of the Apprentices since their Manumission? Have they fallen into the practice of working for Wages or not?", and "Can they [the former owners] hire domestics or field labourers easily and what is their Average rate of hire?"

At George Town, Chief Magistrate John Drayton rather grandly said that since his "old Servants all remain with me as usual without hire or bargain" he could not "answer for the bargains of others". Samuel Parsons, though, claimed that in his experience most ex-apprentices were willing to work as long as they were guaranteed good wages. He himself hired many, including house servants, whom he paid £10 a year. Very few were hired for any length of time as outside workers, but their daily rates varied from 1s 8d to 2s 6d, and even more for skilled work. Another George Town master, William James Bodden, stated "that many are very unwilling to work for hire". That very day he had "asked a number of Individuals and offered a half dollar

& more but they would not take it". This he expressed with "a good deal of picque [sic] and passionate feeling," reported Thompson. At this there was "Murmur throughout a whole host of listening Negros, and only repressed by respect for my Orders". Magistrate Drayton then observed that "if the ex-apprentices were more punctually paid, perhaps they might be more ready to work".[43]

At Spotts and Bodden Town, the would-be employers spoke with a more common voice. Most of the ex-apprentices, they claimed, far from showing gratitude or loyalty, could not be persuaded to work in exchange for free use of their houses and grounds or by sharecropping arrangements. Even at high wages they did not work well. Nathaniel Glover admitted that "A few instances have occurred where the late Apprentices are willing to hire for Wages, by the Month or by the Year." But he added that for day labour they demanded such exorbitant rates that very few of their former masters were willing or able to hire them. Hiring domestics was particularly difficult. Few were willing to be bound for a stated period, and most left, without notice or explanation, after a few weeks or even days – despite wages as high as £5 to £8 a year. Field labourers were able to command from 2s 6d to 3s 4d a day, and "Canoe Negroes" as much as 6s 8d. Yet none were willing to work before 8 a.m., and they expected to go home at 4 p.m.

The previous night, while staying with William Eden Jr. at Pedro St. James, Robert Thompson had heard an even more plaintive tale. Eden had made a will in which he left a portion of his land to each of his former slaves, on condition that they stayed with him. He had also allowed them to keep their houses and provision grounds, and allotted them a third of his stock animals. In return, they were asked only to take care of Eden's grounds and provide him and his wife with provisions. Rather than being grateful, many of the ex-slaves had deserted the estate altogether. Those who chose to stay in what they regarded as their own grounds would not work for their former master and would not even bring him a pail of water unless he paid fivepence for it. The few domestics who chose to stay and serve in the great house were said to live as poorly as he lived himself.[44]

In contrast, SM Thompson recounted three complaints made by ex-apprentices at Bodden Town after the ex-owners finished their testimony. A Negro man named Loring Carter accused his former master, Richard Carter, of having callously stripped him of house and grounds that were rightly his. Thompson knew from personal experience that Carter was "an exceedingly ill-tempered Master". But when he heard that the case had already been decided against Loring Carter in court, he declined to proceed with the complaint for fear of undermining the Magistrates' authority. However, he wrote that he "knew very well that there was many cases in that district where the Houses & Grounds of the late Slaves were by right of possession their own,

having been made by them in their own time on free Kings Lands, with which their Masters had nothing to do and could have no claim, and from everything I learnt this might be one case".[45]

The second complainant was an ex-slave named Morant, who spoke only broken English. He had also had problems with both Richard Carter and the local court. Fined forty shillings on very questionable grounds, he had been saved from jail when one of the Wood brothers paid the fine. He had to work for weeks to pay it back. Thompson felt somewhat guilty about this case, because he had punished the same person on a previous occasion when Richard Carter had charged him on equally flimsy grounds.

Outside the meeting place, Thompson was approached by a woman who complained that she had been assaulted by Nathaniel Glover, who had given her seven licks with his whip in the open street. Thompson advised her to make her complaint to him in court at George Town the following day. But apparently Glover found some means of making private amends, and neither he nor the woman appeared.[46]

Other responses to the questionnaire, together with Thompson's account of what happened outside of court, paint a picture of rapid socio-economic change and a community still adjusting to new circumstances. Asked what work the ex-apprentices did for themselves and what work the ex-masters were able to extract from them, most respondents said that the blacks grew nothing but provisions, and then only enough to sustain their own families. Those who had to leave their grounds went further into the interior, but most stayed where they were. The masters had given up hope of producing cotton for export as before, because of the decline in raw-cotton prices and the high cost of labour. Instead, they too grew only provision crops and tried to raise livestock, given a work force that demanded high wages and gave unreliable service in return.

One question asked whether there was a noticeable change in the ex-apprentices' "habits, dress, or conduct since they have become free Persons". In reply, Richard Phelan echoed others in stating that "as to obtaining house Servants he finds a very considerable difficulty. He can get people to cut down and clear lands for Provisions but when they work one Week they take themselves off and loiter about and squander away their time until necessitated to come out and work for more Wages." He added that "with respect to their dress many have improved, and go more Gaudy and Showy". Magistrate Thompson agreed with Phelan, though he doubted that many of the ex-apprentices were improved "with respect to their Clothing, Food or other comforts" any more than in their habits and behaviour.

In this section of his report, SM Thompson provided vivid vignettes of the behaviour and demeanour of the newly freed, as well as of the plight of their former masters. "In consequence of their not being willing to work for Wages

The evening entertainment of two former slaves.

which the means of their former owners could afford to give," he wrote,

> . . . many of them are going about unoccupied and in the Evenings and nights assemble together at some place where they indulge in their rude & noisy amusements, so noisy as to render it impossible for those who happen to be in their neighbourhood to obtain any rest. I stole in by a bye path to look on one of these nightly carousings, and I found one fellow drunk dancing alone most fantastically Savage before a Sable figure equally tipsey rattling away on an old tin Vessel for a drum, the noise of which directed one for more than a half Mile to the place. When I spoke to them to be still, a younger negro Man attempted modestly to appologize when the Dancer interrupted immediately telling him it was his premises and none had a right to speak but him. Some whispered "Magistrate," which he seemed not to hear, but on the word being passed "Magistrate Thompson from Jamaica," he almost bolted thro' the enclosures of the place, affrighted as if he had seen a Phantom. It was not a house but a little clearing among the Bushes, with a Thatched Shed on one side and underneath a few cross Sticks for him to lie on, and on the other side a few logs and sticks for seats to sit around the fire, the place of which was now occupied with dancing.

"With all the earnestness of which I was capable I reasoned with them to cease drinking and such Savage customs," Thompson went on, "to work for hire, to rent houses and not to sink into that indolent, drunken & debasing mode of Life of which the present group was to the Eye of an European too debasing a Spectacle. Yes Massa was all the reply."[47]

Riding along the road to Bodden Town, Thompson "observed that those largest herds of Cows which were formerly attended by a number of Negroes were now attended by one or two White Boys, the children of the Owners". At Bodden Town itself he "learned that many helpless and poor people who depended upon one or two Negros Work as Slaves and Apprentices, being now deprived of that means of support were left destitute and helpless". To him the most pathetic case was that of "a very delicate Widow Woman who formerly owned thirty five Slaves nearly the greatest number in the Island" (presumably Mrs. Mary Bodden of Bodden Town, who actually owned forty-three slaves in 1834).

> She told me that only one Woman and one Man out of them all remained with her, and those she had rewarded liberally . . . she had to pay at the highest price for provisions which they carried to her out of her own lands and grounds, charging her as if they were theirs and not hers, and every where the [white] females who had never before done any Work of a rough description declared they had to cook their own Victuals, Wash their own Clothes and carry their own Water, and for a small bundle of Wood for the Fire gathered on their own lands they were obliged to pay as high as people who lived in Towns did for their Wood, fivepence and tenpence per bundle.[48]

The one occupation in which ex-slaves and ex-masters had come to fruitful accommodation was in the business of turtling. To many this seemed to offer the most promising economic future. The lion's share of any profits went to the boat owner, of course, while the captain took a major share as well as having almost absolute authority at sea. Yet opportunities for non-white crewmen had apparently increased since emancipation. In response to the question "What alteration of terms has taken place in the bargains or Wages of those employed in the Turtle fishery?" the scrupulous Custos John Drayton testified as follows:

> The Crew gets the one half of the profits and the owner the other. All the hands have share and share alike whether Black or White, excepting the Commander who has a different allowance out of the owners share. Formerly they [the slaves] had what their Masters chose to give them; some one quarter, some one third of what White hired hands had. But since they have become free they share alike and there is no difficulty in obtaining hands.[49]

In the post-slavery economy, conditions were determined by economic realities, and by the will of former slaves as much as by the wishes of their former owners. Restoring anything like a plantation economy in the Cayman Islands was clearly impossible. All parties alike relied on a subsistence economy and the extension of the turtling industry – along with shipbuilding and what might come in from the chancier business of combing wrecks.

The former slaveowners had, of course, received compensation when the slaves were freed. But the impact of this money on the economy is hard to trace. The amount received was less than half the official valuation, which itself was lower than the slaveowners had hoped for. As in other former slave colonies, much of the money was doubtless already spent in anticipation of its receipt, or swallowed up by existing debts. Yet in an economy whose annual turnover was measured in hundreds rather than thousands of pounds, the sudden infusion of almost £20,000 must have had a relatively dramatic impact. Not only did it soften the economic impact of losing slave labour, it stimulated a wage-labour system and promoted an economy based on cash. Compensation allowed the wealthier owners, now that there were no more

plantations, to explore other ventures such as shipowning, shipbuilding, turtling, and shopkeeping.[50]

In some respects, conditions in the immediate post-slavery era may have hardened rather than softened racial and class divisions. To a degree, as elsewhere, "money lightened", so that an economically successful non-white might be absorbed into the ranks of the powerful. Generally, however, it was easier for poor but ambitious white newcomers, such as Richard Phelan and Nathaniel Glover, to move into the ranks of the leading inhabitants than it was for a non-white Caymanian. The end of slavery removed the "privilege" associated with slave ownership by both white and free coloured masters. But it did not bring equality to either the former slaves or the poorest whites.

Difficulties between ex-slaves and former masters may have led in certain cases to a complete sundering of personal ties. Some ex-slaves continued to serve their former owners. Others continued to live in the same places – nearby, but more separately than before. The rest (perhaps the majority) tended to separate themselves from their former masters and locations as completely as circumstances allowed.

CHURCH AND SCHOOL

Parallel to these major political and economic changes, the revolution of the 1830s was seen and felt in two key institutions that made their first appearance during this decade: churches and schools. The challenges arising from a Slave Society were a catalyst for those who brought these institutions to Cayman. In the years immediately after emancipation, those taking the lead in education and religious life were keen observers of – and even participants in – the ensuing upheavals.

The first clergyman in the Cayman Islands, Rev. Thomas Sharpe, arrived in December 1831, the same month that the new legislature convened in Cayman. Sharpe's arrival was part of the planned expansion of the established Church of England following the appointment of Jamaica's first bishop, Christopher Lipscomb, in 1824. But it was also a response to the oft-expressed desire by Caymanians for a resident minister.[51]

From the time of George Gauld's survey in 1773, Caymanians had wished for the services of a "clergyman".[52] By 1802, a "small place of worship" existed in Bodden Town, according to Edward Corbet. The person who officiated was "not an ordained Clergyman, but a respectable Inhabitant" – perhaps one of the Magistrates. The congregation probably included respectable white inhabitants, free persons of colour, and at least some slaves.[53] This arrangement served to combine some spiritual guidance with secular leadership in the society. But although the Magistrates could perform marriages, register births, and conduct burials, there was no one to administer the sacraments

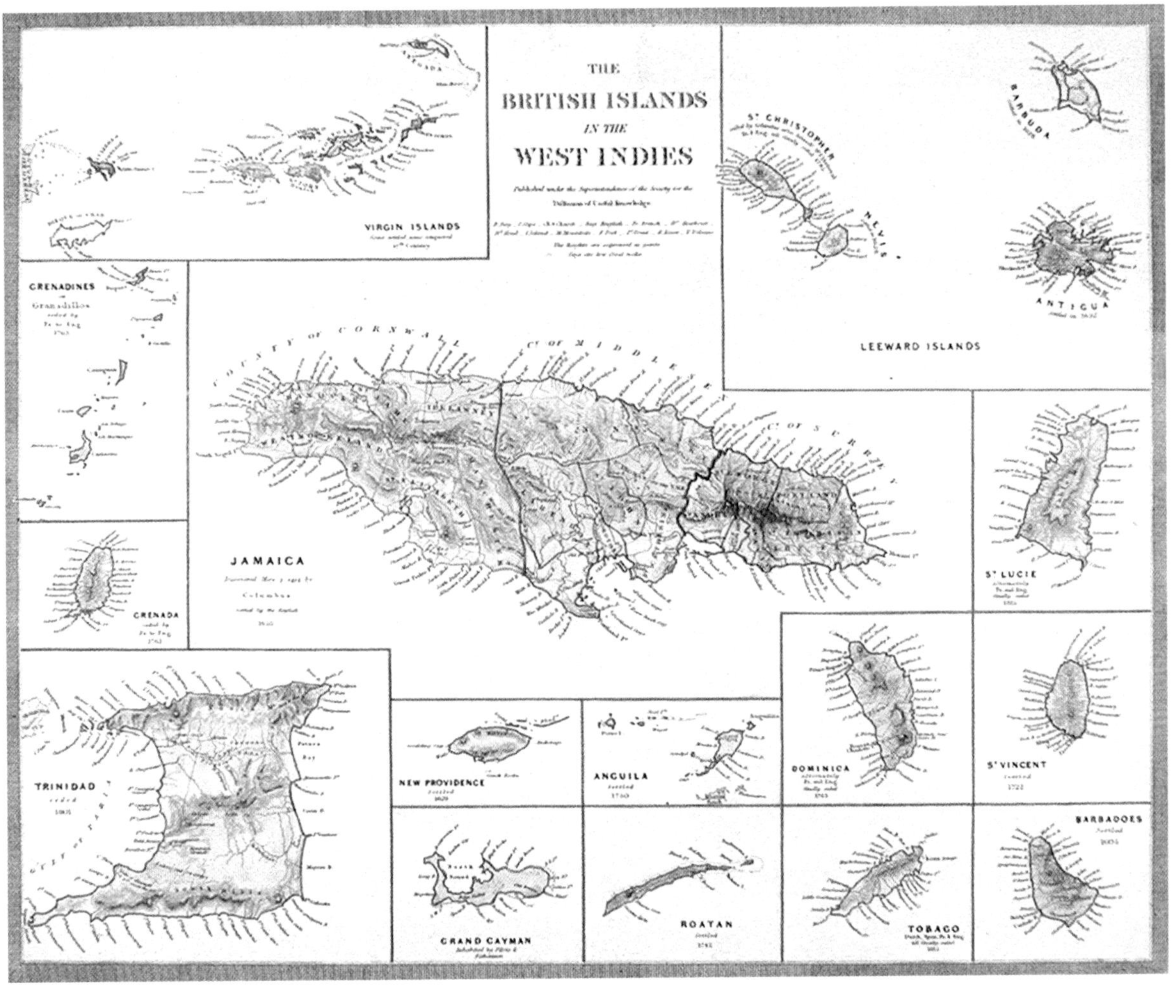

Map of British islands in the West Indies in the 1830s.

or to provide the kind of schoolteaching expected of ministers of the established Anglican Church.

One obstacle to starting churches and schools was the difficulty of providing an adequate stipend and accommodation. Another may have been a certain hesitancy about the pastoral motivation of Bishop Lipscomb. The Anglican Church in the colonies was under the authority of the Bishop of London and supported by financial help from the Society for the Propagation of the Gospel (SPG). It had always believed that its duty was to serve white settlers first, native inhabitants second, and slaves third. The creation of special bishoprics for Barbados and Jamaica, however, marked a significant change. The established church and the SPG now wanted to minister to the entire population of the colonies, including the slaves. To a degree this signified a change of heart, led by anti-slavery evangelicals in Britain. But it was also motivated by a desire to stem the influence of nonconformist missionaries, such as Baptists or Wesleyans, whose main goal was to convert slaves.[54] In the years leading up to emancipation, Caymanians were eager for an ordained minister, and they were willing to try to support one financially. But

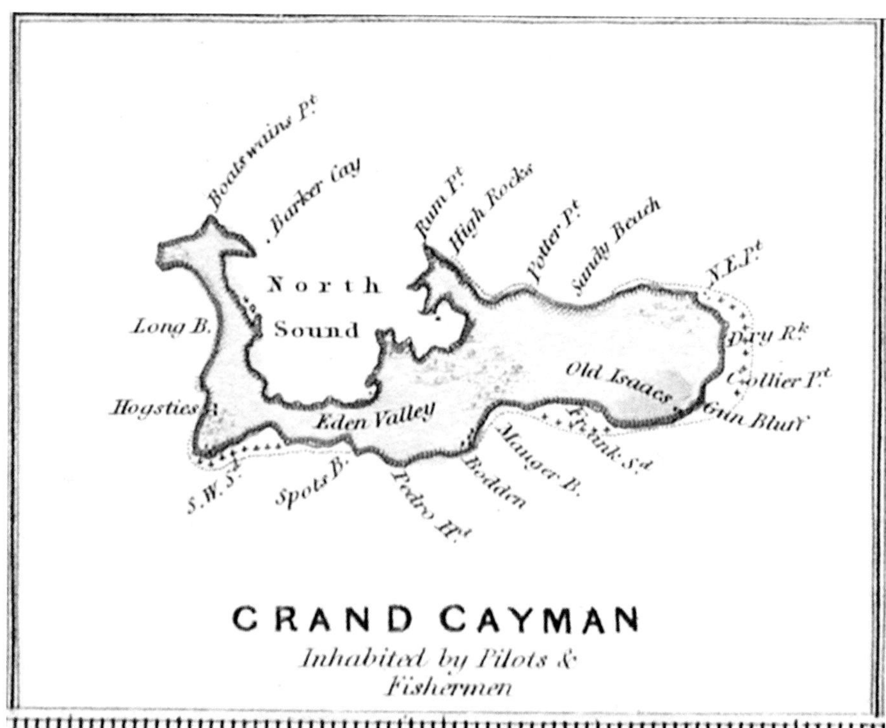

Map of Grand Cayman (detail from map on previous page).

they would have assumed that his functions inclined toward maintaining the social order and training slaves in what were regarded as "civilised" values.

In November 1825, Bishop Lipscomb signalled to the Cayman authorities his intention of sending down a delegate to test the local situation and to appoint a resident clergyman if a stipend and accommodation were assured. Bishop Lipscomb himself visited Grand Cayman in 1826 on his way to Belize, deploring that the island had "neither Clergyman, Lawyer or Apothecary". It was not until March 1832 that Governor Lord Belmore was able to report that most difficulties had been ironed out and that a resident clergyman had been installed.[55]

This person was Thomas Sharpe, who arrived at George Town on 23 December 1831 and held his first service on Christmas Day. Sharpe was, in a sense, on probation. Still a deacon, he was not fully ordained until 1834. He was provided with places of worship at George Town and Bodden Town, and a small sum was voted to build a parsonage. As the whole island's budget was around £70, however, financial support was difficult. In February 1834, the bishop visited Grand Cayman and was generally encouraged by the progress Sharpe had made. He noted with dismay, however, that the £100 promised by the Assembly in 1831 towards his stipend had not been forthcoming. In October 1834, Sharpe resigned to take up a curacy in Westmoreland, Jamaica.[56]

Grand Cayman was without a minister until June 1836, when Sharpe was succeeded for a year by the Rev. David Wilson. The Assembly had voted £50

for a stipend in January 1836, but Wilson received three-quarters of his financial support from the SPG and the Bishop. Though still a deacon, Wilson did what he could. As he explained in a report to the SPG in June 1837, he "performed full Services, with a Sermon, morning and Evening" at George Town and Prospect on alternate Sundays, and occasionally preached at Spotts and Bodden Town during the week. Wilson preached to congregations of 280 at George Town and 200 at Prospect, with 30 attending Sunday School in each place. He employed a young man to teach a day school with twenty scholars, and during the year he performed thirty-eight baptisms, eleven marriages, and nine burials.[57]

Rev. Wilson left Grand Cayman to be ordained in Jamaica in June 1837, returning only once for a short spell in 1838. Grand Cayman was struck by hurricanes in September and October 1837, which virtually destroyed both churches and the parsonage, along with a hundred other buildings. To help in this crisis, the Bishop sent back Rev. Sharpe, bearing a letter that promised £100 to rebuild the church in George Town. The Bishop also offered to help build a schoolhouse and to provide half the salary of a certified schoolmaster from the training college in Jamaica. For their part, the Assembly thanked the Bishop and voted the remaining half of the teacher's salary, and £50 towards the building of a schoolhouse "forty feet by thirty at George Town". This was to be "vested in the Lord Bishop of Jamaica and the officiating Minister of Grand Cayman for the time being".[58]

St. George's Church in George Town was rebuilt within five months. The former day school in George Town was revived, and a new one was started in Bodden Town. Trained teachers supported by the Mico Charity came to Cayman. But the enthusiasm of the local whites soon evaporated when it was discovered that outside funding was temporary and that educational opportunities would be available to all Caymanians, including ex-slaves. By the middle of 1839 both Thomas Sharpe and David Wilson had left for good. More than a century was to elapse before another Anglican minister resided in Cayman.[59]

The two Mico teachers, despite marked successes, remained for just over two years. Andrew Malcolm arrived in August 1838 and opened the first school at Bodden Town that November. The school began with only twenty-three pupils. Fees of sixpence a week for children under six years of age and tenpence for older children must have kept numbers down. Observing that very few families could afford fees (or even payment in kind in ground provisions), Malcolm abolished them on his own initiative. Within six months, enrolment had grown to ninety-seven, with almost equal proportions of white and non-white children.[60]

Malcolm suffered from social isolation, heat, and mosquitoes, but chiefly from opposition by former slaveowners. The issue was Malcolm's determi-

Andrew Malcolm teaching his students in Bodden Town.

nation not to separate the non-whites from the whites in class. As he wrote in a letter to the Mico Trustees in London in May 1839,

> The White population have a most inveterate hatered against the blacks, they have told me that I must erect 2 Gallaries one for the white children and the other for the black children, that I must make a distinction in my school, but I have invariable [*sic*] told them I would not. I have told my children that I would make no distinction between black and white, and that a good boy, is a good boy whether he be black or white, and that I would respect him because he was a good boy, and not because he was a white boy.[61]

The preferred solution of the local regime was to set up a second Mico school in George Town in which white children would be in the majority, leaving the Bodden Town school predominantly for non-whites. The General Superintendent of the Mico schools in Jamaica, Rev. Edmund Wallbridge, visited Grand Cayman in August 1839 in an attempt to resolve the dilemma. Originally he had planned to send a "native" teacher from Jamaica. Now he diplomatically told the Assembly that he was "induced to believe that a European Teacher sent out from the Mother Country would prove a far more efficient mode of procedure". However, with the limited funds it was difficult to support such a candidate, let alone forgo fees at the George Town school, without local support. He particularly requested a schoolhouse and teacher accommodation, rent-free, in both George Town and Bodden Town. The Assembly responded on 28 August. They were happy to provide the buildings in George Town, which they had built and owned, free of rent for at least three years. The Bodden Town buildings, though, were privately owned, and the Assembly "deeply regretted [that] the impoverished State of the Island Treasury" made it impossible for them to subsidise their rental.[62]

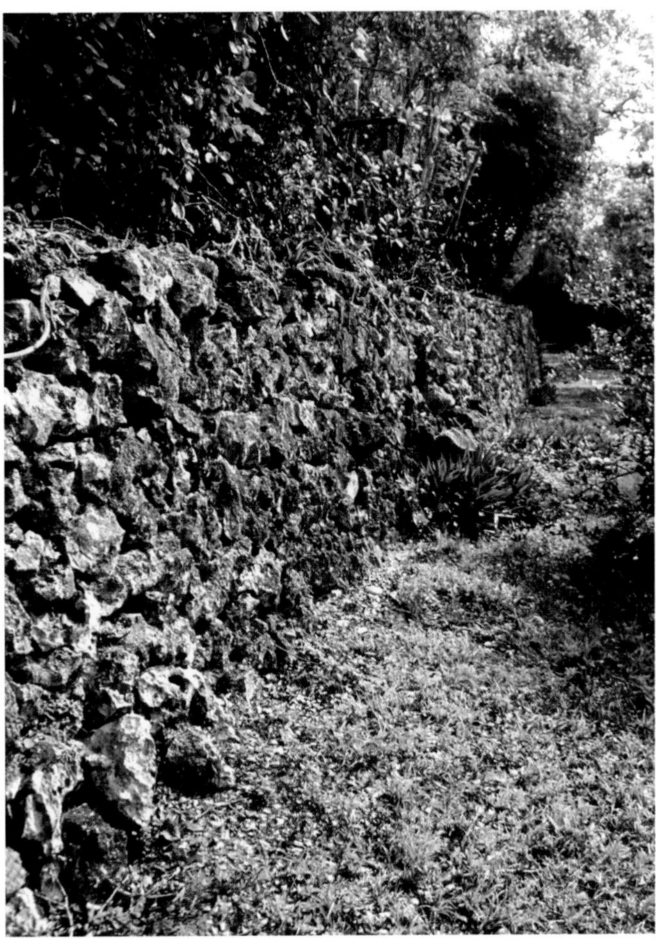

The "slave wall" in Bodden Town, 2002.

At its peak Andrew Malcolm's school had an enrolment of 130, most of them non-whites. But it proved too heavy a burden for both the Mico Charity and its teacher. When Malcolm left Grand Cayman in the summer of 1840, eighty parents of his non-white pupils (only eight of whom could sign their names) sent a heartfelt and revealing petition to the Mico trustees in London pleading for his return. "We the Black and Brown people in or about B-Town beg leave to return our sinceer thanks for your great kindness in sending amongst us our beloved teacher Mr. Malcom," it began. "Was it not for your Honourable Charity and the attention of Mr. Malcom, we would have been this day as we were 6 years back."

Malcolm was described as a "good and great man" who not only taught their children but attended the sick and, in the absence of an ordained minister, preached twice each Sunday. "We are sorry that he has a great many enemies," the petition continued, "but they are not among our class. He is persecuted by a greater part of the whites, but with out a cause, and we are affraid that his troubles and persecutions will drive him off the Island."[63] If Andrew Malcolm did return from Jamaica, it was for no more than a few months. The other Mico teacher, John Ross in George Town, a Presbyterian Scot, engendered less conflict with the local whites and was also a valued lay preacher. But he was withdrawn by the Mico authorities towards the end of 1841 as part of a general retrenchment. The Mico legacy was to continue, however, in the person of John Jarrett Wood, who became the first qualified Caymanian teacher three years later and the first of many to be trained at Mico College in Jamaica.

Christmas 1910: elderly Caymanians in Bodden Town who had been born into slavery.

Between 1837 and 1844, the Wesleyan Missionary Society tried to fill the gaps left by the Anglicans. Their pioneer was Rev. James Atkins, who made an exploratory visit in May 1837, just as Rev. David Wilson was leaving for ordination in Jamaica. Atkins wrote gratefully of Wilson's ecumenical friendliness. But he was scathing about the condition of the church buildings (which were "built of the ruffest materials") and concerned about the spiritual condition of people of all classes and conditions. They were, he said, "living without God or hope in the world". Atkins also stressed the separation, both

cultural and physical, that still existed between the former masters and the former slaves. For example, whites and respectable coloureds were buried with decorum in a neat graveyard annexed to the church; but the "Negro burial ground" was separate, unkempt, and without grave markers, and the burial rites of blacks, according to Atkins, were "distinguished only by dancing, fidling, drunkenness and rioting".[64]

Following Atkins's encouraging report to Wesleyan Missionary House in London, Rev. Mark Bird was seconded from Jamaica in July 1839. Bird found the ministry difficult and stayed no more than a few months. Over the following five years he was succeeded by six other Wesleyan missionaries, who ministered, according to the Wesleyan circuit system, for relatively short periods.[65] Their dutiful letters to London told much the same tale. The cautious good will of most of the Magistrates and the eagerness of many Caymanians to hear and read the word of God were offset by the difficulties of building permanent congregations and preventing backsliding in the missionaries' absence.

The high point of the Wesleyan mission to Grand Cayman was probably the nine-month tenure of Rev. John Mearns in 1842. Congregations as large as 140 were reported in George Town, and in Grand Cayman as a whole there were said to be 120 "class members". Mearns preached and administered communion in five places on the island, riding fifty miles a week on horseback. The first Wesleyan chapel was built at West Bay, and another was started at Prospect. The legislature allowed Mearns to live in the parsonage built for the Anglicans and even to use the court-house for services, though a motion to provide a meagre subsidy of £5 a quarter from public funds was defeated by nine votes to eight.[66]

The difficulties of ministering to a scattered population were compounded by the loneliness of the posting (especially for single men), the frequent change of ministers, and the periods without one. Some leading Caymanians were still resistant to the populist preaching of the Methodists and would have preferred a minister from the established Anglican Church. But the biggest challenges were shortage of funds and the tendency of many families likely to become Wesleyans to leave Grand Cayman altogether.[67]

These factors were stressed in the letters sent by the last Wesleyan missionary, Rev. John Green, who spent a few months in Grand Cayman in the summer of 1844. Green appreciated the use of the parsonage in George Town but pointed out that he would have to vacate it if the services of an Anglican minister were obtained. None of those who attended the Wesleyan services gave as much as sixpence per quarter in contributions, and some became angry or embarrassed when urged to give more. Just as worrisome, in the interim before Green arrived, one of the church "leaders" had taken it on himself to expel a member on his own authority. Soon after being chided by Green, he

and his family left Grand Cayman for Roatán – not out of pique but because the Bay Islands offered much better opportunities. "He had long wished to go thither and so had many other working people," admitted Green; ". . . the soil of that Island is richer than this and a livelihood is more easily obtained . . . the soil of this Country is so impoverished it won't yield sufficient quantity of provisions."[68]

Drawn by opportunities elsewhere, such as those described by Rev. Green, and stirred by the traumatic changes of the 1830s, many former slaves and slaveowners decided to migrate. Their destinations included the unoccupied parts of Grand Cayman, the two other Cayman Islands, the Bay Islands and other islands within range of sail, and the undeveloped Miskito Coast of Nicaragua. These migrations are the central theme of Chapter Six. Viewed from a longer perspective, it might be said that, after slavery ended, many Caymanians chose to live elsewhere until time, and changing times, reminded them that the Cayman Islands were their home. Even those who remained in Cayman lived apart until they learned over time what they had in common and the ways in which they were an interdependent people. Only then could the bitter memories of slavery fade away, allowing slavery itself to become, by the twentieth century, no more than a bad dream best forgotten.

Catherine Susanna Connolly of East End, born 1 May 1838.

CHAPTER 6

Slavery's Aftermath and the First Caymanian Migrations ......

EMANCIPATION IN THE BRITISH WEST INDIES led to a sharp decline in the importance of colonies with sugar plantations. At the same time, economic policy in Britain was increasingly being shaped by the idea of free trade rather than protectionism. As a result, British interests began to switch from her colonies to the world at large. In the Western Hemisphere, for example, Britain was commercially involved in Brazil and Cuba. Britain also sought to cooperate rather than compete with the United States, whose importance in the region was increasing fast.[1]

With less attention being paid to colonies like Jamaica, the Cayman Islands became even more isolated. The prevailing philosophy of *laissez-faire* promoted the belief that colonies should support themselves. This affected even missionary activity. Mainly because of the islanders' poverty, the organisations that came to Cayman in the 1830s – the Anglican Church, the Wesleyan missionaries, and the Mico Charity teachers – were all withdrawn by the mid-1840s.

In the wider world, a revolution in communications was under way, first through steamships and then through submarine cables. This revolution, however, passed the Cayman Islands by. Steamships needed fewer stops than sailing vessels and were much less likely to include Cayman on the homeward journey to Europe. Both steamships and telegraph cables were introduced only on the most profitable and direct routes. Though the Cayman Islands lay close to one of the busiest sea channels, they were avoided because of their

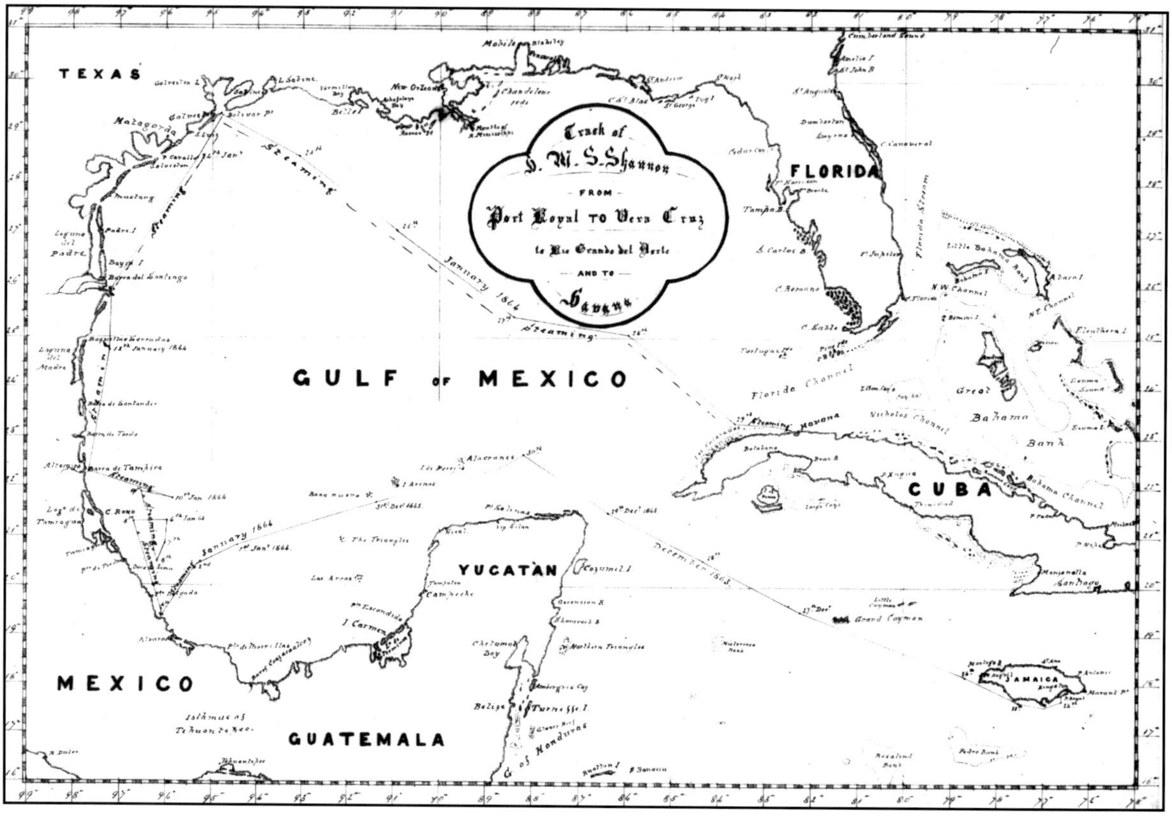

The age of sail gives way to steam: tracking map showing the route of the steamship HMS Shannon *as it passed by the Cayman Islands in 1863.*

dangerous reefs. At best, passing steamships slowed or stopped to take on turtles from islanders waiting in their boats, often far out of sight of home.

This isolation reinforced a rugged self-reliance in the Caymanian people, who became, of necessity, almost totally self-sufficient. At home they were subsistence farmers and fishermen, turtlers and boatbuilders. But they also began to explore other possibilities by spreading more widely over the region – first to the unoccupied parts of Grand Cayman and to the other Cayman Islands, then to the Bay Islands, and by the end of the century to many other destinations within sailing distance of their original home. The most promising avenue of expansion was closed off in 1859, when the British surrendered the short-lived Crown Colony of the Bay Islands to Honduras. To the many Caymanians who had migrated there, this seemed an act of desertion by the British government.

PERMANENT SETTLEMENT IN THE SISTER ISLANDS

Following emancipation in the Cayman Islands, many ex-slaves, eager to possess and work land of their own, settled in the underpopulated eastern and northern areas of Grand Cayman. The same period saw the beginning of the permanent settlement (or the resettlement) of Cayman Brac and Little Cayman,

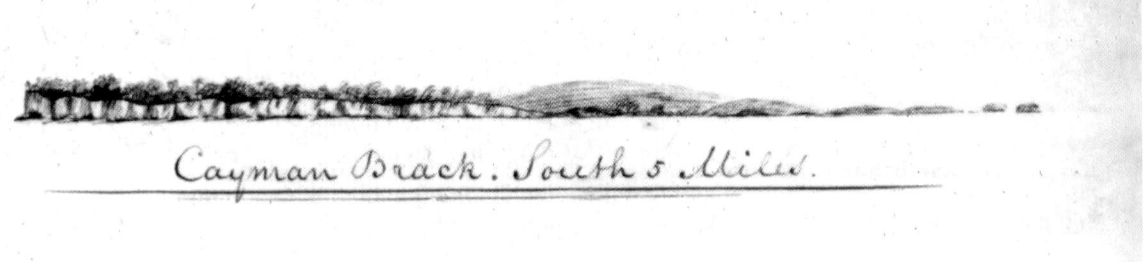

Sketch of Cayman Brac from HMS Sybille, *ca. 1820.*

largely by whites who had never held slaves. The peopling of the Sister Islands was probably a steady but unsystematic process. Their combined population in 1850 was less than one hundred. It had reached more than a thousand by 1900. During most of the next century, however, the increase levelled off, and the combined population was rarely more than fifteen hundred.[2]

It is almost certain that there was no long-term settlement of the Sister Islands between their desertion in the 1670s and the 1830s. Edward Corbet reported in 1802 that both islands were "altogether uninhabited", being visited only by turtlers "in the summer season". A few years later, in 1818, the captain of a passing Royal Navy ship saw a boat coming off from Little Cayman and noticed an abandoned hut on the western end of Cayman Brac. He concluded, however, that "there were no regular Inhabitants, but only Fishermen who stay there in the Season".[3]

In 1831, the Royal Navy survey ship HMS *Blossom* visited the Sister Islands and prepared the first simple "maps" or surveys of them. These maps, drawn by surveyor Richard Owen, show essential soundings around the

First survey of the Sister Islands, by HMS Blossom, *1831.*

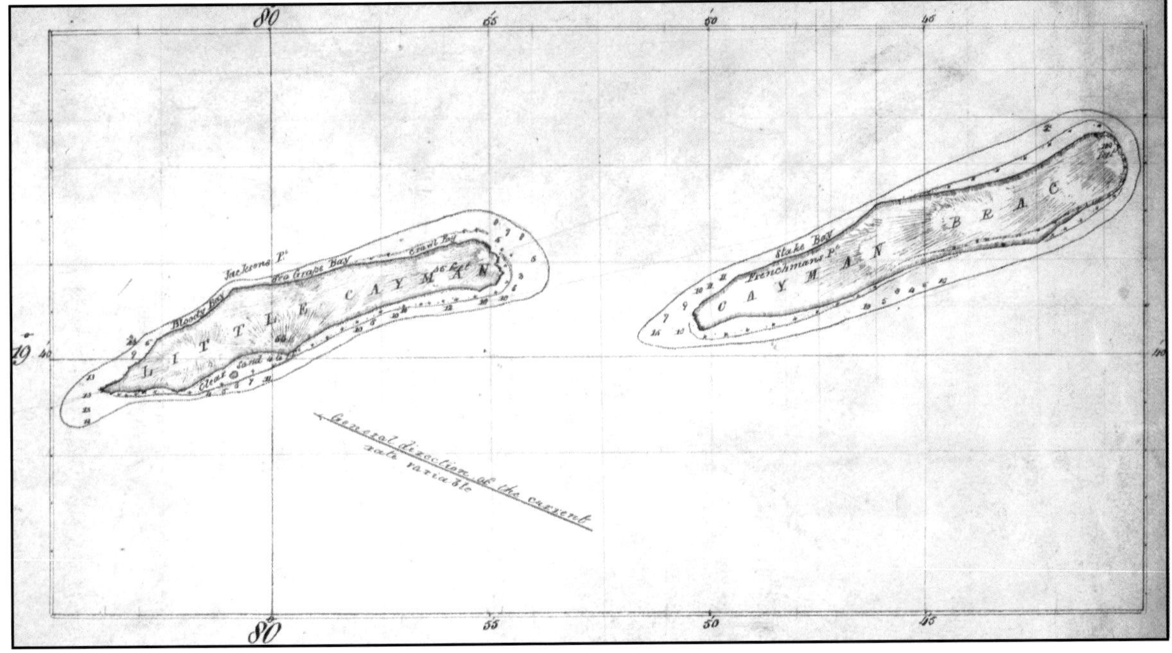

islands and elevations of land on them, but contain no indication of settlements. It is interesting to note, however, that Owen marks the names Stake Bay and Frenchmans Point on Cayman Brac, and Bloody Bay, Sea Grape Bay, Crawl Bay, and Jackson's Point along the northern shore of Little Cayman. It would appear that these were established names and that Owen was able to draw upon local sources of information – very possibly a pilot from Grand Cayman who assisted in the survey. Another Navy ship visited the Sister Islands in 1833, and a crew member drew rough sketches of both islands from a mile or more offshore to the south. But no sign of houses or inhabitants can be gleaned from these sketches.[4]

Our first certain knowledge of the settlement of the Sister Islands during the 1830s comes from records dealing with slave registration in 1834 and emancipation in 1835. James Minot's slave census in 1834 recorded that William Page was living on Little Cayman with six slaves. The following May, Captain Pack read the Emancipation Proclamation in Little Cayman to Page and his slaves. But this small group may well have left soon afterwards, because they are barely mentioned in accounts by later inhabitants.[5]

One of the fullest early accounts of the settlement of Cayman Brac was given by H.W. Rutty, J.P., Collector of Customs at Cayman Brac, in 1908. "As far as can be gathered from a few of the oldest folks," he wrote,

> the first settlements were made in 1833 when three families bearing the names of Ritch, Foster, and Scott respectively, from Grand Cayman removed here and took up their abode. After that others dropped in, chiefly from Grand Cayman and a few from Jamaica, but very largely the present population is composed of descendants of those three first families. The only industry then was turtle-catching. . . . The island [Cayman Brac] was then an uncultivated wilderness, but the enterprising settlers soon started to cut down the woods and make clearings in order to cultivate for their needs.[6]

Of the traditional founding families of the Sister Islands, the Fosters and their close relatives, the Ryans, have the fullest available genealogical and oral records. George Hirst speculated that the founder of the Caymanian Foster clan was the William Foster who patented land in Grand Cayman in 1741.[7] Instead, it seems pretty certain that the founder was an Englishman, Stephen Taylor Foster, born at Brighton in 1805. He was said to have been wrecked as a teenage cabin boy on one of the southern Cuban cays around 1819 and brought by Caymanian wreckers to Grand Cayman. There he was taken in by (or took up with) a widow named Elizabeth Sarah Christian, with whom he had a daughter and three sons, without the benefit of formal marriage, between 1820 and 1828. Working as a seaman on far-ranging turtling boats, Stephen Foster was reported to have died of dysentery and been buried at Viviarero Cay, Honduras, in 1834.[8]

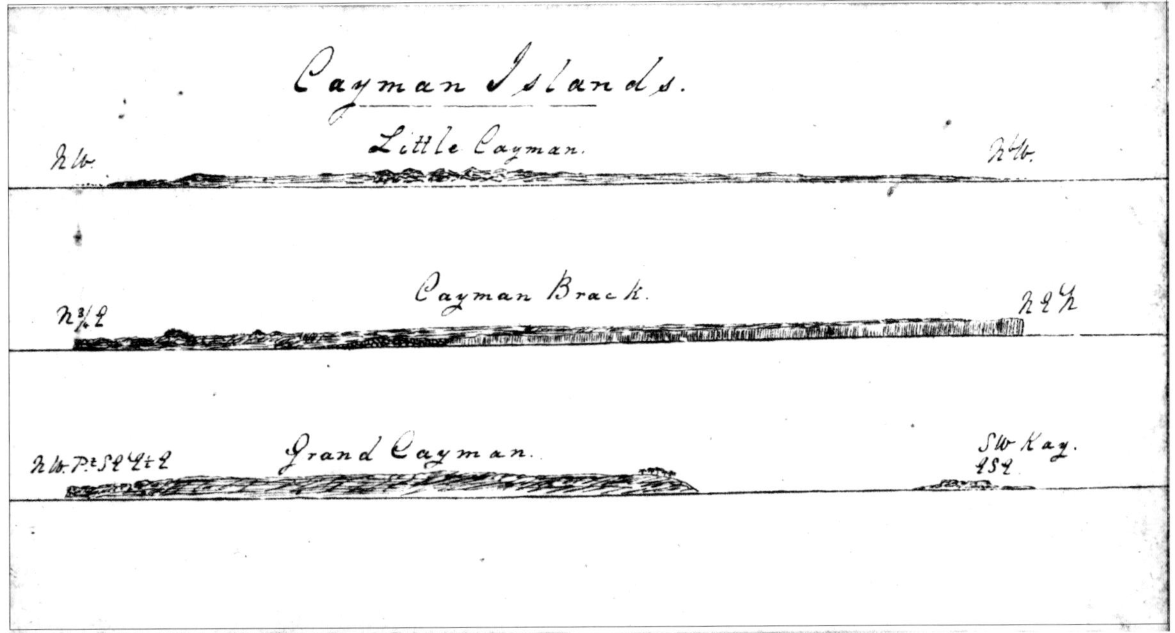

Sketches of the Cayman Islands by a sailor on a Royal Navy vessel, ca. 1833.

According to the strongest oral tradition, around 1833, two Grand Cayman men, one a Scott and the other a Ritch, who were familiar with the Sister Islands from fishing trips, rowed their families the eighty-odd miles in open canoes to the Sister Islands. They settled at Bloody Bay and South Hole in Little Cayman, where "Page" was said to be the lone inhabitant. After Stephen Foster's death, the intrepid Mrs. Christian followed the Scotts and Ritches with her children, settling first at Little Cayman and then at Stake Bay, Cayman Brac, by 1840.[9]

Life in the Sister Islands, though harsh, was healthy. All three of the Foster boys married Scotts and the daughter a Ryan. Between them, the four Foster children of Widow Christian had seventeen sons and twelve daughters. These children, in their turn, had produced 150 grandchildren by 1875.[10] This prolific brood often did not look far to find their partners. Even by the second generation, cousin marriage was common, and well into the twentieth century the society of the Sister Islands must have seemed at times like a large extended family. Wider connections arose, however, as the mariners found wives on their travels to Grand Cayman, the Bay Islands, and other settlements within the Caymanian orbit, and as the women found partners among unexpected immigrants, such as shipwrecked mariners, who occasionally landed in the Sister Islands.

One newcomer was the Irishman William Wallace Ryan. According to Moody H. Ryan, his Irish ancestor was born in or near Dublin in 1812 and migrated first to New York around 1833, where he worked as a longshoreman. He was said to have been shanghaied aboard a French merchantman, but managed to jump ship at Cartagena, Colombia. There he encountered

William Foster, who spoke glowingly of the Sister Islands and the Foster family. William Ryan found his way from Cartagena to Jamaica, walked all the way from Kingston to Montego Bay, and worked his way to Cayman Brac sometime before 1837. There he married Sarah, the only daughter of Elizabeth Christian and William Foster, who was then seventeen years old.

The first of William and Sarah Ryan's four sons was born in Cayman Brac in 1838. The other three were born in Roatán, to which the ever-restless William Ryan moved his family around 1840. After William's death, Sarah Ryan went to Belize and then returned to Cayman Brac with her four boys. One of them married a Hunter from Grand Cayman, one married an Ally from Belize, and two married Scotts. Sarah Ryan is also said to have brought with her from Belize an impoverished carpenter named William Kirkconnell, who helped to build the first schooner in Cayman Brac. Whether Kirkconnell came with Sarah Ryan or arrived in Cayman Brac independently, they certainly had a son, born out of wedlock, named Walter Kirkconnell, who went on to found one of the most prominent Bracker families.[11]

Although we do not know with certainty the identity of the first member of each of the four founding families, the Scotts, Ritches, Fosters, and Ryans

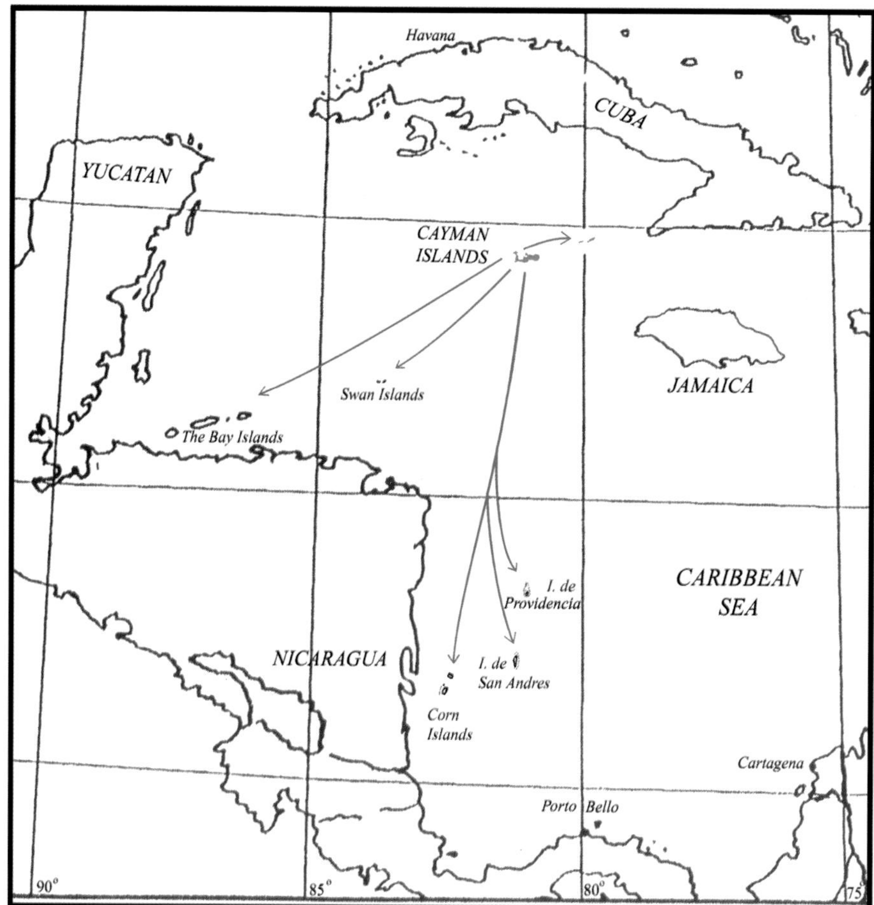

Migrations of Caymanians from the 1830s to the 1860s.

all seem to have been descended from early nineteenth-century immigrants.[12] Probably they came in search of free, plantable land.[13]

By several accounts, the first blacks to make Cayman Brac home may have been runaway slaves from Cuba called Barba and Mateo, who settled at Watering Place on the island's northeastern shore. The former is commemorated in the name of Barbour's Well. Barba and Mateo are said to have been "adopted" by Robert Scott and one of the Ritches, changing their names to Ben Scott and Thomas Mathias Ritch. Later they were known as "Old Daddy Ben" and "Old Dick". There is also a legend that when the first whites came to Cayman Brac, they found a slave already living on the island, who had run away by canoe from Grand Cayman.[14]

It seems very likely that the first permanent settlers of the Sister Islands were followed by a small but growing flow of non-white settlers, mainly from Grand Cayman. Whites and non-whites probably kept largely to themselves, not unlike the pattern in Grand Cayman after emancipation.[15]

As in Grand Cayman, the non-white settlers of the Sister Islands probably did not enjoy the same opportunities, either in landholding or in other economic respects, as whites or ex-slaveowners. Everyone in the Sister Islands was (or at least started) poor. Whites, however, prospered most and soonest. Black or coloured skippers, fishermen, and builders may have been among those who settled in the Sister Islands. But as the thorough account in the 1908 *Handbook of the Cayman Islands* shows, it was whites or near-whites who at that point owned the best land and were the chief shipbuilders, shipowners, and shopkeepers in the Sister Islands.

Prosperity did not come easily or quickly for anyone in the Sister Islands. At first, subsistence farming and local fishing were the only options. They remained the mainstay of poor people well into the twentieth century, though there was no active local market for provisions, and turtle stocks around the two islands were being steadily depleted. As H.W. Rutty commented in 1908, "The first comers, like the 'Pilgrim Fathers' of America, endured many hardships and inconveniences, having to depend on Grand Cayman schooners that very seldom visited the island as the means for taking to market their slender produce and in return for it bringing back supplies." Mariners had to rely on ships from elsewhere for employment. Jamaica was closest to Cayman Brac and provided a good market for turtle and tortoiseshell – and possibly other means of employment. But real progress came only when the Sister Islanders began to build boats larger than dugout canoes and sloops. The first locally built schooner, a 26-footer, was probably the one launched in 1850. It was the forerunner of more than 150 that were to be constructed over the next 120 years.[16]

The population of the Sister Islands in the first decades after 1833 remained small. It may also have fluctuated as settlers moved back and forth between

the Sister Islands and the Bay Islands or Grand Cayman. In 1854 William Eden, the Chief Magistrate on Grand Cayman, reported to the Governor of Jamaica that the Sister Islands were inhabited at that time by only "two or three families of turtle catchers". This report followed a period, however, when a large numbers of Caymanians – including, perhaps, some from the Sister Islands – had been migrating to the Bay Islands. Four years later, when Governor Darling visited the Sister Islands in June 1858, he reported that the population of Little Cayman was about one hundred and that there were only "very few temporary sojourners" on Cayman Brac. By coincidence, that same year James Elmslie preached on Little Cayman on his way home to furlough in Scotland. In the following year on the return voyage to Grand Cayman, he stopped to preach at Cayman Brac. Elmslie's report suggests that both islands were settled with families because their inhabitants were "longing for some person to teach their children".[17]

The Sister Islands' population probably increased after 1859, when the Bay Islands became part of Honduras, prompting some Caymanians who had settled there to migrate back to the Cayman Islands. Over the next four decades the population grew as local opportunities developed, notably in the occupations of turtling and shipbuilding. By 1900, when the population of the Sister Islands had passed a thousand, there were a dozen locally built and owned schooners, some of them three-masted. The largest, the *Clara C. Scott*, displaced 300 tons. By this time, the men of the Sister Islands had a reputation not just as expert boatbuilders but as some of the finest seamen and navigators in the region. H.W. Rutty attributed this to the first regular schoolteacher, a castaway named William Johnston who settled in Cayman Brac in 1863. Johnston taught navigation as well as the basic "three Rs", and included many grown men among his pupils. In 1908 there were twenty-one master mariners, as well as fifteen skilled shipwrights. Of the nine shipowners recorded by Rutty, six were also listed as shopkeepers (out of a total of eleven shopkeepers) and one as a shipowner/boatbuilder. There were also three schoolteachers on the Sister Islands, along with one Baptist minister and one medical practitioner, described as a homeopathic doctor.[18]

Of the sixty-one notable persons listed in the 1908 *Handbook*, all but one (a schoolmistress) were men, and the great majority were drawn from the white founding families. These included thirteen Scotts, nine Fosters, seven Boddens, three Kirkconnells, three Tibbettses, two Ryans, two Hunters, and two McLaughlins. The senior Magistrate, William Stephen Ryan (son of William and Sarah Ryan and grandson of Stephen Taylor Foster and Elizabeth Christian), was said to have been "the second-born native, the first to be married here, the first to go master mariner and the first to receive the appointment of Magistrate".[19]

THE BAY ISLANDS SETTLEMENTS

More rapid and dramatic than the settlement of the Sister Islands was the migration of hundreds of Caymanians to the Bay Islands after 1831. Close to the northern shore of Honduras, the Bay Islands consist of three substantial islands – Utila, Roatán, and Guanaja (or Bonacca) – and three islets – Helene, Barbaret, and Morat. In the wake of emancipation in Cayman, they must have seemed to many Caymanians unusually attractive. The Bay Islands were scenic, with forested hills abounding in game and fertile land that had not yet been cultivated. They were set amid excellent fishing and turtling grounds, and ideally located for trade in the Bay of Honduras.

The British had shown an intermittent interest in the Bay Islands during the seventeenth and eighteenth centuries, most notably when they relocated the fierce Black Caribs, or Garifuna, of St. Vincent there in 1797. Neither the Spanish imperial government nor the Honduran republic sought to develop the islands. By the 1820s they had been abandoned by all but a handful of Garifuna. The rest of the Black Caribs had moved to the nearby mainland, where they eventually established some thirty coastal settlements on the 450-mile stretch between southern Belize and Black River.[20]

While the Bay Islands held much promise for Caymanian migrants, they had definite disadvantages, including tropical disease and racial discord. Ravenous mosquitoes and sandflies, depredations by unfriendly Garifuna, and conflict with local Honduran Spaniards complicated the picture. Worst of all was the failure of the British government, under pressure from the United States, to retain the Bay Islands as a Crown Colony, and the surrender of the islands to the republic of Honduras in 1859.

Caymanians had long been familiar with the Bay Islands from fishing visits and voyages to and from Belize. Roatán, the largest of the islands, was to

A sketch of the Bay Islands in 1842: Bonacca, as seen from Half Moon Cay.

French Harbour, Roatán.

become the predominant settlement, much like Grand Cayman. The first Caymanian settler, however, came to the sister island of Utila. Joseph Cooper was a white man who owned no slaves. He arrived, with his wife and six of their children, at Suc-Suc Cay, Utila, sometime between 1831 and 1836.[21] Cooper found two Americans who had already been settled for some years on Utila. One of these, a Mr. Warren, helped Cooper and his two sons clear their first ground, and later married Cooper's daughter Elizabeth, with whom he had seven children. The Coopers themselves had two more children in Utila. Their oldest daughter, Jane, stayed behind in Grand Cayman and married a Captain Thompson, who brought her and their first two children to the Bay Islands a few years later. The Cooper, Warren, and Thompson clans still formed the bulk of the predominantly white population of Utila more than sixty years later, when Richard H. Rose published his *Utilla: Past and Present*.[22]

Another Cooper, Joseph's brother, was the Caymanian pioneer on Roatán. He settled with his family at the secure anchorage at the southwest tip of the island named Coxen's Hole. The Coopers were followed within a year by six more white Caymanian families, and by 1844 there were some thirty white Caymanian families in the Bay Islands – more than 250 people in all. This influx had already raised concern among the Honduran authorities. In 1839 the Commandant at Trujillo sent a number of convicts, guarded by a detachment of troops, to Port Royal, Roatán, to establish Honduran sovereignty. In response, the bellicose Superintendent of Belize, Colonel Alexander McDonald, sailed to Roatán in the sloop-of-war HMS *Rover*, hauled down the flag of the Central American Federation, raised the Union Jack, and sent the handful of soldiers and convicts back to Trujillo.[23]

The British government eventually disavowed this action, but the settlers were greatly encouraged by it. They briefly renamed Coxen's Hole Port McDonald and began to establish a system of formal land tenure. The process was described in a long report by Captain R.C. Michell of HMS *Arachne*, who visited Roatán in 1850. "Each among the first settlers who came here from the Caymans chose whatever land or spot he liked which he appropriated to himself," he wrote. "From the few on the island no one disputed his possession, and his labour and occupation of the spot gave him a claim." By 1844, so many Caymanians, including non-whites, were arriving that constant disagreements were taking place. A general meeting was therefore convened.

"They agreed to hold possession of what each had at the time," noted Michell, but "from and after that date every person might claim 300 yards of back land, with a frontage of 150 yards." A public surveyor was appointed to measure off the land, with a certain quantity of waste land allocated to lie between each property. "Every man seems now to have his own plantation," Michell concluded.[24]

On the surface this seemed a hopeful situation, and Captain Michell went on to make some flattering remarks about the most enterprising settlers. He was especially complimentary about the ex-slaves:

> The mass of the population is a fine race; they are strong, active, and athletic; temperate, quiet, and regular in their habits, not given to excess; the sexes are equally divided, and the old who have lived with women in the days of slavery evince a disposition to be married. I should say they have fewer vices than one usually meets amongst their class. . . . Without being able to read or write I was particularly struck with the sound common sense and good information of the people; they speak the English language remarkably well beyond that of any of their race I have ever met, and quite free from the accent and dialect of the African.

Michell went on to praise their skill in planting and fishing, and the way that necessity had made them competent craftsmen: "Every man erects his own dwelling, plants and lays out his ground. Most are carpenters, some good rope-makers. They have knowledge of boats and ship building, the making of line . . . and other useful attainments. Their dwellings are well and comfortably made."[25]

Captain Michell's description of land tenure and his admiring comments on the ex-slaves did not tell the whole story. By the 1840s, the white pioneers in Roatán and the near-white former slaveowners who followed on their heels must have felt in danger of being swamped by non-white Caymanians. The 1844 land regulations ensured that land was available to the newcomers with fairly secure title. But this was only in certain locations, in a certain configuration, and up to a certain limit (300 by 150 yards is about 9.3 acres). Within a short while the non-white newcomers greatly outnumbered the white and near-white pioneers. Yet a disproportionate amount of the most fertile land in the best locations already belonged to the first comers. They had established them-

Evangelist's Meeting House, French Harbour.

selves as the chief boatbuilders and shopkeepers and were constituting themselves into a ruling elite.

Captain Michell alluded to this when he commented that the group of "European" migrants, "though small in number exercises a great influence over the minds of the community". Their number included some who had "sought this remote island, some in their old, and others in their middle age, either to commence again or to retrieve their broken fortunes, or to speculate in an imaginary construction of wealth". Observing another small group of near-whites, Michell reported:

> A small portion of the inhabitants are coloured people also natives of that island [Grand Cayman] and formerly slave owners. These latter people seem to be the most wretched on the Island; unaccustomed to labour and having lost their property and their slaves or squandered away what they obtained for them, they no longer had any means of existence; from a false feeling of pride so universal in man and found alike in all countries, they were unwilling to labour in a small Island where they were once regarded with comparative consequence, they emigrated and sought their fortunes on the unpeopled shores of Ruatan.[26]

By 1858, when a full census was taken, the Bay Islands had a population of 1,548 – not much less than the population left in the Cayman Islands. Six hundred of these settlers had been born in the Cayman Islands and about another three hundred born in the Bay Islands to Caymanian parents. The remainder included a handful of Garifuna, "Spanish" natives of Central America, people born in Belize, Jamaica, and other parts of the British West Indies, and immigrants from the British Isles, Africa, and the United States.[27] Eighty-nine per cent lived in Roatán. Though the majority were Caymanians, the population was much more diverse than that of Cayman.

Overall it was a balanced population in terms of sex, ages, and families. It was a society divided, however, by colour and class – much more so than the population of Cayman. The 319 whites were outnumbered by 1,229 non-whites. The overall ratio of four to one (non-whites to whites) was even higher in Roatán, where it was six to one. It was whites, however, who occupied the prime sites in the chief settlement of Coxen's Hole and elsewhere, while the small populations of Utila and Guanaja were overwhelmingly white.

The economy and society of the Bay Islands were strongly influenced by what the Caymanians brought from their home islands but were also shaped by the new environment. For instance, their houses were built close to the sea in a fashion said to be based on Caymanian models. Yet within a short while nearly all houses were being built on stilts and located over the shallow waters along the shore, a style not found in the Cayman Islands. This design was possible because all the settlements were located on the southern, or leeward, side of the Islands.

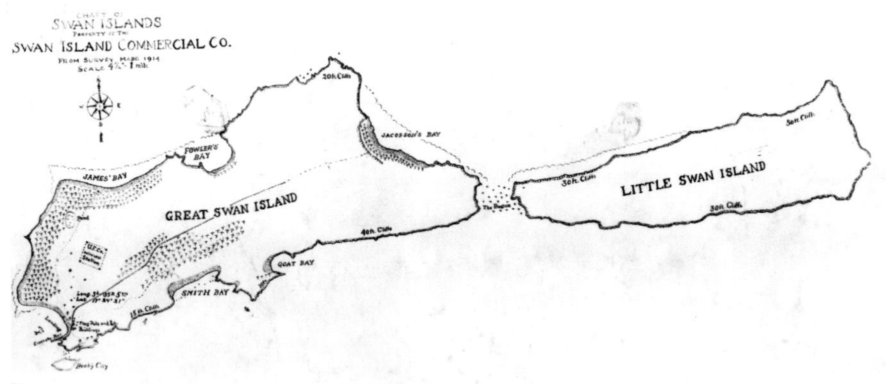

Map of the Swan Islands, ca. mid-1900s.

The newcomers cleared land for crops, and fished and turtled as best they could. But the excellent soils and the tropical climate made it difficult to keep provision grounds clear and enabled plant diseases and pests to flourish. Cultivation was also hampered by raids on outlying provision grounds by Garifuna from the adjacent mainland. In general, it was only the more substantial landowners who could afford to hire the labour necessary to produce surplus crops for export. They were also the only people with the resources to build the boats needed for a successful export trade and turtling industry. The black settlers, like most British West Indian ex-slaves, preferred the life of subsistence farming and fishing. Few wanted to accept employment from the would-be planters, who instead employed workers from the Honduran mainland.

A moderately prosperous export economy developed in the Bay Islands during the 1850s, creating a healthy balance between exports and imports by 1856.[28] The trade was very different from that in Cayman, however. While hundreds of turtles were caught each year for export, turtle fishing never became the mainstay of the economy. Instead, trade consisted mainly of coconut oil, corn, and ground provisions shipped to Belize and consignments of coconuts, bananas, and plantains sent to New Orleans. Trade with the Cayman Islands was negligible, but trade with the United States increased and became more important than that with Belize.[29] The economic shift towards the United States and away from the rest of the Caribbean had important cultural and political implications for the islands.

The whole fate of the Bay Islands settlements hinged on the relative shifts of British and United States influence in the region. Britain's general tendency in an age of free trade and *laissez-faire* was to ignore unprofitable imperial ventures. There was a tacit agreement between Britain and the United States to cooperate rather than compete, and to pay lip service, at least, to the ideals of Latin American independence. Britain was willing to make concessions to United States expansionism, but not to give up long-established possessions. This meant that while British Honduras (Belize) would remain

The Swan Islands: harvesting coconuts.

a British colony, the future of all other recent British settlements was extremely insecure. The situation was complicated by a persistent failure by the Foreign Office, the Colonial Office, and the Royal Navy to communicate with one another.[30]

The Caymanian settlers in the Bay Islands obviously wished to formalise their status. In 1841 they heartily approved when Superintendent McDonald sent a Senior Magistrate from Belize to the Bay Islands with authority to appoint local J.P.s. This action was officially disowned after London received complaints from Honduras and the United States. Yet the settlers later claimed that their Magistrates had endorsed McDonald's successor, Sir John Fancourt, in 1844. They even set up an elected assembly in that year, modelled on the local legislature developed in the Cayman Islands during the 1830s.[31]

In September 1849, three local J.P.s and a Clerk of the Courts sent a plea for the Bay Islands to come officially under British protection. When this drew no immediate response, the principal inhabitants sent a Memorial to Governor Sir Charles Grey of Jamaica in January 1850, asking whether the Bay Islands were recognised as a British colony, if its inhabitants were still British subjects, and if they could appeal for help and protection through British Honduras.[32]

Because most communication was still by sailing ship, events moved slowly. But in August 1851, the Belize Superintendent, Philip Wodehouse, visited Roatán and then wrote to Governor Grey of his intention to set up a more formal system of government for the Bay Islands. His plan was apparently endorsed by Grey in a despatch to the Colonial Office, and by June 1852 he was able to send to Wodehouse Letters Patent and a Commission under the Great Seal (dated March 1852 in London) for the formal creation of a Crown Colony of the Bay Islands. The Governor of Jamaica would be its governor, and the Superintendent at Belize its lieutenant-governor. The local government was to consist of a Presiding Magistrate and a legislative general assembly of twelve men, elected by all males over twenty-one. This news was gladly received in the Bay Islands on 20 June 1852.[33]

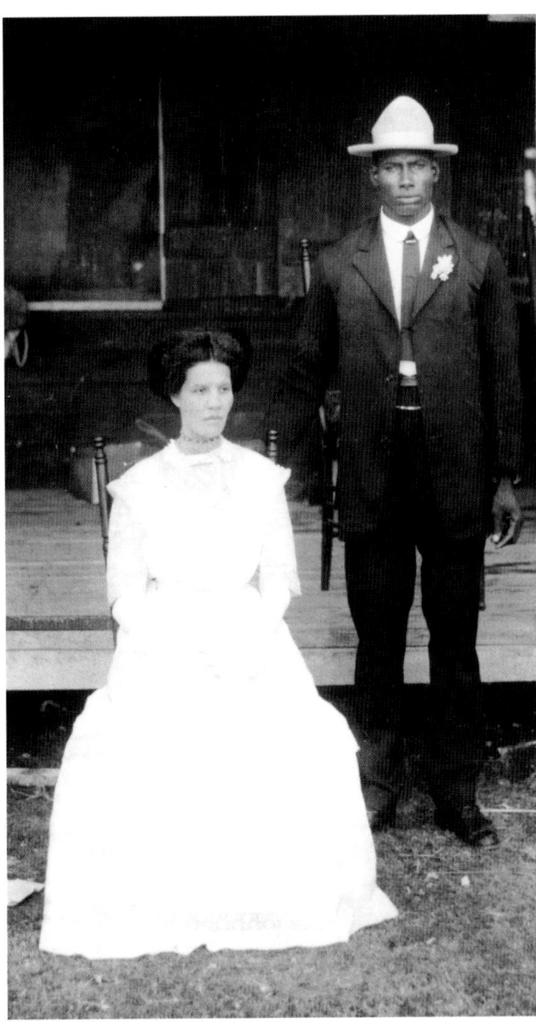

Mr. and Mrs. Tom Ebanks of the Swan Islands.

The short-lived Crown Colony of the Bay Islands had a record of achievement that must have encouraged those in Cayman who may have desired a similar status. Within a short while, an imposing Government House was built on the hill overlooking Coxen's Hole, as well as an assembly building, court-house, and jail. Law and order was kept without a police force or a militia; land ownership was registered; taxes were raised for building roads and bridges. The colony even kept impeccable records in the standard form of Colonial Office Blue Books. None of the expatriate Presiding Magistrates lasted long, however. They fretted about Garifuna raids and other threats from the mainland, and complained about the settlers' squabbles and general sloth. But they were able to report a steadily growing population and a slowly expanding economy.[34]

Alexander Moir, the last Presiding Magistrate, and the lieutenant-governor at Belize, Frederick Seymour, both hoped that the mixed-raced Caymanian migrants might build a unique and viable society in the Bay Islands. Moir wrote on 1 March 1858:

> . . . I think I am correct when I say that no West India Island has the advantage of this, in exhibiting the *ci-devant* [former] slaves, not only in a state of absolute freedom but in the position of a large landed proprietor, indignant at the thought of working as a laborer for others – but himself the employer of hired labor from the State of Spanish Honduras – and that not in isolated instances, but as a general rule. It is true that the largest proprietor here is a white man, but the colored man treads close in his steps, and were it not for the superior intelligence and energy of the former, and the more general credit afforded him, his colored compeers could, with cash, enter the market ahead of him.[35]

The Swan Islands: loggerhead turtle eggs arranged by size.

Moir's report pointed out that the Bay Islands colony was an active Protestant enclave in a Catholic country. Nearly all the Caymanian Bay Islanders were Methodists. In 1858 the Anglican and Presbyterian churches had no presence, but the Methodists could boast an ordained missionary, three chapels with 850 regular attendees, twelve local preachers, fifty-two Sunday school teachers, and seven Sunday schools, of which six were weekday schools as well. Some of their members had been introduced to Methodism fifteen years earlier by missionaries in Grand Cayman, and had brought their faith with them.[36]

Unfortunately, the very existence of this new Crown Colony contradicted the policy pursued by the British Foreign Office. The Clayton-Bulwer Treaty, signed at Washington in April 1850, had already declared that Britain and the United States agreed not "to occupy or fortify or colonise or assume or exercise any dominion over Nicaragua, Costa Rica, the Mosquito Coast or any part of Central America". For Britain this meant a ban only on colonisation after the treaty, thus exempting the colony of British Honduras. But the treaty clearly invalidated the Bay Islands colony, which was set up more than two years later (in addition to raising doubts about the loose British protectorate over the Miskito Coast).

The announcement of the Bay Islands Crown Colony in June 1852 provoked a storm in the American press, which spread to Congress.[37] James Buchanan, the U.S. Ambassador in London, complained vigorously to the Foreign Office, provoking a flurry of dispute and recrimination. To save face, the British, American, and Honduran authorities attempted to establish conventions that would make the Bay Islands a free territory with virtual self-government under the nominal sovereignty of Honduras. These terms were not ratified by Honduras, and were so altered by the U.S. Senate that they became unacceptable to the British.[38]

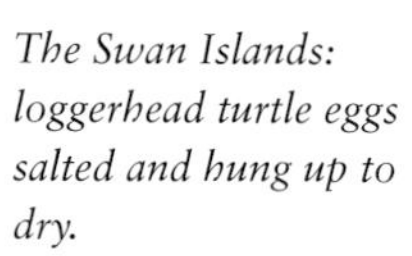

The Swan Islands: loggerhead turtle eggs salted and hung up to dry.

The Bay Islanders themselves did not want to be part of Honduras. Petitions were sent to Queen Victoria pleading for the Bay Islands to remain under her dominion. In March 1857 the visiting lieutenant-governor from Belize, Frederick Seymour, assured the Bay Islanders that "their beautiful islands" would "continue attached to the British Crown". At worst,

he believed, the Bay Islands would become "a free territory, with the exclusive right to manage their own affairs".[39] The decision, however, rested with neither Queen Victoria nor the lieutenant-governor. The British Foreign Secretary, Lord John Russell, was eager to establish good relations with the United States and to clear up the situation in Central America. Without prior consultation with the Colonial Office, he appointed Charles Lennox Wyke as British plenipotentiary in Central America in September 1859. Within a few weeks, treaties with Guatemala, Honduras, and Nicaragua had been concluded. James Buchanan, who by then had become U.S. President, informed Congress in 1860 that these treaties were entirely satisfactory to the United States government.[40]

By the Guatemalan treaty, the borders of British Honduras were clearly defined for the first time. By the treaty with Nicaragua, the rights of the Miskito Indians were protected, and Britain could continue to offer at least some protection to British settlers on the Caribbean coast of Nicaragua for another forty-five years. The Wyke-Cruz Treaty with Honduras, signed at Comayagua on 28 November 1859, however, was nothing short of a disaster for the British settlers of the Bay Islands. The islanders were guaranteed the right to property they already possessed, and freedom of worship and belief. But, far from any mention of a "free territory" or "self-government", the Bay Islands were said to be "in all other respects subject to the laws of the [Honduran] Republic". When a copy of the Honduras official gazette reached Roatán on 13 December, the Bay Islanders immediately realised that they had no guarantee of elective representation or a British system of law, including trial by jury, and no exemption from Honduran taxes or military

A house on Old Providence island in the Colombian Caribbean Archipelago, 2001.

Old Providence: view across the harbour, 2001.

conscription. The only alternative they were offered was to accept free Crown land in any British colony in which they might choose to resettle. To an independent-minded people who had been satisfactorily running their own affairs for two decades, this vague promise must have seemed almost an insult.[41]

The formal takeover of the Bay Islands by Honduras was delayed until June 1861.[42] But the change in political ownership was never fully accepted by the English-speaking settlers or by their descendants. Periodically they petitioned Britain to protect their rights or re-assume control. As late as the 1990s, they still referred to 28 November 1859 as "a sad and bitter day" when "England sold us".[43]

Though the loss of Crown Colony status dashed the Bay Islanders' hopes, there was no immediate exodus. The British government did little or nothing to implement repeated promises to grant Crown lands to those choosing to resettle elsewhere. As the Bay Islands economy steadily declined, and more poor, Spanish-speaking Hondurans arrived, many of the more enterprising settlers moved on to British Honduras. Others moved back to Grand Cayman. Some, following the path of widow Sarah Ryan and her children, moved to the Sister Islands.[44]

During the next fifty years Caymanians migrated from the Bay Islands and directly from the Cayman Islands to settle on the Caribbean coast and offshore islands of Nicaragua. This was an area under the British government's loose protectorate over the Miskito Indians. Small farming, fishing, and trading communities were established at Puerto Cabezas, Prinzapolka, Pearl Lagoon, and other points, as far south as the considerable port of Bluefields.

The security of these settlements was more or less guaranteed by the occasional presence of Royal Navy gunboats. But in 1895 Britain occupied the port of Corinto to enforce reparations for the expulsion of the British consul. A surge of Nicaraguan nationalism and a moderately aggressive U.S. foreign policy greeted this action, and Britain was subsequently persuaded to surrender all claims to its protectorate over the Miskito Coast.[45]

Gravestone of Robert Woodville: born Grand Cayman, 1843; died Utila, 1920.

It was probably during this same half century that Caymanian families formed settlements on the two Corn Islands, fifty miles off the Nicaraguan coast. Others moved to San Andrés and Old Providence (Providencia) to join the English-speaking blacks who either had been left from slavery days or had recolonised these islands. Here they must have seemed even safer from interference. These islands were 150 miles from the coast of Nicaragua and nominally belonged to Colombia, which was 500 miles to the east – farther away even than Jamaica or Cayman.[46] Closer to the Cayman Islands in another direction was the lightly populated Isle of Pines, with which Caymanians had always been familiar. Settlement there before the end of the nineteenth century, however, was probably difficult and rare, as the island was an integral part of Cuba, where slavery did not officially end until 1886, and which remained a Spanish colony until 1898.[47]

The most fortunate of all the outward-looking Caymanians were probably the relatively wealthy shipowners who had a foot in several camps: sailing and trading between the Cayman Islands, the Bay Islands, and Belize, with the possibility of moving even further afield. Such people included Samuel Parsons, at different times a J.P. in Grand Cayman and Roatán. Parsons and two brothers with the surname Eden came to regard the two Swan Islands, midway between Grand Cayman and Roatán, as British. In April 1858 both Samuel Parsons and William Eden described how, some years before, they had left men on the Swan Islands to fish. The men had planted provisions and coconuts, set up a water tank, and established goats, which had multiplied into herds. Now they were outraged to find a camp of Americans on the island, employees of the Atlantic & Pacific Guano Company of New York, busily digging out hundreds of tons of the islands' rich deposits of petrified bird droppings.

Gravestone of Grace Azelda Ebanks in the Bay Islands.

This activity was seen as an intrusion on British soil. Samuel Parsons wrote, with arguments even stronger than might be put for British possession of the Bay Islands:

> It is well known that Swan Islands situate in the Carribean [*sic*] Sea have always been considered British and have been resorted to periodically and occupied by Her majesty's subjects for the last century. . . . The Cayman's people have resorted there for catching Turtle, cutting timber for building their houses and Vessels and cutting Fustick which is plentiful there. They have resided there for months at a time made plantations built their habitations and planted Cocoa Nut Trees.[48]

For those of Caymanian origin who had no option but to stay behind in the Bay Islands, the future was considerably more bleak. They must have felt increasingly stranded between two worlds: making what living they could under growing pressure to conform to Honduran wishes, yet proudly hanging on to their English-speaking identity and Caymanian connections. A census in 1877 showed that "Hondurans" were still only 35 per cent of the people of Coxen's Hole, whereas 60 per cent were listed by the Hondurans themselves as being of British nationality.[49] The Honduran government repeatedly turned down pleas for a separate Bay Islands constitution. Questions of land tenure, conscription, and taxation remained contentious. Riots occurred in the 1880s "caused either by overzealous Honduran officialdom or the sudden appearance of a British ship, or both".[50] Though Spanish was declared the official language in 1872, most of the inhabitants spoke English and regarded themselves as British citizens well into the twentieth century – despite Britain's official repudiation of this claim in 1903.[51]

The English-speaking Bay Islanders probably remained more conscious of both class and colour barriers than their counterparts in Cayman. As we shall see in subsequent chapters, if there were conflicts in post-emancipation Cayman, they tended to be those of class rather than colour. Conflicts of both kinds certainly existed in both communities, but they were less pronounced and easier to resolve in Cayman than in the Bay Islands. Whereas the community in Cayman shared a single language, the issue of language in the Bay Islands was bound to become a point of tension. More important, the community of the Bay Islands was overshadowed by an official Spanish presence that must have bred an increasing sense of isolation amongst English-speakers and may have fostered in them a greater resistance to social change.

Resilience and self-reliance: a common way of life in the 1800s.

CHAPTER 7

Isolation, Neglect, and Self-Reliance, 1845–1898

PROGRESS IN THE CAYMAN ISLANDS between 1845 and 1898 was slow, and notable events were few and far between. Despite the migrations described in Chapter Six, the population tripled within fifty years. But the economy, and with it the islands' treasury, hardly grew at all. This meant that the administration did not expand, and social services remained deficient. Industrialisation and the other modernising features of the long reign of Queen Victoria passed the Cayman Islands by. Although they were formally declared a dependency of Jamaica in 1865, it was not until the 1880s, and particularly with the appointment of the first expatriate Commissioner in 1898, that Jamaica really began to take an interest in the Cayman Islands.

From the perspective of the islands themselves, however, this period was far from uneventful. Jamaican and imperial neglect actually led to the Cayman's evolution as a distinctive people. Periodic complaints and pleas to the mother country or to Jamaica usually fell on deaf ears. But being ignored compelled Caymanians to develop a culture of self-sufficiency and nurtured the features of a unique society. This society remained hierarchical to a degree and varied subtly from island to island and district to district. Boundaries of class and colour continued to exist. But they became much less distinct, with less social tension than almost anywhere else in the Caribbean region. How these formative changes came about is the underlying theme of this and the next four chapters.

Shipwreck off East End, which brought Rev. Hope Waddell to Grand Cayman in January 1845.

A GROWING IDENTITY

A vivid description of Cayman at the start of this period is provided by the Presbyterian missionary Hope Masterton Waddell, who was stranded for ten days on Grand Cayman in January 1845. Waddell's ship was wrecked on the East End reef while carrying him and his family back to England after fifteen years' work in western Jamaica. Sailing smoothly before a gentle wind, the ship struck at midnight. Rushing on deck, Waddell beheld a terrible transformation:

> The breakers were raging and foaming around us, as far as the eye could see ahead, and on both sides, while the vessel was beating and tearing on rocks scarcely below the surface of the water. . . . The vessel fell over on its side, and everything movable fell over too. There was no sitting possible, except on the floor, and there we sat patiently waiting on the Lord. It was grievous to feel and hear the straining and groaning of the poor ship on the rocks, as the swell of the sea lifted it up and cast it down again, with a crash that made everything start, and seemed fit to split it in pieces.
>
> . . . When day dawned, a small low island was visible at some distance, and between it and the reef a lagoon of smooth water. Ere long, to our great joy, canoes were seen coming off from the shore. 'What a benevolent people,' I said; 'see how they hasten to our help.' 'Wreckers,' said our captain; 'that must be their trade. Many vessels have been brought up here all standing;' and he pointed to anchors, chain cables, and fragments of ships lying on the reef, over which the water now lay calm and clear. A fleet of canoes was making for us, and soon surrounded our helpless craft; when a host of wild, reckless-looking coloured men sprang up the sides, like pirates or boarders greedy for prey. The head man, advancing to the captain, with one word of pity and two of business, agreed to take everything ashore, on the usual terms of a half for their trouble.

> Then began the work of despoiling the vessel. The fellows were up the rigging, and over the spars, and everywhere in a moment. Down came the sails and ropes, bundled into the canoes, and off ashore with amazing rapidity. Up came everything from the hold. The cabin doors, fittings, and furnishings, were by fair or foul means torn off and sent away. The people seemed to vie which would do most, the canoes which would go and return most quickly, striving to strip the wreck during the calm of the morning, before the sea breeze rising should impede their operations. Some of them were swearing shockingly until rebuked; when they looked surprised, begged pardon, and then shouted to their companions to mind themselves, as there was a 'parson' on board.

A canoe took the Waddells ashore, where the East End women "received the children into their arms with tenderness and pity". The family was offered the use of the head wrecker's house, the only two-storey building in the settlement, standing amidst "fishermen's huts and hovels of the poorest description". After a few days there was a public sale of the wreck goods, and the Waddells were carried to George Town in one of the schooners attending the sale. George Town, according to Waddell, "presented an attractive appearance in a line of good houses fronting the bay. There we found respectable married families, both white and brown, with whom we had agreeable intercourse during the week we remained. There also were a church and school-house, but neither minister or teacher; nor was any in the island, though it contains about fifteen hundred inhabitants, and is reckoned a parish of Jamaica."[1]

Waddell announced that he would preach on the Sabbath, and was amazed that "several hundred people filled the school-house, white, black, and brown. Between services we had reading classes, and were glad to see the progress many had made, and the desire that all manifested to learn. A good work had been begun among them, and a great work evidently remained to be done. With avidity they received all the books and tracts we had to distribute; and implored us to make known their destitute condition, and procure them a missionary."

From his observations of the island, Waddell added that there was pasturage for cattle, but no farms that he could recognise as such. "Even the bush, which can grow where man cannot labour, is stunted. Yams, cocoas, and plantains are unknown. 'Sweet potatoes will grow in some parts,' said a good woman, 'and we all go a fishing, especially for turtle, to supply the English ships. But to tell you the truth, sir, our main dependence is on wrecks, and we all thank God when a ship comes ashore.'"[2]

The image of the disreputable wrecker, as well as ill-founded rumours of involvement in the illicit slave trade with Cuba, continued through the 1840s and 1850s.[3] Caymanians would doubtless have welcomed Crown Colony status like the Bay Islands, if that had been feasible. But they were hard

pressed by a disastrous hurricane in 1846, by Cuban attacks against their fishermen in the south Cuban cays, and by the general effects of emigration, isolation, and poverty. The Magistrates probably expressed the majority view when they sought a greater degree of imperial or Jamaican control, if it would bring progress and assistance.

In January 1854, two Magistrates, William Eden and John Wood, were delegated to carry a written plea to Governor Sir Henry Barkly. The Cayman Islands, they wrote, were fertile and healthy but underdeveloped. The government lacked funds and the people the means for anything other than building boats, fishing, and subsistence farming. The system of local government, they said, "offer[s] advantages, but is inefficient". The Magistrates asked the Governor to appoint a resident superintendent, who would be in charge of local affairs and subordinate to Jamaica. Funding was needed for local works, especially to create "industrial" schools. Some revenue could be raised through low taxes, if they were collected more efficiently. But in this connection the Magistrates asked that tonnage duties paid by Caymanians to Jamaica (which treated their ships as foreign rather than local vessels) might be returned and for fairer distribution of colonial funds. They also requested that the steamship postal service be extended to Grand Cayman.[4]

Governor Barkly's response was a masterpiece of deflection. More and better schools were certainly desirable, he said, and the Bishop of Jamaica would be contacted to see whether it was possible to reinstate the church-sponsored Mico Charity schools closed some years earlier. The idea of an improved postal service was also a good one and would be passed on to the Jamaican Postmaster General. He reminded the petitioners, however, that the mail was carried by the privately owned Royal Mail Steam Packet Company, which was not likely to make the detour to Grand Cayman on the way between Jamaica and British Honduras.

The Governor indicated that he had no objections to the appointment of a resident superintendent, provided that Caymanians were willing to raise the funds for his salary. If they could do this, he had no objection to "the present vestry" having its powers increased so that it could levy more taxes. There was, however, no possibility that Jamaica would contribute financially or return tonnage duties. Such an action was possible only if the Cayman Islands were completely integrated into Jamaica. This, however, would involve surrendering a degree of independence which the Caymanians seemed to prefer. He concluded by expressing his continued concern for the welfare of the Islands and politely regretting that the pressing affairs of Jamaica prevented his making a visit to Cayman.[5]

Governor Charles Darling, Barkly's successor, did rather better, but with little practical effect. He visited Grand Cayman in June 1858 and wrote a long memorandum to London in October, describing conditions and making recommendations. The population, after the decline of the 1840s, was increasing once more. About a hundred people were now living on the Sister Islands. The population on Grand Cayman had reached twenty-two hundred, of whom nine hundred were said to be blacks, with most of the rest of mixed race. Due to the efforts of two Presbyterian missionaries, James Elmslie and William Whitecross, there were six chapels and Sunday schools, catering to about five hundred pupils of all ages, and three day schools with an attendance of between 150 and 180 children. Yet the islands still lacked both a qualified lawyer and a doctor. There were about fourteen hundred head of cattle and horses on Grand Cayman, though agriculture was limited. While Caymanians still depended on the sale of turtle and other produce to passing ships, the number of wrecks had declined because of navigation aids.

On the positive side, Governor Darling reported that there were twenty-one sailing vessels on Grand Cayman, of which all but one had been built in the islands. He praised the quality of local boatbuilding. One vessel that he saw on the stocks "was commended for mode and strength of construction by a naval officer of experience who was with me". The "moral behaviour" of the people and the low incidence of crime impressed him. Material conditions were less impressive. The few roads on Grand Cayman were little more than bridle paths, since there were no wheeled vehicles. Only one-eighth of the cost of missionary work was raised locally. Government revenue was almost non-existent.

On constitutional and administrative matters, his comments echoed those of Lord Sligo twenty-four years earlier. "The Political and Administrative Condition of the Islands is Unsatisfactory", he noted, especially in its ambiguous connection to Jamaica. The extent of authority by the Governor or government of Jamaica over Cayman was obscure, especially in revenue matters. It was not clear if laws passed by the local legislature were valid and to what extent they could be altered by the laws of Jamaica. The relationship between the courts of Cayman and those of Jamaica badly needed to be clarified.

Having said all this, however, Governor Darling hedged. He admitted that the Caymanian system, though confusing, seemed to work and had the general approval of the inhabitants. Beneficial though a closer connection with Jamaica might be, it would drain Jamaica's limited financial resources. Instead of calling for the appointment of a superintendent as in 1854, the local Magistrates now favoured a Stipendiary Magistrate, funded from abroad. Governor Darling was prepared to recommend the appointment, adding the suggestion that the official appointed should also be Collector of Customs. This would augment his salary and perhaps even increase public revenue in the Islands.[6]

No change was made for another five years. The Colonial Office pointed out that the supposed purpose of the Governor's visit to Grand Cayman had

been to investigate the charge that Caymanians were involved in the Cuban slave trade. The Governor said nothing about this in his despatch, presumably because there was nothing to say. The Colonial Office approved in principle the appointment of a Stipendiary Magistrate, but only if his salary was paid by Jamaica. The Jamaican Assembly, however, angrily rejected any suggestion of subsidising a Stipendiary Magistrate for the Cayman Islands.[7] It took the more forthright Governor Edward Eyre to solve the overarching constitutional dilemma. He steered through the necessary changes so that between June 1863 and March 1865 the islands were at last made a formal dependency of Jamaica.

FORMAL DEPENDENCY STATUS

The formal recognition of the Cayman Islands as a dependency was acceptable to Jamaican legislators as long as it did not prove to be a financial burden. For Cayman, dependency offered distinct advantages. Cayman vessels would no longer pay tonnage dues when entering Jamaican ports. There was a greater chance that Jamaican investment might be attracted, along with professionals such as doctors and teachers. Settling the "dependency question" meant a resolution of constitutional, administrative, and legal tangles without a complete loss of autonomy.

The first seal of the Cayman Islands, devised by the Cayman Vestry in 1865, but disallowed by the Governor of Jamaica. The motto, "Nisi Dominus Frustra", echoes Psalm 127:1: "Unless the Lord builds a house, its builders labour in vain."

The Act for the Government of the Cayman Islands became law on 22 June 1863. It made all British Acts that were valid in Jamaica apply also to the Cayman Islands. It gave the Jamaican legislature the right to pass laws "for the peace, order and good government of the Cayman Islands", and to alter or repeal laws already made in the islands. It allowed the Jamaican legislature to extend to the "Justices and Vestry, or other body or bodies of persons in the said Islands, such power of making Laws and regulations" as it saw fit.[8]

The local legislature in Cayman was thus finally recognised, though certain powers were reserved to Jamaica. The "Justices and Vestry" could continue to make laws that "to them shall seem fit" for their islands. They were specifically empowered to regulate their own powers and procedures, and the powers and duties of public officers, especially J.P.s and officers acting under them. The legislature was in fact made responsible for a wide variety of tasks: "the establishment, maintenance, discipline and powers of the Police . . . The management, occupation, and disposal of the public property, or common land . . . The abatement of nuisances, the construction of works of public utility, the making of roads, the cleansing of streets and houses, and other matters affecting the health or convenience of the community." In line with these powers, it could control the collection, custody, and expenditure of its own revenue. Local laws were to be valid as soon as they were signed by the

Governor of Jamaica, subject only (like all colonial laws) to disallowance by the imperial authorities in Britain.[9]

In two respects only were the Cayman Islands made fully subordinate to Jamaica. The Supreme Court of Jamaica was to have jurisdiction over the islands for any legal action which could not lawfully be tried in Cayman or which could lawfully be referred to the Court for its decision. The Governor of Jamaica was also to exercise authority over the Cayman Islands "as if the same had been part of the Island of Jamaica".[10]

In anticipation of these changes, the Cayman Islands legislature had already passed an important law on 16 June 1863. It ensured that a fair copy of all laws passed in the islands since January 1832 and still operative would be transmitted to the Governor of Jamaica for his approval.[11] This was the first of twenty laws that received the assent of Governor Edward Eyre on 23 March 1865. Other laws of special note were the Act that established the legislature and its procedures (from 2 January 1832), the Act for Land Registration (from 1850); and the Acts for raising a public revenue, for collecting taxes and other dues, and for passing and administering local laws (from 1863). The most significant law from 1864 to be validated was probably the one regarding the Sister Islands. It decreed that the jurisdiction of the Cayman Islands extended also to "the Smaller Cayman Islands".

An Act to Raise an Efficient Police Force (from 1864) actually related to a corps of militia-like volunteers.[12] This law may have been a response to the rising tide of civil unrest in Jamaica in 1864 and 1865. By the time he approved the first official laws of the Cayman Islands in March 1865, Governor Eyre was already embroiled in the troubles that were to erupt at Morant Bay on 7 October. This rebellion and its savage suppression do not seem to have had any direct repercussions in the Cayman Islands. The fortunes of the new dependency were completely overshadowed by the debate in Britain about the situation in Jamaica, including the findings of the Royal Commission, the dismissal of Governor Eyre, and the reconstitution of Jamaica as a directly ruled Crown Colony.[13] What effect these dramatic changes had on the new constitutional arrangements for the Cayman Islands is open to question.

LAND OWNERSHIP

The law governing land registration was extremely significant in the evolution of Caymanian society.[14] It was passed in 1850 and ratified in 1865. Apart from the five land grants of 1735–42, the traditional Caymanian method of acquiring land ownership had been to claim, mark, work, and build on any unused tract. This tradition must have become the norm in the 1700s, because the first land grants had been entirely forgotten by the time Corbet reported on Cayman in 1802.[15] It was assumed that uninterrupted, unchal-

lenged occupation for some years gave the user legal title to land, allowing him to pass on the property to his heirs. The status of sales and transfers to those outside the family was more obscure. There is no evidence of a market in Caymanian land before the mid-nineteenth century. Even wills that were quite precise about the value of property or of shares held in stock, slaves, and ships were vague about the extent and value of lands that were being bequeathed.

This informal system of land ownership appears to have worked well enough for the century or more of settlement in Grand Cayman beginning in the early 1700s. But it could not long survive an expanding population, a cash economy, or the changes that followed emancipation. While slavery lasted, estate owners, whose own land was usually held by custom, had been in the habit of allocating house and garden plots to their slaves. In time, the slaves came to regard these dwellings as their own. With emancipation, conflicts inevitably occurred over land ownership. Many ex-slaves who were not prepared to stay in their customary homes in exchange for work either chose or were forced to move elsewhere. In rarer cases, where the original title or boundaries were vague, former slaveowners were compelled by the Magistrates to concede house and garden property to their former slaves.

Clearly, it was in everyone's interests to have a more precise system. This was the chief motive behind the passage of the original Land Registration Act in September 1850. An official Registrar of Lands was appointed. People wishing to register would first have to reach agreement with their neighbours about boundaries, and the register was to be open to public inspection at request. Registry for five years was "to be deemed a good title against all complaints whatsoever".

Registration, using a special form, was now proof of exactly who owned what and where. The registration form also specified the way in which the land had been acquired. The owner was required to state whether title was claimed through simple occupancy, inheritance, or purchase. The 1850 Act thus served two important purposes: it clarified land ownership and widened

Form for registering land under the Land Registration Act, 1850.

CAYMAN ISLANDS.

Form of Register.

Name of Place.	Proprietor.	Date of Registration.	Location and Boundary.	Title.
				By occupancy. By purchase from By inheritance from

the means of acquiring title to land. These included purchase, as well as the more traditional methods of grant from the Crown, claim, occupancy, or bequest. Many former slaves undoubtedly benefited by obtaining title to their house and garden plots. Large landowners were able to obtain firmer titles, and this may have gradually allowed them to profit in a modest new market in property by subdividing and selling surplus land.

The 1850 Land Registration Act survived for more than a century.[16] Unfortunately, no land registration records have survived from the 1800s, but the system of land registration itself must have fallen into disuse somewhere along the line. The official 1954 Colonial Report for the Cayman Islands made the statement that, besides the absence of any legislation on land tenure and usage: "There is no system of land registration, a fact which gives rise to a certain amount of litigation."[17]

If the new system of land registration fell into disuse within a decade or two, it would suggest that questions about land ownership were no longer pressing or tense. The 1850 Act probably satisfied people who wished to remain in their customary homes and were able to convince their neighbours and the Magistrates that they had authentic title. More important, the population did not increase enough to exhaust the resources of unclaimed land – let alone to develop a competitive market. Those who moved out of the settled areas probably went back to the traditional method of claiming title by occupancy, with no money at all changing hands. This practice may have been common in the "Caymanian frontier" – including the Sister Islands and the northern and eastern parts of Grand Cayman, as well as West Bay. The situation began to change only when the growing population pressed on the available resources of fertile land, as for example, in Cayman Brac in the 1880s. Radical changes in the system of land registration only took place in response to the pressures of modern development in the 1960s.

BENIGN NEGLECT

Compared with Jamaica, where there was enormous conflict over available land after emancipation, the situation in Cayman was relatively peaceful. This fact impressed a succession of Jamaican governors beginning with Sir John Peter Grant (1866–74), who briefly visited Grand Cayman in 1868. Grant was the most reformist of all governors of Jamaica. He was given unprecedented powers under the new Crown Colony status of Jamaica, and charged with remedying the problems that gave rise to the Morant Bay Rebellion. Among other changes, he abolished the Jamaican vestries in favour of parochial boards, instituted district courts, and appointed Stipendiary Magistrates rather than lay justices. He also introduced wide-ranging reforms in education, health, and the economy.[18]

Sir John Peter Grant

None of these changes affected the Cayman Islands for many years. Governor Grant recognised the deficiencies in Cayman's administration, tax collection, and courts, as well as the absence of an organised school system and professional medical care. But his attitude seems to have been that it was a non-system that worked – or at least presented no problems to Jamaica. Reform in the Cayman Islands was not a high priority for Grant's cash-strapped administration, with five hundred times as many people to manage in Jamaica and far greater problems to resolve. In these respects, Grant and his immediate successors could take refuge in the prevailing liberal philosophy of *laissez-faire*. To their way of thinking, Cayman had never really had a plantation economy, and this meant there was relatively little tension between the classes. In contrast to Jamaica, the Caymanian population was also predominantly white or near-white and therefore assumed to be largely capable of handling their own affairs.[19]

The Magistrates and Vestry at Grand Cayman were generally content with this inaction by Jamaica, except when the welfare of the Cayman Islands was directly at risk. Concern arose, for example, when the turtling and wrecking expeditions off the southern coast of Cuba were disrupted as a result of the independence struggle called the Ten Years' War (1868–78). To curtail gun-runners and ships carrying rebel recruits, the Captain-General of Cuba issued a decree defining Spanish territorial waters and authorising the Spanish royal navy to seize vessels that infringed the limits.[20] In February 1871 Custos William Eden sent a plea to Governor Grant about the seizure and detention of the Caymanian turtling schooner *Star* at Cienfuegos. Grant asked the British Consul General in Havana to take action and then informed the Colonial Office, requesting that the matter be passed on to the Foreign Office.[21] But before anything was done, a further decree in October 1871 placed an absolute ban on fishing off the Cuban coast. This gave rise to several more serious incidents.

In January 1872, the Jamaican sloop *Lark* had been properly cleared from Montego Bay to salvage the wreck of a Swedish barque at Cayman Brac. Encountering severe weather, the *Lark* sought refuge in Cuba. After taking on a Cuban pilot, it was boarded and seized by the Spanish warship *Astarte* and towed into Manzanilla. The crew and passengers were thrown into a one-room jail "with 60 others mostly felons and many diseased". The owners of the *Lark* and their Caymanian associates claimed compensation for the loss of potential profit from the Swedish barque, and damages for the seizure of their goods and their disgraceful detention.[22]

In August 1872, Custos Eden sent an urgent petition from "the Magistrates, owners of Vessels, and Principal Freeholders of the Island of Grand Cayman" to Governor Grant, protesting against the Spanish ban on fishing. The petitioners pointed out that Caymanians had always turtled at the Cuban cays.

View of George Town from HMS Eclipse, *1874.*

Their right to do so had been ensured by a treaty between Britain and Spain, backed up by an order in 1849 to protect British vessels fishing more than three miles from the Cuban coast. Grant acknowledged that Caymanians had indeed fished the Cuban cays without interruption from 1850 to 1871. He stated, however, that Caymanians were mistaken in believing that a specific treaty existed, or that as much protection had been promised as they believed.[23]

In his correspondence with London, Governor Grant noted that the Caymanians had made a "solemn protest that no Vessel belonging to or sailing from the Caymans had ever taken Arms, Ammunition or any other articles contraband of War from thence to supply the insurgents in Cuba". He pointed out that the Cuban prohibition pressed "heavily on the industry of these poor people, and [was] in no way of advantage to Cuba". But the most he felt able to recommend was that the Royal Navy continue to defend British vessels outside Spanish territorial waters, and that the Foreign Office request Spain to allow Caymanian fishermen to resume their practice of landing on uninhabited Cuban cays.[24]

In the event, fishing and wrecking off Cuba were halted throughout the Ten Years' War and for some time afterwards. They never regained their former importance. The economic fortunes of the Cayman Islands, and the Jamaican authorities' comparative indifference to them, probably reached a low point during the decade between 1874 and 1883, when Sir William Grey and Sir Anthony Musgrave were governors of Jamaica. Worst of all were the years 1876 and 1877, when Cayman was hit by two disastrous hurricanes, and Jamaica felt able to offer only emergency aid. The hurricane of 1877, for instance, devasted the Caymanian turtling fleet at the Miskito Banks – sinking nine of the twenty turtle boats and drowning sixty-four people, including many fathers of families.

Custos William Eden, who spent much time in Jamaica because of declining health, begged the Governor several times for assistance after the 1876

hurricane. He described the "great loss of life and property" and the starvation and disease that would follow the destruction of crops and the pollution of the water supply. In response, Governor Grey sent HMS *Decoy* to Grand Cayman with emergency food supplies and backed this up with a grant of £200 for further food and clothing. But he instructed Eden to limit relief "strictly to persons who are absolutely in want", and required him to submit an exact accounting of expenditures. Conditions worsened over the following months, and eventually HMS *Bullfinch* was sent down with a doctor aboard. Basic ground provisions valued at £50 were brought in response to Eden's desperate plea, but he was again asked for a detailed report on the distribution of the food.[25]

Even less helpful was Governor Musgrave's response in 1877 to a plea for relief. Sixteen survivors of the ship *Enterprise*, which was Cayman-owned and registered in Jamaica, appealed for help. Their vessel had been wrecked on its regular run between Roatán and Grand Cayman by the same hurricane that had wrought major damage to the turtling fleet off Nicaragua. In a classic example of bureaucratic evasion, Musgrave argued in his despatch to the Colonial Office that Jamaica was under no strict obligation to pay the distressed seamen's expenses.[26]

In August 1878, Governor Musgrave received a further petition from Caymanians who wanted to resume fishing off the Cuban cays now that Cuba was at peace. Representations were duly made through official channels, but no change was made in the decree. Caymanian vessels did return to Cuban waters, but never with their former frequency. Local resistance to Caymanian turtlers continued and redoubled whenever the Cuban struggle for independence revived. An absolute embargo was imposed again during the Spanish-American War of 1898. Thereafter, Caymanian turtlers plied

View of South West Sound from HMS Eclipse, *1874.*

their trade exclusively in the Miskito Cays, where they had fished increasingly since the 1830s.[27]

This gradual change in the principal industry of Cayman went largely unnoticed by the governors of Jamaica. Benign neglect also marked the negotiations by Governors Grant and Musgrave regarding new steamship services for Jamaica. Kingston and Belize were included in a proposed new service in 1871 between New York and Panama, and annual subsidies were earmarked for a direct connection in 1872 between New York and Jamaica, as well as for a coastal steamship service in 1879 connecting Kingston with the Jamaican outports.[28] Throughout these negotiations the Cayman Islands were not even mentioned.

Governor Musgrave was aware of problems in the Cayman Islands but did not visit the islands in person, pleading pressure of Jamaican business and the lack of suitable transportation. In 1879, responding to a report by Commander Boardman of HMS *Griffon*, he wrote:

> . . . the condition of the small local revenue and expenditure of the Caymanese, who receive drawback of duty on goods exported to them from Jamaica and whose produce is on the other hand imported here duty free, is entirely unknown to this Government, and the question of elementary education and of the administration of justice having engaged my attention, and the necessity for the expenditure of public money in these directions and possibly in others, having arisen, I have called for information as to the fiscal and financial position of this portion of the colony. . . . With reference to the allusion to an intention on my part to visit these Islands I may say that the Public business has hitherto prevented me from visiting some important parts of the Colony, but I hope after the prorogation of the Session of the Legislative Council and subject to the Commodore's being able to furnish me with a vessel, to pay a visit to the Islands, taking in the southwestern portion of Jamaica on my way.[29]

Boardman's report had mentioned the threat of epidemics and suggested that the Governor should carry a medical team, including a vaccinator, when he visited the islands. Instead, Musgrave simply arranged for a supply of vaccines to be dropped off at Grand Cayman by an American steamer on its way to Vera Cruz. These were to be administered by "a competent local schoolmaster", a Jamaican named Dennis James, at the rate of a shilling per successful case. Complaints were soon received about James's incompetence, as one vaccinated child died. Before going off on almost a year's leave, the Governor sent "an Officer on whom I can depend to make investigations".[30]

The "officer" turned out to be Musgrave's son and private secretary, Anthony Musgrave Jr. His visit resulted in a detailed and valuable report on Cayman to Edward Newton, the acting Governor. Newton even sent a message to the Senior Magistrate of the Cayman Islands (now William Bodden Webster) referring to the "contemplated effort to be made by this Government

The first chart of all three Cayman Islands, published in 1882 and based on Royal Navy surveys carried out in 1880 and 1881.

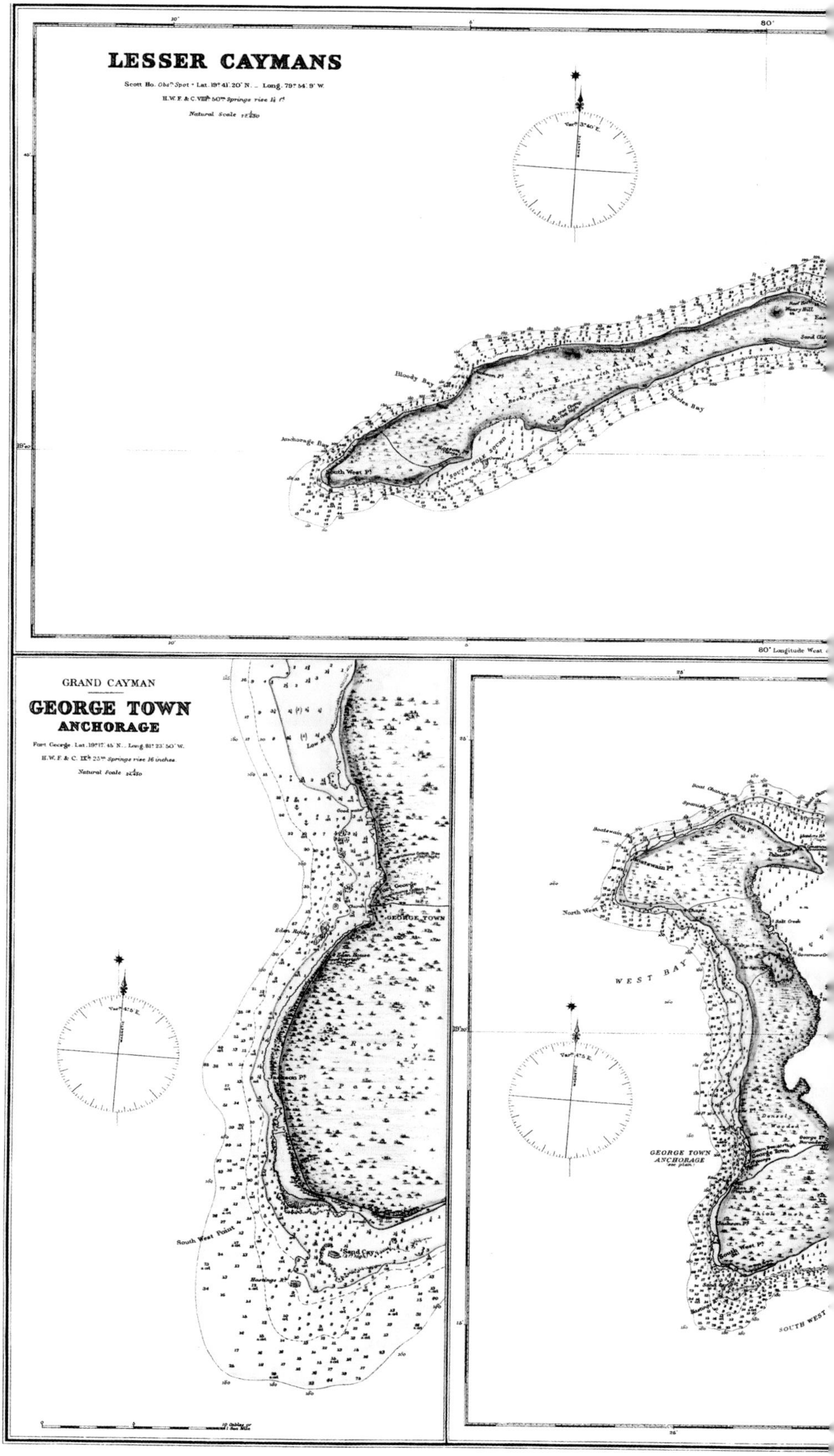

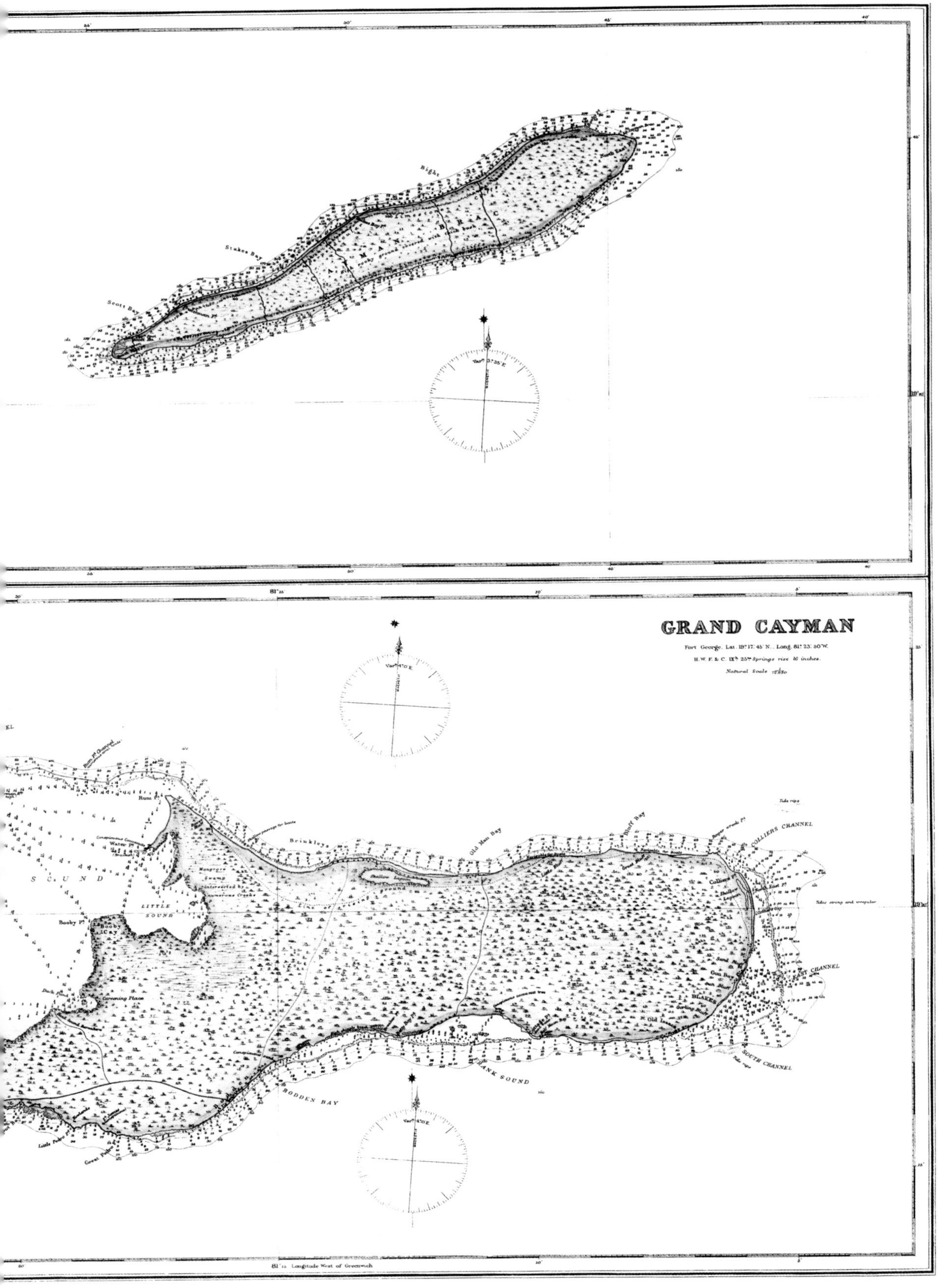

Stakes Bay

Scott Bay

GRAND CAYMAN

Fort George. Lat. 19°17'45" N.. Long. 81°23'30"W.

H. W. F. & C. IX^h 25^m Springs rise 16 inches.

Natural Scale

SOUND

LITTLE SOUND

Booby P^t

Old Man Bay

COLLIERS CHANNEL

EAST CHANNEL

SOUTH CHANNEL

BODDEN BAY

81°15' Longitude West of Greenwich

for the general improvement of the administration of the affairs of that long neglected settlement".[31] But from Governor Musgrave's return in 1880 until his retirement in 1883, the report by his son seems to have fallen into oblivion.

It was during this time that the Royal Navy carried out its first full survey of all three islands, publishing a chart of them in 1882. The surveys were carried out by HMS *Sparrowhawk*, giving its name to Sparrowhawk Hill in Little Cayman. The only previous survey of the Sister Islands had been carried out by Richard Owen, the surveyor from HMS *Blossom*, in 1831. Fifty years later, the surveyors from HMS *Sparrowhawk* apparently were familiar with his work, and it was probably after him that they named Owen Island, the small cay to the south of Little Cayman. The surveys of the Sister Islands in 1880 and Grand Cayman in 1881 were the most detailed to date, as evidenced by the resulting charts and by the notes on the Sister Islands made by Lieutenant Carpenter, the chief surveyor. According to Carpenter, the population of the Sister Islands in 1880 was about three hundred, of whom one hundred were children. The leading families were "Scott's, Foster's, Ryan's and Hunter's". Carpenter describes them as "friendly to strangers and anxious to trade", and continues his description with fascinating glimpses of life on the Sister Islands.

> Their livelihood depends on the capture of turtle, loggerheads being the most common, then hawksbill and the green turtle. The tortoise shell of the hawksbill and the soup meat, and eggs of all are cured and carried to Jamaica markets by schooners. The bush has been cleared in places and yams, bananas, and sugar grown. Only the first of these really flourishes, and they are finer even than the Jamaican yam. The men work in companies turning turtle and fishing at Little Cayman, but residing on Cayman Brac where their plantations are. The turtle nets are buoyed with imitation carved wood turtle and require to be carefully avoided when approaching an anchorage.[32]

GOVERNOR NORMAN'S VISIT

With the publication of the first naval chart of all three islands in 1882, the Cayman Islands would have become more widely known. At the same time, the two governors who followed Mulgrave, Sir Henry Norman and Sir Henry Blake, took a far greater interest in this Jamaican dependency than their predecessors. During their combined tenure, which lasted from 1883 to 1898, they visited all three Cayman Islands and wrote perceptive and interesting reports about them. In addition, Governor Norman sent Laurence R. Fyfe, a senior Jamaican official, to make a thorough examination of the Islands' administration in August 1887. Yet despite this new interest, changes within

the islands came slowly. This was partly because they could not afford them and Jamaica remained unwilling to provide subsidies, but also because both Norman and Blake concluded that the Caymanian system, despite its deficiencies, actually worked to the satisfaction of a people who neither knew nor wished for a better one.[33]

Sir Henry Norman chose to visit the Cayman Islands within a few months of his arrival as Governor of Jamaica. He landed at George Town from HMS *Griffon* on the morning of 14 March 1884. There he noted four or five schooners under construction, which he described as "well-built vessels of from 50 to 90 tons with a beam equal to a third of the length and shallow compared with the modern vessels built [in Britain]". He inspected the schoolhouse, church, court-house, and offices, which he found small but adequately built. He then examined "what records as were forthcoming", given that William Bodden Webster, who was Treasurer as well as Custos, was then absent in Jamaica. Norman concluded that "on the whole the slender revenues of the Island are fairly collected & expended", though he planned to call for a fuller and more regular accounting. On inspecting the available court records, he noted that court cases seemed admirably few in number, but that "in some cases the punishments seemed to me to be unduly severe & in other cases very light. The Magistrates admitted that there was often an inconsistency in their decisions & this is undoubtedly due not only to want of judicial training on the part of the Magistrates but also to their intimate acquaintance with all parties that came before them."[34]

Despite the absence of anything like a general education system, Governor Norman found the men of Grand Cayman lively and intelligent, as well as generally tall, healthy, and comparatively long-lived. Besides meeting with all the available Magistrates, Norman was invited into the homes of several of the principal inhabitants. These houses he found "very comfortable, fairly furnished and with wall decorations of some extraordinary looking paintings and engravings". Some of the ladies, though, "were too bashful to receive His Excellency and made excuses of ill-health although he was taken to their houses by their husbands. At other dwellings a cordial welcome was extended by the fair sex, and those seen were certainly very fine tall women, but without much conversational power."[35]

After two days at George Town, Governor Norman made brief stops at Little Cayman and Cayman Brac. Of the Boddens and Scotts who made up the population of Little Cayman, Norman wrote:

> Here there are no means of regular education for the children nor do I see how any measure [could] be devised, but owing to intermarriages with women from the Grand Cayman there is some rudimentary education on the Island. The people here are as hardy as those at the Grand Cayman but being a very small & isolated community & every male having to work hard for his living there did

> not seem to be as much intelligence as was displayed by the people in the Grand Cayman.[36]

Governor Norman was complimentary about the people of Cayman Brac. Landing at a place called "Scott's Village", he "saw the people of that part of the Island & was much pleased with them". He noted that "out of about 350 inhabitants barely a tenth are blacks & the latter keep much to themselves. The whites seemed intelligent & enterprising". Assessing the need for education and churches, he continued:

> There is no Minister of religion here & no Schoolmaster, but some attempt at education is carried on in families & prayer books & bibles were to be seen in the houses. I am disposed to think that the Islanders wd. welcome a Minister who would also teach their children & I shall endeavour to keep this in view in the hope that some means may be found to provide education for these people who by their fair appearance, their intelligence & their evident pleasure at our visit, excited a warm interest in those of us who went among them, including the Commander & Medical Officer of the "Griffon". Sickness here is very rare & the Island produces an abundance of good cocoa-nuts & a considerable quantity of sugar cane is grown, but the turtle fishery is the main resource of the inhabitants. The revenue which only amounts to a few pounds annually is almost entirely expended under the direction of the three Magistrates in keeping up the roads of the settlement.[37]

Governor Norman was full of praise for Caymanians in general. "My impression of the people was very favourable," he wrote to Colonial Secretary Lord Kimberley,

> and I can assure yr. Ldship that it has been to me a novel & a very pleasant experience to see white men [of] fine physique who are the great grandchildren & in some cases perhaps the great great grandchildren of original settlers retaining within the tropics the energy of there [sic] race & working hard at a dangerous calling contented with their lot, by no means wanting in intelligence & notwithstanding that they have seen little of British power or authority, proud of their allegiance to our Sovereign.[38]

Reporting on the administration of the islands, Governor Norman concluded that there was no immediate need to appoint a Stipendiary Magistrate or Superintendent as some of his predecessors had recommended. With so little to do in such an isolated posting, such an officer would almost certainly deteriorate, and be tempted to interfere in affairs that would best be left alone. Besides, he added, "the cost of such an appointment" would "necessitate at the very least a doubling of the revenue, a measure that [would] be very distasteful to people in whose possession there is at all times very little money". It would be far more useful and acceptable to the inhabitants to appoint a qualified Senior Magistrate, who would visit the Cayman Islands from Jamaica to preside over serious and difficult cases, and who would also look after the interests of the Jamaican government. An appointment like this, however, would face difficulties because "no steamers call at the Caymanas & the communication with Jamaica by means of schooners is uncertain and precarious".[39]

Three years later, Governor Norman sent Laurence Fyfe to make a report on the administration of the Cayman Islands. Fyfe visited only Grand Cayman and stayed no more than a week. But he seems to have met many more people and made more inquiries than Governor Norman, riding out to West Bay, Prospect, and Bodden Town from George Town, and calling in at East End on the way back to Jamaica.

THE FYFE REPORT

Fyfe's report, published in 1887, detailed considerable slackness and inefficiency in administration, as well as some tension between the Magistrates, much of which could be laid at the door of the Custos and island Treasurer, William Bodden Webster. The system of courts and appeals was faulty and not clearly authorised by law. Courts sat irregularly, and the Grand Court had not met for more than two years. Attendance by Magistrates was extremely uneven. Webster was often absent and sometimes threatened to resign because of disputes with other Magistrates. There was no Magistrate who was formally qualified, and the records were clearly deficient. In the important Reconciliation Court, which dealt mainly with disputed land cases, no proceedings or evidence were recorded. Only final decisions were written up, and it was not even clear that the records were complete in this respect. Petty Court records, on the other hand, usually included the evidence taken as well as the decision made. The Grand Court Book contained evidence presented, brief summaries of counsels' arguments, the charge of the "presiding Judge", and the jury's verdict. But rarely was there any authentication by the presiding judge or any other authority.

One of the most unprofessional features of court work was that, in the absence of qual-

The first published report about the Cayman Islands: L.R. Fyfe's report on Grand Cayman, 1887.

GRAND CAYMAN.

REPORT OF OFFICIAL VISIT

BY

MR. L. R. FYFE,

OF THE COLONIAL SECRETARY'S OFFICE, JAMAICA,

PRECEDED BY

MINUTE OF INSTRUCTIONS

BY

HIS EXCELLENCY SIR H. W. NORMAN, G.C.B., G.C.M.G., C.I.E.,

GOVERNOR OF JAMAICA.

1887.

JAMAICA:

GOVERNMENT PRINTING ESTABLISHMENT, 79 DUKE STREET, KINGSTON

1887.

ified persons, Magistrates often stepped down from the bench to act as advocates – sometimes in cases in which they were themselves involved. Custos Webster was especially at fault: he had recently left the bench to defend himself in two cases against other Magistrates. As Treasurer, Webster was also by implication responsible for many of the faults found in the public accounts. The collection of taxes was inefficient, uneven, and open to abuse, and their recording downright casual. Laurence Fyfe estimated that better supervision might increase revenue by up to 50 per cent. No taxes for the current year had yet been collected. Over the previous two years, little more than half the poll tax due had been collected. It was common for imported goods exempted from duty for "private use" to be sold in trade. Collectors were paid by a 12.5 per cent levy on the taxes collected, but they tended to hold monies for a whole year before making account. The whole revenue system was described by Webster himself as "horrible" and was complicated by the shortage of "English currency or its equivalent" and the use of foreign coinage.[40]

Laurence Fyfe gave a much better account of the general condition of the Cayman Islands than of its legal and financial administration. Besides the mainstays of turtling and shipbuilding, some Caymanians were employed by planters on the Miskito Coast for good wages. At least one vessel had been sent to Grand Cayman all the way from Bluefields, Nicaragua, for repairs and refitting. A blight was currently affecting coconut trees, but there was some well-paid work extracting potash on Grand Cayman, developed by a Jamaican firm, and similar work on Swan Island, initiated by the American Guano Company.

"My general impression of the people is that they are a fairly well to do, a self-reliant and loyal community," wrote Fyfe.

> It was impossible not to be struck with the well dressed appearance of the people of all classes and ages on the occasion on which we attended Divine Service on the afternoon of our arrival at George Town. I was told, and as far as my travels extended my own observation bore out the accuracy of the statement, that every head of a family has his house and plot of land for cultivation; and the houses of the laboring and peasant class are comfortable buildings, nicely thatched, often shingled and always floored. They are kept scrupulously clean and otherwise in admirable order. . . . I could hear of no cases of actual poverty or want in the Island. There might perhaps be some cases where, through infirmity from sickness or old age, individuals are unable themselves to earn a livelihood, but the relatives always step in and see that wants are supplied.[41]

Fyfe enclosed a subsidiary report on the conditions of health by George Twigg, surgeon of HMS *Mallard*. The report cited many cases of "dyspepsia" among the elderly, a couple of young people suffering from pulmonary tuberculosis, and single instances of goitre, urethral stricture, and ophthalmia.

Several people suffering from mental ailments were also brought to him. Leprosy, however, was totally absent. There was "no endemic disease that is due to climate or any other local cause", Twigg noted, and epidemics had been defeated early on through the isolation of the sufferers, the benign climate, and healthy nutrition. "Food is plentiful and good, and I think almost equally so for all classes of the community," continued Twigg.

> In any case where I recommended nourishment or diet of a particular nature there was no complaint of inability to obtain it. The people seem to live without care or anxiety of a serious nature; they have no interest beyond the Island; they had no question to ask us when we landed. The houses are of good size, cleanly and well kept, no smells noticeable. The inhabitants, especially the colored people, are extremely tall and of a more spare habit than usual; this may be due to their more intimate association with the white people [causing them] to lead a more active life.

Dr. Twigg concluded, however, that the Caymanians were seriously in need of a qualified resident doctor, "not only to treat sickness but also to lessen ignorant self-treatment".[42]

Fyfe made detailed and specific recommendations to reform the judicial system and the way revenue was collected and spent. He also strongly endorsed Twigg's plea for better medical care through the appointment of a government doctor. His foremost recommendation, however, was to appoint a Stipendiary Magistrate as superintendent, an official who might also act as judge of the Grand Court, senior Collector, and Treasurer. His salary could be paid for by greater efficiency in collecting revenue.

Fyfe frankly acknowledged that there was much local opposition to such a move. He referred to a resolution of the legislature in 1884 which expressed a contrary view, and he enclosed two strongly worded petitions to him and the Governor, which had been signed by fifty-three "principal inhabitants and freeholders in the community of George Town" and thirty-nine "inhabitants of Bodden Town". The petitioners admitted that disputes among the Magistrates had led to a minor crisis, but this could be easily rectified by a reshuffle. The appointment of a superintendent from Jamaica was unnecessary, the petitioners said, and would be an expense with serious local consequences. They fervently pled that Caymanians be allowed to continue to manage their own affairs.

The petition from George Town offers glimpses of life in Grand Cayman not only in 1887 but for some years past. "The Jamaica Government may perhaps not be aware that this Island has no resources or industries whatever by which the people can make a living," the petitioners wrote.

> The very soil, through the cultivation of generations, has become worn out, consequently a great number of the male inhabitants have to seek their living in

> foreign countries and neighbouring Islands, which their own Island cannot afford. Should the Island be burdened with taxes beyond the power or means of the people to pay, in order to pay a Resident Magistrate from Jamaica, we are afraid that in a short time the whole Island would be depopulated, as those who go away and work for the support of their homes (returning after an absence of six months or thereabouts with the fruits of their labour) would eventually take their families away, making their homes in the midst of their labours.
>
> . . . The Island has for generations past been governed by a Custos or Senior Magistrate to the satisfaction of at least the majority of the inhabitants, and we cannot see why the same thing cannot be done now. Surely there are as good men in the island now as then, capable enough to take the management of affairs as those who have gone before. We are glad to say that our Island has been slowly progressing and a marked improvement may be noticed in several ways.
>
> If our present Senior Magistrate wishes to resign his commission surely there is another man among us who could take his place.
>
> We would suggest that His Excellency send some one down here for the next term of the Grand Court, with full power to preside as Judge, to settle up all matters now pending, leaving us with a clear docket. And if there is any difficulty as to the selection of some one to administer affairs afterwards, let it be decided by a majority of the people.
>
> We cannot see why the inhabitants of this Island should be made to suffer because some of our Magistrates cannot get on together.[43]

In response to these petitions, Fyfe recommended gradual change. He noted "the apparent fondness of the Cayman Islanders for existing institutions, and their present prejudice against changes of a radical character". In time, though, he felt it would be possible to work up to the appointment of a superintendent through the appointment of a salaried local Collector and Treasurer, and by sending a judge each year on circuit from Jamaica. The Fyfe Report was printed and widely disseminated, and Governor Norman visited the islands again in May 1888. The only immediate result, however, was the resignation of William Bodden Webster as Custos, Treasurer, and Magistrate. He was replaced by the less abrasive and more efficient Edmund Parsons, who presided as Custos for the next ten years.

THE EDMUND PARSONS YEARS

It was during the administration of Edmund Parsons that the short-lived phosphate industry came to prominence. Indeed, Parsons himself was closely involved in the management of one of the two companies concerned, the Carib Guano Company. In 1883 William Eden had taken some samples of rock from his land in George Town to Jamaica for analysis. The results were encouraging, revealing that the rock had "high grade fertilising properties".[44]

In May 1884 the Grand Cayman Phosphate Company, formed by a prominent Jamaican merchant, began operations. Although the phosphate beds in George Town were soon exhausted, larger beds were discovered in West Bay and at the western end of Cayman Brac. In May 1885, the Carib Guano Company, based in Baltimore, Maryland, began excavations in Grand Cayman and at the western end of Little Cayman, where a "very rich deposit" had been found.[45]

Edmund Parsons, the last Custos (1888–98).

For the next five years exports of phosphate were steady. The new industry provided numerous jobs on all three islands, most of which were filled by Caymanians – although the industry created enough work to employ Jamaican contract labourers as well. All seemed set for continuing success. Owners of the land received a royalty of some five shillings per ton, and as a contemporary observer noted, "there was no need in the Cayman Islands for the word, 'unemployed'". One entrepreneur who exported phosphate from Little Cayman to Baltimore, the grandfather of the late Capt. Theo Bodden, employed as many as 335 men, most of whom came from North Side, East End, and Bodden Town.[46]

Unfortunately, the boom did not last long. Within a few years, much larger phosphate deposits had been discovered in western Florida. Mining phosphate within the U.S. was much more commercially attractive than the extraction and shipment of Cayman deposits. The Grand Cayman Phosphate Company closed down in 1890, and the Carib Guano Company two years later. Though the industry was revived in a limited form on the Sister Islands from the 1920s until at least the 1940s, all that remained of this unusual episode in the commercial history of the islands were sections of the metal tracks, visible for many years, which had borne the trolleys carrying phosphate from the interior to the coast.[47]

Although involved in the phosphate industry, Edmund Parsons is best known as the last Custos and the first paid chief executive of government in Cayman. From his era (1888–98) dates the continuous modern machinery of government, best seen in the clear and consistent records he maintained, including registrations of births, deaths, and marriages and regular correspondence with Jamaica. It was during this time that a post office was first established at George Town and a formal, if irregular, system of letter delivery begun. In the past, outgoing letters had to be carried by ship captains, either to individuals or to the post office at Kingston. Incoming mail had to be handled in Jamaica by an agent for the Cayman Islands, who forwarded it "as opportunity offered, through the courtesy of the captains of schooners touching at Georgetown". From 13 April 1889, Edmund Parsons was officially Postmaster as well as Treasurer and Recorder. Letters were carried by the most convenient vessel. Outgoing mail carried the Grand Cayman cancellation over the Jamaican stamp. Captains were paid a "gratuity" of a

Remnants of phosphate mining in the 1880s: trolley tracks in George Town, 1938.

penny per letter between the Cayman Islands and Jamaica, with letters going further abroad costing fourpence per half ounce.[48]

Custos Parsons also arranged for the Cayman Islands to participate in the important Jamaica Exhibition of March 1891. This was the first formal attempt of any kind by Caymanians to describe their islands to the wider world. William T. Eden, the Commissioner for the Exhibition, and E. Noel McLaughlin, Chief Clerk of the Jamaican Island Record Office, wrote a pamphlet to accompany a display of natural products and crafts from the Cayman Islands. Its purpose was to invite attention "to a small, and little known, but nevertheless important dependency of Jamaica, which in spite of many disadvantages, natural and otherwise, has on this occasion endeavoured to come to the front". This landmark publication praised the "warm but exceedingly healthy" climate, the picturesque villages "skirted by a margin of pure white sand", the quality of life, and the admirable character of the people. "The houses and cottages are models of neatness and substantiality, and the payment of house rent is almost unknown," wrote Eden and McLaughlin.

> The inhabitants take pride in building their own houses, and the humblest peasant is almost certain to be the owner of his own little cottage.

> . . . The population is at present about 4,000. They are a tall, strong, hardy, and very temperate people (the white and colored element preponderating), and almost every one is an expert sailor. They build, equip and man their own vessels, and in this and other respects display an amount of intelligence, skill, and energy, that might well be imitated by larger and more advanced communities. Besides their profession as seamen, however, they are good tillers of the soil, and the same individual is at one period of the year a seaman, braving the perils of the ocean, and at another remains at home and cultivates the soil in order to provide for the wants of his family.[49]

Governor Sir Henry Blake visited the Cayman Islands in June 1892, stopping first at Cayman Brac. He noted that for the Sister Islands, trade connections and other communications were much closer with Jamaica and the United States than with Grand Cayman. They produced half a million coconuts annually, most of which they shipped to Mobile, Alabama, at a price of between £3 and £4 per thousand. The public affairs of the Sister Islands were managed by the three local Magistrates and their own Vestry. Despite this, the Brackers argued strongly for the appointment of an independent Resident Magistrate, who would be able to provide a more even-handed and efficient administration – a very different view from that expressed by the recent petitioners of George Town and Bodden Town.

At Grand Cayman, Governor Blake was impressed with the people and their living conditions. He found that 51 per cent of school-aged children attended school, and 57 per cent of the general population was literate. This made an interesting contrast to Jamaica, where 60 per cent attended school, but only 46 per cent were literate. Having spoken with Custos Parsons and other leading citizens, however, Governor Blake was disappointed to learn that "none of the changes hoped for by Sir Henry Norman had been made". There was still no doctor. The performance of courts and Magistrates was still irregular, and the custom of Magistrates stepping down to act as counsel continued. Foreign coins remained the common currency. Though a Collector

THE ISLAND OF

GRAND CAYMAN

AT THE

JAMAICA EXHIBITION.

Historical Sketch and Descriptive Catalogue:

PREPARED AND COMPILED BY

WILLIAM T. EDEN,

COMMISSIONER FOR GRAND CAYMAN,

AND

E. NOEL McLAUGHLIN,

CHIEF CLERK ISLAND RECORD OFFICE, SPANISH TOWN.

JAMAICA:
DeCordova & Co., Printers, Publishers, Booksellers, &c.,
148, Harbour Street, Kingston.

1891.

The first known publication by a Caymanian: catalogue for the Jamaica Exhibition of 1891.

General had been appointed, there was still no clear customs law, and tax collection and management of public expenditure were still in confusion.

After receiving a formal address from the people and making a short tour, Governor Blake addressed the Magistrates and Vestry bluntly and at length. He especially impressed upon them "the advisability of having a Medical Man on the island, and of making provision for the payment of a Resident Magistrate". He chastised the Magistrates for their continued unprofessional conduct. Blake then withdrew to allow the legislature to discuss the issues without interference, but was disappointed to learn that, while a salary for a doctor and periodic visits from a circuit judge had been approved, the idea of a Stipendiary Superintendent was rejected once more.[50]

The local administration continued to run its own affairs for a further six years, with Custos Edmund Parsons doing as much as he could. He presided over the revision and reprinting of the local laws and made minor reforms in the systems of tax and customs collection and public accounting. Unlike his predecessors, he corresponded regularly with Jamaica and sent in annual estimates and accounts of revenue and expenditure. During his regime, several doctors took up the challenge of working in Grand Cayman, but gave up when they found the rewards of private practice insufficient to augment their small salary. For two or three years, a senior judge from Jamaica, Arthur L. Vendryes, made periodic visits to preside over the Grand Court and settle appeals. But he was severely hampered by the lack of a regular steamship service and the discomforts and delays of travel by schooner.[51]

Although Sir Henry Blake returned to the Cayman Islands in 1896, he was again unable to persuade the Vestry to accept the appointment of a Commissioner.[52] His successor, Sir Augustus William Lawson-Hemming, was much more prepared to take the bull by the horns. Soon after his arrival in Jamaica, Governor Hemming took up Blake's chief recommendation and appointed Frederick Shedden Sanguinetti, a long-serving English civil servant from the Colonial Service in Jamaica, to be the first Commissioner of the Cayman Islands, at a salary of £300 a year. By December 1898, Hemming was able to report that the hitherto reluctant Caymanian Justices and Vestry had unanimously approved the provisions in the Estimates both to pay the Commissioner's salary and to build him a house.[53]

KICKAPOO MEDICINES

	s.	d.
SAGWA per Bot.	2	6
COUGH CURE " "	1	3
WORM KILLER "	1	3
KICKAPOO OIL "	1	3
SUPPOSITORIES "	2	6
SALVE per tin	1	3
SOAP 6d per cake or 3 for	1	3
HAIR TONIC	2	6

Sole Agents for

CAYMAN ISLANDS,

T. COE & SON.

George Town.

H. O. MERREN & CO.

SHEDDEN ROAD.

General Merchants and Importers of

Dry Goods, Ironmongery, Paints, Oils, Canned Goods, (English and American) Flour, Rice, Confectionery, Crockery, Etc.

Our aim is to provide the best article at the lowest price in the future as we have always done in the past, and so continue increasing our already large circle of Patrons.

HONESTY THE BEST POLICY IS OUR MOTTO.

GEORGE TOWN.

GRAND CAYMAN.

CHEMISTS

T. COE & SON,

George Town, Grand Cayman,

also at NORTH SIDE and EAST END.

GENERAL MERCHANTS AND SHIP CATERERS

PATENT MEDICINES (English and American.)

CANNED GOODS.

OUR PRICES ARE THE LOWEST IN TOWN

For EVERYTHING.

Caymanian merchants advertise their wares in the early 1900s.

CHAPTER 8

Change and Resistance

The First Commissioners, 1898–1914

THE NEW FULL-TIME COMMISSIONER COMBINED the roles of Treasurer, Chief Justice, and President of the Legislative Council. The appointment improved the efficiency of both financial and judicial affairs and led to an increase in the islands' revenue. Expenses also rose, however, as the Commissioner and a slowly growing number of other public servants had to be paid. Custos Edmund Parsons (1888–98) had introduced orderly administration and sound record-keeping, and under Commissioner Sanguinetti the professionalism and energy of the local administration blossomed.

The innovations of this period reflected the determination of the first two Commissioners, Frederick Sanguinetti and George Hirst, to do what they could to improve the welfare of the islands. Their commitment and professionalism can be seen in advances large and small – for instance, in Sanguinetti's introduction of the typewriter for outgoing correspondence, and in the series of annual reports about Cayman that were published from 1907. Likewise, Hirst's tenure was distinguished by the energy with which he compiled statistics and promoted the islands in his *Handbook of the Cayman Islands* (1907, 1908), the detailed census published in 1911, and especially his *Notes on the History of the Cayman Islands* (1910).[1]

Frederick Shedden Sanguinetti was hard-working and popular. During his regime he repeatedly sought ways to expand and diversify the Caymanian economy, but unfortunately these attempts did not meet with success. A list of the projects and the reasons for their failure makes disheartening reading,

George Town Harbour, 1906.

even today. A cure for the disease that had blighted the coconut palms of Grand Cayman was not found. A proposal to establish a salt industry was a non-starter because rainfall was too heavy. A search for clays suitable for making bricks proved vain. It was greatly hoped that the phosphate industry might be expanded, but the existing beds were becoming depleted, and extracts from other locations proved disappointing. Samples of local wild cotton were sent away in the hope of reviving the cotton industry that had ended with slavery. But the Imperial Department of Agriculture in Barbados reported that "from neglect and long cultivation without selection of seed the staple has become short and discoloured", while the Cotton Growing Association of Manchester advised that cotton of this kind would not earn more than fivepence a pound. A cotton gin and baler were imported, but nothing came of the project. The commercial production of sisal fibre from the agave plant was also explored, but experts in New York reported that it was not strong and tended to stretch, and would be uneconomic to produce.[2]

Encouraged by Governor Olivier, Sanguinetti explored the possibility of introducing compulsory education. But the discovery that local taxes would have to be doubled to accomplish this aim aroused opposition, and he felt compelled to retreat. In fact, both Sanguinetti and Hirst frequently complained about low levels of taxation and government revenue. The lack of revenue to fund projects was compounded by high prices and wages in Cayman, which were two or three times as high as in Jamaica and the rest of the British West Indies.[3] The landowners, shopkeepers, and shipowners who dominated the legislature made sure that there was almost no direct taxation. Most of the revenue came from a 5 per cent duty on imports and a levy of four shillings a gallon on distilled spirits. These, like the poll tax of six shillings on each male aged eighteen to sixty, affected ordinary Caymanians more than those who were relatively well off. During Sanguinetti's tenure, government revenue rarely rose above £2,000 a year and was often exceeded by government expenditure. Under Commissioner Hirst, however, the national debt of £649 in 1905 was wiped out by careful economic measures and a rise in revenue to about £4,000.[4]

Lack of funds made it difficult for Sanguinetti to attract and keep a competent Medical Officer. At one time advertisements were sent as far as Montreal. Several doctors came, but they were discouraged by the terms of employment, the difficulty of travel within the islands, and the impossibility of earning anything like the £300 that had been promised from private patients.[5] The most memorable of these physicians was the observant and adventurous Richard Keatinge, who stayed through most of 1906 and left only because of pressing matters in England. The first two chapters of his book, *Life and Adventure in the West Indies*, published in 1914, provide a fascinating account of social and medical conditions in the Cayman Islands. Keatinge wrote with amused detachment of the Commissioner's role and his relation to local "white aristocrats", as he called them: the shopkeepers, shipowners, and major landowners, whom he titled "Merchant Princes, Vikings, and Grass Dukes". According to Keatinge, the "Vikings" or shipowners were opposed to the establishment of a steamship service between Jamaica and Grand Cayman because they feared losing their monopoly of the "carrying trade".[6]

No contract for a regular steamship service was obtained during Commissioner Sanguinetti's time – though more because of its cost than in response to opposition by shipowners. Postal services expanded greatly, however, largely because of the great potential for revenue in stamps. A second Caymanian post office was opened at Stake Bay, Cayman Brac, in 1898. In the same year, the Cayman Islands became an independent member of the Universal Postal Union and was allowed to issue its own stamps. An initial order for special Cayman Islands stamps was placed through the Crown Agents for the Colonies in London in 1900. These stamps were first officially used on 19 February 1901 – more than sixty years after special stamps were issued for Jamaica and the Bahamas.[7] Because of the infrequency of vessels connecting the islands, however, most letters between the islands still had to go through Jamaica, and there was no formal inland postal service on Grand Cayman.

Because the Cayman Islands automatically took part in the Imperial Penny Post agreement of 1899, the first batch of Cayman Island stamps consisted only of penny and halfpenny values. These stamps bore the image of Queen Victoria, even though the elderly monarch had passed away the month before they were issued. This anomaly immediately gave them a curiosity value for

A selection of Cayman Islands postage stamps.

collectors. Indeed, philatelists worldwide rapidly began to show an interest in the stamp varieties and misprints that issued from the islands.[8]

In 1907, through miscalculation, the local stock of halfpenny stamps became almost exhausted. Very reluctantly, Jamaica gave permission for an overprint, made in the Government Printing Office in Kingston, on the stocks of the King's head penny issue (now of Edward VII).[9] As the authorities had feared, this halfpenny-on-penny variety was immediately popular with philatelists and speculative dealers. Two later overprints, however, generated far more interest and aroused suspicions in high places. In November 1907 the Postmistress in Grand Cayman, Miss Gwendolyn Parsons, facing a temporary shortage of the most common values, overprinted the penny and halfpenny values on sheets of the five-shilling stamps. The overprint immediately became one of the most sought-after Caymanian varieties. Another overprinting was carried out in February 1908 by the Inspector of Police, John H. Sullivan. No more than half of the overprinted stamps were used for authentic postage; the rest were acquired *en bloc* as a canny investment. After an official inquiry, Commissioner Hirst was exonerated of willful wrongdoing. Miss Parsons was replaced as senior postal officer by W.G. McCausland in October 1908.[10]

With a few exceptions, no more Caymanian overprints were made. But it was clear that postage stamps could generate serious revenue. Largely because of strong interest by stamp collectors and dealers around the globe, the Cayman Islands depended heavily on the sale of stamps for decades. Subsidiary post offices were established in East End and Bodden Town, and a regular system of deliveries on Grand Cayman was set up in 1907. When the local letter rate was reduced in 1908, use of the post office soared. The local mail service was carrying twenty thousand items a year by 1914. Partly because so many Caymanians lived abroad, and partly because the retail and wholesale distribution on the island was undeveloped, letters and packages carried by the external mail service exceeded fifty thousand a year by that time. Even during Gwendolyn Parsons's time, revenue from postal services equalled the revenue from direct taxation. It rose after that from £769 in 1909–10 to £2,750 in 1913–14, when it represented no less than 53.4 per cent of government's total revenue.[11]

THE COCONUT INDUSTRY IN THE SISTER ISLANDS

During his time as Commissioner (1898–1906), Sanguinetti visited the Sister Islands on several occasions. "Everything," he noted after a visit in 1902, "betokened an orderly, contented community." What struck him most was the industry and prosperity of the small population. Ten years earlier Governor

Blake had reported that the cultivation and export of coconuts was the main industry on the Sister Islands, and Sanguinetti observed that the industry was now flourishing.

> Business seemed brisk. There has been a very large coconut crop, such as has not borne for years, and the carrying capacity of the Island vessels to deal with the export of nuts has been scarcely sufficient. . . . I estimate that 1,000,000 nuts have been shipped between October and February last. . . . A sudden increase in price has further stimulated the trade, a large portion of which is done with Mobile.

The Commissioner added that "a recent find of Treasure on the Banner Reef off the Pedro Bank by Vessels from these islands is a stroke of luck", the profit from which he noted, would be used to construct "more Vessels" – this being the usual "direction in which the Cayman Islanders invest Capital". Sanguinetti was full of admiration for the examples of shipbuilding he witnessed:

> There are at present three vessels on the Stocks at Cayman Brac, beautiful models of sailing craft. One of these vessels will be of 290 tons, the largest ever built in Caymanas. I am glad to notice that many of the smaller vessels built from time to time are sailed over to Cuba and sold at paying prices for the local coasting trade and fishery. The large quantity of native lumber encourages the enterprise.[12]

Five years later, Acting Commissioner Slader was able to report "that both Cayman Brac and Little Cayman are in a prosperous condition, the inhabitants are contented and there is practically no poverty". The coconut industry had expanded: "[T]he coconut plantations are rapidly being enlarged.

Catboats on Little Cayman, 1938.

Large tracts of hitherto unused land have been brought into cultivation." Nor were the traditional maritime occupations being neglected. Slader was struck by the inventiveness of the turtlers on the Sister Islands and by their recent design of the Cayman catboat.

> The natives of Cayman Brac have made considerable progress in the development of the industry of fishing for the Hawks Bill turtles. They use a more ingenious fishing net than the fisherman of Grand Cayman, and have introduced a new type of fishing boat, locally called a cat boat, in the place of the old canoes. The catch of the hawksbill has increased largely, and the price for shell is now the highest yet obtained.[13]

The coconut industry in the Sister Islands continued to thrive for another ten years. One can well imagine that, as recorded in oral history accounts at one time it was possible to walk along most of the northern side of Cayman Brac in the shade of coconut palms. In 1906, the total number of nuts exported was 1,558,000. "The whole of these cocoanuts were exported from the lesser Cayman Islands," noted the Annual Report, "as nearly all the cocoanut trees on Grand Cayman have been killed by a cocoanut disease." The export of nuts that year was valued at £6,232. The industry was so successful that government decided to raise revenue from it by imposing a special "export duty" of 1s per 1,000 nuts. In 1906 this tax brought £77 18s 10d into the government Treasury.[14]

The heyday of the coconut industry in the Sister Islands appears to have been between 1890 and 1915. Exports up until that year held steady at 1,000,000 nuts per year or more. But on Friday, 13 August 1915, "[A] hurricane of unprecedented severity devastated the island of Cayman Brac within the period of one hour, rendering the inhabitants homeless and in many cases

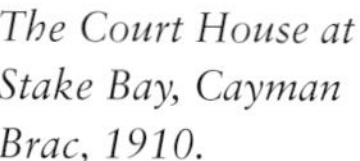

The Court House at Stake Bay, Cayman Brac, 1910.

destitute." Amazingly, only one death was recorded. But 75 per cent of the houses were "totally destroyed", while 98 per cent of the coconut trees on Cayman Brac and 40 percent of those on Little Cayman were blown down. Recovery from this devastation was very slow. To add to the problem, coconut disease, which had not previously affected the Sister Islands, was introduced from Grand Cayman about the same time. Later on, during the 1920s and 1930s, there were modest efforts to revive the coconut industry, and even after World War Two, this aspect of agriculture on the Sister Islands remained significant. But the volume of coconuts produced and the economic value of the industry to the Sister Islands never approached what they were during the boom before World War One.[15]

THE TURTLING DISPUTE

One of the most significant events of the late nineteenth century was the diplomatic storm caused by Nicaragua's sudden interruption of turtling on the Miskito Banks. The controversy continued throughout Sanguinetti's regime and into Hirst's. Caymanians had fished the Miskito Banks at least since the 1830s. But the restrictions of the 1870s on sailing in Cuban waters, re-imposed by Spain in 1895 and still in effect during the Spanish-American War of 1898, concentrated virtually the entire Caymanian fishing fleet on the Miskito Banks. At the peak of the fishery there, some thirty Caymanian schooners and sloops were harvesting up to four thousand green and hawksbill turtles a year. Their catch was worth more than £7,000 – over half the total value of Caymanian exports. Tensions with Nicaragua were compounded by Nicaraguan nationalism, which was aggressively pursued by the Liberal dictator José Santos Zelaya (1894–1909). In response, the British had surrendered all claims to protecting the Miskito Coast in 1895.[16]

Caymanians had been involved in disputes over the Miskito Cays almost since Nicaragua had been granted its independence by Spain in 1850.[17] As early as 1869, the Nicaraguan government had issued a decree authorising the Commandante at Cape Gracias a Dios to collect a licence fee of ten dollars from foreign turtle fishers, and to levy a fine of thirty dollars on fishermen who resisted. Caymanians, however, continued to challenge this jurisdiction and to use cays like Miskito Big Cay. In 1883, when the schooner *Mary Ellen* was anchored at the cay, the ship was boarded by a party of armed Nicaraguans claiming to represent the Commandante at Cape Gracias. They demanded a thirty-dollar fee, and when Captain Ebenezer Jennett refused, they "brutally assaulted" him and the crew and scuttled the ship.

After lengthy diplomatic exchanges, Captain Jennett was compensated by the Nicaraguan government. But the British Foreign Office informed

Caymanians that they had no territorial claim over Miskito Big Cay or any other of the nearby cays or rocks above sea level. These were said to belong unequivocally to Nicaragua. Reluctantly, the Caymanian fishermen began to pay small fees for turtles caught close to the cays or kept alive in crawls built next to dry land. But they refused to pay for turtles caught in the open sea more than three miles from land, or kept in crawls erected on rocks or reefs awash at high tide. For their part, the Nicaraguans set higher fees and penalties after 1895, established a permanent post on Miskito Big Cay, and patrolled the fishing grounds rigorously, often treating Caymanian fishermen roughly.

In 1899 the Nicaraguan Commandante began demanding the turtle fee in gold rather than silver coin – in effect doubling it. After repeated complaints from the fishermen, Commissioner Sanguinetti asked London to arrange for Caymanians to pay a lease for their fishing grounds. The amount suggested was £200 a year, but the Nicaraguan government flatly turned down the proposal. In January 1903, the Nicaraguan government raised the stakes to an intolerable level. They decreed that besides paying fifty cents (U.S.) in gold per turtle, all fishing boats had to be registered at a Nicaraguan port. They would also have to obtain a licence, renewable every fifteen days, at a cost of two dollars for each crewman on board.[18]

The Caymanians responded by sailing in convoy for protection. They avoided Miskito Big Cay and were scrupulous about keeping their crawls on the shoals near Sucre Cay. This, they maintained, could not be deemed Nicaraguan territory because it was overwashed by the sea. Early in April 1904, however, armed Nicaraguan patrol boats seized five Caymanian vessels off Sucre Cay. They were carried first to Cape Gracias a Dios, where the captains and crews were brought before a court and sentenced to heavy fines. Afterwards the boats were sailed to Bluefields and impounded, and the captains and crews were thrown into jail.

The Admiralty immediately sprang into action, despatching HMS *Retribution* to the Miskito Banks to investigate. It reported that the turtle boats had been seized some eleven miles from Miskito Big Cay and more than three miles from any land. Representations were made to Managua, demanding the release of boats and men and the cancellation of the fines. Though the Nicaraguan government maintained that the Caymanians had been seized in territorial waters for fishing without a licence, it ordered the release of the boats and crews, which returned to Grand Cayman after an absence of almost six months.[19]

This was not mere gunboat diplomacy, however. Painstaking inquiries were made by British authorities into each side's case: that of the Caymanians through the Colonial Office and that of the Nicaraguans through the Foreign Office. Meanwhile, the Colonial Office ordered the Caymanians to stop

fishing until the issues were resolved. This was a serious blow for most turtlers. To complicate the issue, the chief Caymanian turtle trader, William T. Eden, was prepared to make a private arrangement with the Nicaraguans.[20]

Early in 1905, Britain and Nicaragua agreed to a joint commission of inquiry to examine the situation on site. In April, the two British Commissioners, Sanguinetti and the captain of the HMS *Diamond*, sailed to Nicaragua, took aboard the two Nicaraguan Commissioners, and made a careful survey of the disputed area. A detailed description of the cays, rocks, and shoals of the Miskito Banks was drawn up and included in a report to London and Managua.[21]

Unfortunately, the commission of inquiry resolved nothing, and little changed in practice. Each side adhered to its own interpretation of territorial waters. The Nicaraguans complained that the Caymanians were back at their turtling even before the Colonial Office ban expired. The Caymanians in turn complained that the Nicaraguans continued to demand – sometimes by force of arms – licence fees and royalties wherever turtle fishing and crawling occurred on the Miskito Banks. The dispute was complicated by divisions among the Caymanian fishermen about whether they should pay any turtle taxes at all.[22]

G.S.S. Hirst inherited the problem when he became Commissioner in 1907. He proposed that Caymanian turtlers pay an annual licence fee of ten shillings and a royalty of two shillings on each turtle caught or crawled in Nicaraguan waters. These fees would be collected in the Cayman Islands and sent annually to the Nicaraguan government, less a small commission. This arrangement would save the Nicaraguan government the expense of keeping armed enforcement agents at the Cays, and it would enable Caymanian fishermen to avoid further disputes over fees.[23]

Hirst's plan was eventually accepted, and a treaty between the United Kingdom and Nicaragua was signed in 1916. But the issues of territorial waters and fishing rights simmered as long as the turtle fishery continued, eventually involving Costa Rica and Colombia as well as Nicaragua.[24] For some years, no serious incidents occurred. This was partly because the fall of President Zelaya in 1909 brought an end to Nicaraguan aggression. But it was mainly due to the steady takeover of Nicaraguan affairs by the United States – which included the control of Nicaraguan customs by New York bankers. As a result, the collection of turtle dues was more efficient and harder to evade. At the same time, the United States market for turtle meat began to expand, and from the first decade of the twentieth century most of the turtles caught were sold directly to American traders at the fishing grounds. There was, therefore, less need to keep turtles in crawls on disputed cays. In addition, profits were greater because less meat was wasted than before, when voyages to market went by way of the Cayman Islands. Together, these

changes tended to make the Caymanian fishermen less reluctant to pay Nicaraguan taxes.

THE HIRST YEARS

During the last months of his tenure, Commissioner Sanguinetti suffered from cancer of the tongue. In June 1906 he retired to England for treatment and died there just four months later. There was a brief interregnum, during which acting Commissioner C.H. Yorke Slader brought out the first separate Annual Report for the Cayman Islands, covering 1905 and 1906.[25] The post was filled in March 1907 by George Stephenson Shirt Hirst. Hirst was a qualified doctor. He was expected to combine the duties of government Medical Officer with those of Commissioner, President of the Council, Chief Justice, and (after 1909) Registrar General. An Englishman educated at Edinburgh University, he had served as Medical Officer first in the Gold Coast and then in the Turks and Caicos Islands, where he had also demonstrated his administrative capabilities as acting Commissioner.

Commissioner Hirst with his two daughters, ca. 1910.

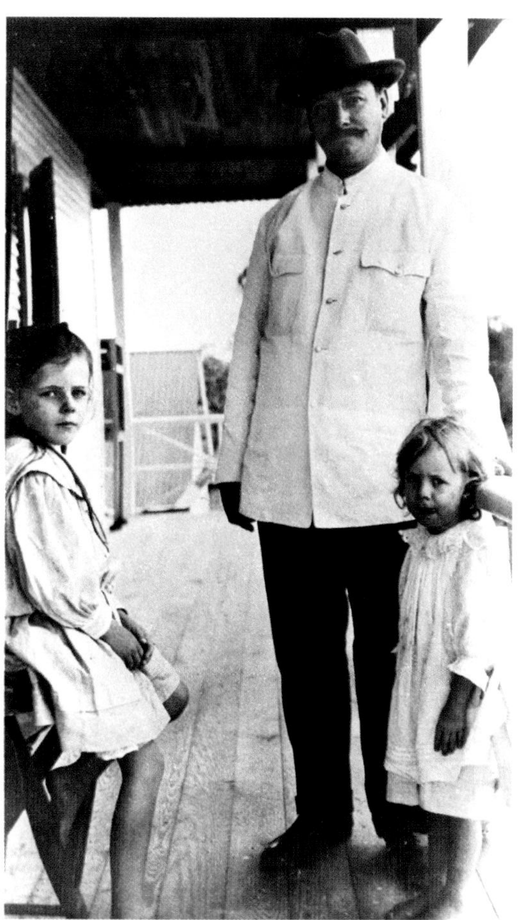

Hirst inherited a modest surplus in the Cayman Islands' treasury. This advantage was immediately cancelled out by an increase in the Commissioner's salary from £350 to £500 and the construction of a relatively grand government residence and set of offices. These buildings were to Hirst's own design (on land purchased from Albert Panton for £40) for a total cost of £830. Nonetheless, thanks to sound management of the continuing small increase in the revenue – particularly from the post office – Hirst was able to undertake many improvements in administration, public works, and services, and to attempt others that proved less successful. He made George Town into a recognisable colonial capital and laid the foundation of Grand Cayman's modern road system.

Two of Commissioner Hirst's first achievements were the establishment of a proper police force and an internal postal service for Grand Cayman. Previously, one policeman had carried the title Sergeant Major of Police, while district constables were paid only when they were called to duty. By an Act passed in September 1907, the Sergeant Major was redesignated Inspector, and four permanently paid constables and eight district constables were enrolled. To keep costs down, all policemen served as

postmen and were employed on customs and other duties when required. The Inspector combined his duties with those of Tide Waiter (chief customs officer) and visiting officer for such matters as school truancy. A small police station and public works depot were built next to the new Government House on Elgin Avenue – a new road named after the British Colonial Secretary at the time. The police compound included a three-cell jail, which replaced the former lock-up. The court-house itself was spruced up: the old lock-up was converted into a government warehouse, and the former Commissioner's office became the sorting-room of the now much more active post office.[26]

The new jail was hardly used. The Annual Report for 1914 stated "There are no prisons in the Dependency. Prisoners sentenced to more than six months' imprisonment are sent to Jamaica. . . . There is very little crime, and offences are of a trivial nature, in most cases the result of excessive drinking." A new five-bed cottage hospital, proudly announced in 1908, also fell into disuse. By 1914 it was being used only to isolate cases of infectious disease.[27]

Other innovations by Hirst were more lasting. The produce and fish market on the Hogsties waterfront was reconstructed and regulated, so that for the first time George Town became the essential trade hub for island fishermen and farmers. A branch of the Jamaican Agricultural Society was set up, holding its annual show in December. The Commissioner's wife, along with Miss Amy Bodden, was instrumental in creating a Grand Cayman Benevolent Society for Women, and in planning a Benevolent Hall that would combine four services hitherto lacking in George Town: reading room, lending library, club room, and concert hall.[28]

George Town had become an official Port of Registry in 1903, and the number of vessels registered there in Hirst's time increased from eighteen in 1909 to thirty-eight in 1913. Because there was no commercial bank, a government savings bank was established in May 1908. Previously, it was said, a considerable amount of gold was privately held, but was often buried in the ground for safety. Now depositors were offered 2 per cent interest on their funds – a figure raised to 2.5 per cent in 1911. The bank attracted only three depositors (and £5) in 1908, but had grown to eighteen depositors (and £90) in 1909. By 1914 the amount on deposit was £554.[29]

Since the Cayman Islands were not covered by the Imperial Lighthouse Service, Commissioners Sanguinetti and Hirst supervised the erection of small oil-fuelled beacons at George Town, Gun Bay, and Cayman Brac. These lights were said to be visible at twelve miles. Hirst also had a new seawall and dock built at George Town, as well as piers at Bodden Town, George Town barcadere, and Batabano. The last two greatly improved connections between George Town, West Bay, and North Side.

Hirst's achievements as a roadbuilder were even more notable. He widened and resurfaced the road along George Town's waterfront as well as Shedden Road, which was named in honour of his predecessor, Frederick Shedden Sanguinetti. He was responsible for laying out Mary Street on the north side of George Town as well as Elgin Avenue to the south. He established George Town's first public park, which was named in honour of Queen Victoria and faced the new Government House on Elgin Avenue. The park hosted the annual Agricultural Show and even boasted a tennis court by 1909.[30]

Most important were the improvements to the roads that connected George Town to the rest of Grand Cayman. For the first time, a drivable road was constructed to cover the seven miles to West Bay, with an extension to North Sound at Batabano. Shedden Road was extended through the bushy and swampy interior, to cut two and a half miles off the coastal route to Bodden Town. The new extension was called Crewe Road, after Lord Elgin's successor as British Colonial Secretary. An offshoot from the road to Bodden Town was also built, leading from Savannah to the isolated hamlet of Newlands. The highway connecting George Town and Bodden Town was the scene of the Cayman Islands' first recorded formal sporting event, a bicycle race held on Boxing Day, 1909.[31]

Despite his many achievements, Commissioner Hirst was a difficult man in some respects. A British chauvinist who could be both irascible and tactless – with a reputation as a drinker – Hirst refused to be treated as a public servant, especially when acting as a doctor.[32] He was a Roman Catholic living in a population of Protestant nonconformists, who tended to equate Catholicism with the distrusted "Spaniards" of other countries in the region. The smouldering conflict between Commissioner Hirst and the most conservative elements in Caymanian society broke into flames during the annual

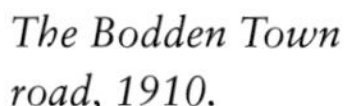

The Bodden Town road, 1910.

meetings of the Magistrates and Vestry in 1909 and 1910. The clash was partly a difference of views, but Hirst's abrasive personality certainly made the situation worse.

As one official in London commented, the minutes of the annual meetings of the Caymanian Assembly during Hirst's regime read almost like the script for a Gilbert and Sullivan operetta. In November 1909, a clique led by C.J.H. Goring, a black Barbadian who had settled in Grand Cayman in 1901, challenged each of Hirst's suggestions and complained of the Commissioner's behaviour in the bluntest terms. Hirst responded, and the session degenerated into verbal warfare. After an adjournment, Hirst sternly lectured the Assembly that the attack was an insult to his office and admonished Goring and his followers to "fear God and honour the King". When Goring responded that he spoke "for the people", Hirst pointed out that as one of the appointed "Justices" Goring was not an elected representative. His duty was therefore to support, not to attack, the government. It was the elected Vestrymen rather than the J.P.s who represented the people – and with one Vestryman for every 140 persons in the population, the Cayman Islands possessed the most democratic system to be found anywhere in the world.[33]

After the biennial general election held on 21 September 1911, Hirst had greater hopes for the new Assembly. But they proved an illusion. Reporting to Governor Olivier that the election had been quiet, Hirst attributed this to the absence of Goring's most active allies and "to the fact that the voting [in George Town] took place in the office attached to the Court House and not in the Court House itself. By this arrangement," Hirst noted, "voters were able to record their votes secretly. This did not meet with the approval of a certain small section, but was agreeable to all those who did not wish to be shouted into voting for Mr. Goring." The elected Vestrymen, however, were

Early legislators: Commissioner Hirst with Justices and Vestrymen, 1911.

a disappointment to the Commissioner. Two "good men" would not stand, several of those he thought favourable to the administration were defeated, and many of the rest were either frequently absent or people whom Hirst regarded as ignorant men, easily swayed. As the election returns showed, the whole body was open to ridicule, with thirty-eight candidates standing for twenty-seven seats and voted for by a grand total of 127 electors. Only in George Town was there anything like a true election, with ten candidates for five seats and sixty-one voters. At the other extreme, Prospect also had five seats, but only fifteen electors.[34]

Hirst planned a complete reorganisation of the system of representation. The number of Vestrymen, he suggested, should be reduced from twenty-seven to a dozen, in proportions closer to the population of each constituency. This would mean three for George Town, two each for Bodden Town, West Bay, and the Sister Islands, and one apiece for Prospect, East End, and North Side. With a normal slate of fifteen J.P.s, this might appear to give a majority to the "nominated" members – that is, the Justices. But since the five J.P.s from the Sister Islands rarely attended, the numbers would usually be more balanced. The change was discussed in the Assembly on 21 September 1910, and the motion passed by seventeen votes to two.[35] Curiously, though, nothing more was done, and the old system of representation remained the same for the next fifty years.

As we shall see in Chapter Eleven, Commissioner Hirst was able to make significant improvements in the schools' curricula. But he was thwarted in what was potentially the most important of all his proposed changes, the introduction of a system of free, compulsory public education. That development had to wait another decade. The major sticking point was the potential cost and the related fear of increased taxation. As far as Hirst was concerned, however, it was one more local obstruction to his administration.

Tensions and opposition to Hirst gradually increased, until Governor Olivier felt obliged to undertake an inquiry in person during December 1911. Olivier's confidential report to the Colonial Office, dated 20 March 1912, was judicious, but definitely more sympathetic to the Commissioner than to the Cayman Islanders.[36]

"The whole situation in the Cayman Islands in regard to the existing discontent is very difficult to judge of or to deal with clearly," wrote Olivier.

> The community is a small society of ill-educated and narrow minded persons, intricately interconnected by family ties, with a considerable amount of vigour and temperament. . . . The prevailing religious persuasions are the Presbyterian and certain independent Revivalist sects of bigoted evangelical or free Christian tendencies. The Commissioner is a Roman Catholic and is accordingly subject to the suspicion and hostility which all evangelical churches foster in regard to

Government House, built in 1907.

> Papists and which I fear there is reason to believe, there is a strong tendency on the part of even the Presbyterian Ministers to foment. . . . Mr. Hirst, as I have had occasion to report in previous Despatches, is a man with a good deal of energy and initiative: but he is inclined to be autocratic. He is singularly devoid of tact and is disposed to be, if not vengeful, at least resentful and even apparently spiteful in his methods of dealing with those who attempt to thwart him.[37]

"The most serious allegation made against the Commissioner is that he drinks to excess," Olivier added. "He has in fact the appearance and odour of a 'soaker'." Hirst certainly drank far too much, as the amounts delivered to Government House by his grocer testified. "At present he and his wife live practically in social solitude," reported the Governor,

> although Mrs Hirst's activities in the many directions in which she exercises them are most admirable and beneficial. . . . Most certainly the island of Grand Cayman is not a place where any man, except of a very sound and equable temperament, can be expected to live for long without danger of deterioration. . . . Dr Hirst, as I have said, is energetic and deserves credit for much that he has done, but he would be far better placed in such administration as Montserrat or the Virgin Islands, and I should fear that unless some such transfer can be made he will steadily deteriorate and his good qualities will be thrown away.[38]

Events overtook Olivier's good intentions. The Colonial Office took no action except to send a message to Hirst on 9 May warning him to moderate his drinking habits. Shortly afterwards, the news reached London of the Commissioner's death on 16 June 1912, at the age of forty.[39] With financial help from friends, his widow and her two young daughters left Jamaica for England on the SS *Chagres* on 13 November 1912. They apparently carried in their luggage the manuscript of a full history of the Cayman Islands, left unfinished by George Hirst, which Mrs. Hirst intended to complete and publish – but which has, unfortunately, since disappeared.[40]

George Hirst's regime had its comic and ultimately tragic aspects, but, as Governor Olivier acknowledged, the Commissioner's energy and commitment to modernisation bore fruit. In spite of persistent local opposition and the lack of any financial aid from either Jamaica or Britain, Hirst increased and deployed the islands' meagre finances, and his improvements and achievements outlasted him.

Despite this progress, however, communications with the outside world continued to be limited and slow. Several attempts were made before World War One to establish regular steamship communications between Cayman and Jamaica, but none lasted more than a few months.[41] Radio communication with the rest of the world via Jamaica was explored as early as 1907, but the cost, which would have been a shilling a word, made it impractical.[42]

Although Hirst had an evident affection for the printed word, the Cayman Islands did not have their own printing facility until well after World War One. The annual Colonial Reports were printed in London. Hirst's own *Handbook of the Cayman Islands* (published twice, in 1907 and 1908) and his better-known *Notes on the History of the Cayman Islands* (1910) were both printed in Kingston. So too was Cayman's first newspaper, the *Caymanian*, which appeared in March 1908 but ceased publication in December 1909 after twenty-two issues.[43] "Hirst's *Notes*", as it is still known, remains by far the most important of these publications. It contains some of the earliest reliable information about Caymanian family history, and it reproduces valuable nineteenth-century documents, many of which have since been lost. As a compilation of all that the Commissioner discovered about Cayman during his very busy administration, it is probably the most memorable of his achievements.

Early photographs – some of which were taken by Hirst and his young daughters – reveal that George Town was beginning to take on the appearance of a proper town by 1914. But it still lingered in the nineteenth century, while other districts were little changed from an even earlier era. Forty years after the invention of the telephone, thirty-five years after the invention of the light-bulb and the introduction of large-scale electricity generators, and a quarter of a century after the application of the internal combustion engine to automobiles, the Cayman Islands still lived in the age of the horse, buggy, and cart. A kerosene lantern provided the best light, ice was a rare and costly imported commodity, and messages could be conveyed only by letter or in person. At the outbreak of World War One, the most significant change was the recent introduction of corrugated galvanised iron (or "tin") sheeting for roofs, in place of shingle or thatch. Tin provided more watertight, long-lasting, and trim-looking roofs, and a more efficient and sanitary way of collecting water in cisterns. This simple but important innovation, introduced under the first Commissioners, often encapsulates the past for modern Caymanians: the time when their ancestors lived "under tin roofs".[44]

MONEY TROUBLES?

You look worn out!

Yes, I haven't slept a wink for weeks. We are saving up to build a new house, and there is such a lot of money now I just dread something terrible happening - a fire, a thief, a rat, or something.

Good Grief! Why don't you put it in the Government Savings Bank, and sleep confident in the knowledge that your money is absolutely safe, and, what's more, earning its own keep in interest?

I know all that, but I have to work, and the only time I get off is at lunch-time when the bank is closed.

Oh, well, I have good news for you! If you can manage to pull through Christmas and the New Year you will be able to bank your money without trouble.

How is that?

From the 2nd of January the Government Savings Bank is going to be open through the lunch hour.

Glory be! I shall sleep from the 3rd of January to the end of the month, and if the boss objects I shall just snore at him!

Don't forget that the Government Savings Bank is there for YOUR convenience:

Look at these 5 stars ---

* Constant rate of interest (2½%)
* Capital guaranteed by the Cayman Islands Government
* Interest paid all the time on all deposits up to £1,000
* Convenient situation near the Post Office
* Prompt attention and a minimum of RED TAPE

and now look at the new star --

* Hours of business from 2nd January, 1959 --
  Monday to Friday - 9 a.m. to 3 p.m.
  Saturday - 9 a.m. to 12 noon.

Advertisement from Cayman Brac for the Government Savings Bank (started in 1908).

CHAPTER 9

A Growing Society

Population Trends and Social Change, 1860–1914

EARLY PHOTOGRAPHS PROVIDE ONE WINDOW on the world that the Caymanians created for themselves in the century between the end of slavery and the onset of modernisation. Another window is offered by the first accurate censuses, taken in 1881, 1891, and 1911. To these can be added a growing number of visitors' accounts, as well as recorded memories about the conditions of life at the turn of the twentieth century. These resources enable us to understand how that era of material poverty, hardship, and isolation helped to shape Caymanian society into what it is today.[1]

Early census data reveal certain distinct characteristics about traditional Caymanian society. It was a remarkably healthy community, when measured by life expectancy, the rate of growth, and the proportion of young to old. It was a family-oriented society with a comparatively low rate of illegitimacy. Up to a third of the working-age men were absent at any one time – a factor that influenced gender roles in the community. And the proportions of those identifying themselves as whites, coloureds, and blacks were more nearly equal than anywhere else in the Caribbean.

In the century or so after Edward Corbet's census, the total population increased from 933 in 1802 to some 6,200 in 1911.[2] This means that it grew at an average rate of about 2 per cent per year, despite migrations in the 1830s and 1840s to the Bay Islands and later movements to places such as Cuba. The population growth came about largely by natural increase, since immigration was never more than a trickle. In 1881, only 83 of the 3,066 persons counted in Grand Cayman (or 2.7 per cent) had been born outside

Cayman. Their numbers included forty-eight born in Jamaica, eight each born in Africa and Central America, and seven each born in the United Kingdom and the United States. By 1911 the total number of foreign-born people living in Cayman had risen to 275 out of 5,518 (5.0 per cent). Of these, 133 were Jamaican-born people living on the Sister Islands, where they made up 10.4 per cent of the local population.

In the first two decades of the twentieth century, Cayman had a healthy annual rate of natural increase, amounting to 21.4 people per thousand. Births varied between 114 and 206 per year, while deaths varied between 39 and 58, according to registered figures. Overall, this points to an annual birth rate of 29.7 and a death rate of 8.3 per thousand. The healthy rate of 21.4 per thousand contrasts sharply with Jamaica, where the rate of natural increase was 14.7 per thousand between 1861 and 1881 and even lower for the period 1881–1911.[3] Because of its natural increase, and the absence of many men in the middle age range, the Cayman population at home had much higher proportions of the young and the old. People under the age of twenty made up 56.6 per cent of the population in Cayman in 1911, while 12.8 per cent were of over the age of fifty-five. By contrast, in Jamaica 49.5 per cent of the population was under twenty and only 7.9 per cent was over fifty-five. Infant mortality in Cayman was low, and life expectancy (at age one) was as high as sixty years for women and fifty-five for men. Again, the contrast with the rest of the Caribbean is sharp: infant mortality was generally much higher in the region, while life expectancy was less than fifty for women and forty-five for men.[4]

The healthy rate of natural increase in Cayman was caused by several factors. The most important was that formal marriages were preferred over temporary or casual liaisons. But it was also significant that women of child-bearing age outnumbered men and that they usually remained in Cayman. There were at least three women for every two men in the age range 20–45.[5] The tendency to marry young, especially among women, and to have large families were also contributing factors. Absent fathers did not mean small families: those families in Cayman with fathers who regularly went to sea were at least as large as those in which both partners were permanently present.

Missionaries in the 1830s and 1840s lamented a tendency towards common-law marriage amongst some ordinary Caymanians. Early church leaders also disapproved of births outside of wedlock.[6] By the end of the nineteenth century, however, formal marriage was the norm, and promiscuity and illegitimacy were low by Caribbean standards. The 1911 census suggests that about 62 per cent of the eligible population was married, and about 72 per cent either was or had been married.

The real figure was probably even higher, because many men absent at the time of the census were also married. The census recorded 861 married

women but only 643 married men. This means that over 65 per cent of the adult population was currently married: about 56 per cent of the available women and about 78 per cent of the men. There were also two hundred widows (12.7 percent of the women) and forty-four widowers (roughly 5 per cent of the men). Again, the contrast with Jamaica is instructive: only 39.9 per cent of the men and 34.8 per cent of the women over twenty in Jamaica were married, while 10 per cent were widows and 4.2 per cent widowers.[7]

Different districts in Cayman showed small but significant variations in the marriage rate. At one extreme was George Town, where only 46.6 per cent of the women aged over twenty were currently married. A closer look shows that 438 females were counted there, compared with only 196 males, and 70 of the women were widows. In West Bay and Prospect, however, where the distribution of males and females counted was similar to George Town's, 62.4 per cent of the eligible women were married. Bodden Town, the second largest settlement in Grand Cayman, had a rate of 53.4 per cent.

Seven ladies from Grand Cayman, 1906. Dr. Keatinge, the photographer, who was the government doctor, commented: "Commandeered three types of the Island's beauty, but seven appeared from a sense of duty."

The census figures demonstrate that, in general, the lowest marriage rates were in districts where there were high proportions of women and where more men were absent. Conversely, the highest marriage rates were in the districts where the sexes were more evenly balanced and there were comparatively few absent men. However, the figures for the more isolated districts suggest that social factors also came into play. In East End and North Side combined, for example, there were 210 women to 139 men aged over twenty, and 59.0 per cent of the women were married. This suggests the economic advantages of stable families in isolated subsistence farming communities. The figures for the Sister Islands point to the influence of both social pressure and the Baptist Church. In 1911 women over twenty in the Sister Islands outnumbered men by 333 to 260, but no fewer than 224 (or 67.3 per cent) of the eligible women were married. Even today, Sister Islanders retain a reputation for having large and stable families.

The high marriage rate in the Cayman Islands led to a low illegitimacy rate. Of the 1,070 births recorded between 1907 and 1915, only 167 (or 15.6 per cent) were said to be illegitimate. Though more than twice the rate in the United Kingdom, this was only a fraction of that in Jamaica, where at least two-thirds of the children were born outside of formal wedlock.[8]

RACIAL DISTRIBUTION

The touchy subject of the mixing of the races, or miscegenation, in the Cayman Islands and its consequences were examined by the "cultural geographer" Edwin Beale Doran forty years later, in 1950. Doran wrote that there was traditionally

> . . . a strong feeling among the whites against miscegenation which involves white women, although relationships between white men and colored or black women are frequent. A similar but less strong feeling is felt by colored people in relation to black; colored male–black female mixing is of more frequent occurrence than black male–colored female. As a result of these cultural preferences it can be seen that almost all progeny of white women will be white, that colored to light-colored offspring will be produced by colored women, and that black to colored offspring will be born to black women. Hence, with birthrates, deathrates, and emigration assumed equal, the whites maintain themselves, the colored increase, and the blacks decrease in proportion.[9]

The process that Doran describes was quite possibly at work throughout the nineteenth and early twentieth centuries. His generalisations are reflected in the censuses of 1802–1943, which distinguished between the black, coloured, and white segments of the Caymanian population.

In 1802, blacks (whether slave or free) outnumbered whites by three to two, with the "coloureds" (people of mixed race) comprising about 8 per cent of the total. By about 1870, however, the Caymanian population was probably unique in the region (if not the world) in having almost exactly equal proportions of all three groups. By 1911 the proportion of blacks had decreased to less than 20 per cent, with the numbers of whites and coloureds equal at about 40 per cent each. In the next thirty years the coloured population increased to about 55 per cent of the total in 1943. In the same period the proportion of whites dropped to 27 per cent and of blacks to 18 per cent.10 This left the Cayman Islands with proportionally fewer blacks than any other territory in the region.[11]

In fact, the Cayman Islands differed from other British West Indian territories in two key respects: they had a uniquely high proportion of non-blacks and a relatively relaxed attitude towards racially integrated neighbourhoods and intermarriage. They were not entirely free of distinctions based on wealth, class, or race, however, nor of residential segregation or variations in material conditions. Unlike the Bahamas, there were no all-white communities, all-black islands or sectors, or strictly split settlements.[12] But there were marked differences among the areas where whites, blacks, and coloureds predominated in the Cayman Islands. And these areas correlated with differences in occupations and material well-being.

The Caymanian population in 1911 was made up of 41.7 per cent whites, 39.7 per cent coloureds, and 18.5 per cent blacks. George Town came closest to having a profile similar to the general population, with 45.6 per cent white, 31.0 per cent black, and 23.2 per cent coloured. Describing George Town, Dr. Keatinge noted that the whites and the more prosperous coloureds had their houses lining "the sea front for a mile on the each side of the Courthouse, while the negroes live in the bush behind".[13]

In other districts, the proportions of the racial groups were very different. Other than George Town, only Prospect, the Sister Islands, and West Bay had proportions of whites above or near the Caymanian average. The proportions for North Side, Bodden Town, and East End were 17.4, 16.9, and 2.3 per cent respectively. The proportion of people identifying themselves as coloureds ranged from 79.7 per cent in East End, 68.2 per cent in North Side, and 52.8 per cent in West Bay to 42.9 per cent in Bodden Town, 32.2 per cent in the Sister Islands, 23.2 per cent in George Town, and 20.2 per cent in Prospect. Those who identified themselves as blacks were most numerous in Bodden Town (40.2 per cent) and George Town (31.0 per cent). Only East End, at 18 per cent, was close to the Caymanian average of 18.5 per cent, and all other districts had far lower proportions of black residents.[14]

HOUSING

One important feature of life that can be measured from censuses and other accounts is the quality of Caymanian housing. In 1854, it was reported that there were 385 houses in Grand Cayman, inhabited by 1,989 persons. In other words, there were 5.2 persons per household. By 1911, the average household consisted of 5.4 persons (or about 5.8, if absent males are included). In the Sister Islands, there were 1,436 persons living in 283 houses, an average of 5.0 persons per house.

Between 1890 and 1911 housing improved, albeit in small ways. In 1891 only 6 of the 633 houses in Grand Cayman had metal roofs, while 208 were shingled and 366 were thatched. By 1911, of the 766 houses in Grand Cayman 159 had metal roofs, 282 were shingled, and 325 were thatched. The tin-roof revolution had not yet reached the Sister Islands, where 201 of the 283 houses were shingled and 75 were thatched, but only 7 had roofs of corrugated iron. Flooring is another measure of improvements during this period. In 1891 there were seventy-one houses in Cayman with dirt floors. Twenty years later, there were nine. All other houses in 1911 had board floors.

The standard of living was generally modest, with small variations from place to place. This is suggested both by the quality of housing and the number of rooms and occupants in each house. Generally speaking, the number of rooms per house remained low and the number of persons to each room

The doctor's house and pony, 1906.

relatively high. George Town headed the list for the largest houses and the lowest number of persons per room. The proportion of houses in the capital with five or more rooms (61 out of 253) was equalled only by Cayman Brac's (63 out of 254). Prospect was similar to George Town in having relatively larger houses and a lower occupation density. In Bodden Town, East End, and North Side, however, the average house was much smaller and the number of occupants higher. These districts also had a far higher proportion of thatched roofs (59.8 per cent) than the rest of Grand Cayman (32.2 per cent). For the Cayman Islands as a whole, more than a third of the houses (384 of 1,048) contained only one or two rooms, and 83.0 per cent had four or fewer rooms. Eleven per cent had five rooms, and only sixty-two (6 per cent) had more than five.

In general, the quality of housing was lower in those areas away from George Town that had a higher proportion of darker-complexioned residents. West Bay, however, appeared to be an exception. It had comparatively few blacks and a high ratio of whites and lighter coloureds. But it also had the simplest houses (averaging 2.6 rooms) and the densest occupancy (averaging 2.07 persons per room) of all the districts. It would seem that poorer whites and lighter coloureds tended to concentrate in West Bay, and this may correlate with the level of literacy in that district in 1911. The level of literacy in West Bay (67.5 per cent) was lower than for either Bodden Town (73.4 per cent) or George Town (72.3 per cent).[15]

Dr. Keatinge's descriptions of Cayman in 1906 underscore the connection between housing and social class. "Vacant houses are very scarce things in Grand Cayman," he noted. "The man of the family may indeed be absent for

months at a time in the pursuit of his calling as a sailor or a fisherman; the house, however, remains inhabited by the wife and children." Keatinge eventually managed to rent a house, which he described and photographed "because it was a good sample of one of the better-class buildings in these Islands".[16]

This house, with its fence and flowers in the yard and its separate kitchen, or "cookrum", could have been a typical middle- to upper-class Caymanian home at that time. Of the four rooms at Keatinge's disposal, the largest room in the front was called the "dignity room". A small room behind this was set up as a dispensary and consulting room, and Keatinge used the remaining two rooms as his bedroom and sitting-room. The so-called dignity room, formerly used as a sitting-room, had interesting social implications. "I found before long that the principal people of the place, who were white, or at least light-coloured, announced themselves at the front door and expected to sit down in the 'dignity room' until I was ready to see them, while the poor black people were generally quite satisfied with presenting themselves at the back door, where they waited until they could be attended in the dispensary."[17]

Keatinge enjoyed a doctor's privileged access to people's houses and lives throughout the islands. He visited all the districts: West Bay and East End on horseback, North Side by canoe, and the Sister Islands on the deck of a 9-ton sloop. He describes a hardy and independent people, much preferring to work for themselves rather than for others, and achieving a remarkable level of self-sufficiency within their families.

Evidence of wealth, such as expensive clothing and more elaborate housing, was rarer away from George Town. Living standards and lifestyles var-

South Sound scene, 1906.

ied according to whether a family was receiving credit or giving it, or managing to live outside the credit system. The seafaring life in particular usually involved relying on credit. It affected the poorest whites at least as much as the descendants of slaves. Cayman Islanders generally bore a good name as a steady and law-abiding people, wrote Keatinge. But they had a tendency to defer their debts. If a sailor was absent on a long voyage, he left his family on shore without sufficient money to buy the necessities of life. These were furnished partly by the natural resources of their home and partly on the credit system. Almost every family owned the piece of land on which their cottage was built, and their ground usually produced "a sufficiency of the more hardy kinds of tropical vegetables". Families generally kept fowl and other small domestic animals, and since all the settlements were on the sea, the boys learned to be expert fishermen at an early age. Certain items, however, such as flour, sugar, and cloth, had to be bought from the stores on the credit system and booked to the name of the absent man, who was expected to settle the account on his return.

WORK

The first official to collect precise details of Caymanians' working lives was Custos Edmund Parsons in the census of 1891. Further information was gathered and published by Commissioner G.S.S. Hirst in his 1908 *Handbook* and 1910 *Notes*, and in the 1911 census over which he presided.[18]

The census of 1891 was the first to tabulate occupations for all three islands. An earlier census in 1881 had covered only Grand Cayman and listed only a few occupations. These included public officers (12), ministers of religion (1), merchants and shopkeepers (11), clerks (5), mechanics (49), mariners (87), and agricultural labourers (332). Women were not included, except for the 28 who were listed as agricultural labourers. The 1891 tabulation was a great improvement, although it was difficult to apply British colonial categories of work to a small island society that did not fit the model.

Occupations in the 1891 census were divided into the somewhat awkward categories of Professional, Domestic, Commercial, Agricultural, and Industrial Workers (as well as "Indefinite and Non-Productive") used for Jamaica. Regrettably, the numbers were not broken down by islands or districts. The census listed the following numbers in these categories: "professionals" (26), merchants and shopkeepers (20), commercial clerks (13), farmers, graziers, and penkeepers (34), agricultural labourers (25), and provision planters (96 men and 5 women). The number of mariners was understated through not listing those at sea at census time. Unfortunately, too, no distinction was made, among the 155 seamen and 19 fishermen, between masters and ordinary mariners – a significant oversight when trying to assess

the turtling industry. In the category of industrial workers, however, there were 88 males and 173 females, the latter including 76 washerwomen and laundresses as well as 83 milliners and seamstresses. These categories were distinguished from domestic workers, who included 31 women and 9 men, and from general labourers, a group with 144 men and 12 women.

The 1891 census (unlike later censuses) gave the age as well as gender of each person. Although many more women were listed as gainfully occupied than had been the case ten years earlier, there was a huge gender imbalance in the adult labour force. For the entire age range between twenty and seventy-five, only 179 women were listed as working in occupations, compared with 566 men. A mere 48 males were listed as "Indefinite and Non-Productive", compared with 860 females. This contrasted markedly with Jamaica, where the numbers of males and females in the "Indefinite and Non-Productive" category were much more nearly equal (143,376 females and 122,598 males).

The 1911 census revealed still more about occupations. It showed considerable growth in the administration, and it suggested that the "upper class" and wage earners had both increased in number. Yet the figures reveal, too, that the basic composition of Caymanian society had changed very little over the previous twenty years. A detailed look at these figures provides a fairly accurate view of the socio-economic situation in the Cayman Islands in the last years before World War One.

Between 1891 and 1911, while the overall population increased by less than 30 per cent, the number of Caymanians who were termed "professionals" more than doubled, from twenty-six to sixty. This category, however, still represented only 1 per cent of the total population, and these "professionals"

The schooner Rainbow *unloading turtle at Kingston, Jamaica, 1906.*

Shipbuilding in Grand Cayman, 1906.

generally had few qualifications. The number of people employed in and by the administration remained tiny: the doctor-Commissioner, a chemist, a Clerk of the Courts, an accountant, three Collectors of Customs, five full-time policemen, and a mailman. The "professionals" included nineteen teachers, fifteen nurses (mainly midwives), four ministers (two Presbyterian and two Baptist), four "law agents", and three notaries.

"Employers" were more numerous and more clearly defined than before. At the top were the forty-four men listed as merchants and storekeepers: thirty-three in Grand Cayman and eleven in the Sister Islands. Among these were several of the Vestrymen and many owners of the forty-nine vessels listed in the 1908 *Handbook* as owned, registered, and (usually) built in the Cayman Islands. Twenty men were listed as farmers and planters, including several Vestrymen and boatowners. Thirty-nine men were listed as cultivators of coconuts, all of them working in the Sister Islands. Their status is harder to determine, but given the volume of coconuts produced and their value, these men were probably closer to being planters than subsistence farmers.[19]

Eight men were listed as shipwrights. These were senior craftsmen who also probably employed most of the eighty-three men listed as carpenters (in boat-building) along with the five specialist sailmakers and two caulkers. Among others listed as carpenters, there were probably some who were contractual house-builders, as well as wage-earning carpenters employed by them. The 1911 census made a much clearer distinction among the seamen: there were 36 master mariners (some being owners or part-owners of vessels), 244 ordinary seamen, 40 fishermen (35 in Cayman Brac), and 3 ship's cooks.

Twenty people (nineteen of them men) were listed as wage-earning clerks. But other than the ninety carpenters and shipbuilders, there was a mere handful of male craftsmen and specialists. These included eight ropemakers, four shoemakers, three stonemasons, three phosphate miners (compared with twenty-six in 1891), three butchers, three hat and basket makers, and one man each listed as a blacksmith, a painter, a mechanic, a photographer, a colporteur, and a naturalist. Most of these specialists were probably self-employed.

In 1911, eighty-seven Caymanian women were listed in what had been called "industrial occupations" in 1891, compared with 120 men. These occupations, though, were distinctly gender-related. There were no women carpenters or shipbuilders and no women engaged in the other crafts listed above, with the notable exception of ropemaking, in which women outnumbered men by thirty-nine to eight. The remaining female craftsmen listed were forty-eight dressmakers and needlewomen. This last figure is surprising, as it was a considerable reduction from the eighty-three milliners and seamstresses recorded in 1891. In fact, it probably illustrates how British colonial categories of work were really not appropriate to Cayman in the early twentieth century.

The largest category of employed women was that of domestic workers. Ninety-three of these were described as domestic servants (forty-five in Grand Cayman, forty in Cayman Brac, and eight in Little Cayman), forty-five as

House, family, and provisions in Grand Cayman: a typical scene from a century ago.

cooks (forty of them in Grand Cayman), and eleven as housekeepers. There were no fewer than 106 laundresses, most of them presumably employed on a casual basis and many of them probably doing seamstress work as well. All told, the 363 women in paid employment amounted to about 23 per cent of the women over the age of twenty. They included 15 nurses, 5 teachers, 1 clerk, 87 craftspersons, and 255 in some kind of domestic work.

Not surprisingly, a higher proportion of men than women was listed as in paid employment. They totalled as many as 750, or 62 per cent of all males aged over twenty. The breakdown included some 450 seamen, 120 craftsmen, 80 "professionals" and store clerks, and fewer than 100 wage labourers. As Commissioner Hirst remarked in 1907:

> The wages compared with other places appear very high, but the Caymanian is as a rule a good, conscientious, and hard-working man, and carpenters especially will put in as much work in a day as is expected from carpenters elsewhere in two days. . . . The wages are high because anything like continuous employment is rarely to be had, and consequently all hands have to make the most they can when the opportunity offers.[20]

By 1911, two-thirds of the men (and probably as many households) relied to some extent on wages and cash, though labour and goods were still often exchanged by barter. Most other adult males were listed as provision cultivators (229 in Grand Cayman and 39 in the Sister Islands).

In a community as small and self-reliant as Cayman, however, there was much overlapping of occupations, and Caymanians knew how to "make do" in a variety of ways. Many subsistence farmers, for example, also fished. So did those who were principally engaged in shipbuilding and other forms of wage labour. On the other hand, those whose main occupation was turtling would turn their attention to the land and its occupations once the turtling season was over. This interweaving of lifestyles and ways of work a century ago is the subject of Chapter Ten.

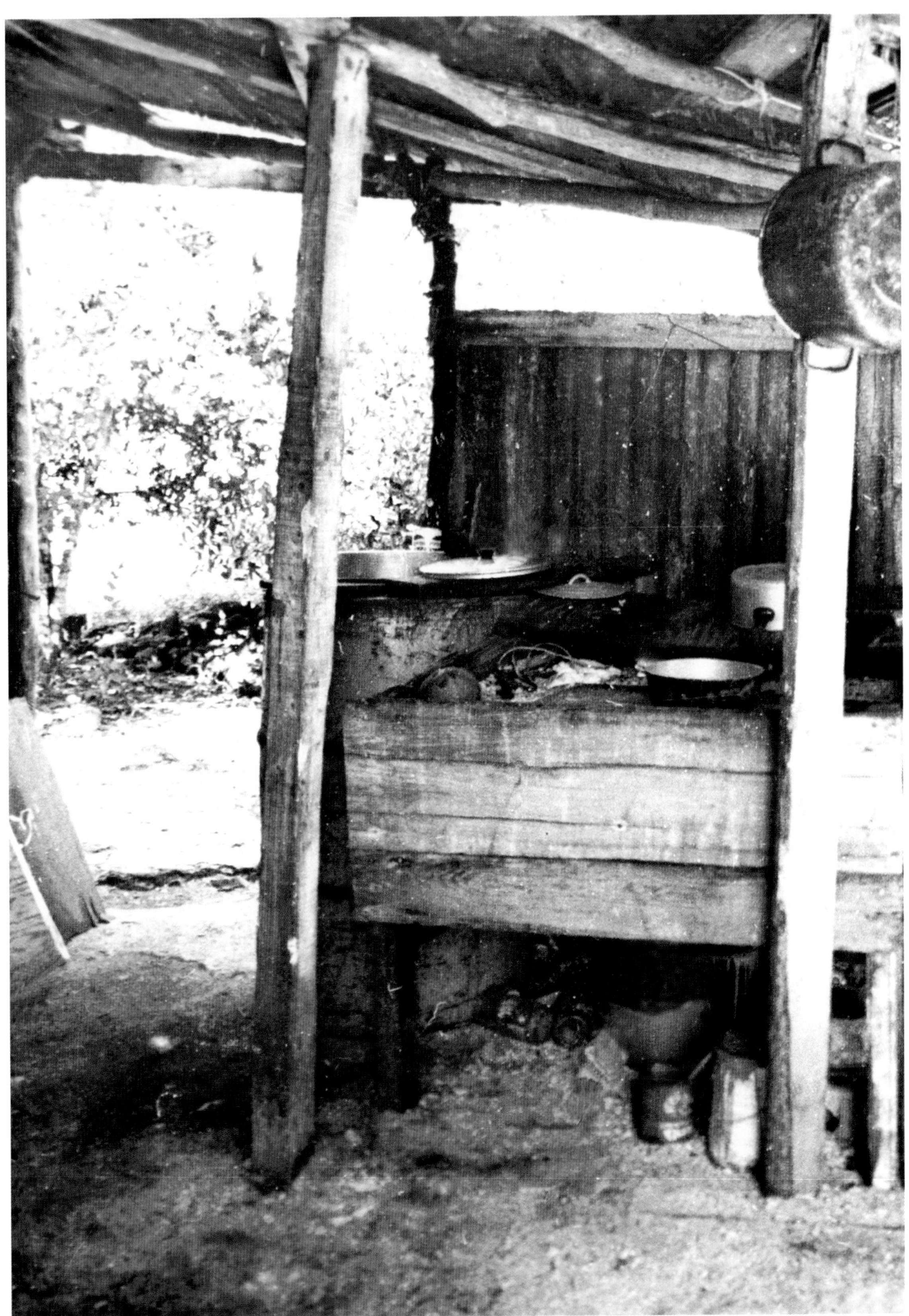

A caboose: the traditional way to cook, used until the 1960s.

CHAPTER 10

Making a World of Their Own

Caymanian Livelihoods and Lifestyles before World War One

As the early census data showed, most men in Cayman about a century ago worked as subsistence farmers, or in occupations such as fishing, turtling, or boatbuilding. Yet very few people, men or women, young or old, had the luxury of pursuing only one livelihood. Everyone in the society had to have multiple skills to survive – a fact that escaped the rigid categories of the census. Certain occupations, especially subsistence farming and fishing, demanded the efforts of all family members, including the children almost as soon as they could walk. Life in Cayman at the beginning of the twentieth century was often hard and lacking in material comfort. Yet it was healthy and bred a spirit of self-reliance. The challenges faced by Caymanians nurtured their distinct character, but they also made each new generation hope for an easier way of life.

THE FARMER-FISHERMEN

The traditional Caymanian families that farmed and fished for a living were descended from both Africans and Europeans and lived in simple wattle-and-daub cottages with thatched roofs, built by themselves from local materials. The family may have had their own landholding, or they may have farmed on land they did not own, paying "rent" for it with a share of the crops they grew. They might also have farmed in both ways – working their own provision grounds as well as someone else's. Families like this were as self-

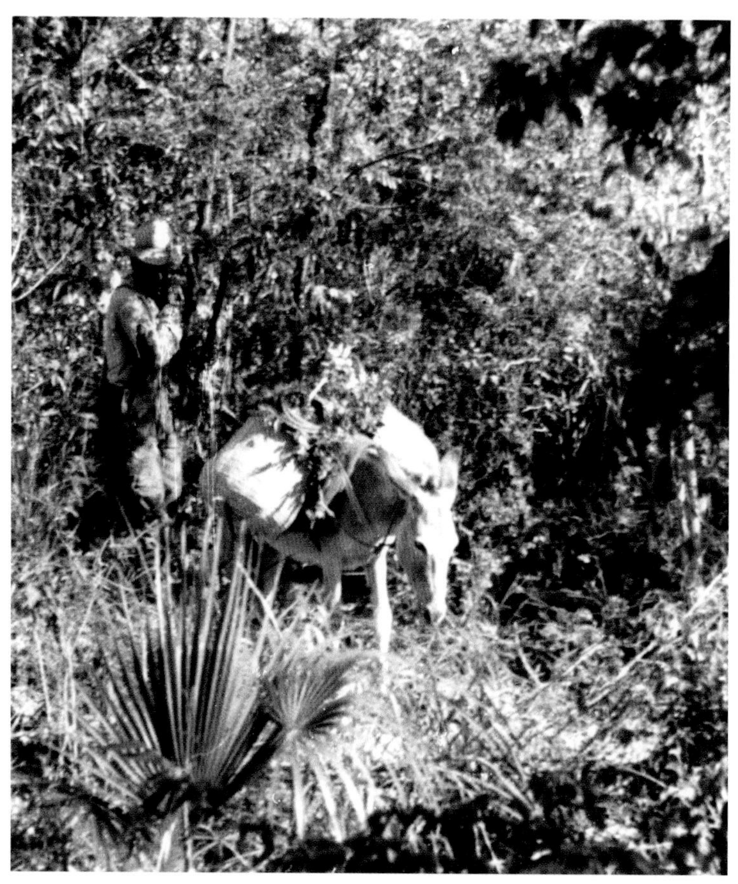

A farmer returns from working his land in the bush.

sufficient as conditions allowed. Ideally, they would have had easy access to the sea to obtain their "meat kind", as well as to the bush, from which they took firewood, lumber, and thatch.

More fortunate subsistence farmers might have owned one of the tough island-bred ponies that were said to live "practically on nothing but guinea grass". Such ponies cost between £4 and £5 apiece a century ago. The family might have had a small canoe, but usually they moved on foot, carrying their wood on their shoulders and their produce in homemade straw baskets. Unlike Jamaicans, who carried even the heaviest burdens on their heads, Caymanians traditionally "backed" their loads in baskets supported by a broad strap around their foreheads.

Most of the two hundred riding horses estimated to be in the Cayman Islands in 1907 belonged to the more prosperous islanders. Similarly, most of the twelve hundred head of cattle were owned by proprietors of the comparatively rich "grass-pieces" in the centre of Grand Cayman. Raising beef was not practical for smallholders, and keeping cows for milk was something of a luxury. Animals for ploughing were of no value to farmers whose rocky, root-choked soils had to be worked by hoe and machete. Most farmers kept a few free-running pigs and chickens. The pigs were said to resemble the lean Berkshires of England, but they grew much faster on a diet of guinea grass, guavas, and breadfruit. Chickens were kept more for the pot than for their eggs. Goats were apparently rare.[1]

Though protein could be obtained from wild birds, land crabs in season, and the occasional agouti, meat was not a common item. Fish and conch were much more plentiful, especially to people with their own small boats. As for starch foods, or "bread kind", which made up the bulk of the diet, flour and rice had to be imported and were luxuries. Families relied instead on their "ground provisions". These included tubers such as cassava, and potatoes of different kinds; varieties of corn, beans, and pumpkins (squash); and many kinds of African and Asian yams, cocos, and eddoes. To these were added

breadfruit, bananas, plantains, coconuts, sugarcane, and fruit from trees growing in the household yard or nearby bush.

Working a provision ground.

It took the efforts of the whole family to raise enough food and to produce, when possible, a small surplus to barter or carry to market. The sea was a vital source of food. Men usually did the fishing, assisted by their sons as soon as they were old enough. Men also looked after the hardest physical tasks – cutting wood, clearing bush, digging, and carrying heavy loads – as well as building homes and maintaining tools. Yet the women performed an even greater range of tasks and duties. Besides bearing and rearing children and running the household, preparing food, and making, washing, and mending clothes, women made most of the baskets, hats, and rope. They were usually in charge of the kitchen garden and involved in what marketing there was. When their men were away, they and their children were responsible for maintaining the provision grounds in addition to other duties.

Though the 1911 census listed all children as Non-Productive, from an early age children had to do household chores such as sweeping. Later they carried water, helped prepare cassava flour, ground corn, and stripped thatch leaves and "twisted the strand". Before they were eight years old they also had outside duties – for example, weeding, caring for animals, and collecting firewood. Children usually tended the green-bush fires that were kept smouldering day and night to ward off mosquitoes, the smoke from which often made people red-eyed. During planting and gathering

A farmer's hut on his provision ground.

times – which were spread over much of the year – men, women, and children toiled together. This pattern alone (apart from the shortage of schools) restricted formal education.

Wompers (everyday footwear).

Households of all kinds grew some of their own provisions and kept domestic animals for food and milk. If the opportunity arose, smallholding farmers might work for wages. Some seamen and turtlers spent part of the year away and the rest as smallholding farmers.[2] But provision cultivators (as the 1911 census called them) generally lived outside the system of wages and cash. Nearly all of them had to produce a crop surplus, or some other product that could be bartered or sold, in order to obtain the basic items that they could not produce for themselves. More and more of these items became available as the Cayman Islands were gradually affected by the wider world of industrial production and exchange. By the early twentieth century, they included cutlery, crockery, and glassware; lanterns and liquid fuel to replace candlewood torches; imported sugar and coffee beans as alternatives to cane syrup and bush teas; patent medicines to supplement bush remedies; flour, rice, canned meat, and even ready-made clothes.

One indication that a cash economy was becoming more common was the construction of a market building at George Town around the turn of the century, and the regulation making it the official mart in 1906.[3] Some people earned a modest income by "barking" – stripping red mangrove trees of bark, which was exported as well as used locally to make a dye used in tanning leather.[4] The main marketable product, however, was Caymanian rope made from the leaves of the silver thatch palm. This was highly regarded for its durability and strength.

Plaiting "strings" of silver thatch for a basket or hat.

The silver thatch palm *Coccothrinax proctorii*, native only to the Cayman Islands, was the most useful and versatile of Caymanian trees. For roofing houses, its open leaves were claimed by William Eden in 1891 to be "the best article of its kind known".[5] The ribs of the leaves made useful brooms. The unopened leaf spikes, or "tops", were woven into excellent hats, for which there was a small market in Central America, as well as mats, fans, and baskets for carrying provisions.

By far the most important product of silver thatch, however, was rope. It was made mainly in West Bay, North Side, East End, Cayman Brac, and Little Cayman. The fibre was first stripped into varying widths (called "strings"), then twisted into strands by hand. Then, by means of a homemade wooden winder (a "cart and winch"), the rope was "layed" into lengths of 25 fathoms (a "half-coil"). Three strands were twisted together for each length of rope. The rope was made into different sizes, determined by the width of the strings. Thatch ropes were used by all local fishermen, as well as those in Jamaica, to tether fish pots and nets. Thin-gauge thatch rope was also used for knitting the various types of net used in turtle fishing, until it was

replaced by cheap imported twine. Ropes of different thicknesses suitable for ships' rigging and mooring were much in demand outside the Cayman Islands. Cayman rope was stronger and more resistant to seawater than ropes made of hemp or any other natural fibres. Thatch rope continued to find a market in Jamaica for several decades despite being undercut in price by machine-laid ropes after about 1910. By the 1950s, though, synthetic-fibre rope had taken over the market.

Rope may not have generated a large profit, but for those involved in this livelihood, it was vital – especially for women. For many, ropemaking meant the difference between economic survival and destitution, and for many years it represented an admirable and successful effort to maintain economic independence. The income itself was a small return for the intricate and time-consuming labours of cutting, carrying, drying, and stripping the thatch leaves, twisting the strands, laying the rope, and getting it to the shopkeepers. The rope was usually bartered to local merchants at a rate of about ninepence per hundred yards.

Twisting strand: twisting "strings" of silver thatch into a single strand for ropemaking.

Laying rope, using a cart and winch to twist three strands together.

However, with flour at ninepence a gallon (six pounds), kerosene at sixpence per bottle, sugar at a penny per pound, and cloth at ninepence per yard, ropemaking was considered a worthwhile endeavour, even though it was labour-intensive.[6]

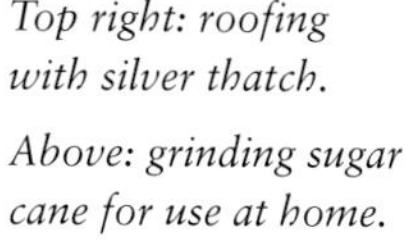

Top right: roofing with silver thatch.

Above: grinding sugar cane for use at home.

SHIPBUILDING

Shipbuilding and its related activities of woodcutting, ropemaking, and sail-making were among the earliest forms of livelihood in Cayman. For about two hundred years, shipbuilding was one of the proudest achievements of Caymanians and a key part of their distinctive way of life.

Shipbuilders in the Cayman Islands, though always eager to learn from other seafaring peoples, developed the industry in a unique way, according to local needs. The original all-purpose boat in the region was the shallop, derived from the Dutch *chaloupe*. This was a double-ended vessel with a shallow draft, no deck, and a single mast, measuring up to twenty-six feet long, eight feet four inches across, and three feet three inches deep.[7] The first turtling craft in Caymanian waters were probably sloops with decks and one or two masts, of a type originating in Jamaica and later developed in Bermuda.[8] Vessels of this kind could travel in deeper waters and on longer voyages.

When Caymanians began to build sloops of their own after about 1770, they were concerned only with comparatively short voyages within the Caribbean to carry on turtling and trade with Jamaica. They did not have the pliable, tough, and self-lubricating Bermudian cedar used for the Bermuda sloop. Instead they built larger, more workmanlike sloops: shallow-drafted, two-masted, and rigged to beat upwind and against the current to Jamaica. They were probably capable of carrying as many as fifty turtles on their decks and were armed only in wartime for their own defence.

Schooners proved more suitable than sloops, however, once turtle fishing was concentrated on the coasts of Central America. By 1907, the Cayman Islands boasted thirty schooners, averaging 67 tons, and seventeen sloops, averaging 31 tons.[9] Caymanian schooners, with at least two masts and displacing up to 200 tons or more, were capable of carrying large cargoes and crews on voyages that might take months. Their size was useful in the growing trade with the United States, especially for carrying lumber. They had deck space to carry the small boats used in locating and netting turtles. These boats were dugout canoes until the early twentieth century, when Caymanian boatbuilders developed the most distinctive of all their vessels, the agile catboat.

Transporting bananas in a dory.

Like Jamaicans, Caymanians probably learned to make dugout canoes from the natives of the Central American coast. Consisting of a hollowed-out mahogany or cedar trunk, the larger of the two main types was called a dory. The Honduran dories were between twenty-five and fifty feet in length and nine in breadth; the pitpan, preferred by the Miskito Indians, was built of the same materials but was smaller and faster than the dory. The canoes adapted for turtling by Caymanians, typically twenty-two feet long and six in beam, may have been an adaptation of the pitpan. Propelled by oars or a simple mainsail and jib on an eighteen-foot mast, canoes were quite seaworthy in capable hands. They may have been used for journeys between Grand Cayman and the Sister Islands, as well as in turtling and salvaging local wrecks. Though useful for netting green turtles, they were much less suitable for catching hawksbill turtles (using "trap-nets") because they were too unwieldy to turn quickly.[10]

The ultimate vessel for pursuing the turtle was a distinctive product of Caymanian boatbuilding and turtling history. In 1904, Daniel Jervis, a Cayman Brac turtling captain and boatbuilder, produced the prototype Caymanian catboat. This model, named *Terror*, was so obviously an improvement on the dugout canoe that it was copied in all three islands. The typical catboat was sixteen feet long and four feet in breadth, and drew no more than eighteen inches of water. It was double-ended and carried a mast and rudder for sailing. At the turtling grounds

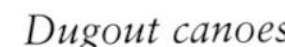

Dugout canoes.

Captain Rayal Bodden with a half-model of a vessel.

it was propelled and steered by a pair of oars called sculls, a long paddle (and sometimes short paddles as well), or a long pole for shallow water. Unlike sloops and schooners, which were painted white or green, catboats were usually painted a distinctive bright "catboat blue". The colour provided an effective camouflage when seen from below, allowing the crew to approach turtles undetected.[11]

The skills required to build schooners, sloops, and catboats became almost instinctive among Caymanians. Well into the twentieth century, the boats were constructed on a suitable piece of shady foreshore, often in George Town or on Cayman Brac. Boats were also built at West Bay, Prospect, East End, and North Side, and on Little Cayman. Boatbuilders did not work from plans or drawings but from what was called a "half-model". This was a hand-carved wooden replica (1:10, 1:12, or 1:15 in scale), cut in half from prow to stern to show the correct curvature of the ribs and planks of the

A boatyard in George Town.

The launching of the F.A. Marie *in 1917.*

desired vessel. These half-models, very few of which have survived, were refined examples of the boatbuilders' inventiveness, unerring eye, and delicate carving skills.[12]

Once builder and owner were satisfied, orders would go out to logcutters to obtain hardwoods of the right shape and size for the keel, ribs, and stem and sternpost. Mahogany and cedar were the most commonly used woods, but pompero, jasmine, whitewood, plopnut, fiddlewood, sea grape, wild sapodilla, and bitter plum were all used at times.[13] The logcutters were familiar with every hardwood tree in the Caymanian bush: those tall enough and the right shape for keels, and those with the right curve for posts, ribs, and knee-pieces. Curved woods were bent into different shapes by the prevailing winds, particularly at the edge of the Bluff, or else bent deliberately by woodsmen a generation or more earlier, when the trees were saplings. Particularly for sappy woods, the preferred time for cutting was during the period of the "old" or waning moon, because timber cut during the waxing moon was believed to be susceptible to worms. The selected timbers were dragged, often over rough ground, to the nearest road or barcadere and then carried by either boat or horse and cart to the building site.[14]

Catboat in South Hole Sound, Little Cayman.

Pine from Nicaragua or the southern United States was imported for the planking, decks, rudder, hatches, masts, booms, and cabin and interior fittings. The imported timber was generally brought in as it was needed, and the tackle, ropes, and sails were obtained last of all. Building a ship might take from six months to more than a year, depending on the resources of

the builder or client. Generally the demand was constant, and specialist boatbuilders were kept fully employed.[15]

Launching a schooner was a community celebration. It was a symbolic, joyous, and hopeful occasion for a seagoing community whose members were well aware of the perils of the sea. When a launching was announced, men, women, and children of all classes and colours would gather from distant parts of the island wearing their best clothes. To the shouting of orders – "Walk away back with the rope now!" – all would join in and pull. To the noise of grunts, shouts, and laughter, the finished boat inched across rollers made of thatch-palm trunks and into its natural element with a mighty splash. A lady would then christen the boat by breaking a bottle against the stern and calling its name with an appropriate blessing: "From rocks and seas in foreign lands, may God protect thee." The whole process might take all day. A plentiful spread of food and drink was provided throughout by the owner, and there was usually music and dancing.[16]

The majority of schooners and sloops built in the Cayman Islands before World War One were designed for turtling. Others were designed for carrying freight or "freighting". At times as many as a third of Caymanian sloops and schooners may have been engaged in trade with Jamaica, as well as trips farther afield. Smaller sailboats and canoes were used for inshore fishing or for transportation between various points in the three islands. Other vessels were constructed to be sold overseas, mainly in Cuba or Central America. A century ago, shipwrights in the Sister Islands, according to Commissioner Sanguinetti, would regularly sail "smaller vessels" they had built to Cuba, where they would be "sold at paying prices for the local Coasting trade and Fishery".[17]

In relation to their small population, the Sister Islands retained a striking record in shipbuilding. From the days in 1850 when the early settlers – said to number thirty-six at the time – launched a vessel with a 26-foot keel, to the construction fifty years later of vessels displacing 300 tons or more, such as the *Clara C. Scott* – built when the population of both islands was still only eleven hundred – Sister Islanders earned a unique reputation in this occupation. In addition to their fame as shipwrights, Caymanians from all three islands were widely sought after throughout the region as seamen. In the early 1900s, many vessels built in Cayman but owned abroad and flying the flag of Cuba or one of the Central American republics, were "manned entirely" by Caymanians, who sent their earnings home to support their families.[18]

A TRULY SEAGOING PEOPLE

If there was a permanent mariner class, it consisted of the captains and crews involved in trading. Unlike the turtlers, who were normally paid on a share system, these captains and crewmen often received wages. The wages were supplemented, at least in the case of the captain and mate, with bonus provisions and the right to carry a portion of the cargo on their own account. Frequently, the captain was also the owner or part-owner of the vessel. This situation was generally popular with the crew because it was in their captain's interest to ensure that a voyage was profitable and safely completed.

By 1900 at least half of the sailing vessels calling at Cayman were registered and based in Jamaica. But as many as a dozen other ships were registered in Cayman and were being used to carry goods rather than for turtling expeditions. All together, probably 120 Caymanian men were permanently involved in trade. In a typical year, some twenty different freight vessels would call at the Cayman Islands, entering and clearing George Town or Cayman Brac about a hundred times in all. Most were on their way to or from Jamaica. At least half were simply calling at the Cayman Islands as part of a longer voyage – to and from the Isle of Pines, Tampa, or Mobile, sometimes to the Bay Islands and Belize, and occasionally to mainland Honduras or Nicaragua.

Vessels trading exclusively with Jamaica might make six or seven round trips annually, while other vessels might call only once or twice a year. Because of the weather, the service was irregular and unpredictable. As late as 1919, Commissioner Hutchings noted that the interval between incoming mail deliveries could be anywhere from two to twenty-eight days, and outgoing mail might wait as long as forty-one days. For Cayman Brac the service was even less satisfactory. The direct service to Jamaica was far less frequent, and there was no regular service between Cayman Brac and Grand Cayman at all.[19]

THE LAST DAYS OF THE WRECKING TRADE

At the end of the nineteenth century, turtling and trading involved about four hundred Caymanians out of a population of perhaps fifteen hundred able-bodied men. But with their strong maritime heritage, many Caymanian men would be drawn to a wreck, especially if it occurred on a nearby reef. Wrecks were increasingly rare after 1870 because of improvements in navigation. Two instances fourteen years apart illustrate the eagerness with which Caymanians descended on a wreck, sometimes risking their own lives in the process. They also show the difficulties faced by the authorities in curbing this behaviour, despite growing public disapproval and an ever more vigilant imperial government and insurance system.

At 2:30 a.m. on 9 April 1874, the 750-ton British barque *Iphigenia*, under the command of Captain Joseph Boase, crashed over the reef at Bodden Town. A naval board of inquiry was held aboard HMS *Eclipse* eight days later. It determined that Bodden Town residents were almost immediately alerted,

and despite heavy surf, all available canoes were launched. Within twenty minutes the two Bodden Town Magistrates, James C. Panton and William B. Webster, went aboard at the head of a huge group of men, said to number up to 350. The barque's back had not been broken and its hull was not even holed. The Magistrates, however, told the captain that its condition was hopeless. No one would be persuaded to help put out kedging anchors, and the captain would be well advised to give them salvage rights, at the customary rate of 50 per cent of the proceeds of sale. The captain refused, asking to speak to the local authorities and the local Lloyd's agent. Panton and Webster responded that the Lloyd's agent was off the island, and that since Custos William Eden was in Jamaica, they themselves were the local authority.[20]

The captain accordingly asked Panton and Webster to stop the local population from pillaging the ship. But the Magistrates made only token remonstrances as unauthorised wreckers cut down and carried off all the rigging and sails, purloined the loose ship's stores, and threatened to invade the officers' quarters and below decks. A third Magistrate, William Eden Jr., the son of the absent Custos, appeared on the scene but was no more effective in stopping the plunder. The captain felt compelled to accept the proposed terms, and awarded salvage to the three Magistrates as a partnership.

The three-man tribunal aboard HMS *Eclipse* decided that Captain Boase had done what he could to save his vessel, but that he had been careless in his navigation and should therefore have his master's license suspended for three months. They exonerated Panton and Eden, but castigated Webster. The Board of Trade later endorsed the criticism of Webster. He appeared to them "not only to have failed to assist in the endeavours to protect the property, but . . . also from his own evidence desired from the first to wreck the ship, and . . . is therefore clearly an unfit person to perform the duties of his Office".[21]

As a direct consequence of the *Iphigenia* case, the Jamaican government passed a Wrecking and Salvage Law in 1875, aimed at protecting "the interests of shipowners and insurers . . . and giv[ing] adequate redress to persons injured by wrecking". Its main provision was for the appointment of Receivers of Wreck in the Cayman Islands, the Turks and Caicos Islands, and Jamaica.[22] Despite local appointments of this kind in Grand Cayman and Cayman Brac, however, it seems unlikely that the new law had any noticeable effect on Caymanian behaviour and practice.[23]

A similar event occurred fourteen years later. On its way from Montevideo to the Mississippi River in ballast, the 939-ton Norwegian barque *Juga*, captained by Christian Jacobsen with thirteen crew, went on the reef off Old Isaac's Point at 3:55 a.m on 17 September 1888. Within five minutes a canoe was alongside, offering assistance. This was declined. Shortly afterwards,

the East End Magistrate Erskine Connolly arrived with seventeen men and persuaded the captain to agree to salvage of all but personal belongings, on the usual 50:50 terms. Connolly then allowed a hundred men (almost the entire adult male population of East End) to go aboard, efficiently cleaning the barque down to its hull and bare poles. Predictably, arguments broke out. At one stage Captain Jacobsen discharged two blanks from a pistol in defence of his possessions. But the most vigorous confrontation seems to have been between the wreckers themselves, particularly between Erskine Connolly and his men and the groups led by Connolly's fellow Magistrates Bodden and Woods, who arrived later.[24]

The wrecking of the *Juga* was investigated by Captain E. Rolfe of HMS *Pylades*. No Receiver of Wreck is mentioned in Rolfe's account, but a sale was held at East End on 20 September. This realised just £122 for the removed goods plus £50 for the hull – despite the fact that the ship was insured at Lloyd's for about £4,000. "Wrecking is one of the principal industries of the Cayman Islands, and one which they appear thoroughly to understand and to conduct in a straightforward and equitable manner," concluded Captain Rolfe.[25]

Wrecking as a trade was pretty well a thing of the past by the end of the first decade of the twentieth century, although wrecks as recent as the *Ridgefield* in the 1960s stirred excitement throughout the islands. Turtling, however, was a significant Caymanian economic activity well into the middle of the twentieth century.[26]

TURTLING

The practice of turtling differed between Grand Cayman and Cayman Brac, but it was equally arduous and dangerous for all turtlers. Before 1700, turtle could be caught off all three Cayman Islands relatively easily. During the later 1700s the focus for hunting turtle shifted to the Sister Islands as supplies around Grand Cayman became depleted. Much turtle was sold to passing ships whose usual route lay closer to Grand Cayman than to the Sister Islands. The turtlers of Grand Cayman specialised in hunting the green turtle, first off Cuba and then off Nicaragua. The turtlers of Cayman Brac came to specialise in the hawksbill, although they caught some green turtle in addition to loggerhead and leatherback. Hawksbill turtle was

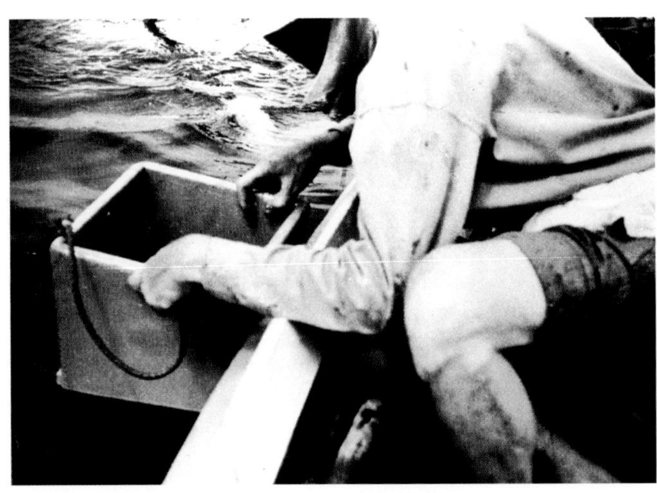

Using a waterglass to spot hawksbill turtles.

Hawksbill turtle nets in Little Cayman.

prized for its shell: each turtle produced as much as six pounds, which was worth about 20 shillings a pound a century ago.[27]

Fishing for hawksbill turtle was literally more of a pursuit than fishing for green turtle. Cayman Brackers, in their agile canoes and catboats, were adept at seeking out hawksbills. With the help of homemade waterglasses, they could detect the elusive prey in water as deep as twenty fathoms. Hawksbill were caught in specially weighted trap-nets, brought to the surface, and later slaughtered. Virtually all the meat was either eaten immediately or dried for later consumption. The shells were carefully stored in crocus bags. For years, Brackers found sufficient hawksbills close to home. But with the increase in demand and the decline in stocks around the Sister Islands and the southern Cuban cays, they ventured further and further afield. They sailed to the Rosalind, Serranilla, Serrana, and Quito Sueño banks (owned by Colombia). As their boats increased in number, they also sailed to the Miskito Banks off Nicaragua, alongside the green-turtle fishermen of Grand Cayman.[28]

Grand Cayman's turtling trade developed similarly. Years of growth were followed by a process of gradual decline. After the mid-nineteenth century, the most productive fishing grounds were increasingly those at the Miskito Banks. Caymanian turtlers came to know the habits and movements of their prey, as well as every rock, shoal, and passage in the two thousand square miles of the Banks. Turtling sloops and schooners (sometimes as many as ten together) would anchor at a favourite shoal – ideally one with plenty of turtle grass. The turtlers would construct an enclosure of mangrove stakes called a "crawl". Canoes and catboats, belonging to the larger vessels or to the independent turtlers called "rangers", went out each day that the weather

Turtle crawl at Ned Thomas Cay on the Miskito Banks, off Nicaragua, 1905.

allowed. Venturing twenty miles or more, they would set their swing-nets at twilight, at carefully chosen spots where turtles were likely to spend the night. In the morning they hauled up the nets and removed the turtles that had become entangled during the night.

Each small boat, carrying two or three men, would set up to forty nets. An exceptional morning would find eight or ten green turtles lying on the surface, ensnared in the nets. To find a hawksbill was a happy bonus. The discovery of an entrapped loggerhead or leatherback, however, was unwelcome, for their flesh and carapace were almost worthless, and they often damaged the net beyond repair. Once on board the schooner, the green turtles were laid on their backs, sometimes tied together by their flippers to keep them still on the deck, and marked with the turtler's initials cut into the bottom plate.[29] Returning to the schooners, the men would release the green turtles into the crawl. This process went on until the captain considered that the total catch was sufficient. This might be anything from 100 to 350 turtles. In earlier years, it might have taken no more than a month to secure a catch of this size. But by the early twentieth century, with fewer turtles left to catch and more vessels involved, the stay could be two months, ten weeks, or more. Round-trip voyages lasted as long as three months, and turtlers rarely made more than two trips in a year.

When winds were southerly, the turtle vessels might carry their catch directly to Kingston, Jamaica. There the turtles were sold to agents and kept in crawls – a few for local sales, but most to be carried to England in the steamers of the Royal Mail Line. Normally, however, the turtles were carried back to Grand Cayman. There they were usually crawled at North Sound (where

Crew relaxing aboard the schooner Banks.

there were good supplies of turtle grass) while awaiting shipment to Jamaica or Florida or sale to passing ships. In later years, some captains took their catch directly to Key West. During voyages, the turtles were turned on their backs, below decks or in shade if possible, and regularly doused with seawater. Although some died during the journey, most arrived in good shape.

The average weight of a green turtle was about 150 pounds, of which half or more might be edible meat. The common practice in 1900 was to ship the turtles to Jamaica and the southern United States, the price being "45 shillings for females and 24 shillings for males". But within a few years this practice began to decline as American turtle agents at the Miskito Cays or in Nicaraguan ports began to offer higher prices, and the turtlers began to sell directly to them. Sales like this, where the agent sent the turtle on to Key West or New Orleans, eventually became the norm. This arrangement benefited the turtlers, who were paid for their work more quickly and could continue on the fishing grounds for longer periods because they did not have to transport their catch back to Cayman.[30]

At the start of the twentieth century, despite the relatively small returns it brought to the fishermen, there were always more Caymanian mariners willing to sail than there were berths available. This meant the captains could select the hardiest and most reliable men. About 450 men were regularly employed. Captains and crews were drawn most heavily from West Bay, George Town, and East End in Grand Cayman, and throughout the Sister Islands.

The complement of a typical turtling schooner would be the captain, mate, cook, and a crew of five to seven. To these might be added up to a dozen "rangers", transported on their own terms, with their own boats carried on the deck along with the schooner's own boats. Usually, turtlers were not paid wages but received a share of the sales from the voyage. Half of this amount normally went "to the ship" – that is, to its owner, who was responsible for providing all the ship's equipment and fishing gear. The remainder was divided equally among the crew, except for the captain, who received a share and three-quarters (unless, as was often the case, he was owner or part-owner of the vessel), and the mate, who was given a share and a quarter.[31] Food supplies for the voyage – flour, corn meal, ground provisions, and some coffee and sugar – were provided by the crew, most of it purchased on credit from shopkeepers (some of whom were also the shipowners). These supplies would be paid for after the voyage was finished and the turtle was sold.

In between signing on and sailing, turtlers made and mended turtle nets, using bales of twine from Jamaica. This was a social time when the crew gathered, usually in the captain's yard, and worked together, chewing tobacco and telling tales. The captain supervised the work, and a meal was prepared for the men. A "gang" of twenty-one nets was the usual unit for each ranger. The turtlers also had to stock up on food and negotiate credit with retail shops to provide for their families left behind. Transactions like this would be made with merchants who very often owned the vessels involved.[32] For the merchants, financing a voyage could be risky: if the voyage failed for any reason, the merchant faced a complete loss of his investment.

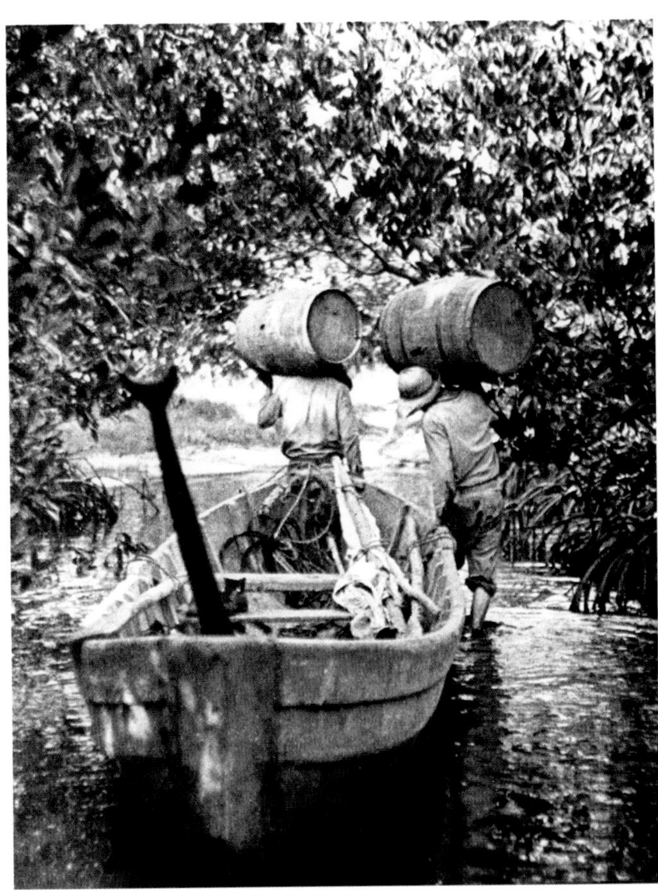

Turtlers replenishing water casks at the Miskito Cays.

Departure time was a sombre family occasion, with a large crowd gathered at the waterfront if several vessels went off together, and prayers sometimes offered by a minister of the district. Families knew that at best it would be months before their menfolk would return, and the possibility always existed that they might never see them again. In the early days, navigation was primitive, dependent on the sun and the stars and a notched stick to determine direction. Mariners also learned to "read" the prevailing currents, the directions of wind and waves, sea colour, the flight of birds, and distant banks of cloud. By the twentieth century, however, many captains were master mariners or even "paper captains" – that is, having some form of certification.[33] Such captains owned and could use a sextant, a compass, and a barometer. An eye on the barometer was vital, for a steady fall in pressure warned of the approach of a tropical storm or a hurricane. Some captains carried well-worn charts of the Banks. Unfortunately, few appear to have kept sailing logs. Since each captain was his own boss, he did not need to report or keep strict records.

Description of Caymanians turtling off the Miskito Cays, 1842.

> The Cape is often visited by small schooners, from the Grand Cayman's island, near Jamaica, to fish for turtle near the Mosquito Kays, about forty or fifty miles from the Cape, and which seldom return without a rich harvest. They supply the Balize and Jamaica markets with the finest green turtle, and often obtain in a season, several backs of hawk's-bill turtle-shell;* as the Mosquito Kays are very much the resort of that species, as well as of the green turtle. Numbers of the Mosquito Indians sail in their doreys from the Cape, Sandy Bay, Duckwarra, Warner Sound, &c., to fish there. When they find the turtle on the beach, they turn them upon their backs, or spear them as they float on the top of the water. The crews of the Cayman's schooners, like the crews of the whale ships, go in shares; at all times they are on the alert, and are as much pleased on hearing of the capture of a fine she green turtle, as the crews of the whalers on the welcome announcement of a fall.† Though the Cayman's schooners are sometimes seven, eight, or ten weeks on a cruize, they seldom or ever take any meat with them, depending upon their own skill in fishing, and the abundance of fish in the waters of this coast, to say nothing of the turtle from which they cut steaks,—from one part quite equal to beef, and from another part resembling veal; so that with the fins, the calli-pash and callipe to make soup, with a few plantains, and flour for what are termed Johnny cakes, they live well, and at a trifling cost.

Life at the Banks was harsh but companionable. Except for one or two trips to the coast to take on fresh water and vegetables and fruit, or to pay licence fees, the schooners anchored close to the fishing grounds and remained there during the week. The turtlers ate and slept aboard – the crew in cramped bunks below. On the voyage out to the Banks and back to Cayman, the rangers slept on deck, under sail canvas when it rained. Once they arrived at the Banks, however, the rangers were dropped off at various cays, where they camped in simple huts until the return voyage.

Caymanian turtlers gained a reputation for being hard-working, sober, and God-fearing. Captain John Hurlston in 1990 recalled that in his day, in the 1930s, rum was never carried on turtling vessels, "but nearly everybody carried the Bible". The Sabbath was always rigidly observed. In contrast to the exhausting labours of the five-day working week, minimal work was done on a Saturday, while Sundays were entirely given over to rest and relax-

The polished shell of the hawksbill turtle, along with finished products made from the beautiful shell.

ation. Several schooners might gather on Saturdays, for example at Miskito Big Cay. On Sunday the turtlers would visit from boat to boat, eat, smoke, and talk, tell stories or riddles, and sing familiar songs and hymns to the accompaniment of mouth organ, banjo, or guitar. This included the rangers, who used Saturdays to replenish their water casks from Miskito Big Cay. At times, if the captain was especially religious or when bad events threatened, one of those aboard would read aloud from the Bible or lead the others in prayer.[34]

With a good voyage and in a good year, the return to an owner-shopkeeper might allow him to maintain his status and even to expand his operations. But at its best, the amount earned by the crewmen bore little relation to the hard work and dangers endured. Though the number of turtles caught increased steadily, it did not keep pace with the greater number of ships and men involved. In 1901, sixteen vessels brought an average of 198 green turtle into Grand Cayman. Seven years later, the twenty-eight vessels turtling in 1908 landed an average of only 145. These were sold for an average of 35 shillings a head. Even if this represented only a half of the total received, it meant that the average return (adding the amount from direct sales at the Banks) was no more than £254 to each boat-owner and as little as £28 to each crew member, much of which was already committed to a retailer for credit previously advanced. Profits from the sale of hawksbill shell at the time were not much greater. In general, however, turtlers from the Brac felt that hawksbill fishing was more profitable than fishing for green turtle.[35]

There was no such thing as personal or even ship insurance. If a vessel was lost, it was a disaster for all involved, including the owner. Turtling boats were occasionally seized by Central American authorities. But hurricanes posed a far greater and more frequent threat. The hurricane of 1876 destroyed almost all vessels at Grand Cayman, and it was followed less than a year later by one at the Miskito Banks that sank nine Caymanian turtlers with the loss of sixty-four lives.[36] These devastating losses severely damaged the turtling industry. Two hurricanes that coincided with the outbreak of World War One in 1914 were equally traumatic. And people still vividly remember the loss of the *Majestic*, which went down on the Cays in a hurricane in 1941, taking the lives of twenty-one men. Despite the inherent risks, the long tradition of turtling continued until the 1960s, a testament to the stoic and resilient nature of all those engaged in this most Caymanian of livelihoods.

1946

Strawrope industry pledge:—

I do solemnly pledge my mind and hands to produce standard quality of straw rope for the promotion of trade and for one common Good."

Sign By the producers.

Major Northside.

	Mavis Tatum
Olive Powery.	Amy Ebanks
Isabel Tatum	Nell Ebanks
Merleen Ebanks	Harold Ebanks
Reta Ebanks	Robert Ebanks
Rhena Ebanks	Novah Malaughlin
Everell Ebank	Amanda Pouchie.
Lucy Connolly	Ewina Browne
Lorena Connolly	Earlyn Ebanks
Merrice Rivers	

"Strawrope Industry Pledge": Northsiders pledge to produce quality rope for export.

CHAPTER 11

Caymanian Churches and Schooling, 1846–1920

THE EARLY HISTORY OF THE Presbyterian mission to the Cayman Islands, as told by successive ministers, had heroic parallels with the spread of early Christianity in the Mediterranean. It included shipwrecks like the one survived by St. Paul at the island of Malta, conflict with unfriendly authorities, and struggles against ungodly customs. The first Presbyterian minister to comment on Cayman, Hope Masterton Waddell, arrived in Grand Cayman by chance, wrecked at East End in January 1845. During his brief stay, he was as impressed by the people's essential goodness and hunger for organised religion as by their poverty, roughness, and rudeness of language. While in Scotland before his posting to Calabar in Nigeria, he urged the Scottish Missionary Society to establish a mission to the Cayman Islands, but without direct result.[1]

The efforts of Rev. William Niven, the second missionary sent to Jamaica by the Secession and United Presbyterian Church, were more effective. Niven had been a pastor at Stirling, in Westmoreland parish, since 1836. Calling at Grand Cayman on his way home to Britain on leave in the summer of 1845, Niven was shocked to find the local men paddling out to sell turtle and other foodstuffs on the Sabbath – though they claimed they would have been in church had there been a minister. In England, Niven ascertained that the Wesleyan Missionary Society had indeed given up their Caymanian mission. Although the Presbyterian Board in Scotland was unable to send out a missionary, it gave Niven a document authorising the recruitment of one in Jamaica.[2]

In July 1846, William Niven made a passionate plea for a Caymanian mission before the Jamaican Presbytery at Montego Bay. He recounted how he had first become aware of the need through two Mico teachers in Grand Cayman, John Ross and the Caymanian John Jarrett Wood. Niven told how he had recently encountered a black Caymanian schooner captain at Negril, whose dearest possession was a psalter given him by the Rev. Hope Waddell, and who begged to participate in a Presbyterian communion service that Niven was holding. The captain proved to be a Wesleyan, though his membership ticket was almost two years old – dating from the last time a Wesleyan minister had been resident in the islands. At the conclusion of his speech to the Presbytery, Niven quoted the prophet Isaiah: "Whom shall I send, and who will go for us?" After a dramatic pause, the Rev. James Elmslie, pastor of Green Island, Hanover, offered himself, and the Presbytery voted money to charter a schooner and provide an initial grant.[3]

Rev. James Elmslie

In several ways, Elmslie was a surprising candidate. Born at Aberdeen in 1796, he was already fifty years old and well established at Green Island. Though he had arrived in Jamaica in 1838 as a catechist, he had been ordained in 1840. He energetically built up the mainly black congregation at Green Island from unpromising beginnings until it included 950 persons, 230 of them full members and 200 regular attenders at Sunday School. Elmslie's reputation was that of a sincere pastor who could be a dour and unbending puritan. He set out with his family in September 1846 in the chartered Jamaican schooner *Wave*, accompanied by his friend William Niven, who had agreed to help him get started.[4]

The Presbyterian ministers arrived at Grand Cayman on 11 September 1846 to a mixed reception. William Niven stayed three weeks, while the captain of the *Wave* impatiently sat out contrary winds. On 6 October they set sail despite local predictions of an impending storm. Two days later, one of the worst hurricanes in living memory ripped through the western Caribbean, sinking the *Wave* without survivors, and leaving no trace except an upturned longboat. Fearing the worst and with dwindling hopes, the young Mrs. Niven developed a fever in childbirth and died with her infant son.[5]

Meanwhile, James Elmslie was surviving his own tribulations. Even before the hurricane of October 1846, the islanders were in a wretched and demoralised condition. "Many of them said, 'We do not want any black coats'," Elmslie later wrote. "They knew the Sabbath from the rest of the days, and they made it a distinguished day for rioting and drunkenness, and all manner of secret and open wickedness; cultivating their grounds, fishing, fowling, and even they [*sic*] had a public sale on the Lord's day after I came to the island."[6]

"For about a year little good was done to all appearances," recalled Elmslie. "A good many came to hear God's word, and many resolved not to come at all." The most obdurate opponent was the Custos, James Coe Jr. Perhaps plagued by a guilty conscience, he believed that Elmslie's hellfire sermons were aimed directly at himself. He once had to be restrained by his fellow Magistrates from angrily confronting Elmslie after a service. He was persuaded to write Elmslie a letter instead, but the minister's conciliatory reply was ineffectual. "Another day, when Custos Coe came out of the church," recounted Elmslie, "he said, 'What new doctrine is this which we are getting now? Nothing but sin, sin at all times; and when we do anything out of the way, it is cast up into our teeth on the Sabbath.'"

The turning point came several months later. One Sunday, James Coe waylaid James Elmslie on his way home by the wharf. The Custos told the pastor that he had heard several ministers before him, but acknowledged that they had had no practical effect. "I can now see why you have preached the way you have done," he stated. "If you had not done so, you would not have been faithful. We thought we were all well; and we believed that our fathers and forefathers had all died happy; but I am afraid they are all lost. You have kindled a light in this island that will not be extinguished when you are mouldering in the dust." Shortly afterwards, James Coe became a formal member of Elmslie's church and later an elder, and remained steadfast to the end of his life.[7]

After Custos Coe's conversion, there was no looking back. For more than ten years, the ageing but tireless Elmslie travelled alone all over Grand Cayman, by foot, on horse, and canoe, making converts everywhere. At first, the people of Bodden Town were the most resistant. But in July 1851 Elmslie reported great victories for the Gospel among them, and by 1854 he regarded the Bodden Town congregation as more ardent and dutiful than the other four to which he ministered, at West Bay, George Town, Prospect, and East End.[8]

Rev. William Whitecross

After eleven years of pioneering work, Elmslie was joined in 1857 by Rev. William Whitecross. The new minister was assigned the eastern half of Grand Cayman, including North Side as well as Bodden Town and East End. Whitecross, who seems to have been even stricter than Elmslie, was complimentary enough at first about the churchgoers under his care. But soon he was complaining about the activities of the predominantly black population, especially the people of Bodden Town. He said they were still given over to "heathenish" practices, to promiscuity and drinking, and to profaning the Sabbath.[9]

In 1862, when Whitecross returned from sick leave, he discovered that the Bodden Town church had come under assault from a rival sect. A group of "revivalists" from Honduras had used the church building despite the opposition of the elders, and conducted services which included fervent singing, clapping of hands, and stomping of feet. Whitecross cautiously praised the spirit engendered, but outlawed the clapping and stomping – to the relief of

Rev. John Smith

some members. It was some months, however, before enthusiasm for the revival atmosphere faded away and Presbyterian sobriety reasserted itself.10

By 1863, Elmslie was worn out by age and Whitecross by recurrent sickness. Both returned to their Scottish homeland, where they died in the following year. There was to be a gap of four years between Elmslie's successor, H.B. Newhall (1863–5), and the arrival of John Smith (1869–84). Grand Cayman would not enjoy the regular ministry of two pastors again until the time of John E. Martin and Thomas Redpath (1896–1905).

It is clear that the foundation of Presbyterian ministry laid by Elmslie and Whitecross was a resounding success. As early as 1855, two Presbyterian ministers, Aird and Thompson, were asked to report on the work in Grand Cayman. They observed

> . . . that the divine blessing had, in a signal manner, attended Mr. Elmslie's labours – always spoken of as indefatigable – and that a great reformation in the character and habits of the people at large, had, in consequence, taken place. All the Magistrates in the island, with two exceptions, are members, and four of them are elders, of the church. . . . The total membership of the churches is 274 – all of whom have been admitted by Mr. Elmslie, and most of whom have been brought to the knowledge of the truth as it is in Jesus, during the period of his ministry. The converted have exercised a restraining and salutary influence on those of their fellow countrymen who are still, in the Bible sense of the words, 'far from God and far from righteousness'.[11]

Aird and Thompson rejoiced that the Sabbath was far less profaned than formerly, "at least externally", and that probably half of the population were to be found in church each Sunday. Intemperance, "which was formerly extremely prevalent", was greatly diminished: some members of the various

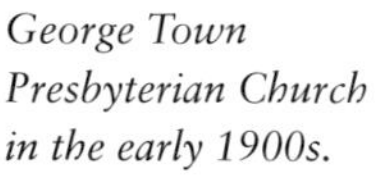

George Town Presbyterian Church in the early 1900s.

churches were reformed drunkards. "Scenes of midnight revelry, which were formerly very frequent," were now comparatively rare, "several of the musicians and other principal performers on these infamous occasions having discovered a more excellent way of spending their time and seeking their enjoyment." Just as notably, "the abominable crimes of *fornication* and *adultery*, which were formerly as common here as elsewhere, alas! In the West Indies," had greatly decreased, being confined "to a few of the more degraded of the inhabitants". Marriage was "increasingly regarded as 'honourable in all, and the bed undefiled'," and, according to the elders, family worship was "engaged in with commendable regularity" by church members.

Reinforcing their findings with statistics, Aird and Thompson mentioned that thirty-four persons, eleven of them adults, had been baptised in the previous year (1854). Of the 1,989 inhabitants of Grand Cayman (of whom 1,129 were said to be under the age of twenty), 578 were, or had been, married, and only 36 were "living in concubinage or fornication". Despite the fact that 1,277 residents were said to be unable to read or write, Bibles or New Testaments were found in 247 of the 385 houses on the island.[12] Five years later, in the most complete summary of his and Whitecross's ministry, James Elmslie was able to claim that in each of the island's six "stations" (North Side having been added), there were churches built by the people themselves. "There are at all the stations," he wrote, "400 members, 60 catechumens [candidates preparing for baptism], two weekly prayer meetings at each station, besides one monthly prayer meeting for the spread of the gospel; six Sabbath schools superintended by forty-eight teachers, and attended by about 500 scholars. There are also three day schools, attended by upward of 200 scholars."[13]

Rev. John Edmond Martin

Despite setbacks such as the hurricane of 1876, which blew down all six churches, and the shortage or absence of ministers, the Presbyterian Church in Grand Cayman came to occupy a dominant role in the social as well as the spiritual life of the people well into the twentieth century. This was not just because of lack of competition, for formal membership in the Presbyterian churches surged to a peak at the same time that the Adventist and Holiness missionaries made their first incursions, roughly fifty years after Elmslie's arrival. Presbyterianism evidently met the spiritual needs of most Grand Caymanians. When Elmslie and Whitecross retired, one-third of all adults in Grand Cayman were full church members. This level of membership remained steady through the solitary ministry of Rev. John Smith, and rose from about six hundred communicant members to more than a thousand between 1888 and 1904, representing almost half of the population over the age of twenty.[14]

Rev. Thomas Redpath

Average Sunday attendance in the Presbyterian churches as a whole at the turn of the century was over fifteen hundred, with more than eight hundred adults and children attending Sunday School and about five hundred adults

Rev. William Pouchie, the first trained minister from the Cayman Islands.

taking part in more than twenty mid-week prayer meetings. These activities were supervised by the two Scottish ministers, John E. Martin at George Town (1896–1905) and Thomas Redpath at Bodden Town (1896–1908). The first Caymanian minister, William Pouchie of North Side, was appointed to succeed Redpath at Bodden Town in 1909. In 1913, a third minister, the Englishman John Blackman, was added to serve the greatly expanded congregation at West Bay, where he ministered, with a break between 1927 and 1935, until 1948. These hard-working ministers were assisted by eighty-five elders and other "office bearers", and some sixty-five Sunday School teachers.[15]

In keeping with Presbyterian practice at the time, the church elders were exclusively male. As the earliest photographs testify, they represented all complexions, roughly in proportion to the district population. For example, the group portrait of the nineteen members of the West Bay church hierarchy in 1913 – ten of them Ebankses – shows three blacks, five browns, and nine whites, besides the two white expatriate ministers (Robert Young and his successor, John Blackman).[16] For Bodden Town, presumably, the ratio would have been the reverse – with blacks in the majority and Boddens as numerous as the Ebankses at West Bay. Throughout the island, the Sunday School teachers represented a similarly typical local range of skin colour, and probably by that time between one-third and one-half of them would have been women.

The Presbyterian Church owed its success in part to its willingness to adapt to local conditions, including colour and class distinctions. Similarly,

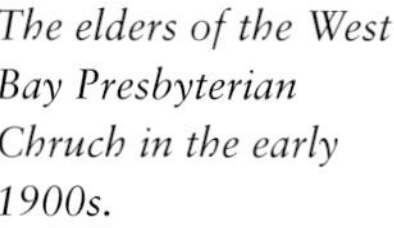

The elders of the West Bay Presbyterian Chruch in the early 1900s.

The North Side Presbyterian Church.

it reserved its moral condemnation mainly for what it saw as the most glaring sins: fornication, adultery, intemperance, profanity, and breaking the Sabbath. It was especially successful with regard to the latter two. In 1890, the Moderator of the Jamaican Presbytery, Rev. William Boyd, making the charge to Rev. J.L. Martin on his appointment to Bodden Town, stated that the Caymanian church had the advantage of not being established by the state. Nor, he said, were the Cayman Islands "over churched" with too many denominations, like Jamaica. "You do not go to a heathen land, but to one that has been for nearly fifty years under Christian influences," said Boyd. "You will find not a few of the people indifferent to spiritual things – their hearts set on this world – with no higher object than its fleeting advantages. You will find many living sinful lives, indulging the lusts and desires of the flesh. But you will find many who have begun the Christian life, and who will support you with their sympathy, and uphold you with their prayers." Boyd quoted a recent visitor to Grand Cayman, an officer aboard the Australian steamer *Orient*, who said its inhabitants "were amongst the most consistent Christians with whom he had come in contact. They stoutly refused to load their turtle on the Sabbath, and he never once heard them use profane language."[17]

Caymanian funerals were always conducted with decorum, but pastors could not completely discourage the public lamenting (probably an African tradition) with which Caymanians attended the dead on their passage from the material world to that of the spirits. Obeah was feared – and legally prohibited – as satanic ritual, rather than as sorcery medicine used for good as

The Presbyterian Mission Council, Jamaica, with representatives from Cayman: Rev. George Hicks (back row, second from left) and Rev. Robert Young (back row, second from right).

The marriage of Bentley Ross and Leila McTaggart (Leila Ross-Shier) in 1915.

well as evil. One minister rejoiced that he had convinced a young black Caymanian woman on her deathbed that she was not a victim of obeah, so that she could die happily in the Lord.[18] But no Presbyterian minister was ever able to exorcise totally the persistent belief in the spirits Caymanians called "duppies".[19]

THE SISTER ISLANDS

The spread of organised religion to the Sister Islands showed many parallels with that in Grand Cayman, except that it was the work of Baptist rather than Presbyterian missionaries and started some forty years later. Until 1885 no house of worship existed in Cayman Brac or Little Cayman, and the religious practice and understanding of the inhabitants consisted of what they had learned in Grand Cayman or on their travels to Jamaica and further afield. When the schooner from Kingston carrying Rev. Andrew Baillie and Rev. John Smith for Smith's induction at George Town stopped briefly at Cayman Brac on Sunday, 21 February 1869, Baillie reckoned (though wrongly) that they were the first ministers ever to have stepped ashore there.[20] They were impressed with the fact that the Brackers who came out in their canoes were wearing their better clothes and observing the Sabbath as a day of rest, though they lacked both minister and church and owned only a few Bibles among them.[21]

Presbyterian Church at Prospect, Grand Cayman, ca. 1915.

The congregation of the Baptist Church on Little Cayman, 1938.

The Brackers were eager for news of friends and relatives in Jamaica and Grand Cayman, and of events in Cuba and Haiti. But they were most interested in the two ministers aboard. One Bracker asked Baillie if he would marry him to his fiancée. Baillie agreed, on condition that the man would be kind to his wife, which "he most ardently engaged to be". A canoe was sent ashore, and boys were seen scurrying through the coconut groves with the news. The schooner anchored at Stake Bay, off the centre of the island, and the ceremony was held within an hour of the request, attended by some fifty people, "all handsomely attired". Following the ceremony, reported Baillie, "we had a service, when Mr. Smith and I endeavoured to give a simple statement of gospel truth, and invited them to accept Christ as their Saviour. We urged on them the duty, and the benefit to themselves, of all gathering together every Sabbath to read the word of God, and be united in praise and prayer."[22]

Baillie and Smith encountered no non-white Brackers, but found that among the whites the older generation were mostly illiterate, having had no opportunity to attend school. The "rising generation", though, was being rather crudely tutored "by a shipwrecked English sailor of good education". This presumably was the Johnston said to have arrived in 1863. He, unfortunately, was reported to be "a slave to strong drink whenever he can get it; and he too often manages to do so, though such a vast tract of ocean is between him and any rum-shop". What a benefit it would be, concluded Baillie, "if these islanders had a godly man for their teacher – one whose life would be a power for godliness, and who could gather all around him on a Sabbath and feed them with the word of life!"[23]

The Brackers did not have such an opportunity for almost twenty years. On his visit in 1884, Governor Norman reported that the Sister Islands still possessed neither a school nor a place of worship.[24] But in the following year, Rev. J.H. Sobey, minister of the second Baptist Church of Montego Bay, visited Cayman Brac at the "earnest invitations" of Brac seamen whom he had met in Montego Bay. He was welcomed enthusiastically when he arrived in May 1885. During the week he spent on Cayman Brac, he went into "every house" and saw "every individual". He reported that the total population was about 440, of whom 40 lived on Little Cayman. His round of visitations and meetings enabled him to gauge accurately how Sister Islanders would respond to the establishment of Baptist churches.

Graves in Grand Cayman dating from the early 1800s.

> The people hungered after the Word of Life. The first service was held in one of the largest houses, which was crowded. Next day, under my direction, a tent was erected with poles, ropes, and sails, which made a splendid shelter from the sun and rain. Here for seven days the Word of God was proclaimed. I visited from one end of the island to another. Either on horseback or by sea in a canoe; entered every house, saw every individual, and ministered to the sick. The greatest attention was paid whilst I preached and sang to them the "wonderful words of life". . . . I presume more than two thirds of the people had never heard the Gospel preached until from my lips. . . . They earnestly entreated me to try and get them a missionary. . . . If a suitable brother can be found . . . I am sure he would be very liberally supported. The people are able and willing, and have promised to do it.[25]

On his return to Jamaica, Sobey contacted the Jamaica Baptist Missionary Society, who sought a missionary to establish a new work on the Sister Islands. In 1886, Sobey returned with Rev. E.J. Hewett, secretary of the JBMS, to introduce Rev. H.W. Rutty, a white Jamaican minister, as the Brac's first missionary worker. (Rev. Rutty's son and grandson were later Cayman Brac's Collector and chief J.P.) Baptisms were performed and congregations started in various settlements. Work was begun on building two chapels, at Stake Bay and Creek. Six months later, Hewett returned to visit Rutty, this time accompanied by the Rev. A.G. Kirkham. Rutty was formally ordained as a permanent missionary, and the work was extended to West End and "East End" on Cayman Brac and "South Harbour" on Little Cayman.[26]

The Baptist mission in the Sister Islands flourished as successfully as had the Presbyterian mission in Grand Cayman. During H.W. Rutty's pastorate, which lasted until 1894, five chapels were completed and a large parsonage built at Stake Bay. This became the centre of Rutty's ministry, in which he was energetically assisted by his wife. Baptist practice was more participatory and less formal than the Presbyterian, and lay preachers, readers, and Sunday School teachers were easily recruited. Rutty served each chapel in weekly sequence, attended additional prayer and Bible-reading classes on different days each week, and visited Little Cayman about once a month.

After Rutty's retirement because of poor health, a series of three missionary pastors (Stephen Witt, Hay Owens, and Joseph Thrift) ably carried on the work for approximately three years each. This situation lasted until Rev.

Charles Barron, who had visited the Sister Islands in 1895, was appointed as pastor in 1906. Barron found that his predecessors had been active. Vestries had been added to each of the chapels, which had been enlarged, roofed with shingles instead of thatch, and provided with elegant woodwork, bells, and organs. By 1907, there were schoolrooms near the chapels at Stake Bay, Creek, and Little Cayman, and by 1908 they were staffed by two relatively qualified day schoolmasters and a schoolmistress. In that year, the five chapels had a combined seating capacity of 950 – almost the total population of the Sister Islands. Though members numbered about two hundred, almost the entire population attended Sunday services, with the pastor or visiting ministers often preaching to packed churches.[27]

In the 1911 census, 969 of the 1,436 inhabitants of the Sister Islands (67.5 per cent) were said to be adherents of the Baptist Church, compared with 118 (8.2 per cent) who belonged to other denominations and 297 (20.7 per cent) with no stated religion. These figures were not far off those for Grand Cayman, where 3,212 (77.8 per cent) of the 4,128 inhabitants were listed as Presbyterians, while other denominations accounted for 319 people (7.7 per cent), and those with no stated religion totalled 584 (14.1 per cent).[28] The Baptist Church held a central position in Sister Islands society just as the Presbyterian Church did in Grand Cayman, and in very similar ways. The minister and his helpers were the community leaders, and the chapels, vestries, and schoolrooms were the only common meeting places. The church buildings were the site of not only church services, prayer meetings, and Sunday Schools, but also regular choir practices, and meetings of organisations such as the International Bible Reading Association and the Young People's Society for Christian Endeavour. Women's Guilds were founded in both Grand Cayman and Cayman Brac from about 1910.

OTHER EARLY CHURCHES

Until the end of the nineteenth century, the Presbyterians in Grand Cayman and the Baptists in the Sister Islands had the only churches on the islands. Other denominations, reflecting new forms of worship that originated in the United States, eventually made inroads into the Cayman Islands. Their presence was one indication of the increasing contact between the islands and their huge northern neighbour. The first newcomers, apparently in 1896, seem to have been Seventh-Day Adventists. In 1907, the Adventist evangelist Rev. F. Hall (who had arrived with his wife and daughter in November 1905) wrote that he had been preceded by an Elder W.W. Eastman, who had been sent by the Adventist Conference in Washington, D.C., in 1896 and had spent fifteen months in Grand Cayman. Eastman himself may have been preceded by Captain Gilbert McLaughlin of East End. A former Presbyterian and

Methodist who had been drawn to the local Adventist mission church while in the Bay Island of Bonacca, McLaughlin had been commanded by a vision to carry the word to his home village. He spent more than fifty years as an Adventist elder and lay preacher in Grand Cayman and the Bay Islands, until his death in 1947. By that time, the denomination boasted six substantial churches throughout the islands.[29]

The early Adventists were hardy souls. But their doctrines, strict dietary restrictions, and Saturday observance of the Sabbath did not gain ground rapidly among the conservative Caymanians. By 1908, Hall claimed "stations" at George Town, East End, and North Side and meetings on Sunday, Wednesday, and Friday evenings, as well as the Saturday Sabbath services. This was besides "Cottage Meetings when convenient, also a Bible Class for women and a meeting conducted by Mrs and Miss Hall once a week, for the purpose of imparting religious, moral and hygienic principles". Total Adventist membership, however, was no more than sixteen. Only fourteen were noted in the 1911 census – of whom nine were at East End, four at George Town, and one at North Side.[30]

The American evangelists who led what the Caymanians named the Holiness Movement were much more immediately successful than the Adventists. These were members of various branches of the Church of God from the southern and midwestern United States. Their original missionary was the self-ordained Joseph E. Carswell of Kansas, who arrived in Grand Cayman "in or about the year 1898". He was followed a few years later by one Richard Russell. By 1907 the movement was more or less led by a local convert, William Coe of West Bay, who claimed two hundred adherents, a well-built "tabernacle" at West Bay, and another under construction at George Town. Two years later, however, Commissioner Hirst reported four tabernacles, and the 1911 census counted 357 Caymanian members of the Church of God. There were 82 at West Bay, 77 at George Town, 36 at Prospect, and 56 at North Side, and 8 apiece at Bodden Town and East End. There were also 90 members in the Sister Islands, 82 of them on Cayman Brac.[31]

As described by Pastor William Coe in 1907, the Holiness Movement claimed to be "purely unsectarian, having no creed or dogma, simply declaring the Gospel in all its purity, holding up Jesus as a Saviour from all sin and through whom salvation, present and full, free and for all, can be obtained". This was especially attractive to those who craved a simple and spontaneous Bible-based religion, unmediated by a ministerial hierarchy. Holiness adherents did not favour a formal theology, particularly one that stressed (as Presbyterianism did) the doctrine of predestination. As in the United States, the Holiness Movement appealed primarily to poor, relatively uneducated whites who felt a special affinity for teaching about the person of the Holy

Spirit. Holiness seems also to have struck a chord among those of African heritage who craved a more spontaneous form of worship, including fervent singing, call-and-response, and even speaking in tongues.[32]

THE BEGINNINGS OF EDUCATION IN GRAND CAYMAN

The earliest schooling in the Cayman Islands was apparently provided by private individuals who, in family groupings and sometimes for small fees, passed on the basics of reading, writing, and arithmetic before there were churches in the islands. But churches and education were inseparable in Cayman from the time the first Christian missions were established until an effective, public Board of Education was created, between 1908 and 1920. For one thing, there was a shortage of funds to create government schools. For another, Caymanians wanted an education system that would instill Christian virtues and values. This gave the churches a powerful influence on society that remained strong for many decades and whose influence can still be felt today. At the same time, the shortage of qualified local teachers meant that that schools would be defined throughout this period as much by Jamaican and British influences as by local conditions and needs.

The first trained schoolmaster in the Cayman Islands after the withdrawal of the Mico teachers in 1841 was the Caymanian-born John Jarrett Wood, who arrived to open a school at Bodden Town in 1844. Wood was trained in Jamaica, first by the Congregationalist London Missionary Society and then at the interdenominational Mico Normal College. He was employed by Rev. James Elmslie in 1846 to open a school in George Town in conjunction with the Presbyterian mission. This school, competing with several small classes held by private teachers, was not successful, and Wood returned to Bodden Town. By 1851 he was teaching ninety-five pupils there, "of whom 35 were able to read the Scriptures and 25 were learning arithmetic".[33] The fees were between threepence and ninepence a week, according to the pupil's grade. But these were paid "mostly in labour and provisions", and, despite receiving a subsidy from the Mission Board of the United Presbyterian Church of Scotland, in 1854 Wood left for a somewhat more lucrative career in Jamaica.

Left to right: Frederick S. McTaggart, one of the first trained teachers in Grand Cayman; Antoinette McTaggart, Roy McTaggart, and Leila McTaggart (later Leila Ross-Shier), ca. 1900.

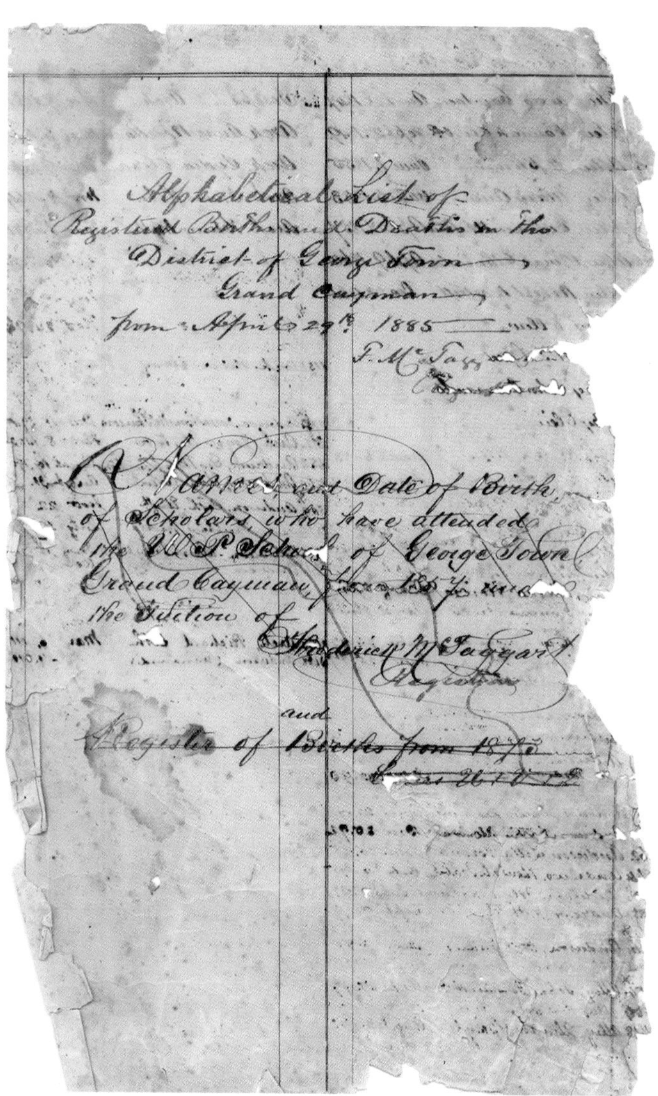

Alphabetical List of
Registered Births and Deaths in the
District of George Town
Grand Cayman
from April 27th 1885
F. McTaggart
Registrar

Names and Date of Birth
of Scholars who have attended
the U.P. School of George Town
Grand Cayman from 1857 and
the Tuition of
Frederick McTaggart
Registrar
and
Register of Births from 1878

Cover page from F.S. McTaggart's school register, dating from 1857.

Wood was followed by a long line of Jamaican teachers. All of them struggled with the shortage of supplies and the difficulties of collecting fees, but were narrowly sustained by continuing grants from the Scottish Presbyterians. Wood's immediate successors at Bodden Town, named Drummond and Grant, seem to have made little impact. The influence of two others, however, was far greater and long remembered. Both graduates of Montego Bay Academy, James C. Panton (whose father had been a missionary at Calabar and married an African) and Frederick S. McTaggart (a Jamaican of Scottish ancestry) arrived in Grand Cayman towards the end of Elmslie's ministry, to teach on behalf of the Presbyterian Church. Panton taught first at Prospect, but moved to Bodden Town following the death of Mr. Grant. McTaggart was appointed to the George Town school, where he remained until he became a full-time elder and lay preacher in 1888, after which Panton took his place and served until his death in 1897. Both men became deeply involved in local affairs and established notable Caymanian families.[34]

When making his survey of conditions in Grand Cayman in August 1887, Laurence Fyfe gave a detailed and generally favourable account of Frederick McTaggart's work. McTaggart's school, catering almost exclusively to boys, was being held in the Presbyterian chapel, though a purpose-built schoolroom was under construction. As in all the island's schools, there was "an absence of such school appliances as maps, blackboards, &c." There were 106 pupils on the roll, though average attendance was no more than 70. McTaggart received a salary of £25 a year from the United Presbyterian Mission, and the school was voted the meagre sum of £5 a year by the Vestry, on condition that places were found for a certain number of fatherless boys free of charge. For the others, the fees were sixpence a week for "those boys sufficiently advanced to do writing in copy books and arithmetic", and threepence a week for the rest. Though he was prepared to accept provisions in lieu of fees, McTaggart acknowledged that the parents' inability or unwillingness to pay fees was

the cause of poor attendance. It also explained why so many school-aged children in the district were not enrolled at all.

Despite his difficulties, Frederick McTaggart earned esteem as a strict but able teacher. Laurence Fyfe found that the children in the highest class, whose ages averaged about thirteen, were reading fluently in the Fifth Royal Reader, at least up to the standard found in Jamaica. "I heard most of the scholars in each of the other classes read in the Royal Readers from the Fourth downwards," reported Fyfe, "and most of them read fluently and well, but a little too fast. I also saw some capital specimens of handwriting: and generally there was gratifying evidence of good work being done by Mr. McTaggart in this School."[35]

McTaggart's school focused mainly on boys, but George Town also had a private school exclusively for girls, with twenty-five enrolled. This was taught by a Miss McDermott, the Jamaican sister-in-law of the Presbyterian minister Rev. H.L. McMillan (1884–96). Elsewhere on the island, the schools were coeducational, though boys had the first call on what facilities were available. The school that most sparked Laurence Fyfe's enthusiasm was the one recently opened in the Presbyterian chapel at West Bay by Miss McDermott's brother Thomas, a graduate of the Collegiate School in Kingston. Thomas McDermott, who taught for almost ten years at West Bay, later became a well-known Jamaican newspaper editor, poet, and short-story writer under the pen name Tom Redcam. In 1887 his school, which had been granted £2 10s a year by the Vestry, already had forty-five pupils enrolled, all of whom paid their fees in cash and on time. "I was struck by the bright and cheerful look of the children in this School," wrote Fyfe, "and the intelligent manner in which they answered questions I put to them; and it was a strange experience to find that

Smiley Connolly's school in George Town in the early 1900s.

they refused a half holiday which was offered to them at my request. Mr. McDermott, who is fond of teaching, and who evidently takes great interest in the work of education, will, I feel sure, in time make the School a great blessing to the District."[36]

Laurence Fyfe was less enthusiastic about the other schools in Grand Cayman. At Bodden Town, J.C. Panton had been succeeded by another graduate of Montego Bay Academy called Hislop. But he died shortly afterwards, and the school was run, with limited success, first by Hislop's widow, then by an Englishman named Roberts, and finally by a person whom Rev. Thomas Redpath later described as a "ship-wrecked sailor".[37] The only other sizeable school was at East End. It had been kept in the Presbyterian chapel since 1883 by the only Caymanian teacher, a Mr. Connolly, who was also the registrar of births and deaths. Despite having to subsist on fees of threepence a week, rarely paid in cash, and a measly grant of £3 a year from the Vestry, Connolly had between seventy-five and eighty regular attendees at his school, including sixteen fatherless children who were taught free. Connolly reckoned, however, that there were as many as 300 children of school age in the East End District and another 170 at North Side who were not attending school.

In general, Laurence Fyfe was pleased at the level of literacy attained with such limited resources, and gave credit to the Presbyterian Church and the Jamaican teachers. He deplored the lack of facilities and cash that kept so many children away from school and limited the education of those who did attend. He recommended that more public funds be spent on schools and that the Jamaican school system be adopted in Cayman. Presumably this meant the inclusion of more free places for needy pupils, standardised grades, syllabuses, and examinations, and regular visits from inspectors.[38]

THE BEGINNINGS OF EDUCATION IN THE SISTER ISLANDS

Education in the Sister Islands probably began informally within families – as it had in Grand Cayman in earlier generations. Matters took a step forward when, as we have seen, a mariner named Johnston was shipwrecked on Cayman Brac in 1863 and started a school. Johnston taught navigation in addition to instructing schoolchildren. Education was apparently sought after by adults, and even "grown men" attended his school. When Governor Norman visited Cayman Brac in 1884, he reported that the island had "no school and no place of worship", but presumably the traditions promoted by Johnston lived on in some form. In 1891 Henry Hewitt, a Jamaican, set up a school in Cayman Brac. This was probably the "private school" described by Governor Blake when he visited Cayman Brac in 1892. Established at Stake Bay, it charged fees of "nine pence per week". Attendance was "somewhat irregular", though it was supported by the people of Stake Bay and Scott Bay, whom the Governor described as "well to do, and intelligent".[39]

The schoolhouse at Creek, Cayman Brac.

It was undoubtedly the influence of the Baptist Church, however, that broadened and deepened educational opportunities in the Sister Islands. When he visited in 1885, Rev. Sobey had seen the need for day schools that would be taught by the missionary pastor "three days a week". Arrangements of this kind probably developed as churches became firmly established on both islands during the later 1880s and early 1890s. In 1896 or shortly thereafter, the chapel at the Creek saw the addition of "a large schoolhouse, with cottage attached, for the use of the Missionary Pastor". During the next ten years two more schoolrooms were added to the chapels in Stake Bay and Little Cayman. According to pastor Charles Barron, these schools were kept "more or less constantly for the benefit of the young people of the islands", while in the other settlements, "the chapels or vestries are sometimes used for a similar purpose". Pioneer efforts by Baptists and others bore fruit. "At the present time," wrote H.W. Rutty in 1907, "two or three of the more ambitious young men are studying the higher branches of education in prominent places of instruction in the United States of America" – setting a precedent that would be followed by many from the Sister Islands in later years.[40]

In all three islands, early educational efforts were promoted from time to time by the fortuitous arrival of shipwrecked mariners. One notable example was the young sailor Samuel Sydney Saunders, who chose to remain in the Sister Islands after his ship, the *Prince Frederick*, wrecked off the south coast of Cayman Brac in 1895. Saunders taught on both Cayman Brac and Little Cayman, eventually marrying into a Caymanian family. J. C. Lazzari recalls going to the school that his father helped Saunders to start in North East Bay. Saunders was also brought over to Little Cayman by some of the more prosperous families connected with the coconut industry to start a private school. For some years he apparently served as a district constable in the Sister Islands; he later lived in the United States. After the 1932 storm, he was invited to return to Cayman Brac by the Kirkconnell family and he started another school in Stake Bay, so that a second generation of Sister Islanders benefited from his instruction. Capt. Charles Kirkconnell attended this school in the 1930s, just as his father had attended Saunders' school in Little Cayman a generation earlier. Saunders was not highly educated, but as the writer

Miss Izzy Powell's schoolhouse, West Bay.

Hiram Dixon notes in *Cayman Brac: Land of my Birth*, his accidental arrival in 1895 helped "to dawn a brighter day for education" in the Sister Islands.[41]

PRIVATE SCHOOLING OVERSEAS

Despite the recommendations made by Laurence Fyfe in his report in 1887, the changes needed to make education available to all children throughout the Cayman Islands, including increased public funding, were slow in coming. It was not, in fact, until the turn of the century that any such developments took place. In the meantime, local legislators were reluctant to increase taxation, while those who elected them were reasonably satisfied with the education that was available. Caymanian voters of the time were, generally speaking, the people most capable of paying the few pence a week that more or less guaranteed a basic primary schooling. They also included those few relatively affluent Caymanians who had the means to send their children to Jamaica for secondary (and even tertiary) education.

From the mid-nineteenth century, the few long-established secondary schools found in major West Indian colonies were transformed into boys' boarding schools modelled on the English "public school".[42] Likewise, Jamaica's parochial schools, originally established as charitable trusts to educate poorer white boys, were changed into fee-paying schools for the white and near-white sons of Jamaican planters, merchants, and professionals. These schools also attracted a small number of students from well-to-do families in the Jamaican dependencies.[43]

Alhough this practice actually produced a Caymanian Rhodes scholar, George Webster, in the 1920s,[44] the system of schooling abroad was generally alien to the Caymanian way of life. Something of this was conveyed in the reminiscences of Lee A. Ebanks, J.P., of West Bay, in 1985. In the absence of a high school in Grand Cayman, Ebanks was sent by his parents to Calabar High School in Kingston in 1920. He graphically described the five-day voyage in the schooner commanded by his father; the impact of seeing for the first time mountains and rivers, as well as crowded and clamorous streets and slums; the tears he shed when he said goodbye to his father; the shock of meeting boys from all over Jamaica; the strange school routines and strict discipline; and the homesickness that he initially suffered.[45]

Over the years, a tiny number of exceptionally talented students found their way, against the odds, to British universities and colleges. A few more had the will, talent, and means to take advantage of the many post-secondary institutions in the United States and Canada. Until the 1920s, though, the only opportunities for tertiary education open to Caymanians were at the three teacher training colleges in Jamaica. These were Mico (dating from 1834), Calabar (mainly a theological school for Baptist trainees, founded in 1843), and Shortwood (1885), the first training college for girls. All three colleges were church-oriented, with a strong emphasis upon religious and moral instruction. They were geared to produce the qualified native teachers that the Cayman Islands sorely needed.[46]

THE DEVELOPMENT OF PUBLIC EDUCATION

Pressures for a more progressive and comprehensive system of education in the Cayman Islands gradually increased during the first twenty years of the twentieth century. They came ultimately from Britain, which had initiated compulsory, free schooling from the 1870s and had nominally introduced this system to Jamaica by the 1890s. The Commissioners in Cayman sought to follow this lead and were joined by a few local supporters of a better education system. But they were frustrated by three factors. These were the belief that a more developed system of education was unnecessary, especially for girls; the legislature's reluctance to vote the necessary funds; and the churches' desire to retain control over what was taught.

It took almost two decades, the efforts of the first four Commissioners, and three Acts of the legislature to achieve a system of primary education in the Cayman Islands equivalent to that in Jamaica. Commissioner Sanguinetti arrived with encouragement to push for compulsory education under government supervision, but was soon made aware of the difficulties posed by the cost and by the opposition of the Presbyterian Church. Prodded by Governor

Olivier, however, he steered the first Cayman Education Act through the legislature early in 1902.

Although the new Act was modest in its aims, these were not realised. It sought to establish at least one government-sponsored elementary school in each district, under the supervision of a Board of Education appointed by the Commissioner.[47] Government funds of up to £200 could be used to support schools, but most operating costs were to come from a fee of five shillings a year for each child enrolled. The Board of Education's duties were only vaguely defined, and the new schools continued to rely on church support for buildings and subsidies for teachers. Education was not made compulsory, and almost half of all children went without schooling.[48] The crucial problem was funding, and between 1904 and 1906 the system broke down altogether. The total collected in school fees in 1904, for example, was less than £18, to which was added £25 from what were called education rates. In the following year it was worse: nothing at all was collected for fees, and a mere £8 in education rates. Revenue depended on attendance, and for the island as a whole, attendance in the eight so-called government schools fell from 404 in 1904–5 to 256 in 1905–6.[49]

Rescuing and improving the education system was one of Commissioner Hirst's priorities.[50] Soon after his appointment in 1907, Hirst submitted to Jamaica a plan for compulsory education for all children aged six to fourteen, with properly qualified and licensed teachers, in recognised government schools. He claimed that this system could be funded without special taxation and would be approved by the Vestry. The Jamaican education authorities generally endorsed the plan, while stipulating that more requirements for registering schools, licensing teachers, and standardising the curriculum would be needed.[51]

After a public meeting calling for a free, government-run system, and heated debates in the legislature, a new Education Act was passed in 1908. But it, too, proved less than satisfactory. The Act's provisions did not extend beyond Grand Cayman. Fees were not abolished. The Act did mandate that schools had to be registered, and that those up to standard with properly licensed teachers would be "recognised" by the government and awarded a grant. But matters such as teacher licensing, syllabuses, examinations, inspections, and the functions of the Board of Education were still ill-defined. Hirst did his best to implement the new Act, even vigorously assuming the role of Schools Inspector, but eventually public inertia and personal opposition caused him to turn his attention to other interests.[52]

The Annual Report for 1911–12, published just after Hirst's death, recorded that the amount spent on education had fallen to £243 in 1910 and £283 in 1911. In the annual inspection of 1911, carried out by Rev. R.C. Young, only 359 pupils (out of 441 enrolled) were found to be present in the "recog-

nised" schools. "No opportunity offered for the inspection of several private schools, and no schools were visited in the Lesser Islands." It was reckoned, however, that there were "in the Dependency about one thousand children of school age, but hardly more than two-thirds are within reach of ordinary educational advantages". It was claimed that "efforts by many interested in progress are now being directed towards the establishment of a system of free and compulsory education". Such a move, though, would "entail special taxation".[53]

The situation did not improve in the three years before World War One or during the war itself. The official report on education written by Commissioner Arthur Robinson in 1914 was bleak. "The state of education in the Dependency is far from satisfactory, especially in the country districts," he wrote.

> The conditions obtaining at the present time do not offer any attractions to good and reliable teachers. . . . While the Government grant is of great assistance to the teachers, they are largely dependent on the collection of fees from private individuals, who cannot always be relied on to pay, and in a large number of cases offer payment in kind instead of cash. The result is that teachers, whether fit or unfit, must be tolerated or the schools must close, as in the case of North Side, Gun Bay and East End, where children are growing up in ignorance.

Robinson noted that the there was no enforcement of the regulation that all children aged six to fourteen living within two miles of a school must attend 75 per cent of the time. There were estimated to be 1,030 children of school age in Grand Cayman, of whom probably fewer than half were meeting this requirement. The problem stemmed partly from lack of interest by parents. "There are many", he wrote, "who attach no importance whatsoever to the education of their children, and who do not consider even reading and writing as in any way essential to a child's future welfare."[54]

It would be six more years before the long-needed Education Act of 1920 was passed with the support of an enthusiastic new Commissioner, H.H. Hutchings.[55] By then the economy had improved. In 1919 a new law increasing import duties was passed, with the income specifically earmarked for education. The 1920 Education Act finally introduced the first practicable system of compulsory education throughout the islands.[56] Private schools were still allowed, fees were still required, and the age range for compulsory education was set at seven to fourteen instead of six to fourteen. The government was now completely responsible for all schools and was required to ensure that there were enough schools for all eligible children, in the Sister Islands as well as Grand Cayman. The crucial factor in delivering this new system was a Board of Education with precisely defined and real powers, including control of a budget that was sufficient to back them up.

The School Inspector (Rev. George Hicks) visits the school at George Town.

The new Board of Education, with the Commissioner as Chairman, comprised between seven and eleven members, with three members from the Sister Islands. Its role was to set policy, inspect and license all schools and teachers, and design and enforce the general curriculum. It was to ensure that all public schools had buildings that were maintained and adequately furnished, and to provide teaching supplies. It was responsible for hiring and paying all public school teachers, for assigning their duties and disciplining them when necessary, and for awarding scholarships to promising students interested in a teaching career.[57] Because of the difficulties of inter-island communication and the special conditions in Cayman Brac and Little Cayman, a separate committee, consisting entirely of local residents, was set up to supervise the quality of education in the Sister Islands.

The Board of Education had a budget of at least £1,500 a year, £300 of it for the Sister Islands. This budget was in addition to school fees, which were actually raised from five to ten shillings a year per pupil. Teachers were to submit half-yearly reports to the Board listing all children in their school and relevant particulars, especially attendance. The police were to draw up a list of all children living within two miles of a public school, though no provision was actually made to control truancy.

The Act acknowledged that while government schools would predominate, the system would continue to rely on private schools, most of which had a strong religious affiliation. The curriculum would be modelled on Jamaica's. Bible study was to be included, though the Act stated that no school would be allowed to impose a sectarian form of Christian teaching, or to discriminate against any pupil on account of religious affiliation. These conditions

could only be enforced by an inspectorate, of course, and the continuing influence of the churches was virtually guaranteed by the fact that the Inspector of Schools was almost always a Presbyterian minister from the 1920s through the 1950s.[58]

The effects of the 1920 Education Act were immediate and dramatic. The number of public schools had already risen from four to six in anticipation of the Act. With the increase in government expenditure on education from £328 in 1920 to £1,875 in 1921, the number immediately soared to eleven, including one each in Cayman Brac and Little Cayman. These schools had a total of 778 pupils enrolled, almost double the pre-war figures, though boys in public schools still outnumbered girls by 432 to 346. Six private schools were still registered, with 134 pupils in all – 73 girls and 61 boys. By 1923, when government funding for education had stabilised at £1,500, the total enrolment in all schools had reached 1,067, of whom 881 were in public and 186 in private schools. Some 80 per cent of all eligible children in the Cayman Islands were now being educated.[59]

In addition to a spurt of school building projects, the Board of Education was able to offer contracts and salaries of up to £98 a year, plus either housing or rent assistance, to the head teachers in each of their schools. This was enough to staff the new system, but barely so. The problem of keeping teachers and training local replacements persisted for decades. The board did its best to install the Jamaican curriculum, but without Jamaican examinations and inspectors, the results were patchy. The development of secondary, let alone tertiary, education in the islands was still a long way off.

The most remarkable thing about the 1920 Education Act was that it set up a system that stayed in place, basically unchanged, until 1968. A generous view of this is that the 1920 Act was sufficiently flexible to accommodate changes arising from international events, such as the Great Depression and World War Two, that affected the islands. A more critical evaluation might blame indifference and inertia: satisfaction with a system that, if basic, seemed to work well enough, and a continuing unwillingness to spend more on education if it meant a higher level of taxation.

Meanwhile, the Board of Education did what it could with its limited resources, which became even sparser during the years of the Great Depression and World War Two. Nothing illustrated this better than the pupil-teacher system, in which senior pupils assisted in teaching junior ones, and untrained pupil-teachers were even given charge of small schools on their own.

The Cayman Islands Board of Education made a virtue out of this necessity. The first general examinations adopted from Jamaica were for pupils identified as pupil-teachers (from years 5, 6, and 7). These examinations were held annually in eight subjects, all of which had to be passed for three successive years to achieve success. If they were successful, pupil-teachers had their

school fees refunded. At the end of three years, they had a good chance of being awarded government sponsorship to Mico or Shortwood Colleges in Jamaica. Fewer than 10 per cent of students reached this level. But even so, the system produced more pupil-teachers than were required for teaching. The special course of instruction pupil-teachers were given represented the beginnings of secondary education in the Cayman Islands.[60]

More fundamental changes would have to wait until the 1960s and a new era of economic prosperity. In the meantime, when proper secondary schooling began after World War Two, it was not started by government but by private interests with a marked religious affiliation and with strong influences, through the Church of God, from the United States.

A youngster eyes a distant schooner from the ironshore.

CHAPTER 12

Caymanians on the Move

Early Decades of the Twentieth Century

THE CAYMAN ISLANDS CAME TO be called "the islands that time forgot" during the first half of the twentieth century.[1] The description was coined by visitors and was catchy, but it was not fully accurate. While Caymanian society may have seemed to outsiders to be innocent of the materialistic hurly-burly of the developed world, it was not standing still. Changes were taking place within the Islands, while in the wider world Caymanians were establishing permanent connections with the United States and other places through migration. This era brought its own challenges, in particular those of World War One, the Great Depression that began in 1929, and the devastating hurricane of 1932, which was probably the worst natural disaster in Cayman's history. Nevertheless, Caymanians continued to make the best of their isolation and lack of natural resources, as well as the limited aid available to a dependency of Jamaica. They introduced what changes they could afford, travelled farther afield to make a livelihood, and in many cases moved elsewhere with their families in search of an easier life.

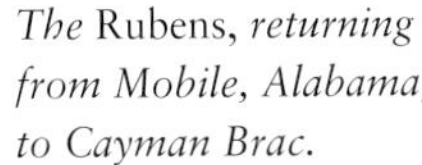

The Rubens, *returning from Mobile, Alabama, to Cayman Brac.*

A SECOND WAVE OF MIGRATION

During the first third of the twentieth century, improvements in sea communications, World War One, and the worldwide boom in the early 1920s increased opportunities to travel, work, and settle abroad. As a result, Caymanians were again on the move, migrating principally to the United States and Cuba but also to places in Central America such as Nicaragua. This "second wave" of migration sprang from the same basic desire for a better life that fuelled the first wave in the 1830s and 1840s, following emancipation. Towards the end of the 1920s this second migration slowed and even reversed. The United States began to tighten its immigration restrictions, and this factor, coupled with the effects of the Great Depression, cut off various opportunities abroad. Some Caymanians returned home, while others hoping to migrate found that they had to remain in the islands.

Although Jamaica was responsible for Cayman during this period, it provided few opportunities for ordinary Caymanians. A handful of fortunate Caymanians followed up a Jamaican education by marrying into the Jamaican landed class or pursuing a career in the Jamaican public service. James S. Webster, for example, settled in Kingston and eventually became a prosperous wholesale and retail merchant, manufacturer, and the owner of a small shipping line by the 1930s.[2] But for the vast majority of Caymanians, Jamaica offered little prospect of a better life. Much more attractive opportunities were afforded by the United States.

The spread of American influence throughout the Caribbean region after the Spanish-American War of 1898 helped to make other destinations promising for Caymanians. A few Caymanians, for example, joined the flood of British West Indians who went to work on the Panama Canal, built by the Americans between 1904 and 1914. Some settled in the Canal Zone, which had become a U.S. protectorate. Others moved to Nicaragua, which became a virtual protectorate of the United States in 1912. They worked in the American-owned plantations and mines or as logcutters, smallholding farmers, shopkeepers, or clerks in the rickety townships of the Caribbean coast. A few also settled as farmer-fishermen and boatbuilders on the Corn Islands, which Nicaragua ceded to the United States under a 99-year lease in 1916.[3] The close connection between the Cayman Islands and the Bay Islands of Honduras continued, with a large number of Caymanian families having branches in both places. With few exceptions, however, the Caymanian presence in the Bay Islands did not spill over onto the Honduran mainland because of continuing differences of language and culture.[4]

Far more promising for Caymanians wishing to migrate were the destinations of Florida and other Gulf Coast states of the U.S. The opening up of southeastern Florida provided jobs and opportunities. Caymanians went there to work on the East Coast Railroad, which reached Miami in 1896 and joined Key West to the mainland by 1912. They also found employment in the citrus orchards or in the industries that built Miami and other cities. As this corner of Florida became more prosperous, it became increasingly attractive to Caymanians, despite tough competition from the thousands of impoverished Bahamians who were also flocking there.[5]

At first the most attractive locations were the U.S. ports on the Gulf of Mexico, especially Tampa (Florida), Mobile (Alabama), and Port Arthur (Texas), each of which developed a Caymanian community. First and foremost was Tampa. It had excellent shipping and railroad connections with the rest of the United States, plentiful supplies of lumber within easy reach, citrus groves and early-vegetable farms, wholesale and retail businesses, and a growing number of factories. Mobile, a far older port than Tampa, had much the same resources but on a lesser scale. From the first decade of the twentieth century, Mobile and Port Arthur also offered work in oilfields and refineries, as well as employment on the freighters and tankers sailing to and from distant parts of the world. Later, as it developed into a great metropolis on the Texas coast, Houston drew many second- and third-generation Caymanian-Americans. In Florida, Miami and Jacksonville also developed sizeable Caymanian communities.

CARIBBEAN CRUISES

CARIBBEAN MOTORBOAT COMPANY

FREIGHT and PASSENGER SERVICE from TAMPA, FLORIDA
to
NEUVA GERONA, I. P. CUBA and GRAND CAYMAN, B. W. I.

Captain Charles G. Farrington, Manager and Operator of the British Motorship "NOCA" announces the completion of a new and larger motorship to be placed in service by above named company on or about

JUNE 1, 1932

This service offers the most economical vacation voyage in Southern Waters, calling at two of the most unique and picturesque spots in the Caribbean Sea.

Passenger rates to Nueva Gerona and Grand Cayman:
Adults (one way)....................................$20.00
Children, under 12 years (one way)........ 10.00
Infants, under 1 year...............................FREE

Freight rates and information as to proposed sailings cheerfully furnished on request.

Address all inquiries to:
FLORIDA FORWARDING AGENCY
P. O. Box No. 246
TAMPA, FLORIDA, U. S. A.

Advertisement for the Noca, *passenger boat linking Grand Cayman, the Isle of Pines, and Tampa.*

The closest destination for the second wave of migration from Cayman was the Isle of Pines, off the southern coast of Cuba. Caymanian mariners had always been familiar with its waters and with the nearby port of Batabanó on the Cuban mainland, which provided the easiest overland access to Havana. Brackers would visit the isolated southern shore of the Isle of Pines seeking turtles and coconuts, and some may have stayed there seasonally. But the island as a whole was not attractive for Caymanian settlement during the Spanish colonial period. Until Cuban slavery officially ended in 1886, the tra-

Aarona Booker Kohlman on the Isle of Pines, waiting to board a boat to Grand Cayman, ca. 1930s.

ditional distrust of the Spanish authorities was probably mixed, for non-whites, with the fear that they might be enslaved. The island itself remained largely undeveloped by the Spaniards.

Conditions on the Isle of Pines changed dramatically, however, after the American victory in the Spanish-American War of 1898. The Isle of Pines became almost as much an American possession as Puerto Rico and its offshore islands of Vieques and Culebra. Though treaties in 1903 and 1904 declared the Isle of Pines Cuban territory, there was such a wave of American investment and settlers that the American press campaigned to have the island annexed. Even after 1907, when the U.S. Supreme Court declared that the island was Cuban, the American flood continued. In its wake came first dozens, then hundreds, of Caymanians. They sought to enjoy the benefits of American investments and protection, without harassment from the Spanish authorities. They were attracted by the prospect of employment and free or cheap farmland.[6]

American property developers were selling large lots of land at bargain prices through brochures, primarily to midwestern farmers expecting an agricultural bonanza. In fact, the land was completely undeveloped. The immigrants built small communities and planted the first citrus groves. By 1919 nearly a quarter of the island's population were United States citizens. Under the American umbrella, many Caymanians, along with a good number of Jamaicans, flocked to the more settled parts of the Isle of Pines. For the men, there were opportunities as craftsmen, dockworkers, and fishermen in the port town of Nueva Gerona, and as grapefruit pickers and general farmhands in the countryside. The women found employment as domestics, working in hotels or for American families better off than themselves. Most migrants aspired to build their own houses and acquire land to support their families.

The Isle of Pines proved a transient dream for Americans. The U.S. Senate finally ratified the 1903 and 1904 Cuban treaties in 1925, and this action, together with the effects of the Great Depression in 1929, completely deflated the Cuban property venture. What was failure for American midwesterners, however, could be relative prosperity for Caymanians, especially if they could combine farming or labour in the citrus groves with livelihoods based on the sea. None became rich. But they enjoyed the amenities of Nueva Gerona, a township much larger than George Town. A few families even migrated on to Havana. But Caymanian *pineros* (as residents of the Isle of Pines are called)

always valued the regular motor-boat and schooner services connecting them to their homeland.

The number of American settlers on the Isle of Pines steadily declined after 1925. The Caymanian population, however, actually grew right up to the time of the Cuban Revolution of 1959. Caymanians in the Isle of Pines were more willing to intermarry and to use Spanish than those in the Bay Islands, though they still tenaciously kept their English language, Protestant religion, and Caymanian culture and identity. They were helped by the activity of American Lutheran missionaries, whose congregations they eagerly joined and to whose English-language schools they sent their children.[7]

A view of the Isle of Pines in the 1930s.

At their peak in 1959 the Caymanian *pineros* may have numbered two thousand – roughly twice the population of Cayman Brac. Probably two-thirds of them lived in the townships of Nueva Gerona and Santa Fé, and another quarter were scattered through the rural parts of the island. The rest lived in the almost purely Caymanian fishing and farming village of Jacksonville. This town was situated on the isolated southwestern shore – looking towards the Cayman Islands, and just two days' sail away. Of all migrant communities in the Isle of Pines, this was both the most self-contained and the one that best retained its Caymanian identity.

A plaque erected in Jacksonville in 1998 notes that the hamlet was founded by a Bracker, Watkin Jackson Hydes (1866–1949), who brought his family there some time in the late 1880s or early 1890s.[8] The Jacksons, after whom the village was named, were joined within a couple of decades by other Caymanian families. Almost all of these new arrivals were from Cayman Brac: the family names included Ebanks, Tatum, Rivers, Hydes, Eden, and Forbes. Unlike those Caymanians drawn to the more settled parts of the Isle of Pines (the area called "the island" by the inhabitants of Jacksonville), the villagers were subsistence farmers from the start. They cut mahogany, made charcoal, and caught turtle and fish for export to other parts of Cuba, the Cayman Islands, and Jamaica.

The population of Jacksonville has remained steady at about three hundred since the first decade of the twentieth century, though its Caymanian identity has faded considerably since the 1959 revolution. Many Caymanian *pineros* from both Jacksonville and "the island" took advantage of periodic relaxations of the Cuban ban on emigration to return to the Cayman Islands, where some remained while others moved on to Florida. By the late 1990s,

Spanish was the only language in the Jacksonville school, and the Lutheran Church had been turned into accommodation for four families recently arrived from "the island". Though poor by Caymanian standards, few of the villagers were openly critical of the Castro regime. But the Caymanian connection remained apparent. Those with Caymanian surnames, though a minority, were still distinguishable from those whom they referred to as "Cubians". The differences were most noticeable in their use of English, their soft voices and retiring dispositions, their Caymanian customs and turns of speech, and their continuing nostalgia for their Caymanian origins and kinfolk.[9]

A particularly interesting Caymanian *pinero* is the popular singer-songwriter Arnold Dixon Robinson, commonly known as Sonny-Boy. Half Jamaican and half Caymanian, he is the best-known performer of the music called *suco-suco*. This is a mixture of Cuban music with Jamaican reggae and Trinidadian calypso, to which, in performance, Sonny-Boy adds Caymanian folksongs handed down to him in his youth. His music is a vibrant illustration of one aspect of the Caymanian migration – the melding of cultural traditions.[10]

THOSE WHO LEFT

It is impossible to know precisely how many people left the Cayman Islands in the migrations of the first third of the twentieth century. But as many as 3,500 people may have left between 1891 and 1931, during a period when the islands' resident population rose only from 4,322 to 5,930. This estimate is based on calculations from the censuses of 1891, 1911, 1921, and 1934, and from the figures for persons arriving in and leaving the islands in the 1920s and 1930s. Emigration was highest between 1911 and 1921, with further peaks in 1924 and 1927–9. Later, between 1931 and 1934, there was a reverse flow of migration back to Cayman.[11]

Between 1891 and 1911, the resident population of the Cayman Islands rose from 4,322 to 5,564. If we assume a healthy rate of natural increase of around 2 per cent, this suggests that some 730 people emigrated from Cayman during these twenty years. During the decade from 1911 to 1921, however, the resident population actually declined from 5,564 to 5,253, during a time when the figures for births and deaths showed a natural increase of 2.3 per cent per year.[12] This suggests that some 1,732 people emigrated from Cayman during this ten-year period. The numbers of women and men in the 1921 census were much more even than those in the 1891 and 1911 censuses, which show a much higher proportion of women. This suggests that a high proportion of the 1,732 presumed emigrants were families rather than single men.[13]

When we examine the next period, using the censuses of 1921 and 1934, we find that the resident population increased moderately, from 5,253 to 5,981. But (based on the rate of natural increase) this figure would normally have been higher by at least 1,085. Emigration presumably accounts for this difference. In fact, the number of migrants was probably even higher because the 1934 census figures included 321 people who returned between 1931 and 1934 due to worsening economic conditions and tighter immigration controls in the U.S. Between 1921 and 1931, in fact, 1,641 more persons were recorded as having departed from the Cayman Islands than had arrived, with a peak of 391 in the single year 1924, and a total of 760 in the three years 1927–29.[14]

Of the perhaps 3,500 Caymanians who emigrated between 1891 and 1931, probably two-thirds were headed for the United States. As Commissioner Hutchings noted in the later 1920s, the flow towards the United States continued for a long time despite increasing immigration restrictions beginning in 1917.[15] Caymanians probably benefited from a preference on the part of U.S. immigration authorities for lighter-skinned West Indians. They were also more likely than many other would-be immigrants to be literate, and so were less affected by the rules excluding those unable to read and write.[16] But the main factor assisting them was that Caymanians could often prove family connections to persons with bona fide United States citizenship. The relative willingness of Caymanians to marry Americans, and vice versa, also explains the comparatively rapid growth of Caymanian communities in the United States.

From the first decade of the twentieth century onward, there was scarcely a Caymanian family that did not have a branch in the United States. This represented a sharp change of focus in the overseas Caymanian network that began with the first migrations in the 1830s, after emancipation. The movements of the first two generations of Kirkconnells during the earlier period, for example, as represented by William Kirkconnell and his son Walter, were normally within the western Caribbean, including Cayman, Jamaica, Honduras, and Belize. The generation that followed was more closely linked to the United States. Four of Walter's sons migrated to Tampa after World War One, leaving their sister, Gyda, to run the family grocery store on Cayman Brac with her husband. From Tampa the brothers ran a small fleet of large schooners, some built on Cayman Brac, the rest bought in Jamaica or the United States. The Depression hit them hard, however, and all returned to Cayman Brac not long after the island had been devastated by the 1932 hurricane.

Stronger ties between Cayman and the United States meant an increase in the influence that the U.S. exerted upon the Cayman Islands and their people. Despite this, Caymanians continued to regard Cayman as their true

home and heartland, however far or long they ventured abroad. They remained loyal to the British Empire and its monarchy. This outlook was amply demonstrated during this era by their response to the outbreak of World War One and by their continuing belief in the empire during the 1920s and 1930s – even as parts of that empire, including Jamaica, were witnessing the first steps towards independence.

THE WAR YEARS

News of the outbreak of war on 4 August 1914 did not reach the Cayman Islands for more than a week, and the war itself was to have almost no direct impact on the islands. But the response to Britain's decision to fight was unequivocal. At the opening of the Legislative Assembly on 16 September 1914, the Justices and Vestry passed a unanimous motion

> . . . most respectfully to convey to His Excellency the Governor, and through him to the Right Honourable the Secretary of State for the Colonies, an expression of the unswerving loyalty and devotion of the inhabitants of these Islands to the Throne and Person of their Sovereign Lord King George V, whom God preserve, and their earnest sympathy with His Majesty and the mother country in the terrible war forced upon them by the German Empire, in which they recognize that the British Government is defending its treaty obligations and its honour. God save the King.[17]

This motion was backed up with the vote of a hundred guineas in aid of the War Fund. Further donations were made, and by the war's end Cayman's total contribution amounted to £450 – about 10 per cent of government revenues for the year 1918.[18]

There was no system of conscription in the British West Indies. But unlike the other British colonies and dependencies, the Cayman Islands did not send a contingent to join the British West India Regiment in Jamaica. A few Caymanians abroad – in Jamaica, Canada, and the United States (when they entered the war in April 1917) – chose to enlist. In January 1916, however, some three hundred Caymanians signed up when a government notice asked for the names, addresses, and qualifications of white and coloured seamen willing to serve in the British merchant navy for the duration of the war – though registration by itself did not guarantee immediate employment.[19] It was not until the German submarine campaign intensified and the United States entered the war that such opportunities were realised.

Indirectly, the first three years of war brought considerable hardship to the Cayman Islands, which was intensified by serious hurricanes in 1915 and 1917. The modest government surplus for 1913–14 was soon wiped out, as the value of exports fell from £8,600 to £1,800 during the next year. The trade in tortoiseshell, which was mostly to mainland Europe, collapsed, while the trade in live turtles was hit by the difficulties of getting the animals to market. The steamship service between Jamaica and Tampa was discontinued. Within a year, the value of imports fell from £26,000 to £17,000. An additional blow was the loss of sales of postage stamps to philatelists.[20]

Commissioner Robinson did what he could to improve conditions, with limited success. He pushed ahead with pre-war plans to set up a turtle canning factory at George Town. This enterprise was sponsored by the local merchant Timothy McTaggart with capital from a New York importer. "It is to be hoped that this will be but the beginning of still further undertakings," wrote Robinson, "which will be the means of introducing capital together with new and progressive ideas among a far too conservative race of people who seem afraid to deviate one iota from the beaten track and whom it is most difficult to move from their apparent lethargy."[21] The factory was built in June 1915, and in its first month of operation five hundred turtles were processed, producing 960 cases of twenty-four cans apiece. In November 1915, though, Robinson had to report that sales were disappointing. Shipments to Europe were out of the question, and two-thirds of all cans remained unsold at New York.[22]

Commissioner Robinson encouraged Caymanian farmers to make the islands more self-sufficient in foodstuffs. He also hoped to improve the production of coconuts and introduce the cultivation of sisal and citrus fruit, in view of wartime demands for copra, rope, and lime juice. But he later had to report that bud-rot made it virtually impossible to grow coconuts in Grand Cayman, and that crops were being damaged by "rabbits" (agoutis) and land crabs. Worse still were the effects of two hurricanes. The first, in August 1915, destroyed almost all the bananas and ground provisions in all three islands. But the 1917 hurricane was even more devastating. It flooded Grand Cayman, and in the Sister Islands it stripped the vegetation bare and destroyed 98 per cent of the seven thousand or so coconut trees, as well as three-quarters of the houses.[23]

Wartime deprivation was also reported in the first proper medical survey of the islands, carried out between April and June 1917 by Dr. John Lee Hydrick of the International Health Board of New York. His work was backed up by the reports of Dr. George N. Overton, the able new Chief Medical Officer. Hydrick had set out to study hookworm disease, but his 49-page report covered much more. It described

The turtle canning factory in George Town, 1917.

all three islands and included useful photographs and comments on wartime conditions. "There is a great scarcity of ground provisions throughout [Grand Cayman] at present," he wrote, "and we are threatened with a meat famine. On two recent market days there was no meat of any kind. With the entry of America into the war, the price of wheat flour and meals has begun to show an upward tendency, and there is danger of shorter and more uncertain supplies."[24]

The most glaring issues identified in the report were ignorance of hygiene, the unsanitary condition of toilet facilities and water supplies, and the mosquitoes. "After a heavy rain," wrote Hydrick, "the [mosquitoes], including *Anopheles*, *Culex* and *Stegomyia*, appear in such quantities that if one ventures out of a screened house after sunset he must wear a head-net and gloves for comfort." A law of 1912 had provided for the construction of a latrine for every house in George Town, but this had not been enforced or extended to other districts. Given these conditions, it was surprising that typhoid and malaria were not more common than they were.[25]

Unsanitary toilets and polluted water supplies caused widespread worm infestations, with ankylostomiasis (hookworms) affecting 20 per cent of the population overall. The prevalence was lowest in East End, Bodden Town, Spotts, and Little Cayman, where facilities were better than adequate, and highest in North Side and West Bay. West Bay had few latrines and polluted groundwater, and 38 per cent of its residents had hookworm disease.[26]

Dr. Overton at first identified the mosquito as the worst health menace, though he later became concerned about the effects of worm infestations. The malaria-carrying *Anopheles* mosquito was almost non-existent. But the *Culex* remained "an intolerable pest", and the cost of eradicating it by draining the swamps was quite beyond the islands' treasury. Both the CMO and the Commissioner advocated the more general use of screens, which had only

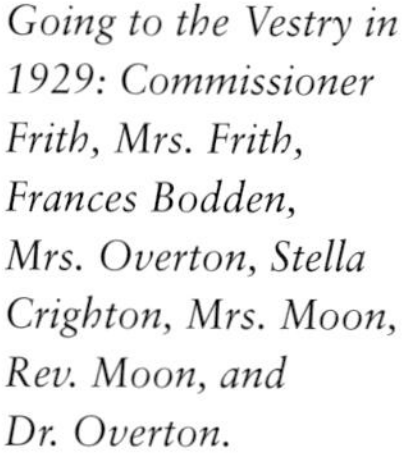

Going to the Vestry in 1929: Commissioner Frith, Mrs. Frith, Frances Bodden, Mrs. Overton, Stella Crighton, Mrs. Moon, Rev. Moon, and Dr. Overton.

recently been introduced into the houses of the well-to-do. Dr. Overton was a keen advocate of hygiene, noting that "the mass of the people is still mediaeval in their ideas of what conduces to health, and the preaching of the hygienist will meet a violent opponent in their deep-seated traditions". Most shocking of all, though, was his report of dental conditions. He claimed that "70–75% of the people wear false teeth . . . which is largely the result of a spongy disorder of the gums, causing the teeth to loosen and in many instances necessitating complete extraction of the sound ones." This affliction, he surmised, was evidence of incipient scurvy.[27] More positively, the islands' isolation often preserved them from epidemics – for example, the devastating effects of the worldwide influenza epidemic of 1918.[28]

THE HUTCHINGS REGIME

Commissioner Robinson was followed, after a brief interim, by Hugh Houston Hutchings, who was to be the longest-serving of all Caymanian Commissioners (1919–31). Bluff, outspoken, and generally easygoing, Hutchings was above all a realist. Born in Turks and Caicos, he was already fifty years old in 1919, with ten children, the youngest of whom was four. He had agreed to take up the Commissioner's post only after it was made pensionable and the salary raised from £300 to £400 a year. Once he arrived, he was shocked to find that the cost of living had doubled since 1913, and he felt bound to negotiate a further salary increase.[29]

One positive aspect of recent inflation was that it doubled the value of government revenue from imports and the sale of postage stamps. The islands' budget remained comfortably balanced throughout the 1920s, ranging between £6,000 and £8,000 a year.[30] As a result, official salaries were increased and the plan for compulsory education was finally implemented in 1920.

Commissioner H.H. Hutchings.

The Town Hall, George Town: venue for official meetings and social occasions, 1938.

Funds were also found to construct a "simple but commodious building" as a Peace Memorial in George Town, which served as court-house, Assembly room, and town hall. Construction was completed at a cost of £2,000 and the building was formally opened on Armistice Day, 11 November 1926.

The ending of World War One did not lead to any rapid local changes, and the dreamy ambience of this period has been well captured by Aarona Booker Kohlman in her book *Under Tin Roofs*.[31] But both the war and its aftermath expanded horizons for many Caymanians. This experience was generally positive, without the heightened awareness of racial and colonial oppression that led West Indians elsewhere to mutiny, riot, and join radical political movements.[32] Caymanians, by contrast, seemed prepared to accept conditions in the Cayman Islands during the decade after the war, rather than agitate for change.

Living standards during the 1920s improved, due to remittances from Caymanians settled abroad, and to the wages and consumer goods brought back by temporary migrants. Imports were worth two or three times the value of exports. More motor cars and trucks were imported (the first car having been introduced in 1914), so that by the mid-1930s there were "41 cars and seven lorries and five motor cycles. The main roads, however, remained sandy lanes and other roads were bridle paths." By 1922 there was a daily mail service between West Bay, George Town, and Bodden Town in a gov-

Two kinds of transport meet on the road from Newlands to George Town in the 1920s.

ernment truck, which doubled as a nine-passenger bus. Individuals brought in electricity generators and even a small ice plant, but the government did not install a central generating plant. George Town obtained a modest telephone network with lines extended to West Bay and Bodden Town, and a private line also ran the length of Cayman Brac. But the proposal that the Cayman Islands should be linked to the outside world by radio was once more turned down on the grounds of cost and lack of sufficient demand.[33]

Shipping communications were very slow to improve. By the mid-1920s, ten of the fifty-nine sailing vessels registered in the Cayman Islands were powered by auxiliary engines. Well over two hundred vessels entered and cleared the islands each year, and steamships stopped two or three times a year in each direction.[34] The inter-island boats provided a service that was intermittent, unreliable, and, for passengers, extremely uncomfortable.

It was not that the needs of the Cayman Islands were unclear, or that there were no men of enterprise willing to propose solutions. In 1921, a committee consisting of E.S. Parsons, Dr. Roy McTaggart, and Rayal Bodden explored the possibility of a regular, subsidised service for mail, freight, and passengers. This would connect all three Cayman Islands with Kingston and Tampa, including a stop at the Isle of Pines. But the project foundered when it was learned that constructing an adequate vessel in Grand Cayman would cost at least £7,000, and that the only bid they had received required an annual subsidy of £720 a year. To pay for the project, import duties would have to be raised from 8.5 to 10 per cent. The committee doubted that the service would be commercially viable.[35]

Throughout the early 1920s, Commissioner Hutchings pressed for a regular, subsidised service. The solution was not found until the means existed to construct a custom-built boat through private enterprise, and until the Jamaican government offered to match a £300 subsidy from the Vestry. In 1926, Dr. McTaggart and others established the Cayman Islands Motor Boat Company, which, with a guaranteed subsidy of £600 a year, commissioned Rayal Bodden to build a 120-ton motor ship at his George Town yard on North Church Street. Launched to great rejoicing early in 1927, the handsome *Cimboco* (named after the company's initials) was to become the best-known locally built motor vessel in Caymanian history.[36]

The arrival of the motorboat Cimboco, *1938.*

Carrying twenty first-class passengers, twelve deck passengers, and a crew of eleven besides the captain, the *Cimboco*

The launching of the Lady Slater, *1934.*

ran a three-weekly service between Grand Cayman, Little Cayman, Cayman Brac, and Kingston, Jamaica. It maintained this schedule with admirable regularity for two decades. The success of the *Cimboco* led to the construction of two other motor vessels to serve the Cayman Islands: the *Lady Slater* (also built by Rayal Bodden for the same company) and the *Nunoca* (built by Heber Arch Sr.). Though both concentrated on the Kingston–Grand Cayman–Tampa route, they were to an extent competitors to the *Cimboco*. The older vessel, however, outlasted them both. The *Nunoca* was mysteriously lost at sea with all hands in July 1936, and the *Lady Slater* burned in Kingston Harbour in September 1940.[37] The *Cimboco* was the first – and for a long time the only – vessel to provide a regular and reliable service linking all three islands with each other and with Jamaica.

PROHIBITION – THE CAYMANIAN APPROACH

Given that Caymanians traditionally took advantage of whatever chance offered – even if it sometimes pushed the limits of legality – it is not surprising that the opportunity to smuggle liquor through the U.S. blockade during Prohibition (1919–33) held a certain local attraction. Commissioner Hutchings looked with apparent favour on such activities as a way of enriching the island treasury. Official revenue figures in fact showed dramatic effects for a couple of years, and unofficial sources point to an illicit flow over a longer period. Nevertheless, Caymanians were never rum-runners on the scale of Bahamians, Cubans, or Bermudians, and the effects of rum-running on the Cayman Islands were nowhere near as significant as in those islands. This was primarily the result of local opposition on moral grounds, led by forces in the Presbyterian and Baptist churches.

Located as close as fifty miles to the United States coast, the Bahamas led the way in the bootlegging business. By 1921 there were more than thirty bonded warehouses in Nassau, Bimini, and Grand Bahama, owned by two dozen new liquor firms. Government revenue from re-exports of liquor rose from almost zero in 1918 to more than a million pounds in 1923, and remained above half a million until 1930. Profits for the main operators were several times these amounts. Many hundreds of men and women were

employed as crewmen, packers, and stevedores, and the effects amounted to one of the most frenetic economic booms in Bahamian history. However, as critics pointed out, rum-running was accompanied by public disorder, rising crime, and, according to local pastors, moral breakdown in society.[38]

Early in 1923, an American named Sanford visited George Town and persuaded Commissioner Hutchings and certain merchants to allow Grand Cayman to become a liquor entrepôt, or storage site for goods in transit. Liquor could be legally imported into the island from any part of the world, held in bond, and then transshipped at the bootleggers' convenience, upon payment of a reasonable export duty. The benefits of charging a fee merely for providing a service to foreign traders seemed indisputable.

Accordingly, Hutchings and his allies easily persuaded the Assembly to pass Law No. 2 of 1923, which allowed the free entry of "all wines, spirits and spirituous liquors", subject only to a duty of two shillings and sixpence a gallon upon their re-export. The immediate results were startling. The official value of Caymanian imports in 1923 and 1924 (£139,746) was twice what it had been in the two previous years, and the value of exports (£69,670) almost three times as much. These figures were accounted for entirely by a hundredfold increase in the import of liquor and its subsequent re-export. The benefit to the treasury was not quite so dramatic, some £750 a year. But, as Commissioner Hutchings argued, this more than made up the shortfall from other sources, particularly the sale of postage stamps.[39]

The normal procedure was for the liquor to arrive from Cuba, Haiti, or Jamaica in bulk. It was held in bond on the wharf, repackaged in smaller barrels or cases of bottles, and then, its duty paid, shipped off in small vessels towards the United States. These vessels would be cleared either for the Bahamas or simply for "the high seas". The former was preferable because, in case of detention by U.S. coastal patrols, the captain could give an authentic destination that was still within the bootlegging network.

But the shocking presence of so much liquor piled on George Town's waterfront galvanised some Caymanians. A vigorous campaign led by the Presbyterian ministers R.N. Dickson and J.S. Blackman and the Senior Magistrate W.C. Watler, a Presbyterian elder, argued that "wives and daughters will be unable to walk the streets" because of the presence of disreputable bootleggers, that "young men will be made drunkards", and that "only a few will benefit, and the mass of the people will get nothing".[40] The campaign was successful, at least on the surface. Official imports and exports plummeted in 1925, with the numbers of vessels cleared for either the Bahamas or "the high seas" falling from dozens to zero.[41]

Hutchings and Parsons, though, did not give up. In 1925 they proposed that the transshipment trade be encouraged by the construction of a substantial bonded warehouse that would control the traffic more efficiently

and shield the liquor from the public's sight. The general election of 1926 was fought on the issue, with the anti-bootlegging forces putting up candidates in all the key constituencies. In the heat of debate, Pastor Dickson even accused Hutchings of being in the bootleggers' pay. He evidently went too far, because nearly all the prohibitionist candidates were defeated, and Dickson himself received not a single vote.

This success led Hutchings to write confidentially to the Governor of Jamaica on 18 August 1926, eloquently arguing for a controlled system of liquor re-export. Though the proposal would circumvent Prohibition and might be regarded as smuggling, it was no more than the policy already being followed by the Bahamas, Bermuda, and British Honduras. Hutchings argued that the increase in government revenue would fund much-needed improvements in education and communications. It would also help redress the huge imbalance of trade with the United States. It could even make up for the lack of funds from Caymanians who would not be able to migrate to the United States if immigration restrictions were tightened.

Perhaps surprisingly, Commissioner Hutchings and his allies did not win their case. On a visit to Jamaica late in 1926, Hutchings was apparently persuaded by Governor Edward Stubbs to drop the plans to make Grand Cayman a rum-running entrepôt. The proposed bonded warehouse was not built, and the official imports of liquor fell to no more than the few hundred gallons needed for local consumption, with no re-exports at all. The prohibitionists found some justification for their views: indictable crimes, which had doubled from 56 in 1920–21 to 110 in 1922–3, fell back to 52 in 1924–5.[42]

TURNING TO THE LAND

Many Caymanians held out hopes during the 1920s that their islands might yield profits in the form of oil deposits. This proved a delusion. But it did make Caymanians aware for the first time of the potential value of the land on which they lived, and of the chaotic state of land tenure, ownership, surveying, and registration.

The internal combustion engine and the military requirements of World War One had intensified the demand for oil, especially close to the United States. The Cayman Islands, at the fractured edge of a vast limestone peneplain, seemed to entrepreneurs to be a promising source. As early as December 1920, an American named Hiram W. Hixon requested permission from the Commissioner and Assembly to prospect for oil and to be granted rights to any that he found. A persuasive negotiator, over the next two years he obtained an agreement and moved ahead. The scheme, however, provoked consternation in the Colonial Office. Who owned the land? Was anything at all known of the geology of the islands? Commissioner Hutchings explained the system of landholding and the nature of the proposal. "It is a curious situation," he wrote on 17 November 1922.

> The Cayman Islands are roughly four-fifths in the hands of small proprietors, and one-fifth in Crown possession. An American prospector has recently visited the Island and wishes to prospect for oil. The landowners (being the electorate) met together informally under the presidency of the Commissioner and drafted an agreement, under which the prospector was to have the lease of the entire sub soil rights of the Island and be free to enter any lands for the purpose of prospecting, drilling etc.
>
> In return for this the prospector was to pay a certain percentage of the market price of the petroleum exported into the Treasury, and the Treasury, after paying the expenses of a survey so as to determine the boundaries of the landowners' property, would divide the proceeds proportional among the various landowners, retaining a certain percentage for the proportion due on Crown property.[43]

After Commissioner Hutchings received tentative approval from Governor Probyn in January 1923, Hixon designed and circulated copies of an oil lease agreement. He gave 490 copies to individuals in Grand Cayman and 400 to Collector Aston Rutty for distribution in the Sister Islands. The documents, which called for the number of acres claimed and their precise location, immediately led to disputes, mainly over the extent and boundaries of the claimed land.

The original land grants of 1735–41 suggested that landowners held rights to all minerals except gold and silver, subject only to a royalty of 5 per cent. Reviewing these documents, the Colonial Office raised a number of tricky questions. Did people who held land tenure simply by "squatter's rights" also hold mineral rights? Was the proposed plan legal and properly approved? Would the signing of agreements by a majority of landowners give the Commissioner authority to sign for the rest? Who owned the shallow waters around the islands, and could they too be leased? What recourse would a lessee have if landowners repudiated their signatures once oil was discovered, or if new claimants to the land appeared?[44] Despite these doubts, the Board of Trade gave approval in principle in March 1923.[45]

Accordingly, the Caymanian Assembly passed a carefully worded Oil Exploration Law (No. 5 of 1924), which included a 28-page set of Oil Mining Regulations. Early in 1924, the Assembly invited the government geologist of Jamaica, Dr. C.A. Matley, to survey the islands' geology and prospects for oil. Matley's report was carefully noncommittal. Nonetheless, the Commissioner wrote in the 1924 Annual Report that islanders were encouraged by the fact that "there have been found for many years, and more recently in increasing quantities, on the shores of the islands or floating nearby, a semi-liquid bituminous material supposed by some to be exudations from a submarine vent in the adjacent ocean". Others, he added, thought that

these were merely "the slowly solidifying bunker cleanings of oil-burning ships traversing the surrounding Caribbean".[46]

Hiram Hixon pursued his explorations for some time. He was eventually joined by another American, G.D. Nash, and an American firm misleadingly called Trinidad Leaseholds Limited.[47] But all drillings came up absolutely dry. With the failure of the hoped-for bonanza, the value of the land evaporated, leaving the questions of land tenure and precise surveys unresolved for another fifty years.

By August 1926, Commissioner Hutchings was expressing his concern to the Governor of Jamaica about the tightening of United States immigration restrictions. He told of three schooners that had recently returned from Tampa and the Gulf ports, each carrying thirty-five would-be labourers, that had been "warned out" by the immigration authorities. Although emigration to the United States continued, within another two years the restrictions had become much tighter. Caymanians, who "because of their industry, sobriety, and general good behaviour" had previously been "well received as dock and barge labourers, mechanics and clerks in the seaports of the Gulf of Mexico", were no longer welcome. "Emigration, save that of seamen who find deep-sea employment in the ports of the Gulf, is now restricted to small numbers who seek work in Honduras and other Central American Republics."[48]

The Great Depression that followed the stock market collapse in October 1929 sharply reduced employment opportunities on ocean-going vessels out of American ports. It also affected employment on American-owned plantations and mines in Central America. And the new hard times, of course, affected Caymanians who had settled in the United States. When Commissioner Hutchings retired in 1931, Caymanian men were almost unable to migrate to the United States for work, while some of those who had been employed there were trickling back home, placing a heavy pressure on the islands' limited resources. This was the sombre situation when the hurricane of November 1932 struck the islands with sickening force.[49]

THE STORM OF '32

Despite ominous barometric signs, the onslaught was not expected because of a strongly held belief that the hurricane season ended on 20 October. In addition, the storm was preceded by a week of gales, rain, and high seas from the southeast as the storm gradually crossed the Caribbean well to the south of the islands. At that point, however, it turned and travelled northeast until it struck Cayman. "None of the old sea captains would agree that it was coming here," noted Captain Keith Tibbetts, "because it never had been known for a hurricane to travel on a course east of north."[50]

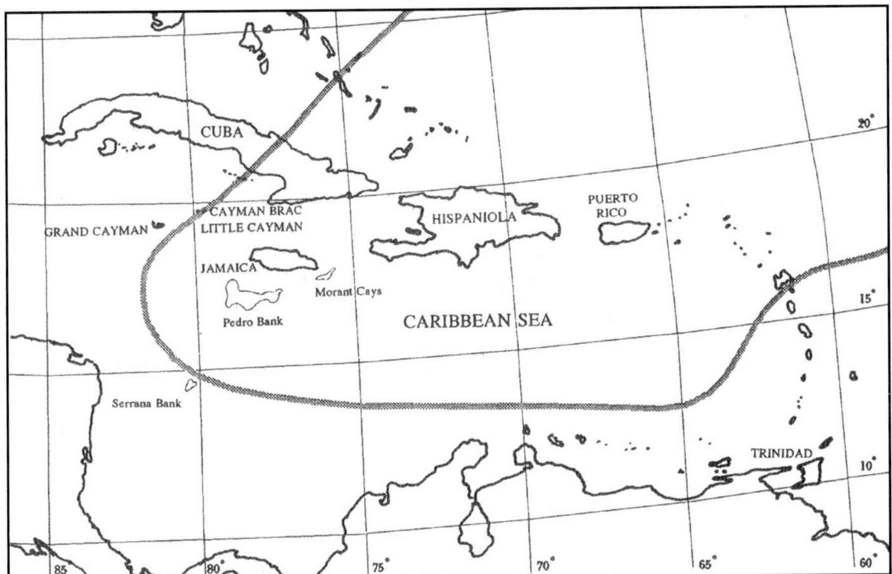

The path of the 1932 hurricane between 31 October and 12 November.

The hurricane struck first at Grand Cayman at dawn on Monday, 7 November. Its impact was worst along the south coast, with huge waves washing over the land and magnifying the damage caused by the wind. Only one life was lost, but some sixty houses were destroyed and 250 people made homeless. Two-thirds of all provision grounds were said to be ruined. The steamship *Balboa*, seeking shelter on a voyage from Port Arthur, Texas, to Jamaica with a cargo of lumber, kerosene, and motor oils, foundered and sank off George Town. Three schooners in South Sound, the *Diamond, Klosking*, and *William Bloomfield*, were also total losses. Yet what hit Grand Cayman was only the fringe of a greater tempest. Even as they counted their losses, some knowledgeable people feared that the fate of the Sister Islands would be worse. Commenting on the awful boiling thunderclouds and flickering lightning on the horizon, one elderly man said, "Well, I'm afraid, when you hear from Cayman Brac it will be a sad tale."[51]

This was no understatement. By the time the hurricane reached the Sister Islands, winds were as high as two hundred miles per hour, and waves were washing far up the 140-foot Bluff on Cayman Brac. Though after the event Brackers told of ominous signs – the arrival of many exhausted seabirds on the south side and the march of myriad young crabs up to the Bluff – the people were almost unprepared for their ordeal. Most had made no move to flee to what shelter the island offered. Nearly all the houses on Cayman Brac were strung along the north coastal ridge, sheltered from the south by the Bluff, and separated from the Bluff by an inland hollow. The wind struck first from the southeast on the evening of Tuesday, 8 November, awesome in its power. But it was as nothing compared with the fury that followed. At midnight it was dead calm as the eye passed directly overhead. Then the winds turned, and hit the island again from the north. Around two in the morning, winds

Fleeing the storm surge on Cayman Brac.

and waves of unimagined ferocity struck the north side of Cayman Brac, blowing the wooden houses away like chaff while flooding the inland hollow and cutting the survivors off from safety.

Those who took shelter in the sturdiest houses fared among the worst, for huge ocean rollers battered the most strongly built structures to pieces, crushing as well as drowning people. Halfway through the storm's most violent phase, it was clear that the only salvation lay in the caves in the Bluff, where the most prudent had taken shelter during the midnight lull. Crouching low in a wind that threatened to blow people into the air like kites, trying to judge the troughs of the huge inland waves, and swimming and scrambling as best they could, families tried to cross the few hundred yards of debris-laden water that lay between them and safety. Those who were successful huddled together in half a dozen caves, bruised, bedraggled, grieving for those they knew were dead, and fearful for those whom they had lost track of in their flight.[52]

The hurricane was to cause greater loss of life when it passed on to the more populous island of Cuba, but the devastation it left in the Sister Islands was almost complete. Virtually all of the houses in Cayman Brac, and most of those in Little Cayman, were uninhabitable. All the trees left standing were stripped bare, and all the provision grounds ruined. Of just over a thousand persons then resident on Cayman Brac, sixty-nine were dead: forty-nine drowned, eleven crushed, five dead from injuries and wounds, and four "not found". Twenty-nine of the dead were children under ten, including eight babes in arms. Some of the bodies were buried in a mass grave. Others, found later and already decomposing, were burned under the orders of the resolute Collector Aston Rutty.[53]

View of Spot Bay from inside Peter's Cave.

Nor was this the complete toll. Many Caymanian boats were out at sea and encountered the hurricane at the Serrana Banks and the Pedro Cays, and off the coast of Cuba. After an agony of waiting, three vessels were found to have been lost with all hands. These were the turtling schooner *Carmena*, captained

by Nelson Jackson, with twenty-five crewmen and rangers aboard, the yawl *Melpomene*, captained by James Ryan, with six crewmen, and the schooner *Fernwood*, captained by C.P. McLaughlin, with five crewmen and a stewardess. Besides the eight to twelve seamen "missing and believed dead" off Cuba, Cayman Brac alone had lost 108 people, including about one in five of the community's adult males.[54]

Almost miraculously, there had been no loss of life on Little Cayman. But the survivors of the storm there were in little better shape than those on Cayman Brac – without shelter, fresh food, or drinkable water. In such a small and interrelated community as the Sister Islands, mourning was shared along with privation. Like many Brackers of her generation, almost sixty years later Eleanor Grant Bodden of Cayman Brac mourned the loss of nineteen of her family, most of them buried in a common grave.[55] Little Cayman confronted another horror. The storm excavated the cemetery, disinterring the dead and scattering their bodies along the shore, and even into wells and cisterns. For days the people faced the anguish and grief of collecting, identifying, and reburying the dismembered remains of family members who had died in previous months and years.[56]

As the islands had no means of communication with each other or with the outside world except by ship, news of the disaster was delayed. Although help came as quickly as possible, the Sister Islanders were left in the direst straits for almost a week. The first ship to arrive was the Webster steamer *Husvik*, stopping at Cayman Brac while on its way to check on the fate of its sister ship *Balboa*. The *Husvik* transmitted the news on its wireless, so it reached Jamaica and even England before reaching Grand Cayman. Commissioner Ernest Weston in George Town did not learn of the devastation on the Sister Islands until the morning of Saturday, 12 November, when he was on the point of leaving in the chartered *Nunoca* to inspect the damage and bring help to East End. Immediately the *Nunoca*, with relief supplies including fresh water, was redirected to Cayman Brac.[57]

Commissioner E.A. Weston.

By this time, help was also on its way from Jamaica. The *Cimboco*, whose Captain, Ashlan Foster, was a Bracker, had remained in Kingston while the hurricane threatened. Now he made full speed for Cayman Brac. There (finding his house destroyed but his family alive) Foster ordered all the food and other supplies on the *Cimboco* to be landed, including the majority consigned to Grand Cayman. The Royal Mail Line steamer *Loch Katrine* arrived soon afterward, directed at the request of acting Governor Jelf, with further relief supplies. Between them, the *Cimboco* and *Loch Katrine* carried to Kingston more than fifty refugees from the Sister Islands who had relatives in Jamaica.[58]

Nor was the British government remiss. Alerted from Jamaica at its base in Bermuda, the cruiser HMS *Dragon* arrived off Cayman Brac on the morn-

Mr. Aston Rutty, M.B.E., Mrs. Rutty, and son, Burns.

ing of 17 November. It bore messages of condolence from the King and Colonial Office and, more practically, much-needed medical supplies, tents, and fresh water. The *Dragon's* doctor and medical orderlies helped the over-worked CMO Dr. Overton and Dr. Murray of the *Loch Katrine* to treat the hundred casualties, carrying the four most seriously injured on with them to Jamaica. The sailors used the ship's pumps to sluice out polluted cisterns and helped build temporary accommodations.

The captain found the food situation already well in hand, was full of praise for the work of Collector Rutty (who was later awarded the M.B.E. for his efforts), and was impressed in general by the people's spirit. "All who have come in contact with them have been much struck by the fortitude, courage, and cheerfulness displayed by the inhabitants, many of whom have seen their homes and belongings completely washed away," he wrote in his report. "This island [Cayman Brac] has been reduced to a desert. The road is a slope of loose coral, not a tree carries a leaf, the cultivated land is salted, many boats have been lost, of twenty motor cars one remains." What struck him most was the complete absence of radio or cable communication on the islands. He pointed out that even the most isolated islands of the Bahamas had wireless-telegraphy radio sets, and fresh batteries were brought in by every mailboat.[59]

The *Dragon's* captain was particularly touched by the fifty or sixty people of Little Cayman, who were camping out in the remains of the four houses left standing. After Guy Banks, the local J.P., had offered an address of gratitude, the people bravely sang the National Anthem. Further help came, including a grant of £1,000 from the imperial government and nearly as much from relief funds set up in Jamaica, Belize, and Trinidad. The garrison in Jamaica sent tents and blankets, and Messrs. J.S. Webster a hundred barrels of flour. Commissioner Weston came twice, Dr. Overton stayed as long as he was needed, and the builder Loxley Arch was sent from Grand Cayman to make a report of the damage and provide what help he could in rebuilding. Even before Arch's report came in, consignments of planking, nails, and other building materials were on their way from Grand Cayman.

Most significant for all three Cayman Islands was the way people forgot their differences and worked together to overcome the disaster. Though hard hit themselves, people in Grand Cayman sent materials and even went up to the Sister Islands to lend a hand without pay. As for the Sister Islanders, the memories of selfless cooperation were as lasting as those of the horrors of the storm. More than a half century later, Mrs. Veronica Smith recalled:

It was a long time before they started to get things back together, you know to get homes built up. . . . And everybody working together, helping one another build back homes and all like that. . . . and when they began, the ships would have to come bring lumber. You didn't buy it then, you know, Government gave you the lumber to get your home, and then the carpenters would all volunteer to try build one another's houses, because the island was poor, distressed, no money-making. Nobody could go out to work and say they're going to bring in a paycheck. Everyone had to live in love and unity and help one another get a shelter.[60]

But even if, as was frequently said, the storm made the community stronger by testing it so severely, the trauma, mental as well as material, took years to mend. Among the losses were almost all the official records stored in the Collector's office at Cayman Brac. This was one of the reasons that no Annual Report was published for 1932. The Annual Report for 1933 stated that Cayman Brac was "still only just recovering from the effects of the visitation" in terms of rebuilding houses and roads and replanting farms, and that all the islands were still suffering severe health problems. Apart from those killed by the storm, there had been more than the usual number of deaths, both among the very young and the very old. Twenty-five infants died in 1933, compared with only thirty-one for the three years 1929–31, and forty-six people over the age of seventy-five died that year. In all, the death rate for 1933 was 29 per thousand, nearly three times the average over the previous decade.[61]

"No reason for the deterioration can be offered other than the hurricane of November 1932," stated the annual report for 1933. Polluted water supplies and insufficient and poor food had led to a huge increase in intestinal complaints. In May 1933 the government dispenser in Cayman Brac reported ten times the usual number of gastrointestinal cases, and of 107 persons whom Dr. Overton examined on his annual visit, "72 showed chronic intestinal ailments, while the remainder were cases presenting functional disturbances caused by exposure to wet and cold". Grand Cayman suffered equally badly. There were forty cases of typhoid (compared to six in 1932 and fourteen in 1931) and no fewer than eight hundred cases of what Dr. Overton called "intestinal catarrh, ranging in clinical significance from a mild gastro-enteritis to a severe colitis". Many of the cases, "though of short duration presented alarming symptoms from the outset, with manifestations more pronounced in the very aged and the young".[62]

After the storm: the R.B. Leitch home, West End, Cayman Brac.

Dr. Overton also sensed that there was a psychosomatic malaise underlying the medical symptoms. He noted that "even at the end of 1933 the people of Cayman Brac were still suffering from a severe 'hurricane complex'". He concluded that in due course the level of health would improve "as the mental balance of those who experienced the assaults of the hurricane becomes restored". The level of general health did indeed improve, but the psychological effects of the '32 Storm lingered far longer. The events and losses of November 1932 remained etched on the minds of those who endured them for the rest of their lives. In 1990 Eleanor Grant Bodden, for example, reported that she still had nightmares about the storm and the deaths of loved ones. This was not an unusual reaction.[63]

The '32 Storm was a symbolic as well as a traumatic event for all Caymanians. It served, and still serves, as a benchmark of the disasters and privations of island living, and of the spirit of endurance and cooperation in adversity that is part of being Caymanian. In retrospect, the '32 Storm also marked a turning point, when the islands' fortunes were at their lowest ebb. Though the recovery at first was agonisingly slow, from November 1932, the way onward for the Cayman Islands in the twentieth century was almost bound to be upward.

Boyd Hydes, part of the long tradition of Caymanian music.

CHAPTER 13

Rhythms of Change in Peace and War

COMMISSIONER WESTON RETIRED PREMATURELY TOWARDS the end of 1933, a year or so after the terrible hurricane of 1932. His replacement, Allen Wolsey Cardinall, turned out to be among the most capable, vigorous, and eloquent of all Cayman's Commissioners. Cardinall steered the Cayman Islands through the Great Depression amidst the rising political unrest that was sweeping through British West Indian colonies in the late 1930s. Over the seven years of his administration (1934–41), he was tireless in the cause of modernising Cayman. He was the first Commissioner to promote tourism, and he oversaw the introduction of daily radio communication with the rest of the world. Though the outbreak of another world war curtailed some of his achievements, these were amply recognised in the form of a knighthood in 1943. His enthusiasm and accomplishments served as a model for postwar development in Cayman, while inspiring patriotism and hope during World War Two.

Allen Cardinall was by no means a typical colonial civil servant. He was a gentleman and a scholar who had gained a wide range of experience before entering the colonial service. Born in 1887, he was educated at Winchester, one of Britain's oldest and most prestigious private schools, and in Europe, where he became fluent in French and German. After working as a schoolmaster, he explored careers in stockbroking and journalism, working in Vancouver, Canada, and in Hawaii. He then joined the Colonial Office. At the outbreak of World War One he was sent to the Gold Coast as an Assistant District Commissioner, and he served there for eighteen years (1914–32).

Unmarried and with a reputation as something of an eccentric loner, Cardinall was described by the Gold Coast's Governor Guggisberg as "an able but difficult officer . . . not fit for promotion". His immediate superior, however, the Chief Commissioner of the Northern Territory, gave a different assessment: "He is an efficient District Commissioner, and takes a great interest in the Native customs and habits, which he writes about. He had his people, when in the Northern Province, under very good control, and he is decidedly a favourite with them. He is not a tidy man, either in his house or in his dress, and his ideas of discipline are nil. That is all there is against him, otherwise he is decidedly good."[1]

In 1932, when the Colonial Office was "retrenching", Cardinall was prematurely retired at the age of forty-five, on a paltry pension. His application for the Cayman Islands post occasioned a revealing exchange of confidential comments in the Colonial Office. "This is a dismal appointment to offer anyone except possibly a (healthy) pensioner with private means – and unmarried," wrote one official. Another commented: "This post is so full of drawbacks that any competent man who wants it at once becomes a strong candidate." Allen Cardinall was offered the post on 19 December 1933. He immediately accepted it, and arrived in George Town on 14 February 1934.[2]

Allen Cardinall's tenure confounded the pessimists and disarmed his detractors. Like his predecessors, he had problems with the Assembly and devised plans for its reform, but in the end he cannily preferred to leave it as it was. Cardinall thought that the Assembly was cumbersome and should be reduced to a quarter of its size. The members, he said, "will generally pass everything placed before them", even though they "often criticise the measures amongst themselves outside the Assembly once they have voted for them". Like Commissioner Weston, Cardinall seems to have concluded that the Assembly provided a useful sounding board that gave Caymanians a sense of democracy while presenting no serious obstacle to policies that the Commissioner wished to pursue.[3]

Cardinall won allies with a combination of candour, concessions, and charm. This approach is evident in an exchange of confidential letters with Aston Rutty, his deputy in the Sister Islands. Cardinall had visited Cayman Brac and Little Cayman in March 1934, shortly after his arrival. Later that year, Rutty complained of the difficulties of his official position when passing on complaints of governmental neglect. Cardinall accused him of "trivial parochialism", priggishness, and even self-pity. Rutty's role, said Cardinall, was not as the Brackers' representative but as spokesman for the government. He should be firmer and stronger. After his chiding, Cardinall changed tack. He apologised for his brusqueness, expressed some sympathy, and sent compliments to Mrs. Rutty. He also made some minor financial concessions to the Sister Islands, and confided in Rutty his general policy: belt-tightening measures were necessary to raise the credit of the Cayman Islands, with the aim of obtaining substantial imperial loans. He told Rutty to explain this to the Sister Islanders in his own words. He might even, wrote Cardinall magnanimously, hint that the policy came as much from himself as from the Commissioner.[4]

Thereafter, Commissioner Cardinall and Collector Rutty seem to have enjoyed mutual understanding and respect. Rutty was a spectator when several Brac boats and crews participated in the first Cayman Islands Regatta, held at George Town in January 1935. This was the beginning of Cardinall's imaginative plans for Caymanian development. As an avid sportsman, Cardinall foresaw that an annual regatta would showcase the superb boatbuilding and sailing skills of Caymanians, while bringing the islands and islanders together in friendly competition. Foreign yachtsmen might be attracted as spectators and in turn become customers for locally built vessels. Now that the turtling industry was suffering from depressed world prices and declining catches, opportunities like this needed to be explored.

Commissioner A. W. Cardinall (centre) with dignitaries in front of the Town Hall, George Town (left to right: Aston Rutty, Bertie Panton, Inspector Roddy Watler, Rev. Douce, Rev Hicks, Dr. Overton, Edgar Lyons, and unidentified man), ca 1936.

PROMOTING THE CAYMAN ISLANDS

With the enthusiastic cooperation of Edmund S. Parsons and Lieutenant-Colonel B. P. Dobson, one of the first expatriate part-time residents, Commissioner Cardinall formed the Cayman Islands Yacht and Sailing Club. The club's chief purpose was to organise the annual regatta. Within a few months, the CIYSC boasted seventy-three members, including thirty-four women. The members had put up eleven challenge cups as regatta trophies.[5] By the time of the third regatta in 1937, CIYSC membership had risen to 134. Dobson and Cardinall also revived the local Boy Scouts (started during the time of Commissioner Hirst) by re-forming them as two troops of Sea Scouts, one in George Town and the other in West Bay. By 1937 the two troops totalled eighty-two boys, with fifty-nine more in two packs of Cubs.[6]

Cardinall's annual regattas generated keen competition. Certain vessels, such as Conwell Watler's schooner *Goldfield* (built by H.E. Arch and Sons),

The George Town scout troop, ca. 1930s.

gained fame for their sleek lines and racing qualities. Each year before World War Two, the races were attended by Cuban and Canadian as well as British naval vessels and by increasing numbers of cruising yachtsmen. Some showed an interest in ordering island-built boats. "In my wanderings through the West Indies I have found that the schooners from your island were all of fine lines and admirably suited to my needs," wrote a wealthy New Yorker in April 1934 asking for an estimate. "Your reputation has travelled far as you may see." He added, "I am further activated in this request by the fact that you are known to build boats reasonably."[7]

Similar inquiries came from the Virgin Islands, the Bahamas, and the United Kingdom, and from as far afield as Kenya and the Gold Coast. However, despite extremely low construction costs – as little as £25 per foot for a completed vessel – few of the potential commissions came to fruition. Because of leisurely business and construction methods, lack of working capital, and the cost of delivery to distant parts, an official subsidy of some kind proved necessary, at least until the industry was more developed. For example, the 10-ton sailing vessel *Cayman* and the 20-ton motor schooner *Caymania* were ordered by a customer in England in 1936. They were not completed until 1938, and by the time they were shipped to England, they had cost 50 per cent more than their respective contracted prices of £900 and £1,000. Although the government provided a £300 subsidy, the project still lost £300.[8]

The schooner Rembro *and the* Caymanian *compete during the annual regatta.*

This experience did not quench Cardinall's enthusiasm for Caymanian boats or his eagerness to promote the Cayman Islands. His most original scheme was a plan for two Caymanian schooners to race each other across the Atlantic, arriving in the Clyde for the opening of the 1938 British Empire Exhibition in Glasgow. The plans got so far as to have an official in the Colonial Office comment: "The crazy idea, though probably quite impractical, is so attractive that I should not like to give it a cold shower bath until it has had a run." Apparently there were captains and crews willing to volunteer, but logistical problems and the deteriorating political situation in Europe scotched the venture.[9]

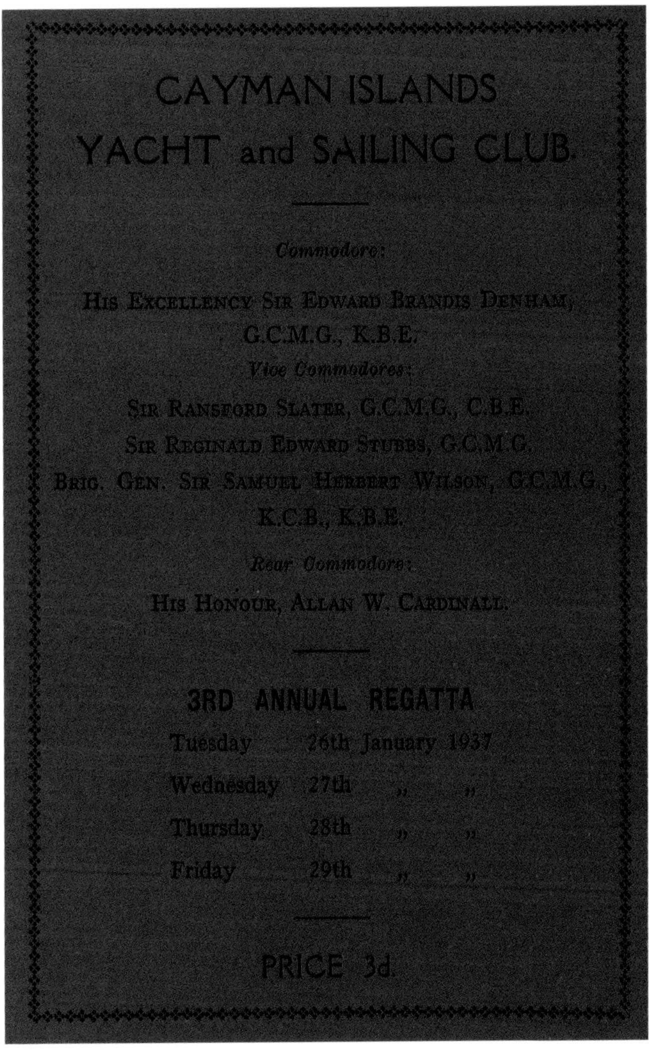

CAYMAN ISLANDS
YACHT and SAILING CLUB.

Commodore:

His Excellency Sir Edward Brandis Denham, G.C.M.G., K.B.E.

Vice Commodores:

Sir Ransford Slater, G.C.M.G., C.B.E.
Sir Reginald Edward Stubbs, G.C.M.G.
Brig. Gen. Sir Samuel Herbert Wilson, G.C.M.G., K.C.B., K.B.E.

Rear Commodore:

His Honour, Allan W. Cardinall.

3RD ANNUAL REGATTA

Tuesday 26th January 1937
Wednesday 27th " "
Thursday 28th " "
Friday 29th " "

PRICE 3d.

The programme of the Third Annual Regatta in 1937.

Cardinall's plans to promote tourism were more practical. He founded a Chamber of Commerce in 1935, to attract visitors and develop local business. He persuaded the Assembly to allocate a small sum for advertising. During his 1936 home leave he wrote articles about the islands and arranged for the first-ever visit of a cruise liner, the 16,000-ton SS *Atlantis*. This very successful event occurred on 22 February 1937. More than 340 of the 450 well-heeled passengers came ashore for the day. For the mostly elderly passengers, noted Cardinall, "Landing at a wharf such as we possess was deemed . . . the highest of adventures." Once safely on shore, they could view the island's sights (which included parrots, iguanas, a turtle crawl, and a working catboat), bathe in the sea, and sit in deck chairs on the beach under sunshades. They were regaled with rum cocktails, beer, and ice cream. Souvenirs of various kinds were on sale: tortoiseshell, sharkskin, and thatch-work, specially made picture postcards, and Spanish gold and silver coins said to have been recently unearthed in Cayman Brac.[10]

Under Commissioner Cardinall, the first law to encourage hotel development was passed. This was a visionary action that anticipated later tourism. The Cayman Islands Hotels Aid Law, 1937, allowed anyone building or extending hotel accommodation to import essential materials duty-free.

Despite much talk, however, no one took advantage of the legislation until after World War Two.

In order to supplement turtling, Cardinall actively encouraged shark fishing. The nurse shark, which abounded off the Central American coasts, was the main quarry. Sharks were snagged using nets operated by three-man teams usually working from catboats, which were carried to the fishing grounds on the decks of schooners. The season ran from July to November. By 1935, three hundred men and ninety catboats were engaged in shark fishing, producing about twelve thousand skins, which commanded from $1.50 to $2.50 each in the United States.[11]

Cardinall tried to develop this industry. He sought to improve sharkskin preparation, to market the parts of the shark that were usually thrown away, and to promote the sale of shark products in the United Kingdom and Europe. In 1936 he consulted with the manager of the main sharkskin importing firm in the City of London, Mr. A.R. Cotton, who informed him that skins treated only with salt could not be preserved on the long journey to Europe. Cotton recommended a more thorough method of curing using a German chemical preparation. He also put Cardinall in touch with a New Orleans firm that offered a market for the whole shark. Its oil and liver could be used for medicinal purposes, the best parts of the back meat for human consumption, the belly meat for pet food or fish meal, the intestines for making a special kind of glove, and the rest dried and ground up as fertiliser.[12]

Sharking in the 1930s: a man pulling a nurse shark into a dory.

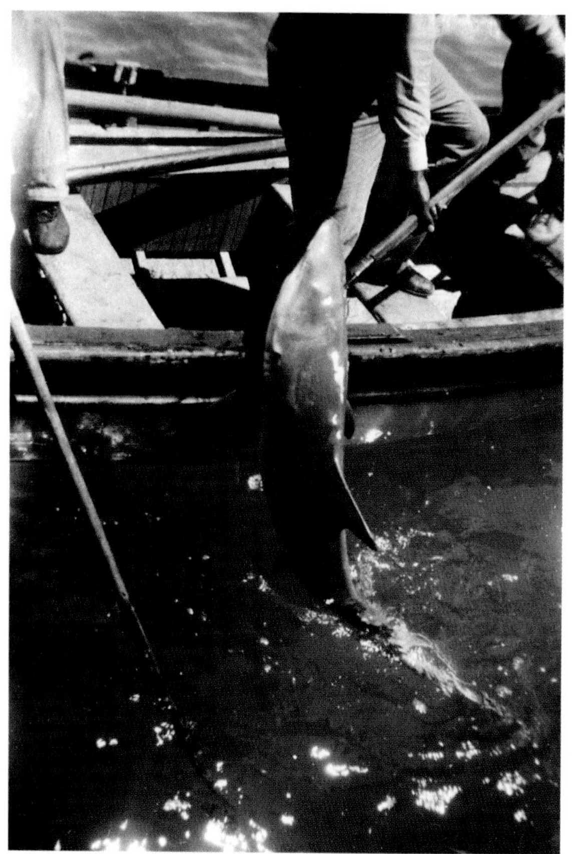

Shark fishing continued for more than a decade. In its best years, the exported skins earned half as much as the turtling industry or more. But the grounds were soon over-fished, and the fishermen found the trade increasingly difficult and dangerous. Because the fishing grounds were so far away and there was no local processing plant, Caymanians continued to export mainly the skins. Unfortunately, the market for skins, after a slight improvement in the later 1930s, was undercut first by the war and then by competition from plastics.[13]

Cardinall's efforts to promote shark fishing, along with several other small industries, helped to quicken the recovery of Cayman Brac and Little Cayman after the '32 Storm. Sister Islanders also fished for shark, at the same time as pursuing their traditional preference for hawksbill turtle. They brought back the sharkskins, cured with salt, directly to Cayman Brac. From there they were shipped via Jamaica to the Ocean Leather Corporation of New York, who employed Wardwill Lazarri of North East Bay as their local agent. According to Isaac Tatum, the company would purchase as many sharkskins as the fishermen could supply, provided that the skins were over 35 inches in length. The longer the skin, the more valuable it would be, and one good skin could mean "a week's food" for the family.[14]

A 1929 Ford, one of ten cars on Cayman Brac in 1938.

In the years after the '32 Storm, "egging", which had been a steady occupation amongst some Sister Islanders for a decade or more, also provided a much-needed source of income. This unusual livelihood involved sailing hundreds of miles to the Serrana, Pedro, or Morant Cays to the southwest and southeast of Cayman, constructing huts as temporary dwellings on the cays, and collecting birds' eggs over a number of weeks or months. The eggs were shipped directly from the cays for sale in the Jamaican markets, where they were considered something of a delicacy. Thousands of eggs were collected in a single day, and hundreds of thousands during a season, with 291,000 being a record. The eggs fetched £4 per thousand in Jamaica, which meant that egging proved a valuable livelihood for quite a few families.[15]

Unique to Cayman Brac was the small tanning trade maintained during this period and well into the 1950s by the Lazzari family at North East Bay. J.C. Lazzari's father set up the operation, bringing his knowledge and experience of tanning from Cuba to Cayman Brac in the late 1800s. At one time, the family's tanning operation was large enough to treat all of the cattle and goat hides produced in the Sister Islands. Its leather products, including handmade shoes, supplied the needs of the Sister Islands, and the surplus was sufficient for export to Jamaica as well as for sale in Grand Cayman.[16]

MODERN COMMUNICATIONS

One major initiative during Cardinall's era changed the Cayman Islands irrevocably. This was the installation of the first radio stations, on Grand Cayman in 1935 and on Cayman Brac in 1936. The George Town facility was a joint venture with the Cuban government of Fulgencio Batista – at that time regarded as a progressive moderniser rather than a repressive military dictator. During the first half of 1932 the Cubans had lost their main "listening post" for hurricanes in the western Caribbean, the U.S. station on Swan

The opening of the wireless station in George Town, November 1935.

Island. They immediately approached Cayman, via Jamaica, to explore the possibility of a radio station on Cayman. The British strongly supported the idea. The radio could be used to relay meteorological reports as well as for two-way telephone and telegraph communication. Tragically, events moved too slowly for it to be operational before the '32 Storm. But in the wake of the high death toll in Cuba and Cayman, the vital importance of the station was all the more evident. The Cubans constructed the building at their own expense and maintained their own operator in Grand Cayman. The equipment was installed at a cost of £1,000. One-third of the cost was raised from subscribers, while the rest came from Cable & Wireless Ltd., which controlled commercial traffic. The Caymanian operator was trained by Cable & Wireless but paid by the Cayman Islands government.

The George Town radio station was opened on 23 November 1935, in a ceremony attended by a huge local crowd and by representatives of the Cuban and Jamaican governments. A clear voice message was received from Governor Sir Edward Denham, and a loyal telegraph message was transmitted to King George V, who "graciously replied". Other Morse code messages were exchanged with Australia, Canada, South Africa, Ceylon, and the Falkland Islands, as well as most of the British West Indian colonies. The service was considered sufficiently promising for a short-range transmitter/receiver to be installed on Cayman Brac.[17] This station was officially opened on 22 August 1936, in time for the more dangerous part of the hurricane season. Its operator, R.W. Foster, maintained a twice-daily schedule of transmissions between Cayman Brac and Grand Cayman.

It was a long time, however, before the Cayman Islands saw a return on this new investment. At the end of 1937, Commissioner Cardinall reported 1,097 inward and 1,420 outward transmissions, compared with a total of 1,882 for 1936. Even at the rate of a shilling a word, this made no profit for

anyone except Cable & Wireless. Receipts for 1937 were £340, but the company's share was £206. After subtracting the Cayman Islands' expenditure of £291, there was a net loss of £157. Cardinall, however, reported these figures with characteristic optimism: "The growth of the traffic was much more than originally estimated so that the station may, in the near future, prove a profitable investment. But it must be remembered that in the first instance these installations were erected to maintain communication in the event of hurricanes."[18]

Equally vital was the installation in 1937–8 of modern navigational beacons at six points: East End, South West Point, George Town, and North West Point on Grand Cayman, the westernmost point of Little Cayman, and the easternmost point of Cayman Brac. The project was made possible through an outright grant of £3,100 (two-thirds of the cost) from the Colonial Development Fund. The beacons were automatic, and only needed to be tended every six months. They were as valuable to Caribbean navigation as to the Cayman Islands themselves.[19]

Like Commissioner Hirst, Cardinall was a dedicated builder of roads and public buildings, despite an annual revenue that never exceeded £18,000 during his tenure. Inhabitants of outlying areas such as Breezy Castle in George Town and Birch Tree Hill in West Bay frequently complained that their byroads were neglected.[20] Cardinall oversaw the construction of the first drivable roads along the length of Cayman Brac, and on Grand Cayman from Bodden Town to East End and from Frank Sound across the island to North Side – places that previously could be reached only by boat, by horse or mule, or on foot. These vital improvements were celebrated, along with the Silver Jubilee of King George V, in May 1935.[21]

For many building projects, Commissioner Cardinall relied on the talented shipwright and builder Rayal B. Bodden. In the 1920s, this ingenious and skilled craftsman had built the wooden Peace Memorial town hall and the concrete-block and wood Elmslie Memorial Church. He developed a distinctive style, using both local and imported materials and local skills. In the six important public buildings that he designed during the 1930s, Bodden combined native hardwoods with hand-moulded concrete blocks, made with Jamaican cement. They proved to be strong and durable – some of them outlasting much later buildings.[22]

The first of Commissioner Cardinall's new buildings was a small hospital in George Town, built by the Public Works Department and officially opened on King George VI's Coronation Day, 12 May 1937. It was partly funded by a bequest of £383 from a Miss Helen Lambert. The hospital contained four beds, an operating theatre, a dispensary, and a consulting room. It was in use until 1953, when it was replaced by a 24-bed facility. Two other buildings associated with Rayal Bodden still lend a distinctive character to George Town's

centre. One is the Public Library, which was opened in 1939, with Miss Alice V. Bodden as the full-time librarian. It superseded the public reading room initiated by Rev. H.L. McMillan in 1888 and the subscription library started by Commissioner Hutchings in 1920. The second building was the new Post Office, which opened in 1939 and for many years also housed the offices of Treasury and Customs.[23]

The George Town buildings were paid for partly out of the surplus revenue from the sale of postage stamps, including the Coronation issue of 1937. But the other four major buildings begun in 1938 and finished in the months before the outbreak of World War Two depended on the raising of short-term loans. They were the town halls constructed in West Bay, Bodden Town, East End, and North Side. These substantial buildings were also used as schools and hurricane shelters. Projects like these provided much-needed work for the unemployed and gave a sense of progress at the height of the Depression.

In the Annual Report for 1935, Cardinall reported that there were no formal provisions for orphans, the aged, or the sick, and that cases of real distress, even destitution, existed in the Cayman Islands. "Conditions of general poverty obtained everywhere in the Dependency," he wrote. "The aged people who depended on remittances from their sons abroad were left without that aid. Young mothers with families likewise dependent on money from outside were equally stranded." At a time when wages were low, "the fall in the value of thatch rope affected directly the poorer classes, who have found themselves more and more involved in a variety of the 'truck system' which enforces payment in kind in exchange for produce that is not readily marketable".[24]

Yet Caymanians were not without resources. Families rallied round in difficult times, many fell back on subsistence farming, and the more affluent,

West Bay Town Hall in the late 1930s.

particularly the women, did what they could to supplement the small grants voted by the Assembly. Relief to paupers had always consisted of tiny cash payments, recommended by local J.P.s. But in 1935 the Assembly chose to disburse relief in the form of flour, sugar, and tobacco, which could be imported duty-free. The distribution was entrusted to a newly formed Friendly Society, consisting of "ladies in the various districts". Cardinall hoped that the new measure would "ensure a larger and more regular distribution of necessities, the visiting of the poor, and at the same time provide an outlet for the naturally charitable inclinations of the women".[25]

Using homemade equipment: the 1938 scientific expedition from Oxford University.

Commissioner Cardinall was relieved to note the absence of organised discontent among the lower classes. On a visit to Jamaica in May 1938, he was horrified by the escalating disorder, and he was anxious to prevent a spillover to the Cayman Islands. He seems to have been unaware of the depth and breadth of the workers' movement, led by William Alexander Bustamante and others, that marked the beginning of Jamaica's journey towards independence.[26]

Cardinall had little to fear in his own domain. There was no labour organisation in the Cayman Islands, let alone political disaffection led by organised labour. In Jamaica an enquiry into labour conditions was set up, while the West Indies Commission under Lord Moyne examined the interrelationship of social, economic, and political conditions there and throughout the British West Indies. These official bodies did not include the Cayman Islands in their investigations. The only outside group of note to visit Cayman at this time was a small scientific expedition that carried out research in all three islands for six months in 1938. Organised by Oxford University and strongly encouraged by Cardinall, it concentrated on medical and sanitation problems, gathering a wide range of scientific data and taking photographs and films.[27]

Off to work: the Oxford scientific expedition, 1938.

Cardinall was well aware that Caymanians were proud and loyal subjects of the British Empire, and he fostered these sentiments. In 1935 he declared Trafalgar Day (21 October) a public holiday and offered

prizes to schoolchildren for the best essays on Nelson's great victory. The winning efforts were remarkably well researched and reflected heartfelt imperial sentiments. "Well may the 21st of October be celebrated throughout the British Empire as a great day," wrote Sylvia Stewart of the Fifth Standard at Bodden Town School, "for on that day our memory is carried back to a great and noble man, Horatio Nelson, England's greatest sailor, and to that great and terrible battle of 'Trafalgar'. Not only England's, but the whole British Empire's fate depended on that battle. Had it not been won, Britain would not be reigning over the seas now. 'Long may she reign.'"[28]

The following year Cardinall delivered a stirring speech at the Remembrance Day ceremony on 11 November. Thanks to his efforts, the remains of a Caymanian airman who had died in France in World War One had been disinterred and brought back to his homeland. Reminding his hearers that they shared a solemn commemoration of the war with multitudes throughout the British Empire, he concluded: "We are part and parcel of our native land; the dust to which our bones will some day turn is the dust of the land which gave us birth. Belief in this is deep-rooted; but the thought lies more or less unspoken until the horrors of war shaped it into human words."[29]

WORLD WAR TWO

It was undoubtedly in this spirit of patriotism that Caymanians reacted to the outbreak of the Second World War on Sunday, 3 September 1939. While Caymanians rallied to the British cause out of loyalty, they also became aware of the new employment opportunities it brought. Even before the war escalated in 1940 and 1941, many Caymanian men had gone away to wartime work, both inside and outside the armed forces. Some enlisted in the Army (especially the Jamaica Defence Force), the Royal Navy, and the Royal Air Force. But the majority enrolled in the British Merchant Service as civilian seamen. Some saw action, hardship, and even death. Keith Tibbetts of Cayman Brac, for example, serving on a Jamaican banana boat, was present at the evacuation of Dunkirk and was later torpedoed off Puerto Rico. Elgin Scott, another Bracker, was unlucky enough at the age of nineteen to be captured with his ship. He was a prisoner of war for more than five years, first in Stalag 17 in Poland, then in a non-combatants' camp near Bremen, along with five fellow-Caymanians.[30]

By mid-1942, many able-bodied Caymanian men had been mobilised. The men they left behind included the Home Guard, government employees, and those engaged in the turtling and shipbuilding industries. A good number of Caymanians found employment in and around the American bases in the Canal Zone, and some took their families along. Those who joined the

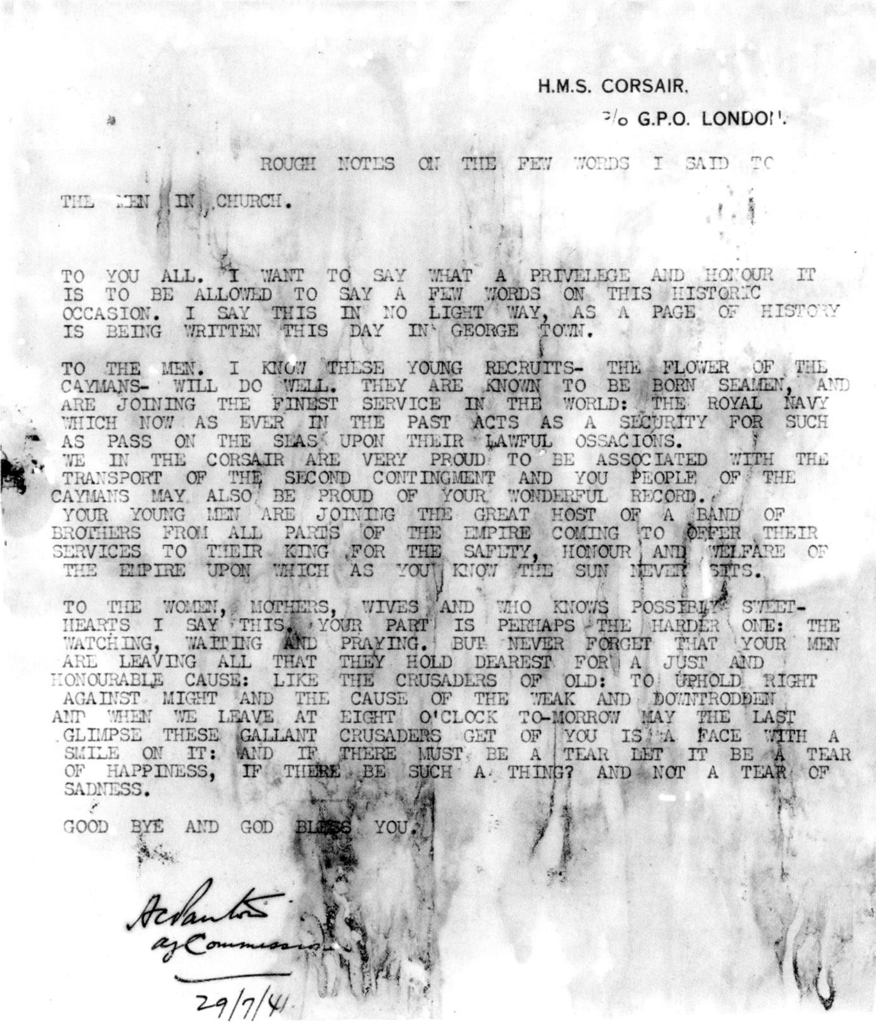

H.M.S. CORSAIR.
c/o G.P.O. LONDON.

ROUGH NOTES ON THE FEW WORDS I SAID TO THE MEN IN CHURCH.

TO YOU ALL. I WANT TO SAY WHAT A PRIVELEGE AND HONOUR IT IS TO BE ALLOWED TO SAY A FEW WORDS ON THIS HISTORIC OCCASION. I SAY THIS IN NO LIGHT WAY, AS A PAGE OF HISTORY IS BEING WRITTEN THIS DAY IN GEORGE TOWN.

TO THE MEN. I KNOW THESE YOUNG RECRUITS- THE FLOWER OF THE CAYMANS- WILL DO WELL. THEY ARE KNOWN TO BE BORN SEAMEN, AND ARE JOINING THE FINEST SERVICE IN THE WORLD: THE ROYAL NAVY WHICH NOW AS EVER IN THE PAST ACTS AS A SECURITY FOR SUCH AS PASS ON THE SEAS UPON THEIR LAWFUL OSSACIONS.
WE IN THE CORSAIR ARE VERY PROUD TO BE ASSOCIATED WITH THE TRANSPORT OF THE SECOND CONTINGMENT AND YOU PEOPLE OF THE CAYMANS MAY ALSO BE PROUD OF YOUR WONDERFUL RECORD.
YOUR YOUNG MEN ARE JOINING THE GREAT HOST OF A BAND OF BROTHERS FROM ALL PARTS OF THE EMPIRE COMING TO OFFER THEIR SERVICES TO THEIR KING FOR THE SAFETY, HONOUR AND WELFARE OF THE EMPIRE UPON WHICH AS YOU KNOW THE SUN NEVER SITS.

TO THE WOMEN, MOTHERS, WIVES AND WHO KNOWS POSSIBLY SWEET-HEARTS I SAY THIS. YOUR PART IS PERHAPS THE HARDER ONE: THE WATCHING, WAITING AND PRAYING. BUT NEVER FORGET THAT YOUR MEN ARE LEAVING ALL THAT THEY HOLD DEAREST FOR A JUST AND HONOURABLE CAUSE: LIKE THE CRUSADERS OF OLD: TO UPHOLD RIGHT AGAINST MIGHT AND THE CAUSE OF THE WEAK AND DOWNTRODDEN AND WHEN WE LEAVE AT EIGHT O'CLOCK TO-MORROW MAY THE LAST GLIMPSE THESE GALLANT CRUSADERS GET OF YOU IS A FACE WITH A SMILE ON IT: AND IF THERE MUST BE A TEAR LET IT BE A TEAR OF HAPPINESS, IF THERE BE SUCH A THING? AND NOT A TEAR OF SADNESS.

GOOD BYE AND GOD BLESS YOU.

29/7/41.

Address by the Captain of HMS Corsair *to the second contingent of Caymanian volunteers, the day before they left George Town to join the Trinidad Royal Naval Volunteer Reserve, 1941 (copy given to A.C. Panton, Acting Commissioner).*

Trinidad Royal Naval Volunteer Reserve were directly involved in the war effort, and were separated from their homes and families for long periods. Beginning with a first draft of fifty recruited in mid-1942, these eventually numbered more than two hundred – of whom no fewer than forty bore the surname Ebanks.[31] After initial training at the U.S. base at Chaguaramas, Trinidad, most became crewmen on the flotilla of converted yachts, tugs, and trawlers used for U-boat patrols in the eastern Caribbean. Others became gunners on merchant ships that ventured into more distant and dangerous waters.[32]

Altogether, it is reckoned that at least a thousand Caymanian men – two-thirds of the adult male population – saw active service during World War Two, and that between twenty-five and forty perished. In 1992, Captain Keith Tibbetts computed that the Sister Islands, with a combined population of 1,200, had sent 331 men to war, of whom 23 did not return. This level of commitment and loss, he noted, was the same as or even higher than that

West Bay volunteer for the TRNVR, Ewart Ebanks, on duty in Bermuda, 1941.

found in any other British colony.[33] The absence of so many able-bodied men also had important effects on those at home. On the positive side, the men serving abroad acquired new skills and experience, and most were able to send much-needed money to their families at home. However, separation also created stress within the families left behind and sorely stretched the islands' traditional economy.

The islands were probably never a target for enemy attack, despite their strategic position close to Allied shipping lanes. This was especially true after an American base was established in Grand Cayman in 1942. Long before Pearl Harbor, the U.S. had sought to bolster its security in the Caribbean from threats such as those posed by German U-boats. In September 1940 President Roosevelt accepted Prime Minister Churchill's offer of the use of seven British West Indian colonies for military bases, in return for fifty moth-balled World War One destroyers. The Cayman Islands were not included in this deal, but various circumstances soon highlighted their strategic location and led to the establishment of a small American base at George Town between 1942 and 1945. Grand Cayman was situated almost within sight of the main east-west shipping route across the Caribbean. It was also centrally located for aircraft patrols throughout the western Caribbean, and could serve as a refuelling base for small anti-submarine vessels and medium-range seaplanes operating between the major American naval bases in Florida, Puerto Rico, the Canal Zone, and Guantanamo Bay, Cuba.

Given the absence of so many Caymanian men, the local economy was not as hard hit by the war as it might have been. The islands never suffered serious shortages of food or other supplies because lines of communication between the Cayman Islands, Jamaica, and the United States were protected by American forces. Financially, the first two years of the war were the worst. The revenue for 1939 and 1940 combined equalled that for 1938, though expenditures remained the same. Catches of turtle and shark declined throughout the war, although the prices of these items actually rose. The rope industry, which was carried on mostly by women, positively boomed, as wartime demand almost tripled prices. Shipbuilding suffered from the absence of men to cut timbers and the difficulties of importing pine planking, but in 1944 Rayal Bodden received commissions to build two 162-ton minesweepers for the Royal Navy. The value of imported products rose as a result of the demands of the U.S. Navy base and funds sent by Caymanians abroad. Helped by imports, government revenue recovered to its pre-war level in 1941, and doubled by the end of the war. In 1946 Commissioner Jones could boast a healthy surplus of government funds.[34]

Commissoner Jones had no doubt that the American presence in Grand Cayman between 1942 and 1945 was wholly beneficial. When he arrived to take over from Allen Cardinall in 1941, the German U-boat campaign in

Members of the Cayman Home Guard, ca. 1943.

the Caribbean was intensifying. There were almost daily reports by radio of merchant vessels being sunk, some of them near the Cayman Islands. The most dramatic of these was the torpedoing of the United Fruit Company's steamer *Camayagua* within sight of George Town on 14 May 1942. Ignoring the danger, Commissioner Jones ordered Captain Eugene Thompson of the *Cimboco* to go to the rescue. Many survivors were brought in, some of them badly burned. Two later died in the George Town hospital.[35]

After the *Camayagua* incident, it was decided that the small police force, which had kept a lookout for enemy shipping, should be supplemented by a "Home Guard". In due course, forty-two men were recruited, drawn from those in "reserved" occupations and those who were too young or too old for overseas service. Supplies were sent from the garrison stores at Up Park Camp in Kingston, Jamaica. The men wore khaki uniforms, complete with solar topees, shorts, and puttees. They were equipped with World War One rifles and Lewis guns, three antiquated small naval guns, much telephone equipment, and a notoriously temperamental Leyland motor wagon. Their monthly pay was fairly generous – more than double that of soldiers in the British regular army: £7 15s for privates, £10 for corporals, and £15 for a sergeant.

The unit was officially subordinate to Jamaica, though directly under the orders of the U.S. base commander, and was commanded by a Lieutenant Craig from the Jamaican Home Guard. Basic training was in the hands of a tough Canadian sergeant-major, Ernie Highfield, who put the recruits through a rigorous one-month training regimen, including marching and rifle drill, route marches, and simulated hand-to-hand fighting.

Once the U.S. Navy was firmly established, the Home Guard focused on the essential but humdrum role of maintaining coastal lookouts. Six posts were established at the highest points around Grand Cayman. The most notable

The Home Guard lookout above Fort George during World War Two.

was the lookout consisting of a wooden platform and hut sixty feet up in the giant silk cotton tree by Fort George. The others were at Palmetto Point (Barker's), North West Point, Pedro Bluff, Gorling Bluff (East End), and North Side. Each post was manned round the clock, with anything suspicious being reported by telephone to the headquarters in George Town. Sightings included floating mines and derelict lifeboats, and the watchers during the night were often certain that they had heard a submarine discharging its water ballast and running on the surface. On a couple of occasions, it was even rumoured that uniformed sailors had come ashore in rowboats.[36]

On 22 May 1942, the U.S. Navy detachment arrived at George Town from the Canal Zone in the form of an advance party in two armed supply vessels. This was just a week after the sinking of the *Camayagua*, at the very time that the Home Guard was being formed. The original USN detachment consisted of three officers and thirty men, which soon became a permanent complement of forty-six men and five officers. They were commanded for the first two years by a reservist from the Midwest, George R. Roy, USNR. Their orders were to set up an Advanced Air Base, code-named Baldpate, as a unit of the command called Gulf Sea Frontier, headquartered in Miami.[37]

Warmly welcomed by the Commissioner and the leading citizens of George Town, the Americans were given the use of the town hall and allocated a large vacant area behind the library in which to set up their permanent quarters. This placed them closer to the local population than almost any other U.S. forces posted to the Caribbean. Within a very short time, with the eager help of well-paid local labourers, carpenters, and provisioners, they had created an enclave of comparative comfort.

The main building was a combined barracks, mess hall, and galley for the men. It was made of wood, and had a tin roof and louvred windows with mosquito screens. In front of it was a neat array of khaki canvas tents, each sixteen feet square. Each officer had a tent as his personal "cabin". Other tents constituted the officers' mess, the captain's office, a dispensary, and a miniature hospital. One shed served as the radio shack, another as the base's "brig" or lock-up. A small concrete-block building was the storeroom and armoury. The base had a continuous supply of electricity, a distillation plant for drinking-water, and running water from its own well for showers.

Aerial view of the U.S. Navy Base, George Town, ca. 1942.

Two miles away on the North Sound, the Americans constructed a fuel depot, an ammunition store, a firing range, and a new jetty. Seaplanes that landed in the sound were serviced by ferry-boats, fuel lighters, and a fire-boat operating from the jetty. Local men were employed to improve the road to the Sound and to build the jetty. Caymanians also worked as dock labourers, handymen, and mess servants around the downtown facility, and as laundresses, cooks, and bakers.

The first flying boat arrived on 31 May 1942. It was the forerunner of hundreds of seaplanes that used Grand Cayman as a base for anti-submarine patrols, for refuelling, or as a refuge from storms. A third of the planes were the comparatively nimble and elegant PBY Consolidated Catalinas. But the workhorse of the anti-submarine campaign was the lumbering and thunderous PBM Martin Mariner, with its nine-man crew, four gun turrets, and awesome array of bombs and depth charges.[38]

The flying patrols were immediately effective. But it was not until they were joined by a Caribbean-wide network of ship patrols in 1943 that the subma-

Men from the U.S. Navy Base, George Town, ca. 1942.

rine menace was removed. Surface operations in the western Caribbean and Gulf of Mexico were largely the responsibility of the U.S. Coast Guard. Grand Cayman was an important link in a chain of temporary bases that extended from southern Florida along the entire length of Cuba. In June 1943 the first flotilla of four small USCG patrol boats arrived at George Town, staying a week to test local facilities and set up a refuelling and re-arming depot. Thereafter until the end of the war, similar flotillas regularly stopped by in a patrol circuit that included Key West, La Fé in western Cuba, the Cayman Islands, and Guantanamo Bay.[39]

The air and sea traffic to and from Cayman kept the base fairly busy. Nevertheless, the posting to Grand Cayman was probably viewed by the servicemen as being unusually safe and even boring at times – far from the war's real action. Some of the men may have been surprised by the absence of strict racial segregation. For their part, the people of Grand Cayman accepted this sudden influx of Americans in good spirit. The Baldpate base represented an exciting visitation from an unfamiliar outside world – a revelation of American energy, enterprise, and materialism, as well as a chance to acquire a healthy infusion of American dollars. Nevertheless, there were tensions from time to time, especially as the American presence entered its third year and the war in the Caribbean sphere was winding down.[40]

Three members of the Cayman Home Guard, ca. 1943.

Though they had a regular round of duties, the American sailors and airmen had plenty of opportunities to interact with locals in off-duty hours. Most of these encounters were amicable and peaceful, and some were romantic. The officers were occasionally entertained at informal private parties, held, for example, at "Petra Plantation", now the home of the Grand Old

A PBM Mariner in the North Sound, Grand Cayman, 1943.

House on South Church Street. For the enlisted men, one respectable meeting point was the Hislops' ice-cream parlour, another the Tea Shoppe run by Madeline and Myrtle Ebanks, in the centre of George Town near the base. From time to time the base was visited by a naval chaplain. In addition, a local Presbyterian minister, Rev. George Hicks, was appointed honorary chaplain to the base, and encouraged the men to attend Elmslie Memorial Church. Several romances blossomed there, including the one between Lilian Bodden, the daughter of Captain Rayal, and Chief Warrant Officer Jack Howard, who were married towards the end of 1942.[41]

Tensions predictably arose occurred when young Caymanian women were thought to be too friendly to the American servicemen – for instance, when they accepted invitations to film shows on the base or dances at the town hall for the enlisted men. On several occasions words, and sometimes blows, were exchanged outside the town hall. The most serious incident occurred around Christmas 1943, when forty young men of the TRNVR were home from Trinidad on leave. Members of the Home Guard were occasionally involved in arguments or fights as well. Civilian and naval authorities attributed these encounters to over-consumption of liquor by individuals predisposed to be troublemakers. But undoubtedly jealousy and boredom played their parts.[42]

The Baldpate base was wound down during the last year of the war. From January to July 1945, the U.S. Navy was replaced by the U.S. Coast Guard. With the removal of a small American meteorological unit in December 1945, the installation finally closed. Victory in Europe had already been hailed in May earlier that year. The surrender of Japan four months later was celebrated with even more enthusiasm in Cayman because it coincided with the return from Trinidad of nearly all of the Caymanians from the disbanded TRNVR. Their homecoming brought a sense of relief and reinvigoration.

Marriage of Lillian Bodden to Chief Warrant Officer Jack Howard of the U.S. Navy at Elmslie Church in 1942.

Families were reunited, postponed marriages celebrated, and (as in most Allied countries) nine months later there was a surge in the number of children born. The only concern was whether there would be enough employment for the men who returned.

AFTER THE WAR

Happily, this fear proved to be unfounded. Local wartime job vacancies were quickly filled, and many servicemen had no difficulty in finding maritime employment abroad. One traditional occupation that drew Caymanians, especially Cayman Brackers, overseas from the 1930s to the 1950s was employment in the shipyards in Jamaica, notably in the Belmont Dry Dock, as well as with Cayman Boats Limited, a boat-construction company started after the war by Sir Anthony Jenkison and managed by the Bracker Arnold "Cappy" Foster. Building on the reputation they had earned during the war, Caymanians also benefited from the postwar boom in shipping, particularly in the use of oil tankers and other bulk carriers. More jobs than ever before were available on American vessels. Although wartime damage had crippled the mercantile might of Britain and other Allies, the United States was expanding fast. In the immediate postwar years, Caymanian seamen found work on the boats of the revived United Fruit Company, the Booth American Line, and the Lago Oil and Transport Company, headquartered in Aruba. But the great majority of Caymanian mariners from 1950 until the 1970s were employed by Daniel K. Ludwig's giant shipping line, National Bulk Carriers.[43]

Beginning with a handful of converted wartime Liberty ships bought at bargain prices, Ludwig had encouraged shipyards in several countries besides the United States to continue building at wartime levels. For more than a decade he owned the largest mercantile fleet in the world, including the biggest bulk carriers before the age of the supertanker. Ludwig's employment tactics were equally astute. He preferred to hire foreign crewmen because they were usually not unionised and were happy to work for wages that, while lower than American rates, were far higher than they could earn in their homelands.

Of all the mariners that Ludwig had encountered, he considered Caymanians, along with the inhabitants of the island of Bequia, off St. Vincent, the most intelligent, reliable, hard-working, and untroublesome. The fact that they spoke English was a bonus.

Ludwig's NBC offered long-term, easily renewable contracts and excellent prospects for internal promotion. The voyages offered plentiful opportunities to study for professional examinations. Beginning as deckhands, engine-

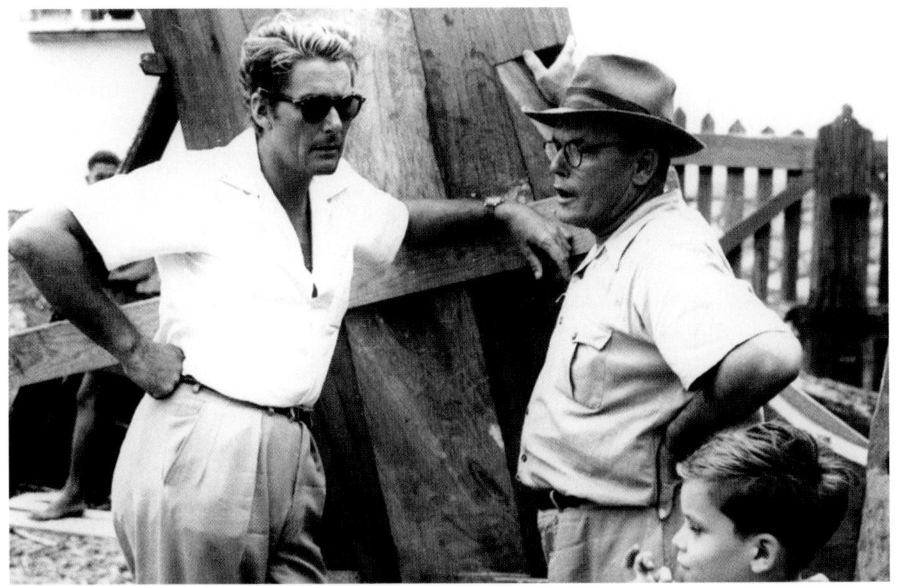

Above: Arnold A. "Cappy" Foster at his boatyard, Cayman Boats Ltd., in Jamaica in the 1940s.

Middle: Boats under construction at Cayman Boats Ltd.

Below: Cappy Foster and Errol Flynn discuss boatbuilding techniques (Trevor Foster in foreground).

Daniel K. Ludwig

room oilers, or stewards, most long-serving Caymanians obtained formal qualifications and rose steadily through the NBC ranks. Later, as NBC declined in relative importance, some found even better jobs with other companies. Of the nearly one thousand Caymanians employed by NBC, more than fifty obtained master's or chief engineer's certificates. Exceptional mariners, such as Paul Hurlston and Harris McCoy of Grand Cayman and Darwin Tibbetts of Cayman Brac, ended their careers in command of supertankers and giant container-carriers sailing the ocean lanes of the world.[44] The NBC connection to Cayman was strengthened by the fact that at one time the captain of D.K. Ludwig's private yacht was from Cayman Brac, while another Bracker was an important recruiter in NBC's New York head office.

A key development at this time was the visa waiver concession obtained for Caymanian seamen from the United States government in 1949. Before that point, even those sailing from American ports had to obtain their visas from one of the U.S. consulates in Kingston or Cuba – a process that generally required a week's residence. On a motion in the Caymanian Vestry by the young politician Ormond Panton, formal application was made to Washington for the appointment of a United States consul in the Cayman Islands. An American official named Wilson visited George Town and concluded that the appointment of a separate consul was not justified. But Wilson was so impressed by his hosts that he recommended instead that the Commissioner be authorised to issue a visa waiver to any applicant holding a Caymanian passport who had no criminal record. This concession, unique to all foreign colonies, was formally endorsed by the U.S. Senate, and has lasted to the present day.[45]

THE TIDE OF CHANGE

Despite the impact of World War Two and the continuing opportunities of the immediate postwar years, at the beginning of the 1950s the Cayman Islands still retained the aura of a previous age, especially to outsiders. A typical article, written by John Maloney and published in the *Saturday Evening Post* in April 1950, bore the title "The Islands Time Forgot". Its heading asked American readers: "In this Caribbean paradise a furnished house and three servants cost forty dollars a month, and you can make a good living as a beachcomber. Are these the islands you have dreamed about?" The Cayman Islands still lacked a commercial bank, an efficient and reliable supply of electricity and water, and a public telephone service. There was no airfield or regular air service, and only one or two guest-houses. The price of freehold land varied from £15 to £40 an acre, according to location. Even lots fronting the incomparable stretch of Seven Mile Beach cost no more

than £2 a front foot (with depth varying from 100 to 200 feet) – or less than £220 per acre.[46] Turtle and shark fishing, boat-building, and the making of thatch rope were still the economic mainstays of the island. The colonial administration, with its eight-man police force and its dozen civil servants sharing some forty posts, operated comfortably on a balanced budget of less than £40,000 a year.[47]

The impression of living in a time warp was misleading, however. Various factors were working to make change both inevitable and irreversible. For visitors in the 1940s and 1950s, one of the attractions of the Cayman Islands was the absence of the poverty often seen in other Caribbean territories. Cayman's relative prosperity reflected the general brightening of the economic situation since the Depression. Funds sent home by Caymanians overseas during and after the war were built into modest reserves of capital. They improved the standard of living and created the potential for an economic take-off.

CAYMAN ISLANDS.

GOVERNMENT NOTICE.

No. 66/45.

Georgetown, 1[illegible]th. August, 1945.

T. R. N. V. R.

It is hereby notified for general information that the following T.R.N.V.R. Ratings, on leave prior to demobilization, are expected to arrive at Georgetown on Saturday 18th, August, 1945:-

1.	S. MARTIN	Leading Seaman.	32.	H. ANDERSON	A.B.
2.	A. THOMPSON	Do.	33.	A. L. EBANKS	Do.
3.	T. HYDES	Do.	34.	T. E. EBANKS	Do.
4.	D. D. EBANKS	Do.	35.	C. EBANKS	Do.
5.	E. L. PEARSON	Do.	36.	H. R. EBANKS	Do.
6.	C. FLOWERS	Do.	37.	H. L. BAZAAR	Do.
7.	E. W. EBANKS	Do.	38.	J. J. BODDEN	Do.
8.	S. WATLER	Do.	39.	S. EBANKS	Do.
9.	J. R. BODDEN	Do.	40.	M. C. EBANKS	Do.
10.	C. W. EBANKS	Do.	41.	E. A. HYDES	Do.
11.	C. V. GLIDDEN	Do.	42.	K. SMITH	Do.
12.	J. L. EBANKS	Do.	43.	E. TATUM	Do.
13.	H. D. EBANKS	Do.	44.	L. GARVIN	Do.
14.	C. EBANKS	Do.	45.	B. BERRY	Do.
15.	J. M. C. HYDES	A.B.	46.	V. G. EBANKS	Do.
16.	H. C. HYDES	Do.	47.	H. MCCOY	Do.
17.	V. EBANKS	Do.	48.	H. SMITH	Do.
18.	W. HENNING	Do.	49.	L. SMITH	Do.
19.	C. W. EBANKS	Do.	50.	F. HISLOP	Do.
20.	A. WHITTAKER	Do.	51.	E. JACKSON	Do.
21.	M. W. EBANKS	Do.	52.	A. FREDERICK	Do.
22.	A. JACKSON	Do.	53.	W. PRENDERGRAST	Do.
23.	W. H. EBANKS	Do.	54.	J. YATES	Do.
24.	A. O. MOORE	Do.	55.	J. JACKSON	Do.
25.	D. R. HYDES	Do.	56.	O. M. BODDEN	Do.
26.	E. BANKS	Do.	57.	H. C. EBANKS	SIG.
27.	A. WHITTAKER	Do.	58.	L. CHRISTIAN	L/TEL.
28.	W. HYDES	Do.	59.	E. BODDEN	TEL.
29.	B. E. HILL	Do.	60.	J. BARNES	
30.	H. S. EBANKS	Do.	61.	B. NAVIS	COOK.
31.	C. CONOLLY	Do.	62.	S. L. EBANKS	St. [illegible]

A Public reception will be given in their honour at the Town Hall Georgetown on the day of their arrival. A further notice regarding this will be published later.

A. C. PANTON,
Acting Commissioner.

Government notice announcing the return of Caymanians from the TRNVR to George Town, August 1945.

The records of the Government Savings Bank – then the only bank in the islands – reveal the increasing wealth after the war. The number of depositors had risen from 180 with some £4,000 in 1937, to 478 with £15,000 in 1941. By 1950 there were 1,570 depositors with £117,000 in savings. When sterling (in the Jamaican form) was declared the only legal tender in 1949 and dollars were called in, $35,000 was exchanged.[48]

Caymanians were increasingly able to stay in the Cayman Islands rather than migrating. The new wave of maritime employment, of course, kept men away for a year or even two years at a time. But heads of families were willing to accept these absences – far longer than those experienced by traditional turtlers – in exchange for the much greater benefits. Many young men seized the opportunity to make enough money abroad to buy land and build a house in their homeland before marrying and starting a family. Even those who found it advantageous to live in the United States for a while kept close family connections, visited frequently, and sometimes chose to return when they had made enough money to do so.

The war had given Caymanians a wider experience of the world than most of their fathers had known. They returned from overseas and their wartime occupations with increased enterprise, ambition, and expertise. They had also seen what political change could accomplish. And they began to see that improved communications and air transportation held out new opportunities for their previously isolated homeland.

Perhaps the new era was foretold by the words of acting Commissioner A.C. Panton when he greeted the sixty-two veterans of the TRNVR at their homecoming on 10 August 1945. "We rejoice in your safe return to the old Rock, the land of your birth, the land to which you have brought renown by reason of your conduct at the place of duty. . . . You'll always look back with pride on the fact that you wore the King's uniform when our Empire's existence was at stake," he began.

> I remember when I was demobilised after World War One – my one thought was to get home. Today that is the thought uppermost in [the] minds of all servicemen: Home and the comforts of home and the Freedom of home. We want the homes of Cayman to be the happiest homes in the whole Empire. . . . We are expecting great improvements in our islands' life in the near future and we believe that our war veterans will make a valuable contribution toward the creation of a better Cayman. Let us work together in [the] spirit of co-operation and comradeship. You have been shipmates together and you have learned the value of comradeship. Keep up that spirit of unity and self- sacrifice and give your hearty support to every cause that will benefit Cayman.[49]

What ensured that the Cayman Islands and its people would experience change in the near future were external events affecting the British Empire. Immediately after World War Two, people in many British colonies began thinking about – and in some cases demanding – independence. Britain's ability to sustain its Empire and its will to do so were in decline. The world was changing. However strong their loyalty and conservatism, Caymanians were led by new realities within their region to explore change. Between 1944, when Jamaica achieved universal adult suffrage and established political parties, and 1962, when the British West Indies Federation failed and Jamaica chose independence, change was in the wind, and the Cayman Islands could not but be affected.

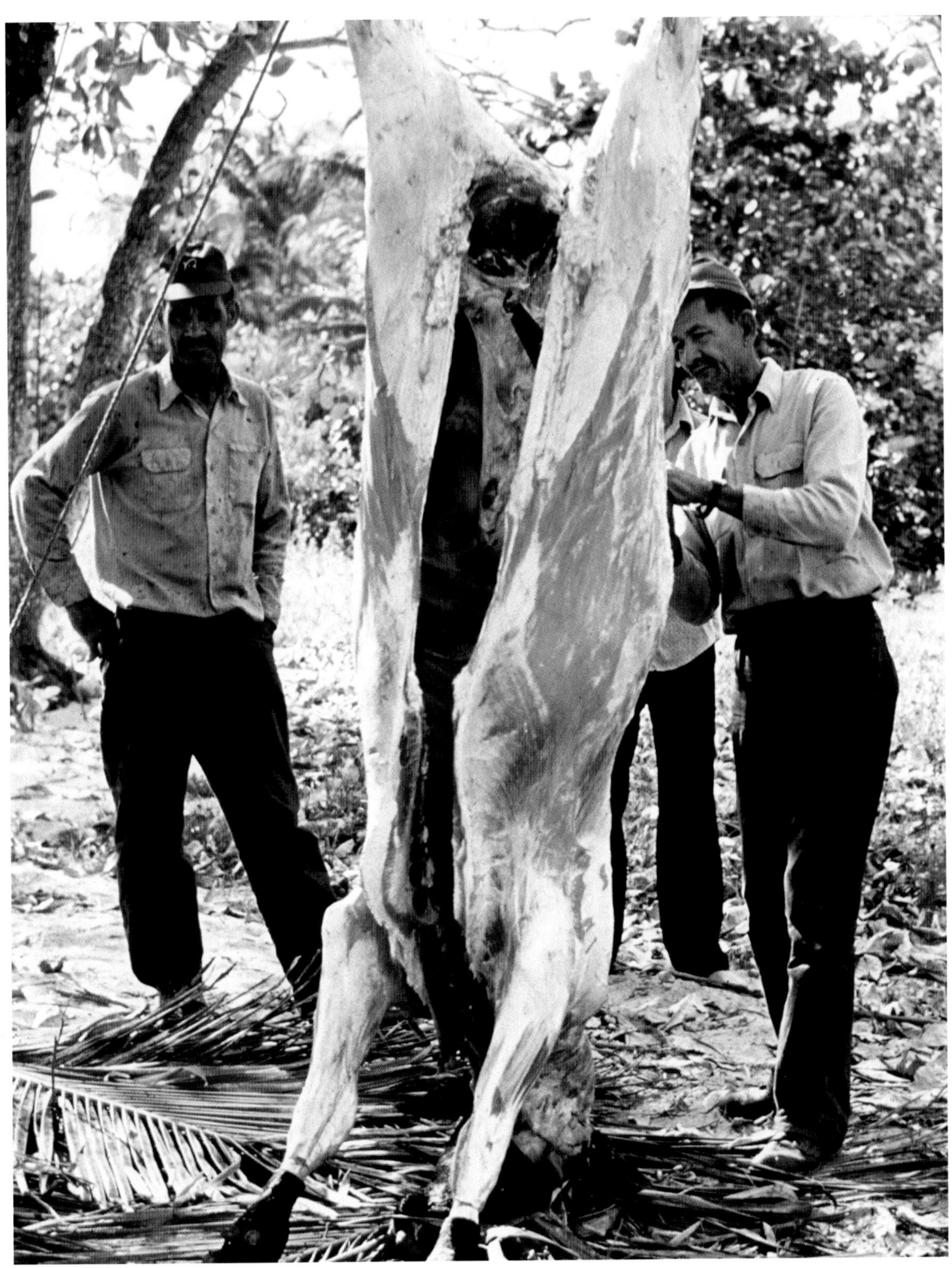

Christmas Beef: a seasonal delicacy before the days of imported beef.

CHAPTER 14

Declining Dependency

Constitutional, Political, and Administrative Changes, 1944–2000

BETWEEN THE END OF WORLD WAR TWO and the close of the twentieth century, the Cayman Islands experienced significant constitutional, political, and administrative changes. Although these changes were triggered by external events, they were increasingly the product of Caymanian choices. Caymanians had learned over the previous century or more that they could enjoy a large measure of control over their own internal affairs, partly because of their reputation among the higher authorities for not creating problems or demanding attention. An equally pragmatic approach enabled them to adapt to the very different conditions of the postwar era. As a result, the political, administrative, and legal systems of the islands evolved in response to changing circumstances and growing prosperity.

The Cayman Islands and its people entered the twenty-first century without organised political parties and apparently content with their status as an Overseas Territory. Caymanians were loyal to the British Crown and unmoved by the regional political ferment that led, after World War Two, to demands for independence in many British West Indian colonies. Once Jamaica began to take the various steps toward colonial devolution and independence, however, Caymanians had to respond to the new regional situation with their own choices.

The Caymanian approach in the second half of the century was generally to buck the regional trend. In 1962 the Cayman Islands chose to separate from

Jamaica and remain a British Crown Colony. This crucial decision proved both astute and profitable. Not inclined to make sudden changes or under pressure to do so, Caymanians sought by gradual means to shape a constitution, administration, and legal system that reflected their character and needs.

This process was generally peaceful. Only occasionally did proposals provoke heated debate or threaten to lead to entrenched political parties. The chief issues were the Cayman Islands' role in the British West Indies Federation, the direction they should take once Jamaica achieved independence, and the role of the British-appointed head of the Cayman Islands executive. The political status of women was a continuing question until they obtained the rights to vote and stand for election in 1958. As we shall see in Chapter Sixteen, there was also controversy over the need for planning controls and the consequences of establishing a foolproof system of land registration. These disputes, however, were relatively short-lived. The general picture is of a society guided by a lively sense of self-interest, well aware of outside pressures for change, but cautious and prudent about acceding too readily to them.

THE WEST INDIES FEDERATION AND CONSTITUTIONAL DEVELOPMENT

The new constitution granted to Jamaica in November 1944 had important implications for the Cayman Islands, though it had little direct impact. Jamaica now had universal adult suffrage and a limited form of ministerial government, as well as political parties based on trade unions. The Cayman Islands, in contrast, had no written constitution. The Caymanian legislature consisted of twenty-seven Vestrymen, elected only by taxpaying adult males, and an equal number of nominated J.P.s. There were no political parties or trade unions, and the leading figure was an appointed Commissioner, who was the chief executive as well as chairman of the legislature and Chief Justice.

During the 1940s and 1950s, the gap between the Jamaican and Caymanian political systems became apparent. In theory, the Jamaican legislature could pass laws applying to the Cayman Islands without consulting Caymanians. The Jamaican cabinet of ministers also had the right to govern the islands without consulting Cayman. Only the Governor of Jamaica had the authority to intercede, if need be, on Cayman's behalf.

Legislators in Cayman gradually became aware of the implications of these changes and the need to adjust to them. The first Jamaican general election, in December 1944, had resulted in a smashing victory for the Jamaican Labour Party under its populist leader, Alexander Bustamante. He

became Jamaica's first Chief Minister in 1953 during the movement towards full cabinet government, which was completed by July 1959. By that time, the socialist People's National Party held the reins of power, under the leadership of Norman Manley, Bustamante's cousin. Jamaica was the most important member in the British West Indies Federation, the mechanism that Britain favoured for her Caribbean colonies to gain independence.[1]

Alexander Bustamante visiting Cayman in the 1950s.

Caymanian legislators entered this political arena when two Assemblymen, Ernest Panton and Willie Farrington, attended the first meeting to discuss the proposed West Indies Federation, held at Montego Bay, Jamaica, in September 1947. The Cayman delegates (though attending only as observers) made it clear that their Assembly would agree to join only if the Cayman Islands had direct representation in the Federation legislature. This position was rejected by the Standing Closer Association Committee, which in 1949 recommended that the Cayman Islands should continue as a dependency under the administration of the Governor-General of the Federation. This solution was seen as impractical and unacceptable in two further organisational meetings, held in London in 1953 and 1956. The position of Cayman was still unresolved when the Federation was formally launched on 3 January 1958.

Meanwhile, Cayman had responded to the constitutional changes in Jamaica and the creation of the Federation. On 7 April 1955, six Assemblymen (who constituted the Advisory Executive Council) sent a petition to the Colonial Secretary through the Governor of Jamaica. It asked that the Cayman Islands be given the right to control its own affairs, subject only to the powers of the Jamaican Governor, once Jamaica reached the stage of fully responsible government. It wanted the special position of the Cayman Islands to be protected. "While . . . we look forward to strengthening ties both with Jamaica and with the other territories of the British Caribbean," wrote the petitioners, "we wish to restate as clearly and strongly as we can three main aims. First, we wish to retain the right to control entry to our islands. Secondly, we wish to retain our rights to decide what taxes should be imposed upon us. Thirdly, we wish to retain our right to maintain our established channels of trade and employment overseas."[2] Two weeks later, with the intention of increasing the elected proportion of the legislature, the Assembly passed a resolution to reduce the number of sitting J.P.s to "about ten".

Vestrymen elected for the districts of Grand Cayman in August 1944.

CAYMAN ISLANDS.

Government Notice.

COMMISSIONER'S OFFICE,

No. 85/44.

Georgetown, 23rd. AUGUST, 1944.

ASSEMBLY OF JUSTICES AND VESTRY.

ELECTION OF VESTRYMEN, 1944.

It is notified for general information that, at the recent election, the following VESTRYMEN were elected for the period 1944-46.

GRAND CAYMAN.

GEORGETOWN	James Ashford Panton	Merchant.
	James Ausley Webster	Landowner.
	Edgar Ducan Merren	Company Director.
	Ronald Joscelyn Watler	Law Agent.
	Royal Douglas Watler	Shipowner.
WEST BAY	James Stafford Banks	Merchant.
	Charles Garfield Farrington	Master Mariner.
	John Samuel Smith	Road Foreman.
	William Redfern	Merchant.
	Samuel McNee Farrington	Master Mariner.
PROSPECT	Valentine Hurlston	Carpenter.
	Alexander Selwyn Eden	Farmer.
	Winston Watler	Seaman.
BODDENTOWN	Edgar Leopold Waite	Minister of Religion.
	John Bodden	Farmer.
	A. Biddle Bodden	Merchant.
	Malcolm Eden	Farmer.
	William Thomas Bodden	Barber.
EAST END.	Warren Conolly	Car Proprietor.
	Theophilus Watler	Seaman.
	Ennis McLaughlin	Merchant.
NORTHSIDE	Henry Glenn	Master Mariner.
	W. A. Smith	Ship's Cook.

COMMISSIONER.

197/44

The Jamaican Governor and the Colonial Office gave qualified support to these moves. The proposal to reduce the number of J.P.s, according to one official, was "mainly window dressing" designed "to give a slightly more democratic appearance to the Caymans system of government". Its real aim was for Caymanians to continue "their virtual internal autonomy in the face of increasing self-government in Jamaica and the advent of a British Caribbean Federation . . ." This official pointed to the wisdom of a continuing relationship with the Governor of Jamaica rather than with the Jamaican government. "I do not think interference by Jamaican politicians, which is not likely to be

altruistic, would really benefit the inarticulate majority in the Caymans," he wrote. "I think this little society, full of blemishes as it is, is best left to work out its own salvation, for as long as possible under the guidance of the Commissioner and the Governor."[3]

Cayman representatives at the second conference on the British West Indies Federation. Left to right: Frank Hill (second), E.O. Panton (fourth), T.W. Farrington (sixth), O.L. Panton (seventh), E.D. Merren (tenth).

Before any decision could be made, the complex relationships between the Cayman Islands, Jamaica, and the proposed Federation had to be sorted out. Any new relationship had to be accepted both by the Premier of Jamaica and by the politicians of the Cayman Islands. Premier Manley was content to let the Jamaican Governor resolve the Cayman Islands question. Locally, however, it was a contentious matter that involved a number of political views and several very distinct personalities.

On the official side, two judicious Governors, Hugh Foot and Kenneth Blackburne, were represented by three successive Commissioners who had limited success in pouring oil on troubled waters: Andrew Gerrard, Alan Donald, and Jack Rose. Amongst Caymanians, opinions were sharply divided, mainly between the white merchants led by E. Ducan Merren, and those claiming to represent the near-white and black majority, led by the outspoken Ormond L. Panton. An important factor to weigh was the views adopted by the Sister Islands, whose inhabitants made up a fifth of the population.

Ducan Merren had spent some years working for an oil company in Louisiana, and had returned before World War Two to take charge of the commercial family empire founded by his father, Henry O. Merren, in 1906. His influence and wealth were described by Governor Foot in a confidential memo in November 1956:

> Ducan Merren is the most active member of the large Merren family which runs the biggest trading company operating in the Caymans and particularly since the war he and his many brothers have made tremendous profits. They own one of the ships which brings supplies to the Caymans and though there are one or two other traders (principally the McTaggart family) the Merrens in fact fix all retail prices in the Caymans and there is no other merchant strong enough to stand against them. The amount of profit which they obtain from their retail sales is prodigious and with so much development going on in Grand Cayman and no income tax they have been rapidly making a fortune. Amongst other enterprises they run the Pageant Beach Hotel and it is the Merrens, acting with some of their United States associates, who have been carrying out exploration for oil.[4]

Sir Kenneth Blackburne addressing a public meeting in the Town Hall, George Town, ca. 1960.

Ducan Merren and his allies stood resolutely for local control over Caymanian interests. They were especially keen that the Assembly control revenue and expenditure and prevent higher taxes. This could best be achieved, in their view, by maintaining the British connection. They opposed Cayman's affiliation with the Federation and closer ties with Jamaica.

Ormond Panton, the youngest Caymanian delegate at the Federation discussions, and one of the most vocal, claimed to represent a different constituency – the poorer and non-white segments of society – and took a different stance. Panton regarded himself as a maverick, though he was the son and nephew of prominent members of the Caymanian administration, who were also engaged in shopkeeping and trading. He favoured a break with Britain and a closer relationship with Jamaica within the framework of the Federation, as long as it involved a greater degree of self-government.[5]

The Cayman Islands received their first written constitution by a royal order-in-council on 4 July 1959. This was the first step in political advancement. They were specifically exempted from the control of the Jamaican legislature and placed directly under the authority of the Governor of Jamaica, who was instructed to visit them at least once a year. The Commissioner was retitled "Administrator" but retained almost all of the executive, legislative, and judicial powers held by the Commissioner. The Administrator was to be guided by the Governor and to keep him informed, corresponding directly with the Colonial Office only with the Governor's authorisation.

The changes to the legislature in the 1959 constitution were much more radical. After 129 years, the unique body of Vestrymen and Justices was replaced by a Legislative Assembly and an Executive Council. The Legislative Assembly was reduced from about thirty-five to eighteen Members – twelve elected, three nominated, and three official. The Administrator functioned as both chairman and speaker, and presided over an Executive Council consisting of two official, one nominated, and two elected Members. The Executive Council was "normally" to be consulted on matters of policy, but there was "provision for dispensing with the need to consult them, or for their advice not to be followed, in certain specified circumstances". The Governor of Jamaica had "a general reserved legislative power", and the Crown could still disallow any legislation that it did not favour.[6]

Perhaps the most significant change for the average person was that all adult Caymanians were given the rights to vote and to stand for election. The order-in-council decreed that all British persons over the age of twenty-one who had been resident at least a year could vote, and that all Britishers over twenty-one who had lived in the islands for five years or more could stand for election. Though not stated specifically, this was taken to mean that women as well as men had the right to vote and sit in the legislature. The change came thirty-three years after such rights had been extended in the

United Kingdom, and fifteen years later than Jamaica. As a result, women voted in the first general election held under the new constitution, on 23 September 1959.

POLITICAL RIGHTS FOR WOMEN

No women were elected (or even stood) in 1959. Miss Sybil McLaughlin, however, was appointed Clerk of the new Assembly – perhaps the first woman in the Commonwealth to hold this post. The first woman to be elected to the legislature was Miss Evelyn Wood, a midwife and active church worker, who was one of the two Members for Bodden Town in November 1962. At the same time Miss Annie Huldah Bodden was selected by Commissioner Rose as one of the three nominated Members of the Legislative Assembly. Miss Wood was defeated in the next election in 1965, but Miss Bodden stood successfully for election in George Town as an independent and went on to a long and distinguished political career.[7]

Miss Annie Huldah Bodden, MLA for George Town, 1961–84.

These advances came about remarkably smoothly, considering that the role of women in politics and public office had been a hot issue, off and on, since the late 1940s. On 19 August 1948, twenty-four George Town women had sent a strongly worded letter to the Commissioner, saying that since there was nothing in the constitution of the Cayman Islands denying women the vote, they intended to exercise their right to do so at the forthcoming general election. "Should this privilege be denied us by the Officials in Charge of the Election," they stated, "we shall demand the Government give just reasons for making of no effect the Laws it has sworn to uphold." There is no record of the Commissioner's response, but apparently no women actually voted in the 1948 general election.[8]

In 1954, Mrs. E. Cook-Bodden, an Englishwoman married to a Caymanian, signified her intention to stand for election. She buttonholed Commissioner Gerrard and attempted to speak with Governor Foot regarding her right to stand. Gerrard privately wrote that, in his opinion, women were not excluded from voting, but that custom had always decreed that they did not. If this were altered, little would change in practice. Few women would choose to stand, and those that did had small chance for election. Mrs. Cook-Bodden herself would have practically no hope at all, if only because she was not a Caymanian. "However," he concluded, "as the principal electioneering weapon is rum, it is unwise to make any predictions whatsoever!"[9]

Governor Foot privately agreed with Gerrard, but pointed out that allowing women to stand for election was probably illegal. The Attorney General of Jamaica advised that whereas the 1865 Act did not specifically exclude women, the fact that it did not specifically *include* them had the same effect,

Women's petition seeking to exercise the right to vote, 1948.

Georgetown,
Grand Cayman.

Aug. 19, 1948.

His Hon. The Commissioner,
Government House,
Georgetown.

Sir:

We, the undersigned, residents of the District of Georgetown, having examined and obtained Legal advice on the Constitution of the Cayman Islands, find nothing therein which denies women the fundamental Human Right of taking part in deciding who shall govern us.

Therefore, we declare that it is our intention to exercise our Constutional Right to vote today, August 19th, 1948, according to our conscience, in the Election of Vestrymen for the District of Georgetown.

Should this privilege be denied us by the Officials in Charge of the Election we shall demand the Government give just reasons for making of no effect the Laws it has sworn to uphold.

We have the honour to be, Sir,

Olive M. Hinds.	Dareen V. Merren
Valda L. Bodden.	Mrs. Winston Walter
Ermyn Merren	Roselyn Merren
Carolyn Hinds	Veta C. M. Bodden.
Pansy A. Thompson.	R. Virginia Bodden.
Sunbeam Thompson	Ena Coe
Mrs Carley Merren.	Mrs R J Waller
Georgette U. Hurlston	Eva Merren
Violet Thompson	Sylvia E. Coe
Mrs. Geo. A. Merren.	Goldie D Banks
Rosie E. Bodden.	Isabelle Granger
Effie Anderson	Mrs. Pershing Merren

Commissioner's Office
19 AUG 1948
CAYMAN

given the general status of women then. This was borne out by what he believed was an unspoken Caymanian custom of excluding women. If Caymanian women were to be given the vote and allowed to stand for election, they would need a positive law to say so – as had happened in the United Kingdom and other jurisdictions where women now enjoyed such rights.[10]

The issue subsided until 1957. In that year, Caymanian women mobilised to demand their political rights. Their cause was both helped and hindered by their chief male advocate, a Jamaican pharmacist popularly called "Dr."

Rose, who had lived in Grand Cayman for seven years and wanted to inject Jamaican-style politics through an organisation styled the Vanguard Progressive Party. Rose's character, style, and agenda enraged and scared Ducan Merren. He drafted a legislative resolution to raise property and residence qualifications to exclude such "slick" Jamaicans, and also to deny women's suffrage "since women were not politically educated" – to a chorus of approval from his fellow Assemblymen.[11]

Mrs. Sybil Mclaughlin, National Hero, attired as Clerk of the Legislative Assembly (1959–84). She was Speaker of the Legislative Assembly from 1991 to 1996.

The women of Grand Cayman, undeterred, bombarded the Assembly with petitions. On 29 May 1957, identically worded requests from seven different districts were placed before the legislature. The petitions asked for the rights to vote in elections and hold any public office, "so that we be not regarded by you or by the world as less worthy than the women of other lands who have been accorded those rights". They were signed by 358 women of all classes and from all areas of Grand Cayman.[12] The petitions were referred to a Select Committee of Assemblymen, including Ducan Merren. The committee delayed for more than a year, saying that the matter was being considered in higher quarters. On 31 May 1958, ten men from George Town who were not legislators attempted to press the issue by nominating Mrs. Ena Watler as a candidate for the upcoming general election in August 1958. On 5 June, Commissioner Donald rejected Mrs. Watler's nomination on legal grounds, though he held out the hope that "within a year or thereabouts the position will have changed".[13]

This was not good enough for the more activist women, who demonstrated vociferously during and after the August 1958 election. Governor Blackburne and Commissioner Donald alike were concerned. "The only way to control female demonstrations such as that which recently occurred in Georgetown," wrote Blackburne to Donald on 10 September, "is by the grant of a vote to all women who can thus express their feelings in a sensible manner." Accordingly, on 20 September the Governor forwarded a draft bill for a Cayman Islands Sex Disqualification (Removal) Law, almost an exact copy of the Jamaican equivalent passed in 1950. He asked the Commissioner to ease its passage if he could, but hinted that he would exercise his reserved powers to impose it if the Assembly refused to pass it.[14]

The hint proved unnecessary. On 16 October (as the details of the proposed new constitution were also being published), the Select Committee unanimously recommended that the petition by 358 women be granted.[15] The Sex Disqualification (Removal) bill was introduced in the Assembly four days later and was passed into law on 8 December 1958.[16]

THE CAYMAN ISLANDS AND THE END OF FEDERATION

In the 1959 constitution, the relationship of the Cayman Islands to the West Indies Federation was left vague. The islands were said to be "part of" the Federation, though they made no financial contribution and were not represented in the Federation legislature. No Federation laws were to apply to them unless "expressly stated to do so". However, the relationship became a pressing issue as Federation moved closer to its planned goal of independence and Dominion status within the British Commonwealth. Five delegates – Ducan Merren, Roy McTaggart, Willie Farrington, Ormond Panton, and Administrator Jack Rose – were chosen by the Caymanian Assembly to participate in a series of conferences held between September 1959 and June 1961. Their purpose was to address unresolved aspects of the Federation's constitution, including the Cayman Islands' position within it. In the process (in Panton's view), the Cayman Islands were almost granted complete internal self-government in association with the West Indies Federation.[17]

In July 1961, Governor Kenneth Blackburne came to Grand Cayman to announce the proposals that had been drafted in June. The details were outlined at a public meeting. Once the Federation became independent, he explained, Cayman would cease to be a British dependency, though it would remain a member of the Commonwealth. It would enjoy internal self-government. The Governor of Jamaica would no longer have any responsibility for the Cayman Islands. Foreign affairs and defence would be Federation responsibilities and Cayman would have to contribute to their costs. Cayman would also retain links with Jamaica through the University of the West Indies, through medical and prison services, and through various types of technical assistance.

Administrator Jack Rose with Colonial Office officials at the Lancaster conference on the West Indies Federation , 1961.

Administratively, the proposed arrangements would mean that the Cayman Islands would have a Lieutenant-Governor as head of state, appointed by the British government. This person would normally preside in the "Council of Ministers", but he would have no vote and would have to follow the Council's advice. There would be a Chief Minister, appointed by the Lieutenant-Governor. The Council of Ministers would comprise the Lieutenant-Governor, the Chief Minister, two legislators selected by the Chief Minister, and an Attorney General

chosen by a Public Service Commission. Each member of the Council would have specific responsibilities in areas such as immigration, education and health. The Chief Minister, for example, would be responsible for finance and development and the appointment of J.P.s.

Governor Blackburne pointed out that these arrangements would not be final. The proposal set out a trial period of five years. After that, a review would be carried out by the Federation and Cayman governments to decide whether the islands should continue in an associated relationship or become a unit territory. If the Cayman Islands decided to withdraw from the Federation, they could petition the Crown to revert to colony status. The U.K. government gave an assurance that in these circumstances, subject to Parliamentary approval, it would resume responsibility for the Cayman Islands.[18]

These proposals would probably have been the central issue in the election that was set for the beginning of 1962. It was assumed that at least two political parties would operate in the new Legislative Assembly. Accordingly, Ormond Panton and his chief ally, Warren Conolly of East End, moved to form what became the National Democratic Party and began campaigning. These moves proved to be premature, however, because the proposals for self -government under a full ministerial system were about to receive a total setback from the Federation itself.

In September 1961, Norman Manley's ruling party held a referendum to decide whether Jamaica should remain in the West Indies Federation. To Manley's own surprise, the Jamaican electorate voted narrowly to withdraw from the Federation. Manley therefore obtained an assurance from the British government that they would allow Jamaica to become independent and then withdrew Jamaica from the Federation on 21 March 1962. Jamaica's withdrawal, closely followed by that of Trinidad and Tobago, sounded the death knell of the regional government. The Federation was formally dissolved on 31 May 1962, and Jamaica became an independent nation on 6 August of the same year.

PARTY POLITICS AND THE IDEA OF SELF-GOVERNMENT

The Federation's collapse and Jamaican independence left the proposed self-governing Cayman Islands an orphan. In the wake of these events, political activity in Cayman increased, as would-be leaders considered the options. Ormond Panton, Warren Conolly, and the NDP wanted internal self-government above all. Most of the party thought this could be achieved under a Jamaican umbrella far better than as a British dependency. Targeting the

non-whites and the newly enfranchised women, the NDP formed local branches. Evelyn Wood and Sam Powery were as active in Bodden Town and North Side as Warren Conolly and Ormond Panton were in East End and George Town. At its peak, the NDP had more than a thousand signed-up members. A strongly worded manifesto was printed, vociferous speeches were made at public meetings, and marches were held. Supporters composed a song with the refrain, "We will follow Ormond Panton 'til we die." The NDP also recruited two influential businessmen who wished to remain independent of the Merren influence in George Town. These were Captain Eldon Kirkconnell, a Bracker who was expanding his family's business in Grand Cayman, and Dr. Roy McTaggart. McTaggart, however, strongly favoured a British over a Jamaican link and did not care for Ormond Panton's claim to be the Caymanian "Little Bustamante".[19]

To counter the NDP, the conservative forces led by Ducan Merren of George Town, Willie Farrington of West Bay, and Burns Rutty, son of the Deputy Commissioner in Cayman Brac, formed the Christian Democratic Party. It too favoured internal self-government, and most of its ideas differed little from those of the NDP. But the CDP resolutely supported links with Britain rather than Jamaica. It tapped into the islanders' traditional respect for British institutions and leadership and their commitment to Christian values. Above all, it appealed to Caymanians' fear of being dominated by a Jamaica whose standard of living was rapidly falling behind that of the Cayman Islands, and whose population was a hundred times larger and overwhelmingly black.

Jack Rose and Kenneth Blackburne came close to campaigning for a British rather than a Jamaican connection and against rapid constitutional advance. At the beginning of January 1962, Rose stated publicly that Britain would not grant internal self-government, and that the Cayman Islands' only chance of obtaining it would be to join Jamaica. This polarised Caymanian opinion and greatly raised the temperature of public debate, at the same time throwing the party alignments into disarray.

On 17 January 1962, Governor Blackburne came to George Town to try to resolve the impasse. Throughout the following day, he presided at a meeting of the Assembly attended by some five hundred members of the public, inside and outside the town hall. In his opening speech, Blackburne eloquently and fairly put both sides of the issue. He somewhat defused Administrator Rose's earlier pronouncement by stating that association with Britain did not rule out internal self-government altogether – though it would be neither automatic nor immediate. A majority of the Assembly spoke for continuing association with Britain, whatever the cost. Three Members (Panton, Farrington, and, strangely, Ducan Merren) advocated self-government, with Jamaica handling foreign affairs and defence.[20]

Of no small importance in the deliberations was the position taken by the MLAs from the Sister Islands, Capt. Keith Tibbetts and Nolan Foster. They brought a petition signed by 345 of the 435 registered voters on the Sister Islands. The petition expressed the wish to remain linked to Britain in the strongest possible terms: if Grand Cayman chose to remain with an independent Jamaica, the Sister Islands would seek separate Crown Colony status under Britain. When Tibbetts presented the petition to the Governor at the Town Hall, Blackburne scrupulously inquired if the petitioners were registered voters. "Yes, Your Honour," Tibbetts replied, producing a registered voters list from his pocket. Turning to Commissioner Rose, Blackburne was heard to remark, "Do we need to go further? . . . This can't be overlooked."[21]

At the climax of the afternoon session, the crowd avidly listened to impassioned speeches by the leading proponents of each side. Ormond Panton put the case for a Jamaican connection, and his NDP colleague Roy McTaggart spoke for the British link. In a memorable judgement that Ormond Panton was later to call one of the "most undemocratic and dictatorial steps ever taken in the British Commonwealth", Governor Blackburne wound up the meeting by announcing that, having listened to the volume of applause given by the people to the two speakers, he believed that the British case had clearly won.[22]

The following day, the Assembly, including (to Governor Blackburne's surprise) Panton, Farrington, and Merren, unanimously passed the following resolution: "It is the wish of the Cayman Islands: 1. To continue their present association with Her Majesty's Government in the United Kingdom; 2. To negotiate with Her Majesty's Government in the United Kingdom for internal self-government, taking into account the wishes of the people of the Cayman Islands as to timing."[23]

In a final speech to the Caymanian public, the Governor spelled out the implications. The people's representatives had chosen to remain a British colony. Caymanians would continue to carry United Kingdom passports with the Cayman Islands stamp on the front, to fly the Union Jack, and to sing the British National Anthem. Britain would keep responsibility for defence, foreign affairs, internal security, and other matters, and the powers of the Administrator would most likely increase once there was no longer a British-appointed Governor of Jamaica.

One very significant change was the adoption of the so-called Membership system. This was not yet ministerial government, as Governor Blackburne pointed out, but it was one step towards it. Two or three representatives would be invited by the Administrator "to become what is called 'Member' for some subject or other". They would be expected to take "a keen and personal interest" in their subjects, and to deal with all the relevant govern-

ment papers. They would be consulted for advice before decisions were made, but the final decision would still rest with the Administrator and the Governor. In the future, the Assembly and the people would be free to send a delegation to London to "negotiate the conditions, and the terms, and the type of Constitution for internal self-government". Meanwhile, the Cayman Islands would continue to use Jamaican currency. A further delegation should be sent to Jamaica to ensure that Jamaica would continue to provide the services, staff, and technical specialists that the Cayman Islands could not yet provide for themselves.[24] Arrangements of this kind were in fact made by October 1962.[25]

The amendments to the constitution that came into force on 6 August of that year changed only the Administrator's role. The legislature remained the same, without even the formal institution of the Member system. A majority of the Assembly passed a motion in June 1962 that "it was the wish of the people of the Cayman Islands that a Constitution providing for full internal self-government be granted immediately after the forthcoming General Elections". This motion was turned down by the British government, pending the outcome of the election itself.[26] The question of internal self-government was therefore the major focus of the November 1962 general election. The NDP were confident that, after their victory, they could install responsible government under a two-party system and press for the appointment of a Chief Minister and a cabinet. This would bring about at least internal self-government, if not complete self-rule.

Initially, the election seemed a resounding victory for the NDP and Ormond Panton. But the outcome was actually a crushing blow to the party's aims and to its leader's ambitions. With the support of Dr. Roy McTaggart and Captain Eldon Kirkconnell, the NDP won seven seats to the CDP's five. Administrator Rose, however, used the composition of the legislature to ensure that it was the CDP that effectively formed the government. Rose chose people sympathetic to the CDP as the three nominated Members. These three, along with the five CDP Members, then voted for their leader, Willie Farrington, as one of the two elected Members of the Executive Council. The other elected Member was Roy McTaggart, which meant that Ormond Panton was kept out of power. Panton tried to persuade the NDP Members to resign as a bloc, but failed. McTaggart himself chose to resign – but more through disenchantment with local politics than in an act of party solidarity.[27]

Ormond Panton remained in politics, though embittered by the experience. The NDP and the CDP gradually faded away as more and more legislators declared themselves independents. Internal self-government was still an issue in the next general election in 1965. But it was no longer such a live partisan cause, and most of the independents actively opposed it. In the colony

at large, burgeoning prosperity and the energy needed to sustain it made politics and political change seem less and less necessary.[28]

FURTHER CONSTITUTIONAL CHANGE

Select committees of the legislature were appointed to consider constitutional change in 1966, 1967, and 1969, but nothing was achieved until 1972. In response to a request of the Assembly in June 1970, a British constitutional expert, the Earl of Oxford and Asquith, was sent the following January by the Foreign and Commonwealth Office to examine the situation and make recommendations. Lord Asquith stayed a month and interviewed about a hundred Caymanians. He discovered that very few people favoured radical change and that about a third were satisfied with the current situation. Even the half who favoured some changes stopped short of wanting a ministerial system. A majority called for greater participation by elected representatives in government business, the abolition of nominated Members in both ExCo and the Legislative Assembly, and some reduction in the powers of the Administrator. They also asked for a better flow of information to the public about policy decisions, and the protection of Caymanians against the flood of immigrants, including those of Caymanian origin returning from abroad.

Lord Asquith noted the moderate nature of these demands. He also commented that the absence of distinct political parties might make it difficult to set up a ministerial system on the British model. There were no truly divergent ideologies. Everyone seemed to agree that continued prosperity depended on "external confidence in the political stability of the Islands and in the good faith of the Government in honouring commercial undertakings". What was required was greater efficiency, as well as the assurance that sudden or radical political change was not going to happen. Many people acknowledged that the colony's administrative framework had been unable to keep pace with economic development. Too many decisions were made on an *ad hoc* basis, and too many responsibilities were left to the Administrator. The lack of a daily newspaper or local broadcasting service left the public uninformed about what decisions were made and how they were carried out. This contributed to the impression that the Administrator's role was more controlling than it actually was.

As Asquith astutely observed, the position of the people of the Sister Islands was subtly different from those of Grand Cayman. Though they constituted only 10 per cent of the population, they had strong views. Conservative by nature, they were generally content with the existing constitution. However, they felt neglected. At the very least they wanted one of

their two elected Members in the Assembly to be guaranteed a place on an expanded Executive Council.

On the positive side, Lord Asquith concluded that Caymanian society in general was comparatively harmonious. "There is at present no marked stratification of society by colour, age, wealth, class or education," he wrote. "Among the many people of all types whom I interviewed it was noticeable that these factors had little or no bearing on the political opinions expressed." Relations between Caymanians and non-Caymanians were relatively cordial, and, as long as proper safeguards could be introduced, were not likely to deteriorate. "The presence in large numbers of tourists and the sale of land to expatriates are both so profitable that they have so far given rise to no resentment," wrote Asquith. "Although these land sales may provide seeds of future discontent when the land is gone, it must be remembered that much of the land now being sold and developed is uncultivable swamp or rock and the expense of its conversion to usefulness would not be undertaken by developers unless a foreign market were assured."[29]

The new constitution, based on the Asquith report, came into force on 22 August 1972. It made some significant changes, but stopped far short of the degree of self-government that the NDP had sought a decade earlier. Asquith's non-political recommendations were steadily implemented in a series of administrative and judicial changes. The wisdom of a gradual approach was attested to by the Cayman Islands' reputation for political stability and their almost uninterrupted economic growth. It was to be almost three decades before there was any pressing demand for further constitutional change.

No new parties or charismatic leaders emerged during this period. The only possible successors to the NDP and CDP, the "Unity" and "Dignity" teams of the 1970s and 1980s, were loose and often short-lived coalitions of indi-

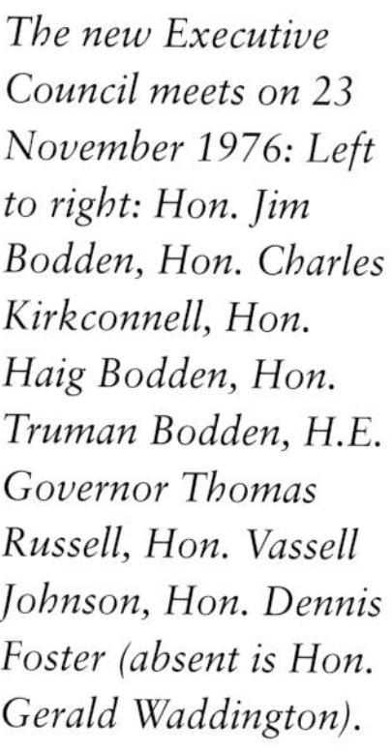

The new Executive Council meets on 23 November 1976: Left to right: Hon. Jim Bodden, Hon. Charles Kirkconnell, Hon. Haig Bodden, Hon. Truman Bodden, H.E. Governor Thomas Russell, Hon. Vassell Johnson, Hon. Dennis Foster (absent is Hon. Gerald Waddington).

viduals. In general, the teams often held similar political ideas and pursued similar policies, with prominence given to the development of the islands and the protection afforded to Caymanian interests. Likewise, the "National Team", which swept into power in 1992 with thirteen seats out of fifteen, found it progressively difficult to maintain its unity over eight years and two administrations. Throughout this time, internal self-government was not promoted by any team or leader.

In 1971, during the tenure of Mr. Athelstan Long, the title of the chief executive was changed from Administrator to Governor, though this was essentially a paper change. The 1972 constitution did away with the system of nominated Members. However, three official Members appointed by the Governor – the Chief Secretary, the Financial Secretary, and the Attorney General – continued to sit with the twelve elected Members in the Legislative Assembly, over which the Governor presided. As president of the Assembly, the Governor could be replaced by a Speaker once this change was voted by a majority of the Assembly. But as late as May 1989, when a private Member made a motion to this effect and the voting was tied, the Governor used his tie-breaking vote to maintain the status quo. The following year, the Assembly voted to replace the Governor as president, and the veteran civil servant and parliamentarian Ms. Sybil McLaughlin became the first Speaker.

As chairman and president of the Executive Council, the Governor remained the Cayman Islands' chief executive. From 1972 the Legislative Assembly elected four of its Members to serve on the Executive Council. These were balanced by the Governor's three appointed officials and the Governor himself. Of the official Members, the Chief Secretary (who was the Governor's deputy) was responsible for internal and external affairs, the Attorney General for legal administration, and the Financial Secretary for all matters of finance and development. The four elected Members were each assigned "portfolios" by the Governor. In 1972 these were the portfolios of health, education, and social services; agriculture, lands, and natural resources; communications and works; and tourism, aviation, and trade. Combinations of these subjects, with others added over time, made up the portfolios and ministries during the next thirty years.

The Governor was normally required to act on the advice of the Executive Council except in matters of defence, external affairs, internal security, the police, and the civil service, for which he had sole responsibility. The Governor could go against ExCo's advice if he considered it in the public interest, and in emergencies he was permitted to do this without prior approval from London. In certain other respects the Governor could act without consulting the Council – though he was obliged to report his actions to ExCo afterward. Members of ExCo were bound by "collective responsibility" to support all its decisions in the Assembly.

Captain Mabry Kirkconnell, MLA for the Sister Islands (1980–2000), attired as Speaker of the Legislative Assembly (1996–2001).

The Sister Islands continued to be represented by two Members of the Assembly, although their population represented only a tenth of the total in 1972 and no more than a twentieth by 2000. Whenever possible, the Sister Islands were given a voice on ExCo, as happened during the 1970s and 1980s through the steady presence of Captain Charles Kirkconnell. In 1997 one of the two elected representatives for Cayman Brac and Little Cayman, Julianna O'Connor-Connolly, became the first woman to sit in ExCo, as Minister for Community Affairs, Sports, Women, Youth and Culture. The other Sister Islands Member, Captain Mabry S. Kirkconnell, succeeded Sybil McLaughlin as Speaker of the Legislative Assembly in 1996.[30]

Under the 1972 constitution, the term of the Assembly was extended from three to four years. This change was intended to give the elected house greater stability and to attach more weight to the general election process. The reduction of the voting age from twenty-one to eighteen was particularly significant. A larger electorate helped to offset the political influence of recent immigrants, who at that time became eligible to vote after a relatively brief residency. Voting by non-Caymanians was reviewed again in the 1980s, and a constitutional amendment passed in 1987 tightened the qualifications for both voting and candidacy for the Assembly. It enabled control of the legislature to remain in the hands of Caymanians.

In 1991, at the request of the Assembly, the 1972 constitution was reviewed by two commissioners appointed by the FCO: Sir Frederick Smith and Mr. Walter Wallace.[31] As a result of their report and the subsequent debate by the legislature, the Secretary of State submitted, in July 1992, a draft new constitution that included a full ministerial system and virtual self-government. This was circulated to the public before the general election scheduled for November 1992. Prior to the election, the number of elected Members in the Assembly was raised from twelve to fifteen.

The National Team government elected in 1992, however, did not advocate major political change. In 1993 it "shelved the draft constitution and proposed instead certain amendments to the 1972 constitution". One of these was adoption of an authentic ministerial system. Another provided for the appointment of a fifth elected Member to the Executive Council, which gave elected Members a majority. The amendments did not include the appointment of a Chief Minister. Elected Members of the Executive Council continued to head formal ministries, each with its permanent secretary to implement policy and oversee the administration of the departments included in the ministry. Passed by the legislature in November 1993 and approved by the Privy Council in the following month, the amendments were implemented in 1994. These were the last constitutional changes effected before the end of the century.[32]

ADMINISTRATIVE CHANGES

The transformation of the Caymanian civil service during the postwar period contrasted with the slow and cautious pace of constitutional change. In the second half of the twentieth century, the administration expanded from a few dozen individuals in a handful of departments to more than three thousand posts in over sixty departments, units, and sections and an additional sixty-nine statutory authorities, boards, and committees. The challenge to the public service was to keep up with the demands of a modern country operating in a global economy. As the economy flourished, some of the ablest and most ambitious Caymanians gravitated towards the private sector. For that and other reasons, it was often difficult to find Caymanians with the specialised skills and experience for technical and professional positions. This put a premium on training Caymanians, but it also meant that the government necessarily depended on expatriates in order to operate a growing range of services.

Both the size and the structure of the civil service have developed dramatically. As recently as 1955, the Commissioner was head of all three branches of government. The Civil Service totalled about eighty staff, or about 1 per cent of the population. Beginning with the division of Customs, Post Office, and Treasury into three separate bodies in 1955, some government functions became separate departments. Some departments naturally grew faster than others, such as those responsible for education, health, policing, and financial matters. A few were reshuffled or changed their focus. The strongest trend from the 1960s to the 1990s was towards new departments, boards, and semi-autonomous bodies. As the economy expanded and Cayman's links with the world became more sophisticated, a growing degree of specialisation was required of the public service.[33]

Among the new government bodies were the Planning Department and Central Planning Authority, the Port Authority, the Mosquito Research and Control Unit, the Departments of Tourism, Agriculture, and Labour, the Department of Lands and Survey, and Radio Cayman. The expansion of the civil service created a need for a Public Service Commission, a Personnel Department, and a Pensions Board. By the end of the twentieth century, the Cayman Islands Government had become truly "national" in the sense that its numerous departments and committees had responsibilities as wide as those of many other national governments. The public

The Legislative Assembly in the 1970s.

Senior civil servants with Governor Thomas Russell, in front of the new Government Administration Building, 1976.

service had increased in size by thirty times, with over 8 per cent of the population now working for government. Concerns were being expressed that the sheer size of government was making it harder for departments to respond properly to market forces. Accordingly, in 1996, Governor John Owen initiated a "reinvention" project, with the stated aim of making the public service "more customer-focused and result-oriented". The exercise was based on widely praised programmes of reinvention elsewhere, especially in New Zealand.[34]

The Caymanian legal and public safety systems adapted well to the inevitable social problems generated by rapid change from the 1960s onward. While gaining in professional skills and efficiency, the police and the courts remained scrupulously independent from political pressures and influence. The *Annual Report & Official Handbook* for 1997 could justifiably claim: "The Cayman Islands continues to be one of the most tranquil places on earth. Despite having to deal with many of the social and other problems brought on by rapid development, the level of crime remains relatively low, the detection and prosecution rates are high and justice is swift."[35]

The 1974 opening of the Grand Court at the new Courts Building, George Town.

Before the 1950s the Cayman Islands had an extremely simple court structure. Litigation was carried out by self-trained "law agents", and justice was administered by J.P.s chosen from among the chief citizens. The Commissioner served as chief justice as well as chief executive and president of the legislature. At the lowest level were the Petty Session

The Government Administration Building, Cayman Brac, ca. 1960.

Courts, in which two J.P.s dealt with minor summary offences and preliminary examinations. At the intermediate level was the Quarterly Petty Court, presided over by either two J.P.s, or one J.P. with a jury of three to five persons. The Grand Court, which sat just twice a year, tried all criminal cases, including capital crimes, as well as civil disputes involving claims over £10. For the rare capital cases, a judge was brought in from Jamaica to hear the case before a jury of twelve people. Appeals could go from the Petty Courts to the Grand Court, from there to the Court of Appeal in Jamaica, and ultimately to the Judicial Committee of the Privy Council in London.[36]

In 1948, the Grand Court dealt with only ten criminal and seventeen civil cases and four judgement summons.[37] But as the number and complexity of cases steadily increased throughout the 1950s and 1960s, it became necessary to enlarge the courts and make them more professional. The separation of the judiciary from the executive and legislative branches of government became essential. The first move was the appointment of a Stipendiary Magistrate in 1957. This person took over the Commissioner's judicial functions.[38]

The principle of the separation of powers – legislative, judicial, and executive – was the crux of an important appeal case in Jamaica in 1967, *Re Cayman Islands Public Service Co. Ltd.* The Stipendiary Magistrate, acting as judge of the Grand Court, had made a judgement in favour of the government. This was held to represent a conflict of interest, since the SM was also the only Member of the Executive Council with legal responsibilities.[39] It was largely to resolve this dilemma that the post of Attorney General was created, later in the same year. This person, invariably an expatriate skilled in

On parade: the Grand Cayman police force, ca. 1940s.

the operation of the British judiciary, played a key role in the expansion and restructuring of the Caymanian legal system.

Between the 1970s and the 1990s, substantial changes were made in the structure and workings of the courts. The Petty Courts were reformulated as Summary Jurisdiction Courts, sitting under one or two qualified Magistrates or, in minor cases, two J.P.s. A separate Youth Court was created, reflecting the growth in cases of this kind. By 1998 there were two Stipendiary Magistrates and ninety-four J.P.s.[40]

As the numbers of complex civil cases and indictable crimes grew, the Grand Court expanded in size and activity. It sat under either a chief justice or one of two subordinate puisne judges appointed by the Governor, and had its own administrator and a growing staff of clerks and recorders. Appeals from the Grand Court went to the Jamaican Appeals Court. In 1984, however, a separate Cayman Islands Court of Appeal was instituted, under four distinguished expatriate judges, appointed not by the Governor but by the Secretary of State for Commonwealth Affairs. Final appeals could still be made to the Judicial Committee of the Privy Council in London.[41]

The work of the Attorney General's office was also expanding during this period, along with the judicial system in general. As a result, the Attorney General delegated a number of functions, while concentrating on his primary work as a Member of the Legislative Assembly and a Member of Executive Council. A separate legal draftsman was first appointed in 1970.

A separate office of Solicitor General was created in 1990, reflecting both the rapid increase in cases during the 1980s and the amount of legal advice required by government. The Solicitor General and his staff in the Legal Department are responsible for conducting criminal and civil cases and giving specialist advice to support the myriad functions of government.[42]

Working in tandem with the Attorney General and his staff was a growing police force. From a single officer and a handful of constables in the 1940s and 1950s, the police had developed into a force with 20 civilians and 260 police officers by the late 1990s. Renamed the Royal Cayman Islands Police Service at the time of the official visit of Queen Elizabeth II in 1983, it grew to include separate units for CID, highway, emergency response, commercial fraud, and drugs. According to the Annual Report for 1997, the level of crime was "still relatively low compared to most Caribbean countries, and residents and visitors alike enjoy a generally safe and secure environment". A total of 3,307 crimes were reported during the year, though with commendable detection and conviction rates of 74 per cent and over 50 per cent, respectively.

In 1981 a new prison was opened at Northward, in the centre of Grand Cayman. It was based on progressive principles of rehabilitation rather than on punishment and retribution. In 1997, its average population of 216 inmates received excellent educational, vocational, religious, health, and counselling services. The most trustworthy inmates were allowed to volunteer for community projects. The buildings had originally been designed, however, for 130 inmates, and there were complaints from the inside about overcrowding, as well as public concerns about security. A major alarm occurred when four of the most serious offenders escaped and were at large for several days in

The Post Office at Hell, West Bay, 1973.

December 1997. An even more disturbing event happened in October 1999, when the number of prisoners exceeded three hundred. A riot involving some sixty inmates got out of control, and fires were started that caused damage estimated to cost more than a million dollars.[43] Over the next twelve months the facility was rebuilt and order restored with the leadership of an experienced prison governor from the U.K.

All in all, the Cayman Islands has a well-established reputation for political stability, personal security, and the rule of law. This has been a major factor in ensuring prosperity by attracting investment, tourists, and non-Caymanian residents. Most people maintain that the British principles of an independent judiciary and a police force free from political influence have been critical in achieving this fortunate state of affairs. A majority would probably maintain that it has been assured by the continuing constitutional link with Britain. Oversight of the judiciary and control of the police have continued to be reserved to the Governor, for example, rather than allocated to elected representatives.

One striking feature of the judicial system at the end of the twentieth century was the continuing dependence on non-Caymanian judges, lawyers, and legal experts. The Cayman Islands Law School is gradually changing this profile. Founded in 1982 as an affiliate of the University of Liverpool, it was equipped with an excellent small law library and provided with a six-member faculty. Besides a diploma in legal studies, it provided tuition for the courses that lead to the Bachelor of Laws (Honours) degree of the University of Liverpool, and qualification as an attorney-at-law in the Cayman Islands. The first LL.B. (Hons.) candidates graduated in 1994. The following year saw the first graduating class from the professional practice course, the members of which could become fully qualified as local attorneys-at-law after a further eighteen-month period of practical training.

By the year 2000 the Cayman Islands could therefore boast a legal system whose structure and workings were at least as sophisticated, efficient, and self-sufficient as those of Jamaica, Barbados, and the Bahamas. Although the Cayman Islands had not chosen the path to independence followed by those countries after the demise of the West Indies Federation, they had nevertheless witnessed significant political and administrative developments, which had played a key part in their growing prosperity. Their legal system was every bit as robust as that of their independent neighbours in the region, while being admirably suited to their unique needs and to the political constitution of their choice.[44]

Mr. Tomlinson, a visiting member of the legal profession from Jamaica, consults his books, ca. 1930.

CHAPTER 15

The Engineered Miracle

Economic Development, 1950–2000

......

In less than half a lifetime, the Cayman Islands changed almost beyond recognition. A sleepy backwater, with a few dozen foreign visitors a year and without a single commercial bank, was transformed into one of the Caribbean's favourite tourist destinations and the world's fifth-largest financial centre. This did not happen by chance. Tourists were drawn by the climate, the beaches and reefs, and the islands' proximity to the United States, from which most of the visitors came. The islands combined the exotic with the familiar, and were safe. For bankers and investors, the Cayman Islands enjoyed many advantages. They were strategically located between the dollar bloc and the financial centres of the rest of the world's major currencies. They offered the stability and security of British institutions, while at the same time being far enough from Great Britain and the United States to minimise financial scrutiny.

By themselves, however, these advantages were not enough to bring about the transformation. The Cayman Islands had to be linked to the outside world by commercial flights and telecommunications. Before land could be sold to hoteliers, developers, and foreign owners, it had to be accurately surveyed and its ownership established and registered. Finally, few outsiders of any kind would be attracted for long until the scourge of the mosquito had been sharply reduced.

The tourism and banking industries were the product of skilful cooperation among all those who stood to benefit. On one side of the table were American, Canadian, and British entrepreneurs eager for profitable invest-

Seven Mile Beach, with the new Galleon Beach Hotel, ca. 1956.

ment; on the other, British officials wishing to place the Cayman Islands on a sound economic footing. In between, and most significant for the future of the islands, were Caymanians themselves. Among the most dynamic and astute were retired sea captains, returned migrants, and Cayman Brackers. But Caymanians as a whole were willing to embark on a new kind of voyage towards what promised to be a strong economic future. They sought advice, attracted capital, and welcomed reputable people seeking residence. At the same time, they guarded the right to Caymanian citizenship, strove to exclude undesirable elements, and made sure that Caymanians controlled the process of change and shared in the ultimate rewards.

TAKING TO THE SKIES

World War Two brought home to the Cayman Islands the full potential of air transportation. The first air carriers were seaplanes that landed on Grand Cayman's North Sound. Most of them were converted Catalina amphibians like those used at the Baldpate base during the war. Further progress required airfields, which were constructed in Grand Cayman and Cayman Brac in the 1950s and in Little Cayman in the early 1960s. Major expansion became necessary from the 1960s onwards, when turbo-props and jetliners superseded propeller planes. When the handsome new terminal building at Owen Roberts airport was officially opened in 1984, a British Airways Concorde floated in over Hog Sty Bay to make its first-ever landing in Cayman – a fitting symbol of how far air travel in the Cayman Islands had come.

Air transportation grew with tourism but also required government investment. Even after public air transport was established, the costs of buying

and maintaining aircraft and operating facilities always outpaced the immediate returns. Private enterprise tended to be attracted to places where facilities already existed, and to routes and schedules that guaranteed profits. This meant that government, which was concerned with general, long-term benefits, had to offer start-up investment and subsidies, as well as ensuring that commercial carriers took the economic rough with the smooth. As in other Caribbean countries, debate about a national airline brought these issues into sharp focus.

The two pioneers of Caymanian air travel were swashbuckling Royal Air Force veterans of World War Two. King Parker Jr. was an American living in Tampa who had ferried bombers across the Atlantic for RAF Transport Command. Early in 1946, with several other ex–RAF pilots, he purchased six surplus aircraft – PBY Catalinas, or flying boats – from the Canadian government and went looking for work in the Caribbean. The first passenger flights to Grand Cayman originated in Tampa, with Parker as pilot and his wife as stewardess. The normal flight time was five hours, and delays and cancellations due to mechanical problems and the weather were frequent.

When King Parker was offered the franchise for a regular service between Kingston and Montego Bay, he formed Jamaica Air Transport Ltd. In November 1946 he added a weekly service between Kingston, Grand Cayman, and Cayman Brac. Parker negotiated a mail contract with the Cayman Islands government in return for a small subsidy and promptly reorganised his company as Cayman Island Airways. The prominent businessman-politician Ducan Merren became a director, and many Caymanians took out ten-shilling shares in the company. The inaugural flight was on 20 October 1947. The shoestring airline, however, had difficulties finding enough passengers, keeping up with U.S. regulations, and maintaining its ageing aircraft. To avoid landing in choppy seas, the crew sometimes pushed mailbags and other freight out

The Santa Maria, *a PBY Catalina, disembarking passengers in the North Sound, ca. 1950.*

of an open window as the aircraft flew low over Grand Cayman or Cayman Brac.[1]

Wing Commander Owen Roberts.

In December 1947, King Parker sold out to a small group headed by a former RAF wing commander, Owen "Bobby" Roberts. Though his airline was grandly named Caribbean International Airlines, Roberts centred his operations on the Cayman Islands. By 1950, he had established a fairly regular service to Tampa, Kingston, and Belize. A man of vision as well as charm, Owen Roberts saw the need for airfields that could accommodate airliners with far greater capacity and reliability than his fourteen-seat amphibious Catalinas. He spearheaded a tireless lobbying campaign for proper airfields, directed through Commissioners Smith and Gerrard to the authorities in London.

The construction of the airfield at George Town in the early 1950s was by far the largest project undertaken in the Cayman Islands up to that time. To build a runway 150 feet wide and 6,000 feet long, the government had to purchase land, re-route the island's main east-west road, and hire considerable labour to level the limestone rock and fill in the swamps. The estimated cost was £93,000 – almost twice the entire revenue of the islands in 1950. After much debate and negotiation, the money was raised by using £12,500 of the islands' modestly expanding reserve funds, applying for a Colonial Development and Welfare grant of £25,000, and borrowing £55,000 from the Colonial Development Corporation. The work itself could not have been accomplished without the generous loan of trained engineers and heavy equipment by the Jamaican government.[2]

To construct the airfield and oversee its operations, a new body called the Cayman Islands Corporation was created in late 1951. Actual work began in August 1952, and on 28 November, before an enthusiastic local crowd, Owen Roberts's Catalina *Santa Maria* made a perfect landing on the not-quite-finished runway. With his company still seriously short of funds but within sight of his goal, Roberts went to the United States and purchased two used

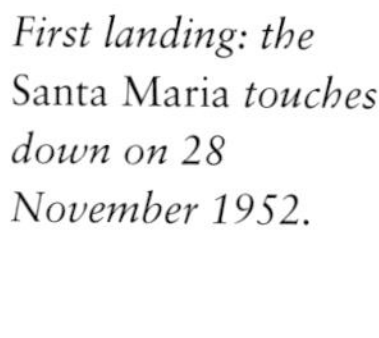

First landing: the Santa Maria *touches down on 28 November 1952.*

Lockheed Lodestar airliners. Then tragedy struck. On its inaugural flight from Kingston to Grand Cayman on 10 April 1953, one of the Lodestars crashed on take-off from Palisadoes Airport. Owen Roberts was killed, along with thirteen passengers and crew.[3]

Construction of the George Town airport was completed in August 1953. It was officially opened in March 1954 by Governor Sir Hugh Foot, in the presence of Jamaican Chief Minister Alexander Bustamante, the British naval Commander-in-Chief in the West Indies, and an honour guard of Royal Marines from the flagship HMS *Sheffield*. The airport was named Owen Roberts Field. "His memory is revered in the Cayman Islands," noted the Annual Report, "both for his invaluable pioneering work (without which it is doubtful if there would be any air services today) and for his humorous and happy temperament which caused him to be regarded with great affection as the epitome of the English gentleman-adventurer."[4]

The death of Owen Roberts proved to be the end of his company, and for many months the Cayman Islands lacked a regular air service. The gap was eventually filled by the fledgling British West India Airways, which included Grand Cayman as an intermediate stop in its weekly service between Kingston and Belize. For a time, U.S. licensing obstacles meant that it could go no further than Havana. But BWIA eventually established the vital connection out of Miami, which was fast becoming the air gateway to the Caribbean. At the same time, LACSA, the Costa Rican national airline, recognized the advantages of making a refuelling stop at Grand Cayman between Miami, San José, and Panama, and obtained rights for a weekly flight. By the end of 1954 the Cayman Islands thus enjoyed two passenger flights a week to Kingston, two to Miami, one to Belize, and one to Costa Rica and Panama.[5] Steadily increasing demand led to growth in the number of flights in and out of Grand Cayman.

Regular air service to the Sister Islands, in typical Brac fashion, started as a community initiative. In 1954, a group of Bracker volunteers hacked out the first 1,200 feet of an airstrip with picks and shovels and levelled it with a heavy roller borrowed from Jamaica, for a total cost of £1,600.[6] Modest grants, obtained as a result of the Commissioners' pleas to London, enabled the strip to be extended to 2,400 feet and covered in asphalt. The runway was completed in 1955 and named the Gerrard-Smith Airport in honour of the two Commissioners who had encouraged its construction. At first Cayman Brac was served

Cattle being unloaded from a LACSA plane, ca. 1960s.

twice a week by a company called Cayman Brac Airways (a LACSA subsidiary), which had only a six-seat Cessna and was supported by an annual government subsidy of £4,000.[7]

Air service to the Sister Islands steadily expanded. The Gerrard-Smith runway was extended first to 2,800 and then to 3,500 feet, to accommodate larger planes and even small jets. In 1962 a small grass airfield was built on Little Cayman with private money on parcels of land owned by a number of different individuals.[8] The service to the Sister Islands frequently needed government subsidies and barely covered its costs. But its importance to the development of the islands was recognized, and in 1968 Cayman Brac Airways was reconstituted as Cayman Island Airways, owned 49 per cent by LACSA and 51 per cent by the Cayman Islands government.[9] In 1977 the government took it over completely. Meanwhile, the needs of the Sister Islands continued to be served by private enterprise. During the 1970s and 1980s, a series of companies, including Trans-Island Airways, Red Carpet Airlines, and Executive Air Services, offered flights either into Cayman Brac from the U.S. or else between the islands – a precursor, in the latter case, of the daily schedule of inter-island flights that Island Air began to offer from the early 1990s.[10]

All three airports became busier as passenger flights (both scheduled and charter), cargo flights, and traffic in private airplanes increased. From handling 2,164 arriving aircraft bringing in 7,283 passengers in 1964, Owen Roberts Airport was accommodating 8,733 planes carrying 121,561 passengers by 1979. The traffic at the two Sister Island airfields in the 1970s rose from fewer than a thousand take-offs and landings with about 3,000 passengers to as many as 3,600 flights carrying 8,000 passengers a year. By 1997, the three airports combined handled 22,000 arrivals and departures and almost a million passengers.[11]

Official opening of the terminal at Edward Bodden Airfield, Little Cayman, 1962.

Underlying this successful growth over thirty years, however, is a more complex story. There were recurrent crises and reorganisations, and conflicts between private carriers and the national airline, as well as between U.S. regulatory authorities and the Cayman Islands government. Within the islands, there were policy disagreements about cost and efficiency between those who favoured government control and the advocates of free enterprise.

Hon. James Bodden, National Hero, MLA for Bodden Town (1972–89), Member with responsibility for Tourism, Aviation and Trade (1976–84).

In 1968 a newly created Civil Aviation Authority took over from the Cayman Islands Corporation shortly after the airport facilities at Owen Roberts had been upgraded and the runway resurfaced. In the same year, Cayman Airways was created. Besides serving the Sister Islands, it became an international carrier when it took over the Kingston–Grand Cayman–Miami service discontinued by BWIA in 1971.[12] But Cayman Airways faced powerful competition from U.S. carriers. These airlines had far greater resources and better access to the aviation authorities which assigned air routes and regulated the industry. The Cayman Islands therefore found themselves facing a perennial dilemma. They wanted to attract an ever-increasing flow of tourists. But in order to maintain a viable national carrier, they had to balance the high cost of local services with more lucrative international flights.

A key figure in this unfolding story was James Manoah Bodden, who served from 1976 to 1984 as the Member of the Executive Council responsible for tourism, aviation, and trade. "Mr. Jim", as he was known, was the first Caymanian to be designated a National Hero, six years after his early

Inter-island service provided by Cayman Brac Airways during the 1960s.

death in 1988. He is the best known of the Caymanian returnees who revitalised the islands during the 1970s and 1980s. Born in 1930 at Lower Valley, Grand Cayman, the son of a seaman, he migrated to Port Arthur, Texas, at the age of seventeen. For two years he worked for a two-boat tanker company started by another Caymanian, Eddingstone Ambrose, before settling ashore, marrying an American, and becoming a U.S. citizen. Over the next dozen years he worked as a private detective, started and sold a costume-jewellery and novelty business and a taxicab company, and became general manager of a frozen-foods company in Beaumont, Texas. Jim Bodden returned to Grand Cayman in the 1960s with plans to start a hotel. When his plans fell through, he went back to sea for a time. Later he became involved in a charter-boat business and started a real estate company. In 1972 he entered politics, winning a seat for Bodden Town. He and Haig Bodden, the other member for Bodden Town and his long-term political ally, became energetic back-benchers.[13]

From 1976, when Jim Bodden became the Member responsible for tourism, the budget allocations for aviation greatly increased. Cayman Airways and the airports were supplied with up-to-date equipment, and energetic promotional campaigns were undertaken. Foreign carriers were encouraged, but not at the expense of the national airline. By negotiation, the vital passenger link with Jamaica was shared equally with Air Jamaica, which (in cooperation with Air Canada) succeeded BWIA in the western Caribbean. The long stand-off and eventual settlement with the U.S. carriers was even more critical. Three airlines, Pan Am, Eastern, and Northwest, were already well established. In the early 1980s the Cayman Islands government declared a moratorium on further expansion, claiming that Cayman Airways was being unfairly excluded from the wider U.S. market. The impasse was resolved in 1986. In return for opening up the islands to additional U.S. airlines, Cayman Airways was allowed routes to Atlanta and other American gateway cities besides Miami.[14]

By the late 1990s, the air passenger business had become even more competitive. An impressive array of airlines and charter companies met the needs of tourists and Caymanian residents. The people of the Sister Islands were also well served through competition. In addition to regular Cayman Airways flights to the Brac, Island Air operated twin-engine aircraft that seated from eight to twenty people, stopping at the grass airstrip on Little Cayman as well as the more substantial facility on Cayman Brac.

In 1998, besides the services of Cayman Airways, six U.S. airlines provided scheduled service to and from seven U.S. gateway cities: Miami, Tampa, Orlando, Houston, Atlanta, Charlotte, and St. Louis. At least eight charter companies also flew passengers from various North American cities, including Newark, Boston, Chicago, Cincinnati, Indianapolis, Minneapolis, Dallas, and Toronto. Within the Caribbean itself, apart from the service to Jamaica

offered by Cayman Airways and Air Jamaica, Cubana flew charter flights to Havana, and occasional charter flights were organised to Belize, San Andrés, and other Central American destinations. Throughout the 1990s, British Airways provided thrice-weekly flights between the U.K. and Grand Cayman. In addition, more and more private aircraft, including company jets, visited the islands.[15]

PROBLEMS ON LAND

Questions about land ownership in the Cayman Islands had long been settled in a fairly informal manner. The purchase of land for the airports on Grand Cayman and Cayman Brac, however, brought into focus the deficiencies of this system. As the value of beachfront land escalated during the 1950s and 1960s, more and more ownership questions arose. It was increasingly clear that the system of land registration and the absence of local surveying facilities were unacceptable. Ownership was often claimed simply by customary usage, with boundaries indicated by axe-cuts on trees or other impermanent landmarks. When land was bought, sold, bequeathed, or mortgaged, the relevant documents were supposed to be lodged with the Public Recorder. But even when this was done, the land plats were rarely more than freehand sketches.

Two key examples illustrated the main problems. In 1949, when the Englishman Benson Greenall sought an unequivocal land title in order to build the first hotel on Seven Mile Beach, he had to employ Jamaican lawyers and surveyors – a move that was likely to stir up fears of foreign exploitation. And when ownership of the land for the Cayman Brac airstrip was being established, there were more than thirty claims for compensation, most of them overlapping. Any registered documents that might have existed had apparently been destroyed in the 1932 hurricane.[16]

Throughout the 1950s, the Annual Reports deplored the lack of clear land registration, each year repeating the complaints almost word for word. Apart from creating confusion, the situation tied up land that was ripe for development, either because ownership could not be determined or because speculators had bought up large plots for long-term gain. "The general trend," Commissioner Andrew Gerrard wrote

Benson Greenall (second left) and staff, unloading a washing machine for the Galleon Beach Hotel, ca. 1955.

in 1952, "is for more and more land to pass into fewer hands, in many cases absentee proprietors who permit the land to go to waste . . . consideration must inevitably be given to whether legislation should be enacted in regard to land usage and development." Land speculation nevertheless continued, and by 1956 the value of land had risen considerably, especially beach property and land for building. But in the absence of appropriate legislation, a good deal of valuable land was lying fallow, hindering development.[17]

Attempts were made to resolve the problem, but in 1965 Administrator Jack Rose still regarded it as critical. A 1960 law made the registration of all land transactions compulsory. But, "without the backing of accurate survey . . . the registration of land is of limited value", wrote Rose in 1965. "Although Caymanians generally respect existing land titles, the increasing value of land is reflected in the growing number of land disputes between Caymanians which result in litigation before the courts". Government had recently appointed a committee to examine the need for new laws on the subject. Rose hoped that their work would lead to "an appropriate law" before the end of 1966.[18]

It took five more years, however, and three separate laws to provide for proper land registration. The process provoked one of the most prolonged and serious political debates – accompanied by public demonstrations – in modern Caymanian history. The trouble was not the innovations themselves, but the fact that they originated largely in London and were poorly explained to the Caymanian public. There was widespread concern about the effects of the changes and suspicion that they were part of a British trend towards increasing the Administrator's authority.

The rumblings started with the introduction of the first set of planning controls. According to Administrator A.C.E. Long, there was a need "to intro-

A Ruston electrical generator for use by government being unloaded at George Town dock, ca. 1960s.

duce some order and control over the pace and extent and nature of development projects both private and public". A Land Development Control Board was set up by law in 1968. Early the following year, it issued detailed regulations, drafted by committees of the Assembly, to govern planning permissions and zoning.[19] Public protest meetings and a march on the government offices led to the regulations being temporarily rescinded. Administrator Long was compelled to defend the moves. Another Select Committee of the Assembly was appointed, which, after "long and careful examination", allowed the re-introduction of the regulations " in an almost identical form to the original". By 1971, Long was able to report, "They are now generally accepted and their usefulness recognised."[20]

The public reaction in 1969 was mild, however, compared with the storm following the introduction in March 1971 of the Land Adjudication, Land Surveyors', and Registered Land laws. The controversy affected the discussions leading up to the new constitution in 1972. There was strong support for a change that would, as Long said, "give every owner clear title to his land and introduce a modern system of registration to make dealings in real estate much simpler".[21] But the sudden change from a system of land ownership based simply on traditional documentation to one based upon a new comprehensive survey was hard to accept. Those pressing most for this "cadastral" system were the Overseas Development Administration and the Directorate of Overseas Services in London. It had already been adopted by the Bahamas, and was being introduced without opposition in the Turks and Caicos and British Virgin Islands.

Some Caymanians suspected a plan by the Crown to claim all lands to which the owners could not prove title. Many feared that the new system was designed to introduce taxes on land. As opponents were quick to point out, the word "cadastral" in its original form means "a survey for the purpose of taxation". There were also concerns about the cost and about bringing in a whole new set of outside experts.

To allay fears, Long introduced the new legislation in his Throne Speech only after he had dealt with three other laws that he knew would be popular. These were the Caymanian Protection Law, the Local Companies (Control) Law, and the Trades and Businesses Licensing Law.[22] Turning to the new land legislation, the Administrator argued strongly that it was needed and tried to calm local anxieties. Far from being deprived of land, he claimed, only under the new system would Caymanians obtain clear title. A claimant to a piece of land would now have to prove uninterrupted occupation for only twelve years, not sixty years, as previously. The Crown wished to establish what land was and was not privately owned. It did not want to extend its own landholdings. The cadastral survey would be carried out without cost to landholders, and government had no intention of imposing taxes on land. A team of sur-

veyors from the Directorate of Overseas Services would carry out the work, Long concluded. Their work would be complete within eighteen months and paid for solely by the British government.[23]

The Assembly, perhaps wary of public reaction, declined even to debate the land bills. Confronted by this refusal, and summoned by the Secretary of State, Administrator Long immediately flew off to London. He returned with a sternly worded message from Sir Alec Douglas-Home, the Foreign and Commonwealth Secretary, which Long read to the Assembly on 9 May 1971. Experts were brought in from England and other parts of the West Indies to explain the workings of the intended system. A delegation was sent to the Turks and Caicos Islands to observe it in operation. After much discussion in committee and a diminishing chorus of public protest, all three bills were passed into law in September 1971.[24]

The survey team began its work in conjunction with the new Lands and Survey Department in 1972. But the cadastral process proved more complex, time-consuming, and costly than promised. The surveyors began with George Town, which was a jigsaw of different-sized parcels, some of them tiny. The swampy, rocky parts of the islands proved equally challenging. The surveyors considered the interior the most difficult terrain they had ever encountered. Cayman Brac offered the challenges of vague titles, overlapping claims, and disagreements that occasionally became violent.[25]

Instead of eighteen months, the cadastral process took more than five years. As early as March 1973 there was a minor storm when it was revealed that the Cayman Islands Government was being held responsible for $33,000 of the CI$120,000 total cost for the year. Governor Crook was forced to apologise for the previous underestimate, and it became clear that costs would exceed revenues until the whole process was complete.[26]

In September 1977 the project officially came to an end. The last surveys were handed over to the Director of the Lands and Survey Department, who combined the roles of Chief Surveyor and Registrar of Lands. A small branch office of Lands and Survey was opened in Cayman Brac during the year. Nearly all Caymanian landholdings were now accurately incorporated into the master cadastral plan: some 13,500 parcels in all, of which at least 650 had been disputed and resolved. In October 1977, an aerial survey was carried out under the supervision of the DOS. This, along with the cadastral survey, allowed the first really accurate maps of the islands to be drafted.[27]

By this time, Governor Russell could claim that the Lands and Survey Department had fulfilled predictions. "Most if not all of the opposition to the laws has ceased," he reported, "and they are now accepted as necessary for the determination of ownership and systematic land transactions." By now, too, the financial rewards were becoming evident. In 1977, the Department spent just under $100,000 but brought in nine times as much. The great

bulk of this was from stamp duty on land transactions.[28] Thereafter, income for the Lands and Survey Department grew in tandem with the economy, exceeding $25 million a year within twenty years. In the last three decades, the department has been a key player in facilitating the development of the Cayman Islands.

THE MOSQUITO WAR

Throughout the 1950s and early 1960s, the Cayman Islands were becoming better known. But as all residents knew and visitors soon learned, the chief adversary in this "paradise" was the tiny but pesky mosquito. Its control was essential if development was to succeed. Defeating the mosquito required determination and planning on the part of Caymanians, and cooperation with agencies and experts from many parts of the world. It was also extremely costly in relation to local resources. Victory took years of dedicated effort. It was achieved, for the most part, in the 1970s, when the Cayman Islands were poised for their greatest economic expansion.

The first serious campaign against the mosquito followed a report by Dr. George Giglioli, a renowned Italian entomologist long resident in British Guiana, who visited the Cayman Islands on behalf of the World Health Organisation in 1948. The campaign was carried out between 1949 and 1951 under the supervision of the energetic government health officer, H.O. "Bertie" Ebanks. Mr. Ebanks had travelled to British Guiana to observe Dr. Giglioli's successful methods of combating the disease-carrying mosquitos there. Spraying equipment and large quantities of the new insecticide DDT were obtained through a Colonial Development and Welfare grant, and almost all houses throughout the islands were regularly sprayed over a three-year period. The programme is credited with removing the threats of yellow fever and malaria by eradicating the species of mosquitoes which carried them. However, the most troublesome pests, the swamp and pastureland species, continued to swarm in staggering numbers, especially in the summer rainy season.[29]

MRCU fogger in action in the 1970s.

A second campaign in the later 1950s achieved a similar level of success. The government purchased an impressive machine called the Todd Insectidal Fog Applicator. It was mounted on the back of a truck and delivered a noxious mist of DDT-impregnated diesel oil. As the Annual Report for 1955–6 noted, mos-

Dr. Marco Giglioli, first director of the Mosquito Control and Research Unit.

quitoes in the vicinity were "annihilated for a period of 24 hours" and "severely discouraged for several following days". Though not a cure-all, the report continued, fogging was "a reasonably cheap method of suppressing a nuisance, and keeping it within reasonable bounds. Within these limits the results are gratifying, and if further funds can be provided there is no reason why the mosquito nuisance cannot be kept under permanent control."[30]

These early efforts in the 1950s were eventually replaced by a much more systematic approach that relied on scientific research to increase the effectiveness of control operations. The Mosquito Research and Control Unit was created in January 1966, and Dr. Marco E.C. Giglioli, George Giglioli's son, was appointed to direct it. By the Mosquito (Research and Control) Law passed in November 1966, the unit was given wide powers to operate throughout the Cayman Islands, with the right to designate "any part of or a whole island" either as an "experimental control" or a "control" area.[31]

The hero of the Caymanian mosquito wars was ideally suited to the task. Following his early education in Italy and British Guiana, Marco Giglioli earned doctorates from McGill University in Canada and the London School of Hygiene and Tropical Medicine and gained field experience in British Guiana, Canada, Liberia, and Gambia. He was also a person of almost Napoleonic energy and self-confidence, with a clear sense of mission.

From the beginning, Marco Giglioli sought local involvement in the enterprise. He encouraged the formation of a Volunteer Foggers unit, which assisted the MRCU for a decade under the enthusiastic leadership of Capt. Theo Bodden. Giglioli was tireless in promoting the MRCU. He raised funds from the Caymanian and British governments and from international bodies such as the World Health Organisation. He attracted expatriate volunteers, including young scientists working on their doctoral theses and workers from the U.K.'s Voluntary Service Overseas programme. The MRCU earned a reputation for solid research, and Giglioli and his co-workers were in demand as consultants to other mosquito-plagued countries. Marco Giglioli also played a role in the 1974 creation of the Natural Resources Laboratory, which ultimately evolved into the Department of the Environment.

MRCU Thrush Commander spraying mosquito breeding grounds in the 1970s.

As a result of its research, the MRCU perfected a many-pronged attack upon its enemy. MRCU workers sprayed all ships coming into the islands in order to prevent entry of the mosquitoes that carried yellow fever, malaria, and dengue

Controlling mosquitoes: aerial view of dykes and canals created at Salt Creek by the MRCU, 1975.

fever. The work was extended to Cayman Brac and Little Cayman, with the yellow fever mosquito being eradicated in Cayman Brac by the early 1970s.[32] Spraying of the main breeding grounds in the swamps was initiated and fine-tuned to target larvae as well as mature insects. When the environmental dangers of DDT were discovered in the late 1960s, and the mosquitoes developed resistance to the first alternatives, the MRCU widened its range of insecticides and larvicides. Indeed, the department pioneered research into the

general problem of insect and larval resistance and later experimented with bacterial and hormonal agents that were effective against mosquitoes.

MRCU's most ambitious enterprise was to construct a network of canals through the mangrove swamps in Grand Cayman. The canals had a twofold purpose. They allowed high tides to inundate the swamps more completely and reduce the areas of mud in which the eggs were laid. Rainwater could also drain into the sea more quickly, giving the larvae insufficient time to develop into mature mosquitoes. How well the canals worked is unknown. A plan to encourage the breeding of mosquito-eating fish was unsuccessful. No fish could be found that could live in both the brackish and freshwater ponds where the larvae flourished.[33]

From the early 1970s, the number of tourists rose as the mosquito problem came under control. MRCU used its carefully compiled statistics of insect densities to argue first for the intensification of the campaign and then for its continuation. The unit obtained its first sprayer aircraft in 1971 and a second three years later. The laboratories and workshops were continually upgraded and eventually housed in custom-built headquarters named the Marco Giglioli Centre.[34] When he died in 1984 at the age of fifty-six, Dr. Giglioli presided over a prestigious entity, amply justified by its success.

By 1993 it was claimed that the mosquito had practically been eliminated from the main tourist and business areas and had been reduced by 95 per cent since 1966 in the islands overall. Attention was being turned to eliminating the sandflies on the beaches, with considerable success.[35] But the victories were not so complete that the MRCU could relax its vigilance.[36] The dawn and dusk patrols of the two spray aircraft and the foggers' periodic visits to built-up areas continue, reminding residents and visitors alike of the ongoing commitment required in this "war" to keep the islands attractive and livable.

WELCOMING THE OUTSIDE WORLD

Defeating the mosquito, developing air services, and facilitating land sales were not the only factors involved in attracting tourists and investors. Hotel construction had to be encouraged and infrastructure provided, at least on a temporary basis. The building boom required architects, builders, and construction workers, as well as investors, and imported materials and equipment. A major restructuring of port facilities would eventually be required if the cruise-ship industry continued to grow.

During the 1970s, more formal promotion of the islands became essential, especially as competition with other Caribbean tourist destinations grew. From the beginning, the Cayman Islands targeted the middle and "high end" segments of the tourist market. Promotions emphasised sunbathing, swimming, sailing, and scuba diving, rather than nightclubs and casinos.

In the years immediately after World War Two, the colonial government did not build on the tourism initiatives made by Commissioner Cardinall in the late 1930s. The modest ten-year Sketch Development Plan for the Cayman Islands published in June 1946 made no mention of tourism. Colonial funds were used for improving education, building health and social welfare facilities, and supporting agriculture, rather than for tourism. As late as 1949, the islands boasted just two small guest-houses in George Town, the Bay View and the Turtle Inn.[37]

Fresh impetus came from the private sector. The catalyst was a wealthy English visitor, Benson Greenall. Like his compatriot Billy Butlin in Grand Bahama, Greenall recognized that the future of West Indian tourism lay in the American rather than British market. Both men saw in the American postwar boom a chance to escape the damp economic climate created by an austere British Labour government.

In 1949, Benson Greenall bought land on Grand Cayman's empty West Bay Beach. The parcel was one-tenth the size of Butlin's on Grand Bahama, and ten times as far from Florida, but the beach was splendid. There Greenall built the first phase of what he called the Galleon Beach Hotel, with a dozen rooms. It opened in time for the winter season of 1950–51, and was designed for "the wealthier class of tourist".[38] Greenall and his allies were instrumental in influencing the passage of the Caymanian Hotels Aid Law of 1950, which revived legislation passed under Commissioner Cardinall in 1937. This provided exemptions from import duties and taxes for anyone building a hotel with more than ten rooms.[39]

The first fruits of the 1950 Hotels Aid Law included not just Greenall's Galleon Beach Hotel but the Merrens' Seaview Lodge, which opened in 1951 and doubled in size for the 1952 season. After Owen Roberts Airport opened, the airlines carefully monitored the availability of accommodation before increasing their services, and there was a small spurt of building in the mid-

The Galleon Beach Hotel, 1956.

The Buccaneer's Inn, Cayman Brac, in the mid-1960s.

dle and late 1950s. In 1954 the Merrens built the Pageant Beach Hotel, with room for thirty-six guests. Benson Greenall in turn spent £200,000 on the second stage of his hotel, with luxury accommodations for eighty-four. When it opened on 1 January 1956, it was described as "one of the finest hotel buildings in the West Indies".[40]

In 1957 and 1958 four new tourist establishments were opened: the modest Coral Caymanian hotel and three smaller facilities. The new air service to Cayman Brac encouraged the building of the Sister Islands' first guest-house, the Buccaneer's Inn, which could accommodate twenty-four people. Little Cayman's first tourist facility, the privately owned Southern Cross Club, opened in 1960, though at the time it was little more than a fishing camp.[41]

By 1960 there were nine hotels, clubs, and guest-houses, seven of which were open all year. Between them they had only three hundred beds, with daily rates that ranged from £2 3s at the Seaview Lodge in summer to £15 15s at the Galleon Beach Hotel in winter. Although it was claimed that "those who enjoy a simple holiday of the kind offered by the Cayman Islands return time and again", occupancy rates remained low, with scarcely a trickle of visitors venturing to the Sister Islands.[42] This may have been due to the lack of services. The islands still had unreliable water and electricity supplies, and no radio station or daily newspaper. There were almost no shops catering to tourists, or restaurants outside the hotels, and only one open-air cinema – at which the human patrons were greatly outnumbered by mosquitoes.

During the 1960s the government left the promotion of tourism largely to private enterprise. A Hotel Association was formed in 1964, which persuaded the government to set up a Tourist Board two years later. It was chaired on a voluntary basis by an expatriate club owner, Eric Bergstrom, and its advertising was funded by interested local businesses. Within government, the most active proponent was Warren Conolly of East End, who as a member of the Tourist Board argued for government subsidies for advertisement and promotion. In 1969 he was appointed the Member responsible for Tourism. He obtained a budget to extend advertising abroad and establish the first overseas tourist office, in Miami. The number of guest accommodations rose from nine to twelve during the 1960s, but by 1970 the total number of rooms was still around three hundred. Scuba diving had already begun, due almost entirely to the enterprise of a single individual, Bob Soto.[43]

Tourism and its support services took off in the early 1970s. The new constitution in 1972 placed the direction of development firmly in the hands of the Executive Council. In 1974, after considerable debate, a comprehensive Tourism Law was passed. This set up a government Department of Tourism in place of the Tourist Board, with Eric Bergstrom as the first director. The department was given a generous budget of $370,000 in its first year.[44] Warren Conolly remained responsible for tourism in the Assembly until 1976, when he was replaced by Jim Bodden, who served as the Member of ExCo responsible for Tourism, Aviation, and Trade for the next eight years. Building on Conolly's pioneer work, Jim Bodden brought his own vision and energy to the position. He understood that tourism and all other forms of development were interconnected, and he was a tireless advocate of the right marriage between public and private sectors.

After 1972, new legislation increased concessions to hotel builders. It also extended them to others willing to invest in tourist and visitor services, including builders of condominiums and private homes for wealthy foreign residents. Newcomers were given every encouragement to stay. The new Immigration Department's guidelines allocated work permits generously for architects and contractors, craftsmen and specialised hotel workers, as well as for construction labourers and domestics, according to need. The Port Authority, created in 1973, promoted improved harbour facilities to service visiting cruise ships and to unload construction and other materials swiftly and efficiently.[45]

The first sign of a new era was the construction of the Holiday Inn in the centre of Seven Mile Beach, still largely undeveloped. The first phase, with 125 rooms, was opened in time for the 1972–3 winter season. When completed during 1973, it boasted 250 rooms and full conference facilities. For a time it had no rival. Affected by the general recession, tourism remained steady through the middle and late 1970s. By 1979 there were still only sixteen hotels, totalling 653 rooms and 1,305 beds. A similar amount of accommodation was available in holiday cottages and apartments.[46] After this point, though, the hospitality industry began to grow rapidly.

The first Holiday Inn, 1973.

As early as 1978, in its first year of operation, the Central Planning Authority reported applications for building projects totalling $40 million. One was Cayman's first major commercial complex, the Anchorage Centre in central George Town, with 16,000 square feet of office space, multi-storey parking for 130 cars, and an arcade of upscale shops geared to tourists. Other large projects added villas and mari-

An early advertising poster for fishing trips with Capt. Ertis Ebanks.

nas to hotels. The grandest of these was the Palm Heights project, approved in May 1978. Besides a 200-room hotel facing Seven Mile Beach, the plans included eighty-four luxury condominiums and a golf course and marina on a 77-acre lot across West Bay Road, fronting North Sound. In 1987, after several design changes, the complex became the 240-room Hyatt Regency Hotel, Britannia Villas and Golf Course. This was the model of what was later called "the condominium boom of the 1980s".[47]

In 1980, building applications to the Central Planning Authority reached such a peak that the government decided to apply a brake – and tap the source – by levying a 4 per cent tax on the value of future condominiums. This slowed growth somewhat. But the 1980s and 1990s still saw steady building that filled almost the entire sweep of Seven Mile Beach with a dozen large hotels, an equal number of diving facilities, and some thirty-five luxury condominium projects. At the same time, more than half of the swampy and rocky ground on the eastern side of West Bay Road had been dredged and filled to make hundreds of marina slips, luxurious villa sites, and Cayman's second golf course.[48]

These developments were not limited to Seven Mile Beach. Cayman Brac saw the construction during this period of two notable hotels with diving facilities, the Brac Reef Beach Resort and the Divi Tiara Beach Resort. On Grand Cayman, large hotels located away from Seven Mile Beach and George Town's shops and airport seemed impractical. But smaller establishments attracted divers and fishermen, while residential estates catered to those who wished to combine luxurious living with privacy.

At the same time, George Town was being transformed by the number of visiting cruise ships. It was not until the late 1960s that the first postwar cruise ships stopped in the Cayman Islands. But once the Florida-based cruise business developed, Grand Cayman was seen as an ideal location for several Caribbean itineraries. Cruise liners had to anchor offshore, or else near Spotts on the south coast during nor'westers. Piloting, landing, and taxiing facilities steadily improved, however, and immigration formalities were kept to a minimum. Every effort was made to ensure that the town was attractive, colourful, and clean. Passengers familiar with more garish Caribbean resorts appreciated the absence of brash advertising, cheapjack street stalls, and pushy vendors. Grand Cayman immediately struck visitors as friendly, pretty, and safe.

The Stella Polaris, *an early cruise ship, off George Town, ca 1960.*

In the first half of the 1970s, when the number of tourists arriving by air was rising from 23,000 to 53,000, there was a maximum of eight cruise-ship visits to Grand Cayman in any one year, bringing some 2,500 passengers. In 1975, the number of cruise-ship calls suddenly jumped to thirty-three, with 22,500 passengers. Four years later, ninety-eight calls were made, bringing 59,000 passengers. The number of tourists arriving by air also increased during the same period but at a far slower rate, from 54,000 in 1975 to 100,600 in 1979.[49] The number of cruise-ship visitors equalled those coming by air in the mid-1980s, when the combined total was around 270,000. During the 1990s, however, the phenomenal growth in the cruise-ship industry meant that the numbers arriving by sea far outstripped air arrivals. Between 1992 and 1997, air arrivals rose from 242,000 to 381,000. Over the same period, cruise-ship visitors increased from 613,000 to 865,000 per year.[50]

The annual total of visitors by air and sea reached a million in 1994 and passed 1,250,000 in 1997. This represented roughly thirty-five visitors for every resident in the islands – by far the highest ratio of any country in the world.[51] During the winter season, the arrival of up to five cruise ships at a time transformed George Town and its commercial economy. Altogether it was reckoned that the cruise-ship business injected about

Cruise-ship passengers on Harbour Drive, 2001.

CI$100 million a year into the economy, translating into about $10 million in government revenue. Far more revenue was generated by stay-over tourists arriving by air, however, and by property owners who spent at least part of the year in the islands.[52]

All in all, by the year 2000, tourists, longer-term visitors, and permanent residents generated more than half a billion dollars a year for the Caymanian economy and brought some $50 million a year into the Treasury. Thirty years earlier, by contrast, the hospitality industry had brought about $1 million into the economy and $100,000 into the Islands' Treasury.[53]

THE GROWTH OF THE FINANCIAL SECTOR

The tourism business was one of two economic wands that almost magically transformed the Cayman Islands in the last third of the twentieth century. The second was Cayman's financial industry, which grew alongside tourism and eventually surpassed it in economic value. Again, much of the impetus and expertise came from outside. But Cayman provided an attractive environment that was stable, secure, well regulated, and discreet. Although few if any Caymanians had any previous experience of high finance, they proved good listeners and fast learners.

Given the international financial centre they were to become, it is almost incredible that the Cayman Islands did not have a single proper bank until 1953. The Government Savings Bank (founded in 1908) could not carry out commercial transactions or solve temporary shortages of currency in the islands. Merchants had to bank by post in either Jamaica or Miami. The banks operating in Jamaica ignored appeals by the Governor to open a branch in the Cayman Islands until Barclays DCO took up the challenge in March 1953. Their first office was housed in Dr. Roy McTaggart's dental parlour on South Church Street in George Town, with a staff of two. In 1957, when Dr. McTaggart built the Rembro Building on Cardinall Avenue, Barclays leased half of the ground floor. The new bank had no competition until the Royal Bank of Canada opened a branch in George Town in 1963. The Sister Islands' first commercial bank was the Cayman Brac branch of Barclays, which opened in 1964.[54]

The first Royal Bank building, 1965.

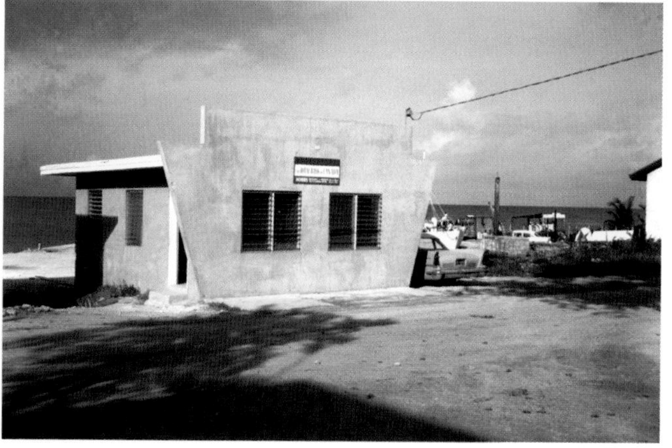

Bermuda and the Bahamas had already shown that small island colonies could become offshore financial centres. In both cases, the attractions were a stable government run by people with

strong commercial instincts, the absence of direct taxes, and the guarantee of confidentiality. It was also assumed that expatriate experts would be welcome, competent local staff would be available, and communications would improve as needed. The Cayman Islands attempted to follow the lead of Bermuda and the Bahamas, though it had neither self-government nor a commercial ruling class.

The Banks and Trust Companies Regulation Law of 1966 was the key. It created two levels of licensing and supervision for banking and trust company operations: those conducting business in the islands (Category A) and those conducting only offshore business (Category B). Naturally, the banks in the first category were more closely regulated. But even the far more numerous companies in the second category had to maintain authentic offices in the islands, list all their officers, and make their records available to local (though confidential) inspection. "Suitcase" companies, which required less office space and fewer local employees, were still a good source of fees. These companies were very willing to pay for an offshore operating address in a friendly and secure environment.

The consistent, steady hand behind the Cayman Islands' transformation into one of the world's leading financial centres was Vassel G. Johnson, who rose through the ranks of the civil service and, after a career spanning almost fifty years, became the first Caymanian to be knighted, in February 1994. Sir Vassel started as an outsider who had to make his way by his own efforts and abilities. He was born of East Indian parents at Golden Grove in eastern Jamaica in 1922, and moved to the Isle of Pines with his family at the age of four. It was there that he met Caymanians for the first time. At the height of the Depression in 1934, his mother moved to Grand Cayman, supporting her children with domestic work.

Vassel Johnson performed outstandingly well at school. He was one of the few students to pass all of the pupil-teachers' examinations at George Town Primary. He seemed destined to be one more in Cayman's long line of teachers trained in Jamaica. Instead, he went to work in the civil service in 1942 as the lowliest clerk in the office of the courts. After war service in the local Home Guard and the Jamaican defence force, he rejoined the Caymanian civil service in 1945, as a clerical assistant in the tiny department that combined the functions of Treasury, Customs, and Post Office.

In the next thirty years, Vassel Johnson rose steadily to the top of the expanding civil service. He built a reputation for capability and forethought in financial matters, and for combining ambition and hard work with absolute integrity. In 1972 he was appointed as the first Financial Secretary, the ExCo Member for Finance and Development, a post he held for ten years. At the end of the century, Sir Vassel Johnson was still on the board of the Monetary Authority.[55]

Sir Vassel Johnson being knighted by H.M. The Queen on the steps of the Legislative Assembly building during her visit in February 1994.

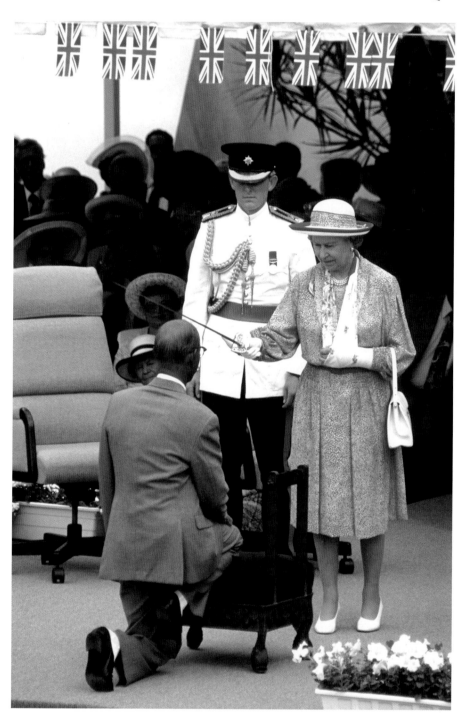

"He was determined to work at establishing the economic environment to create jobs for Caymanians," wrote the *Caymanian Compass* in praise of Vassel Johnson at the time of his knighthood. "[He] began to scan the horizon of the financial future of the Cayman Islands. He had a dream to create a leading offshore financial centre."[56] The Cayman Islands were fortunate to have a person of Johnson's calibre in charge of finance at a time when international financiers were seeking assurance that the islands had the necessary qualities to become a successful financial centre. Johnson himself gave much of the credit to expatriate professionals such as James McDonald and William Grundy, who were the architects, respectively, of the landmark Companies Law of 1960 and the Bank and Trust Companies Law of 1966. Once the start had been made, though, Vassel Johnson became the model and inspiration for a younger generation of Caymanians determined to promote their country's new source of prosperity.[57]

The development of the Cayman Islands in all areas required proper telecommunications. This need was largely met from the 1960s onward by Cable & Wireless Ltd. The company negotiated terms with the government that guaranteed them a monopoly to the end of the century. Operations began in December 1967 with an initial investment of £250,000 and a domestic capacity of 450 lines. Full capacity was predicted to take twenty years but in fact was reached in two. Within five years Cable & Wireless had invested £900,000. Bodden Town as well as George Town had major exchanges with a capacity of twenty thousand lines, and West Bay, East End, and Cayman Brac had radio-linked exchanges. An international telex service was established in August 1969, and in 1973 a cable was laid between Grand Cayman and Jamaica to hook up with an Earth satellite station being constructed there.[58]

Telecommunications expanded from the 1970s to the 1990s, until the Cayman Islands had one of the most complete and efficient systems in the world. By 1990, they had their own satellite Earth station. In 1996 a fibre-optic cable was laid between Grand Cayman, Cayman Brac, and Jamaica at a cost of some $28 million.[59] By 1998 there were twenty-five thousand telephone lines in use in the Cayman Islands and some four thousand cellular-telephone users. The internal telephone service was entirely digitised, and international direct dialling was available to 175 countries around the globe. The C&W monopoly and the islands' prosperity combined to make the rates for all telecommunications services among the highest anywhere. This produced a consumer backlash and a rising demand to reschedule the C&W franchise and re-examine the monopoly. Following the formation of a government regulatory body, OFTEL, in 1996, C&W began to respond. They reduced Internet charges by more than 50 per cent and stressed their commitment to training local staff and their contributions to community programmes.[60]

Already by 1970 the Annual Report could claim that the Cayman Islands were a well-recognised tax haven, at the forefront of the rapidly expanding field of mutual-fund operations. Financiers were drawn by the absence of direct taxation and by favourable legislation, as well as by the growing infrastructure, especially in telecommunications. The offshore industry was more than justified by the income it generated both directly and indirectly. Besides five other Category A banks that now competed with Barclays and Royal

The Cayman National Bank building in 2002.

Bank, there were more than three hundred Category B banks and trust companies with local offices, and two thousand registered offshore companies. All of these paid initial registration and annual operating fees. For banks and trust companies in 1970, fees were £500 per annum to operate within the islands, and £250 to operate outside the islands. "Indirectly the international finance business generates considerable traffic of business men visiting the Islands and contributing to the tourist economy," the report noted. It went on to mention the other more or less indirect benefits of local employment, construction, leasing of premises, and the increase in government revenue from consequent fees and import duties. In sum, the financial industry was already considered, "in conjunction with tourism . . . the main economy of the Islands".[61]

This was only a foretaste of what was to come. The Cayman Islands had already benefited somewhat from the decline in confidence in the Bahamas as a tax haven, following the coming to power of the black majority there in 1967–8. The migration of banks, trust companies, and other offshore operations suddenly accelerated when the Bahamas achieved full independence in October 1973. This was due to a combination of factors. Internal opposition to Bahamian independence carried the threat of political instability. The parliamentary opposition accused the ruling party of mismanagement, if not outright corruption. This negative picture was given substance by a serious downturn in the Bahamian economy (reflecting a worldwide recession), the failure of several Bahamas-based banks, and the regime's willingness to shelter the flamboyant financial buccaneer Robert Vesco. Offshore businesses feared both an increase in government fees and an erosion of their image of discretion and respectability. Finally, there was the accent on Bahamianisation. Expatriate staff felt increasingly insecure, while offshore companies feared having to hire poorly qualified local staff.[62]

Part of the Cable & Wireless complex, George Town, 2002.

In contrast, the Cayman Islands (like Bermuda) offered the advantages not only of a small country determined to retain its political stability but also of being a British dependency with its own laws governing offshore financial business. Unlike Bermuda, though, there were no marked political or ideological divisions in the Cayman Islands. The Cayman Islands offered reliable local employees, as well as the assurance that, because of its small population and the rapid growth of financial services, there would be few restraints on recruiting expatriates. The movement of business to Cayman was undoubtedly helped by the Caymanian Bank Secrecy Law, passed in 1976. This law made it a crime for a bank or its officers to reveal to anyone, inside or outside the islands, anything about a customer's dealings with the bank.[63]

From the mid-1970s, the growth of financial business in the Cayman Islands was rapid. A large number of operations shifted to the Cayman Islands altogether, and many others opened Caymanian branches as a hedge against further deterioration in conditions in the Bahamas or elsewhere. Favourable experiences in the Cayman Islands led many businesses gradually to shift their principal operations there. At the same time, the benefits of the financial boom encouraged the Caymanian legislature to enhance the financial environment. As the original forms of business expanded, they attracted others. One of these was ship registration, which grew steadily over the next two decades. The Cayman Islands by the mid-1990s boasted a nominal fleet of a thousand vessels and posed a challenge to such traditional leaders in the flags-of-convenience field as Liberia, Panama, and the Bahamas.[64] They were also emerging as the premier centre for offshore operations by insurance companies. Within a decade of its beginning, this industry involved some 450 companies (83 per cent of them U.S.–based), managing billions of dollars in assets.[65]

Underpinning the Cayman Islands' reputation as a financial centre was the strength and stability of its currency. This involved the creation of a separate Caymanian currency, its gradual detachment from sterling, and its formal link to the U.S. dollar. Until the 1960s, the situation was both confused and unfavourable to the Cayman Islands. Officially, the local currency was Jamaican, which was on par with the British pound. After the savage British devaluation of 1948, however, the preferred currency had always been the U.S. dollar. Transactions made in other regional currencies were invariably related to the dollar rather than the pound.

Some stability was achieved with the passage of the local Exchange Control Law in 1966. But there was increasing dissatisfaction with the link to sterling through Jamaica, especially because of Jamaica's political instability and the decline in its economy. In May 1969 the Caymanian government appointed a Currency Committee, which sought advice from the Bank of England and the Crown Agents for the Colonies. The committee recommended a separate Caymanian decimal currency, but decided that it should still be pegged to the pound, at the existing rate between the U.S. dollar and the pound of 2.4 to 1. This money went into circulation in 1972. The new currency worked well, at least until Britain herself removed all currency-exchange controls and allowed the pound to float in the early 1970s.[66]

Fluctuations in the pound, especially downwards, did not help the stability of the new currency. As a result, the Currency Board (as it was reconstituted) decided to peg the Cayman dollar to the U.S. dollar in 1974.[67] The board astutely fixed the ratio at CI$1.20 to the U.S. dollar rather than basing the rate on the current value of the pound, which (at US$1.60 to the pound) would have been 80 cents. This decision was to have an very beneficial effect on Caymanian income levels, though at the cost of making Cayman one of the region's most expensive destinations.

All that the Cayman Islands lacked in the year 2000 in comparison with the Bahamas, Bermuda, and other larger and longer-established Caribbean countries was a national central bank. In its place, the Caymanian government effected a marriage of mutual convenience between the public and private sectors. On all matters involving currency and foreign exchange, the Monetary Authority worked with the premier local bank and six of the strongest international Category A retail banks operating in the islands. These were Cayman National Bank (founded in 1985), Barclays, Bank of Nova Scotia, Canadian Imperial Bank of Commerce, Royal Bank of Canada, British-American Bank, and Bermuda's Bank of Butterfield International.[68]

By the mid-1980s, the financial sector was generally considered to have overtaken tourism in economic importance. The Cayman Islands had been transformed into a kind of tropical Switzerland, with George Town a low-rise version of Zurich. The business traffic had become so huge and complex

that there was a growing demand to rationalise the machinery of supervision and control. It was equally important to allay rising concern in the United States, Britain, and other countries about the flight of financial resources to the Cayman Islands – not just through legal tax avoidance schemes, but through laundering money derived from criminal activities, particularly the drug trade.

With some trepidation (at a time of temporary worldwide recession), the Cayman Islands signed the Narcotics Agreement with the United States and Great Britain in 1984, and a Mutual Legal Assistance Treaty two years later. By these means, the governments agreed to share information about known drug traffickers and money launderers and to provide assistance to apprehend offenders. Cayman undertook to give information about the flow of money from suspect sources, under strict conditions that would not breach the general rule of confidentiality. Contrary to the predictions of pessimists, these moves did not have a negative effect on the islands' banking industry, which continued to grow steadily through the late 1980s and 1990s.[69]

In 1995 the Cayman Islands became the first member of a Caribbean Financial Action Task Force to voluntarily put its financial services and practices under the scrutiny of a panel of legal, financial, and law enforcement experts. The panel's report, formally accepted by the Cayman Islands government in October 1996, concluded: "The Cayman Islands' adoption of a progressive attitude towards countering money laundering demonstrates that such policies are compatible with a developing offshore financial centre." Already in September 1996, the Cayman Islands had become the first British dependent territory to adopt a more stringent measure against international financial criminals, the Proceeds of Criminal Conduct Law.[70]

More important in this respect was the passage of the Monetary Authority Law, which came into effect on 1 January 1997. This brought together, under the Cayman Islands Monetary Authority, the very different activities of the Currency Board and the Financial Services Supervision Department. The authority's board was chaired by the Financial Secretary, while a managing director who was a professional financial expert oversaw four specialist divisions: Banking, Insurance, Research, and Administration.[71]

This reorganisation may have assisted in bringing about the disclosures that led to the collapse of First Cayman Bank in October 1997. It certainly made a repetition unlikely – not least by sparking new regulatory legislation. Category A banks in particular were given tighter rules governing the relationship between head offices and branches, the responsibilities of board members, and the monitoring of assets to guarantee that sufficient funds were available in the Cayman Islands to protect the interests of local investors.[72] As a whole, the Cayman Islands entered the twenty-first century

as a model financial centre of its kind, and a shining example of what a clean financial industry can do for a tiny country and its fortunate people.

In 1997, 594 banks and trust companies were licensed in the Cayman Islands, thirty of which held A licences. Since 1970 the number of banks and trust companies had doubled, and the increase in insurance operations was far greater. Most striking of all was the twentyfold surge in the number of companies registered in the Cayman Islands. More than eight thousand new registrations in 1997 brought the total to forty-one thousand. All in all, the financial industry was calculated to contribute CI$142 million a year to the Cayman Islands' gross domestic product of CI$920 million. The currency in circulation was over CI$40 million, and per capita income was calculated at US$31,000, by far the highest in the region and one of the highest in the world.[73]

The Cayman Stock Exchange (CSX), which began operations in July 1997, was a further sign of prosperity and sophistication. It also symbolised the successful marriage between the public and the private sectors. From its earliest days, it illustrated the determination of the Cayman Islands to consolidate its position as a financial hub at the cutting edge of international financial developments. Set up by a special law in 1996, the CSX was a private limited company with a board made up of senior financiers from private businesses, but wholly owned by the Cayman Islands government. Though it operated independently, it came under the watchful eye of a Stock Exchange Authority, chaired by the Financial Secretary.

Within a year the CSX could boast significant listings, a dozen approved listing agents, and three local broker members. Not surprisingly, offshore mutual funds dominated the early listings. Already by the end of 1997 they included "the entire offshore mutual funds portfolio of Unibanco Asset Management, one of the largest asset managers in Brazil, eleven Canadian Imperial Bank of Commerce funds which are managed out of Toronto, and Maverick Fund Ltd., one of the largest hedge funds in the world".[74] In 1998 the CSX also moved into the Eurobond trading market, successfully adopting "a more pragmatic approach than other Eurobond exchanges as regards the documentation required for a listing".[75]

Together with all other aspects of a vibrant financial industry, the operations of the CSX underlined the fact that the Cayman Islands had matured within a half century. From a little-known though proud dependency, they had become a significant actor on the world's financial stage. The new voyage Caymanians had embarked on in the 1950s and 1960s had carried them much farther than they had anticipated. The twin industries of financial services and tourism had brought opportunities and rewards greater than even the most far-sighted of them could have dreamed.

Sweeping the sand yard with a rosemary broom.

CHAPTER 16

Change and Adjustment

Population Changes and Immigration, 1950–2000

THE REMARKABLE ECONOMIC GROWTH OF the Cayman Islands during the second half of the twentieth century was mirrored by a rapid increase in population. The number of people living in the Cayman Islands doubled between 1960 and 1980, and more than doubled again by 1999. This astonishing growth was due as much to immigration as to a natural increase in the Caymanian population. Population growth fuelled the economic engine, and most of those attracted by Cayman's success benefited – whether they were at the front of the economic train or nearer the back. Underneath the bare figures of population growth, however, were the human dimensions of immigration and education, housing conditions, and social welfare. This chapter and Chapter Seventeen explore these dimensions.

The population of the Cayman Islands at the beginning of the twenty-first century was not just different from what it had been. It was different in certain respects from almost all other populations. It was in a state of flux. With more than half the population born outside the islands and drawn from many countries, the old homogeneity of "the islands time forgot" was fast disappearing. The great majority of newcomers were in the 20-to-40 age range, and the numbers of men and women were roughly equal. Most were not permanent residents. Single people greatly outnumbered married couples, and there were relatively few children. The expatriate portion of the population was therefore quite different from the Caymanian.

Before the surge of development: the road to East End in 1949.

Amongst expatriates there were also marked differences of ethnic origin and class. Broadly speaking, about half of them were whites from developed countries, either wealthy foreign residents or relatively well paid white-collar workers and their young families. The other half were mainly black or coloured workers in blue-collar jobs, who came from developing countries in the region, principally Jamaica and Central America. These workers were attracted by wages that were good in comparison to those in their own countries. They were rarely able to bring their families with them, and quite a few spoke limited English or had unfamiliar accents.

In the past the Cayman Islands had been able to assimilate a trickle of new immigrants and had been invigorated by them. Now the flood of newcomers could seem overwhelming. As the numbers grew, immigration restrictions tightened and social tensions increased. For expatriates, there were frustrations and jealousies; for Caymanians, there was the fear of being swamped by outsiders. Rapid development coupled with a traditional political philosophy of *laissez-faire* led to sharp disparities in wealth. Caymanians looked with pride on the virtual absence of poverty in their society, and on the relatively easy access to education, medical care, and other social services. Nevertheless, the best facilities usually went to those best able to pay. Meanwhile, a significant number of people were economically insecure or unsure that they would be able to remain in Cayman. With competing concerns and worries like these, it is hardly surprising that by the end of the century people of all backgrounds acknowledged an increase in social disharmony. Cayman had became a somewhat fractured society, evolving in directions that were not easy to define, let alone plan for.

A growing demand for goods: the opening of Comart Ltd., 1968.

THE NUMBERS

The population "story" can be traced in the census figures. The official censuses between 1943 and 1999 reveal a marked upward curve. The very thorough wartime census of 1943 – the first that included men temporarily absent from the islands – counted a total population of 6,670. Of these, nearly 80 per cent (5,311) lived in Grand Cayman, 19.4 per cent (1,296) lived in Cayman Brac, and fewer than 1 per cent (63) lived in Little Cayman. Seventeen years later in 1960, at the time of the first postwar census, the total population had risen 27.6 per cent to 8,511. This represented a low average increase of just 108 people per year. The population of the Sister Islands had increased even more slowly and was now 17.5 per cent (1,486) of the total.[1]

According to censuses taken roughly every ten years, the total resident population rose from 8,511 in 1960 to 39,410 in 1999. The growth was uneven, increasing by about 18 per cent in the 1960s, 74 per cent in the 1970s, just under 50 per cent in the 1980s, and 55 per cent in the 1990s. The overall increase in the forty years after 1960 was about 30,900, or 363 per cent, with an average of 156 newcomers per year arriving in the 1960s, 734 in the 1970s, 868 in the 1780s, and 1,406 in the 1990s.[2]

The situation in the Sister Islands was very different from that in Grand Cayman. The population of the Brac and Little Cayman increased by 30.3 per cent between 1960 and 1999, from 1,486 to about 1,937. It actually fell to 1,309 in 1970. Despite determined efforts by the government to promote the Sister Islands, their proportion of the total population fell from 17.5 per cent in 1960 to less than 5 per cent in 1999.

In an extreme example of the "metropolitan effect" seen in other Caribbean countries, George Town saw its population rise sharply. The population of the capital grew from 2,705 in 1960 (some 32 per cent of the Cayman Islands total), to 20,626 (52 per cent) in 1999. The numbers of people living in all other districts of Grand Cayman also rose steadily over the same period, but in every district except George Town the *proportion* of the total population declined – although by much less than that of the Sister Islands.[3]

Less than half of the expansion of the Caymanian population was due to natural increase – that is, the excess of births over deaths. The remainder came from immigration. In 1999, the number of residents born in the islands, 16,052, was considerably outnumbered by the 22,968 (59 per cent) born elsewhere. In stark contrast, in 1943 only 312 residents out of 6,670 (less than 5 per cent) were listed as born outside the islands – including 106 from the British West Indies, 104 from Central America, 60 from the non-British West Indies, 27 from the United States, and 6 from the British Isles. The foreign-born residents in 1999 were drawn from a hundred different countries, the largest numbers being from Jamaica (10,152), the United States (2,895), the United Kingdom (2,239), Canada (1,484), and Honduras (1,373).[4] The number of residents born in Jamaica had more than doubled since 1989, and now made up more than a quarter of the entire population.

Of the 22,968 residents of the Cayman Islands in 1999 who had been born elsewhere, 2,166 had received Caymanian status through parentage and 2,909 through granted application on other grounds. The remaining 17,893 were non-Caymanians. Of these, no fewer than 10,790 (58.4 per cent) had arrived since 1995. A further 3,976 (21.4 per cent) had been resident since 1990, making a total of 80 per cent with less than ten years' residence. Only 552 non-Caymanians had been living in the Islands since the 1970s, and a mere 118 since the 1960s.[5]

Age was a major difference between Caymanian and non-Caymanian residents. In 1999, 55 per cent of the non-Caymanian residents were between the ages of thirty and forty-nine. In contrast, only 28 per cent of Caymanian residents were within that range. Most of the very young and the old were Caymanian. In the same census, only 8.6 per cent of non-Caymanian residents were under the age of fifteen, compared with 29.2 per cent of Caymanians. Likewise, only 2.0 per cent of non-Caymanians were over sixty-five, compared with 8.9 per cent of Caymanians.[6]

Mainly as a result of immigration requirements, the expatriate population consisted mostly of single people of working age. When we distinguish between newcomers by their country of origin, however, we notice substantial variations. Those from the mainly black and poor countries of the Caribbean region show a much less equal distribution of ages than those from North America and Europe. Because of the different method of enumer-

ation these features were much more apparent in the 1989 than in the 1999 census. The most extreme case was that of the 4,829 Jamaica-born residents recorded in 1989 (whose numbers more than doubled in the following decade), 73 per cent of whom were between the ages of twenty and fifty.[7]

Unlike most other immigrants, Jamaican women outnumbered men, making up 58 per cent of those aged twenty-five to fifty in 1989. Though relatively well educated by their country's standards (as immigration restrictions require literacy and numeracy), Jamaican women nearly all worked as domestic helpers in private homes, as cleaners in hotels, or as shop assistants. Jamaican men were for the most part manual labourers, hotel workers, or semi-skilled mechanics. The same was true of immigrants from the Spanish-speaking countries of Central America, especially Honduras and Nicaragua (though Jamaicans outnumbered them by a factor of six).

People of working age also made up the majority of residents from the United Kingdom, Europe, and Canada. Most had good educational qualifications, and many were in well-paid white-collar jobs or professional employment. Some held medium-wage jobs as skilled artisans, office workers, policemen, shop clerks, hotel desk clerks, and food service workers. In general, these residents were more likely to be accompanied by young families than Jamaicans and Central Americans.

The more than two thousand Americans living in Cayman between 1989 and 1999 included a sizeable proportion of wealthy permanent residents, and quite a few working people accompanied by their families. The numbers of men and women were almost equal. The majority were between twenty and fifty years old, and there were fair proportions of children and older people. The 1989 figures, in fact, show that children under the age of fifteen constituted almost a quarter of the American population, compared with only 13.5 per cent of the British expatriates and 7.3 per cent of the Jamaican residents.[8]

Opportunities for employment in the Cayman Islands accounted for the massive influx of new workers. Caymanian-first hiring policies meant that the non-Caymanians occupied vacancies in the job market that Caymanians were unwilling to fill, or for which there was an insufficient number of qualified Caymanians.

In 1999 the entire workforce was computed to include 25,506 persons, of whom 14,862 (58.3 per cent) were non-Caymanians and only 10,630 (41.7 per cent) Caymanians. Among "service workers" and those in "elementary occupations", only 1,969 of 7,752 workers, or 25.4 per cent, were Caymanians. Similarly, in the hotels and restaurants, non-Caymanian employees outnumbered Caymanians by more than two to one – in the case of men, by three to one. In the field of construction work, 2,285 of the 3,798 persons employed (60.2 per cent) were non-Caymanians – mainly occupying

the more menial positions. In the artisanal ranks, Caymanians were much better represented, especially in the more skilled and responsible (and better paid) positions. For instance, in the all-male category of "plant and machine operators and assemblers" Caymanians outnumbered non-Caymanians by 467 to 356. In the relatively well-paid fields of transport and communications 914 Caymanians were employed but only 359 non-Caymanians (28.2 per cent).[9]

In education and health care, the Cayman Islands were dependent on expatriates at all levels. In 1999, non-Caymanians occupied 1,205 of 1,776 jobs (67.8 per cent) in these categories. In the clerical, technical, and minor managerial categories, however, Caymanians were dominant, both in numbers and in positions of responsibility. Of 3,016 workers in the general category of "clerk", 2,017 (66.9 per cent) were Caymanians. In the fields of finance and insurance, the relative proportions were almost exactly the same: 1,673 to 859 (66.0 per cent).[10]

At the upper end of the employment scale, however, the distribution looked very different. Despite the understandable desire of Caymanians to fill the ranks of "senior officials and managers", 46 per cent of this category were non-Caymanians in 1999. This was despite the inclusion of "legislators" in this category – all of whom would, of course, have to be Caymanians. Cayman depended most heavily on expatriates in the ranks of fully qualified professionals. In 1999 non-Caymanians made up 61.8 per cent of the professional workforce of 2,665. Despite a resolute policy of Caymanisation, this proportion had been reduced by only 4.2 per cent since 1989, when the census showed a non-Caymanian majority in other important professions – for example, 56 per cent of nurses and midwives, 70 per cent of teachers, and 73 per cent of doctors, dentists, and veterinarians.[11]

Workers from poorer countries on short-term renewable work permits were apparently likely to stay longer than those from the more developed countries. They were also more likely to apply for permanent residency. For example, among those from Jamaica and Central and South America, about 45 per cent had been in Cayman less than five years, 45.5 per cent between five and twenty years, and about 8 per cent more than twenty years. In contrast, about 62 per cent of the Americans had been in the Cayman Islands less than five years, about 84 per cent less than ten years, and fewer than 5 per cent more than twenty years.[12]

The unique ethnic and age mixtures in the Caymanian population were the consequence of Caymanian immigration policy. This policy was subject to much official tinkering as conditions changed and as successive governments pondered what kind of policy was needed to reshape Caymanian society. The immigration issue and its associated questions raised uncertainties and insecurities for Caymanian and non-Caymanian alike.

IMMIGRATION POLICY AND LAW

The search for a suitable immigration policy was by no means a modern development. In 1934, at the height of the Great Depression, a 1916 law designed to prevent entry into the islands of non-Caymanian paupers was repealed and a far more detailed Regulation of Immigration Law passed in its place.[13] The 1934 law foreshadowed many aspects of future immigration policy. It also gave the first legal definition of a Caymanian: "a person born in the Cayman Islands or of parents born therein or of parents, British subjects and resident more than twelve months therein . . .". Besides Caymanians so defined, unrestricted entry was permitted to British officers and officials, to non-resident Britishers who owned property within the Islands worth at least £100, and to those who were admitted at the Governor's or Commissioner's discretion. Bona fide tourists were also allowed free entry, but passengers in transit and visiting seamen were subject to specific regulations.

Totally excluded were non-Caymanians who were lunatics, mentally deficient, convicted criminals, prostitutes, persons deemed by the Medical Officer to be suffering from a dangerous disease, or anyone who was in any way "deemed by the Commissioner . . . to be an unsuitable person for admission into the Cayman Islands". No non-Caymanian was allowed to land without a valid passport, and he or she might be required to produce a cash deposit or security up to £50 to defray the possible cost of deportation. Any non-Caymanian who had entered or stayed illegally, who was convicted of a crime within the Islands, or who was "found wandering without visible means of subsistence" could be deported for these reasons, or, indeed, "for any reason . . . conducive to the public good".[14]

The 1934 law was sufficient until the Cayman Islands became a magnet for foreign workers. The Aliens Law of 1961 required that a foreigner wish-

Moving to the Cayman Islands: the Immigration Department building, 2002.

ing to stay had to prove that "he was in a position to support himself and his dependents". If he wanted to work, the proof consisted of an employment permit issued by the Administrator to the would-be employer. Immigrants had to have a valid visa, unless coming from a country from which no visa was required. Other regulations could be applied, and any foreigner could be prohibited from landing by the Administrator without a reason being given.[15]

The Caymanian Protection Law of 1971 was a comprehensive immigration law intended to protect the interests of Caymanians and the integrity of the Caymanian way of life. It was passed because the recent influx of foreign workers and "private and business settlers" was thought to be approaching a critical level.[16] It was almost an exact copy of the Bermudian Protection Law. But it did not have the restrictions of the Bermuda law on foreigners acquiring land or setting up businesses. In fact, later legislation in Cayman made it relatively easy for non-Caymanians to acquire Caymanian land, and allowed foreigners to own up to 40 per cent of local businesses.

The main administrative changes in the 1971 Caymanian Protection Act were the appointment of a Chief Immigration Officer, the creation of a Protection Board, and the establishment of an appeals procedure. The definition of Caymanian status was now more precise and narrow, and the terms under which non-Caymanians could work and live in Cayman were spelled out. Caymanian status was limited to British subjects and came automatically only to those who were born in the Islands, were married to a Caymanian, or had a Caymanian parent or grandparent and resided in the Islands. Adult British subjects could apply to the Protection Board for Caymanian status after submitting proof that they had been resident for the previous five years and satisfying the board that they were of good character, that they intended to

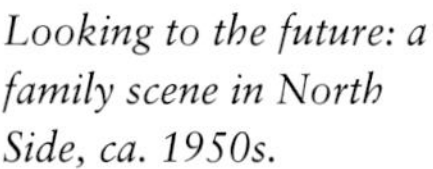

Looking to the future: a family scene in North Side, ca. 1950s.

stay in Cayman, and that their continuing presence was not "contrary to the public interest".[17]

Non-Caymanians who wished to reside permanently in the Cayman Islands had to come in first as visitors. Provided they were not in any of the excluded categories (more or less unchanged since 1934) or on the Protection Board's specific "stop list", they were given permission to stay for six months. This period could be extended for further six-month periods. After at least a year in the Islands, the would-be resident could apply through the Chief Immigration Officer to the Governor for a certificate of permanent residence. This could be granted with or without conditions or refused without reasons being given. It was harder, in fact, for foreigners with permanent residence to get permission to work in the Islands than it was for those on work permits to be granted permanent residence or Caymanian status.[18]

The 1971 Protection Act defined the terms under which non-Caymanians could work in the Cayman Islands, though some areas remained ambiguous. Non-Caymanians had to apply to the Protection Board for a "gainful occupation licence" (work permit) either in person or through their prospective employer. Work permits in 1971 were valid for either one or two years, and a new application was required for renewal.

In judging the application for a work permit, the board had to be satisfied on a daunting number of grounds. These included the "character, reputation and health of the applicant, and, where relevant, of any member of his household", the applicant's "professional or technical qualifications", and "the sufficiency of the applicant's resources or proposed salary". The board had to make sure, in addition, that no one already resident in the Islands was available to do the job, and had to consider both "the protection of local interest" and "the economic and social benefit which the applicant may bring to the Islands or enhance by his presence". The Protection Board could "either refuse or grant the application subject to any condition or limitation, without assigning any reason for that decision". If it refused to grant a work permit, it had to inform the applicant of the right of appeal to the Governor in Council.[19]

The Caymanian Protection Law was reformulated in 1984 and rewritten as the Immigration Law in 1992, with further revisions made in 1997. The main features of the law, however, remained as they had been laid down in 1971. The Protection Board was renamed the Immigration Board in October 1992.[20] It was provided with a full-time Secretariat, though its members, including the chairman, were not paid.

The 1992 law aimed to facilitate permanent residence for well-heeled foreigners, to slow the process of granting Caymanian status, and to place selective barriers against the free flow of persons on work permits. In due course, employers were required to advertise all job vacancies, inviting Caymanian

applicants; to re-advertise when applying for work permit extensions; and to show proof that they were offering training to Caymanians.

Quotas for work permits and grants of status were sometimes applied. At one time the guideline for grants of Caymanian status was twelve per year, but the number of actual grants varied between six and sixty in different years. In 1987 there was a resolute attempt to spread the allocation of work permits. Six regions of origin were designated, and a regulation decreed that the numbers of persons from any one region could not exceed those from the next most numerous by more than 20 per cent. Such quotas, however, were hard to enforce.[21]

Other regulations were more effective. The normal tenure of work permits was reduced from two years to one. Unskilled workers and domestics were especially affected by this rule and were also not allowed to bring any dependents with them, whereas other workers could bring up to three dependents.

RUMBLINGS OF DISCONTENT

The 1990s saw Caymanian society becoming increasingly wealthy but also increasingly divided. The "local/expat issue", as it was dubbed by the magazine *Newstar*, was only the most obvious facet of a situation that involved Caymanian social services, education, religion, and the media.[22]

As a *Newstar* article in September 1989 shockingly revealed, the glossy façade of an international financial centre with a high GDP concealed the existence of actual slums and real poverty in Grand Cayman. Hidden enclaves of George Town – for example, Dog City, Rock Hole, and Meringue Town – contained jumbles of wooden shacks. "For those who are financially confined to these impoverished areas," continued the report, "commonplace items like sinks, showers, and even toilets are considered unaffordable luxuries. They depend upon their own ingenuity, collecting bits of refuse here and

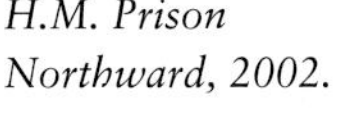
H.M. Prison Northward, 2002.

there in order to better deal with their predicament; a small cardboard box is converted into a nightstand, a scrap of plastic covers holes in the roof." An official of the Environmental Health Department admitted, "We have places in West Bay you'd never think were sub-standard, but you go in the back and there are 42 people living on a property that is 128 by 140 feet. Seventy-five percent of the property is occupied by little shacks which measure about 12 by 15 feet – and families are living in these."[23]

Most of the inhabitants of these slums were black immigrants. Some were illegal "overstayers" without regular work, while others had legal work permits but illegal dependents. A few were Caymanian indigents. The public, while turning a blind eye to the slum areas, suspected that they were breeding grounds for disease and crime. Officials from the Departments of Environmental Health and Planning, as well as the police, visited the areas and were familiar with the problems. But beyond filing reports and making the occasional arrest, they did little to address the underlying causes or to anticipate what this growing new "underclass" might mean for the future.

A unique episode of temporary "immigration" in August 1994 forced Caymanians to think about their relationship to regional migrations. This was the sudden descent upon Grand Cayman of more than a thousand Cuban refugees. In 1993, President Clinton's administration closed the door on Cuban migration to the United States. As a result, a growing number of Cuban "boat people" began to find their way to the Cayman Islands. During the latter part of that year, the situation became uncomfortable but remained manageable. Dozens of small boats arrived, carrying hundreds of people. Those arriving on the Sister Islands were transferred to Grand Cayman, where a small transit camp was set up in George Town. The more seaworthy boats belonging to the Cubans were patched up, and the occupants were given provisions and sent on their way.

In August 1994, however, the flow became a flood. Once again the Sister Islands bore the brunt of receiving "wave after wave" of new arrivals, totalling well over two hundred at times.[24] Although the resources of Cayman Brac, with its population of twelve hundred, were often taxed, authorities and residents alike handled the crisis with remarkable calm. Within weeks, as the newcomers were transferred to the larger island, Grand Cayman became the unwilling host to almost twelve hundred ostensible refugees. Mainly at its own expense (though with help from the British government and the United

Vessels used by Cuban boat people to reach Cayman Brac, 1994.

Managing the crisis: District Administrator for the Sister Islands, Oswell Rankine, with Cuban boats, 1994.

Nations Committee for Refugees), the Cayman Islands was forced to house, feed, and care for this huge influx. As one official graphically described it, the situation was equivalent to 3,300,000 refugees landing at Gatwick Airport in England within a three-week period. The temporary accommodation in George Town was hastily enlarged, and the small refugee camp became known as "Tent City". Financial and human resources were stretched to the limit, and tempers sometimes deteriorated on both sides.[25] Although Caymanians were willing to support their government in a crisis, some resented the amount of money being spent on the boat people and the freedom of movement they apparently enjoyed. For their part, some of the Cubans, including a small criminal element, complained that their conditions and treatment were comparable to those of a concentration camp. In the midst of an acutely difficult situation, numerous officials and volunteers quietly did what they could to help, often working long hours at no notice.

Meanwhile, urgent negotiations were going on between the Foreign Office and the U.S. State Department about easing American restrictions. For months, however, Washington refused to change direction. Tensions reached a climax in November, when three hundred Cubans left Tent City to demonstrate in front of the Government Administration Building. A Cuban Crisis Committee was formed. Governor Gore and the Commissioner of Police drafted in forty-five British policemen to help keep the peace and ensure that the Cubans stayed within the Tent City confines.

The situation was not remedied until early 1995, when Washington suddenly relented. All Cubans who wished to do so would be allowed to enter the U.S. enclaves of Guantanamo Bay in eastern Cuba and the Panama Canal Zone. They were assured that these centres would be way-stations on the path to the United States. Almost all of the Cubans took up this offer, and Tent City finally closed, to much relief, at the end of 1995.[26]

The Cuban refugee experience, like the reluctant recognition of some appalling social conditions in Grand Cayman and the riots at Northward Prison a few years later, proved something of a wake-up call for many in Cayman. "The islands time forgot", as they had been called in 1950, now faced challenges springing from an era of rapid growth and material prosperity. Such challenges placed new strains upon the social, educational, and religious institutions of the Cayman Islands. How they responded is the subject of Chapter Seventeen.

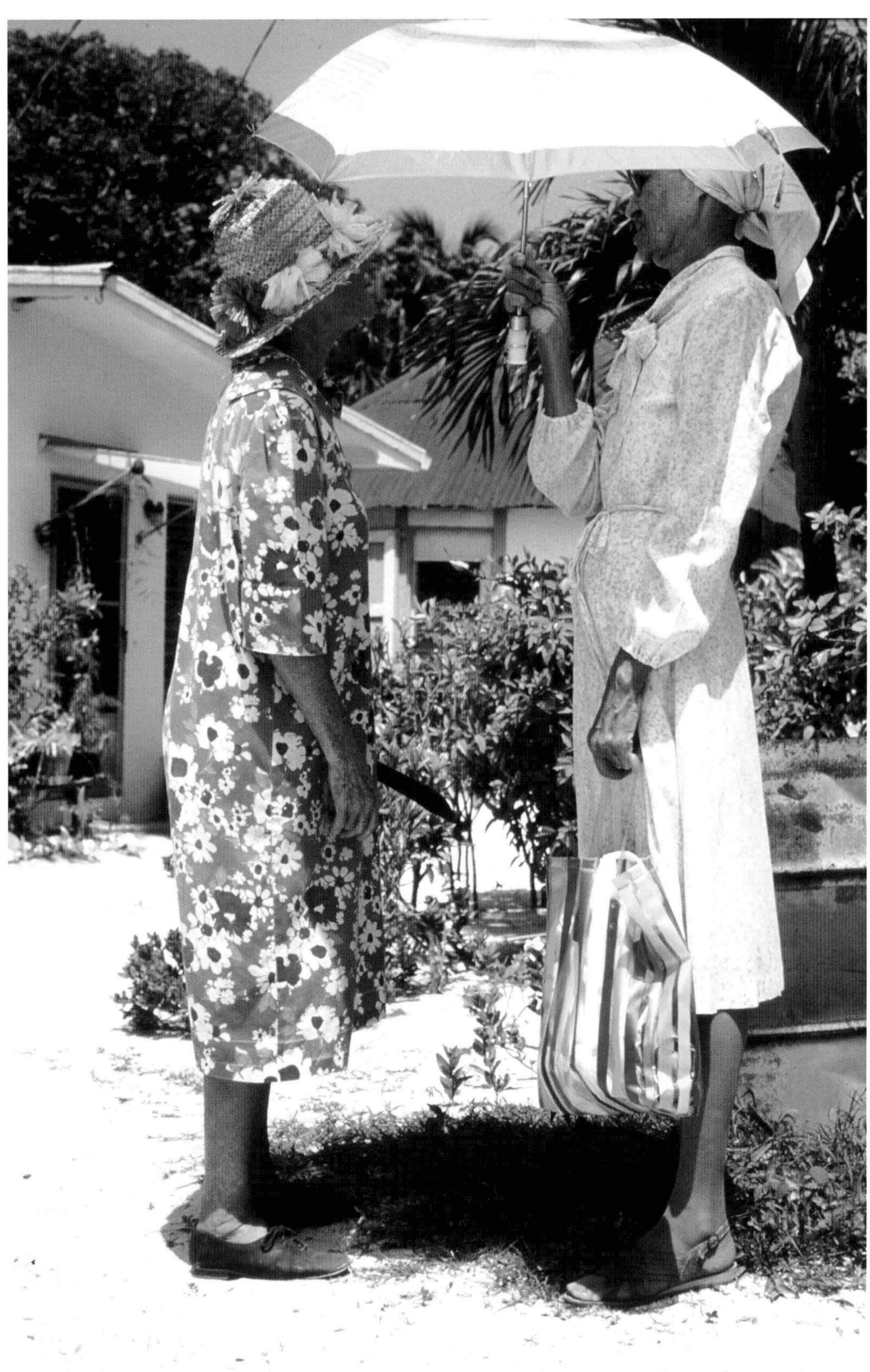

Pausing to chat in the midday sun.

CHAPTER 17

Social Development

Health, Education, the Churches, and the Media, 1950–2000

The Cayman Islands faced major challenges in three broad areas of social development during the latter part of the twentieth century: social services, health, and education. As the growing population required more resources, it was clear that while private enterprise and voluntary organisations still had important roles to play, they could no longer fill all of the gaps in these areas. Churches had long been involved in education and the provision of social services, for example, and they were anxious to retain their influence, especially in the schools. Yet the churches themselves faced new pressures both from within Caymanian society and from outside. Many new voluntary organisations came into being during the last three decades of the century in order to address a variety of needs. Nevertheless, the accent during this time was increasingly on government taking a central role to promote education, social services, and health care, along with other social amenities expected by a modern society.

SOCIAL SERVICES

Caymanians take well-deserved pride in the way that families have customarily looked after their own. There is a long-standing tradition that the more affluent members of the community voluntarily contribute to the less fortu-

The Steering Committee appointed to set up the National Council of Social Services in 1974.

nate. These traditions could hardly cope with the effects of modern development, however, especially given the influx of immigrants from areas far poorer than the Cayman Islands. As a result, government increasingly found itself responding to a widening spectrum of social needs.

The variety and depth of these needs can be measured in part by the growth of government's commitments through the Social Services Department. The department was originally formed as the Probation and Welfare Unit in 1964. In that year the unit was staffed by one Welfare Officer; a second was added in 1968. In 1964 a total of £2,240 was spent on all items related to social services, including the burial of paupers. Almost twenty years later, the unit had grown to a staff of fifteen, and amongst its responsibilities was Bonaventure House, a boys' home built by the Rotary Club but operated by government. In 1982 the unit was transformed into the present Social Services Department and was given a budget the following year of some $500,000. By 1986 the department had a staff complement of twenty-nine with a budget of $1 million. During the next fourteen years, the department's responsibilities broadened considerably, and it witnessed a tremendous increase in its caseload. By 2000, the staff involved in delivering its services, including those on the Sister Islands, totalled more than two hundred, and the budget for their work exceeded $12 million. Despite this rapid growth, there were still needs that could not be met. As recently as 1989, for example, funds were available to assist only 176 needy people in Grand Cayman – all of them Caymanians. Each received between $50 and $85 a month, for a total outlay of no more than $10,000. "This is not expected by any means to meet all of their needs," admitted the Deputy Director of Social Services. "This is a supplement in addition to what their families can contribute."[1]

A recent Annual Report lists numerous "areas of focus" for the Department of Social Services: "counselling, child protection, juvenile delinquency, custody, foster care and adoption, financial services, residential placement services for adults and children, probation and aftercare for adults, and community development". The list indicates the breadth of social problems facing modern Caymanian society. The department's activities included providing aid to the desperately needy, finding homes for the elderly poor and for unwanted and problem children, counselling juvenile offenders and prisoners on probation, and providing a young parents' programme for unwed mothers still in school. The department also offered a national parent training programme

Lions and Leos on Cayman Brac prepare to distribute gifts, Christmas 2001.

designed "to develop and enhance parenting skills in adults of all ages, who would be responsible for the care, supervision and guidance of children".[2]

The range of services provided under the umbrella of the National Council of Voluntary Organisations was even broader than that provided by government. The NCVO had originally been established in January 1975 as the Cayman Islands National Council of Social Services to coordinate all existing voluntary organisations that sought "to meet the social needs of the community". Its first chairman was Benson Ebanks, the ExCo Member responsible for social services. Different board members represented the churches, service organisations, sports clubs, youth groups, and cultural and other organisations. The NCVO (as it became known in 1992) was sustained by donations and membership fees and relied heavily on the community support it received in its annual radiothon and telethon appeals. By 1998 it had a permanent staff of four and was the coordinating body for a variety of organisations. Some overlapped and supplemented the activities of the DSS, while others worked independently.

Among those in the first category were services for children, the elderly, and the otherwise needy. These included the Pink Ladies Volunteer Corps, the Caring Cousins welfare scheme, the Lifeline telephone counselling service, the Big Brothers and Big Sisters programmes, and the John Gray Memorial Scholarship Fund. NCVO donations and volunteers largely helped to sustain the Jack and Jill Nursery, the Nadine Andreas Children's Centre, the Lighthouse School for disabled children, The Pines home for the elderly, and the ancillary services of the George Town Hospital. The NCVO worked

closely alongside the Cayman Islands Cancer Service, the Humane Society, and the Cayman Horse Association, and helped to coordinate the social service activities of the Rotary, Lions, and Kiwanis clubs and their ladies' and juniors' auxiliaries, the Business and Professional Women's Club, the United Church Women's Fellowship, the Scouts and Guides, the Boys' and Girls' Brigades, and the Duke of Edinburgh's Award programme. It also worked in conjunction with two other vital organisations, the Cayman Islands Red Cross and Cayman Against Substance Abuse (CASA), the anti–drug and alcohol abuse action group.[3]

HEALTH CARE

Historically, medical care in the Cayman Islands was very limited. The healthfulness of the climate and the islands' freedom from epidemics enabled the population to remain relatively healthy despite the lack of services. As elsewhere in the modern world, calls for medical attention increased with material prosperity. From the 1970s on, the generally satisfactory level of health care services was aided by two factors: the authorities' mandate to deny entry to unhealthy immigrants, and the ability of more and more residents to seek medical attention outside the islands.

One of the least understood medical problems was congenital defects resulting from close-cousin marriage. There were cases of polydactylism (extra fingers or toes), cleft palate, and congenital blindness, and a relatively high frequency of congenital deaf-mutism. Pathologists visiting the Cayman Islands in the 1970s identified two indigenous varieties of genetic disease, transmitted by parents who both carried recessive genes. "Cayman Disease", as it was sometimes known, was described as "a rare combination of mental retardation and nerve and muscular disorder, the latter affecting the lower extremities of the body, the former limiting eye movements". It was easily identified at birth, and its victims were said generally to live to a very mature age.

The George Town Hospital in the 1950s.

The lethal affliction termed Cayman Storage Disease was more traumatic. Children with this condition were said to be completely normal during the first eighteen months of life. They then began "to show evidence of enlargement of the abdomen, indicative of the accumulation of an abnormal substance in the body". By age two they had "lost the ability to sit or walk, with mental retardation setting in by age four". Life expectancy was no more than fourteen years.[4]

The incidence of genetic birth defects decreased with careful public health education and counselling. Better facilities were also being created for treating the deaf and mute, blind, and mentally handicapped. Gradually the causes and prevention of genetic disabilities became more widely understood. The Lighthouse School, established in 1976, provided much-needed care for disabled children.[5]

Two other widespread problems were also practically eradicated. As we saw in Chapter Fifteen, the Mosquito Research and Control Unit removed the chief misery of life in the Cayman Islands, reducing almost to zero the likelihood of epidemics of yellow fever and dengue fever and the chance of acquiring malaria. At the same time, the introduction of clean water supplies and flush toilets, coupled with health education and effective medicines, virtually wiped out the worm infestations that were common before the 1950s.

Poor dental health was also addressed. This problem stemmed as much from deficiencies in diet and water supplies as from neglect. Public awareness and better diet certainly helped. But the great improvement from mid-century resulted mainly from better dental care and many more local dentists. As late as 1950 there was never more than one dentist in the islands, and for long periods none at all. A dentist seconded from Jamaica for six months in 1950 commented unfavourably on local dental conditions. He recommended that a full-time government dentist be appointed to carry out a three-year programme of dental care and education. He also urged that attempts be made to improve the quality of cistern water used for drinking, and that the people's diet be improved through "a wider consumption of milk, vegetables and fruits".[6]

By 1960, there was a government dental clinic served by a dentist, a dental nurse, and a dental technician. By the end of that decade, Dr. Edlin Merren, one of the first Caymanian dentists in private practice, had opened his office. By 1979, two dentists and a "dental auxiliary" served Grand Cayman, and a dental auxiliary was located in Cayman Brac. The following two decades saw rapid expansion, and by 1998 the Cayman Islands had the services of four government dentists and a government orthodontist; twelve dentists, orthodontists, and periodontists in private practice; and an equal number of trained dental nurses and dental technicians. A "dental caravan" donated by the Rotary Club of Grand Cayman regularly toured the schools, and the

government dental unit alone performed twenty-two thousand treatments during the year.[7]

Other medical and hospital services grew even faster. At the end of World War Two, the islands' seven thousand people were served by a single doctor, a dispenser (stationed at Cayman Brac), a sanitary inspector, a "general and maternity trained nurse", and a four-bed hospital in Grand Cayman. Serious cases and people needing X-rays had to be sent to Jamaica.[8] In 1953, a 28-bed hospital was built in George Town, thanks to a Colonial Development and Welfare grant of £37,000 and public and private local contributions totalling £10,000. Commissioner Gerrard proudly stated that "considering the size of both the Dependency and the hospital, the islands possess one of the best equipped and most efficiently run hospitals in the West Indies". Staffing, though, posed a major problem. The hospital staff consisted of the matron, five nurses, and an X-ray and laboratory technician. A dispenser and a midwife served Cayman Brac. But there was still only one qualified doctor, and the Islands depended on the voluntary part-time services of a gynaecologist and a specialist surgeon from Jamaica.[9]

Health services began to develop rapidly in the 1970s, as the growing economy generated funds and as responsibility for health care came under a Member of ExCo. In 1971 an eight-bed hospital was built in Cayman Brac. In keeping with the Brac tradition of self-sufficiency, it was financed largely by local subscriptions and donations and built with local labour, and was fittingly named Faith Hospital. The government then took over its operation and appointed a full-time doctor for the Sister Islands. Altogether, by 1979 the fifteen thousand residents of the Cayman Islands had the services of a Chief Medical Officer, six other full-time and three consultant government doctors, and another eight doctors in private practice. This amounted to one qualified doctor for every 833 inhabitants. In addition, experts in health education, family life education, genetics, and epidemiology visited periodically from the World Health Organisation and the Caribbean Epidemiology Centre. Meanwhile, more and more Caymanians were going to Britain and the United States to be trained in nursing, medical technology, and pharmacy.[10]

Faith Hospital, Cayman Brac, in the 1970s.

The dramatic expansion of health services continued throughout the 1980s and 1990s, as the budget for health tripled within a decade and increased by a factor of ten over twenty years. By 1987 the George Town hospital had expanded to fifty-two beds and Faith Hospital to twelve, a small clinic had been established in Little Cayman, and four district clinics were operating in Grand Cayman. Special facilities existed for infants, the elderly, and psychiatric patients. Regular clinics raised public awareness about hypertension, kidney disease, cancer, and HIV/AIDS. An annual programme of sight conservation, sponsored by the Lions Club since 1972, provided free vision testing for all children. There was a total of fifteen doctors in government service, two of whom were based in Cayman Brac, as well as eighteen doctors in private practice, with a further sixteen specialists visiting regularly. It was computed that there was now a resident doctor in the Cayman Islands for every 650 inhabitants – roughly the same ratio as in the United Kingdom. The total staff for the Health Department in the three islands was 322, of whom 127 came under the command of the Chief Nursing Officer.[11]

In the late 1990s, George Town Hospital was transformed into the Cayman Islands Health Services Complex, at a cost of more than $26 million. The number of hospital beds was raised to 146, of which 18 were in Cayman Brac. Grand Cayman boasted separate maternity, paediatric, and intensive care wards, and up-to-date operating, radiology, laboratory, pharmaceutical, physiotherapy, and mental-health facilities. There were now thirty-six doctors in government service, including four in Cayman Brac, and thirty-seven in private practice, along with 146 other professional medical specialists and 226 nurses. Faith Hospital in Cayman Brac was served by a Chief Medical Officer, a resident obstetrician/gynaecologist, an anaesthetist, and a general practitioner, and fifty-seven other staff members, including a full-time physiotherapist. The Kirkconnell Community Care Centre, a modern rest home named for Captain R.B. Kirkconnell, had been constructed next door to the hospital to serve the elderly residents of the Sister Islands who could not be cared for at home.[12]

Public health services made rapid progress too. Immunisation programmes were carried out throughout the islands – for polio, diphtheria, whooping cough, tetanus, measles, mumps, rubella, tuberculosis, and influenza – covering between 91 and 94 per cent of the resident population. The great plague of the late twentieth century, AIDS, seemed to have been kept largely at bay, at least in comparison with other countries in the Caribbean region. By 1998 AIDS had led to eighteen deaths in the islands. Six people were said to have the active disease, and another eighteen were infected with HIV, but no new cases were reported among residents during that year.[13]

By the year 2000, the Cayman Islands could rightly claim to be one of the healthiest places in the world to live. Its annual death rate was between three

and four per thousand, the infant mortality rate was seven per thousand, and life expectancy at birth was seventy-seven years. The rate of natural increase was moderate. These statistics are partly accounted for by demography and by the Islands' general prosperity. Any population with a disproportionate number of young adults, a majority of whom are for one reason or another unmarried, is bound to have both a low death rate and a comparatively low birth rate. In addition, couples in prospering economies tend to limit the size of their families by choice.

In the area of social planning, the Cayman Islands faced a complex dilemma. The fact that half of its resident population was expatriate posed a challenge to the creation of an integrated society. Yet Cayman's general prosperity, including its financing of health and social services, depended heavily on the same expatriates. The overall demographic measures of health were excellent partly because the expatriates were largely of working age and healthy – as required by immigration regulations. The longer expatriates stayed, though, the more they would be represented in both the very young and the old sectors of the population. Such changes threatened to increase the cost of health and social services over the long term.

EDUCATION

Education in the Cayman Islands has come to be characterised by a variety of approaches and models: private and public; religious and secular; British, American, and West Indian. This variety emerged in less than four decades and contrasted sharply with the educational scene before 1960.

The Caymanian school system changed little for thirty years after the passage of the 1920 Education Act. Limited to primary education in all-age schools, it was controlled by the government but underfunded. It relied heavily on private institutions, most of them church-oriented. Education in public schools was free after 1920, but fortunately for the government, church affiliation kept at least some private schools in business and relieved pressure on the education budget. Schooling was compulsory for children between the ages of seven and fourteen. The 1920 budget allocation of £1,500 a year for education was not increased for twenty-five years. Even the slight postwar surge took it only to £3,040, in 1946. In that year, there were eight government primary schools in Grand Cayman, four

The school at Spot Bay, Cayman Brac, 1938.

in Cayman Brac, and one in Little Cayman, catering to eight hundred pupils in all and employing twenty-one teachers, three of whom were college-trained. As late as 1960 the government allocation for education reached only £18,109. This represented 9 per cent of the budget, at a time when Jamaica was spending 30 per cent of its annual budget on education.[14]

Given the challenges it faced, it is remarkable that the Caymanian education system achieved what it did. The adult literacy rate as early as 1943 was over 90 per cent. Being able to read and write, though, was as far as education went for the great majority. In 1943, only 128 (or 2.5 per cent) of the 5,142 Caymanians could claim any schooling beyond the elementary level. Of these, 82 had at least some secondary education (almost all obtained in Jamaica), and 35 some practical or pre-professional training. Only 11 people were counted as trained professionals.[15] Some legislators felt that the Cayman Islands could not afford and did not need public education beyond the primary level. Even the Colonial Office poured cold water on the education proposals made in the 1949 Cayman Islands Ten Year Plan for Development and Welfare. The suggested improvements were held to be beyond the financial means of the colony, and the Colonial Office advised that a proposed government senior school be postponed.[16]

The churches, however, had already begun to remedy the lack of secondary school facilities. As early as 1941, two members of the prominent Merren family, members of the Church of God, asked their church's headquarters in Anderson, Indiana, to send a missionary who could also teach school. The first classes began that year, with ten pupils, four of them Merrens. They were taught by Nina Ratzlaff, the wife of the Church of God missionary to the Cayman Islands. From the beginning, the school aimed at secondary as well as elementary teaching, with a strong Christian emphasis and adherence to the American rather than British models of organisation and curriculum. Within two years, the school had acquired two more classes and a distinctive name. Chosen by the pupils in a ballot, it was Creative Christian Character, popularly known thereafter as "Triple C".

Although it received no government aid, Triple C School steadily prospered. Its success was attributable to the dedication of its staff, moderate financial help from the Church of God, and the ability and willingness of its pupils' parents to pay its modest fees. The school managed in a succession of temporary quarters until 1963, when it acquired and built on a three-acre site off George Town's Hospital Road. Though it gradually became overcrowded, this building was used for thirty years, until funds were raised to buy nine acres on Bobby Thompson Way and construct a 50,000-square-foot, thoroughly modern facility.

By the mid-1990s Triple C School had almost five hundred pupils of all ages, and twenty-five teachers. Many of its graduates planned to go on to ter-

Rev. George Hicks receiving the M.B.E. from the Governor of Jamaica, Sir Hugh Foot, 1952.

tiary education, usually in the United States. Its teachers were required to be committed Christians, and Bible teaching was a vital element in the curriculum. In other respects, the curriculum was recognisably American and included a range of practical subjects and electives. Despite fees of three to five thousand dollars a year, the school's intake remained selective.[17]

The energy of those behind the genesis of Triple C School was matched by those in another denomination at the end of the 1940s. The idea of a Presbyterian high school was first broached during the centennial celebrations of the church's mission to the Cayman Islands in 1946. Two years later, the Moderator of the Jamaica Synod, Rev. Henry Ward – himself a teacher and educational pioneer in Jamaica – persuaded the local Presbytery to proceed with the project. Rev. George Hicks, who had often acted as Inspector of Schools, negotiated with the government for an annual grant of £500 and the free use of the site and buildings of the disused U.S. base in George Town. The school, called the Cayman High School (CHS), enrolled its first pupils at the beginning of 1949. Hicks acted as headmaster until the Synod sent Rev. John Gray to take over the headship and serve in the West Bay church in September 1949. At the same time a preparatory department was set up under Miss Ercel Connor, one of the first college-trained Caymanian teachers. The school attracted eighty-nine pupils within its first year.[18]

In contrast to Triple C, CHS followed the British system, preparing its first candidates for the Cambridge Overseas School Certificate in 1951. The government grant to CHS was doubled in 1955. But this was a stopgap measure, as the Board of Education struggled to satisfy the growing demand for secondary education. Charles A. Hunter, a Caymanian who had studied school management in Jamaica, was appointed the Cayman Islands' first Supervisory Teacher (later called Chief Education Officer) in 1950. The forceful Hunter made many improvements in the Islands' all-age schools during his tenure. Even so, results in the Jamaican Local Examinations (the only external examinations held in the government schools) deteriorated to a level unacceptable to the government and the public alike.

In 1959, the government accepted a new five-year plan, prepared by Hunter. It proposed a combination of the Jamaican and English systems as they had developed since World War Two. The plan called for the division of primary education into infant schools for those aged five to seven, and jun-

ior schools for children aged eight to twelve. Secondary schools would be instituted under a system of streaming according to abilities. On the basis of an "eleven-plus" examination, children would be assigned either to a high school (based on the English grammar school model) or to a senior school, concentrating on commercial and technical subjects (like English Secondary Modern Schools). It was recommended that the CHS should become the government's official high school and that Caymanian infant-school teachers be trained at Caledonia College in Jamaica.[19]

Aerial view of Triple C School (centre), 1964.

The 1959 recommendations were only gradually and partially adopted. The period that followed was one of experimentation, confusion, and considerable demoralisation – among teachers, parents, and children alike. The government subsidy to CHS was almost doubled to £1,800, but the only substantial venture was the building of a senior school in George Town, later called the Secondary Modern School. This was not a success: few people understood its purpose, and bussing senior children from all over Grand Cayman proved both troublesome and expensive.[20]

In 1964, two years after Jamaican independence, the Jamaican Local Examination was discontinued, and the government assumed full responsi-

Students and staff of the Cayman High School and its preparatory department, when it opened in 1949.

Rev. John Gray, Headmaster, with the staff of the Cayman High School, ca. 1950.

bility for the CHS, which was renamed the Cayman Islands High School. There were attempts to establish a British-style eleven-plus Common Entrance Examination, set by Moray House in Scotland. The plan was that the top forty candidates would be awarded places at the High School, while the remainder would attend the Secondary Modern School. This never worked as intended. To the dismay of the Board of Education, no more than a third of the eligible children ever sat the Common Entrance Examination. The private schools did not enter any candidates, and teachers at the public schools weeded out (without authorisation) those who did not seem to be promising candidates.

The dual system of public secondary education limped on for six years. But the system that replaced it was only marginally more successful. A new Education Act was passed in 1968, modelled on one from Kenya. This added an Education Council, a Department of Education, and a separate Lesser Islands Education Board to the existing Board of Education. It also extended the period of compulsory education to include all children aged five to fifteen.

A radical switch was made in September 1970, to the comprehensive system of education then in vogue in Britain. This followed a highly critical survey and recommendations made earlier that year by Dr. Gordon Williams of the United Kingdom and Dr. Phyllis Macpherson of the University of the West Indies. Streaming and the eleven-plus examination were abolished. CIHS and the former Secondary Modern School in George Town were combined and opened to all children over the age of twelve. The result was near-chaos. Staff struggled to cope with pupils of all levels of ability, and the sudden rise in enrolment posed an almost insurmountable challenge. Williams and Macpherson had projected an enrolment of 1,050 by 1975, but that number was reached within three years.[21]

Over the next twenty-five years, increasing amounts of money were spent on education. In 1967 a high school was established on Cayman Brac, which children entered directly from primary school. The new facility meant that students from Cayman Brac who wished to continue their studies in the higher grades no longer had to transfer to the high school in Grand Cayman – unless they wanted to take A levels, which were never offered on Cayman Brac. In 1979 compulsory schooling throughout the Cayman Islands was extended to cover children from the age of four years, nine months to sixteen years. A further important initiative was the construction of a Middle School

in Grand Cayman in September 1979, for all children between the ages of ten and thirteen. This modified junior high school, which had an enrolment of 230 students in its first year, was designed to "strengthen the primary base of students entering the Cayman Islands High School" by focusing on the needs of this age group in a separate environment.[22]

Students play basketball during lunch break, Cayman Brac High School, 2002.

By 1982, there were 2,728 children enrolled in the government schools, compared with 1,168 in private schools. There were 1,129 pupils in nine public primary schools (now with a favourable teacher-to-pupil ratio of 1:19) and almost 50 per cent more in the public secondary schools. The Middle School began its fourth year of operation with 770 pupils and 45 teachers, and at its first graduation exercises in July 1982 passed on 265 students to CIHS. The High School had an enrolment of 806, of whom 46 were in the sixth form. Cayman Brac High School had 180 pupils, with a sixth form of 14. The high schools entered students for the British external examinations, with solid if not stellar results.[23]

A Community College was started in 1976 to meet the need for continuing education. Between five hundred and six hundred students were enrolled in 1982 at its headquarters in George Town and its branches at East End and on Cayman Brac. It replaced the Hotel, Marine Training, and Building and Trade schools, founded in 1977, 1979, and 1980 respectively, and was intended to develop into a true tertiary institution. Its aim was to provide a government-supported college to meet a variety of adult educational needs. Eventually its tertiary curriculum would prove a challenge to the privately funded, American-oriented International College of the Cayman Islands, established at Newlands, Grand Cayman, in 1970. The only other tertiary institution in 1982 was the fledgling Cayman Islands Law School, which opened in September of that year.[24]

All told, the government spent $6.23 million on education in 1982, or 15.5 per cent of the total budget. By 1998, expenditure had increased five times and represented a slightly larger share of the budget. Yet progress had not completely borne out the guarded optimism of earlier years. Much money had been spent on buildings and equipment, including air conditioning in almost all schools and a computer for every three secondary pupils in the public system. The number of teachers in the government schools had increased almost in proportion to the number of students, and teachers' salaries were higher than in the private schools. But teachers' pay could not compete with salaries

in the private business sector. Even with generous government bursaries for teacher training, few Caymanians saw teaching as a rewarding career. The consequences were a continuing dependence on expatriate teachers and, at times, low morale, which was worsened by declining standards of student discipline and behaviour.[25]

A further challenge was choosing what form of external examinations should be taken. For a long time there was a preference for the British examinations, beginning with the Overseas School Certificate and Higher Certificate, set by various regional boards, including Cambridge. This was followed in the 1960s by the General Certificate of Education, both O and A levels. This in turn was replaced in the 1970s by the General Certificate of Secondary Education, together with exams offered by the Welsh Board consisting of the Certificate of Education (C of E) and Certificate of Secondary Education (CSE). The GCSE was eventually superseded by its international equivalent, the International General Certificate of Secondary Education (IGCSE). During the 1980s Cayman chose not to adopt examinations set by the Caribbean Examination Council (CXC), which had been established in the Commonwealth Caribbean in the 1970s. It was felt by some that CXC was regionally slanted and did not give enough opportunity for local input. In 1992, however, John Gray High School introduced CXC, entering its first candidates in 1994 with notable success. By the end of the 1990s, a flexible approach to examinations had emerged in which schools offered a mixture of IGCSE and CXC subjects, with teachers given the option of selecting the one that best suited their subjects and students.[26]

In 1995 the High School and Middle School were renamed John Gray High School and George Hicks High School respectively, after the two pioneer educators of the 1940s. In the same year, the Community College, with a new George Town campus, took over the sixth form from John Gray High School. The aim was to groom its students more effectively for the college's projected Associate of Arts, Sciences, and Applied Sciences degrees.

Not everyone was fully satisfied with the advances made by public education, however, and in some quarters concerns were expressed about deteriorating standards, student disorder, and alleged drug use at the secondary schools. For this and other reasons, parental demand for private schools remained strong, especially for schools with a firm moral basis to their teaching. In the 1980s and 1990s both the Catholic and the United churches added higher grades to their schools, and in 1997, the First Baptist Church included a school in its

The Community College of the Cayman Islands, 2002.

large new complex on Crewe Road. Government itself took the view that private schools relieved the pressure on public education. As a result, they provided subsidies to all private schools on a prorated basis, depending on enrolment.

At the end of the century, Caymanian education faced complexities that were a world away from the few schools that existed in 1900. In response, public and private educational institutions were seeking to draw on a wide range of resources to meet the challenges of providing education in a rapidly changing society. In 1998 there were 3,869 pupils enrolled in the fourteen government schools, compared with 2,093 in the ten private schools. The private schools' share in primary education was significantly greater, however: there were 2,090 children in reception and primary classes in public schools, compared with 1,553 in private schools.[27] In part, these figures reflected the traditional Caymanian interest in private alternatives in education, which stemmed back almost a century. They also reflected the wealth of modern Cayman and the fact that many more Caymanians could afford a private education for their children. Two other contributing factors were the increasing number of expatriates in the population, and a government policy during the mid-1990s that required expatriates to use private schools because the public schools were full.

Among the developments of the 1990s, three in particular held out promise for the long-term future of education. The first was the national *Education Development Plan 1995–1999*, the product of a lengthy strategic planning process and the basis for later "site-based" plans created by individual schools. Approved by the Legislative Assembly in March 1995, the education plan gave rise to two further key developments: a Schools Inspectorate and the National Curriculum. The Inspectorate was established in 1996 with a mandate to evaluate the quality of education and pupil performance in all schools, private as well as public. By the middle of 2000, ten schools had been inspected and summary reports on them made public, while an even larger number of schools had been trained in self-evaluation – an integral part of the inspection model.[28] Work on creating a National Curriculum began in 1997. One of its main goals was to infuse Caymanian culture into subjects throughout the curriculum. Although progress in this respect was slow, much work was done to rewrite the curriculum in the core subjects of mathematics, science, and language arts, and by 2000 the first three textbooks in a new series in social studies had been published.[29]

THE CHURCHES

The churches in Cayman confronted much the same challenges as the Caymanian education system: tumultuous change, increasing diversification,

and powerful external influences. Cayman's traditional ties to Britain through Jamaica gradually weakened following Jamaican independence. At the same time, Caymanians were progressively exposed to influences from the United States, Latin America, and beyond. Caymanian society remained resolutely and proudly Christian, resisting to a remarkable degree the undermining of the religious impulse that accompanied materialism and prosperity elsewhere. But it is debatable whether the multiplication of churches, each with its ardent adherents, constituted a strengthening of religious life in the society.

Leading the way in the process of change was the Presbyterian Church, traditionally the steadfast moral rock on which society in Grand Cayman was based. With its Synod in Jamaica and its historic ties to the Scottish missionary societies, the Caymanian Presbyterian Church was naturally vulnerable at a time when imperial ties and financial supports were weakening. By the 1950s and 1960s the links with Scotland were almost gone, while those with Jamaica were gradually being strengthened.

As early as 1951 the Jamaican Presbyterians and some other established Protestant denominations felt that their ministries were critically weakened by competition with each other, and met to discuss a possible ecumenical union. In 1953 a Jamaica Church Union Commission was set up, combining the Presbyterians, Congregationalists, Moravians, Disciples of Christ, and Methodists. It went so far as to produce a draft plan of union in 1957. The plan foundered, largely on the issues of episcopacy and the form of baptism. But in December 1965, three years after Jamaica gained its political independence, the governing bodies of two of the churches, the Presbyterians and the Congregationalists, agreed to unite as the United Church in Jamaica and the Cayman Islands.[30]

The union provoked lasting debate in the Cayman Islands. It was accepted, however, partly because a majority did not want to break the historic ties with

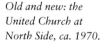

Old and new: the United Church at North Side, ca. 1970.

Jamaica and partly because it was felt that the Caymanian church was probably no longer viable on its own. The fact that there were no Congregationalists in the Cayman Islands was seen by some as a weakness. But others argued that it was a positive factor, in that the Presbyterian Church in Cayman would be able to continue almost as before, despite the change of name. This proved largely true, even after the exclusively Jamaican Disciples of Christ were accepted into the New United Church in Jamaica and the Cayman Islands, in December 1992.[31]

The new constitution of the United Church did not differ radically from the old one. It incorporated a simple all-encompassing article of faith, and neatly combined Congregationalist and Presbyterian principles of church organisation – along with a subtle tendency towards greater democracy already in evidence in each of the churches. Congregational meetings were more frequent and more important. Within each church the functions of the elders and deacons were now combined into that of a single Congregational Board of Elders, whose members were elected every three years. The local Presbytery was renamed the Area Council and comprised ministers and lay pastors, together with lay representatives of each church including some younger members. The governing Synod consisted of all members of Area Councils and met every second year.[32]

Despite this astute blending of authority and democracy, the United Church gradually lost its primacy after 1970. Elmslie Memorial on the George Town waterfront is still considered the Islands' outstanding church building and is often used for official government functions that require a church setting. But traditional Presbyterians lamented the erosion of the church's central role, which some attributed to the strengthening of links with Jamaica.

The Anglican Church in the Cayman Islands faced similar challenges, but even more acutely – to the point that it split into two bodies. One body was subordinate to Jamaica, while the other professed allegiance directly to England. In the 1970s, the Anglican Church had only recently been revived in the Cayman Islands, and almost all of its members were Jamaican and British expatriates. At times, then, the disagreement may have had national overtones.

The Church of England in Jamaica had given up its pastoral work in the Cayman Islands after 1839, first to the Methodists and then to the Presbyterians. The Church of England in Jamaica was actually disestablished in 1870. A century later, in the 1960s, the movement for independence throughout the British West Indies spilled over into a demand to be released from the direct authority of the Archbishop of Canterbury. In February 1964, the Anglican Synod in Jamaica made a "Declaration of Principles" that effectively broke the direct jurisdictional tie with England. At the same time, there was concern among some Anglicans in Jamaica that they should support an

Anglican presence in Cayman. It was two decades later, however, that the Diocese of Jamaica was able to take the Cayman Islands fully under its pastoral care.[33]

The expatriate Anglican community in Cayman grew steadily during the 1960s. It consisted of a majority of West Indians, and a smaller number of British and American residents. They met in private homes and hotels whenever a priest visited the Islands, although they were also allowed to use the Elmslie Memorial Church and the Catholic Church of St. Ignatius. In 1970 the Cayman Islands were formally declared part of the Deanery of Kingston, and Bishop Swaby of Jamaica visited George Town for confirmations. In 1973, the Bishop appointed the Jamaican Laurence Small as the first resident catechist in the Cayman Islands. Progress was slow because of the Jamaican diocese's lack of resources and also because some Anglicans in Grand Cayman were hesitant about the Jamaican link. But a site for the church was acquired in 1976, and the completed church building was eventually dedicated as St. George's in April 1979. The Rev. Harris Spence from Jamaica was appointed the first priest-in-charge in September 1984. St. George's was formally consecrated in September 1987, when it was declared a "settled congregation".[34]

The Caymanian Anglicans as a whole, however, were far from settled. In 1983, an Anglican priest, Rev. Nicholas J.G. Sykes, and others began to meet separately. They formed St. Alban's church in George Town, and eventually St. Mary's, a daughter church in Cayman Brac. Sykes and his followers denied the episcopal authority of Jamaica over the Cayman Islands and wished to establish direct pastoral ties with the Church of England. They received neither endorsement nor financial support from the Archbishop of Canterbury, however. Theologically traditional, they were also disturbed by certain movements in the English church, including the General Synod's decision in 1992 to allow the ordination of women as priests.[35] Accordingly, in 1993, after several years without a bishop's oversight and care, they petitioned the Presiding Bishop of the Episcopal Missionary Church, an American group that had separated from the Episcopal Church after the 1992 General Synod.[36] Insisting that this was only a temporary measure forced upon them, they affirmed their allegiance to the Queen as Supreme Governor and their belief that they were and remained part of the Church of England.

Like the Anglicans, the Roman Catholic Church also catered mainly to expatriates at first. The first resident priest was an American Jesuit, Father Francis Jackmauh, who arrived in 1955 and set up a church named for St. Ignatius Loyola. Its stated purpose was not to make converts but to serve the growing number of Catholics from other parts of the world, especially from Central America. Like other churches serving immigrant communities, many of its members were relatively poor. Those who were more prosperous were mainly white Catholics from other developed countries. Its style was essen-

tially conservative. The Cayman church escaped radical influences, such as Liberation Theology, that were so divisive in the Catholic Church throughout Latin America.[37]

In 1955, Fr. Jackmauh ministered to just thirty Catholics, and even by 1970 there were no more than sixty. In that year, however, the Catholics started a primary school, open to all, taught by Franciscan nuns. It flourished. By the 1990s, it had added secondary years, with lay and non-Catholic teachers, and, as St. Ignatius High School, had become one of the most prestigious local schools. By that time, the Catholic congregation in Grand Cayman had expanded to many hundreds.[38]

Many churches in Cayman were increasingly open to American influence, not least through television, which reached most households by the 1990s. We have already seen how the Seventh-Day Adventists, the Holiness Movement, and various Churches of God, originating in the United States, made inroads into Grand Cayman between the 1890s and 1930s.[39] As the Caymanian population expanded and became more prosperous and diverse, these congregations grew, while a succession of new churches arose. Some were led by American-style preachers, serving those who sought a different, more personal and simple religious experience. From the early 1970s, various attempts were made to coordinate the religious diversity in Cayman by means of a Ministerial Association, frequent interdenominational meetings, and non-sectarian revivals. A number of non-denominational churches have come into existence, as well as a branch of the unity-oriented Baha'i faith.[40]

By the 1990s Grand Cayman had an impressive variety of churches. In addition to the United Church (with its dozen places of worship), the two Catholic and three Anglican (or Episcopalian) churches, there were eight Adventist churches, at least five different Baptist churches, and eight Church of God or Holiness congregations, besides many other independent evangelical or fundamentalist bodies. Two other denominations originating in the United States were also represented: the Jehovah's Witnesses and the Mormons. Cayman Brac, with a population of fewer than fourteen hundred souls, boasted ten active churches including two Holiness, one Adventist, one United, and several Baptist congregations, as well as a retired priest, Msgr. John Meany, who ministered to the island's Catholic population. A small Baptist Church was located on Little Cayman.

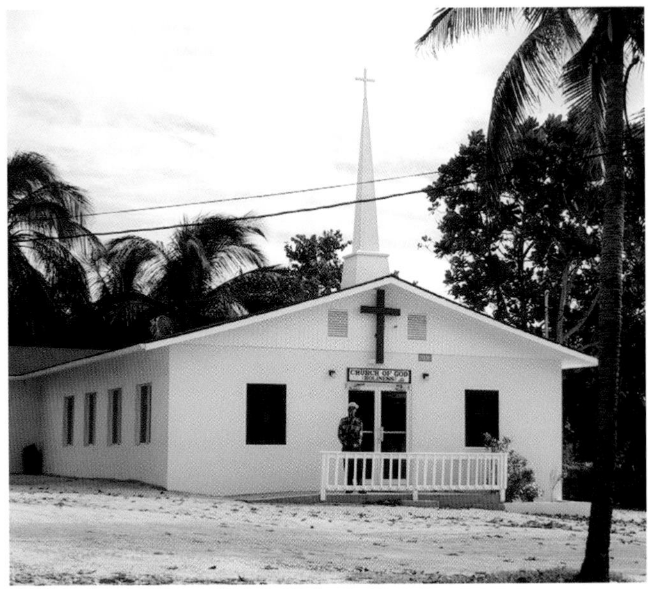

Church of God Holiness, Watering Place, Cayman Brac, 2002.

THE MASS MEDIA

One of the principal tools with which the modern evangelist delivers his or her message is the mass media. This is not new. The early Presbyterian missionaries used newsletters to promote their activities and to raise support. In the twentieth century, the very first newspaper printed in the Cayman Islands was *The Gospel of the Kingdom*, a monthly that first appeared in January 1945 and lasted until 1987, edited and printed by Will T. Bodden. It promoted the Church of God but was also a popular source of local news.[41]

As for the secular press, in March 1908 a monthly paper, *The Caymanian*, had been started by a Jamaican entrepreneur, Fred Myers, with encouragement from Commissioner Hirst. Copy was put together in George Town and sent down to Kingston on the SS *Oteri*. There it was edited by P.A. Myers, Fred's son, printed in newspaper format, and sent back on the *Oteri*'s next voyage. It had a very small circulation and only survived for twenty-two issues.[42]

Further advances in the news media were delayed for at least half a century. Although a local paper called the *Cayman Times* was published for a brief period from December 1956, it was not until December 1964 that the Cayman Islands gained its own regular newspaper, with the launching of the weekly *Tradewinds*. A rival, the *Caymanian Weekly*, started up in October 1965. The 1961–65 Annual Report wrote optimistically, "Both papers have successfully maintained sound standards of journalism, comment and criticism, with attractive layouts and clear printing on good quality newsprint." But the market proved too small for both of them, and the *Tradewinds* soon folded. The *Caymanian Compass* was formed from the *Caymanian Weekly* and the *Cayman Compass* (both weekly papers) on 20 June 1974. It became a bi-weekly paper on 4 May 1976, published on Tuesdays and Fridays. The *Caymanian Compass* began to publish daily on Tuesday, 6 October 1981, the sixteenth birthday of the newspaper's parent company, Cayman Free Press.[43] Sold for twenty-

The first print shop in Cayman: outside and inside the Cayman Gospel Press, ca. 1950s.

five cents, by 1995 it boasted a steady circulation of ten thousand and was being produced by a permanent staff of forty-one.

The *Compass* adequately covered local news, and made admirable efforts to provide regional and worldwide coverage. But it depended heavily on news agencies with an American slant. The choice of international newspapers brought in by air showed an even more marked bias towards the U.S. media. Some 75 per cent of all newspapers and magazines came in from the United States, with 15 per cent from the United Kingdom, 5 per cent from Jamaica, and 5 per cent from the rest of the world. Although some fine newsmagazines were published locally between 1970 and 1995, none survived to the end of the century.[44] Local news coverage received a boost in April 2000, when Desmond Seales, well known as the publisher of the popular *Nor'wester* (1971–84), launched a weekly newspaper, *Cayman Net News*, and an associated daily Internet newsmagazine.

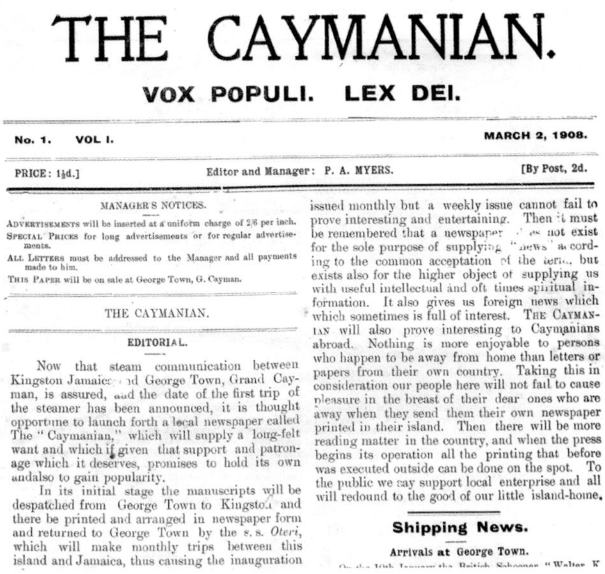

THE CAYMANIAN.

VOX POPULI. LEX DEI.

No. 1. VOL I. MARCH 2, 1908.

PRICE: 1½d.] Editor and Manager: P. A. MYERS. [By Post, 2d.

MANAGER'S NOTICES.

ADVERTISEMENTS will be inserted at a uniform charge of 2/6 per inch.

SPECIAL PRICES for long advertisements or for regular advertisements.

ALL LETTERS must be addressed to the Manager and all payments made to him.

THIS PAPER will be on sale at George Town, G. Cayman.

THE CAYMANIAN.

EDITORIAL.

Now that steam communication between Kingston Jamaica and George Town, Grand Cayman, is assured, and the date of the first trip of the steamer has been announced, it is thought opportune to launch forth a local newspaper called The "Caymanian," which will supply a long-felt want and which if given that support and patronage which it deserves, promises to hold its own andalso to gain popularity.

In its initial stage the manuscripts will be despatched from George Town to Kingston and there be printed and arranged in newspaper form and returned to George Town by the s. s. *Oteri*, which will make monthly trips between this island and Jamaica, thus causing the inauguration issued monthly but a weekly issue cannot fail to prove interesting and entertaining. Then it must be remembered that a newspaper does not exist for the sole purpose of supplying "news" according to the common acceptation of the term, but exists also for the higher object of supplying us with useful intellectual and oft times spiritual information. It also gives us foreign news which which sometimes is full of interest. THE CAYMANIAN will also prove interesting to Caymanians abroad. Nothing is more enjoyable to persons who happen to be away from home than letters or papers from their own country. Taking this in consideration our people here will not fail to cause pleasure in the breast of their dear ones who are away when they send them their own newspaper printed in their island. Then there will be more reading matter in the country, and when the press begins its operation all the printing that before was executed outside can be done on the spot. To the public we say support local enterprise and all will redound to the good of our little island-home.

Shipping News.

Arrivals at George Town.

GRAND CAYMAN B.W.I.

Tradewinds

VOL. I NO. I DECEMBER 17, 1964 PRICE 6d

FIRECRACKERS

Annual Danger

Once again we are reminded that it is Christmas, not by the Herald Angels or sleigh bells but by the sharp report and thunderous crack of Cannon and Firecrackers. These can, of course, be fun - especially for small boys - when used in safe places and under circumstances where they can cause no danger to persons and property.

Here in Cayman, however the misuse of these dangerous fireworks is appalling as they are thrown about carelessly causing the public and animals to be in danger of serious injury. On Christmas Eve last year it was horrifying to see boys attempting to throw lighted firecrackers underneath car engines, despite warnings from adults and the Police.

PLEASE make this Christmas Eve more pleasant for us all by keeping these explosives off the Main Streets and around Shopping Centres so that small children (and adults!)

Cayman Officials with the Leader of the Commonwealth Parliamentary Delegation of 25 who paid a one day visit to Grand Cayman on the 14th November.

(From left to right) Mr. E.O. Panton, Mr. Spurgeon Ebanks, Mr. P.E. Lucock (Australia) and His Honour the Administrator.

CAPITAL PUNISHMENT FOR MURDER TO BE ABOLISHED.

By a majority of 185 votes, The House of Commons in Britain, yesterday passed a Private Members' Bill, introduced by Mr. Sidney Silverman M.P., to abolish capital punishment for murder.

Gospel Hall & West Bay Gospel Hall on 25th December at 7p.m. and George Town Gospel Hall on 26th December at 7p.m.

CHRISTMAS SHOW FROM JAMAICA COMES TO CAYMAN

Two Big Shows are to be staged in Grand Cayman

AN APOLOGY

Tradewinds Publishing Ltd. very much regrets that, due to technical difficulties this first issue is a little late in reaching you. We take this opportunity to wish all our readers a very Happy Christmas and a Prosperous New Year.

STOWAWAY ABOARD THE "MERCO".

The Captain of the "Merco" reports that when his ship reached Cayman Brac on its way from Jamaica to Grand Cayman, a stowaway was discovered aboard. He is now in the George Town jail.

WEDDING

The Church of God Chapel was beautifully decorated for the wedding of MR. HURLEY MERREN and MISS LEONIE EDEN on Sunday the 20th December commencing at 5:30 p.m. The ceremony was performed by the Rev. C.D. Holm.

The Maid of Honour was Miss Trilee Parsons who sang "Wedding Prayer" during the signing of the Register. The Bridesmaids were Maxine and Maureen Bodden and Betty Sue

First Tourists Arrive Here

Quite a good welcoming party of Caymanians were at the Airport on Saturday the 21st of November when the Pacific Western plane, chartered by Elgin Investments Ltd., touched down at 11:55 a.m. bringing 88 passengers for a two week stay.

First off the plane was a young man with a camera and he was seen taking shots of the Calypso Band, McField and his Mashyiannes, who were present to give a musical welcome. They were well applauded and one lady began to sway as soon as she caught the rhythm and almost danced her way from the aircraft to the Terminal Building.

All agreed that it had been a very smooth flight and the Stewardesses found their complement all ideal passengers. A comment was made to one lady who was well clad in

First editions: The Caymanian, *a monthly newspaper started in 1908 (top);* Tradewinds, *a weekly newspaper started in 1964 (below).*

Until 1973 the Cayman Islands did not have a radio station of its own. Local radio receivers easily picked up broadcasts from the region – often in Spanish, from Cuba and Central America, as well as English-language programming from Jamaica and Florida. In 1973, local broadcasting began with the FM student-training facility at ICCI. In December 1976, Radio Cayman began broadcasting, with a single channel operating seventeen and a half hours a day. Owned by government, its mandate was "to meet the needs for information, education, religion, culture and entertainment". By the 1990s it had added a second channel and operated around the clock, with a staff of twenty. In 1992 the first private radio station was authorised, Z99.9 FM, broadcasting music twenty-four hours a day and designed to be "particularly attractive to a younger listening audience". A fourth radio station was added in 1997, a private FM station called Heaven 97, offering "round-the-clock Christian music, with a contemporary emphasis".[45]

Broadcasting House: the home of Radio Cayman, ca. 1977.

One of the most powerful external influences on the Cayman Islands from the 1980s onwards was television. Interest began in the mid-1970s with the start of the first videotape club, and accelerated with the installation of the first satellite dishes in 1982. Within a further decade there were a dozen video clubs and six thousand satellite receivers. By that time there were also four privately owned local television stations and a rapidly expanding cable facility. The Cayman International Television Network (CITN) started in October 1992, and its sister network Cayman Television Service (CTS) one year later. Between them they offered "24-hour daily transmission of local, Caribbean and international news, complemented by U.S. news and entertainment programmes". In January 1993, CITN and CTS began a subscription cable service, with twenty channels of largely American programmes.

Besides these two predominantly secular operations, the Cayman Broadcasting Authority licensed two religious stations. Cayman Christian Television (CCT) re-transmitted satellite programmes from the U.S.-based Trinity Broadcasting Network and did not offer any local programming. The more sectarian Cayman Adventist Television Network (CATN/TV-30) began broadcasting in July 1996. Though it provided some local programmes, the bulk of its 24-hour coverage was re-transmitted directly from the Three Angels Broadcasting network in the United States.

Before television: the Islander Theatre, George Town, popular during the 1950s and 1960s.

Television is probably the most influential medium in modern Caymanian society. As the Annual Report for 1994 acknowledged, "the proliferation of TV-watching in the Islands . . . has left its mark on conversation and usage, as well as prompting some misgivings about its effects on culture."[46] Such effects have continued to multiply, aided by other forms of the modern media. At the same time, during the 1980s and 1990s Caymanians became more keenly aware of their history and national identity. They took positive steps to preserve aspects of their culture and to promote its development. It is to issues such as these that we turn in the concluding chapter.

Heroes Square on the first Heroes Day: Monday 27 January 2003.

CHAPTER 18

A Caymanian Nation

Out of the Past and into the Future

THROUGHOUT THE DAY DURING THE 1990s a steady stream of dump trucks thundered to and fro along the road from East End to George Town. They carried rocks and gravel quarried from the eastern district to fill the low ground adjoining both sides of the Seven Mile Beach road to West Bay. At the same time, the western side of the North Sound was scraped, dredged, and filled to build luxury condominiums and sumptuous private homes, often with their own yacht moorings. A network of canals was created, with the bare limestone in between grassed and carefully landscaped. Meanwhile, George Town was being transformed into a miniature city of concrete and glass, with a commercial harbour in place of the old anchorage of Hog Sty Bay. On Cayman Brac, too, and even on Little Cayman – long considered the most tranquil of the three islands – familiar landscapes gave way to modern façades. From their earliest beginnings, Caymanians had been shaped by their environment. The sea and the land had, in many ways, defined them. Yet from the start they had also worked to shape their physical environment: first with machete and mattock, now, 300 years later, with bulldozer and backhoe.

As environmentalists were quick to point out, the changes represented loss as well as gain. Quarrying and filling disfigured the landscape and endangered the natural forest with its native birds, animals, and flowers. Draglines made the waters of the North Sound turbid and upset its fragile ecology. The clearing of more and more land and the disposal of a modern community's waste products threatened the mangrove swamps that protected the island

George Town port in operation at night, 2001.

from the worst storm damage. At sea, cruise-ship anchors threatened the once-pristine reefs that were the Cayman Islands' main attractions.

Marco Giglioli, the leader of the war against the mosquito, was among the first to sound the alarm. Giglioli's Mosquito Research and Control Unit increasingly concerned itself with conservation, and by the mid-1990s its Environmental Research Unit had become the Department of Environment. From 1986, marine conservation legislation set up a government board with powers to designate marine park zones and protected areas, to protect certain species, to control fishing methods, and to contain pollution and physical damage. Parallel initiatives led to the formation of the National Trust for the Cayman Islands, which was given extensive powers of preservation and protection by a law passed in 1987.[1]

By the 1990s, more than a third of the three islands' shorelines were designated either Marine Parks or Replenishment Zones. The eastern side of Grand Cayman's North Sound was designated an Environmental Zone and almost closed off. Four pond areas, including the nesting site of the Red-footed Booby and the Magnificent Frigatebird on Little Cayman, were designated Animal Sanctuaries. Similar legislation gave some protection to the Grand Cayman and Cayman Brac parrots, the Cayman blue iguana, and other threatened or endangered species of animals and plants. Fines for violations, limited to $500 in 1978, had been raised to a maximum of $500,000 by 1998, though the law was rarely enforced. As greater ecological awareness swelled its membership, the National Trust increased its nature reserves by purchase and donation. Development continued to threaten sensitive habitats near private land, however, and no legal protection was in place for woodlands or mangrove swamps. In a joint effort with government, the

National Trust created a national Botanic Park in the very centre of Grand Cayman, which was opened by Queen Elizabeth II and named in her honour in February 1994.[2]

No one seriously challenged the moves to protect the marine environment. But the idea of controlling private land development eventually stirred up bitter opposition. In the late 1990s, a storm erupted over the Central Planning Authority's decision to adopt the recommendation of the Department of Environment and National Trust to extend the Environmental Zones on Grand Cayman. In such areas no land could be sold, altered, or built upon. The principal area involved was the Central Mangrove wetland, covering almost a third of the island east of North Sound. The National Trust was also eager to add to the protected tracts that it had already acquired, especially the area near North Side called the Mountain. The distinguished botanist George R. Proctor had described this area as "native forest that has never been disturbed . . . the last example of sea level dry forest in the West Indies".[3]

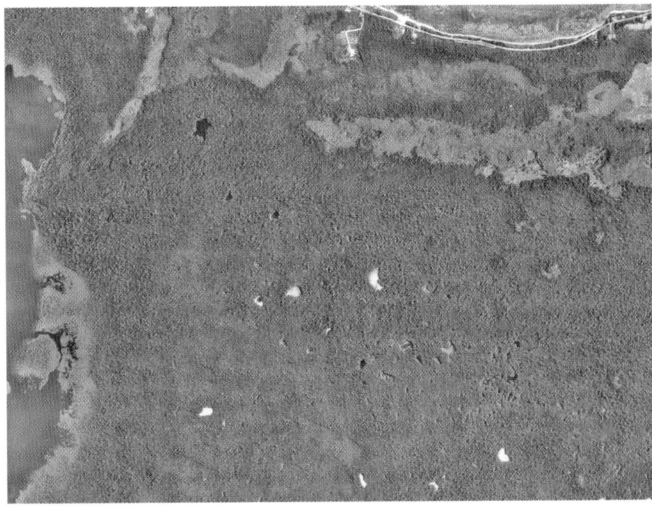

The Central Mangrove wetlands (with the North Side and North Sound coasts visible), 1999.

Most of the land in question was owned by people from North Side and Bodden Town, who felt that the new regulations infringed their right to profit from its development. Led by their political representatives, they angrily campaigned with public meetings, marches, slogans, and a petition bearing 1,750 names. In the letters column of the *Caymanian Compass*, fervent arguments for environmental protection were met with accusations of discrimination. Landowners from the unfashionable two-thirds of Grand Cayman, it was claimed, were being denied opportunities for profit by controls that were ignored on the richer third of the island. In broad terms, it was a clash between the interests of development and those seeking to preserve Cayman's heritage.[4]

Although this modern debate about the use of land was unprecedented in its vigour, Caymanians were no strangers to conservation issues. They had encountered them in a different sphere thirty years before, as commercial turtling came to an end. Conservation was one, though by no means the only, reason for the demise of turtle fishing. What had always

Hon. John McLean, M.L.A. for East End, accompanies H.M. The Queen on her visit to his constituency, February 1994.

been a hard trade was made even tougher when the Nicaraguan government tightened fishing regulations. By the late 1960s, no new schooners were being built, and fewer and fewer Caymanian mariners were willing to head for the Miskito Banks when there were easier and more lucrative jobs available at home. But a crucial factor was the depletion of the turtle stocks through over-fishing, plundering of eggs, and destruction of nesting sites throughout the Caribbean. To concerned experts like Archie Carr, it seemed that some, if not all, turtle species were in danger of extinction – and that Caymanian turtlers had contributed to their demise.

THE TURTLE FARM

In 1968, two Americans and an Englishman came up with a plan to breed and raise green turtles in the Cayman Islands. The aim was to replenish turtle stocks in the wild and to profit from the sale of meat, calipee, oil, leather, and shell. Irwin Naylor was a Pennsylvania entrepreneur who, while water-skiing and scuba diving in the Florida Keys, met a local marine biologist, Robert Schroeder. Schroeder had written an article called "The Buffalo of the Seas", which argued that turtle farming was the best way to save the species. This idea won the endorsement of Archie Carr (the premier world expert on sea turtles), who recommended the Cayman Islands as the most suitable location.[5]

Within a year, the partners had incorporated a company called Mariculture Ltd. and negotiated a site with the Caymanian government at Salt Creek, on the west side of North Sound. A Turtle Protection Act was passed, which limited the catching of wild turtles and endorsed Mariculture's operation. Naylor

Mariculture Ltd. at Salt Creek, North Sound, during the 1960s.

and Schroeder contracted to obtain fifteen thousand turtle eggs from Boca de Tortuguero, Costa Rica, in return for a promise to bring back or release five thousand yearlings. The eggs were hatched in Styrofoam containers and the hatchlings corralled in plastic pools. One- and two-year-olds were tagged for scientific study, and the remainder were fattened for slaughter or for breeding.

In 1971 Mariculture Ltd. moved to its permanent location at North West Point. By 1973, its turtle meat and shell were available for sale, and the first eggs were being produced by captive-bred females. But then adversity struck. The international conservation agency CITES declared the green turtle first a threatened and then an endangered species. The United States passed an Endangered Species Act, which banned the import of all turtle products. Cut off from its chief market, Mariculture Ltd. went into receivership in 1975.

A somewhat surprising saviour appeared in the person of Heinz Mittag, a retired German millionaire. Mittag bought out the company in 1976 for CI$2 million and renamed it Cayman Turtle Farm Inc. He then started a campaign to convince CITES and the U.S. government that the operation not only had scientific validity but was the green turtle's best hope for survival. By 1978 the CTF could claim to be self-sustaining, in that its own captive females were producing all the eggs needed. But in the following year, the U.S. government, influenced by the conservationist lobby, denied CTF's application for a revision of the turtle-products ban. A further blow was the defection of Archie Carr, who had begun to doubt that captive-raised turtles could survive and breed once returned to the wild.

After seven years Mittag had spent $10 million on the venture and was more than ready to give it up. At this point, the Cayman Islands government stepped in. The Turtle Farm's value as a tourist attraction and a heritage facility was already apparent. In 1983 the government purchased the Turtle Farm from Mittag for US$1.5 million.[6] With dynamic management, the Turtle Farm's fortunes turned around. It continued its scientific tag-and-release programme, while butchering and selling meat on the local market and shipping tortoiseshell to countries that did not ban its importation. But it was first and foremost a tourist-oriented operation, eventually attracting up to 300,000 visitors a year. From 1988 on, the operation made a healthy annual profit. Visitors could see Caymanian iguanas, agoutis, hiccatees, and parrots, in addition to various turtles in all stages of development, as well as a separate display of traditional turtling tools and methods, aptly reflecting the slogan: "Turtle Farm – cultivating Cayman's history".[7]

The Turtle Farm is an admirable and effective attempt to marry development with preservation. Whatever the benefits of modernisation, however, other changes in the last thirty years have threatened to obscure the history and traditions of the islands. This threat has aroused the desire to honour the

past and to rediscover and celebrate aspects of Cayman's traditional culture on all three islands.

THE IMPORTANCE OF SYMBOLS

Probably the first modern effort to show what their country, their past, and their culture signify for Caymanians was the adoption of the official coat of arms in 1958. The design was submitted by a non-Caymanian, James Ford, but it was discussed and accepted by a committee of the legislature.[8] Like all such insignia, the coat of arms is rich in symbols. In the centre of the shield, floating on wavy lines of white and blue which represent the sea, are three green stars with golden borders. These are the three islands, united but distinct. Above them, on a ground of regal red, is the British lion in a watchful and protective stance. Below the shield is the Caymanian motto: "He hath founded it upon the seas." Taken from Psalm 24, it refers to the Islands' marine environment, its people's traditional livelihoods, and their profound faith in the Creator.

The official coat of arms of the Cayman Islands, 1958.

Symbolic "achievements" surmount the shield. Pride of place goes to the green turtle, the creature that first attracted European visitors and which sustained the economy for over two hundred years. The turtle stands on a coil of rope made from the leaves of the silver thatch palm, unique to Cayman and later declared the national tree. Along with the distinctive Caymanian schooners and catboats, thatch rope was the most famous item Caymanians made and an important supplement to many household incomes down to modern times. A pineapple tops the crest. Since the pineapple featured prominently in Jamaica's coat of arms at the time, it aptly represents the Cayman Islands' 300-year ties with her nearest Caribbean neighbour.

More recently, other symbols have joined the crest as official expressions of Caymanian identity. In 1993 "Beloved Isle Cayman" by Leila Ross-Shier was designated as the national song. In 1996 three popular icons were designated as national symbols: the silver thatch palm (national tree), the wild banana orchid (national flower), and the Cayman Parrot (national bird).[9]

THE SISTER ISLANDS

Two of the stars on the crest represent the Sister Islands. The second half of the twentieth century was to witness an ever-closer relationship between the Sister Islands and Grand Cayman, both because of modern travel and because Brackers often sought to make a living on Grand Cayman. Yet the Sister Islands have always felt historically distinct, with cultural characteristics and a way of life that was their own. They were the first islands seen by Europeans,

the first to be settled (if only temporarily), and an early destination in the migrations from Grand Cayman that followed the end of slavery. Caymanians from the Sister Islands have always displayed an unusual willingness to seize new opportunities, and during the past fifty years they became noted as entrepreneurs in ways that echoed their early pioneering spirit.

Remembrance Day ceremony at Stake Bay, Cayman Brac, 2002.

From the mid-1800s, the Sister Islanders developed their own economy, based almost exclusively on the sea and on the pursuit of the hawksbill rather than the green turtle. Their men were active and inventive boatbuilders. They culled native hardwoods from their own islands or Grand Cayman, and roamed farther afield for planking timber. They vigorously sought out wrecks for masts, riggings, and fittings – not to mention the useful cargoes they were carrying. Conservative and naturally religious, they became Baptists through missionaries whose non-conformist message resonated with their own style and ways of thought. Their churches were more autonomous and their families even more tightly knit than those of Grand Cayman.

Though isolated, the Sister Islanders were every bit as loyal as other Caymanians. In World War Two half of their menfolk served the British cause abroad, and one in twelve did not return. When there was talk of joining Jamaica in 1962, pro-Jamaican campaigners from Grand Cayman were warned off with shotgun blasts in the night. Sister Islanders threatened that they would declare their own independence rather than be yoked to Jamaica. They have consistently worked to keep their own identity and their fair share of the prosperity that Providence has showered upon the Cayman Islands as a whole.

Ship-to-ship oil transfer off Little Cayman, ca. 1980.

The Sister Islanders' sense of independence, self-reliance, and enterprise was sharpened by necessity. Great venturers abroad, they always hankered to return to their own small islands. Grand Cayman proved a land of comparative opportunity for some from the Sister Islands, especially in the era of modern development. From the mid-twentieth century on, Brackers were among the most active entrepreneurs on Grand Cayman.[10]

Yet new opportunities were also available within the Sister Islands, as tourism increased and other amenities, such as branch banks and shops, opened. One unusual venture was the work provided by the oil transshipment company Cayman Energy Ltd. Government signed an agreement with Cayman Energy in March 1977, permitting them to carry out ship-to-ship transfers within Cayman waters. This location meant that supertankers could deliver their cargo closer to their destinations in the Gulf, with consequent savings. The first transfer took place in August 1977, and over the next six years some of the world's largest ships could be seen off Little Cayman, as oil from giant supertankers was transferred to shallow-draft tankers capable of entering U.S. ports. The agreement provided revenue for government and jobs for Cayman Brackers. In 1980, for example, over 80 million barrels of oil was transferred – work that employed about sixty local people earning a million dollars in wages. Cayman Energy paid $800,000 in royalties, amounting to 2.5% of government revenue. Unfortunately, 1980 turned out to be the peak year of operation. During the next three years, a combination of economic challenges, environmental concerns, and development of alternatives for transferring oil to Gulf ports led to the demise of what had originally been viewed as a very promising enterprise.[11]

Cayman Brac and Little Cayman are now known as the Sister Islands, the older name of "Lesser Islands" having been officially discontinued in 1990.[12] Their status has been underscored through frequent visits by the Governor and by the occasional meeting of the Legislative Assembly in Cayman Brac. But the Sister Islands' importance was also shown by their distinctive representation in the legislature (with two MLAs representing 5 per cent of the population), by the regular election of one of their MLAs to ExCo, by a large group of government employees, and by higher per capita government spending. Cayman Brac has a hospital and a high school as fine, for the size of their community, as any in the Commonwealth Caribbean.

For more than a century, the Sister Islands have had their own local administration headed by a District Commissioner, who has usually been from the Sister Islands. The Government Administration Building at Stake Bay in Cayman Brac has housed separate customs, postal, surveying, and immigration sections. The local Port Authority and Public Works Department has operated with a measure of autonomy. From time to time, the Sister Islands have also been given import duty concessions on building materials, aimed at attracting foreign investment, wealthy settlers, and useful expatriates. In the 1990s, however, Brackers faced a continuing significant challenge. Because of the lack of opportunity for young people beginning their careers, the tradition of migration has continued, mostly to Grand Cayman and the United States.

RELATIONS WITH THE MOTHER COUNTRY

The Sister Islanders share with all other Caymanians a continuing attachment to the British motherland. In the past, the connection brought benefits without undue interference. In recent years, the relationship seems to have grown even stronger, and it will surely continue as long as the advantages outweigh any disadvantages.

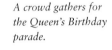

HMS Zest *visits George Town in May 1967.*

What do Caymanians perceive as the benefits? They include military and diplomatic protection. The foreign policy interests of the Cayman Islands are the responsibility of Britain, and Cayman does not have the trouble and expense of creating its own diplomatic corps. Internal security is ultimately assured by Britain's continuing involvement in policing matters. British institutions and principles provide certain forms of security, among them constitutional monarchy, the parliamentary system, democracy and the rule of law, the separation of powers, and British Common Law.

For Caymanians, however, loyalty to the monarch is central. The visits of members of the Royal Family have been widely celebrated events, including two visits by the Queen herself, in 1983 and 1994, when she held investitures and read the Speech from the Throne to the Legislature.[13] Every year there are symbolic ceremonies – the formal opening of the Legislature and of the Supreme Court, the celebration of the Queen's Birthday with its honours and awards, investitures at Government House, and Remembrance Day.

Patriotism remained strong and even grew in the last four decades of the twentieth century. In 1962, the Cayman Islands chose overwhelmingly to remain a British colony. In August 1969, Warren Conolly moved a resolution that the Islands celebrate the three-hundredth anniversary of the Treaty of Madrid, which was Cayman's first formal link to Britain, with the publication in 1970 of the first official history.[14]

A crowd gathers for the Queen's Birthday parade.

Since 1962 there have been no serious proposals to break away. In 1977, the United Nations Committee on Decolonisation sent a fact-finding mission to the Islands. When asked whether they wanted independence, some Caymanians simply answered by singing "God Save the Queen". In 1982, when Britain went to

war with Argentina over ownership of the Falkland Islands, Caymanians started a special fund and donated half a million pounds to the cause. At the end of the century, the only cloud on the horizon was the British Labour Government's White Paper of 1998, the purpose of which was to bring Britain's remaining Overseas Territories into compliance with European Community standards in various areas, including environmental protection, human rights, and regulation of financial services. Many Caymanians felt that the White Paper represented unwarranted interference in their internal affairs. In part, this feeling reflects the fact that their historic ties are to Britain, rather than to the European Community.[15]

DEFINING THE CAYMANIAN IDENTITY

Patriotism is an important aspect of the Caymanian identity and sense of self. Recent decades have seen a growing preoccupation with Caymanian identity – with recognising, preserving, and celebrating it. The preoccupation is reflected in the recent creation of organisations dedicated to these ends, all of which carry the word "national" in their titles: the National Trust, the National Archive, the National Museum, the National Gallery, and the National Cultural Foundation.

Several factors complicated the process of defining Caymanian identity and sustaining authentic Caymanian culture. Like many tourist destinations, the Cayman Islands sought to project an image of their past which would be attractive to tourists. But like other destinations, they discovered that such projections can distort the past and ignore the harsher realities of history.

The official programme for the first Pirates Week, 1977.

One example of a controversial effort to cultivate the Caymanian past in order to attract tourists was the exploitation of the pirate image, represented by Pirates Week, an annual event first held in October 1977. The person most responsible for starting Pirates Week was Jim Bodden, ExCo Member for tourism at that time. He explained it as the equivalent of a Mexican fiesta, Trinidad's Carnival, or Goombay Summer in the Bahamas. "If we are to keep abreast of the progress made by other island destinations of comparative size and attractions, we know we must do something special each year, particularly during the traditionally lean months," Jim Bodden wrote in the first souvenir programme. "Pirates Week is not only intended to give tourists a little fun and excitement, it is intended that residents as well should get involved, participate in the various events and generally thoroughly enjoy themselves."[16]

Ignoring the fact that the Cayman Islands were never a true pirate lair, many Caymanians enthusiastically embraced the opportunity for an annual super-party. By its second year the "week" had been stretched to eleven days, and it went from strength to strength over the following quarter century. But

Pirates Week owed its longevity and continued success to its gradual evolution into an authentic national cultural festival. From the beginning, all three islands were involved, and from the second year every district had its own day for celebration. Soon these were re-christened District Heritage Days, each with its own displays of traditional crafts, music, dancing, and cooking. In George Town, the annual display of fireworks grew more splendid each year. The festival also featured performances by local artists and concerts by well-known regional musicians, week-long shows of local arts and crafts, and performances of local plays.[17]

As Governor A.J. Scott wrote in the 1991 souvenir programme, "Today the festival is still strongly identified with its original theme, but it has embraced the larger objective of strengthening Caymanian cultural identity. Visitors will find that each district has a character and flavour of its own, springing as they did from villages whose relative isolation has melted away only during the last 50 years." In 1998 Governor John Owen urged visitors and residents alike "to take advantage of this time, of our Community Heritage Days, to get involved, and reflect on the rich traditions – and hardships – that represented daily life for earlier generations of Caymanians. Pirates Week is always a time for light-hearted revelry," he went on, "but it is also an opportunity to appreciate the customs and values that add continuity and character to contemporary Cayman."[18]

Another concerted effort to combine a showcase of Caymanian history with a tourist attraction was the restoration of Pedro St. James. The project centred on the scrupulous restoration and presentation of the only surviving stone "great house" in the Islands, popularly known as Pedro Castle. The house was built in 1780 by the English settler William Eden, on a low bluff overlooking the southern approaches to Grand Cayman.[19] Probably because of its substantial nature and central location, Pedro St. James served in the 1820s and 1830s as a rallying point for the local militia, as a court-house, and as a meeting place for the island's decision-makers. It was where leading inhabitants decided, on 5 December 1831, to hold the first district elections for an island legislature, and it was one of the places where the Emancipation Proclamation was read in May 1835.[20]

After emancipation, Pedro St. James gradually decayed, along with the fortunes of the Eden estate. The main building was reduced to its stone core by a fire in 1870, leaving the Eden descendants to live in wood, wattle, and thatch homes in the surrounding yard. By the twentieth century, the building was no more than a picturesque ruin, a picnic spot, and a source of imaginative local legends. Indeed, it was during the twentieth century that it came to be called a "castle".

In 1954 an enterprising American named Thomas Hubbell bought the property, intending to turn it into a restaurant and tourist attraction. He

Pedro St. James, shortly before its official opening as a National Historic Site on 5 December 1998.

added battlements to the main building to make it look more like a typical castle, carved the date 1631 on the entrance arch, and promoted the idea that it was built by a Spaniard named Pedro Gomez, whose "castle" had once housed the buccaneer Henry Morgan. A second fire destroyed Hubbell's plans, and by the late 1980s, after an unsuccessful attempt to turn it into a restaurant and bar, Pedro St. James was derelict once more.

In the 1990s, however, the ministries responsible for tourism and culture collaborated in the restoration of Pedro St. James. Under the auspices of the Historic Sites Committee, comprising organisations such as the National Archive, National Museum, and National Trust, the site was thoroughly researched. With the expertise of a highly professional Canadian team, the original building was restored and furnished. Detailed signage was placed on the site to guide visitors through its history, and a first-class multi-media show was created for the theatre, housed in an elegant visitors' centre. The restoration was designed to be both a National Historic Site and a visitor attraction, intended to accommodate 100,000 visitors per year. After a six-year programme of restoration, it was officially opened in December 1998.

There were other efforts in the 1980s and 1990s to explore and promote Caymanian culture. Parallel to these, and part of the development of Cayman's modern culture, was the increasing popularity of competitive sports. In the past, Caymanians had had few opportunities for organised or competitive sports. Commissioners Hirst and Cardinall initiated bicycle races and a sailing regatta, but these annual events had petered out long before modern times.

All this changed in the second half of the twentieth century, as greater prosperity and more leisure time allowed sports to flourish. The Cayman Islands boasted more than a hundred tennis courts by the year 2000, along with three golf courses on Grand Cayman. Sailing and swimming came naturally, but they became more popular and competitive. The annual Easter Regatta was revived in 1968, and at the end of the twentieth century there was a determined attempt to revive catboat racing.[21] Cycling caught on in a way that would have gladdened Commissioner Hirst's heart. Supported by ample encouragement in the schools, expatriates' enthusiasm and skills, and ever-improving facilities, Caymanians became involved in a remarkable range of competitive sports. By the time the spacious Truman Bodden National Sport Complex was opened in 1996, the Cayman Islands could field highly competent teams in soccer, rugby, and squash. With sponsorship from Cable & Wireless Ltd., the Cayman Islands also strengthened its cricket league and fielded a national cricket team, leading to a resurgence of one of the oldest competitive sports in Cayman.

The Truman Bodden Sports Centre, George Town, 2002.

Having sent their first competitors to the Commonwealth Games and Olympics only in 1975, by 1995 the Cayman Islands had hosted and won medals at the CARIFTA Games and had participated in a wide range of other regional tournaments. Being a small country, they did not achieve wonders on the world scene. But wearing the uniform of their homeland and marching behind their flag at international competitions reinforced a sense of national pride, as well as bringing recognition to the Cayman Islands.

In the realm of creative arts, an early encouragement was a Festival of Arts, organised twice in the early to mid-1970s. Interest in drama and the visual arts gave birth eventually to the Cayman National Cultural Foundation, initiated in 1984, and the National Art Gallery, started in 1996. From 1995 the CNCF promoted an annual festival of the arts called Cayfest. The Education Department was also involved in the encouragement of creative expression through the National Children's Festival of the Arts, initiated in 1982 and held annually to popular acclaim.[22]

During the time when isolation and hardship bred invention, the traditional Caymanian songs were narrative ballads, sea shanties, and launching songs. Such folk music was rarely heard once sailing days ended. The distinctive Caymanian folk-dance was a local variant of the European quadrille, danced to the music of a small band using locally constructed instruments, in which the fiddle led and an African resonance lingered. During the 1980s and 1990s the quadrille was revived among a number of school groups, inspired especially by the survival of the tradition at East End. During the same period, the one remaining traditional band, Radley Gourzong and his Happy Boys (fiddle, guitar, tambourine, maracas, grater, and cowskin drum), was giving its last performances.[23] Alongside these traditional sounds, popular and classical singing was performed by groups such as the Cayman Singers, formed in the late 1960s, and the National Choir, formed in the mid-1970s.[24]

Despite the proximity of Cuba and other hispanic countries (whose music was often picked up on early radio sets), Latin American music had limited influence in the Cayman Islands. At the end of the century, pop music from the United States dominated the airwaves, along with reggae and soca. Country-and-western music had always been a strong favourite, reflecting long

ties with the southern United States. Radio, television, and disco DJs promoted current American hits, adolescents listened avidly to rap music, and the latest West Indian songs boomed loudly from stereos and car radios. These different styles coexisted without approaching a Caymanian fusion. The best-known performer in the Cayman Islands during the last three decades of the twentieth century was George Novak, the "Barefoot Man". His music was a mélange of contemporary pop hits, old country-and-western favourites, and familiar calypso and reggae tunes.[25]

With the exception of community and church events, the writing arts did not have a strong place in traditional Caymanian culture, partly because of the lack of any local newspapers and magazines until the 1960s. But this began to change in the 1970s, as an awakening interest in play writing, performance, and short-story writing built on the vigorous Caymanian tradition of informal drama. From at least the beginning of the twentieth century there were church pageants and Christmas skits. Those put on by members of Christian Endeavour youth groups are remembered with particular fondness. Since the 1960s various amateur dramatic groups have been formed, the best known of which is probably the Cayman Drama Society, originally formed in 1970.

An important catalyst in the development of Caymanian drama was the Inn Theatre, which included local players and writers and put on performances at the Royal Palms Hotel from the late 1970s. The Inn Theatre's members included Frank McField, whose plays, especially *Time Longer Dan Rope* and *Downside Up*, explored aspects of Caymanian family life and class and race relations, using authentic Caymanian dialect.[26] A further step forward was the formation of the Cayman National Theatre Company in the 1980s. It held workshops where it could, until it was able to move into the Harquail Theatre. This splendid theatre and arts centre opened in 1986 and immediately became the headquarters for the Cayman National Cultural Foundation. In 1991, the CNCF instituted an annual National Playwriting Competition, encouraging works with Caymanian themes. The best submissions were performed at the Harquail Theatre, though the CNCF also strove to acquaint the Caymanian public with the cultural riches developed elsewhere in the Caribbean.

Strong encouragement for writing poetry and fiction came from educators. As early as 1982 the Department of Education started an annual National Children's Festival of the Arts, and beginning in 1990 published an anthology of the best poems, stories, essays, and playlets submitted each year. In 1992 the work of students from John Gray High School was published in a literary potpourri called *Our Voice*, while the same year another group of students at the ICCI produced a similar collection of poetry and short stories called *In Our Own Write*.[27] A number of Caymanians, such as Joy Brandon

and Curtis Barnett, have published individual anthologies of their poetry and fiction.[28]

In the visual arts, local painters were striving for a distinctively Caymanian form of expression, if not aiming to found a recognisable Caymanian school. They were starting late in a medium that had few if any local roots. When the American artist and craftsman Ed Oliver first visited Grand Cayman in the late 1950s, there were no art teachers, nor were artists' materials locally available. The nearest thing to visual art was sign-painting, much of it fairly primitive, with one or two practitioners trying their hand at pictures, using ordinary house paints. Ed Oliver settled in Grand Cayman in 1969, rented a loft for $35 a month, started an informal gallery, sold materials, and gave free lessons. He carried on for more than thirty years, by which time he reckoned that over five hundred people had attended his informal classes, many of them young Caymanians.[29]

From the late 1970s on, however, other encouragement was plentiful. In 1979, the Visual Arts Society was founded, largely by expatriates, and gave as many as three shows a year in local hotels. Beginning in 1986, the Cayman National Cultural Foundation promoted workshops and exhibitions, and in the 1990s, the National Museum undertook a policy of collecting the best of local art. During the early 1990s much preparatory work went into the creation of a National Gallery, which was established in temporary headquarters in 1996.[30]

The best-known Caymanian artist is probably Bendel Hydes, born in West Bay in 1952. One of the early stars of Ed Oliver's workshop, Hydes went on to study at Liverpool and Canterbury in England and at Clark University in Massachusetts. His work was exhibited in the 1980 VAS summer show. He was also the main artist exhibited in the McField Square Gallery, when it opened in a renovated family home on Mary Street, George Town, in 1981. But the venture was not a financial success, and in 1982 Hydes migrated to New York.[31] Since then, his work has been increasingly recognised and sought after by residents and local businesses.

Homage to Cayos Miskitos I, *by Bendel Hydes, 1993: a tribute to Cayman's long turtling tradition.*

During the last twenty years, the Cayman Islands has continued to attract accomplished non-Caymanian artists, whose works have been exhibited fre-

Peace Be Still, *Jesus calming the storm: a typical painting with a strong Biblical theme, by Gladwyn K. Bush (Miss Lassie).*

quently by the Visual Arts Society and elsewhere. Of the young Caymanian artists who stayed at home, the most prominent were the quartet who called themselves "Native Sons" and began to give group shows in 1996: Miguel Powery, Ray Banker, Allie Ebanks, and Horacio Esteban.

The most unusual Caymanian artist to emerge in recent years was a visionary intuitive painter named Gladwyn K. Bush, commonly known as "Miss Lassie". Born in South Sound, Grand Cayman, in 1914, she had never been off her native island until she was seventy-nine years old. Her earliest artistic impulses were stifled by her Barbadian teacher, who punished her for drawing duppies on her slate. The daughter of a master mariner and boatbuilder of modest means, she lived a hard, conventional life. She worked as a nurse, and her church was the focus of her activities. In 1984, as a widow of sixty-nine, Miss Lassie had a series of visions commanding her to paint, providing specific patterns and themes in vivid colours. She began with all the flat surfaces of her little wooden house, using ordinary house paints, until she had turned her dwelling into a magical place, inside and out. She called her work her "markings".

Once tapped, Miss Lassie's inspiration knew no limits. She transformed almost every mundane object in her house: seat cushions, mirrors, water jugs, her guitar. She also produced first dozens and then hundreds of thematic pictures on every available piece of paper, board, and wood. Only later did friends provide her with artists' paints and canvas. In time, Miss Lassie's work was discovered by the CNCF, which produced a beautifully illustrated book called *My Markings: The Art of Gladwyn K. Bush* in 1994.[32] Requests for shows and commissioned pieces followed, as did sales, at ever escalating prices. Her house was declared a national treasure.

VISION OF THE FUTURE

National artists are, by definition, those who best expound a nation's view of itself. It is, however, the people and their leaders who must come to terms with the realities of contemporary life and plan for the nation's future. These imperatives were what led the Caymanian government to involve all three islands in the development of a national strategic plan, designed to see the

Cayman Islands through the first decade of the new millennium and beyond. It was called Vision 2008.

The "Visioning Process" was launched by Governor John Owen in February 1998. The Hon. Truman Bodden, Leader of Government Business, was given overall responsibility for the process, while Mrs. Joy Basdeo, his Permanent Secretary in the Ministry of Education, was appointed executive director.

The new Vision 2008 office made steady and efficient progress. Between March and May 1998 more than two thousand people put forward ideas for consideration. MLAs and senior civil servants held "Visioning retreats". Public meetings took place in every district on all three islands. The population was polled, and residents enthusiastically submitted their views by letter, e-mail, fax, telephone, and even personal visits to the Vision 2008 office. In June 1998, a thirty-member Planning Team was appointed, consisting of Caymanians and expatriate long-term residents, "reflecting the composition of the community". After three days of intensive discussion, it had produced a framework for the plan: a Statement of Beliefs, a general Vision Statement, lists of Parameters and Objectives, and a set of sixteen implementation Strategies.[33] The Statement of Beliefs was something of a national credo.

WE BELIEVE

- *In God and traditional Christian values.*
- *That all people are created with equal worth and are entitled to basic human rights.*
- *That all people have a responsibility to contribute to the good of the community.*
- *That a healthy natural and built environment and a balance between the two, is essential for social, economic and political well-being and prosperity.*
- *In freedom of speech.*
- *That respect for Caymanian and non-Caymanian culture is important for social harmony.*
- *In the importance of a strong family unit.*
- *That people are responsible and accountable for their own actions.*
- *In striving towards a society that is free from crime and drug abuse.*
- *In lifelong education for everyone which embraces social and life skills.*[34]

The Vision Statement fleshed out the bold assertions in this Statement of Beliefs. It gave first place to the belief in God and Christian values, adding that Cayman should be a "caring community based on mutual respect for all

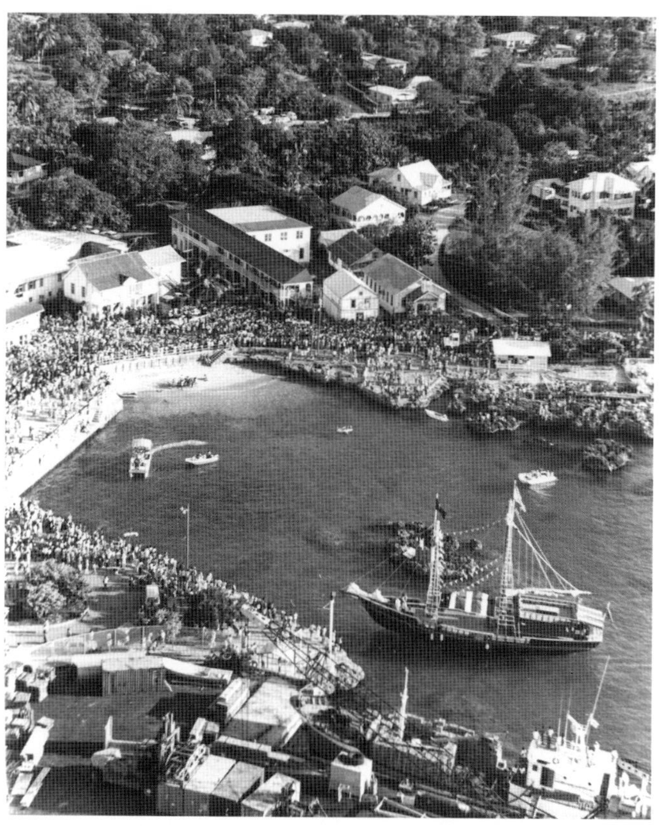

Hogsty Bay at the start of Pirates Week, 1977.

individuals". It promised "a comprehensive health-care system" and an education system that would enable all persons "to reach their full potential and productivity". It aimed for a diversified economy with full employment and balanced growth, which would nevertheless protect Cayman's "social and natural environment". Politically, its goal was "open, responsible, and accountable" government with a "working partnership with the private sector" and "beneficial ties with the United Kingdom". It called for an immigration policy to protect Caymanians yet give security to "long-term residents". It sought to preserve "traditional Caymanian heritage and the family unit", and to practice a policy of "zero tolerance for crime and drug abuse". It pledged separate plans to address the "uniqueness, special needs, and concerns" of the Sister Islands.[35]

Vision 2008 then invited 250 members of the general public to join one of sixteen Roundtables, each of which researched a particular "strategy" on subjects like culture or the environment, and held intensive discussions from October 1998 to February 1999. The results of their work were carefully reviewed by the Planning Team, who published their conclusions on 7 April. In all, 205 Action Plans had been drawn up, each of which had up to fifteen Action Steps. The Sister Islands examined their own issues, and their two Roundtables drew up twenty-six Action Plans for Cayman Brac and twenty-seven for Little Cayman.[36]

The Vision 2008 master plan was tabled in the Legislative Assembly on 6 June 1999, with a strong endorsement from the new Governor, Peter Smith. The most difficult stages – dealing with priorities, implementation, and costs – still lay ahead. But all in all, the Vision 2008 process showed how resolutely the Cayman Islanders were accepting the challenges that confronted them, attempting to discern what they needed as a nation, and recognising what in their history and culture made them what they were. As the new millennium was celebrated with speeches, fanfares, and fireworks at midnight on 31 December 1999, the Cayman Islands and its people could feel pride and optimism. If they were not yet quite a fully fashioned nation, they were firmly on their way.

Celebration fireworks over Hog Sty Bay.

Notes

N.B. The abbreviation PRO refers to documents in the United Kingdom Public Record Office; ADM refers to the Admiralty group of documents, CO to the Colonial Office group, T to the Treasury group, and FO to the Foreign Office group. MODHO refers to the archives of the United Kingdom Ministry of Defence Hydrographic Office; SOAS refers to archives of the School of Oriental and African Studies, London. Unless otherwise specified, *Colonial Report* and *Annual Report* refer to the annual report on the Cayman Islands submitted to the Colonial Office. CINA is the abbreviation for the collections of the Cayman Islands National Archive.

Chapter 1: OVERTURE

1. This book does not examine the geological prehistory of the Cayman Islands, which can be explored in a number of sources, notably in the work of Brian Jones. See, for example, his "Geology of the Cayman Islands," in *The Cayman Islands: Natural History and Biogeography*, ed. M.A. Brunt and J.E. Davies (The Netherlands: Kluwer Academic Publishers, 1994), pp. 13–49. According to geologists, the oldest rocks of the Cayman Islands were formed more than thirty million years ago. As sea levels rose and fell during the intervening millennia, the islands were submerged and exposed many times.

Chapter 2: FIRST COMERS: THE PERIOD BEFORE PERMANENT SETTLEMENT

1. Irving Rouse, *The Tainos: Rise and Decline of the People Who Greeted Columbus* (New Haven: Yale University Press, 1992); David Watts, *The West Indies: Patterns of Development, Culture, and Environmental Change since 1492* (Cambridge: Cambridge University Press, 1987), pp. 41–77; Jesse W. Fewkes, "A Prehistoric Island Culture of America," 34th

Annual Report of the Bureau of American Ethnology (Washington: Government Printing Office, 1922); Peggy Denton and K.C. Smith interview with Mr. Callan Ritch, 12 June 1980, nos. 7 and 8, donated to CINA, 1990.

2. Anne V. Stokes and William F. Keegan, *A Settlement Survey for Prehistoric Archeological Sites on Grand Cayman,* Miscellaneous Project Report no. 52 (Gainesville: Florida Museum of Natural History, 1993). Peter L. Drewett, *Prehistoric Settlements in the Caribbean* (St. Michael: Archetype Publications, 2000), p. 7. See especially chapter 2, "Unoccupied Islands? The Cayman Islands."
3. Julian Granbery, "A Brief History of Bahamian Archeology," *Florida Archeologist* 33 (1980), pp. 83–93; Watts, *West Indies,* pp. 48–51; William F. Keegan, *The People Who Discovered Columbus: The Prehistory of the Bahamas* (Gainesville: University Press of Florida, 1992), pp. 4–8.
4. Samuel Eliot Morison, *Admiral of the Ocean Sea: A Life of Christopher Columbus* (Boston: Little, Brown, 1942).
5. Morison, *Admiral of the Ocean Sea,* pp. 633–6; *The Life of the Admiral Christopher Columbus by His Son Ferdinand,* trans. Benjamin Keen (New Brunswick: Rutgers University Press, 1958), p. 264.
6. Morison, *Admiral of the Ocean Sea,* pp. 636–7, 640–59; *Life of The Admiral Christopher Columbus,* p. 265–8. Columbus died in May 1506, aged only fifty-four. For the best account of his shaky health and disordered mind during the later stages of the fourth voyage, see Felipe Fernandez-Armesto, *Columbus* (Oxford: Oxford University Press, 1991), pp. 153–75.
7. For the Juan de la Cosa, Cantino, Maggiolo, and Turin maps, see Morison, *Admiral of the Ocean Sea,* pp. 144, 286, 408, 413, 467; Kenneth Nebenzahl, *Atlas of Columbus and the Great Discoveries* (Chicago: Rand McNally, 1990), pp. 30–37, 40–47, 58–60. The etymology of the word *cayman* is as interesting as the animal itself, but still not fully resolved. In the 1660s, the pioneer French linguists, the missionary friars Rochefort and Breton, presumed it was simply an Amerindian word for what the Europeans had called the *crocodile* (from a Greek word) since the time of Herodotus, citing the Carib word *Acayoúman.* However, earlier writers had reported the name *cayman* being given to crocodiles by the natives of central Africa. To confuse the issue further, the words *cayman* and *alligator* had become almost but not quite interchangeable. As early as 1577, one Frampton referred to "Caimanes that are called Lagartos [in New Granada]", and in 1648, Thomas Gage mentioned "the great lisarts, or Caimains". *Lagarto* does mean lizard in Spanish, but *El* (or *Al*) *Lagarto,* **the** lizard, was applied only to the American crocodile, or cayman. William Dampier tried to resolve the question in 1699, but with limited success: "At the Isle Grand Caymanes there are Crocodiles but no Alligators. At Pines by Cuba there are abundance of Crocodiles, but I cannot say there are no Alligators. Both kinds are called Caymanes by the Spaniards." *Oxford English Dictionary,* Compact Edition, s.v. "Cayman, caiman"; Roger C. Smith, *The Maritime Heritage of the Cayman Islands* (Gainesville: University Press of Florida, 2000), p. 26.

8. Nebenzahl, *Atlas of Columbus,* pp. 84–7.
9. Arthur Percival Newton, *The European Nations in the West Indies, 1493–1688* (London: A & C Black, 1933), pp. 74, 82, 93–7; John H. Parry, *The Spanish Seaborne Empire* (London: Hutchinson, 1966), pp. 134, 254.
10. Nebenzahl, *Atlas of Columbus,* pp. 112–17; Kenneth R. Andrews, *The Spanish Caribbean: Trade and Plunder, 1530–1630* (New Haven: Yale University Press, 1978), p. 140. Le Testu, an associate of Francis Drake, was killed in 1572 by an arquebus shot during the exploit against Nombre de Dios.
11. Previously it was thought that the first visitor was Drake's cousin, John Hawkins, during one of his three trading voyages between 1563 and 1568. See, for example, John A. Murray, ed., *The Islands and the Sea* (New York: Oxford University Press, 1991), pp. 64–5. Hawkins, like many others, almost certainly knew the Cayman Islands, but none of the extant accounts of his voyages mention his stopping there. Mary Freer Keeler, ed., *Sir Francis Drake's West Indian Voyage, 1585–1586* (London: Hakluyt Society, 1981), pp. 203–4; Nebenzahl, *Atlas of Columbus,* pp. 140–45. Probably a by-product of Drake's visit was the schematic depiction of "L'isle des Cayamans" in an illustrated French manuscript of 1590 entitled "Histoire Naturelle des Indes", acquired with the Clara Peck Collection by the Pierpont Morgan Library in New York in 1983 and exhibited as the centrepiece of a Drake exhibition in 1988. *Sir Francis Drake and the Age of Discovery* (New York: Pierpont Morgan Library, 1988).
12. British Library, Royal MS. 7C, xvi, fols. 166–73, in Keeler, *Drake's West Indian Voyage,* pp. 203–4. Drake's men clearly found nothing of great or permanent value on Grand Cayman. Finding plenty of wood but no easily tapped fresh water, they saw the indigenous fauna simply in terms of their food value. Though Frobisher called the island "a very desert and wilderness", ironically it was the visitors who helped to fulfill this description, killing all the animals they could find and wantonly burning the woods as they left.
13. William King's often-quoted account of a 1592 visit, given in Richard Hakluyt's *Principal Navigations,* does not command absolute credibility, since besides praising the ready availability of turtle and seabirds he speaks of a river of fresh water on Grand Cayman. Richard Hakluyt, *The Principal Navigations, Voyages, Traffiques, & Discoveries of the English Nation,* 8 vols. (1598–1600; reprint, London: Dent, 1907), pp. vii, 154–6, quoted in Kenneth R. Andrews, *English Privateering Voyages to the West Indies, 1588–95* (Cambridge: Cambridge University Press for the Hakluyt Society, 1956), p. 214.
14. Johannes de Laet, *Iaerlyck Verhael van de Verrichtinghen de Geotroyeerde West-Indische Compagnie,* 4 vols. (1644; reprint, 's Gravenhage: Martinus Nijhoff, 1931–37); Cornelius Ch. Goslinga, *The Dutch in the Caribbean and on the Wild Coast, 1580–1680* (Assen: Van Gorcum, 1971), pp. 227–57, 28–31, 152–242.
15. De Laet, *West-Indische Compagnie,* pp. ii, 169–70. Other references to the Caymans in De Laet are in vol. 1, pp. 42, 125, 137–8, 153; vol. 2,

pp. 27, 39–40, 89, 94, 168. Maps of the itineraries of many of the Dutch West India Company's fleets are given in Goslinga, *Dutch in the Caribbean,* pp. 144, 208, 240. Translations from the Dutch provided by Jan Liebaers, Senior Archivist, Cayman Islands National Archive.

16. De Laet, *West-Indische Compagnie,* vol. 2, p. 173. In 1632, as described in vol. 3, p. 119, the Dutch ship *Amersfoort,* commanded by Martin Thijsz, was ordered to call at Grand Cayman to recover the *Dolphijn*'s remaining guns, but found only two. The location of the wreck has not been identified, but it may have taken place on the northern coast of Grand Cayman.
17. Newton, *European Nations in the West Indies,* pp. 193–348; Goslinga, *Dutch in the Caribbean,* pp. 284–338; C.R. Boxer, *The Dutch Seaborne Empire, 1600–1800* (London: Hutchinson, 1965); J. Saintoyant, *La colonisation francaise sous l'ancien regime,* 2 vols. (Paris: La Renaissance du livre, 1929); Nellis M. Crouse, *The French Struggle for the West Indies, 1665–1713* (New York: Columbia University Press, 1943). Already by the 1630s the English, as well as the French and Dutch, had established small island colonies in the Lesser Antilles against Spanish opposition. But they wished to augment and extend them, both as bases from which to exploit the riches of the Spanish empire, and as plantations for growing tobacco, cotton, and, above all, sugar. Particularly active in this phase were the English Puritans who were to come to power under Oliver Cromwell – men in whom imperialistic aims, the profit motive, and anti-Catholic zeal were usefully combined. Robert L. Brenner, *Merchants and Revolution: Commercial Change, Political Conflict, and London Overseas Traders, 1550–1653* (Cambridge: Cambridge University Press, 1995); Arthur Percival Newton, *The Colonizing Activities of the English Puritans* (New Haven: Yale University Press, 1914); Karen Ordahl Kupperman, *Providence Island, 1630–1641: The Other Puritan Colony* (Cambridge: Cambridge University Press, 1993).
18. British Library, Sloane MSS 793; Vincent T. Harlow, ed., *The Voyages of Captain William Jackson (1642–1645),* Camden Miscellany vol. XIII (London: Camden Society, 1923).
19. Samuel J. Hurwitz and Edith F. Hurwitz, *Jamaica: A Historical Portrait* (New York: Praeger, 1971), pp. 3–15; Clinton V. Black, *The Story of Jamaica: From Prehistory to the Present* (London: Collins, 1965), pp. 31–51; S.A.G. Taylor, *The Western Design: An Account of Cromwell's Expedition to the Caribbean* (Kingston: Institute of Jamaica, 1965); C.H. Firth, ed., *The Narrative of General Venables: With an Appendix of Papers Relating to the Expedition to the West Indies and the Conquest of Jamaica, 1654–1655* (London: Longmans, Green for the Royal Historical Society, 1900).
20. PRO, CO 1/14, fols. 125–40.
21. The Instructions to Lord Windsor were also of great importance in laying down the principles and procedures for land tenure and the establishment of courts and of central and local government – in due course for the Cayman Islands as well as Jamaica. "Instructions for Thomas Windsor, Lord Windsor, Governour of our Island of Jamaica in the West Indies, Westminster, 21 March 1662, PRO, CO 138/1, fols. 13–14; George S.S.

Hirst, *Notes on the History of the Cayman Islands* (Kingston: P.A. Benjamin, 1910), p. 17–18, citing the *Calendar of State Papers, 1661–1668,* Item 164, and CO 140/1, fol. 26.

22. Michael Pawson and David Buisseret, *Port Royal, Jamaica* (Oxford: Clarendon Press, 1975), pp. 42–62.
23. C.R. Williams, "Thomas Modyford, Planter-Governor of Barbados and Jamaica, 1620–1679" (Ph.D. diss., University of Kentucky, 1979); Frank Cundall, *The Governors of Jamaica in the Seventeenth Century* (London: West India Committee, 1936); John Ure, *The Quest for Henry Morgan* (London: Constable, 1983); E.A. Cruikshank, *Sir Henry Morgan: His Life and Times* (Toronto: Macmillan, 1935).
24. Goslinga, *Dutch in the Caribbean,* pp. 319–469; Crouse, *French Struggle for the West Indies,* chap. 2 and 3.
25. James Modyford to Governor Modyford, Jamaica, 30 July 1667, PRO, CO 1/21, fols. 106–7.
26. Ure, *Quest for Henry Morgan*; Cruikshank, *Sir Henry Morgan.*
27. Governor Modyford's correspondence over the Rivero Pardal episode, with sundry enclosures, is in PRO, CO 1/25, fols. 153–78. The events were seemingly corroborated by underwater archaeological discoveries made by a team from the Institute of Nautical Archaeology, led by Roger Smith, in 1979. Cayman Islands Survey 1979–80, Kassa's Beach Site, LC 008, and the Turtle Wreck, LC 002.
28. Deposition of Captain Samuel Hutchinson, Jamaica, 16 June 1669, in Modyford to Arlington, PRO, CO 1/25, fol. 178.
29. The challenge is in PRO, CO 138/1, fol. 49. The account of Rivero Pardal's demise is in Browne to Arlington, aboard the frigate *Satisfaction,* Hispaniola, 12 October 1670, CO 1/25, fols. 186–7.
30. Deposition of Cornelius Johnson, 5 June 1670, PRO, CO 1/27. Copies of the Queen Regent's authorisation and the Governor of Cartagena's commission, sent by Modyford to England, are in PRO, CO 1/25, fols. 153–6.
31. Text of the Treaty of Madrid, PRO, CO 1/30, fol. 7.
32. Biblioteque National de Paris, Departement des Manuscrits, Fond Colbert, vol. 31: *Receuil de Relations et Memoires sur l'Espagne, les Indies, etc.* Fol. 622, *Des Isles Caymans.* Original translation by William A. Hart, CINA, MSD/145.
33. Black, *Story of Jamaica,* pp. 52–63. An indication of Lynch's difficulties is that during his first term (1671–4) he was merely Lieutenant Governor, and on their return Morgan and Modyford were made Vice Admiralty Judge and Chief Justice, respectively. Morgan (now Sir Henry) actually served as Lieutenant Governor on three subsequent occasions (1674, 1678, and 1680–2).
34. Resolution of the Jamaica Council, Port Royal, 12 June 1671, PRO, CO 140/1, fols. 223–5. This was passed with only four Councillors present, as a request or suggestion, not as an order. Lynch himself did not arrive until 25 June, and there is no record of any formal proclamation in the terms suggested by the Council.
35. "Instructions for Our Trusty and Wellbeloved Sr. Thomas Lynch Knt. Our Lieutenant Governor of Jamaica. Given att Our Court att Whitehall the

31th. day of December in 22th. yeare of Our Reigne, 1670," PRO, CO 1/25, fols. 269–70.

36. For the romanticised view of piracy, see Philip Gosse, *The History of Piracy* (1932; reprint, New York: Burt Franklin, 1968); George Woodbury, *The Great Days of Piracy in the West Indies* (London: Paul Elek, 1954). For a more scholarly and accurate approach, see Marcus Rediker, *Between the Devil and the Deep Blue Sea: Merchant Seamen, Pirates, and the Anglo-American Maritime World, 1700–1750* (Cambridge: Cambridge University Press, 1987). For piracy in the Bahamas, see Michael Craton and Gail Saunders, *Islanders in the Stream: A History of the Bahamian People*, vol. 1, *From Aboriginal Times to the End of Slavery* (Athens: University of Georgia Press, 1992), pp. 104–19.
37. George Gauld, *The Island of Grand Cayman 1773*. Survey and Remarks. Published by the Hydrographic Office, UK, and Cayman Islands National Archive, 1994.
38. Captain Charles Johnson [Daniel Defoe], *A General History of the Pyrates*, vol. 1, 3rd ed., ed. Philip Gosse (1725; reprint, London: Cayme Press, 1925, 1927), pp. 143–6.
39. Hunter to Lords of Trade, 4 July 1730, 19 September 1730, PRO, CO 137/18, fols. 70–71, 120–22; Proclamation of 26 September 1730, list of treasure, PRO, CO 137/19, fols. 3, 5.
40. Hunter to Lords of Trade, 24 December 1730, PRO, CO 137/19, fols. 37–40.

Chapter 3: PIONEER SETTLERS IN PEACE AND WAR, 1700–1800

1. A Spanish captive later testified that among those captured by Rivero Pardal were four children. PRO, CO 1/25, fol. 65; see also PRO, CO 1/25, fols. 176–8.
2. Gauld, *Grand Cayman 1773*.
3. E.F. Aguilar and P.T. Saunders, *The Cayman Islands: Their Postal History, Postage Stamps, and Postmarks* (Folkestone, Kent: F.J. Parsons, 1962), pp. 8–14; Neville Williams, *A History of the Cayman Islands* (George Town: Government of the Cayman Islands, 1970; George Town: CINA, 1992, 1995, 1998, 2001), pp. 6–7, 39–40; Hirst, *Notes*, pp. 69–70. The letter is quoted (apparently in full) in Aguilar and Saunders. The original (copy available at CINA) is in SOAS, being found on microfiche in IDC Box 13, Methodist Missionary Society Archives (H-2707) fiche #604 and 607; it consists of Glover's original letter and the copy made by Rev. E. Lockyer. Bodden and Watler appear to be distinctively if not exclusively Caymanian surnames. Ebanks is distinctively Caymanian but is also found in Jamaica. Tradition suggests that the founder of the Ebanks clan was really a Banks whose first name began with an E. Later writers followed Glover in believing that the original Walter and Bowden were among those reprobate "soldiers, planters, privateers and others" said to have been recalled to Jamaica in 1671, and that their particular "irregular actions" included desertion. However, if they were indeed real persons, they may not have been Cromwellian veterans. Searches among the sur-

viving (and limited) lists of Cromwell's soldiers in Jamaica have disclosed a Captain Walters but no Bowden, Bodden, or similar name. Apart from the fact that a captain was an unlikely deserter, there is no certain reference to a Walters, Walter, or Watler in the Cayman Islands before 1745, when the earliest traceable ancestor of the present clan, Stephen Watler, is said to have arrived from Jamaica (see Hirst, *Notes,* pp. 69–70). For references to "Watler" see Williams, p. 7, and CO 142/30.

4. From Volume One of the Index to Patents 1661–1825 in the Jamaica Archives (IB/11/1), the following names occur between June 1662 and February 1672: John Bourdon, Thomas Bourdon, John Bowden, and John Boden. The last of these may be the likeliest candidate, since his 106-acre holding was in St. Andrew Parish, adjacent to Port Royal; IB/11/1, p. 106. The earliest map of Jamaica showing landholdings throughout the island, by Charles Bochart and Humphrey Knollis (1684), shows an estate with a sugar mill owned by one Boughton in the far west of Jamaica (the later Hanover Parish) close to the harbour of Lucea, which was often used by vessels going to and from the Cayman Islands. For Glover, see Aguilar and Saunders, *Postal History,* p. 8.
5. Frank Wesley Pitman, *The Development of the British West Indies, 1700–1763* (New Haven: Yale University Press, 1917), pp. 111–26.
6. ". . . and shall keep a number of Whitemen if to be procured proportionable to the number of slaves thereon employed according to the true intent and meaning of an Act of the Governor and Council and Assembly of our said Island entitled an Act for regulating Servants Provided that the said Mary Bodden her heirs or assigns do keep and maintain ten whitemen on the said land pursuant to our instructions of the 1st. July 1735 . . .". Mary Bodden grant, 6 January 1742, signed by Governor Edward Trelawny, quoted in Hirst, *Notes,* pp. 45–6.
7. Island Record Office, Jamaica, Liber Patents 20, fol. 151, Daniel Campbell et al., Enrd., 28th Febry, 1734 [1735]; Hirst, *Notes,* pp. 38–40. Hirst presumed that this grant was made in February 1734, but it was actually 1735, since until the adoption of the Gregorian calendar in 1752, the English new year began on 25 March.
8. Margaret E. Leshikar-Denton, personal communication with Michael Craton, 1998.
9. IRO, Jamaica, Liber 22, Patents, fol. 46, Murray Crymble; fol. 46, William Foster; fol. 47, Samuel Spofforth; fol. 59, Mary Bodden, cited in Hirst, *Notes,* pp. 49–51, 55–8, 61–3, 44–6.
10. The Jamaican Shipping Returns, 1680–1818, PRO, CO 142/15, fols. 37, 39, 47–52, and 73, records Samuel Spofforth as the owner of the Bermudian sloops *Merry Monday, Mary Anne,* and *Experiment,* trading to and from Jamaica between 1742 and 1744.
11. Jamaica Archives, Inventories IB/11/3.
12. Hirst erroneously located the Foster grant at Grand Cayman's East End, mainly because Fosters were said to have lived there before branching to Bodden Town and elsewhere. The north-south alignment of the Foster plat and the fact that the land abutted the sea along its western and southern sides make the Hirst location impossible. Hirst's own sketch of the Foster plat, moreover, clearly shows "Hogstie Bay" at its northern end; Hirst,

Notes, pp. 57, 66, 69. It is possible that William Foster of Kingston was the man of the same name who in 1745 was granted three hundred acres alongside the Great River in Westmoreland, the Jamaican parish nearest to the Cayman Islands. Interestingly, there he would have been a close neighbour of a Daniel Campbell, granted a similar parcel of three hundred acres in Westmoreland in 1729, who may have been one of the three original Grand Cayman patentees of 1735. Jamaica IRO, 1B/11/3, fols. 37, 33–45 (1756), 49, 98 (1770). Jamaica Land Patents, Liber 24, 1745, 4 March 1745 (1746). Ibid., Liber 19, fol. 164, 29 September 1729; Inventories, 1B/11/3, fols. 19, 47.

13. Hirst, *Notes,* pp. 53–5.
14. Jamaica Archives, 1A/3 Chancery Court, Liber 28, fols. 344–52. Photocopy and (inaccurate) transcription in CINA. A key event was the removal of duties on timber from the British plantations in America in 1722. This led to the supplanting of walnut by mahogany. Kenneth E. Ingram, "The West Indian Trade of an English Furniture Firm in the Eighteenth Century," *Jamaican Historical Review* 3 (March 1962): 22–37.
15. An interesting sidelight on the case is provided by the Will Inventories in the Jamaica Archives. In 1740 it was recorded that a certain John Middleton, sawyer, died leaving pitifully few worldly goods. The likelihood that he was the person who shared the first Caymanian land grant five years earlier is strengthened by the fact that besides "A negro man named Jupiter and another named Quamina worth 30 pounds apiece 2 pairs of wheels one old the other not finished worth 7 pounds and 5 whip saws without tillers worth £7.10s.", his only other asset was "A Judgmt. Obtaind August Grand Court last Johnson Exr of Middleton vs Benja. Battersby for £92.12s.6d." Jamaica Archives, Inventories, 1B/11/3, vol. 21 (1740–1), fol. 64.
16. Jamaica Archives, 1B/11/8, Parish Registers: Port Royal, 1733–1808. Copies of selected items in these registers relating to Cayman can be found in CINA, MSD 82; MSD 137; MSD 269. The last in the series of Caymanian marriages in Jamaica traced was that of a William Bodden, widower, to a Mary Watler, spinster, at Montego Bay on 18 November 1808. Possibly the earliest "formal" marriage in the Cayman Islands was performed by William Cartwright (who may have been a Magistrate) between Robert Knowles Clarke and Elizabeth Rivers around 1770. No register survived, but many years later a George Bodden testified that he had been a witness to the ceremony but could not precisely recall the date. Williams, *History of the Cayman Islands,* p. 33.
17. The earliest marriage and baptism entries are in the Registrar General's Department, Jamaica: Port Royal Copy Register, vol. 1, fols. 2ff., 116ff. Gauld, *Grand Cayman 1773.* Hirst, *Notes,* p. 28, cites the Bawden-Lamar entry, but not the earlier Bass wedding.
18. The earliest known baptism is that of Robert Bass, son of Isac and Sarah Bass, baptised the day of their marriage, 29 October 1732. The identity of "Governor" Bodden is somewhat confused because there were several William Boddens. George Gauld in 1773 recorded that the William Bodden who then held a commission from Governor Trelawney of Jamaica (1767–72) and was "generally called Governor of the Caymans"

was the nephew of Isaac Bodden, "descended in a direct line from the Patriarch". George Hirst in 1910 recorded family tradition that "Governor" Bodden was the grandson, not nephew, of Isaac Bodden, but Hirst was not certain of that, suggesting that he might have been the son of Mary Bodden. Hirst also believed that "Governor" Bodden was Chief Magistrate from "about 1775" until "well into the next century". That there were two Chief Magistrates named William Bodden, father and son, both called "Governor", is almost certainly borne out by a brief entry in the London monthly *Gentleman's Magazine and Historical Chronicle,* vol. 59, June 1789, which read: "Deaths . . . April 23. At the Grand Caymanas, aged 67, Wm. Bodden, esq. Chief Magistrate of that island." "Governor" William Bodden Sr. (1773–89) thus may well have been William Price Bodden, the son of Isaac Bodden born in 1732, and his son "Governor" William Bodden Jr. (1789–1823) therefore Old Isaac's grandson, as Hirst recounted. Hirst, *Notes,* p. 123; Gauld, *Grand Cayman 1773.*

19. Port Royal Parish Register, 1765, CINA, MSD 82. *Our Islands' Past,* vol. 1, *Edward Corbet's Report and Census of 1802 on the Cayman Islands* (George Town: Cayman Islands National Archive and Cayman Free Press, 1992), p. 13.
20. Westmoreland (Savanna-la-Mar) Parish Register, 1762–73, CINA, MSD 82; *Our Islands' Past,* vol. 1, pp. 11–13.
21. Hanover (Lucea) Parish Register, 1776–84; St. James (Montego Bay) Parish Register, 1785–1808, CINA, MSD 82; *Our Islands' Past,* vol. 1, pp. 11–13.
22. Richard Pares, *War and Trade in the West Indies, 1739–1763* (Oxford: Oxford University Press, 1936); Pitman, *British West Indies 1700–1763;* Lowell J. Ragatz, *The Fall of the Planter Class in the British Caribbean, 1763–1833* (New York: American Historical Association, 1928); J. Steven Watson, *The Reign of George III, 1760–1815* (Oxford: Clarendon Press, 1960); Michael Duffy, *Soldiers, Sugar, and Seapower: The British Expeditions to the West Indies and the War against Revolutionary France* (Oxford: Clarendon Press, 1987).
23. For patrolling areas and convoying in the war of 1739–48, Pares, *War and Trade,* pp. 300–311. For patrolling areas in the later wars and the activities of the prize courts, see Michael Craton, "Indispensable Agents of Empire: The Caribbean Vice Admiralty Courts, 1713–1815" (Ph.D. diss., McMaster University, 1968). Note that the majority of ships taken around the Cayman Islands were carried to the prize court in Nassau, Bahamas, rather than to Jamaica. Significantly, the route of the Spanish *galeones,* sailing very close to the Cayman Islands, was featured on British maps of the Caribbean as late as the American War of Independence. See, for example, Jeffreys' map in the *West India Atlas* (London: Sayer and Bennett, 1775), which shows the "Gallions Track from Cartagena" passing within sight of Grand Cayman.
24. Sir Alan Burns, *History of the West Indies* (London: Allen and Unwin, 1954), pp. 522–31. The evidence for Spanish attacks during the American War is meagre but convincing. Corbet in 1802 wrote of Grand Cayman, "In the course of the war which has just terminated [that is, the French Revolutionary War, 1793–1801], they have not been annoyed from any

quarter, but in the war which preceded it, it was attacked by the Spaniards from Cuba and totally destroyed. Its desireable situation however for shipping lead [*sic*] to its renewal." *Our Islands' Past,* vol. 1, p. 4. Royal Navy Remark Books mention the absence of any fortifications on Grand Cayman down to the last French War (1802–15), and precious few then, though there is evidence that Fort George in George Town and Prospect Fort were constructed around 1790.

25. Pares, *War and Trade, 1739–1763,* pp. 97–104; Craig L. Dozier, *Nicaragua's Mosquito Shore: The Years of British and American Presence* (Tuscaloosa: University of Alabama Press, 1985), pp. 6–29; Frances Armytage, *The Free Port System in the British West Indies: A Study in Commercial Policy, 1766–1822* (London: Longmans, Green, 1953).
26. Archive of the Indies, Simancas, Spain, Mapas, Planes y Dibujos, XI–165 (1783); CINA, MSD 181; MSC 44; Acc. 123, 524. Robert Hodgson Sr., who had been appointed Superintendent of the Miskito Coast by Governor Trelawney in 1739, wrote the valuable *Some Account of the Mosquito Territory* in 1757 (reprinted Edinburgh, 1822). He was succeeded by his son and namesake around 1776. Captured on his way to England in 1783 and carried to Cartagena, Robert Hodgson Jr. produced his memorandum and sketch-map after his interrogation by the Archbishop of Bogotá and his decision to work for the Spaniards. After years of mixed relations with the Spaniards and local Indians, Hodgson died in Guatemala City in 1791. Archive of the Indies, Seville, Guerra, Legajos, pp. 6945–9, summarised in report by Frank G. Dawson, 1995, CINA, MSD 120.
27. George Metcalf, *Royal Government and Political Conflict in Jamaica, 1729–1783* (London: Longmans for the Royal Commonwealth Society, 1965), pp. 199–228. For the figure of "three hundred" see also MODHO, Miscellaneous Papers, vol. 43, fols. 558–61, Remark Book of HMS *Camilla.*
28. For the career of George Gauld, see John D. Ware and Robert R. Rea, *George Gauld: Surveyor and Cartographer of the Gulf Coast* (Gainesville: University of Florida Press, 1982). Gauld's map of Grand Cayman exists in a number of versions, copies of which are in the CINA. Ministry of Defence (GB), Hydrographic Department, Taunton, q43, Ag. 1; 196 Ag. 1; U 10 Ag. 1; CINA. See also *An Account of the Surveys of Florida, &c. With Directions for Sailing from Jamaica or the West Indies by the West End of Cuba, and through the Gulph of Florida (To accompany Mr. Gauld's Charts)* (London: W. Faden, Geographer to the King, 1790).
29. Jamaican Shipping Returns, 1680–1818, PRO, CO 142/13–29. For the *Experiment* see CO 142/15, fols. 48–9, 73. For the *Sarah* see CO 142/15, fols. 51-2. See also CINA MSD 94.
30. PRO, CO 142/18, fols. 91–2, 95–6, 96–7.
31. PRO, CO 142/18, fols. 138–9. Dr. Philip Pedley, Director of CINA, speculates further that the *Susanna* may have been the renamed 10-ton schooner *Juliana,* built in Jamaica and registered at Savanna-la-Mar in 1765, which made its maiden voyage to Georgia in May 1765 with a cargo of sugar and rum and returned in September. For William Eden, who was said to have been born in Devizes, Wiltshire, England, in 1737

and died at the Pearl Lagoon on the Miskito Coast (where he had migrated) in 1820, and other Caymanian Edens, see CINA MSC 270, and Hirst, *Notes*, pp. 87–91. No record of the marriage of William Eden to Dorothy Bodden has been found in the Savanna-la-Mar parish register.

32. MODHO, Miscellaneous Papers, vol. 2 (1764); vol. 9 (1765); CINA, MSD 174. The Remark Books and the shipping registers for Jamaica are far from complete. The richest period for surviving records relating to Cayman is 1780 to 1820.
33. MODHO, Miscellaneous Papers, vol. 9 (1765); CINA MSD 174. The earliest of all Remark Book references to Grand Cayman, made by the master of HMS *Alarm* in April 1764, provided an even sparser (perhaps slightly exaggerated) picture: "No fortification but good Landing in the Bay . . . Its trade Consist in Mahogany and Turtle which is carried to Jamaica the Inhabitants is very Poor having neither Civil or Military office among them and but 16 familys on the Island at this time and but one small Schooner belonging to the place; MODHO, Miscellaneous Papers, vol. 2 (1764), 4–6, CINA MSD 174.
34. MODHO, Miscellaneous Papers, vol. 43.
35. PRO, CO 142/18, fols. 63–4.
36. PRO, CO 142/20, fols. 64, 110.
37. The famous Jamaican planter-historian Edward Long – who never visited the Cayman Islands and wrote in England – gave a slightly different and idealised description of Caymanian society in his *History of Jamaica*, published in the year following Gauld's survey. By the 1770s the Caymanians may, in fact, have had a Chief Magistrate and other Magistrates, but according to Long they hardly needed them. "They have a Chief or Governor of their own choosing," he wrote, "and regulations of their own framing; they have some Justices of the Peace among them appointed by commission from the Governor of Jamaica, and live very happily without scarcely any form of civil government. Their poverty and smallness of number secure them effectually from the animosities that disturb the peace of larger societies; yet they are not without decorum in their manner of living. Their tranquillity depends much on a due presentation of good order. Their Governor and Magistrates decide any matter of controversy arising among them, without appeal." Edward Long, *The History of Jamaica*, vol. 1 (London: Printed for T. Lowndes, 1774), chap. XII, sect. 1, quoted as an appendix in Hirst, *Notes*, pp. 392–7.
38. Gauld, *Grand Cayman 1773*.
39. *Our Islands' Past*, vol. 1, pp. 10–21. For a fuller discussion and analysis of Corbet's Report and Census, see Chapter 4.
40. As late as 1797, the Spanish Captain Juan Tirri, making an official survey of the Isle of Pines, called the Caymanian and Bahamian mariners "nothing more than sea robbers" who did not hesitate to plunder British as well as Spanish and other foreign wrecks. Tirri even recommended that the Spanish government mount an expedition to wipe out the "pirates' nests" on Grand Cayman and New Providence for good and all. Report of Captain Juan Tirri, 1797, in Records of the *Real Sociedad Patriotica* (Havana, 1838), quoted in H.B.L. Hughes, "Notes on the Cayman Islands," *Jamaican Historical Review* 1 (September 1946): 153–7.

41. For example, the comments of Commander G. Carter, captain of a navy vessel (possibly) HMS *Barossa,* in 1816: "Sail'd from Port Royal, Jamaica on the 17 of March, on the 19th we were in the Latitude and Longitude of the middle part of Grand Cayman, as it is laid down in the Admiralty and other Charts; but could not see the Island – we then shaped our course for the West end of the Isle of Pines; but fell in with the jardines, which, together with missing the island of Grand Cayman, leads us to believe that island [Grand Cayman] is, as reported by many Naval Officers and Masters of Merchant Vessels, laid down full thirty miles to the Eastward of its proper Longitude." MODHO, Remark Books, vol. 41 (1816), p. 115. Gauld was nearly correct in giving the latitude of Grand Cayman's southwest point as 19°11'20" N, but he was silent about longitude. As late as 1828, the Captain of HMS *Nancy* correctly gave the latitude of "the town called the Hogsties" as 19°17'20" N, but reckoned its longitude "by a good Chronometer" at 81°29' W, which was out by some seven miles in the other direction – its real longitude being 81°22'25" W. MODHO Remark Books, vol. 48 (1828), p. 369.
42. Major General Thomas Gage to War Office, 30 January 1768, CO 5/233; Log of HMS *Adventure,* 13–31 January 1768, PRO, Adm 51/52, cited by Smith, *Maritime Heritage,* pp. 31, 198, n.18. Margaret E. Leshikar-Denton and Philip E. Pedley, eds., *Our Islands' Past,* vol. 2, *The Wreck of the Ten Sails* (George Town: Cayman Islands National Archive and Cayman Free Press, 1994). As the editors point out, both Hirst and Williams relied only on oral traditions for the story of the multiple wreck, among other errors misdating it to 1788.
43. Jamaica *Royal Gazette* 15, no. 51 (21 December 1793); petition of eight prominent Caymanians, 12 February 1794; both quoted in Leshikar-Denton and Pedley, *Our Islands' Past,* vol. 2, pp. 9, 77.
44. Letter of Captain John Lawford, dated Grand Cayman, 20 February 1794, read at his court martial, Port Royal, Jamaica, 1 April 1794, PRO ADM 1/5331, quoted in Leshikar-Denton and Pedley, *Our Islands' Past,* vol. 2, p. 39.
45. Ibid., p. 40.
46. Anonymous correspondent (probably Lieutenant Brice, formerly of HMS *Hermione*), Jamaica *Royal Gazette,* 8 March 1794; Leshikar-Denton and Pedley, *Our Islands' Past,* vol. 2, pp. 25–28.
47. Leshikar-Denton and Pedley, *Our Islands' Past,* vol. 2, pp. 9, 15, 16–28. The oft-told story that a member of the British royal family was in the wreck, for the rescue of whom Caymanians were awarded freedom from taxation and conscription in perpetuity, is pure legend. It is not known how it originated, though as Leshikar-Denton and Pedley note, it has certainly served to sustain popular interest in the incident.
48. Considerable archaeological research was carried out by Margaret Leshikar-Denton, which is recorded in "The 1794 'Wreck of the Ten Sail', Cayman Islands, British West Indies: A Historical Study and Archaeological Survey, Vol. 1" (Ph.D. diss., Texas A&M University, 1993).
49. Ibid., pp. xiv–xv, 29–30.
50. Ibid, p. xvii.

Chapter 4: CAYMANIAN SLAVE SOCIETY AND EMANCIPATION

1. Commissioner Hirst (1910) believed the first slaves arrived on a Dutch ship carrying five hundred slaves as booty in 1677. Nathaniel Glover (1841) cited the wreck of a slave ship, the *Nelly*, coming from Africa in 1781. In 1962 "Bertie" Ebanks recalled the oral tradition of such a wreck at a place still called Guinea Man's Reef off Grand Cayman's North Sound "some time around 1805". In the same interview, the near-centenarian Ms. Nettie Levy claimed to know the names of the first slaves in Grand Cayman, Manwe (or Mancoe) and Sopingo, whose tombs she said could still be seen at Bodden Town. Hirst, *Notes*, pp. 25–6, citing Vaughan to Secretary Coventry, 26 June 1677, *Calendar of State Papers, Colonial*. Letter from Mr Nathaniel Glover, U.S. Consul at George Town, Grand Cayman, to Rev. Lockyer, 14 June 1841, quoted in Aguilar and Saunders, *Postal History*, pp. 8–14. Interview with Mr. S.O. (Bertie) Ebanks and Ms. Nettie Levy by Anita Ebanks for National Museum, 1982, in CINA Memory Bank. None of these accounts is independently corroborated. Hirst was searching for an explanation for the apparent anomaly that the later population of slaves "was out of all proportion to the buying capacity of the slave owners". There is no evidence that the Dutch ship did actually reach the Caymans, let alone leave any slaves there. Glover's account does appear to explain the undoubted increase in the slave population in the 1780s, and also to bear out his contention that it was the introduction of slavery that led to the need for laws, courts, and justices and the appointment of the harsh William Cartwright as Chief Magistrate. There was at least one ship called the *Nelly* that carried some slaves to the Caymans, but this was in 1802–4 and in groups of no more than a dozen. Glover's account is further weakened by the fact that Cartwright seems to have been Chief Magistrate long before 1781 (traditionally, 1750–76). Bertie Ebanks's date of "about 1805" is far too late to explain the origins of the Caymanian slave and black population. Nettie Levy's reference to the undoubtedly African-sounding Manwe and Sopingo is undermined by her subsequent confusion as to whether they were in fact the first slaves or Spanish pirates.
2. For the concept of a Slave Society (in the sense that "not only were slaves in the numerical majority and constituted the essential labour force, but that the society of each colony can only be properly understood by demonstrating the interrelationships between all elements in the community, including the black slaves and the non-white freedmen as well as the dominant whites"), see Elsa V. Goveia, *Slave Society in the British Leeward Islands at the End of the Eighteenth Century* (New Haven: Yale University Press, 1965), p. vii. For the present author's interpretations of Caribbean slavery, see Michael Craton, *Searching for the Invisible Man: Slaves and Plantation Life in Jamaica* (Cambridge: Harvard University Press, 1978), pp. 52–253; *Testing the Chains: Resistance to Slavery in the British West Indies* (Ithaca: Cornell University Press, 1982), pp. 41–57; *Empire, Enslavement, and Freedom in the Caribbean* (Kingston: Ian Randle Press, 1997), pp. 147–305.

3. Gauld, *Grand Cayman 1773.*
4. Sir Hans Sloane, *A Voyage to the Islands Madera, Barbados, Nieves, S. Christophers, and Jamaica,* vol. 2 (London: B.M. for the Author, 1707, 1725), p. xlviii.
5. F.G. Davenport and C.O. Paullin, *European Treaties Bearing on the History of the United States and its Dependencies,* vol. 4 (Washington: 1917–37), p. 162. Contemporary descriptions of the English settlements on the Miskito Coast suggest a much larger version of the society and economy of Grand Cayman in the logging era, augmented by some ranching and the beginnings of a plantation economy, with perhaps half a dozen cotton, indigo, and rice plantations with holdings of at least fifty slaves apiece. There is also more than a hint in contemporary accounts of considerable miscegenation between white males and local Indian or black slave women; by 1786 few of even the most prosperous families could claim complexions and features that would have been recognised as "pure white" among the haughtiest Jamaican planters. Evidence of progressive miscegenation was seen, for example, in the gradual creolisation of the descendants of the first Superintendent, Robert Hodgson, and of such patriarchal planters as Gregor McGregor. Dozier, *Nicaragua's Mosquito Shore.*
6. PRO, CO 123/6, fols. 82–4. There is also a request by a John Campbell to be allowed to evacuate with twenty-four slaves to "Caymanes" in Captain Hutt to Commander Gardner, 19 February 1789, PRO, CO 123/6, fol. 70.
7. MODHO, Miscellaneous Papers, vol. 43, fols. 558–61, Remark Book of HMS *Camilla.*
8. The principal inventions relevant to cotton production were Hargreaves's "spinning jenny" (1765), Arkwright's "waterframe" (1769), and Crompton's "mule" (1779), which were all in general use by 1785. British imports of raw cotton were about 3 million pounds a year in 1760 and 5.5 million in 1770, but by 1789 they soared to 32.5 million pounds, of which at least 12 million pounds came from the British West Indies. By 1830, however, 211 million pounds were being imported annually from the United States alone, and only 3.5 million pounds from the British West Indies. The price at Liverpool for the best-quality imported fibre reached 60 pence a pound in 1799 but fell to about 35 pence a pound in 1802, to 20 pence a pound by 1815, and was little more than 5 pence a pound by 1830. Ralph Davis, *The Rise of the Atlantic Economies* (Ithaca: Cornell University Press, 1973), pp. 252–4, 311–16; Watson, *The Reign of George III,* pp. 332–35, 508–12; Ragatz, *The Fall of the Planter Class,* pp. 122, 201–4, 292–4, 301, 371; Lucy Frances Horsfall, "The West Indian Trade," in *The Trade Winds: A Study of British Overseas Trade during the French Wars, 1793–1815,* ed. C. Northcote Parkinson (London: Allen and Unwin, 1948), pp. 171–2.
9. PRO, CO 142/13–29. These are the surviving shipping returns for Jamaica, which include entries related to Cayman.
10. PRO, CO 142/21, fols. 122–3. Quite a few vessels were recorded simply as "plantation built". Many of these may have been built in the Cayman Islands. A likely example was the 15-ton schooner *Susan & Kitty,* owned

and captained by William Bodden, which entered Kingston in January 1786, and was recorded as "Built, Grand Caymanas" in 1783, registered at Montego Bay in June 1785. PRO, CO 142/22, fol. 101.

11. This is based on a price of 18 pence a pound to the primary producer. At this time, the Liverpool price for the best cotton fibre was about 35 pence a pound.
12. Michael Craton and Gail Saunders, *Islanders in the Stream,* vol. 1, pp. 310–12. The Bahamas produced ten times as much cotton in its peak years, from the labour of about three thousand working slaves spread over ten islands.
13. Ibid.
14. *Our Islands' Past,* vol. 1, pp. 10–24.
15. For a detailed description of Caymanian planters' houses, see the letter by Nathaniel Glover in Aguilar and Saunders, *Postal History,* p. 9.
16. A comparison over a ten-year period shows the decline. For example, *Eliza* carried 127 bags to Kingston in 1805, and *Polly & Betsy* carried 65 bags to Montego Bay in 1806, whereas in 1816 *Eliza* carried only 14 bags to Kingston and in 1817 *William & James* carried only 1 bag there. An important factor was competition from the Miskito Coast – for instance, the *Kingston Packet* carried 15,000 pounds of cotton to Jamaica in 1816.
17. PRO, CO 142/27, fol. 47; 142/25, fol. 91.
18. PRO, CO 142/24–29.
19. PRO, CO 137/181, fol. 403, quoted in Brian L. Kieran, *The Lawless Caymanas: A Story of Slavery, Freedom, and the British West India Regiment* (Grand Cayman: privately published, 1992), p. 27.
20. In Barbuda, Anguilla, and the Bahamas, slaves on decayed cotton plantations were left essentially unsupervised to live as subsistence farmers, and the slave populations increased by 25 to 35 per thousand per year. From his exhaustive study comparing colonies and work regimes, along with many other factors, for the period 1807–34, Higman found that mortality rates were more critical than fertility rates (which were more general and gradually improved even on large sugar estates) in accounting for rates of natural increase or decrease. Of mortality rates in Demerara-Essequibo, for example, he concluded, "Of the major crops, sugar was associated with a crude (registered) death rate of about 40 per thousand, compared to 32 on coffee plantations and 26 on cotton plantations. Cattle farms showed mortality similar to that on coffee plantations, while woodcutters had a surprisingly low death rate." The general birth rate for Demerara-Essequibo at that time was some 32 per thousand. Barry W. Higman, *Slave Populations of the British Caribbean, 1807–1834* (Baltimore: Johns Hopkins University Press, 1984), pp. 303–78, especially 325, 355.
21. The information relating to slave returns in the Cayman Islands is in PRO T71, vols. 243, 734, 851, 875, 1026, and 1331.
22. For discussion of slave naming patterns, see Craton, *Searching for the Invisible Man,* pp. 156-61. At Worthy Park, Jamaica, in 1838, 82 per cent of the slaves had surnames. Of the 18 per cent who had single names, only 1.3 per cent were recognisably African. In 1793 the ratios had been 1 per cent surnames, 99 per cent single names, and 9 per cent African. Ibid.
23. Ibid.

24. PRO, T71/243, fols. 13–132. Cuba(h)s aged 79, 60, 26, 24, 3; Quasheba, 70; Juba, 67; Quashees, 60, 18, 18; Congo Tom, 52; Mocho, 50; Mimbas, 46, 7, 3; Congo George, 45; Cuffy, 45; Corta 43, Benebas, 40, 32, 23; Briana, 30; Miana, 28; Statira, 16, 6; Coffee, 10; Elmina, 2 days.
25. See above, Chapter 3. The earliest formal appointment of a Magistrate of which we have a record is 1798; see *Our Islands' Past,* vol. 1, p. 23.
26. Rachel Ebanks/George Bodden transactions, 1816, Public Recorder's Records, vol. I, fols. 25-8.
27. The career of Elizabeth Jane Trusty was well covered in the transcriptions from the Public Recorder's Records in Hirst, *Notes,* pp. 145–57.
28. PRO, T71/1026.
29. For slave family and household patterns, see Barry W. Higman, "Household Structure and Fertility on Jamaican Slave Plantations: A Nineteenth-Century Example," *Population Studies* 27 (1973): 527–50; "The Slave Family and Household in the British West Indies, 1800–1834," *Journal of Interdisciplinary History* 6 (1975): 261–87; and *Slave Populations,* 364–73; and also Michael Craton, "Changing Patterns of Slave Family in the British West Indies" (1978), in *Empire, Enslavement, and Freedom in the Caribbean* (Kingston: Ian Randle Press, 1997), pp. 233–59.
30. PRO, T71/243, fols. 79, 38, 108.
31. PRO, T71/243, fol. 64.
32. One other variant was the household where slaves were to an extent interbred with their owners. Although there is no evidence in the official records, the possibility cannot be ruled out in the Cayman Islands. That miscegenation often occurred during slavery days is attested to by oral tradition. See the Jackson example in Hirst, *Notes,* p. 169, and the testimony of Nurse Annie Bush (aged 89) of South Sound, given to the CINA Memory Bank in October 1990. Ms. Bush claimed descent from a Scots slaveowner, Charles Bush, who had three sons, two of whom married white Caymanians. The other (her grandfather) "married" one of his father's slaves. "So I have a family that is actually cousin to me," said Ms. Bush, "but they're . . . some of them as fair as you [the white interviewer] are. But you see I got . . . the tar brush for me."
33. Copy of will of Thomas Thompson dated 9 May 1811, witnessed by Magistrate James Coe, 11 May 1811, CINA, Public Recorder's Records, vol. I, fols. 15–18. In the 1834 census, two of the bequeathed slaves, Statira Baker, age 42, and Clarissa Thompson, 39, were listed as the property of Robert Knowles Thompson of Prospect, along with three male and six female slaves aged between 1 and 23 years, who may well have been their offspring. If so, the father or fathers were clearly not in that slave group, since the only other slave owned was a 27-year-old male. In the same census, a third of the bequeathed slaves, Juliet Brooks, age 57, was listed as still owned by Thomas Thompson Jr. of Thompson's Bay, Prospect (along with one other slave surnamed Brooks, age 11), and others might well be traced by looking at the slaves owned by the husbands of Thomas Thompson's Sr.'s daughters. T71/243, fols. 53, 69.
34. The male slaveowners away from Grand Cayman in April 1834 were John Bodden, William Bodden Sr., William Bodden, William James Bodden,

William Thomas Bodden, John Bush, William Christopher Bush, William Christopher Collins, William Jonathan Ebanks, Thomas Knowles Eden, James Hind, Thomas John Jennett, George Edward Merren, James Reeves, Edward S. Rivers, William Robert Scott, James C. Tatum, Robert Knowles Thompson, Thomas Thompson, Thomas Lindsay Thompson, and James H. Watler. T71/243.

35. Ibid., fols. 30–31A; see also T71, vols. 734, 851, 875, 1026, and 1331.
36. Ibid.
37. Nathaniel Glover letter, in Aguilar and Saunders, *Postal History*, pp. 12–14. Glover goes on to describe the African influence on Caymanian society in the following terms: "The old Africans brought with them their own peculiar superstitious rites and it is remarkable that many of them were in practice as late as when I came to the island [in 1831]. Their sending an African home as they term it is indeed a singular and I may add a laughable superstition. . . . A lapse of time after the death of the party, and when all others [have] probably forgotten him, one of his countrymen gives out that his friend has appeared to him and expressed himself unhappy and not yet arrived in his own country. Whereupon as many Africans as they can gather together meet at one or other of their houses at sunset and from that hour they commence a singing in their own language, and with dances peculiar to themselves in which they move only their bodies, continue until the dawn or morning accompanied by a rude music which they call a 'Gumbai.' This is an instrument made by drawing the skin of any animal over a box on which they thump with their fingers. In their songs frequent allusions are made to the deceased. At daylight a procession is formed, and, with a little coffin [in which] they say the spirits of their friend is confined, they move in solemn order to a new made grave prepared during the night. The person officiating as Priest, takes with him a White Cock and a Calabash containing rum. They then deposit the coffin in a grave when the Priest cutting the throat of the Cock over the grave and plucking its tail and wing feathers intermingled them with the blood and strews them in the grave uttering some form of prayer (in which he is joined by the whole African party) expressive of the hope that their friend would soon reach his country. He then mixes a portion of the dirt from the grave with the rum, drinks a portion of it himself and gives a portion to a few of his favourites, then he sprinkles the remainder over the coffin uttering a similar prayer. Then filling up the grave they severally depart, under the conviction that the spirit of their departed friend is happy in his own country."
38. PRO, CO 137/189, fol. 247. Quoted in Kieran, *Lawless Caymanas*, pp. 32–3. Coincidentally, the Assembly had issued a notice about "The Police Powers of the Magistrates under the Authority of the Governor of Jamaica," on 14 December 1833. This was very much in tune with the procedures for the strict enforcement of the observance of the Sabbath passed just two weeks later (2 January 1834); PRO, CO 137/367, fols. 336–96.
39. Opinion of Law Officer Lefevre to James Stephen, 3 February 1834, PRO, CO 137/189, fols. 242; Kieran, *Lawless Caymanas*, pp. 34, 180, nn. 56, 57. Governor Lord Sligo to Colonial Secretary, "Private & Confidential,"

20 July 1834, PRO, CO 137/192, fols. 385-6. Technically, the two men successively appointed were not Stipendiary Magistrates as defined by the Colonial Office, but supernumeraries commissioned by Lord Sligo, called either Special Magistrate or Special Justice.

40. Governor Lord Sligo to Colonial Secretary, 30 September 1834, PRO, CO 137/193, fols. 50–52; Kieran, *Lawless Caymanas,* p. 43.
41. Once fully ordained, Rev. Sharpe appears to have spent more time in Jamaica, at Darliston in Westmoreland parish, than in Grand Cayman. Installed there first in December 1834, he seems to have alternated to a degree with another curate, Rev. David Wilson. In December 1837, for instance, it was reported that Wilson was officiating at Darliston for "Rev. T. Sharpe, head curate on leave at the Caymanas". Rev. N.J.G. Sykes, *The Dependency Question: A Study of Church and State in the Cayman Islands* (George Town: The Ecclesiastical Corporation, 1996), pp. 74–5. See below, Chapter 6.
42. Governor Lord Sligo to Colonial Secretary, 14 May 1835, PRO, CO 137/198, fols. 382–6.
43. Ibid. See also Colonial Secretary to Governor Lord Sligo, 27 June 1835, PRO, CO 137/199, fols. 276–7.
44. "Address to the Inhabitants of the Grand Caymanas," 3 May 1835, in Sligo to Colonial Secretary, 27 April 1835, PRO, CO 137/198, fols. 318-19. Printed in full in Kieran, *Lawless Caymanas,* p. 61. This and other key documents relating to emancipation in the Cayman Islands were printed in *Parliamentary Papers*, "Papers Relative to the Abolition of Slavery in the British Colonies".

Chapter 5: EARLY GOVERNMENT AND THE SOCIOPOLITICAL REVOLUTION OF THE 1830S

1. Williams, *History of the Cayman Islands,* pp. 24–5.
2. According to Neville Williams, a few of the Sambos (who were mixed-race descendants of Nicaraguan Indians and African slaves) came to the Cayman Islands as slaves and stayed. One of these, who had been brought to Grand Cayman as a girl, petitioned to be freed, along with her two children, in 1805. Williams, *History of the Cayman Islands,* p. 25.
3. Ibid.
4. *Our Islands' Past,* vol. 1, p. 4.
5. *Our Islands' Past,* vol. 1, pp. 3–8. In what seems to be the only documentary reference to Magistrate Cartwright, an 1820 affidavit by a George Bodden (freedman) testified that he had been witness to the marriage between Robert Knowles Clarke (his first former owner) and Elizabeth Rivers, performed by William Cartwright. This ceremony must have occurred some time between 1780 and 1790 – when, incidentally, it was William Bodden, not William Cartwright, who was styled "Governor". Hirst, *Notes,* p. 158; CINA Public Recorder's Records, vol. I, 1810–86, CR 1/1. For another aspect of George Bodden's life, see above, Chapter 4.
6. Governor Nugent to Colonial Secretary, 20 August 1802, CO 137/108; *Our Islands' Past,* vol. 1, p. 24.

7. Williams, *History of the Cayman Islands,* p. 36; *Our Islands' Past,* vol. 1, pp. 27, 29, viii.
8. Ragatz, *Fall of the Planter Class;* William A. Green, *British Slave Emancipation: The Sugar Colonies and the Great Experiment, 1830–1865* (Oxford: Clarendon Press, 1976), 99–127; Craton, *Testing the Chains.*
9. Hirst, *Notes,* pp. 220–34. In the second case, the accused, James Shearer Jackson, was the nephew of the coroner, James Bodden, and related by marriage to three of the jurors. He was found guilty of manslaughter and fined £60 Jamaican currency. Hirst commented, "I think the reader will agree that Jackson was very severely punished for an act which, to all intents and purposes, found its initiative in self preservation."
10. Hirst, *Notes,* p. 203. The first recorded slave trial occurred in September 1816, just five months after the outbreak of Bussa's Rebellion in distant Barbados. A slave called Primis (or Primus?), belonging to William Bodden, was said to have stealthily entered the cook room of James Coe Sr. (who was to be Bodden's successor as Chief Magistrate) "and there bury . . . an egg for purposes unknown, but supposed to be for the purposes of that diabolical Art termed Obeah". After they had "heard and examined the evidence herein respecting", the twelve white men duly pronounced Primis guilty of practising obeah, and sentenced him "to be transported from this Island, never more to return upon it, under pain of Death". It is not recorded where Primis was shipped, but Belize was most likely, being a favoured destination for slave transportees from other British West Indian colonies. Since the valued of Primis was officially assessed, presumably William Bodden was recompensed for his loss from the island treasury – if only by the meagre £7 5s Jamaican currency of the assessment. That Primis was clearly a senior or trusted slave, belonging to the Chief Magistrate himself, made his misdemeanour all the more serious. This was very much in tune with the disaffection of "confidential" slaves that was so shocking to slaveowners elsewhere, especially in the late slave rebellions of 1815–32 but also at least as early as the Antigua slave conspiracy of 1739.

    A second and more serious obeah case was tried in August 1826. A "Negro Man Slave" named Hannibal was also sentenced to transportation, not just for "pretending to Obeah" but for verbally abusing, threatening, and actually assaulting his mistress, Mrs. Elizabeth Rivers. Hirst, *Notes,* pp. 204, 207. See also Craton, *Testing the Chains,* pp. 115–24, 241–321.
11. Hirst, *Notes,* pp. 205–6.
12. *Our Islands' Past,* vol. 1, p. 7. For an almost comic squabble occasioned by one of Bodden's decrees (involving the erection of gates where Bodden's new road crossed other landowners' property), see "Petition of the Inhabitants to Governor Nugent, December 1804," William Bodden to Governor Nugent, 28 August 1805; Nugent Papers MS72, National Library of Jamaica, Kingston.
13. Hirst, *Notes,* p. 214. What may be the Caymanian prototype law is cited by Hirst under the date "Georgetown, October 12, 1820: In open court this day at Georgetown it is agreed by the court and jury that the public roads shall be henceforth cleaned on the third Monday in October and the

third Monday in April in every year." This was certified as "Approved by the Magistrates" and signed (without clear distinctions) by William Hunter (Foreman), Peter Rodrigues, Waide Bodden, George Edward Bodden, William E. Watler, William Eden, John H. Thomson, William Nixon, William J. Bodden, Thomas Ward, Alexander Watler, Henry Clarke, John Drayton, and William Page. Ibid., pp. 213–14. The main jail was switched from Pedro St. James to Bodden Town by a Resolution (enactment) dated 11 January 1837; PRO, CO 137/367, fol. 369.

14. Hirst, *Notes,* pp. 215–19. The listings are unclear, but the following seem to have been Magistrates in 1824: James Coe Sr. (Chief Magistrate), John Drayton, William Page (listed with Drayton in Hirst, *Notes,* p. 205), Robert S. Watler, James Coe Jr., Joseph Bodden. Between them, the eighteen signatories owned 250 slaves in 1834, more than a quarter of those in the islands, an average of 14 apiece.
15. Ibid., pp. 218–19. Governor Sligo was almost contemptuous about the Caymanian legislators' self-interested control of liquor sales. Concerning an amendment in 1834 against the watering down of rum, he claimed that it was passed when only two merchants, Samuel Parsons and Richard Phelan, still had rum in stock. Phelan had watered his to stretch his profits. The effect of the amended law was to have Phelan's rum poured away, leaving Parsons with a monopoly and the ability to charge almost what he wished. Sligo to Stephen, Spanish Town, 13 December 1834, PRO, CO 137/194, cited in Sykes, *The Dependency Question,* p. 60.
16. Hirst, *Notes,* p. 219. The remainder of the law, presumably dealing with further safeguards, is unfortunately missing. Commissioner Hirst made the tantalising comment: "The rest of this Law has been torn out of the Record Book together with many others."
17. Governor Lord Belmore to Colonial Secretary, 21 November 1831, CO 137/179, fols. 342–8; Belmore Papers, Public Record Office, Northern Ireland, D3007/G/16, fols. 5, 6, copied by CINA as Collection 278.
18. Enclosure in Governor Lord Sligo to Colonial Secretary, 16 November 1834, CO 137/193, fol. 274. The eight Magistrates were John Drayton (Senior Magistrate), Robert Watler, Waide W. Bodden, John S. Jackson, James Coe Jr., Abraham O. Fuertado, Ebin John Parsons, and Nathaniel Glover (for whom William Eden Jr. was soon substituted). The Vestrymen were George W. Wood and James Hunter Wood (Bodden Town), James Coe Sr. and William Eden Jr. (Prospect), John Goodhow (South West Sound), James Parsons Sr., William J. Bodden, and Thomas L. Thomson (George Town), and Samuel Parsons and William Bodden Sr. (West Bay). Only one of these men (John Goodhow) was not a slaveowner in 1834. Between them, they owned 279 slaves, an average of more than 18 apiece. The "Meetings of Magistrates and Representatives" were redesignated "Meetings of Justices and Vestry" by a "Resolution" (that is, Act) dated 6 November 1837 (on the occasion of the taking of the oath to Queen Victoria on her accession). Meetings were held at Bodden Town, Prospect, or George Town, perhaps in rotation. "Local Laws of Grand Cayman," enclosed in Governor of Jamaica to Colonial Office, no. 66, 23 August 1862, PRO, CO 137/367, fols. 336–96.

19. Local enactments concerning the militia were the most numerous on any subject. Eight were passed between 31 December 1831 and 28 September 1841, illustrating both the importance of the militia and its changing role during the emancipation period. An "Act for Enrolling the Late Manumitted Slaves" was passed on 14 March 1836. But a close reading shows that it was merely concerned with controlling the possession of firearms and limiting the personnel of the militia to those regarded as reliable. On threat of stiff penalties, only members of the militia were permitted to possess arms without a licence. Membership in the militia was restricted to those approved by the Magistrates, and its numbers were limited to two hundred – a total smaller than the number of eligible white males. By 1840, the militia was mustered only quarterly rather than every month, and in the following year its annual subsidy and the levy added to the poll tax for its upkeep were both halved. The militia seems to have ceased to exist shortly after 1841 – either because it no longer had any sociopolitical relevance or because it was no longer thought to be necessary or suitable for policing purposes. Similar reasons may explain the decline in significance of the Assembly of Magistrates and Vestry – which seems to have passed no new legislation between September 1841 and 1862. Either its legislation was no longer necessary for the preservation of law and order, or (perhaps and) in an ostensibly more democratic era the dominant class did not welcome input from a wider spectrum of the population. "Local Laws of Grand Cayman," PRO, CO 137/367, fols. 342v–348r.
20. It is not easy to discern what the earliest Acts were, both because local records were patchy and because local enactments had a dubious status in Jamaica and London. Hirst's transcription of laws passed in the 1820s is invaluable but incomplete. Governor Sligo sent a compilation of Local Laws to London in November 1834 (PRO, CO 137/193, fols. 271–86), but the one sent by Governor Eyre in August 1862 (PRO, CO 137/367, fols. 336–96) was much fuller, covering the period 1831–41. The first Acts authorised by the Governor after the Cayman Islands formally became a dependency in 1865 included what was considered essential of the existing laws, but with much revision and sundry additions. See K.C. St.L. Henry and R.C. Laming, eds., *The Laws of the Cayman Islands,* vol. 1 (London: Eyre and Spottiswoode, 1963), p. ix. Though only four Acts were included in the 1834 list of "Local Laws", one to regulate the local Assembly, dated 2 January 1832, was included among the Acts approved by Governor Edward Eyre when reorganising the relations of the Cayman Islands with Jamaica in 1862–3. This ordained that the Justices and Vestry should be convened at least once a year on the third Wednesday in February (later amended first to September, then November), and that Vestrymen should serve two years, after which "Upon requisition of the Custos, or Senior Magistrate, the Magistrates in the Districts shall call the people together, and proceed to elect Vestrymen to serve" a further two years. In contrast to the actual situation in 1832, however, the Act decreed that there would be five Vestrymen each for George Town, Prospect, and Bodden Town and three each for East End and West Bay – with East End taking the place of South West Sound as a constituency district and the

number of elected representatives raised from ten to twenty-one. Five Magistrates and twelve Vestrymen were to constitute a quorum. "Act for the Government of the Cayman Islands," 22 June 1863, PRO, CO 137/392, fols. 560–65.

21. The first constable appointed by the resolution of 14 December 1833 was Edward Maxwell. He was to be paid £12 a year, plus fees. The building of a jail (or guardhouse) at Bodden Town was authorised by a resolution dated 11 January 1837. Another resolution on 12 January 1839 closed the jail at Pedro St. James and transferred the prisoners there to Bodden Town; PRO, CO 137/367, fols. 336–96.
22. Drayton and Thompson to Lord Sligo, 6 February 1835, PRO, CO 137/198, fols. 253–71.
23. For Phelan, Hirst, *Notes,* pp. 190-96; for Chloe, James, and William Parsons as free coloureds, *Our Islands' Past,* vol. 1, p. 15. For details on the Parsons clan other than their colour, see Hirst, *Notes,* pp. 85–7. Phelan is listed as Clerk of Vestry (or "CV") throughout much of the "Local Laws of Grand Cayman" in CO 137, fols. 336–96.
24. SM Thompson to Governor Lord Sligo, 10 March 1835, PRO, CO 137/198, fol. 268; Kieran, *Lawless Caymanas,* pp. 47–9.
25. PRO, CO 137/198, fol. 269.
26. Ibid., fol. 270.
27. Ibid., fol. 270–71.
28. Ibid., fols. 45–56, 265–71.
29. Lord Sligo's despatches to London, dated 13 and 27 April 1835; for comments by Colonial Office officials, see PRO, CO 137/198, fols. 253–63, 305–322A.
30. Pack to Sligo and Thompson to Sligo, 27 June 1835, PRO, CO 137/199, fols. 278-87.
31. Pack to Sligo, 14 June 1835, PRO, CO 137/199, fol. 279. A purely fictitious account of the ex-apprentices of Bodden Town celebrating their freedom, allegedly described by the Rev. Sharpe, is given in Kieran, *Lawless Caymanas,* pp. 63–4. Kieran cited S.O. "Bertie" Ebanks, *Cayman Emerges* (Grand Cayman: Cayman National Bank and Trust Co. Ltd., 1983). Ebanks, in all innocence, derived the account from the imaginative uncirculated historical romance *The Great Crocodile,* written by the Scottish Presbyterian minister Thomas Redpath in his retirement in the 1940s. Rev. Thomas Redpath, *The Great Crocodile: in Tradition, Legend and Records,* 2 vols., (unpublished typescript, reproduced in limited quantity by Mrs. Jane Redpath, 1946, 1949), pp. 330–57. Redpath's invention (including speeches and sermon, a fête, and banners across the road at the entrance to Bodden Town) seems to have been based on Emancipation Day celebrations such as he took part in around the turn of the century. In the Introduction, he wrote: "I need scarcely add that the characters I have attempted to portray bear no reference to anyone now living, but are purely tradition lighted up with imagination."
32. Pack to Sligo, 14 June 1835, CO 137/199, fol. 279.
33. CO 137/199, fols. 280, 279–83.
34. Ibid., fol. 280.

35. Ibid., fol. 285. A "dollar" was regarded as a third of a Jamaican pound, at a time when the Jamaican pound was reckoned as three-fifths of a pound sterling.
36. Ibid.
37. Ibid., fol. 286.
38. Ibid.
39. Ibid.
40. Ibid., fol. 287.
41. For SM Thompson's 1836 report, PRO, CO 137/210, fols. 394–403; Kieran, *Lawless Caymanas,* pp. 93–106.
42. By a coincidence, the new militia law, ostensibly allowing for the enrolling of the ex-slaves, had been passed by the Magistrates and representatives just five days earlier. See note 19, above.
43. PRO, CO 137/210, fol. 396.
44. Ibid., fols. 397–8.
45. Ibid., fol. 399.
46. Ibid., fols. 399–400.
47. Ibid., fol. 400–1.
48. Ibid., fol. 401.
49. Ibid., fol. 395.
50. For the compensation pay-out process, PRO, T71, and above, Chapter 4, n. 21.
51. Rev. J.B. Ellis, *The Diocese of Jamaica: A Short Account of Its History, Growth, and Organisation* (London: Society for Promoting Christian Knowledge, 1913); E. L. Evans, *A History of the Diocese of Jamaica* (Kingston: Diocese of Jamaica, 1976); C.F Pascoe, *Two Hundred Years of the SPG, 1701–1900* (London: Society for the Propagation of the Gospel, 1901).
52. The earliest indications of this desire are found in Gauld, *Grand Cayman 1773* ("they are very desirous of having a clergyman and a surgeon to reside among them") and *Our Islands' Past,* vol. 1, p. 7.
53. *Our Islands' Past,* vol. 1, p. 7. See above, Chapter 4. A letter to Governor Nugent from William Bodden as early as 23 November 1805 suggests that schoolmasters had also provided church services – incidentally shedding a tantalising light both on the earliest schooling in the islands and the connection between religion and education from the earliest years: "there is not, nor has been, Resident in this Island, any person that has taken Holy Orders – Schoolmasters have performed divine service for the benefit of the Rising Generation – and of setting forth the doctrine of Christ – the Magistrate therefore generally performs the office of Marrying – it is sometimes perform'd by those schoolmasters". Library of Jamaica, Nugent Papers, quoted in Hughes, "Notes on the Cayman Islands," pp. 156–7.
54. Mary Turner, *Slaves and Missionaries: The Disintegration of Jamaican Slave Society, 1787–1834* (Urbana: University of Illinois Press, 1982).
55. Belmore to Colonial Office, 19 March 1832, PRO, CO 137/181, fols. 397–403; Sykes, *Dependency Question,* p. 58.
56. Sykes, *Dependency Question,* pp. 61–4, 74–5; CO 137/271, fols. 69A–71; CO 137/272, fols. 8–21.

57. "Report of the Rev'd David Wilson, Stipendiary Curate of the Island of Grand Cayman from the 9th of June 1836 to the 9th of June 1837," SPG Archive, Rhodes House, Oxford, quoted in Sykes, *Dependency Question,* pp. 67–9. Interestingly, the body voting Wilson's stipend in January 1836 called itself a "Court of Sessions" rather than Magistrates and Vestry or Assembly, perhaps because it was dealing with ecclesiastical rather than legislative matters.
58. Sykes, *Dependency Question,* pp. 59–61. When, following the 1837 hurricane, the Assembly sent a petition to the Colonial Office for aid, they were told that £150 had already been allocated to the SPG for a school for 110 children in Grand Cayman. The Assembly ought therefore to apply first to the Bishop in Jamaica. The subsequent correspondence between Grand Cayman and Jamaica, involving the Assembly, the Bishop, and the Mico Charity is described in Sykes, *Dependency Question,* pp. 77–83.
59. Ibid., pp. 75–94.
60. Rhodes House Library, Oxford: Andrew Malcolm to Directors of the Mico Charity, London, Bodden Town, 3 May 1839, MSS Brit. Emp. S20; E1, fols. 271–81. (The letters from Grand Cayman are in E1, vols. 1 and 2.)
61. Ibid., E1/1: 271–81.
62. Rhodes House Library, E1/1: 309–25: Edmund Wallbridge, General Superintendent of Schools under the Mico Charity (Kingston, Jamaica) to Cayman Islands Vestry, n.d. [August 1839]; Richard Phelan, Clerk of Vestry to Wallbridge, 28 August 1839.
63. Bodden Town Petitioners to Honourable Directors of the Mico Charity, London, Bodden Town, Grand Cayman, 8 July 1840, Mico Charity Archive, Rhodes House Library, E1/2: 141–4, 161–2, reproduced in *Three Petitions by Caymanians from 1837 and 1840,* Archive Pack, CINA, Grand Cayman, 1991.
64. Rev. James Atkins to Rev. John Buckam, Wesleyan Missionary Society, 77, Hatton Garden, London, dated Wesley Chapel, Kingston, Jamaica, 24 August 1837, Wesleyan Missionary Society Archives, School of Oriental and African Studies, London, reproduced in *A Wesleyan Missionary in Grand Cayman,* Archive Pack, CINA, Grand Cayman, 1991. Atkins, like Nathaniel Glover four years later, made much of lingering African "superstitions", including the practice of obeah and the preference for African over Christian methods of oath-taking – with which the Magistrates had been forced to comply. See *A Wesleyan Missionary,* p. 14.
65. The turnover of Methodist ministers was due in part to the Wesleyan custom of sending ministers on circuit rather than to permanent assignments. But this did not account for either the short stay of some of the ministers or the long gaps between them. The Wesleyan ministers in Grand Cayman were James Atkins (1837), Mark Bird (1838–9), William Redfern (1840–41), Edward Lockyer (1841), John Mearns (1842–3), George Savery (1843), and John Green (1844). The approximately fifteen letters from these ministers from or about Grand Cayman are in SOAS, Methodist Missionary Society Archives, Fiche Boxes 47 and 48, fiches 2256–311, and Fiche Box 13, fiches 604 and 607 (which contains the long

letter by Nathaniel Glover to Rev. Lockyer dated 1841 and Lockyer's copy of it).

66. Rev. John Mearns, Grand Cayman, to Wesleyan Mission Society, London, 3 October 1842, SOAS, WMMS, Fiche Box 48, fiche 2298.
67. It was probably not entirely by chance that the Caymanians who migrated and settled in the Bay Islands overwhelmingly became Methodists, much as those who went to the Sister Islands became Baptists, and those remaining in Grand Cayman became Presbyterians.
68. Rev. John Green, Grand Cayman, to Wesleyan Missionary Society, London, 18 June, 30 July 1844, SOAS, WMMS, Fiche Box 48, fiche 2311.

Chapter 6: SLAVERY'S AFTERMATH AND THE FIRST CAYMANIAN MIGRATIONS

1. For British imperialism after emancipation, especially in the Caribbean and Latin America, see D.K. Fieldhouse, *The Colonial Empires: A Comparative Survey from the Eighteenth Century* (London: Weidenfeld and Nicolson, 1966), pp. 177–302; W.P. Morrell, *British Colonial Policy in the Age of Peel and Russell* (Oxford: Oxford University Press, 1930); Green, *British Slave Emancipation;* David Eltis, *Economic Growth and the Ending of the Transatlantic Slave Trade* (New York: Oxford University Press, 1987); Thomas C. Holt, *The Problem of Freedom: Race, Labor, and Politics in Jamaica and Britain, 1832–1938 (*Baltimore: Johns Hopkins University Press, 1992); Hilary Beckles and Verene Shepherd, eds., *Caribbean Freedom: Economy and Society from Emancipation to the Present* (Kingston: Ian Randle Press, 1993); Craton, *Empire, Enslavement, and Freedom,* pp. 263–438.
2. The population of the Sister Islands went from 597 in 1891 to 1,436 in 1911. It was 1,357 in 1943, and 1,474 in 1989. Grand Cayman, according to Corbet, had 933 inhabitants in 1802. H. W. Rutty's 1907 statement that the combined population of the Sister Islands in 1850 was only 36 was inaccurate, but it was almost certainly under 100. *Cayman Islands Historical Compendium of Statistics, 1774–1980* (George Town: Government Statistics Office, 1992), p. 45; *Cayman Islands 1989 Census, vol. 1, Commentary and Tabulation of Results* (George Town: Government Statistics Office, 1990), p. 35; H.W. Rutty, "Lesser Caymans," in *Handbook of the Cayman Islands, 1908,* ed. G.S.S. Hirst (Kingston: Times Printery, 1907), pp. 67–72.
3. *Our Islands' Past,* vol. 1, pp. 7–8; HMS *Sybill,* 7 July 1818, MODHO, Miscellaneous Papers, vol. 42, p. 667.
4. Documents from the Hydrographic Office: H 56 (signed "R. Owen" and dated 1831), and OD456, [1830–37], which is Owen's manuscript memoir of his surveys. For the 1833 reference see the "views" of all three islands in Album 8I, West Indies, vol. II, fol. CE, which is dated 1833 but contains no reference to its source; and "Surveyors Letters", vol. 26a, which shows that HMS *Jackdaw* stopped at Grand Cayman on 19 July 1833, taking on "an excellent pilot" in order to survey a "bank", proba-

bly to the west of Grand Cayman. The *Jackdaw* may have visited the Sister Islands at this time.

5. See above, Chapter 4. Captain Pack's 1835 report and the slave registration returns also mention one Daly (Daley or Dealy) who was living with his family and six Negroes on Cayman Brac (which HMS *Serpent* did not visit). CO 137/199, fol. 279. See also T71/1331, which lists a "Daley" on Little Cayman. Nothing is known about what happened to Daly and his ex-slaves, though there is still a Daley's Well on Cayman Brac. William Page is said to have died in Grand Cayman in 1842 and to have had two sons and three daughters. The two daughters who married were wed to a Merren and an Arch in Grand Cayman. The one son who reached adulthood was said to have migrated to Nicaragua. The surname Page is not known in the Cayman Islands today but is common in the Bay Islands – though whether they are descended from William Page's migrant son (William Robert) or from those of his slaves who assumed his surname is unclear. "Genealogy of Merren and Hunter Families. Compiled by Catherine Merren Hunter," typescript, n.d., CINA, Vertical File (Biography, Autobiography, and Genealogy, A–Z).
6. Rutty, "Lesser Caymans," p. 70. In 1993, Hannah Joan Parchman of Cayman Brac, aged 69, gave the CINA Memory Bank a more detailed version of the established tradition: "And then you had three men from Grand Cayman, Foster, Scott and Ritch. They came over and occupied the island, shared the island in three . . . Scott was the west end, Foster was the middle part and Ritch was the east end." CINA Interview with Hannah Joan Parchman, #1–4, 9 December 1993.
7. Hirst, *Notes,* p. 69. See above, Chapter 3. Some Foster descendants have claimed that the English Stephen Taylor Foster was the son or grandson of the Jamaican William Foster, but this is without substantiation.
8. Cayman Brac Foster genealogy, Moody H. Ryan notes, CINA Acc. 58, MSC 28.
9. In one account, the original Scott was said to have been William Robert, a recent migrant from Scotland who had married Judith, the daughter of one of the William Boddens of Grand Cayman. They were said to have gone to Little Cayman with their four young sons and (less plausibly) with "several slaves". Another version claimed that the migrant Scott and Ritch were half-brothers, though how this might have been so is obscure. More substantially, in May 2000, Nolan B. Foster (born 1916) stated that the widow Christian's grave was still to be seen in the southeastern corner of the Stake Bay cemetery on Cayman Brac and that as a boy he had seen the ruins of her house at Stake Bay. "The Widow Mary Bodden by Sarah Hunter Scott," typescript, n.d., CINA, Vertical File (Biography, Autobiography, and Genealogy, A–Z), pp. 2–3; Nolan B. Foster, personal communication with Michael Craton, 1 May 2000.
10. The four children and their spouses were Sarah Foster and William Ryan, who had four sons and twenty-four grandchildren; William Foster and Elizabeth Scott, who had six sons, four daughters, and fifty-two grandchildren; Hemmington Chesse Foster and Anne Scott, who had four sons, six daughters, and forty grandchildren; and Waide Taylor Foster and

Sarah Scott, who had three sons, two daughters, and at least twenty-four grandchildren. CINA, MSC 28.

11. Moody H. Ryan Notes, CINA Acc. 58, MSC 28. For Kirkconnell family history, CINA Vertical File (Biography, Autobiography, and Genealogy, A–Z).
12. PRO/T71/243, fols. 1–116; Hirst, *Handbook, 1908,* pp. 70–74. There are no Ritches, Fosters, or Ryans among the slave returns, but Return #15 concerns "William Roberts Scott, Grand Cayman, who owned three slaves".
13. CINA Interview with Hebe Foster (born 1901), 26 October 1990. Nolan Foster mentioned the legend that his family was descended from a (clearly imaginary) "Foster, King of Flanders." Fascinating claims came from the 1992 oral testimony of Captain William T. Ritch (born 1916). CINA Interview with Captain William Theophilus Ritch, 26 February 1992; Moody H. Ryan, "History of Joseph Daniel Hunter Sr.," unpublished typescript, n.d., Moody Ryan and Linton Tibbetts Collections, CINA Acc. 58, MSC 28; Acc. 36, MSC 23.
14. CINA Interview with Nolan B. Foster (born 1916), 13 August 1991. The emigrant chronicler Rev. H.C. Dixon, author of *Cayman Brac: Land of my Birth,* did not challenge the Barba-Mateo version, though he added a third alleged Cuban runaway called Peter Pascual – whose name is perpetuated by a Peter's Cave and a Peter's Road. More significantly, to explain later independent black arrivals, Dixon did mention a man called Bob Robinson, nicknamed "Governor," who was the first – and for many years the sole – inhabitant of Spot Bay at the far northeastern point, which became the most distinctively black settlement in Cayman Brac. Robinson was said to have married a black woman, Keziah Watler from Gun Bay, Grand Cayman, with whom he had many children. He also had a sister, known as Aunt Bessie, who married the "African" known as "Old Dick" (that is, Thomas Mathias Ritch) and had six sons. All of these blacks, finding the best lowland areas pre-empted by the whites, took up provision and grazing lands on the nearby Bluff. Rev. H.C. Dixon, *Cayman Brac: Land of My Birth* (Brooklyn: Shining Light Survey, n.d. [1955]), p. 16. Nolan Foster and others, however, claim that Peter Pascual was neither black nor a slave but "French" (like Elizabeth Sarah Christian, who was said to have been the daughter of a Frenchman named Chesse). Burnard Tibbetts, personal communication with Michael Craton, May 2000; CINA, Collections 89 (Linton Tibbetts) and 132 (Moody Ryan).
15. By all accounts the non-white settlers were as prolific as the whites, but also had to find their separate socio-economic niches. For various modern accounts of the relations between whites and non-whites, see, for example, CINA Interviews with Nolan Foster, 13 August 1991; Marjorie Tibbetts, #2, 16 March 1995, pp. 12–20; and Hannah Joan Parchman, #3, 9 December 1993; and the account by H.C. Dixon in *Cayman Brac*, p. 16. Nolan Foster, for example, described relations between whites and non-whites in these terms: "The fact is, this is something that's probably amazed a lot of people and I've often thought on it, that the majority of the coloured people on this island lived in the Spot Bay and Watering

Place area. Now perhaps it's changing a bit today [1991], but in my younger days . . . we used to go to Spot Bay 'cause we had property in Spot Bay. We used to go up there and on the Bluff there, and those people'd always invite us in to have something to eat. I mean we were treated as friends. . . . If they came to our place it was the same thing. Nobody sort of took any privileges with the other. . . . They accepted their position as it was. . . . A lot of people have wondered about that, that there's no race prejudice among them. Each one lives in their own community, they accept the other as they are, but they don't try to take any privileges or . . . any liberties with one another."

16. Rutty, "Lesser Caymans," pp. 70–74. Captain Keith P. Tibbetts, *Bits of the Brac: A Brief History of Cayman Brac* (Cayman Brac: Cayman Brac Museum, n.d. [c. 1980]).
17. CO 137/322, fol. 115; CO 137/339, fol. 216; and *Missionary Record of The United Presbyterian Church,* vol. 14, pp. 214–15. (Hereafter cited as *UP Missionary Record.*)
18. See Rutty on "Lesser Caymans" in Hirst, *Handbook, 1908,* pp. 71–4.
19. Rutty, "Lesser Caymans," p. 74; Tibbetts, *Brief History of Cayman Brac.* For the genealogies and other information on the Boddens, Scotts, Fosters, Ryans, Tibbettses, Hunters, McLaughlins, and other Sister Island families, see Hirst, *Notes,* pp. 68–107; CINA, Collections 89, 132; and CINA, Vertical Files (Biography, Autobiography, and Genealogy, A–Z).
20. William V. Davidson, *Historical Geography of the Bay Islands, Honduras: Anglo-Hispanic Conflict in the Western Caribbean,* 3rd ed. (Birmingham, Ala.: Southern University Press, 1988), pp. 65–91. For British policy and actions in the region in general, see Robert A. Naylor, *Penny Ante Imperialism: The Mosquito Shore and the Bay of Honduras. A Case Study in British Informal Empire* (London and Toronto: Associated University Presses, 1989). For an excellent scenic account of the Bay Islands by an English trader, see Orlando W. Roberts, *Narrative of Voyages on the East Coast and in the Interior of Central America* (Edinburgh: Constable, 1827), quoted in Davidson, *Historical Geography of the Bay Islands,* p. 74.
21. The authorities Rose and Davidson give 1836 for the date of Joseph Cooper's arrival, but Cooper, in an 1856 petition, described himself as having been resident in the Bay Islands for twenty-five years, that is, since 1831. Petition of Inhabitants, November 1856, CO 34/5; Richard H. Rose, *Utilla: Past and Present. Including an Article on HMS* Psyche *at the Bay Islands, With Illustrations* (Dansville: F.A. Owen Publishing Co., 1904); Davidson, *Historical Geography of the Bay Islands,* p. 75. The 1834 Minot Cayman Islands Slave Registration list does not include any Cooper slaveowners.
22. Rose, *Utilla,* pp. 20–25.
23. Ibid., pp. 26–8.
24. Report of Captain R.C. Michell of HMS *Arachne* (London: Royal Geographical Society, 1850), pp. 14–15, cited in Davidson, *Historical Geography of the Bay Islands,* p. 78.
25. Report of Captain Michell, pp. 11–14.
26. Ibid., pp. 9-10.

27. Davidson, *Historical Geography of the Bay Islands*, pp. 80–85.
28. In 1855, exports were worth £4,909 and imports £6,026. By 1859, exports were worth £13,874, compared with imports of £11,163; CO 36/1–5, tabulated in Davidson, *Historical Geography of the Bay Islands*, Table 5, p. 85.
29. Ibid. Davidson's table does not include exports of turtle or tortoiseshell, though Presiding Magistrate Moir in 1858 reported that 886 turtle had been officially exported in the previous year; CO 34/7. Davidson's tabulation that trade to and from the Cayman Islands was a mere "trace" also almost certainly disguises a considerable traffic in persons and goods – probably because such voyages went unrecorded and no duties were paid. In 1855 Belize accounted for 58 per cent of Bay Island exports and 85 per cent of imports by value, against 41 and 13 per cent respectively for the United States. But by 1859 the United States was taking 90 per cent of Bay Islands exports and supplying 58 per cent of imports, compared with 9 per cent of exports and 37 per cent of imports to and from Belize.
30. For the operation of British and United States policy in the region, especially in regard to the Monroe Doctrine and its corollaries, see Gordon Ireland, *Boundaries, Possessions, and Conflicts in Central and North America and the Caribbean* (Cambridge: Harvard University Press, 1941); Lester D. Langley, *Struggle for the American Mediterranean: United States–European Rivalry in the Gulf-Caribbean, 1776–1904* (Athens: University of Georgia Press, 1976); Ralph Lee Woodward, "Central America, 1812–1879," in *Cambridge History of Latin America*, vol. 3 (Cambridge: Cambridge University Press, 1985), pp. 471–506; Thomas D. Schoonover, *The United States in Central America, 1860–1911: Episodes of Social Imperialism and Imperial Rivalry in the World System* (Durham, N.C.: Duke University Press, 1991).
31. Report of Captain Michell, p. 15. David Kenneth Evans, "The People of French Harbour: A Study of Conflict and Change on Roatán Island" (Ph.D. diss., University of California, Berkeley, 1957), p. 18, citing CO 34/2.
32. Evans, "French Harbour," p. 20, citing Sir John Burdon, *Archives of Belize*, vol. 3. (London: Praed, 1931–5), p. 128. Curiously, the 1850 petition excluded Utila.
33. PRO CO 34/1. CO 34, vols. 1–10 contain the official correspondence regarding the Bay Islands during the time it was recognised as a British colony. CO 36 contains the Blue Books for the Bay Islands in the same period.
34. PRO CO 34/1–10.
35. Moir to Colonial Office, 1 March 1858, CO 34/7. There were 15 to 20 shopkeepers and 294 freeholders liable to pay direct taxes. The grand total of taxes levied in 1857 was £304 13s 6d.
36. Ibid.
37. Michael Duncan, *The Bay Islands or the Gentle Art of Cutting the Painter* (Warwick: University of Warwick, Centre for Caribbean Studies, n.d.), pp. 2–4.
38. Ibid., p. 4.

39. Ibid., p. 5–6; Public address by Lieutenant-Governor Seymour, 11 March 1857, CO 34/6.
40. Duncan, *The Bay Islands,* pp. 6–7; Robin A. Humphreys, *The Diplomatic History of British Honduras, 1638–1901* (London: Royal Institute of International Affairs and Oxford University Press, 1961), p. 58.
41. Duncan, *The Bay Islands,* p. 8; Humphreys, *British Honduras,* pp. 59–91; Narda Dobson, *A History of Belize* (London: Longman Caribbean, 1973), pp. 179–213; Dozier, *Nicaragua's Mosquito Shore.*
42. Duncan, *The Bay Islands,* pp. 10–12; W.O. Scroggs, *Filibusters and Financiers* (New York: Macmillan, 1916); R.E. May, *The Southern Dream of a Caribbean Empire, 1854–1861* (Baton Rouge: University of Louisiana Press, 1973).
43. Duncan, *The Bay Islands,* pp. 9–13; Heather R. McLaughlin, "A Sad and Bitter Day: Oral Traditions in the Bay Islands of Honduras Surrounding the Wyke Cruz Treaty of 1859," CINA Memory Bank Report, 1994.
44. The demise of the colonial status of the Bay Islands can be traced in CO 34, vols. 8–10.
45. Langley, *Struggle for the American Mediterranean,* pp. 150–60.
46. See Original Documents OD 495 MODHO, which contains the unpublished manuscript of Captain Robert Owen [1829–37] indicating that at that time Corn Island had three hundred inhabitants, San Andrés had six hundred, and Swan Island was planted with coconut trees by "turtlers, who frequent these islands in the fishing season". Rodwell Morgan, *Meet Corn Island* (Kearney, Neb.: Morris Publishing, 1996); James J. Parsons, *San Andrés and Providencia* (Berkeley: University of California, 1956); Peter J. Wilson, *Crab Antics: The Social Anthropology of English-Speaking Negro Societies in the Caribbean* (New Haven: Yale University Press, 1973), pp. 12–43.
47. Ramiro Guerra y Sanchez, ed., *Historia de la nacion cubana,* 10 vols. (Havana: Editorial Historia de la Nacion Cubana, 1952); Rebecca J. Scott, *Slave Emancipation in Cuba: The Transition to Free Labor, 1860–1899* (Princeton: Princeton University Press, 1985).
48. Memoranda of Samuel Parsons and William Eden, 18 and 28 April 1858, CO 34/7.
49. Duncan, *The Bay Islands,* p. 14.
50. Ibid., pp. 13–14.
51. Evans, "People of French Harbour," p. 22.

Chapter 7: ISOLATION, NEGLECT, AND SELF-RELIANCE, 1845–1898

1. Rev. Hope Masterton Waddell, *Twenty-Nine Years in the West Indies and Central Africa: A Review of Missionary Work and Adventure, 1829–1858,* 2nd ed. (London: Frank Cass, 1970), pp. 212–15. The apparent similarity of Cayman to Jamaican parishes was borne out by the existence of a Vestry and the title of Custos for the Chief Magistrates.
2. Ibid., pp. 215–17.
3. For example, letter from Custos John Drayton to Governor Charles Metcalfe, 28 February 1841, stating that he had no knowledge of the

licensing of wreckers and that "from time immemorial" Cayman vessels fishing on the outer cays of Cuba had picked up the cargo and crew of wrecked vessels and taken them to Grand Cayman, where arbitrators had decided the amount of salvage; CO 137/255, fols. 84–6. See also CO 137/280, fols. 1–8, 206–19; 286, 225A–227; 288, 293–9; 289, 266–77; 291, 186–92.

4. William Eden and John Jarrett Wood to W. Austin, Colonial Secretary, Kingston, 6 January 1854, enclosed in Governor Barkly to Newcastle, 9 February 1854, CO 137/322, fols. 120–24.
5. Austin to Eden and Wood, King's House, Kingston, 2 February 1854, ibid., fols. 125–6.
6. Governor Charles Darling to Colonial Secretary E. Bulwer Lytton, King's House, Kingston, 20 October 1858, CO 137/339, fols. 216–37. Though he stressed Governor Barkly's indifference to the Cayman Islands, Neville Williams ignored Governor Darling's 1858 visit, claiming that the only Jamaican governors to visit the Cayman Islands in the nineteenth century were Lord Sligo (1835, wrongly given as 1838), Sir John Grant (1868), and Sir Wylie Norman (1884, 1888). Williams, *History of the Cayman Islands,* p. 60.
7. CO 137/339, fols. 232–3.
8. An Act for the Government of the Cayman Islands, 22 June 1863, 27 Vict. Cap. XXXI, in *Laws of the Cayman Islands up to No. 12 of 1889* (Jamaica: Government Printing Establishment, 1889), pp. 1–4. It should be noted that the legislative authority of the Jamaican legislature over Cayman presumably lapsed when the Jamaican Assembly was abolished in 1866 – though residual legislative authority may have been retained by the Jamaican Governor-in-Council under the system of Crown Colony rules. Hurwitz and Hurwitz, *Jamaica,* pp. 150, 178.
9. *Laws of the Cayman Islands . . . 1889,* p. 2.
10. Ibid., pp. 3–4.
11. An Act authorizing a Revisal of Former Acts, and to Consolidate the Government, 16 June 1863, assented to by Governor Eyre, 23 March 1865, in *Laws of the Cayman Islands . . . 1889,* pp. 5–6.
12. An Act regulating the Courts was also passed, the details of which were not given in the printed *Laws of the Cayman Islands . . . 1889* (it was repealed by Law 3 of 1889). Minor Acts assented to in 1865 included those to appoint a Clerk of the Peace, to prevent debtors leaving Grand Cayman, to license liquor sales, to establish and regulate the animal pound, to control stray animals, to regulate division fences, to repair the public roads, and to prevent public nuisances; *Laws of the Cayman Islands . . . 1889,* pp. 8–19. For the development of the law for land registration (often said to have dated from 1865 rather than 1850), see below.
13. For Governor Eyre and the Morant Bay Rebellion, see Bernard Semmel, *Jamaican Blood and Victorian Conscience: The Governor Eyre Controversy* (Boston: Houghton Mifflin, 1963; Westport, Conn.: Greenwood Press, 1976); Geoffrey Dutton, *The Hero as Murderer: The Life of Edward John Eyre, Australian Explorer and Governor of Jamaica, 1815–1901* (Sydney: Collins, 1967); Mavis Christine Campbell, *The Dynamics of Change in a Slave Society: A Sociopolitical History of the*

Free Coloureds of Jamaica, 1800–1865 (Rutherford, N.J.: Fairleigh Dickinson University Press, 1976); Gad J. Heuman, *Between Black and White: Race, Politics, and the Free Coloreds in Jamaica, 1792–1865* (Westport, Conn.: Greenwood Press, 1981); Holt, *The Problem of Freedom,* pp. 262–309.

14. VII. An Act for Land Registration [5 September 1850], assented to by Governor Edward Eyre, 23 March 1865. *Laws of the Cayman Islands . . . 1889,* pp. 11–12.
15. *Our Islands' Past,* vol. 1, pp. 5–6.
16. One minor amendment in 1889 specified that claimants had to inform their neighbours fifteen days before registering land and to arrange for a Magistrate to confirm the boundaries on the site. Cayman Islands Law 5 of 1889, cited in Tamara Selzer, "Selected Sources for the History of Land Registration in the Cayman Islands" (M.A. thesis, University College, London, 1997), p. 14.
17. *Colonial Report 1953–4,* p. 18.
18. For Grant's administration, see Sydney Olivier, *Jamaica: The Blessed Island* (London: Faber, 1936), pp. 189-91; Black, *The Story of Jamaica,* pp. 183–4, 191, 203–4; Hurwitz and Hurwitz, *Jamaica,* pp. 180–85.
19. Archives of Jamaica, [Governors'] Despatches from Jamaica to England, 1725–1945, IB/5/18, vol. 31, no. 26, p. 207.
20. William Eden to Governor Grant, 9 May 1871, IB/5/18, vol. 33, no. 59, pp. 6–7. See also PRO, CO 137/456, fols. 281–304 (the equivalent despatch in the PRO).
21. Grant to Kimberley, 10 March 1872, IB/5/18, vol. 33, no. 49, p. 320. Also nos. 52, 63, 70, pp. 341, 363, 395; Grant to Kimberley, 23 May 1872, vol. 34, no. 100; 10 December 1872, no. 257, 24 April 1873, no. 70.
22. Grant to Kimberley, 8 November 1873, IB/4/18, vol. 34, no. 188, 22 December 1873, no. 206.
23. Ibid.
24. William Eden to Colonial Secretary, Jamaica, 9 November, 12 December 1876, IB/5/18, vol. 37, no. 212; Musgrave to Colonial Office, 23 March 1877, vol. 37, no. 47.
25. Governor Musgrave to Lord Carnarvon, 5 September 1877, IB/5/18, vol. 37, no. 151.
26. Musgrave to Hicks Beach, 9 August 1878, IB/5/18, vol. 38, no. 165.
27. See Thomas Young, *Narrative of a Residence on the Mosquito Shore* (London: Smith, Elder and Co., 1842), p. 17, which gives a brief, pithy account of Caymanian turtling off the Miskito Cays.
28. IB/5/18, vol. 32, no. 3, pp. 291–9; Grant to Kimberley, 3 and 31 January 1872, nos. 2, 15; Musgrave to Hicks Beach, 1879, vol. 38, no. 196.
29. Musgrave to Hicks Beach, 15 March 1878, IB/5/18, vol. 38, no. 87.
30. Musgrave to Hicks Beach, 23 July 1879, IB/5/18, vol. 38, no. 231.
31. Acting Governor Newton to Hicks Beach, 21 August 1879, IB/5/18, vol. 38, no. 267.
32. CINA MSD/174 (containing a copy of Hydrographic Office document OD 505); *Admiralty Chart of the Cayman Islands, 1882,* published by the U.K. Hydrographic Office and the Cayman Islands National Archive, 1996.

33. For Governors Norman and Blake, see Olivier, *Jamaica: The Blessed Island*, pp. 247–54. Henry Wylie Norman was an Evangelical with more than thirty years' experience in India, later the chairman of the West Indies Commission of 1897. Henry Blake was an Irishman with experience of and sympathy for peasant conditions, exaggeratedly said to be "a pronounced negrophilist". For the Australian account of the 1884 trip (given nine years later), see J.P. Thompson, "A Governor's Cruise in the West Indies in 1884," *Australian Royal Geographical Quarterly* 9 (1893–4): 7–14. For Norman's actual visit and Report, Norman to Lord Derby 10 March, 2 and 3 April 1884, IB/5/18, vol. 46, nos. 102, 128, 130.
34. Norman's Report, 2 April 1884, IB/5/18, vol. 46, no. 128, pp. 2–3.
35. Thompson, "A Governor's Cruise," p. 9. No examples of the "paintings and engravings" are known to have survived.
36. Norman's Report, 1884, p. 7.
37. Ibid., pp. 7–8. The social observations on the Sister Islands by Rev J.H. Sobey, the first Baptist minister to visit them, are also revealing. After a week-long visit to Cayman Brac in 1885, he estimated the total population to be about 440, of whom 40 lived on Little Cayman. He admired the Brackers' houses, which he described as "large, clean, airy and substantial, being built of ironwood, candlewood and various other hard woods. Some roofs are shingled, but most are covered with fan-thatch, a species of palm." The chief occupations, he noted, were "cocoa-nut and yam growing, hook and turtle fishing", with most of their trade being conducted through Montego Bay. See *The Missionary Herald* of the Baptist Missionary Society, 1 November 1886, pp. 514–15.
38. Norman's Report, 1884, pp. 4, 8.
39. Ibid., pp. 4–5.
40. *Grand Cayman: Report of Visit by Mr. L.R. Fyfe of the Colonial Secretary's Office, Jamaica, preceded by Minute of Instructions by His Excellency Sir H.W. Norman, GCB, GCMG, CIE, Governor of Jamaica, 1887* (Kingston: Government Printing Office, 1887). (Hereafter cited as Fyfe, *Report*.)
41. Fyfe, *Report*, pp. 3–9.
42. Fyfe, *Report*, Enclosure no. 10, *Mallard*, at sea, 30 August 1887, p. 18.
43. Ibid., Enclosure no. 7, Grand Cayman, 23 August 1887, Enclosure no. 9 to Governor, n.d., pp. 16–18.
44. Hirst, *Notes*, p. 258.
45. Ibid., p. 259.
46. CINA Interview with Capt. Theophilus Bodden, #1, 7 August 1990, p. 2.
47. Hirst, *Notes*, pp. 259–60; CINA Interviews with Capt. Theophilus Bodden, #1, 7 August 1990, p. 2; Capt. Keith Tibbetts, #3, 26 February 1991, p. 24; Japheth Walton, #2, 2 April 2001, pp. 9–11.
48. D.B. Armstrong, *The Cayman Islands: The Stamps and Post Office* (London: Council of the Junior Philatelic Society (reprinted from *The Stamp Lover*), 1910), p. 5.
49. William T. Eden and E. Noel McLaughlin, *The Island of Grand Cayman at the Jamaica Exhibition: Historical Sketch and Descriptive Catalogue* (Kingston: De Cordova Printers, 1891), pp. 2–3.

50. Governor Blake to Colonial Secretary, 13 September 1892, Archives of Jamaica, 1B/5/18, vol. 47, no. 34, pp. 2–6.
51. CINA, Custos's Correspondence, 1888–1898, AA 1/1, 24 July, 11 August 1893, 25 January 1895, 25 and 31 July 1895, 4 December 1895, original folio numbers 74, 75, 165, 142, 134.
52. CO 137/573, fols. 505–16. Blake lamented that "I observed no difference whatsoever in the condition of the island since my last visit." One reason for his evident frustration was the potential he saw for development, and this is probably the first report of any kind that links Cayman to the nascent industry of tourism. Cayman, Blake observed, was "excellently situated for a possible tourist resort from Tampa, being on the direct route between that port and Jamaica".
53. Governor Hemming to Joseph Chamberlain, 26 April 1898, 9 December 1898, Archives of Jamaica, Governors' Despatches, 1B/5/18, vol. 50, no. 162; vol. 51, no. 565.

Chapter 8: CHANGE AND RESISTANCE: THE FIRST COMMISSIONERS, 1898–1914

1. The work of Sanguinetti and Hirst can also be seen as a filtering down of the influence of the radical Joseph Chamberlain's tenure as Secretary of State for the Colonies (1895–1903), mediated through the most remarkable of all Jamaican officials, the Fabian Socialist Sydney Olivier (later Lord Olivier). Olivier had been Jamaican Colonial Secretary, secretary of the Norman West Indian Commission (1897), and Administrator of Jamaica before his term as Governor (1907–13).
2. CINA, Commissioners' Correspondence, vol. 5 (1903), 26 August 1903, 24 November 1903, nos. 68, 85; vol. 6 (1904), 21 December 1903, no. 1; vol. 9 (1907), 27 September, 10 December 1907; vol. 10 (1908), no. 105.
3. Ibid., vol. 4 (1902), 15 January1902. For the extension of education, see below, Chapter 11. In the first *Colonial Report,* covering the years 1905 and 1906 and published in 1907, it was stated that Caymanian labourers received 3 shillings and carpenters 7 shillings a day, compared with rates of 1s 6d and 3s for Jamaica and Trinidad, 1s and 2s 6d for Barbados, and 10d and 1s 6d for Antigua, *Colonial Report 1905–6,* p. 9.
4. For Caymanian revenue and expenditure 1888–98 and 1898–1907, see CINA, Custos' and Commissioners' Correspondence AA 1/1; for 1907–14, see *Colonial Reports* for these years.
5. For example, CINA, Commissioners' Correspondence, vol. 6 (1904), nos. 86-88; vol. 7 (1905), no. 75.
6. Vaquero [pseud.], *Life and Adventure in the West Indies* (London: Bale and Danielsson, 1914), p. 29. Internal evidence points to Vaquero's being Dr. Keatinge, who was in Grand Cayman for a little less than a year in 1906, rather than a Dr. F.R. Evans, who served for a similarly short period about three years earlier. See Paul G. Boultbee, *Cayman Islands,* vol. 187 of World Bibliographical Series (Oxford, Santa Barbara, Denver: Clio Press, 1996), p. 4.

7. For excellent accounts of the early history of Caymanian postal services, including the overprints "scandal", see Armstrong, *Stamps and Post Office;* Aguilar and Saunders, *Postal History; Stanley Gibbons Postage Stamp Catalogue,* Part 1, *British Commonwealth* (London: Stanley Gibbons, 1969). The relevant official correspondence takes up much space in the Commissioners' and Jamaican Governors' Correspondence for 1898–1908, beginning with Governor Hemming to Joseph Chamberlain, 27 April 1898, IB/5/18, vol. 50, no. 163, p. 523.
8. The variations and misprints were almost certainly the result of local inexperience and inefficiency, though rumour attributed them to deliberate moves to generate revenue far above the stamps' face value. The fullest account of the alleged scandal appeared in an issue of the magazine *Truth* in January 1908, as conveyed to the Colonial Secretary by the Ipswich stamp dealers Messrs. Whitfield King on 31 January and 20 February 1908, enclosure in Elgin to Olivier, 31 March 1908, CINA, Commissioners' Correspondence, vol. 10, no. 64.
9. "My attention has been called to the practice of issuing surcharged postage stamps, and to the temptations which it affords to Post Masters and Treasurers, and other public officers, of making irregular profits by dealings with stamp dealers and collectors. If proper care is taken to maintain a sufficient supply of stamps, the practice of surcharging is unnecessary, and it should never be resorted to unless absolutely required for the convenience of the public, and in every such case the officer responsible for keeping up the supply of stamps should be liable to be fined." Lord Ripon circular to colonies, 18 August 1893. Enclosure in CINA, Commissioners' Correspondence, vol. 10 (1908), no. 64, 21 April 1908. ". . . be so good in future as to refuse to supply the speculative demands of dealers until you have got a new stock . . .", Clarence Bourne, Colonial Secretary of Jamaica to Commissioner Hirst, 26 July 1907, ibid., vol. 9; Armstrong, *Stamps and Post Office,* p. 11. It should be noted that the Turks Islands were among the most active in setting a precedent for provisionally overprinted stamps, between 1881 and 1894; *Stanley Gibbons Stamp Catalogue,* Part 2, pp. 616–17.
10. Armstrong, *Stamps and Post Office,* p. 15. The local overprinting, being done by hand-stamps, meant that no two stamps were identical – making them especially attractive to philatelists. See also PRO, CO 137, vol. 664 (Despatch 302), vol. 666 (Despatch 587), and vols. 668 and 669 (which contain numerous complaints from philatelists).
11. For the extension of postal services in the Cayman Islands, see Aguilar and Saunders, *Postal History,* pp. 29–34. The total revenue in 1913 was £5,044, of which £2,750 came from the sale of postage stamps, while the Post Office Department cost a mere £264 to run. Customs revenue for 1913 was £1,706, and revenue from internal sources, a mere £372. *Colonial Report 1913–14* [Cd.7622-30], p. 4.
12. CO 137/627, Despatch #186, 17 April 1902.
13. CO 137/657, Enclosure in Despatch #170, 14 March 1907.
14. *Colonial Report 1905–6,* p. 4. CINA Interviews with Alta Scott, 11 November 1992, p. 7; Glanston Dilbert, 10 March 1995, p. 13.

15. *Colonial Report 1908–9,* p. 5; *Colonial Report 1913–14,* p. 6; *Colonial Report 1915–16,* p. 4. For the possible effect on shipbuilding, see *Colonial Report 1917–18,* p. 2. For the introduction of coconut disease to the Sister Islands, and the revival of the industry in the 1920s to 1950, see CINA Interviews with Capt. Theophilus Bodden, #1, 7 August 1990, pp. 2–4; #2, 8 August 1990, p. 15; #5, 18 July 1991, pp. 5–6; Capt. Keith Tibbetts #2, 25 October 1990, pp. 11–12; Capt Dillon Kirkconnell, # 1, 13 May 1994, pp. 4, 14 ; Linton Tibbetts, 9 November 1992, pp. 2, 6.
16. For the local effects of the Cuban Revolution and the Spanish-American War, see Hugh Thomas, *Cuba: The Pursuit of Freedom* (London: Eyre and Spottiswood, 1971), pp. 316–435. For the turtle industry at its peak, see Hirst, *Handbook, 1908,* pp. 59–63. For the regime of José Santos Zelaya, see Ralph Lee Woodward, Jr., *Central America: A Nation Divided,* 2nd ed. (Oxford: Oxford University Press, 1985), pp. 151–208.
17. For the Nicaraguan fishing disputes before 1908, see PRO, London, FO 371, vols. 189, 393, 593 (collectively known as "case 614"); CO 137, numerous volumes from 631 to 653, copies of which are available at CINA; Jamaica Archives, Governors' Correspondence, 1904–08, IB/5/18; CINA, Commissioners' Correspondence, vols. 6–10, 1904–08. FO 371/189, pp. 7–9, 275–9, 307–13.
18. FO 371/189, pp. 12–15, 18–19.
19. Ibid., pp. 19–21.
20. Ibid., pp. 20–21.
21. Ibid., pp. 22–3; CINA, Commissioners' Correspondence, vol. 7 (1905), no. 76.
22. Foreign Office Memorandum, 15 November 1906, FO 371/189, pp. 324–9.
23. FO 371/393, pp. 636–7, 681–7; FO 371/593, pp. 151–65, 174–7, 190–92, 197–200, 214–19, 270.
24. In fact, the fishing dispute with the Nicaraguans between 1897 and 1908 was already complicated by the Caymanians' concern about the depredations of locals at the crucial nesting grounds at Turtle Bogue, Costa Rica, and by unsuccessful attempts to lease the area in order to protect it; FO 371/189, pp. 13-15. Disputes continued into the 1950s and 1960s. See, for example, CO 1031, vols. 144, 2663, 2822, and 3808. See also seven files from FO 371, vols. 126556, 132252, 132253, 139619, 139620, 148438, and 156328.
25. *Colonial Report 1907;* CINA, Commissioners' Correspondence, vol. 8 (1906), nos. 77, 78, 86, 109; Hirst, *Notes,* pp. 324–5.
26. Hirst, *Handbook, 1908,* pp. 27–32; *Colonial Report 1910,* pp. 15–20; Hirst, *Notes,* pp. 325–31.
27. *Colonial Report 1914–15,* p. 10.
28. The Benevolent Society for Women offered sickness benefits of ten shillings a week for a maximum of thirteen weeks, and a death benefit of £5; Hirst, *Handbook, 1908,* pp. 29–32; Hirst, *Notes,* pp. 328-30; *Colonial Report 1910,* pp. 10–11.
29. *Colonial Report 1910,* pp. 9–10; *Colonial Report 1911–12,* pp. 5-7; *Colonial Report 1912–13,* pp. 6–7; *Colonial Report 1913–14,* p. 7; *Colonial Report 1914–15,* p. 7.

30. Hirst, *Notes,* 325–31; Hirst, *Handbook, 1908,* p. 30.
31. Laid out by Arthur J. Roberts, Crewe Road was contracted out in 110-yard sections to Timothy Ebanks of West Bay, Joseph Nixon and Panton Thompson of George Town, Rodriguez Watler of Red Bay, and Edward Bennett of Spotts. The wooden bridges were constructed by Millard Russell of George Town and John Miller of North Side. The work was thus judiciously spread throughout Grand Cayman. The road was completed on 19 February 1909, at a cost of £700. A dozen bicycles were imported in 1908, and forty in 1909. Hirst, *Notes,* 327–8; *Colonial Report 1910,* pp. 15–16.
32. For complaints against Hirst as a doctor, see CINA, Commissioners' Correspondence, vol. 10 (1908), no. 1, p. 102.
33. Copy of Minutes of Meetings of Justices and Vestry, 18 August 1909, Commissioners' Correspondence, PRO, CO 857/1, fols. 5–33 (esp.15–16).
34. Hirst to Olivier, 25 October 1911, PRO, CO 137/686, Despatch 393.
35. Ibid.
36. Olivier to Harcourt, Confidential, 20 March 1912, PRO, CO 137/690.
37. Ibid.
38. Ibid.
39. Acting Governor Cork to Harcourt, Confidential, 9 May 1912 (minuted 18 June), PRO, CO 137/691. The local copy of George Hirst's death certificate, dated 17 June 1912, gave his age at last birthday as forty, and the cause of death as "hemorrhage of the stomach" and "heart failure". CINA, Death Registrations, George Town and West Bay, 1885–1923, XH/205/1–8, p. 566.
40. Hirst's thirty-four-year-old widow, Gertrude, with their daughters aged twelve and eight, was stranded. Hirst had no pension, debts almost swallowed his small insurance policies, and there was no paid passage home. Mrs. Hirst applied for a job in the Jamaican government service. But she had no formal qualifications, and even the sympathetic Governor was unable to find her a suitable post. He advised her to return to England for professional training. Gertrude Hirst to Capt. Pretyman, 15 August 1912; Olivier to Harcourt, November 1912, PRO, CO 137/ 690.
41. Hirst, *Handbook, 1908,* p. 32; Hirst, *Notes,* p. 327; *Colonial Report 1912–13,* p. 7; *Colonial Report 1913–14,* p. 7. In 1913, 166 vessels officially entered the port of George Town and 165 cleared the port. While increasingly connecting the Cayman Islands with Kingston and the other Jamaican ports, Bluefields, Nicaragua, Belize City, and the nearby Cuban ports, these were almost exclusively small sailing vessels. In March 1908, the steamship *Oteri* had hopefully begun a regular service between Kingston and George Town, but lack of local support and engine breakdowns on what was an outdated vessel led to its discontinuance within a year. During 1912, steamers of the Seeberg Line stopped at George Town on their way to Jamaica, but this service was unreliable and even more short-lived. No replacement was found until early 1914, when a contract was signed with the Williams Shipping Agency of New York for a steamship to call at George Town en route between Kingston, the Isle of Pines, and New York. But this service was scotched by the outbreak of World War One in August 1914.

42. The traffic needed was estimated at an unrealistic twenty-five messages a week, averaging ten words; CINA, Commissioners' Correspondence, vol. 9 (1907), 4 October 1907.
43. Hirst, *Notes,* p. 329. All twenty-two issues are held by CINA. G.S.S. Hirst is the only Commissioner, Administrator, or Governor buried in the Cayman Islands-in the George Town ("Dixie") cemetery.
44. Aarona Booker Kohlman, *Under Tin Roofs: Cayman in the 1920s* (George Town: Cayman Islands National Museum, 1993).

Chapter 9: A GROWING SOCIETY: POPULATION TRENDS AND SOCIAL CHANGE, 1860–1914

1. Most of the data in this chapter are derived from Jamaica Archives, Printed Works, Censuses: Census of Jamaica and Dependencies, Cayman Islands, 1881, p. 5; 1891, pp. 74–80; 1911; pp. 88–91. See also the unofficial census report for 1855 by Rev. John Aird and Rev. Adam Thompson, printed in *United Presbyterian Missionary Record,* 1 October 1855, pp. 178–81, and 1 November 1855, pp. 190-91. For the fullest and most useful contemporary account see Vaquero, *Life and Adventures,* pp. 13–36.
2. For the figures in this and the next four paragraphs, see *Colonial Reports* 1907–14.
3. The actual Jamaican population increased only from 639,000 to 831,000, an annual rate of barely 10 per thousand. But it was calculated that there had been a net emigration of as many as 43,000 Jamaicans during that period. Including these would bring the annual rate of natural increase to about 14 per thousand; Jamaica Census, 1911, p. 2.
4. George W. Roberts, *The Population of Jamaica* (Cambridge: Cambridge University Press, 1957), pp. 165–215. Kalman Tekse, *Population and Vital Statistics, Jamaica, 1832–1964: A Historical Perspective* (Kingston: Department of Statistics, 1974).
5. Higman, *Slave Populations,* pp. 303–78.
6. See above, Chapter 6, and below, Chapter 11.
7. These percentages exclude men and women under twenty who were already married. The figures for men were also inflated by excluding the married men absent at census time, lowering the married percentage by as much as 15 per cent. The same corrective factors, though, applied largely to Jamaica, validating the comparison. The present calculations are based on the estimate that 450 men (and no women) were absent at census time. In the United Kingdom, fewer than 10 per cent of people aged over twenty had never been married.
8. Roberts, *Population of Jamaica,* 287–94.
9. Edwin Beale Doran, "A Physical and Cultural Geography of the Cayman Islands" (Ph.D. diss., University of California, 1953), p. 201. A copy, together with all the original photographs, is held by CINA.
10. Ibid., pp. 193–210.
11. In contrast, the Jamaican population in 1844 consisted of 78 per cent blacks, 18 per cent coloureds, and 4 per cent whites. These percentages

had only changed to 77 per cent, 20 per cent, and 3 per cent (with 2 per cent "others") by 1911. Roberts, *Population of Jamaica,* pp. 64–70.

12. Michael Craton and Gail Saunders, *Islanders in the Stream: A History of the Bahamian People,* vol. 2, *From the Ending of Slavery to the Twenty-First Century* (Athens: University of Georgia Press, 1998), pp. 131–61.
13. Vaquero, *Life and Adventures,* p. 16.
14. Doran, "Physical and Cultural Geography," pp. 202–10.
15. Census, Cayman Islands, 1911, p. 90.
16. Vaquero, *Life and Adventures,* pp. 14–15.
17. Ibid., p. 15.
18. Cayman Islands Census, 1881, 1891, 1911.
19. For coconut farming in the Sister Islands, see above, Chapter 8.
20. Hirst, *Handbook, 1908,* p. 49.

Chapter 10: MAKING A WORLD OF THEIR OWN: CAYMANIAN LIVELIHOODS AND LIFESTYLES BEFORE WORLD WAR ONE

1. Hirst, *Handbook, 1908,* pp. 38-9. See also the extracts from interviews with Eunice McLaughlin, Ashley Godfrey, and Nettie Wood Levy, extracated in the teaching booklet *Time Was* (George Town: Cayman Islands National Archive and George Hicks High School English Department, 2000), pp. 9–18, 23–6.
2. Numerous oral history interviews in CINA describe traditional farming and the food grown by Caymanians. See, for example, James Earlie Whittaker, #1, 27 November 1990, and #2, 4 December 1990; Marvell McLaughlin, #2, 14 March 2001; Joselyn Rankine, 14 January 1992; Leon Lazzari, #1, 23 April 1997, and J. Ballanger Christian, #1 and #2, 27 October 1990. See also Eden and McLaughlin, *The Island of Grand Cayman,* pp. 2–3.
3. *Colonial Report 1908–9,* pp. 9–10.
4. See, for example, interview with Mr. W.O. Barnett, "When Barking Was an Industry," *Time Was,* pp. 27–30, based on CINA Interview with William O. Barnett, #3, 11 March 1991.
5. Eden and McLaughlin, *The Island of Grand Cayman,* p. 5.
6. Numerous interviews by CINA describe ropemaking. See especially, for example. B. Adinah Ebanks, 25 September 1990; Leticia Ebanks, 7 March 2000; R.H. (Dickie) Black, #1, 1 February 2000; and Ashley Godfrey, #1, 26 November 1990. The Cayman Islands exported 314,000 fathoms (almost two million feet) of rope in 1901–2, increasing to a remarkable peak of 661,000 fathoms in 1908–9. But this was said to have brought in no more than £256 in 1901–2, rising to a maximum of £586 in 1905–6 and actually declining to £496 in 1908–9. *Colonial Report 1905–6,* p. 8; *Colonial Report 1908–9,* pp. 7–8.
7. For Caymanian ships and shipbuilding in general, see Smith, *Maritime Heritage.* For the origins of the shallop, William A. Baker, *Sloops and Shallops* (Barre, Mass.: Barre Publishing Company, 1966), p. 111.
8. Smith, *Maritime Heritage,* p. 115.

9. Hirst, *Handbook, 1908,* pp. 47–9.
10. Smith, *Maritime Heritage,* pp. 121–2.
11. CINA Interviews with Leopold (Lee) Jervis, October 1990, #1, 26 October 1990, pp. 36–41; #2, 26 October 1990, pp. 3–6; and two additional interviews. Leopold Jervis (b. 1907) was the son of Daniel Jervis. He assisted his father with boatbuilding as well as building catboats and other small boats himself. Against some accounts Leopold Jervis denied that his father was influenced directly by Canadian models since he had never visited Canada. Other accounts note the similarities as well as the differences between the Caymanian catboat and both the New England whaleboat and the Newfoundland dory. Smith, *Maritime Heritage,* 122–8.
12. For an excellent description of the construction of the *Goldfield* by one well-known twentieth-century builder, see CINA Interview with Heber Elroy Arch, April 1983, pp. 29–34. Of many other CINA interviews that deal with boatbuilding, see also those with Captain Keith Tibbetts, #1, 25 October 1990; #3, 26 February 1991; #4, 28 August 1991; Leopold Jervis (see above, n. 11), and James Leitch, #1 and #2, 22 January 1993.
13. Smith, *Maritime Heritage,* pp. 123, 129.
14. CINA Interview with Heber Elroy Arch, April 1983, pp. 6–7.
15. The first stage in building a ship was to shape and lay the keel, which for a 75-ton turtling schooner would be seventy feet long, with a slight upward curvature ("sheer") to the fore. Even if exceptional pieces of imported timber were available, this required expert longitudinal jointing ("scarfing") and bolting of four or more segments of timber up to a foot square in cross dimension. To the finished keel were added stem and stern posts, cut with an adze or a saw; they were fixed with mortice-and-tenon joints and either tight-fitting six-inch wooden pegs called treenails, or metal bolts. The most demanding steps followed: cutting and fitting the latitudinal ribbing and the side-planking "strakes". Following the section lines of the half-model with the aid of "eye and mother wit", the builder shaped primary ribs called "floors" and fitted them to the keel at six-foot intervals. Between each of these were added two or three further "futtocks" and "half-timbers" to complete the framing shape of the hull. Then the whole rib cage was fastened and stiffened by a longitudinal timber bolted to the keel, called the keelson. Cutting and fitting the ship's planking was almost as refined an art or craft as designing and constructing the frame. Each strake had to be shaped and chamfered to fit with an even tightness or overlap, and permanently fixed with treenails, to provide a hull that ran smoothly through the water and did not bulge, give, and leak under the ocean's stress. Compared with this, fitting the stern planks, decking the vessel, and adding the other woodwork were more like a superior form of carpentry. Caulking the hull planking seams with cotton, flax, or hemp oakum and putty, and the deck planks with tar, though a specialist activity (for which the men of South Sound were noted), was also fairly routine. More complex were the stepping of the mast (done by hand by means of a "sheer-legs" crane and blocks and tackle) and the installation of the rigging and the anchoring and steering gear. Originally, mast and rigging were fitted and most other gear installed only after launching. But it became normal (and a matter of boatbuilders' pride) for

Caymanian vessels to be so well designed that even without ballast they could be relied upon to enter the water without tipping. Consequently, it became the almost invariable custom to step masts and install rigging while the boats were still on the stocks. Heber Elroy Arch points out the difficulties involved in this; ibid., pp. 29–33. Sails, which had to be made from imported canvas unless they could be salvaged intact from wrecks, were the most valuable parts of a sailboat's equipment. All mariners had to learn skill with the needle and sailcloth, and the well-patched sails of most Caymanian vessels bore evidence of their work. But especially admired were the few specialist sailmakers who could fashion sails that stood up against the ravages of salt spray and all but hurricane winds. Ibid., pp. 33–4.

16. For ship launchings, see Kohlman, *Under Tin Roofs,* pp. 96–101. CINA Interviews with Heber Elroy Arch, 4 September 1990, pp. 4–6; Leopold Jervis, # 1 and #2, 26 October 1990, pp. 27–30.
17. *Colonial Reports* 1908–10; CO 137/627, enclosure in Despatch 186, 21 March 1902.
18. Hirst, *Handbook, 1908,* pp. 68, 71; *Colonial Report 1911–12,* p. 10. See also *Colonial Report 1905–6,* p. 17; *Colonial Report 1912–13,* p. 10; *Colonial Report 1913–14,* p. 10.
19. *Colonial Report 1905–6,* p. 14; *Colonial Report 1918–19,* pp. 5–7.
20. PRO, CO 137/478, fols. 20–77.
21. Ibid., fols. 70–74.
22. PRO, CO 137/479, fols. 345–52.
23. The same William Bodden Webster so roundly criticised in 1874 was elected by the other Magistrates and Vestry and allowed by the Governor to stand as Custos between 1879 and 1888. Later, former Governor Olivier wrote in a private letter that at least one of the Caymanian Custodes had formerly been a wrecker. Olivier to Harcourt, Confidential, 20 March 1912, PRO, CO 137/690.
24. PRO, CO 137/538, fols. 32–42.
25. Ibid., fol. 36.
26. For Caribbean turtles in general, see Archie Carr, *So Excellent a Fish: The Classic Study of the Lives of Sea Turtles* (New York: Scribner's, 1967, 1984). For Caymanian turtling in general, see "Turtle" in Eden and McLaughlin, *The Island of Grand Cayman,* p. 7; F.N. Lambert, "Notes on Turtling," in Hirst, *Handbook, 1908,* pp. 59–63; Edmund Parsons, "Turtle Fishing on the Nicaraguan Coast," in Hirst, *Notes,* pp. 271–6; Smith, *Maritime Heritage,* pp. 60–69, and CINA Interviews with Captain John Hurlston, #1, 11 October 1990, pp. 22–37; Varion Ebanks, #1–4, 11 September, 12 September, 20 September 2000; L. Eddison Ebanks, #1, 2 December 1992; Arturo Bodden, 28 May 1991.
27. *Colonial Report 1905–6,* p. 8.
28. For hawksbill turtling from a Cayman Brac perspective, see, for example, the CINA Interview with Leopold Jervis, #1, 26 October 1990, CINA, pp. 30–40. For harvesting of booby eggs in the Colombian cays by mariners from the Sister Islands, see Chapter 13.
29. Smith, *Maritime Heritage,* p. 71.

30. *Colonial Report 1908–9,* p. 7. Hirst, *Notes,* pp. 271–6. When the American agents started buying at the Banks is not precisely clear from the sources – presumably some time shortly before 1904 and rapidly increasing over the following decade, as the United States increased its grip on Nicaragua.
31. Smith, *Maritime Heritage,* p. 74; Lambert, "Notes on Turtling," p. 61. Edmund Parsons, J.P., in 1910 was particularly censorious of the "truck" system of advances on credit: "On his return," he said of the turtling crewman, "he receives his account which in many instances exceeds the value of the share. Thrift and any attempt on a man's part to keep his 'head above water' are thus ruthlessly discouraged. In the turtling trade, as in many other insular industries, 'truck' is the order of the day, the labourer gradually descends while the employer gradually ascends. Among people who make such loud protestations of Christianity it is hard to understand how they make the truck system coincide with their principles." Parsons, "Turtle Fishing," p. 274.
32. CINA Interview with Captain John Hurlston, #1, 11 October 1990, pp. 27–9.
33. The most prized master's certificate, because it was the most difficult to obtain and involved the most rigorous examination, was that of the British Board of Trade, obtainable in Jamaica. Rather less prestigious, but still worthy, were those obtainable through Panama and Liberia. Least regarded were Honduran certificates, which reputedly could be bought.
34. CINA Interviews with Leopold Jervis, #1, 26 October 1990, pp. 28–9; Captain John Hurlston, #1, 11 October 1990, pp. 36–8.
35. *Colonial Report 1905–6,* pp. 7–8; *Colonial Report 1908–9,* p. 7.
36. Parsons, "Turtle Fishing," p. 272.

Chapter 11: CAYMANIAN CHURCHES AND SCHOOLING, 1846–1920

1. Waddell, *Twenty-Nine Years in the West Indies and Central Africa,* pp. 212–15. See above, Chapter 6.
2. For the best contemporary account, see *Missionary Record of the United, Secession, and Relief Churches,* February 1847, pp. 20–21. Also, see John McKerrow, *History of the Foreign Missions of the Secession and United Presbyterian Church* (Edinburgh: n.p., 1867), p. 308.
3. McKerrow, *Foreign Missions,* pp. 308–9; *Presbyterian Church in Grand Cayman, 1846–1946: Centenary Souvenir* ([Kingston: Presbyterian Church of Jamaica and Grand Cayman], 1946), pp. 9–10.
4. *Centenary Souvenir,* p. 11. Also, see Harwell (Harry) McCoy, O.B.E., B.E.M., J.P., *Journey to Partnership: A History of the Presbyterian (United) Church in Grand Cayman* (George Town: privately printed, 1998), pp. 13–15.
5. *USRC Missionary Record,* February 1847, pp. 21–6.
6. McKerrow, *Foreign Missions,* p. 309. For a more contemporary account of Elmslie's early work, see *UP Missionary Record,* March 1850, pp. 39–40.

7. McKerrow, *Foreign Missions,* pp. 309–10. See also *UP Missionary Record,* July 1851, p. 101.
8. McCoy, *Journey to Partnership,* pp. 2023; *UP Missionary Record,* July 1851, pp. 101–2; January 1859, pp. 7–8.
9. McCoy, *Journey to Partnership,* pp. 13–23; McKerrow, *Foreign Missions,* pp. 356–61.
10. *UP Missionary Record,* 1 August 1862, p. 149.
11. *UP Missionary Record,* November 1855, pp. 190–92.
12. Ibid., p. 190.
13. McKerrow, *Foreign Missions,* pp. 310–11; McCoy, *Journey to Partnership,* pp. 17–18.
14. For the 1876 and 1877 hurricanes and their effects ("By this event we have lost two elders and a good number of adherents"), see *UP Missionary Record,* 1 February 1878, pp. 32–3; and June 1878, pp. 181–2.
15. *UP Missionary Record,* 1847–1920, especially 1904, no. 4: West Indies: Jamaican Mission Council, pp. 103–4.
16. CINA, Photographic Collections: XG/CN/99/BS/C2.
17. *UP Missionary Record,* 1 September 1891[?], pp. 204–5. In other respects, too, the Caymanian presbyters seem to have tempered their expectations to conform to local tradition. They disapproved of dancing and drumming, but they were unable to stifle them completely at celebrations held on days other than the Sabbath. One survival was the popular Christmas festival called Jonkanoo, which in its original form featured African-style "gombay" drumming, masked dancers reminiscent of West African secret societies, and a central "pitchy-patchy" figure, whose name may have derived from the Ewe word for a male sorcerer, *dzonko-nu.* In slavery days, especially in Jamaica, Jonkanoo had actually been encouraged by the masters, as a way for the the slaves to safely let off steam at year's end. Jonkanoo – albeit in a mild form – survived in Grand Cayman well into the twentieth century.
18. Rev. John Smith, *UP Missionary Record,* 2 October 1876, p. 283.
19. For the persistence of obeah practices and belief in duppies, see the numerous references in CINA oral history transcripts, obtained through computer word search facilities, especially *obeah, duppies, tokens,* and *superstitions.*
20. Narrative of Rev. Andrew Baillie, Ebenezer Station, Jamaica, *UP Missionary Record,* 2 August 1869, pp. 419–22. In fact, Rev. James Elmslie at least called at Cayman Brac both going on leave and coming back in 1855 and 1856, and preached at the Sister Islands going to and from furlough in 1858.
21. Ibid., p. 419.
22. Ibid., p. 420.
23. Ibid., pp. 421–2. For Johnston, see above, Chapter 6.
24. J.P. Thompson, "A Governor's Cruise," pp. 10–11.
25. *Missionary Herald* of the Baptist Missionary Society, 1 November 1886, pp. 514–15. There is a misprint in this source regarding the date of Sobey's visit, which is noted as 1881. In fact, the Rev. Joshua Heath Sobey was an Englishman who was ministering in Helston, Cornwall, when he

was accepted by the BMS in December 1882. He arrived in Jamaica in February 1883. See *Missionary Herald,* 1 February 1883, p. 66; and 1 May 1883, p. 174. According to John Best, one of his references, shortly before leaving England Sobey had assisted the famous evangelists, Moody and Sankey, in meetings at Plymouth. Best comments: "He has a fine voice, is a good singer, and delights to praise." Sobey presumably introduced "Sankey" hymns to Cayman Brac. Application file for J.H. Sobey, BMS collections at Angus Library, Regents Park College, Oxford.

26. Rev. Charles Barron, "The Baptist Church in the Lesser Caymans," in Hirst, *Handbook, 1908,* p. 56.
27. Ibid., pp. 56–8.
28. Jamaica Census, 1911, Table 8, p. 92. In Jamaica in 1911, some 23.5 per cent of the population of 831,385 were said to be Baptists and only 6.8 per cent Presbyterians, compared with 32.1 per cent Anglicans, 11.3 per cent Methodists, 4.3 per cent Moravians, 3.0 per cent Roman Catholics, 1.6 per cent Congregationalists, 4.1 per cent other Christian denominations, and 11.5 per cent of no stated religion.
29. Rev. F. Hall, "Seventh Day Adventist Mission," in Hirst, *Handbook, 1908,* pp. 54–5; Dorothy Minchin Comm, "The First Adventist in the Caymans," *Youth's Instruction,* 24 September 1957, pp. 12–14. Commissioner George Hirst mentioned that the first group of Adventist elders who came from Central America in 1896 were thought to have brought yellow fever with them. Hirst, *Notes,* p. 295.
30. Hall, "Adventist Mission," pp. 54–5. In 1911, the Adventists were actually outnumbered by Anglicans (32) and even Wesleyans (16); Jamaica Census, 1911, Table 8, p. 92.
31. James Coe, "The Holiness Movement," in Hirst, *Handbook, 1908,* p. 55; Jamaica Census, 1911, Table 8, p. 92.
32. Coe, "The Holiness Movement," p. 55. The claim of the Holiness Movement to simple poverty and non-sectarianism divided it bitterly not just from the Presbyterian Church and its spokesmen, but increasingly within itself. The same fate was eventually to affect the Baptists of the Sister Islands, once they ceased to be a missionary offshoot of Jamaica and came under the influence of the traditionally autonomous and splintered Baptists of the United States. See below, Chapter 17.
33. Rev. Thomas Redpath, "Notes on Education," in Hirst, *Handbook, 1908,* p. 44. The Wesleyan churches promoted some schooling in the early 1840s, and a J.B. Coe was reputed to be supervising a school with a total of thirty-two children in 1844. *Methodist Missionary Society Archives* on microfiche, IDC Box 47, Fiche #2233.
34. Redpath, "Notes on Education," pp. 44–5.
35. Fyfe, *Report,* pp. 8–9.
36. Ibid., p. 8.
37. Redpath, "Notes on Education," p. 45.
38. Fyfe, *Report,* p. 9.
39. Hirst, *Handbook, 1908,* pp. 56-8; *Proceedings: Transactions of the Queensland Branch of the Royal Geographical Society of Australia* 9 (1893–4), pp. 7–11; H.C. Dixon, *Cayman Brac,* p. 27; CO 137/550, fols. 102–3.

40. *Missionary Herald,* 1 November 1886, p. 514; Hirst, *Handbook, 1908,* pp. 57–8, 71.
41. Smith, *Maritime Heritage,* p. 175; CINA Interviews with J. C. Lazzari, 23 April 1984, p. 11; Capt Charles Kirkconnell, #1, 7 March 1995, p. 10; Capt Dillon Kirkconnell, #2, 13 May 1994, pp. 27–30; Guy Banks, #2, 10 December 1992, p. 17; Capt. Keith Tibbetts, #5, 24 September 1991, p. 37; Dixon, *Cayman Brac,* p. 27.
42. See, for example, Norman Washington Manley, "My Early Years: Fragment of an Autobiography," in *Manley and the New Jamaica: Selected Speeches and Writings, 1938–1968,* ed. Rex Nettleford (London: Longman Caribbean, 1971), p. xcvii.
43. For details of endowed schools in Jamaica, see, for example, *Handbook of Jamaica, 1931* (Jamaica: Government Printing Office, 1931), pp. 288–307.
44. Ibid., pp. 284–6. George E.E. Webster, a pupil of Calabar High School, won the Jamaican Rhodes Scholarship (first awarded in 1909) in 1924.
45. Lee A. Ebanks, M.B.E., J.P., *Lest It Be Lost: Eighty Years in the Life of a Caymanian* (George Town: privately printed, 1985), pp. 26–35. See also Kenneth Pringle, *Waters of the West* (London: Allen and Unwin, 1938), pp. 16–17, for a moving account of another young Caymanian educated in Jamaica.
46. For Mico, Shortwood, and Calabar Colleges, see, for example, *Handbook of Jamaica, 1931,* pp. 275–7, 302–3.
47. "A Law to Provide for Elementary Education throughout the Island of Grand Cayman," Act No. 2 of 1902. CINA, Commissioners' Correspondence, 15 January 1902.
48. Philip E. Pedley, "The Executive Branch of Government in the Cayman Islands before 1960" (M.A. thesis, University College, London, 1990), pp. 49–50; Tamara Selzer, "Administrative History of the Board of Education, 1902–1960" (paper for Administrative History course, University College, London, 1996), pp. 5–6.
49. Redpath, "Notes on Education", p. 45; Selzer, "Board of Education," pp. 7–8; *Colonial Report 1906,* p. 17.
50. Hirst, *Notes,* pp. 326–31.
51. Jamaican Colonial Secretary R.M. Johnstone to Commissioner Hirst, 20 June 1907, CINA, Commissioners' Correspondence, AA1/9.
52. Act No. 7 of 1908 (Education Law, 1908); Selzer, "Board of Education," pp. 8–9; Pedley, "Executive Branch," p. 50; *Colonial Report 1910,* p. 19. Hirst's model syllabus, officially adopted by the Board of Education on 9 January 1911, is in PRO, CO 137/693, Despatch 367.
53. *Colonial Report 1911–12,* p. 10. For a 1911 petition requesting a free system of compulsory education, signed by hundreds, which the Commissioner reported had been "more or less favourably received in the recent Assembly", see PRO, CO 137/694, Despatch 450.
54. *Colonial Report 1912–13,* p. 11. The Blue Book for 1912–13 gave a more precise breakdown. There were only three government schools: West Bay, with 48 boys and 40 girls, and an average attendance of 41 boys and 36 girls; Prospect, with 43 boys and 27 girls, and an average attendance of 43 boys and 25 girls; and Bodden Town, with 77 boys and 67 girls, and an

average attendance of 63 boys and 57 girls. There was no government school in George Town, where 112 boys and 58 girls were in private schools. There was one small private school in Cayman Brac and none in Little Cayman; PRO, CO 651/1, Blue Book for 1912–13.

55. *Colonial Report 1912–13,* p. 11. For the delay due to the war, see PRO, CO 137/708, Despatch 48.
56. Act No. 5 of 1920, Cayman Islands Education Law 1920, passed 13 May 1920.
57. Previously, some candidates had been privately promoted through the Presbyterian Church, such as the three young women sent to Shortwood College through the auspices of Rev. Thomas Redpath of Bodden Town. The first official government candidate seems to have been Thomas A. Farrington, sent to the Mico Normal College in February 1919 with a bursary of £50 a year for two years, after successfully passing the third-year pupil-teacher examination.
58. Most notably Rev. R.N. Dickson (1919–30) and Rev. George Hicks (1936–61).
59. Blue Books, 1920, 1921, CINA AA/4/7 and AA/4/8 (in the PRO these are vols. CO 651/8 and CO 651/9). Pedley, "Executive Branch," p. 77, n. 186. In 1934, it was estimated that 82 per cent of eligible children were actually receiving an education; *Colonial Report 1934,* p. 21.
60. This point was made as early as 1923: "Some 50 pupils by taking a pupil teacher course of four years, have the benefit of secondary training." *Colonial Report 1923,* p. 6. See also *Colonial Report 1934,* pp. 20–21.

Chapter 12: CAYMANIANS ON THE MOVE: EARLY DECADES OF THE TWENTIETH CENTURY

1. The actual phrase may have originated in the title of an article by John Maloney in the 8 April 1950 *Saturday Evening Post* – "The Islands Time Forgot" – but the general idea was not new. See, for example, George Allan England, "Grand Cayman: A Onetime Pirate Island, Far at the Back of Beyond, Where it is Always Afternoon," *Saturday Evening Post,* 21 July 1928.
2. *Cayman Horizons*, May/June 1992, p. 114; *Cayman Islands A–Z Reference,* 4th ed. (George Town: Cayman Islands Public Library, 1996), under "Webster."
3. The way United States protection led to the Somoza dictatorship between 1933 and 1979 helps to explain the generally pro-Somoza sentiments of these Caymanian migrants and their descendants. For the history of Nicaragua in the twentieth century, see Woodward, *Central America,* pp. 195–200, 219–23, 259–67.
4. See above, Chapter 6.
5. Craton and Saunders, *Islanders in the Stream,* vol. 2, pp. 143–4, 218–22.
6. Thomas, *Cuba,* pp. 502–3; Leland Jenks, *Our Cuban Colony: A Study in Sugar* (New York: Vanguard Press, 1928), pp. 148–9; Charles E. Chapman, *A History of the Cuban Republic* (New York: Macmillan, 1927), pp. 157–9.

7. Thomas, *Cuba,* pp. 502–3. Much of the information here on the Isle of Pines and most of that on Jacksonville is derived from Oliver Marshall, personal communications with Michael Craton, April 1999–January 2000.
8. The plaque was erected personally by Henry Jackson, who created the "Jamaican and Caymanian Association" for the purpose. The association had no signed-up members. Oliver Marshall, personal communication, 26 November 1999.
9. Oliver Marshall, personal communication, 21 May 1999.
10. Oliver Marshall, personal communication, 2 September 1999.
11. *Compendium of Statistics,1774–1980,* pp. 42–7.
12. Ibid., Table 10:01, Births, Deaths, Marriages, and Infant Mortality Rates, 1906–65, p. 43.
13. See above, Chapter 9, compared with Cayman Islands figures from Jamaican Census 1921.
14. *Compendium of Statistics, 1774–1980,* Table 10:06, People Moving to and from Cayman Islands, 1921–79, p. 46.
15. *Colonial Report 1926,* p. 3.
16. Howard Johnson, "Late Nineteenth and Early Twentieth Century Labour Migration to Florida," in *The Bahamas in Slavery and Freedom* (Kingston: Ian Randle Press, 1991), pp. 172, 179, nn. 70, 71; Craton and Saunders, *Islanders in the Stream,* vol. 2, p. 236.
17. "Loyal Address of Cayman Islands Vestry and Magistrates," 16 September 1914, PRO, CO 137/705, Despatch 558.
18. PRO, CO 137/716, Despatch 411.
19. Circular of 15 January 1916, PRO, CO 137/716, Despatch 338.
20. The loss in revenue from sales to collectors was only partly recouped once "war tax" overprints were introduced in February 1917 – bringing in more revenue from collectors than from the tax itself. *Colonial Report 1913–14,* p. 5 ("The year under review has been the most prosperous in the annals of this island."); *Colonial Report 1914–15,* pp. 6–7. For the "War Tax" overprints, see *Stanley Gibbons Stamp Catalogue,* Part 1, p. 152.
21. 23 June 1915, PRO, CO 137/710, Despatch 282.
22. 10 November 1915, PRO, CO 137/711, Despatch 511.
23. PRO, CO 137/710, Despatch 266; Cayman Islands Blue Book, 1914–15, PRO, CO 651/3; PRO, CO 137/714, Despatch 64; CO 137/732, Despatch 368.
24. John Lee Hydrick, *Hookworm Survey of the Cayman Islands, April 18, 1917 to June 20, 1917,* no. 7297 (New York: International Health Board, 1917).
25. Twenty-two cases of typhoid were reported in 1918 (mostly in West Bay) as a consequence of the after-effects of the 1917 hurricane. But the only cases of malaria seem to have been originally contracted in the Bay Islands or at other places in Central America. 16 September 1918, PRO, CO 137/728, Despatch 443.
26. Hydrick, *Hookworm Survey,* 35–8.
27. Report by Commissioner Hutchings and Dr. Overton, 30 September 1919, PRO, CO 137/733, Despatch 544.

28. Dr. Overton might deserve some of the credit, issuing a comprehensive set of rules to prevent the spread and worst effects of influenza – though some of his preventive measures illustrated the limited contemporary understanding of the disease. CINA, Commissioners' Correspondence, 29 November 1918, AA/1/31: 858.
29. "Mrs. Elizabeth Hinson Hurlston, Cert. Hon., M.B.E. Recipient," *Caymanian Compass*, 29 June 2001, p. 3. For Hutchings' self-assessment when applying for promotion in 1914, see PRO, CO 137/703, fol. 254. He negotiated the salary up to £500, with annual increments of £25 to a ceiling of £600, along with comparable raises for other local civil servants. From then on the Hutchings family lived in reasonable comfort but unpretentiously, helped out by the fact that two of the daughters, Josephine and Dorothy, ran a small private school in George Town.
30. For data, see *Colonial Reports* 1919–34.
31. Kohlman, *Under Tin Roofs*.
32. A fascinating exception was the case of a black Caymanian named William S. Connolly, who got into trouble with the British authorities in July 1919 for speaking out against racial discrimination from a soapbox in London's Hyde Park. PRO, CO 137/736, under India Office, 15 July 1919. But it is significant that the movement led by Marcus Garvey, the Universal Negro Improvement Association, never made a foothold in Cayman as it did in every other part of the British West Indies.
33. *Colonial Report 1935*, pp. 19–20; *Colonial Report 1922*, p. 7; CINA, AA 669/22.
34. *Colonial Reports* 1922–27.
35. CINA, Commissioners' Correspondence, AA/1/553/21.
36. *Northwester*, November 1972; *Cayman Islands A–Z*, under "Cimboco."
37. Williams, *History of the Cayman Islands*, pp. 73–4, 79.
38. Craton and Saunders, *Islanders in the Stream*, vol. 2, 237–52.
39. Hutchings to Governor of Jamaica, Confidential, 19 June 1926, CINA, Commissioners' Correspondence, Central Registry File 526/26; *Colonial Reports* 1923–25.
40. Hutchings to Governor of Jamaica, Confidential, 18 August 1926, CINA, Central Registry File, 508/26.
41. *Colonial Report 1925*, p. 12.
42. PRO, CO 651/11, fol. 13.
43. Hutchings to Colonial Office, PRO, CO 137/762, Despatch 801.
44. PRO, CO 137/767, Despatch 43.
45. PRO, CO 137/772, Board of Trade to Colonial Office, 12 March 1923.
46. *Colonial Report 1924*, pp. 3–4.
47. PRO, CO 137/780, Despatch 490.
48. *Colonial Report 1926*, p. 3; *Colonial Report 1928*, p. 4. Between 1926 and 1927, efforts were made, largely in vain, to exempt the Cayman Islands from the United States quota system, or at least to separate Cayman's quota from Jamaica's. A Committee of the Assembly, chaired by W.C. Watler, on 26 October 1926 drafted a resolution to petition the U.S. Congress to that effect. Forwarded, with some trepidation, by the Commissioner on 15 November 1926, this resulted in an *aide-memoire* by

the British Embassy in Washington, dated 15 March 1927; CINA, Central Registry File 146/28.

49. For an excellent account of the 1932 hurricane – a model of the interweaving of personal testimonies with official reports, see Heather R. McLaughlin, ed., *The '32 Storm* (George Town: Cayman Islands National Archive, 1994).
50. McLaughlin, *The '32 Storm,* p. 2.
51. Ibid., pp. 2–14. For the wreck of the *Balboa,* see ibid., p. 105; *Northwester,* April 1975, p. 61.
52. McLaughlin, *The '32 Storm,* pp. 15–44.
53. Ibid., pp. 79–89.
54. Ibid., pp. 49–78, 172–3.
55. Ibid., pp. 85, 99.
56. Ibid., pp. 99–101, 155.
57. Commissioner Weston to Assembly, 30 November 1932, ibid., pp. 156–65.
58. Ibid., pp. 90–98.
59. Captain, HMS *Dragon,* to Admiral Drax, 25 November 1932, quoted in McLaughlin, *The '32 Storm,* pp. 153–6.
60. McLaughlin, *The '32 Storm,* pp. 111, 163–4.
61. *Colonial Report 1933,* pp. 3–4, 8–9. The death rate for 1932 alone was, not surprisingly, the highest ever – approximately 40 per thousand.
62. Ibid., pp. 8–9.
63. McLaughlin, *The '32 Storm,* p. 125–7.

Chapter 13: RHYTHMS OF CHANGE IN PEACE AND WAR

1. File on Cardinall's appointment, 1933–4, PRO, CO 137/799/12 (File 16494). Williams, *History of the Cayman Islands,* pp. 76–8.
2. This was despite Governor Stubbs's telegram of 21 November 1933, saying "I do not regard Cardinall suitable for Cayman Islands though he might do for Turks Island." PRO, CO 137/799/12 (File 16494).
3. Cardinall to Beckett at Colonial Office, 30 August 1938, PRO, CO 137/830/68969. For Weston's comments, see PRO, CO 137/800/15 (File 16553).
4. CINA, Central Registry Files 529, 405; CINA Central Registry File 125/34, on Cardinall's visits to all the districts.
5. For CIYSC, see *Colonial Report 1934,* p. 22; *Colonial Report 1936,* p. 16; *Colonial Report 1937,* p. 16. See also the request by the Colonial Secretary in Jamaica for the names and addresses of persons in the "educated classes in the Dependency", CINA, Central Registry File 819/35.
6. The local Scouts were incorporated by the Boy Scout Law, No. 8 of 1934. *Colonial Report 1934,* p. 22; *Colonial Report 1936,* p. 16; *Colonial Report 1937,* p. 18. Commissioner Cardinall reported in 1935 that "the boys are all born sailors, and I believe will soon put on a show which will be quite unique"; CINA, Central Registry File 890/35.
7. CINA, Central Registry File 301/34. For *Goldfield* (depicted on the obverse of the local 25-cent coin), see *Nor'wester,* April 1983, pp. 7–8.

8. Cardinall to Parsons, Winchester, 28 August 1936, Cardinall to McKee, 28 May 1937, CINA, Central Registry File 712/36. Also Cardinall to "Dear Chief", 22 October 1937, CINA, Central Registry File 454/37.
9. PRO, CO 137/828/68906.
10. Cardinall to Parsons as Secretary, Cayman Islands Chamber of Commerce, Winchester, 16 June 1936, CINA, Central Registry File 712/36. *Colonial Report 1937,* p. 14.
11. *Colonial Report 1935,* p. 14.
12. Cardinall to Parsons, 16 June 1936, CINA Central Registry Files 712/36; 320/37; *Colonial Report 1935,* pp. 13–14.
13. The peak year for shark fishing was 1935, when sharkskin exports were valued at £2,352 (compared with £4,652 worth of turtle and tortoiseshell). There were also very modest attempts at sponge fishing, sponsored by Dr. Roy McTagggart; CINA interviews with Reginald Parsons, 8 April 1992, pp. 5–7; Vassel Johnson, 30 July 1992, pp. 7–8. In 1935, 250 hundredweight of sponge was exported to Germany and the United States. None was reported for 1937. *Colonial Report 1935,* pp. 13–14; *Colonial Report 1937,* p. 13.
14. CINA Interview with Isaac Tatum, 13 April 2000, pp. 6–16. The shark industry did not last much beyond the 1930s.
15. CINA Interviews with J. Ballanger Christian, #1, 27 October 1990, pp. 14–26; Valma Hew, #2, 1 December 1997, pp. 2–27; Capt. Theophilus Bodden, #2, 8 August 1990, p. 27; Fredance Ebanks, #1, 9 June 1991, p. 15. "Egging" continued until the 1950s.
16. CINA Interviews with J. Cummings Lazzari and Eslie and Brinsley Lazzari, 23 April 1984, pp. 14–19; Eslie and Brinsley Lazzari, 21 April 1984, pp. 3–16.
17. CINA Central Registry File 183/36, "Wireless for Cayman Brac". See, e.g., fols. 116 and 140.
18. *Colonial Report 1935,* pp. 20–21; *Colonial Report 1936,* p. 17; *Colonial Report 1937,* pp. 19–20.
19. *Colonial Report 1937,* p. 21.
20. Residents of Birch Tree Hill, West Bay, to Cardinall, 7 February 1938; residents of Breezy Castle to Cardinall, 4 November 1937, CINA, Central Registry File 388/36.
21. The cost of the roadbuilding was £874, working out at £58 per mile. *Colonial Report 1935,* p. 19; *Colonial Report 1937,* p. 21. A special issue of Jubilee stamps, coinciding with the issue of the first Caymanian pictorial stamps, resulted in a record revenue for the Post Office that year of £8,694, against an expenditure of only £2,029. Fittingly, the Cayman Islands commemorated the King, who died on 20 January 1936, by erecting a clock tower in the centre of George Town in 1937.
22. For Captain Rayal Brazley Bodden Sr., M.B.E., J.P., and his works, see *Cayman Islands A–Z; Northwester,* November 1972, p. 13; March 1974, p. 6; *Nor'wester,* August 1979; October 1983; *Caymanian Compass,* 6 May 1988.
23. *Colonial Report 1934,* p. 11; *Colonial Report 1937,* p. 21. *Cayman Islands A–Z*; *Nor'wester,* August 1979, p. 6 (library); *Northwester,* December 1974, pp. 12–13 (post office).

24. *Colonial Report 1935*, p. 18.
25. Ibid.
26. Cardinall to Parsons, 25 May 1938, CINA, Central Registry File 712/36.
27. See Collections 6 and 35 (among other materials) in CINA. Two pamphlets were published in 1944 and 1946 under the auspices of a Colonial Development and Welfare grant, ostensibly on the fisheries and forestry resources of the Cayman Islands, but incidentally containing much about general economic, social, and political conditions in the islands. Ernest F. Thompson, *The Fisheries of the Cayman Islands* (Kingston: Development and Welfare in the West Indies, 1944); Christopher Swabey and Bernard C. Lewis, *Forestry in the Cayman Islands* (Kingston: Development and Welfare in the West Indies, 1946).
28. CINA, Central Registry File 706/35.
29. The re-interred remains were those of Lt. Harold Borden, RFC, who was probably the first Caymanian to fly. They were taken from Plot 3, Row B, Grave 8 of the Heath Military Cemetery, Harbonnieres, by the War Graves Commission, and sent to the Cayman Islands at a cost of 90 francs (30 shillings). CINA, Central Registry File 963/36.
30. CINA Interviews with Keith Tibbetts, #1 and #2, 25 October 1990; Elgin Scott, #1 and #2, 23 February 1998.
31. "When 40 Ebanks Went to War," *Northwester,* November 1972, pp. 46–7.
32. CINA Interviews with Keith Tibbetts, #1 and #2, 25 October 1990.
33. Ibid. The exact count of Caymanians who died on active service in World War Two is complicated by several factors. Not only were many men serving in the merchant navy rather than the formal armed services, but several died through illness rather than in action. Some also died in prisoner-of-war camps. The Seamen's Memorial at Fort George on Hog Sty Bay (which includes soldiers and airmen as well as seamen) includes many names, but these are not distinguished by war service, and many are without precise dating. There is a separate war memorial for Brackers outside the Government Administration Building at Stake Bay, Cayman Brac.
34. *Colonial Report 1946*, p. 4.
35. For the *Camayagua* sinking, see CINA Interviews with Clifton Bodden, #1, 13 May 1997; Vassel Johnson, 30 July 1992.
36. For the Home Guard, see CINA Interviews with Bob Soto, #1, 12 April 1994; Vassel Johnson, 30 July 1992; Arthur Ebanks, #3, 1 April 1993; Clifton Bodden, #1, 13 May 1997; Nolan Porter, #2, 23 April 1992; Photo Files XG/CN/152/BS. The figures for monthly pay are from the CINA Interview with Clifton Bodden, #1, 13 May 1997, pp. 6–7.
37. For the U.S. "Baldpate" Base, see CINA, Collection 16 (The George Roy Collection), MSC/1; Photo Files XG/OP/1–129/BS; CINA Interviews with John C. Mitchell, 29 March 1995; Rev. Bob Maase, 8 May 1995; Lewis Jones, #1 and #2, 28 February 1996; Madeline Brown, #1, 18 November 1996; Ella Latter, #3, 17 October 1990.
38. CINA Interview with John C. Mitchell, 29 March 1995; *Janes Encyclopedia of Aviation* (London: Janes' Publishing, 1980), pp. 259, 265, 635.

39. For the USCG, see CINA Interviews with Lewis Jones, #1 and #2, 28 February 1996.
40. This is borne out by collating the 1942–4 journal kept by Commander Roy, Commissioner Jones's correspondence, and the recorded reminiscences of American veterans and elderly Grand Caymanians. See below, n. 42.
41. CINA, Collection 16 (The George Roy Collection), MSC/1.
42. Ibid. In 1944 one officer wrote of the Baldpate base: "Esprit de corps is very hard to get. The men feel remote from the war and from naval affairs. Their work is that of day labourers." Lt. Develey to Cdr. Sedgwick, 2 September 1944, CINA, George Roy Collection. Captain Roy provided perhaps the best summary of the official point of view: "These incidents, when written or told verbally, are apt to take on a seriousness which they do not warrant. For the most part, the naval personnel are well liked by the natives. There are a few natives, as well as naval personnel, who are trouble makers. When they meet it is difficult to prevent trouble, particularly when they are under the influence of liquor. In discussions with the Commissioner we have agreed that it is almost impossible to entirely eliminate trouble when men of two nations and color are stationed. We are also agreed that it is remarkable how little trouble there has been since the establishment of the naval base on this island." Memorandum by Capt. George Roy: "Disturbances and Relations between the Naval Base Personnel and British Subjects, Grand Cayman Island, British West Indies, which happened Dec. 1943–Jan. 1944." Ibid.
43. CINA Interviews with Charles Foster, #1, 1 May 2000, pp. 24–31; Dennis Foster, 3 January 1996, pp. 11–15. According to Dennis Foster, some three hundred Grand Caymanians and Cayman Brackers were employed in these activities at their peak in the late 1940s. See also CINA Interview with Sedley Ritch, 4 March 1996, p. 20.
44. For Caymanian experiences with NBC and other shipping lines, see, for example, CINA Interviews with Rosingdell Bodden, Lemick Bryan, Brent Bush, Ulric Coe, Frank Conolly, Robert Ebanks, Paul Hurlston, Lee Jackson, Arlen McCoy, Audley Scott, Eston Scott, Isaac Tatum, Darwin Tibbetts, and Leroy Tibbetts. Also, *Northwester* series "Our Men at Sea," 1972–75.
45. Dave Martins, *A Special Son: The Biography of Ormond Panton* (George Town: Pansons Ltd., 1994), pp. 72–3.
46. Maloney, "The Islands Time Forgot," pp. 38–39, 83, 86, 89, 91; "Notes on the Cayman Islands, 1949–50," CINA, MSC/35.
47. *Colonial Report 1949–50,* p. 11.
48. *Colonial Report 1937,* p. 23; *Colonial Report 1949–50,* p. 14.
49. "Speech by Acting Commissioner A.C. Panton on Return of Men from Trinidad, August 18, 1945," CINA, Vertical File, War and Military Service File. The item is also found in CINA in an unnumbered file, TRVNR, in Box 21, Transfer 49.

Chapter 14: DECLINING DEPENDENCY: CONSTITUTIONAL, POLITICAL, AND ADMINISTRATIVE CHANGES, 1944–2000

1. For the West Indies Federation, see Sir John Mordecai, *The West Indies: The Federal Negotiations* (London: Allen and Unwin, 1968); Gordon K. Lewis, *The Growth of the Modern West Indies* (New York: Modern Reader Press, 1968), pp. 368-86; Elisabeth Wallace, *The British Caribbean: From the Decline of Colonialism to the End of Federation* (Toronto: University of Toronto Press, 1977), pp. 109–227.
2. Advisory Executive Council (E.D. Merren, W.A. McLaughlin, O.L. Panton, T.W. Farrington, W. Wood, E.O. Panton) to Secretary of State for Colonies, George Town, 7 April 1955. See also CO 1031, vols. 752, 1411, 1697, 2332–8, copies of all of which are held by CINA.
3. Confidentially, the official, summarising reports from Commissioners Smith and Gerrard, was brutally frank about the nature of the Caymanian government. "The truth of the matter is that . . . the Assembly is in the hands of an oligarchy – the white and part-white merchant families. They control by bribery and influence, the election of the 27 Vestrymen and there is little difference between the interests of those 27 and the interests of the 27 Justices. There is in theory universal adult suffrage, the law (of 1865!) stating – 'The Magistrates shall call the people together and proceed to elect the Vestrymen to serve for two years.' By custom however only male tax payers between the ages of 18 and 60 vote. Of these many of the more virile are usually away following their traditional avocation of serving as sailors on ships. So the 'barons' have their way." Confidential memo by Mr. L. Wallace, 25 August 1955, CO 1031/1411. See also the additional sources in note 2.
4. Governor Foot went on to be even blunter about Ducan Merren himself: "He is a pleasant fellow to meet but I think it can fairly be said that most of his influence in the Caymans is bad. He extorts unreasonable profits from the ordinary people, he is opposed to anything which will raise the standard of living of the poorer people (he did his best to kill the project for an elementary school in Georgetown) and we have a good deal of evidence that he will adopt almost any methods in his pursuit of private gain. He has repeatedly intrigued against the Commissioner and his rapidly increasing riches have now given him a touch of megalomania." Governor Sir Hugh Foot to Philip Rogers, Confidential, King's House, Jamaica, 17 November 1955, CSO no. 2572/S25/111, CO 1031/1697.
5. Ormond Panton did not fit the pattern of Presbyterian moral rectitude assumed by the traditional leaders in the society. From his youth he particularly resented the appointed Commissioners, both as representatives of outside authority and as the people at the pinnacle of the petty local society. However, he attributed his own failure to meld into the upper echelons of that society and his comparative lack of success in business ventures to prejudices based on his non-white Jamaican background and his litigation on behalf of ordinary Caymanians, rather than to character flaws or political miscalculation. To an outside observer, he might have

seemed a victim of that small-island syndrome that Peter J. Wilson has called "Crab Antics" – the tendency to bring down those over-ambitious or unorthodox individuals who attempt, like exceptional crabs, to escape from the barrel that encloses them all.

An undoubted Caymanian patriot, Panton was certainly also ambitious. Even before he helped to found the first effective (though short-lived) Caymanian political party in 1961, his hatred of the British and his identification with the poorer and non-white segments of the population inclined him to favour a break with Britain and a closer, though more independent, relationship with Jamaica. His many enemies maintained, however, that this position was based on a calculation that he could parlay leadership of a majority party in the Caymanian legislature into the role of the first Chief Minister or Premier of a virtually independent country. Such an eventuality, though, was scotched by external events if not by Ormond Panton's own behaviour, and the Cayman Islands were little closer to having a Chief Minister or Premier when Panton died in 1992. Martins, *Ormond Panton;* Wilson, *Crab Antics.*

6. *Caribbean and North Atlantic Territories: The Cayman Islands (Constitutional) Order in Council, 1959,* Statutory Instruments, No. 863 (Kingston, Jamaica: Government Printer, 1959); Confidential Colonial Office memo, undated [1959]: Constitutional Development: Jamaica, Cayman Islands and Turks and Caicos Islands, CO 1031/2335.
7. Ulf Hannerz, *Caymanian Politics: Structure and Style in a Changing Island Society* Stockholm: University of Stockholm, 1974), pp. 79, 90–99. Sybil I. McLaughlin, *Development of Parliamentary Government in the Cayman Islands,* Specially Prepared for the Celebration of the 150th Anniversary (George Town, 1982), p. 22.
8. CINA Transfer 14, 202/48. The CINA Interview with ex-Commissioner Ivor Smith, recorded on 27 August 1996, contains no reference to the 1948 women's petition.
9. Commissioner Gerrard to Governor Foot, 4 May 1954, CINA Transfer 68, 94/57.
10. Ibid., Foot to Gerrard, 10 May 1954; Opinion of I.H. Cruchley, Acting Attorney General of Jamaica, 28 May 1954.
11. Ibid., Commissioner Donald to Governor Blackburne, Personal and Confidential, 16 September 1958. Donald's comments on the "anti-feminists" are telling: "Those who oppose are not amenable to reason, because their grounds for opposing are personal: the present set-up allows the extremes of male society only to vote, that is, the merchants on the one hand, and the least enterprising and most feckless on the other, with a small scattering of artisans between. The second group is largely dependent on the first for credit, employment and so on, and is open to bribery. Within itself the first group is subservient to the ship-owners' whip. The merchants know that if they do not control the Assembly they will be in danger of being affected seriously by new measures of taxation, price control and so on (as indeed it is high time they were – under the present iniquitous system so far from *paying* anything for the running of the country they are able to make their own profit on the customs duty which they pass on to their customers). The large group of independent men, whose

money keeps the Islands going, is virtually disenfranchised by being at sea. Once the women are given the vote a very audible voice will be heard from this independent group, and the one that pays the piper will start calling the tune. Vested interest is worried." Merren's resolution called for at least fifteen elected Members in the new Legislative Assembly, and residence for a minimum of seven years both for electors and those elected.

12. Petitions to the Legislative Assembly of Justices and Vestry, 19 March–5 April, placed before the Assembly 29 May 1957. The seven petitions were dated as follows: Crewe Road and North Side 19 March, Gun Bay and West Bay 21 March, Bodden Town 22 March, East End 23 March, George Town 25 March. CINA Transfer 68, 94/57.
13. Ibid., Commissioner Donald's reply, 5 June. The members of the Select Committee were T.W. Farrington (Chairman), Logan Bodden, W.A. McLaughlin, E.D. Merren, H.M. Coe, O.L. Panton, O.G. Hurlston, and Lincoln Bodden. The nominators for Mrs. Watler were Thomas A. Hurlston, Charles Hislop, S.H. Coe, Pat Henderson, T.B. Bodden, A.H. Godfrey, Allen Whittaker, Ralph Lott, Conrad Forbes, and James Arch Jr.
14. Ibid., Blackburne to Donald, 10 September 1958; Acting Chief Secretary, Jamaica, to Donald, Airmail, 20 September 1958; Donald to Select Committee, 6 October 1958. Jamaican Sexual Discrimination (Removal) Ordinance, 24 June 1950.
15. Ibid., Donald to Select Committee, 14 October 1958; Donald to Chief Secretary, Jamaica 14 October 1958; Select Committee to President and Members of the Legislative Assembly, 16 October 1958.
16. Law to Remove Discrimination on Grounds of Sex or Marriage, Number 2 of 1959, consented to by Governor Blackburne, 5 February 1959. Rather curiously, neither the Act of 5 February 1959 nor the Order in Council of 13 May 1959 specifically grants rights to women, though it is implied in both. Consequently, the crucial document may be said to be the Select Committee's 16 October 1958 handwritten acceptance of the 358 women's 1957 petition, which did specify both the right to vote and the right to be elected to public office.
17. Martins, *Ormond Panton,* pp. 103–17.
18. Sybil McLaughlin, *Parliamentary Government,* p. 26, quoting Jamaica *Daily Gleaner,* 12 July 1961; CO 1031/3244.
19. Martins, *Ormond Panton,* pp. 116–30. Hannerz, *Caymanian Politics,* pp. 57–72.
20. See CINA Interviews with Sybil McLaughlin, February 1993, and Jack Rose, May 1999.
21. CINA Interviews with Capt. Keith Tibbetts, #3, pp. 10–14; Nolan Foster, #2, pp. 15-18; Alan Ebanks, "Captain Keith: A Living Brac Legend," *Newstar,* June 1991, pp. 29–32.
22. Martins, *Ormond Panton,* pp. 131–50.
23. Ibid., p. 135. Governor Blackburne to Colonial Office, Personal and Confidential, King's House, Jamaica, 22 January 1962, enclosing Address by the Governor at Public Meeting in the Cayman Islands, 19 January 1962, CO 1031/3244; McLaughlin, *Parliamentary Government,* p. 28.
24. Blackburne to Colonial Office, 22 January 1962, Address, CO 1031/3244.

25. Confidential *Aide-Memoire*: "Further Relations Between Her Majesty's Government in Jamaica and the Governments of the Cayman Islands and the Turks and Caicos Islands." October 1962, CO 1031/3392.
26. *Cayman Islands. Proposals for Constitutional Advance: Report of the Constitutional Commissioner, the Rt. Hon. The Earl of Oxford and Asquith, KCMG,* Foreign and Commonwealth Office (London: HMSO, 1971), p. 7.
27. For the 1962 General Election, see McLaughlin, *Parliamentary Government,* p. 28; Hannerz, *Caymanian Politics,* pp. 76–99; Martins, *Ormond Panton,* pp. 136–47.
28. Hannerz, *Caymanian Politics,* pp. 99-108, 167–84.
29. Asquith Report, pp. 9-13.
30. *Cayman Islands 1997: Annual Report & Official Handbook* (George Town: Government of the Cayman Islands, 1998), pp. 62–7.
31. *Cayman Islands: Report of the Constitutional Commissioners 1991, Sir Frederick Smith, Mr. Walter Wallace* (London: HMSO), Cm 1547, May 1991.
32. *Annual Report & Handbook 1997,* p. 58.
33. Pedley, "Executive Branch," p. 57–8.
34. *Annual Report & Handbook 1997,* pp. 69–75.
35. Ibid., pp. 7, 93.
36. Elizabeth W. Davies, *The Legal System of the Cayman Islands* (Oxford: Law Reports International, 1989), pp. 66–73.
37. Ibid., p. 72.
38. *Colonial Report 1957–8,* p. 28.
39. Davies, *Legal System of the Cayman Islands,* p. 74.
40. *Annual Report & Handbook 1997,* pp. 93–5.
41. Ibid., p. 94.
42. *Annual Report 1990,* p. 112.
43. *Annual Report & Handbook 1997,* pp. 97–8; *Annual Report 1999,* pp. 23, 89.
44. *Annual Report & Handbook 1997,* p. 222.

Chapter 15: THE ENGINEERED MIRACLE: ECONOMIC DEVELOPMENT, 1950–2000

1. *Cayman Horizons,* March/April 1992, 90–92. For a useful chronology of the development of Caymanian aviation, see *Cayman Islands: Economic Development Plan, 1986–90* (George Town: Government of the Cayman Islands, 1986), pp. 49–54.
2. *Colonial Report 1951–2,* pp. 3–4.
3. *Colonial Report 1953–4,* pp. 3–4. "Cayman's Airline Pioneer," *Northwester,* October 1971, pp. 6–9.
4. *Colonial Report 1953–4,* p. 3–4.
5. Ibid.
6. Ibid., 7.
7. *Colonial Report 1955–6,* pp. 4–5.

8. *Colonial Report 1957–8,* pp. 5–6. The airstrip at the southwest end of Little Cayman was built at the instigation of Logan Robertson, the American owner-operator of the Southern Cross Club, on land owned by residents of Little Cayman and levelled by local labourers. Whereas the other two airports were named after the air pioneer and two Commissioners respectively, Robertson named the Little Cayman airfield after Edward Bodden, the local foreman of works. The government's plans to relocate and enlarge the Little Cayman airport generated controversy between pro-development forces and conservationists in the late 1990s.
9. *Cayman Horizons,* January/February 1994, p. 106.
10. Daniel Tibbetts, personal communication with Philip Pedley, 24 April 2002 (in regard to Trans-Island Airways, Red Carpet Airlines, and Executive Air Services), Mervin Cumber and Capt. Tom Guyton, personal communication with Philip Pedley, 7 May 2002 (in regard to Island Air); CINA Interview with Ulric Coe, #2, 7 August 1998, pp. 5–6.
11. The exact figures in 1997 were 21,916 aircraft movements and 947,204 passengers. *Compendium of Statistics, 1774–1980,* pp. 68–9; *Annual Report & Handbook 1997,* pp. 261–2.
12. *Colonial Report 1971,* p. 4.
13. "The Man Who Changed the Face of Cayman," *Statue Memorial Programme* (George Town, 1994). *Cayman Horizons,* March/April 1996, p. 44.
14. *Annual Report 1986,* 25–6.
15. *Annual Report & Handbook 1997,* pp. 261–2.
16. Manton and Hart Law Firm Papers, Jamaica Archives, IB/4/82; Tamara Selzer, "History of Land Registration," p. 49, App. 7.
17. *Colonial Report 1951–2,* p. 16; *Colonial Report 1955–6,* pp. 17–18.
18. Cayman Islands Law No. 16 of 1960; Selzer, "History of Land Registration," p. 21. *Colonial Report 1961–5,* p. 17.
19. *Colonial Report 1966–70,* pp. 3–4. Law to Control the Development and Use of Land . . . pending the Introduction of Comprehensive Planning Legislation, No. 2 of 1959 (17 April 1969). This replaced the Jamaican Regional Planning Law of 1934 (Cap 147), which had nominally set up a regional Planning Board and which had allowed Commissioners Smith, Donald, Rose, and Cumber to make piecemeal zoning regulations in and around George Town in 1951, 1960, and 1967. The new law was much more general, had more regulations (including the control of advertisement hoardings), and required formal permission for any changes. See Regulations, Rules, and Orders of the Cayman Islands, 1967.
20. *Colonial Report 1966–70,* pp. 3–4.
21. Land Adjudication Law, No. 20 of 1971; Registered Land Law, No. 21 of 1971; Land Surveyors' Law, No. 22 of 1971. For Long's speech, *The Caymanian Weekly,* 25 March 1971, Insert, p. 4.
22. *Caymanian Weekly,* 25 March 1971, pp. 1–2, 14, 20. Caymanian Protection Law, No. 23 of 1971, "A Law to consolidate the law affecting persons who do not belong to the Cayman Islands, whereby control is exercised over the entry, residence, engagement in gainful occupation, removal and deportation of such persons, and to make provision with respect to the acquisition and enjoyment by persons who belong to these

islands, of Caymanian status." See above, Chapter 9. Local Companies (Control) Law, No. 24 of 1971, "A Law to prohibit save under licence the carrying on in the Cayman Islands of local businesses by companies which are not under Cayman control." The Trade and Business Licensing Law, No. 25 of 1971. *Colonial Report 1973,* p. 3.

23. *Colonial Report 1973,* p. 3.
24. *Caymanian Weekly,* 13 May 1971, pp. 1, 12.
25. "Answering the 'Who Owns What?' Conundrum," *Northwester,* November 1972, pp. 18–19.
26. "Cadastral Survey Continues Under Heavy Fire," *Northwester,* March 1973, pp. 13–14. John Redman, "Cadastral Survey," *Northwester,* February 1975, pp. 73–6.
27. *Annual Report 1977,* Pt. 4, Chap. 3, Lands and Surveys, pp. 29–33. An aerial survey had been undertaken in 1958, but solely for mapping purposes; *Colonial Report 1957–8,* p. 6.
28. *Annual Report 1977,* p. 30.
29. Yellow fever is carried by *Aedes aegypti* and malaria by *Anopheles* mosquitoes. The swamp and pastureland species (*Culex* spp. and *Aedes taeniorhyncus*) are annoying but not particularly dangerous. Colonial Development and Welfare Grant no. D1213; *Annual Report 1949–50,* p. 5; *Northwester,* June 1975.
30. *Colonial Report 1955–6,* p. 6.
31. "The MRCU Story, Part I," *Northwester,* June 1975, pp. 6–21.
32. Dr. W. Petrie, Director of MRCU, personal communication with Philip Pedley, 24 April 2002.
33. "The MRCU Story, Part II," *Northwester,* July 1975, pp. 27–37; *National Geographic,* June 1985, pp. 818–20.
34. *Annual Report & Handbook 1997,* pp. 246–8.
35. *Cayman Islands Yearbook & Business Directory 1993,* pp. 418–20.
36. In the mid-1990s Grand Cayman had a minor outbreak of dengue fever and two cases of what was said to be indigenously acquired malaria. As a result, a dedicated campaign was undertaken to eliminate any remaining *Anopheles* and *Aedes aegypti* mosquitoes. A similar fate awaited the potentially dangerous Asian tiger mosquito, which made a brief appearance in 1997. *Annual Report & Handbook 1997,* p. 246.
37. *Colonial Report 1946,* p. 5.
38. *Annual Report 1951–2,* p. 5; Michael Craton and Gail Saunders, *Islanders in the Stream,* vol. 2, pp. 302–3, nn. 65, 524.
39. Hotels Aid Law, No. 5 of 1950.
40. *Colonial Report 1955–6,* p. 5.
41. *Colonial Reports 1957–8,* p. 6; *1959–60,* p. 21.
42. *Colonial Report 1959–60,* p. 20.
43. Ibid.; "Tourism: The Problems of Success" and "Mr. Warren: The Hon. W.W. Conolly, Member for Tourism," *Northwester,* May 1974, pp. 5–14. Bob Soto started a small dive centre at the Pageant Beach Hotel in 1957. His operation really took off when he moved to the new Holiday Inn in 1972. Nancy Sefton, "Bob Soto: A Life on the Ocean," *Newstar,* April 1994, pp. 6–8; *Key to Cayman,* Spring 1996, pp. 194–5. See also CINA Interviews with Bob Soto, #1 and #2, 12 April 1994.

44. "Eric Bergstrom Named Director of Tourism," *Northwester,* September 1973, p. 29.
45. The Port Authority Law, Law 15 of 1976.
46. *Colonial Report 1972,* p. 5; Cayman Islands Statistical Abstract, 1981; *Compendium of Statistics, 1774–1980,* Table 13:02, Availability of Tourist Accommodation, 1970–79, p. 56.
47. *Annual Report 1978,* pp. 36–7.
48. Cayman Islands Travelers' Road & Dive Map (George Town: Cayman Islands Department of Tourism and AT&T, 1997).
49. *Compendium of Statistics, 1774–1980,* Table 13:05, Tourists Arriving by Cruise Ship, 1969–79; Table 13:06, Tourists Arriving by Air, by Months, 1970–79, p. 58.
50. *Annual Report & Handbook 1997,* Appendices, Port Statistics, 1993–6, p. 301; Air Traffic, 1995–6, p. 303; Tourism Statistics, 1992–7, p. 305. *1997 Cayman Islands Compendium of Statistics* (George Town: Economics and Statistics Office, 1998), Table 14:02, p. 104.
51. The ratio for the Bahamas was about 12:1, for Bermuda 7:1, for Barbados 2:1, and for Jamaica roughly 1:1.
52. *1997 Compendium of Statistics,* Tables 14:03, 14:04, pp. 106–7.
53. Ibid., Table 14:07, p. 110. The Tourism Department estimated that the average daily expenditure in 1997 of the 381,000 airborne visitors, who stayed an average of 7.3 days, was CI$147 – of which $60 was for accommodation, $35 for food, $14 for transport and tours, $19 for entertainment and watersports, and $19 for shopping – for a total of CI$409 million. The 649,000 cruise-ship passengers, who stayed less than a day, were estimated to spend on average $60, for a total of some $39 million. The amount generated by non-Caymanian long-term residents is incalculable, but would have pushed the grand total well over the half-billion mark.
54. According to the *Northwester,* June 1974, "Rumour and legend have suggested that the merchants of George Town told Barclays that if the bank wanted their accounts, Barclays must not employ Caymanians. No doubt they were worried that news of their affairs would leak out and become public knowledge." Barclays, however, sidestepped this in December 1955 by posting to George Town the Caymanian Benson Ebanks Jr., who was already employed in their Kingston office. It was Benson Ebanks who was appointed the first sub-manager at Cayman Brac. The Cayman Brac branch of Barclays DCO was closed in 1999, despite local protests. *Northwester,* June 1974, pp. 6–13; Benson Ebanks, personal interview by Michael Craton, December 1999. (But see also the CINA Interviews with Benson Ebanks in 1997.)
55. *Cayman Executive,* no. 5 (1994), pp. 52–9, 78; *Cayman Islands A–Z,* under "Johnson, Vassel"; CINA interview with Vassel Johnson, July 1992; *Northwester,* July 1974, pp. 42–4.
56. *Caymanian Compass,* 5 January 1994, pp. 3–5.
57. Sir Vassel Johnson and Benson Ebanks, personal interviews by Michael Craton, December 1999. In 2001 Sir Vassel Johnson published his autobiography, which combines the story of his own life with the development of the financial industry and Cayman's general development from the

1960s to the 1980s. Sir Vassel Johnson, *As I See It: How Cayman Became a Leading Financial Centre* (Sussex: The Book Guild, 2001).

58. *Colonial Report 1966–70,* pp. 44–5.
59. *Annual Report & Handbook 1997,* p. 252.
60. Ibid.
61. *Colonial Report 1966–70,* p. 15.
62. Craton and Saunders, *Islanders in the Stream,* vol. 2, pp. 355–62.
63. Confidential Relationships Law, No. 16 of 1976, 20 April 1976.
64. *Annual Report & Handbook 1997,* p. 141.
65. *Annual Report 1986,* p. 5; *Annual Report & Handbook 1997,* pp. 123–6.
66. *Colonial Report 1972,* pp. 14–15; *Annual Report & Handbook 1997,* pp. 123–5, 305.
67. *Colonial Report 1975,* p. 19.
68. *Annual Report & Handbook 1997,* p. 118.
69. *Annual Report 1986,* p. 4–8.
70. *Annual Report & Handbook 1997,* pp. 35–7.
71. *Yearbook & Business Directory 1999/2000,* pp. 355–7.
72. Ibid.
73. *Annual Report & Handbook 1997,* pp. 113–28.
74. Ibid., p. 127.
75. Ibid., pp. 128; "Wall Street, Cayman Style," *Yearbook & Business Directory 1999/2000,* pp. 252–5.

Chapter 16: CHANGE AND ADJUSTMENT: POPULATION CHANGES AND IMMIGRATION, 1950–2000

1. *Compendium of Statistics, 1774–1980,* Tables 10.03, Censuses of Population, 1773–1979; and 10.05, Estimates of Population, Selected Years, 1931–79, pp. 44–5.
2. *Report of the Cayman Islands 1999 Population & Housing Census* (George Town: Government of the Cayman Islands, 2001), Table 2, p. 12.
3. Ibid. Even in West Bay there was a noticeable proportional decline from 27.8 to 20.9 per cent of the total population, though the actual population of the district almost quadrupled, from 2,370 to 8,243, between 1960 and 1999.
4. *Report of the Cayman Islands 1999 Census*, Tables 7, 8, pp. 20–21; *Cayman Islands 1989 Census: Commentary and Tabulation of Results*, vol. 1 (George Town: Government Statistics Office, 1992), Table 2:1, pp. 54–72.
5. *Report of the Cayman Islands 1999 Census*, Tables 7, 8, 9, pp. 20–25.
6. *Report of the Cayman Islands 1999 Census,* Table 5, p. 18.
7. *Cayman Islands 1989 Census*, Table 2:2, pp. 73-88. Unlike the 1999 Census Report (which used the less revealing cohorts 0–14, 15–29, 30–49, 50–64, and 65+), that of 1989 divided the population into much more useful five-year cohorts. The 1989 Census Report also very usefully divided the population and workforce by country of origin, which that of 1999 did not.
8. *Cayman Islands 1989 Census*, Table 2:2, pp. 73–88.

9. Ibid., Tables 26, 27, pp. 51–3.
10. Ibid.
11. Ibid.; *Cayman Islands 1989 Census*, Table 4:5, pp. 139–41.
12. *Cayman Islands 1989 Census*, Table 2:3, p. 89.
13. Immigration of Paupers (Prevention) Law, No. 5 of 1916, 24 November 1916. This law authorised the Commissioner in Grand Cayman and the Collector in Cayman Brac to deny entry to any person "not a native of or domiciled in these Islands" who could not "produce and show" the sum of five pounds, who was "unable by reason of physical or mental infirmity to maintain himself", or who was "likely, if permitted to land, to become chargeable to the funds provided for the relief of the poor".
14. Regulation of Immigration Law, No. 3 of 1934, 24 January 1934.
15. Aliens Law, No. 8 of 1961, Jamaica cap. 3.
16. Caymanian Protection Law, No. 23 of 1971: "Memorandum of Objects and Reasons. By reason of the tax advantages afforded to many people taking up residence in the Cayman Islands, and the unprecedented prosperity of the tourist industry, there has arisen a grave risk that the social character of the Islands as well as the way of life of the population may be adversely affected by the influx of private and business settlers, and other consequential factors. It is sought to enact legislation calculated to control this situation by affording means of protecting the traditional way of life of the Islanders by cushioning the impact of the establishment of international business interests and the settlement here of people who formerly had no interest in the public and private affairs of these Islands. It is also sought to take advantage of the opportunity to consolidate and bring up to date the law affecting immigration and deportation."
17. Ibid., Part III. Caymanian Status, pp. 13–18.
18. Ibid., Part V. Immigration, Nos. 40, 43, pp. 23, 25.
19. Ibid., Part IV. Gainful Occupation of Persons of Non-Caymanian Status, pp. 18–20.
20. *Annual Report 1992*, p. 134.
21. The Caymanian Protection Law 1984, Section 27 (1) and 72 (3). Directives to the Caymanian Protection Board: Grant and Renewal of Gainful Occupation Licences, August 1987; John Bostock, former Chief Immigration Officer, personal communication with Michael Craton, October 1999. *Annual Report & Handbook 1998*, p. 283.
22. See especially Dave Martins, "Foreign/Local Business Combination," *Newstar*, April 1993, pp. 18–22; "The Local/Expat Issue," *Newstar*, May 1993, pp. 28–9; "The Immigration Tangle," *Newstar*, November 1993, pp. 6–7; "The Expatriate Question," *Newstar*, March 1995, pp. 10–18.
23. Bill Schiller, "The Other Side of Prosperity," *Newstar*, September 1989, pp. 13–18.
24. CINA Interview with Oswell Rankine (then District Commissioner), #1, 28 October 1997, 23; CINA Interview with Audley Scott (then Deputy District Commissioner), #3, 5 March 1996.
25. "Waiting for Freedom: The Cuban Quest for a New Life," *Newstar*, February 1995, pp. 8–21; Omar Lorenzo, *Forbidden Reflections: The True Story of Tent City* (George Town: Casa de Cultura, 1997).
26. Lorenzo, *Forbidden Reflections*, pp. 63–96.

Chapter 17: SOCIAL DEVELOPMENT: EDUCATION, HEALTH, THE CHURCHES, AND THE MEDIA, 1950–2000

1. Alan Ebanks, "Helping the Needy," *Newstar,* September 1989, pp. 19–20; *Annual Report 1983,* p. 73; C.I. Government Estimates of Expenditure and Revenue for the year 1964, p. 62; for the year 1985, p. 103; for the year 2001, p. 85; *Annual Report 2000,* pp. 127–32.
2. *Annual Report & Handbook 1998,* pp. 147–57; *Economic and Development Plan, 1986–90,* pp. 143–4.
3. *Annual Report & Handbook 1998,* pp. 157–72.
4. "Cayman Disease: New Strain Revealed in Genetic Study of In-breeding Problems," *Nor'wester,* July 1977, pp. 33–4; "Second Cayman Disease Found: Genetics Study Confirms High Incidence of Problems," *Nor'wester,* April 1978, pp. 31–2. In the 1943 census, seventeen cases of congenital blindness and twenty-seven of deaf-mutism were recorded.
5. Mrs. Janet Hislop (former head of the genetic counselling service), personal communication with Philip Pedley, 17 February 2002. The Lighthouse School opened, with twenty pupils, on 26 March 1976. It was later taken over by the government and its scope for dealing with the handicapped greatly expanded. In 2000 its enrollment was fifty-six. Handicapped adults were cared for in a separate facility called the Sunrise Training Centre. CINA Interview with Ms. Mary Woodward, 1991; Mary E. Woodward, *The Lighthouse* (George Town: The Ecclesiastical Corporation, 1997).
6. *Annual Report 1949–50,* p. 20.
7. *Annual Report 1959–60,* p. 22; *Annual Report 1979,* p. 37; *Annual Report & Handbook 1998,* pp. 89–91. The first Caymanian trained as a dentist was Dr. Roy McTaggart.
8. *Annual Report 1946,* pp. 18–20.
9. *Annual Report 1955–6,* pp. 22–4.
10. *Annual Report 1979,* pp. 37–8.
11. *Annual Report 1987,* p. 70; *Annual Report & Handbook 1997,* p. 189. The Lions programme culminated in the construction of the Lions Eye Centre, which was opened in 1992 and operated thereafter by government. The club also sponsored a dental hygiene programme in schools.
12. Mary Lawrence, "Brac Rest Home Is a Family Affair", *Nor'wester,* August 1979, pp. 38–41. The Kirkconnell Community Care Centre was the successor to the original rest home established by private donation in 1974 and run by volunteers from local Baptist churches during in the 1970s and 1980s.
13. *Annual Report & Handbook 1998,* pp. 87–96.
14. Timothy ("Teacher") McField, "A Brief History of Education in the Cayman Islands" (Paper for Caribbean Studies III course, University of the West Indies, 1969), pp. 14–25 (available at CINA); *Annual Report 1946,* pp. 17–18; *Annual Report 1959–60,* pp. 21–2.
15. Of the 5,614 persons over the age of seven in 1943, 4,890 could read and write, 197 could read but not write, and 527 were illiterate (277 males and 250 females). Of the 5,142 persons over the age of ten, 394 had never attended school, 734 had only a lower elementary, 1,680 middle elemen-

tary, and 2,201 upper elementary education. 1943 Census, Tables 361, 362, 364, pp. 446–7.

16. McField, "Brief History of Education," p. 22.
17. Alan Ebanks, "Triple C: A Half-Century of Excellence in Education," *Newstar,* December 1991, pp. 29–33. Whether a school receiving government aid could suspend students for bad behaviour or for non-attainment became a public issue in mid-2000. See, for example, "Academic Probation Policy at Triple C School," and covering letter from Director Marjorie Ebanks, *Cayman Net News,* 27 July–2 August 2000, p. 11.
18. McCoy, *Journey to Partnership,* pp. 38–42.
19. Islay Conolly, "A Brief History of Education in the Cayman Islands," in *Cayman Islands: 100 Years of Public Education, 1887–1987* (Grand Cayman: [Cayman Islands Government], 1987), pp. 31–4; *A History of the Development of Education in the Cayman Islands* (Paper for a Diploma in School Management, International College of the Cayman Islands, 1981), pp. 11–12 (both available at CINA).
20. Conolly, "Brief History," p. 34; *History of the Development of Education,* p. 12.
21. *Annual Report 1966–70,* pp. 25–6; Conolly, "Brief History," p. 32; *History of the Development of Education,* pp. 13–14.
22. *Annual Report 1979,* pp. 39–40.
23. *Annual Report 1982,* pp. 27–31.
24. Ibid. See above, Chapter 15.
25. Will Pineau, "Breaking All the Rules," *Newstar*, March 1988, pp. 10–13; "Teachers in Despair," *Newstar*, November 1988, pp. 12–15.
26. Dave Martins, "CXC: Here to Stay," *Newstar,* November 1994, pp. 6–8. In 1998, 122 students were receiving government funding for tertiary education, of whom about 40 were studying abroad; *Annual Report 1998,* p. 144.
27. *Annual Report & Handbook 1998,* p. 136.
28. *Annual Report 1995,* pp. 82–3; *Annual Report & Handbook 1997,* p. 217; *Annual Report & Handbook 1998,* pp. 137, 144–5. Ms. Mary Rodrigues, Chief Inspector of Schools, personal communication with Philip Pedley, February 2002.
29. *Annual Report & Handbook 1997,* p. 218; *Annual Report & Handbook 1998,* pp. 137–9.
30. McCoy, *Journey to Partnership*, pp. 46–67; "Inaugural Synod, December 13th, 1992, Souvenir Magazine," The United Church in Jamaica and the Cayman Islands (Kingston: The Herald Ltd., 1992), pp. 4–6.
31. "Inaugural Synod," pp. 2–3.
32. Ibid., p. 7; Mr. Michael Bowerman (elder and lay preacher at Elmslie United Church), personal communication with Philip Pedley, 16 February 2002.
33. Sykes, *The Dependency Question,* pp. 15–18, 89–94.
34. *The History of the Anglican Church in the Cayman Islands* (Grand Cayman, ca. 1995), [p. 6 (not paginated)].
35. Sykes, *The Dependency Question,* pp. 89–91.
36. Ibid., pp. 88, 90.

37. *New Caymanian,* 4–10 October 1991.
38. CINA Interviews with Monsignor John Meany, #1 and #2, 26 April 1997; *St. Ignatius School* 25th *Anniversary Booklet,* 1996. In July 2000 the Cayman Islands were switched from the jurisdiction of the Archbishop of Jamaica to that of the Archbishop of Detroit, indicating a closer link to North America than to the Caribbean. *Caymanian Compass,* 4 July 2000, pp. 1–2.
39. See above, Chapter 11.
40. See, for example, Ebanks, *Cayman Emerges.*
41. *The Gospel of the Kingdom* carried the admirable subtitle *A Friendly Christian Paper, for the encouragement of the oneness of God's people regardless of race, colour, or creed.* It had first been published in Kentucky in 1913 and survived there and elsewhere in the United States until 1931. Bro. Will T. Bodden, *A Brief History of the Church of God in the Bay Islands of Honduras and the Cayman Islands* (George Town: Will T. Bodden, 1990).
42. *Newstar,* March 1988, p. 16; Hirst, *Notes,* p. 329. All twenty-two issues of *The Caymanian* are held by CINA.
43. *Caymanian Compass,* 20 June 1974, editorial; 4 May 1976, p. 1; Brian Uzzell, publisher, personal communication with Philip Pedley, July 2001.
44. The *Compass,* owned by the Cayman Free Press, survived the competition through astute management and with the profits from a range of auxiliary publications and other printing business. Besides *Tradewinds,* it outlasted the *Cayman Times* (1979–82), *Caymanian Pilot* (1984), and the *New Caymanian* (1990–2). The excellent news magazines *Northwester* (1971–84) and *Newstar* (1987–94) have been succeeded but not replaced by a range of more business- and tourism-oriented magazines, such as *Cayman Executive, Cayman Shopper, Cayman Tourist Weekly, Key to Cayman,* and Cayman Airways' *Cayman Horizons.*
45. *Annual Report 1982,* p. 68; *Annual Report 1987,* pp. 102–3; *Annual Report 1990,* pp. 151–3; *Annual Report 1994,* pp. 303–6; *Annual Report 1995,* pp. 245–6; *Annual Report & Handbook 1997,* p. 208.
46. *Annual Report 1994,* pp. 303–6; *Annual Report & Handbook 1997,* pp. 207–8.

Chapter 18: A CAYMANIAN NATION: OUT OF THE PAST AND INTO THE FUTURE

1. The Marine Conservation Law, 1978, No. 19 of 1978; The National Trust for the Cayman Islands, 1987, No. 22 of 1987.
2. *Annual Report 1994,* pp. 7–11; Programme: Official Opening of Queen Elizabeth II Botanic Park, 27 February 1994 (George Town, 1994). The park itself is owned and operated by government, and the land belongs to the Trust; *Annual Report & Handbook 1997,* pp. 239–41.
3. *Yearbook & Business Directory 1997,* p. 300.
4. *Caymanian Compass,* October-November 1999.

5. Peggy Fosdick and Sam Fosdick, *Last Chance Lost? Can and Should Farming Save the Green Sea Turtle? The Story of Mariculture Ltd. Cayman Turtle Farm* (York, Penn.: Irwin Naylor, 1994), pp. 1–53.
6. Ibid., pp. 54–338.
7. Turtle Farm: Cultivating Cayman's History. [Cayman Islands Turtle Farm pamphlet, ca. 1999].
8. In 1899, the first Commissioner, Frederick Sanguinetti, designed a coat of arms for the Cayman Islands. It featured a silver thatch palm and a schooner, and had the Latin motto *terra marique,* "by land and sea"). But he was firmly told that Cayman would continue to use the Jamaican insignia. See CO 137/603 (Despatch of August 1899). Sixty years later, Commissioner Alan Donald was strongly behind the project. James Ford was advised by a Rev. Saunders, a Jamaican overseas member of the English College of Heraldry. The warrant for the coat of arms was signed by Queen Elizabeth II on 14 May 1958 and inscribed in the records of the College of Arms in London. CO 137/603, Despatch 488, 25 August 1899, Flag for Caymans; *Annual Report 1957–8,* pp. 7–8; CINA, Vertical File, "Ensign."
9. Interestingly, the Jamaican coat of arms, with its five pineapples in the centre of the shield, is surmounted by an alligator or cayman. On the two sides of the shield are a male and a female Amerindian, not slaves. This coat of arms was rejected by the Jamaicans at the time of Independence (1962). For national symbols, see *Annual Report 1996*, pp. 1824. For national song, see The Cayman Islands Coat of Arms, Flag and National Song Law, 1993.
10. A typical example was the Kirkconnell clan, whose history has been well described in "Kirkconnell Brothers Limited: A Century of Service," *Cayman Executive* (3rd Quarter 1996), pp. 41–62; "Kirk Celebrates 100 Years of Service," *Cayman Islands Yearbook 1996*, pp. 35–44; "Kirkconnell Family," CINA, Autobiography and General, Vertical Files. An equally remarkable Bracker success story has been that of Linton Tibbetts, multimillionaire owner of Cox Lumber Co. in Tampa and the Cayman Islands and a founding father of modern Little Cayman: "Linton Tibbetts: Cayman's Most Successful Businessman Ever," *Cayman Executive* (4th Quarter 1993), pp. 58–68, 105–9.
11. John Redman, "Oil Transfer Deal Signed; $3m. a Year Prospect", *Nor'wester,* April 1977, p. 6; Beverly Tatum, "Cayman Energy Adds New Services", *The Bracker and Little Caymanian* (supplement to *Nor'wester*), May 1982, pp. 5–6; "Cayman Energy Expands, *Bracker and Little Caymanian,* Nov–Dec 1982, p. 12; *Annual Report 1980,* p. 25; Johnson, *As I See It,* pp. 202–5. Mr. Thomas Jefferson (Financial Secretary in the 1980s), personal communication with Philip Pedley, 9 May 2002. See also CINA Interviews with Roger Scott, 4 May 1998; Lemick Bryan, #2, 7 March 1996; and Nolan Porter, #2, 13 March 1991.
12. Private Member's Motion No. 6/90, passed by the Legislature on 8 March 1990, resolved that legislation be introduced to repeal the words "Lesser Islands" in all Laws, Regulations and Orders and replace them with the words "Cayman Brac and Little Cayman". The motion was made by Gilbert McLean, the second elected Member for Cayman Brac and Little Cayman at the time. The term "Sister Islands" was never formally adopted but has become common usage.

13. *EIIR Royal Visit to the Cayman Islands, 16th–17th February 1983* (George Town: Progressive Publications, 1983); "Her Majesty the Queen: After 300 Years She Is Really Here," *Nor'wester*, March 1983, pp. 3–37; Programme for the Visit of Her Majesty the Queen and His Royal Highness the Duke of Edinburgh to the Cayman Islands, 26th and 27th of February, 1994 (George Town, 1994); "The Royal Visit," *Newstar,* March 1994, pp. 18–22.
14. See above, Chapter 12; Williams, *History of the Cayman Islands,* p. ix; Warren Conolly, personal interview by Michael Craton, December 1999.
15. *Partnership for Progress and Prosperity: Britain and the Overseas Territories,* Cm 4264 (London: Foreign & Commonwealth Office, March 1999); "White Paper Update Published," *Caymanian Compass,* 31 July 2000, pp. 1, 6–7. The White Paper became a matter of public concern and considerable debate as the November 2000 general election approached. Despite repeated assurances that the principle of non-reciprocity would be upheld, sceptics wondered whether it would withstand legal challenges once Caymanians, as British citizens, became members of the European Union, with its right of free movement within EU countries. The sceptics also feared the extension of EU and British banking and tax evasion laws to the Cayman Islands. The problematic section of the White Paper read: "Regulation of offshore financial service industries in the Overseas Territories needs to be improved to meet internationally accepted standards and to combat financial crime and regulatory abuse. Other measures are needed to ensure that regulators and law enforcers in the Overseas Territories are able to cooperate properly with counterparts elsewhere, and to provide for tighter audit and financial accountability." See Governor Peter Smith's judiciously worded responses to a Chamber of Commerce task force, "Special Report: H.E. the Governor responds to White Paper questions," *Cayman Net News*, 27 July–2 August 2000, p. 11.
16. *Cayman Islands Pirates Week, 29 October–5 November 1977: Official Souvenir Programme* (Grand Cayman: *The Nor'wester,* 1977), p. 3.
17. *Cayman Islands Pirates Week Official Souvenir Programme,* 25 October–1 November, 1980 (Grand Cayman: *The Nor'wester,* 1980). The first play produced during Pirates Week, in 1980, was Frank Swarres McField's social drama *Time Longer Dan Rope* (George Town: Camac Publishing Company, 1979).
18. *Pirates Week 1991 Official Souvenir Programme* (Grand Cayman: Cayman Free Press, 1991), p. 1; *Pirates Week 1998 Official Souvenir Progamme* (Grand Cayman: Cayman Free Press, 1998), p. 1
19. See above, Chapter 5; "Summary History of Pedro St. James," Historical & Site Investigations, Pedro St. James, unpublished report prepared by Commonwealth Historic Resource Management Limited for the Cayman Islands Government, September 1993).
20. *Northwester,* January 1972, p. 7; July 1973, p. 63; February 1974, p. 79; June 1974, p. 80; Colleen Webb, "Pedro St. James: The Oldest Building on the Island is a 17th Century Plantation-Style House on a Seven-Acre National Historic Site," *Key to Cayman*, 1999, pp. 115–17.

21. Those behind both the revival and the racing of the catboat were H.E. Ross and fellow-members of the Cayman Islands Seafarers' Association. See H.E. Ross, ed., *Love's Dance – The Catboat of the Caymanes* (George Town: Cayman Islands Seafarers' Association, 1999).
22. The CNCF is a statutory body, supported by the government. Cultural affairs were made the responsibility of a Ministry of Community Development, Sports, Women's Affairs, Youth and Culture, set up in 1992; *Cayman Islands Annual Report 1995,* pp. 155–68.
23. "The Cayman Quadrille: How a French Ballroom Dance Became a Caribbean Tradition," *Newstar*, May 1990, p. 46. Radley Gourzong died in 1995 at the age of 73.
24. *Annual Report 1995,* pp. 8, 196.
25. "George Novak: He Can't Sing or Play Guitar Very Well, but the Barefoot Man is (Undeniably) a Star," *Newstar,* May 1990, pp. 30–2; H.G. Novak [The Barefoot Man], *The People Time Forgot: A Photographic Portrayal of the People of the Cayman Islands,* 2nd ed. (George Town: Cayman Islands National Museum, 1998 [1987]).
26. Introduction by Rawle Gibbons, University of the West Indies, St. Augustine, Trinidad, in Frank McField, *Two Plays: Downside Up & Time Longer Dan Rope* (George Town: Cayman National Cultural Foundation, 2000), pp. 11–15. See also "Drama Is Life to Him," *Nor'wester,* November 1978, pp. 6–15. Another Caymanian playwright was Arthurlyn Pedley, whose play *Sandman's Peramble* is described in "Arthurlyn Gives Native Drama a Good Start," *Northwester*, February 1980, pp. 32–3.
27. Mary Rodrigues and Roy Murray, eds., *Our Voice: A Collection of Original Poems and Short Stories by Students of the John Gray High School, from 1988–1992* (George Town: Dept. of English, John Gray High School, 1992); *In Our Own Write: A Collection of Poetry and Short Stories* (George Town: The Creative Writers Association of the Cayman Islands, 1992).
28. Joy Brandon, *Island Thoughts: Poems of the Cayman Islands* (George Town: Cayman National Cultural Foundation, 1995). Ms. Brandon, who was also an accomplished playwright, died in 1991. See also Curtis Barnett, *Something About Us* (Grand Cayman: The Northwester Publishing Co., [ca. 1978]) and *Toes in the Sand* (West Bay: CLEB, 1995); Bonnie-Lee E. Webster, *Beyond the Iron Shore* (Grand Cayman: n.p., 1991); Jackie Bodden Webb, *On the Island of Grand Cayman* ([Grand Cayman?]: n.p., 1981).
29. CINA Interviews with Ed Oliver, #1 and #2, 6 January 1994.
30. *National Gallery of the Cayman Islands* (George Town: National Gallery, 1998).
31. *Nor'wester,* August 1980, pp. 46–7; CINA Interviews with Ed Oliver #1 and 2, 6 January 1994.
32. Henry D. Muttoo and Karl "Jerry" Craig, *My Markings: The Art of Gladwyn K. Bush, Caymanian Visionary Intuitive* (George Town: Cayman National Cultural Foundation, 1994).
33. *Vision 2008: The Cayman Islands National Strategic Plan, 1999–2008* (George Town, 1999); *Vision 2008: The Cayman Islands The Key to the*

Future (A Guide to the National Strategic Plan); *Vision 2008: Working Together to Shape Our Future* (George Town: Vision 2008 Secretariat, 1999).

34. *Vision 2008: The Cayman Islands National Strategic Plan,* p. 4.
35. Ibid., p. 5
36. Ibid., pp. 1–116.

Bibliography

MANUSCRIPT AND OTHER PRIMARY SOURCES

Cayman Islands

The Cayman Islands National Archive (CINA)

Birth, Marriage and Death Registrations, 1885–1999 (and continuing).
Blue Books of Statistics, 1912–47.
Custos and Commissioner's Correspondence, 1888–1927.
Central Registry Files, 1917–78.
Collections 1–443 (and continuing), 1992–present. Collections of archives from private sources and copies of records related to the Cayman Islands obtained from archives overseas in the CINA copying programme. They include numerous items from the archives listed below.
Government Notices, 1909–74
Oral History Interviews and Donated Tapes 1–1,220 (and continuing), 1976–present. Most of these items are available as word-searchable transcripts.
Public Recorder's Records, Vols 1–9, 1810–1953.
Vertical Files containing ephemera, genealogical and other materials 1992–present.

England

Public Record Office, Kew

Admiralty
Admiralty and Secretariat Papers ADM 1.
Captains' Logs ADM 51.
Masters' Logs ADM 52.
Ships' Logs ADM 53.
Admiralty and Secretariat Cases ADM 116.

Colonial Office

Colonial Papers, General Series CO 1.
America and West Indies: Original Correspondence CO 5.
Bay Islands: Original Correspondence CO 34.
Bay Islands: Blue Books CO 36.
British Honduras: Original Correspondence CO 123.
Jamaica: Original Correspondence CO 137.
Jamaica: Entry Books CO 138.
Jamaica: Miscellanea CO 142.
Cayman Islands: Acts CO 650.
Cayman Islands: Miscellanea CO 651.
Colonial Office and Predecessors: Maps and Plans: Series 1 CO 700.
Cayman Islands: Sessional Papers CO 857.
Cayman Islands: Gazettes CO 1019.
West Indian Department: Original Correspondence CO 1031.

Foreign Office

General Correspondence before 1906: Nicaragua FO 56.
Embassy and Consular Archives, Cuba: Correspondence FO 277.
Foreign Office, General Correspondence: Political FO 371.

Treasury

Slave Registration and Compensation Commission T71.

Bodleian Library, Oxford
Rhodes House Library

Anti-slavery Papers. MSS Brit. Emp. S20. E1 vols 1–2.

Ministry of Defence Hydrographic Office, Taunton

Albums.
Miscellaneous Papers (Vols. 2–114 contain "Remark Books" referring to the Cayman Islands during the period 1760–1865).
Original Documents.
Sailing Directions.
Surveyors Letters.
Surveys and Charts.
"S" Papers.

Regents Park College (Angus Library), Oxford

Application File for J.H. Sobey.
The Missionary Herald of the Baptist Missionary Society, 1883–1914.

School of Oriental and African Studies, London

Methodist Missionary Society Archives on microfiche. Inter Documentation Company AG, Switzerland. Box 13 (fiche 604, 607), Box 47 (fiche 2249–2274) and Box 48 (fiche 2275–324) contain correspondence from missionaries in Grand Cayman; Box 44 (fiche 2100–2140) contains correspondence from missionaries in the Bay Islands of Honduras.

Jamaica

Jamaica Archives, Spanish Town

Chancery Court 1A/3.
Despatches from Jamaica to England, IB/5/18.
Patents 1B/11/1.
Plat Books 1B/11/2.
Inventories IB/11/3.
Parish Registers 1B/11/18.
Governor General's Office, 1B/34.
Manton and Hart Law Firm Papers. Private Collections, 4/82.

National Library of Jamaica

Nugent Papers, MS 72.

Northern Ireland

Public Record Office

Belmore Papers, D3007/G/16.

France

Bibliothèque National de Paris

Département des Manuscrits
Fond Colbert, vol. 31: *Receuil de Relations et Memoires sur l'Espagne, les Indies, etc.* Fol. 622, *Des Isles Caymans.* (Original translation by William A. Hart available in CINA, MSD/145.)

Scotland

Edinburgh University Library (New College Library)

Missionary Record of The United Presbyterian Church, 1855 and 1858–80.

National Library of Scotland, Edinburgh

Missionary Record of the United Free Church of Scotland. Vols. 1–29, 1901–29.
Missionary Record of The United Presbyterian Church, 1848–54, 1856–7, and 1881–99.
Missionary Record of the United, Secession, and Relief Churches. Vol. 2, 1847.
Missionary Record of the United Secession Church. Vol. 1, 1846.
United Free Church of Scotland. Report on Foreign Missions. Submitted to the General Assembly of the United Free Church, 1901–29. Annual.

Spain

Archivo General, Simancas
"Costa de Mosquitos desde Rio Tinto al Rio Chagre." Drawn by Robert Hodgson Jr. Mapas, Planes y Dibujos, XI–165 (1783). (CINA transparency XG/OT/50/2).

Archivo General de Indias, Seville
Guerra, Legajos, pp. 6945–9.

PERIODICALS, NEWSPAPERS, AND BROCHURES

Cayman Executive, 1993–96. George Town: Cayman Publishing Co., 1993– . Quarterly.

Cayman Horizons, 1992–96. George Town: Progressive Publications Ltd., 1983– . Bimonthly.

Cayman Islands Compendium of Statistics, 1997. George Town: Economics and Statistics Office, 1991– . Annual.

Cayman Islands Pirates Week Official Souvenir Programmes, 1977, 1980, 1991, 1998. Grand Cayman: The Northwester Company Ltd., 1977, 1980; Cayman Free Press Ltd., 1991, 1998.

Cayman Islands Yearbook and Business Directory, 1993–2000. George Town: Cayman Free Press Ltd., 1986– . Annual.

Cayman Net News, 27 July–2 August 2000. George Town: Cayman Net Ltd., 2000– . Daily.

Caymanian Compass, 1988–2001. George Town: Cayman Free Press Ltd., 1965– . Daily.

The Caymanian Weekly, 25 March 1971, 13 May 1971. George Town: Cayman Publishing Company Ltd., 1965–74.

Comm, Dorothy Minchin. "The First Adventist in the Caymans." *Youth's Instruction*, 24 September 1957.

Duncan, David Douglas. "Capturing Giant Turtles in the Caribbean." *The National Geographic Magazine* 84 (August 1943).

EIIR Royal Visit to the Cayman Islands, 16th–17th February 1983. George Town: Progressive Publications, 1983.

England, George Allen. "Grand Cayman: A One-time Pirate Island, Far at the Back of Beyond, Where It Is Always Afternoon." *The Saturday Evening Post* 201, no. 3 (21 July 1928).

Hughes, H.B.L. "Notes on the Cayman Islands." *Jamaican Historical Review* 1 (September 1946).

Ingram, Kenneth E. "The West Indian Trade of an English Furniture Firm in the Eighteenth Century." *Jamaican Historical Review* 3 (March 1962).

Key to Cayman, Spring 1996, Spring 1999. George Town: Cayman Free Press Ltd., 1990– . Biannual.

Maloney, John. "The Islands Time Forgot." *Saturday Evening Post* 222, no. 41 (8 April 1950).

The Man Who Changed the Face of Cayman. Statue Memorial Programme. George Town, 1994.

National Gallery of the Cayman Islands. George Town: National Gallery, 1998.

The New Caymanian, 4–10 October 1991. George Town: Cayman Media Corporation Ltd., 1990– . Weekly.

Newstar, 1988–95. George Town: Cayman Publishing Co., 1987–95. Monthly.

Northwester, 1971–83 [name changed to *Nor'wester* August 1975]. George Town: The Northwester Company Ltd., 1971–83. Monthly.

Presbyterian Church in Grand Cayman, 1846–1946: Centenary Souvenir. [Kingston: Presbyterian Church of Jamaica and Grand Cayman], 1946.

Proceedings: Transactions of the Queensland Branch of the Royal Geographical Society of Australia 9 (1893–4).

Programme for the Visit of Her Majesty the Queen and His Royal Highness the Duke of Edinburgh to the Cayman Islands, 26th and 27th of February, 1994. George Town, 1994.

Programme: Official Opening of Queen Elizabeth II Botanic Park, 27 February 1994. George Town, 1994.

St. Ignatius School 25th Anniversary Booklet, 1996.

Statistical Abstract of the Government of the Cayman Islands. George Town: Government Statistics Office, 1975–90.

United Church in Jamaica and the Cayman Islands. "Inaugural Synod, December 13th, 1992, Souvenir Magazine." Kingston: The Herald Ltd., 1992.

BOOKS

Aguilar, E.F., and P.T. Saunders. *The Cayman Islands: Their Postal History, Postage Stamps, and Postmarks*. Folkestone, Kent: F.J. Parsons, 1962.

An Account of the Surveys of Florida, &c. With Directions for Sailing from Jamaica or the West Indies by the West End of Cuba, and through the Gulph of Florida (To accompany Mr. Gauld's Charts). London: W. Faden, Geographer to the King, 1790.

Andrews, Kenneth R. *The Spanish Caribbean: Trade and Plunder, 1530–1630.* New Haven: Yale University Press, 1978.

Armstrong, D.B. *The Cayman Islands: The Stamps and Post Office*. London: Council of the Junior Philatelic Society (reprinted from *The Stamp Lover*), 1910.

Armytage, Frances. *The Free Port System in the British West Indies: A Study in Commercial Policy, 1766–1822*. London: Longmans, Green, 1953.

Baker, William A. *Sloops and Shallops*. Barre, Mass.: Barre Publishing Company, 1966.

Barnett, Curtis. *Something About Us*. Grand Cayman: Northwester Publishing Co., [ca. 1978]).

———. *Toes in the Sand*. West Bay: CLEB, 1995.

Beckles, Hilary, and Verene Shepherd, eds. *Caribbean Freedom: Economy and Society from Emancipation to the Present*. Kingston: Ian Randle Press, 1993.

Black, Clinton V. *The Story of Jamaica: From Prehistory to the Present*. London: Collins, 1965.

Bodden, Will T. *A Brief History of the Church of God in the Bay Islands of Honduras and the Cayman Islands*. George Town: Will T. Bodden, 1990.

Boultbee, Paul G. *Cayman Islands*. Vol. 187 of World Bibliographical Series. Oxford, Santa Barbara, Denver: Clio Press, 1996.

Brandon, Joy. *Island Thoughts: Poems of the Cayman Islands*. George Town: Cayman National Cultural Foundation, 1995.

Brenner, Robert L. *Merchants and Revolution: Commercial Change, Political Conflict, and London Overseas Traders, 1550–1653*. Cambridge: Cambridge University Press, 1995.

Burns, Sir Alan. *History of the West Indies*. London: Allen and Unwin, 1954.

Campbell, Mavis Christine. *The Dynamics of Change in a Slave Society: A Sociopolitical History of the Free Coloureds of Jamaica, 1800–1865*. Rutherford, N.J.: Fairleigh Dickinson University Press, 1976.

Carr, Archie. *So Excellent a Fish: The Classic Study of the Lives of Sea Turtles*. New York: Scribner's, 1967, 1984.

Cayman Islands 1989 Census. 2 vols. George Town: Government Statistics Office, 1990.

Cayman Islands Annual Report. George Town: Government of the Cayman Islands, 1974– 2000. Annual.

Cayman Islands A–Z Reference. 4th ed. George Town: Cayman Islands Public Library, 1996.

Cayman Islands Census, 1881, 1891, 1911. Jamaica Archives, Printed Works, Censuses: Census of Jamaica and Dependencies, Cayman Islands.

Cayman Islands Colonial Report. London: HMSO, 1907–73.

Cayman Islands Historical Compendium of Statistics, 1774–1980. George Town: Government Statistics Office, 1992.

Cayman Islands. Proposals for Constitutional Advance: Report of the Constitutional Commissioner, the Rt. Hon. The Earl of Oxford and Asquith, KCMG. Foreign and Commonwealth Office. London: HMSO, 1971.

Cayman Islands: Economic Development Plan, 1986–90. George Town: Government of the Cayman Islands, 1986.

Cayman Islands: Report of the Constitutional Commissioners 1991, Sir Frederick Smith, Mr. Walter Wallace. London: HMSO, 1991.

Chapman, Charles E. *A History of the Cuban Republic*. New York: Macmillan, 1927.

Conolly, Islay. "A Brief History of Education in the Cayman Islands." In *Cayman Islands: 100 Years of Public Education, 1887–1987*. Grand Cayman: [Cayman Islands Government], 1987.

Craton, Michael. "Indispensable Agents of Empire: The Caribbean Vice Admiralty Courts, 1713–1815." Ph.D. diss., McMaster University, 1968.

———. *Searching for the Invisible Man: Slaves and Plantation Life in Jamaica*. Cambridge: Harvard University Press, 1978.

———. *Testing the Chains: Resistance to Slavery in the British West Indies*. Ithaca: Cornell University Press, 1982.

———. *Empire, Enslavement, and Freedom in the Caribbean*. Kingston: Ian Randle Press, 1997.

Craton, Michael, and Gail Saunders. *Islanders in the Stream: A History of the Bahamian People*. Vol. 1, *From Aboriginal Times to the End of Slavery*. Athens: University of Georgia Press, 1992.

———. *Islanders in the Stream: A History of the Bahamian People*. Vol. 2, *From the Ending of Slavery to the Twenty-First Century*. Athens: University of Georgia Press, 1998.

Crouse, Nellis M. *The French Struggle for the West Indies, 1665–1713*. New York: Columbia University Press, 1943.

Cruikshank, E.A. *Sir Henry Morgan: His Life and Times*. Toronto: Macmillan, 1935.

Cundall, Frank. *The Governors of Jamaica in the Seventeenth Century*. London: West India Committee, 1936.

Davenport, F.G., and C.O. Paullin. *European Treaties Bearing on the History of the United States and its Dependencies.* Vol. 4. Gloucester, Mass.: P. Smith, 1917–37.

Davidson, William V. *Historical Geography of the Bay Islands, Honduras: Anglo-Hispanic Conflict in the Western Caribbean.* 3rd ed. Birmingham, Ala.: Southern University Press, 1988.

Davies, Elizabeth W. *The Legal System of the Cayman Islands.* Oxford: Law Reports International, 1989.

Davis, Ralph. *The Rise of the Atlantic Economies.* Ithaca: Cornell University Press, 1973.

de Laet, Johannes. *Iaerlyck Verhael van de Verrichtinghen de Geotroyeerde West-Indische Compagnie.* 4 vols. 1644. Reprint, 's Gravenhage: Martinus Nijhoff, 1931–37.

Dixon, H.C. *Cayman Brac: Land of My Birth.* Brooklyn: Shining Light Survey, n.d. [1955].

Dobson, Narda. *A History of Belize.* London: Longman Caribbean, 1973.

Doran, Edwin Beale. "A Physical and Cultural Geography of the Cayman Islands." Ph.D. diss., University of California, 1953.

Dozier, Craig L. *Nicaragua's Mosquito Shore: The Years of British and American Presence.* Tuscaloosa: University of Alabama Press, 1985.

Drewett, Peter L. *Prehistoric Settlements in the Caribbean.* St. Michael: Archetype Publications, 2000.

Duffy, Michael. *Soldiers, Sugar, and Seapower: The British Expeditions to the West Indies and the War against Revolutionary France.* Oxford: Clarendon Press, 1987.

Duncan, Michael. *The Bay Islands or the Gentle Art of Cutting the Painter.* Warwick: University of Warwick, Centre for Caribbean Studies, n.d.

Dutton, Geoffrey. *The Hero as Murderer: The Life of Edward John Eyre, Australian Explorer and Governor of Jamaica, 1815–1901.* Sydney: Collins, 1967.

Ebanks, Lee A. *Lest It Be Lost: Eighty Years in the Life of a Caymanian.* George Town: privately printed, 1985.

Ellis, Rev. J.B. *The Diocese of Jamaica: A Short Account of Its History, Growth, and Organisation.* London: Society for Promoting Christian Knowledge, 1913.

Eltis, David. *Economic Growth and the Ending of the Transatlantic Slave Trade.* New York: Oxford University Press, 1987.

Evans, David Kenneth. "The People of French Harbour: A Study of Conflict and Change on Roatán Island." Ph.D. diss., University of California, Berkeley, 1957.

Evans, E. L. *A History of the Diocese of Jamaica.* Kingston: Diocese of Jamaica, 1976.

Fernandez-Armesto, Felipe. *Columbus.* Oxford: Oxford University Press, 1991.

Fewkes, Jesse W. "A Prehistoric Island Culture of America." 34th Annual Report of the Bureau of American Ethnology. Washington: Government Printing Office, 1922.

Fieldhouse, D.K. *The Colonial Empires: A Comparative Survey from the Eighteenth Century.* London: Weidenfeld and Nicolson, 1966.

Firth, C.H., ed. *The Narrative of General Venables: With an Appendix of Papers Relating to the Expedition to the West Indies and the Conquest of Jamaica, 1654–1655*. London: Longmans, Green for the Royal Historical Society, 1900.

Fosdick, Peggy, and Sam Fosdick. *Last Chance Lost? Can and Should Farming Save the Green Sea Turtle? The Story of Mariculture Ltd. Cayman Turtle Farm*. York, Penn.: Irwin Naylor, 1994.

Gauld, George. *The Island of Grand Cayman 1773*. Survey and Remarks. Published by the Hydrographic Office, UK, and Cayman Islands National Archive, 1994.

Goslinga, Cornelius Ch. *The Dutch in the Caribbean and on the Wild Coast, 1580–1680*. Assen: Van Gorcum, 1971.

Gosse, Philip. *The History of Piracy*. 1932. Reprint, New York: Burt Franklin, 1968.

Goveia, Elsa V. *Slave Society in the British Leeward Islands at the End of the Eighteenth Century*. New Haven: Yale University Press, 1965.

Granbery, Julian. "A Brief History of Bahamian Archeology." *Florida Archeologist* 33 (1980): 83–93.

Grand Cayman: Report of Visit by Mr. L.R. Fyfe of the Colonial Secretary's Office, Jamaica, preceded by Minute of Instructions by His Excellency Sir H.W. Norman, GCB, GCMG, CIE, Governor of Jamaica, 1887. Kingston: Government Printing Office, 1887.

Green, William A. *British Slave Emancipation: The Sugar Colonies and the Great Experiment, 1830–1865*. Oxford: Clarendon Press, 1976.

Guerra y Sanchez, Ramiro, ed. *Historia de la nacion cubana*. 10 vols. Havana: Editorial Historia de la Nacion Cubana, 1952.

Hakluyt, Richard. *The Principal Navigations, Voyages, Traffiques, & Discoveries of the English Nation*. 8 vols. 1598–1600. Reprint, London: Dent, 1907, pp. vii, 154–6. Quoted in Kenneth R. Andrews, *English Privateering Voyages to the West Indies, 1588–95* (Cambridge: Cambridge University Press for the Hakluyt Society, 1956), p. 214.

Handbook of Jamaica, 1931. Jamaica: Government Printing Office, 1931.

Hannerz, Ulf. *Caymanian Politics: Structure and Style in a Changing Island Society*. Stockholm: University of Stockholm, 1974.

Harlow, Vincent T., ed. *The Voyages of Captain William Jackson (1642–1645)*. Camden Miscellany vol. XIII. London: Camden Society, 1923.

Heuman, Gad J. *Between Black and White: Race, Politics, and the Free Coloreds in Jamaica, 1792–1865*. Westport, Conn.: Greenwood Press, 1981.

Higman, Barry W. "Household Structure and Fertility on Jamaican Slave Plantations: A Nineteenth-Century Example." *Population Studies* 27 (1973).

———. "The Slave Family and Household in the British West Indies, 1800–1834." *Journal of Interdisciplinary History* 6 (1975).

———. *Slave Populations of the British Caribbean, 1807–1834*. Baltimore: Johns Hopkins University Press, 1984.

Hirst, George S.S., ed. *Handbook of the Cayman Islands, 1908*. Kingston: Times Printery, 1907.

———. *Notes on the History of the Cayman Islands*. Kingston: P.A. Benjamin, 1910.

A History of the Development of Education in the Cayman Islands. Paper for a Diploma in School Management, International College of the Cayman Islands, 1981.

The History of the Anglican Church in the Cayman Islands. Grand Cayman, ca. 1995.

Hodgson, Robert Sr. *Some Account of the Mosquito Territory.* 1757. Reprint, Edinburgh, 1822.

Holt, Thomas C. *The Problem of Freedom: Race, Labor, and Politics in Jamaica and Britain, 1832–1938.* Baltimore: Johns Hopkins University Press, 1992.

Horsfall, Lucy Frances. "The West Indian Trade." In *The Trade Winds: A Study of British Overseas Trade during the French Wars, 1793–1815,* edited by C. Northcote Parkinson. London: Allen and Unwin, 1948.

Hughes, H.B.L. "Notes on the Cayman Islands." *Jamaican Historical Review* 1 (September 1946).

Humphreys, Robin A. *The Diplomatic History of British Honduras, 1638–1901.* London: Royal Institute of International Affairs and Oxford University Press, 1961.

Hurwitz, Samuel J., and Edith F. Hurwitz. *Jamaica: A Historical Portrait.* New York: Praeger, 1971.

Hydrick, John Lee. *Hookworm Survey of the Cayman Islands, April 18, 1917 to June 20, 1917.* No. 7297. New York: International Health Board, 1917.

In Our Own Write: A Collection of Poetry and Short Stories. George Town: The Creative Writers Association of the Cayman Islands, 1992.

Ireland, Gordon. *Boundaries, Possessions, and Conflicts in Central and North America and the Caribbean.* Cambridge: Harvard University Press, 1941.

Jamaican Parish Registers, 1733–1808. Copies of selected items in these registers relating to Cayman in CINA, MSD 82; MSD 137; MSD 269.

Janes Encyclopedia of Aviation. London: Janes' Publishing, 1980.

Jenks, Leland. *Our Cuban Colony: A Study in Sugar.* New York: Vanguard Press, 1928.

Johnson, Captain Charles [Daniel Defoe]. *A General History of the Pyrates.* 3rd ed. Vol. 1. Edited by Philip Gosse. 1725. Reprint, London: Cayme Press, 1925, 1927.

Johnson, Howard. "Late Nineteenth and Early Twentieth Century Labour Migration to Florida." In *The Bahamas in Slavery and Freedom.* Kingston: Ian Randle Press, 1991.

Johnson, Sir Vassel. *As I See It: How Cayman Became a Leading Financial Centre.* Sussex: The Book Guild, 2001.

Jones, Brian. "Geology of the Cayman Islands." In *The Cayman Islands: Natural History and Biogeography*, edited by M.A. Brunt and J.E. Davies. The Netherlands: Kluwer Academic Publishers, 1994.

Keegan, William F. *The People Who Discovered Columbus: The Prehistory of the Bahamas.* Gainesville: University Press of Florida, 1992.

Keeler, Mary Freer, ed. *Sir Francis Drake's West Indian Voyage, 1585–1586.* London: Hakluyt Society, 1981.

Kieran, Brian L. *The Lawless Caymanas: A Story of Slavery, Freedom, and the British West India Regiment.* Grand Cayman: privately published, 1992.

Kohlman, Aarona Booker. *Under Tin Roofs: Cayman in the 1920s.* George Town: Cayman Islands National Museum, 1993.

Kupperman, Karen Ordahl. *Providence Island, 1630–1641: The Other Puritan Colony.* Cambridge: Cambridge University Press, 1993.

Langley, Lester D. *Struggle for the American Mediterranean: United States–European Rivalry in the Gulf-Caribbean, 1776–1904*. Athens: University of Georgia Press, 1976.

Laws of the Cayman Islands up to No. 12 of 1889. Jamaica: Government Printing Establishment, 1889.

Leshikar-Denton, Margaret E. "The 1794 'Wreck of the Ten Sail', Cayman Islands, British West Indies: A Historical Study and Archaeological Survey, Vol. 1". Ph.D. diss., Tex A&M University, 1993.

———, and Philip E. Pedley, eds. *Our Islands' Past*. Vol. 2. *The Wreck of the Ten Sails*. George Town: Cayman Islands National Archive and Cayman Free Press, 1994.

Lewis, Gordon K. *The Growth of the Modern West Indies*. New York: Modern Reader Press, 1968.

The Life of the Admiral Christopher Columbus by His Son Ferdinand. Translated by Benjamin Keen. New Brunswick: Rutgers University Press, 1958.

Long, Edward. *The History of Jamaica*. Vol. 1, chap. 12, sect. 1. London: Printed for T. Lowndes, 1774. Quoted as an appendix in Hirst, *Notes*, pp. 392–7.

Lorenzo, Omar. *Forbidden Reflections: The True Story of Tent City*. George Town: Casa de Cultura, 1997.

Manley, Norman Washington. "My Early Years: Fragment of an Autobiography." In *Manley and the New Jamaica: Selected Speeches and Writings, 1938–1968*, edited by Rex Nettleford. London: Longman Caribbean, 1971.

Martins, Dave. *A Special Son: The Biography of Ormond Panton*. George Town: Pansons Ltd., 1994.

May, R.E. *The Southern Dream of a Caribbean Empire, 1854–1861*. Baton Rouge: University of Louisiana, 1973.

McCoy, Harwell (Harry). *Journey to Partnership: A History of the Presbyterian (United) Church in Grand Cayman*. George Town: privately printed, 1998.

McField, Frank S. *Two Plays: Downside Up & Time Longer Dan Rope*. George Town: Cayman National Cultural Foundation, 2000.

McField, Timothy ("Teacher"). "A Brief History of Education in the Cayman Islands." Paper for Caribbean Studies III course, University of the West Indies, 1969.

McKerrow, John. *History of the Foreign Missions of the Secession and United Presbyterian Church*. Edinburgh: n.p., 1867.

McLaughlin, Heather R. "A Sad and Bitter Day: Oral Traditions in the Bay Islands of Honduras Surrounding the Wyke Cruz Treaty of 1859." Cayman Islands National Archive. Memory Bank Report, 1994.

———, ed. *The '32 Storm*. George Town: Cayman Islands National Archive, 1994.

McLaughlin, Sybil I. *Development of Parliamentary Government in the Cayman Islands*. Specially Prepared for the Celebration of the 150th Anniversary. George Town, 1982.

Metcalf, George. *Royal Government and Political Conflict in Jamaica, 1729–1783*. London: Longmans for the Royal Commonwealth Society, 1965.

Mordecai, Sir John. *The West Indies: The Federal Negotiations*. London: Allen and Unwin, 1968.

Morgan, Rodwell. *Meet Corn Island*. Kearney, Neb.: Morris Publishing, 1996.

Morison, Samuel Eliot. *Admiral of the Ocean Sea: A Life of Christopher Columbus*. Boston: Little, Brown, 1942.

Morrell, W.P. *British Colonial Policy in the Age of Peel and Russell*. Oxford: Oxford University Press, 1930.

Murray, John A., ed. *The Islands and the Sea*. New York: Oxford University Press, 1991.

Muttoo. Henry D., and Karl "Jerry" Craig. *My Markings: The Art of Gladwyn K. Bush, Caymanian Visionary Intuitive*. George Town: Cayman National Cultural Foundation, 1994.

Naylor, Robert A. *Penny Ante Imperialism: The Mosquito Shore and the Bay of Honduras. A Case Study in British Informal Empire*. London and Toronto: Associated University Presses, 1989.

Nebenzahl, Kenneth. *Atlas of Columbus and the Great Discoveries*. Chicago: Rand McNally, 1990.

Newton, Arthur Percival. *The Colonizing Activities of the English Puritans*. New Haven: Yale University Press, 1914.

———. *The European Nations in the West Indies, 1493–1688*. London: A & C Black, 1933.

Novak, H.G. [The Barefoot Man]. *The People Time Forgot: A Photographic Portrayal of the People of the Cayman Islands*. 2nd ed. George Town: Cayman Islands National Museum, 1998 [1987].

Olivier, Sydney. *Jamaica: The Blessed Island*. London: Faber, 1936.

Our Islands' Past. Vol. 1. *Edward Corbet's Report and Census of 1802 on the Cayman Islands*. George Town: Cayman Islands National Archive and Cayman Free Press, 1992.

Pares, Richard. *War and Trade in the West Indies, 1739–1763*. Oxford: Oxford University Press, 1936.

Parry, John H. *The Spanish Seaborne Empire*. London: Hutchinson, 1966.

Parsons, James J. *San Andrés and Providencia*. Berkeley: University of California, 1956.

Partnership for Progress and Prosperity: Britain and the Overseas Territories. Cm 4264. London: Foreign & Commonwealth Office, 1999.

Pascoe, C.F. *Two Hundred Years of the SPG, 1701–1900*. London: Society for the Propagation of the Gospel, 1901.

Pawson, Michael, and David Buisseret. *Port Royal, Jamaica*. Oxford: Clarendon Press, 1975.

Pedley, Philip E. "The Executive Branch of Government in the Cayman Islands before 1960." M.A. thesis, University College, London, 1990.

Pitman, Frank Wesley. *The Development of the British West Indies, 1700–1763*. New Haven: Yale University Press, 1917.

Pringle, Kenneth. *Waters of the West*. London: Allen and Unwin, 1938.

Ragatz, Lowell J. *The Fall of the Planter Class in the British Caribbean, 1763–1833*. New York: American Historical Association, 1928.

Rediker, Marcus. *Between the Devil and the Deep Blue Sea: Merchant Seamen, Pirates, and the Anglo-American Maritime World, 1700–1750*. Cambridge: Cambridge University Press, 1987.

Redpath, Rev. Thomas. *The Great Crocodile: in Tradition, Legend and Records*. 2 vols. Edinburgh: Unpublished typescript [reproduced in limited quantity by Jane Redpath], 1946, 1949.

Report of the Cayman Islands 1999 Population and Housing Census. George Town: Statistics Office, 2001.

Roberts, George W. *The Population of Jamaica*. Cambridge: Cambridge University Press, 1957.

Roberts, Orlando W. *Narrative of Voyages on the East Coast and in the Interior of Central America*. Edinburgh: Constable, 1827. Quoted in Davidson, *Historical Geography of the Bay Islands*, p. 74.

Rodrigues, Mary, and Roy Murray, eds. *Our Voice: A Collection of Original Poems and Short Stories by Students of the John Gray High School, from 1988–1992*. George Town: Dept. of English, John Gray High School, 1992.

Rose, Richard H. *Utilla: Past and Present. Including an Article on HMS* Psyche *at the Bay Islands, With Illustrations*. Dansville: F.A. Owen Publishing Co., 1904.

Ross, H.E., ed. *Love's Dance – The Catboat of the Caymanes*. George Town: Cayman Islands Seafarers' Association, 1999.

Rouse, Irving. *The Tainos: Rise and Decline of the People Who Greeted Columbus*. New Haven: Yale University Press, 1992.

Saintoyant, J. *La colonisation francaise sous l'ancien regime*. 2 vols. Paris: La Renaissance du livre, 1929.

Schoonover, Thomas D. *The United States in Central America, 1860–1911: Episodes of Social Imperialism and Imperial Rivalry in the World System*. Durham, N.C.: Duke University Press, 1991.

Scott, Rebecca J. *Slave Emancipation in Cuba: The Transition to Free Labor, 1860–1899*. Princeton: Princeton University Press, 1985.

Scroggs, W.O. *Filibusters and Financiers*. New York: Macmillan, 1916.

Selzer, Tamara. "Administrative History of the Board of Education, 1902–1960." Paper for Administrative History course, University College, London, 1996.

———. "Selected Sources for the History of Land Registration in the Cayman Islands." M.A. thesis, University College, London, 1997.

Semmel, Bernard. *Jamaican Blood and Victorian Conscience: The Governor Eyre Controversy. Boston*: Houghton Mifflin, 1963; Westport, Conn.: Greenwood Press, 1976.

Sir Francis Drake and the Age of Discovery. New York: Pierpont Morgan Library, 1988.

Sloane, Sir Hans. A Voyage to the Islands Madera, Barbados, Nieves, S. Christophers, and Jamaica. Vol. 2. London: B.M. for the Author, 1707, 1725.

Smith, Roger C. *The Maritime Heritage of the Cayman Islands*. Gainesville: University Press of Florida, 2000.

Stanley Gibbons Postage Stamp Catalogue. Parts 1 and 2. London: Stanley Gibbons, 1969.

Stokes, Anne V., and William F. Keegan. *A Settlement Survey for Prehistoric Archeological Sites on Grand Cayman*. Miscellaneous Project Report no. 52. Gainesville: Florida Museum of Natural History, 1993.

Swabey, Christopher, and Bernard C. Lewis. *Forestry in the Cayman Islands*. Kingston: Development and Welfare in the West Indies, 1946.

Sykes, Rev. N.J.G. *The Dependency Question: A Study of Church and State in the Cayman Islands*. George Town: The Ecclesiastical Corporation, 1996.

Taylor, S.A.G. *The Western Design: An Account of Cromwell's Expedition to the Caribbean*. Kingston: Institute of Jamaica, 1965.

Tekse, Kalman. *Population and Vital Statistics, Jamaica, 1832–1964: A Historical Perspective*. Kingston: Department of Statistics, 1974.

Thomas, Hugh. *Cuba: The Pursuit of Freedom*. London: Eyre and Spottiswood, 1971.

Thompson, Ernest F. *The Fisheries of the Cayman Islands*. Kingston: Development and Welfare in the West Indies, 1944.

Thompson, J.P. "A Governor's Cruise in the West Indies in 1884." *Australian Royal Geographical Quarterly* 9 (1893–4).

Tibbetts, Captain Keith P. *Bits of the Brac: A Brief History of Cayman Brac*. Cayman Brac: Cayman Brac Museum, n.d. [c. 1980].

Time Was. George Town: Cayman Islands National Archive and George Hicks High School English Department, 2000.

Turner, Mary. *Slaves and Missionaries: The Disintegration of Jamaican Slave Society, 1787–1834*. Urbana: University of Illinois Press, 1982.

Ure, John. *The Quest for Henry Morgan*. London: Constable, 1983.

Vaquero [pseud.]. *Life and Adventure in the West Indies*. London: John Bale, Sons & Danielsson, Ltd., 1914.

Vision 2008 documents: National Strategic Plan, Guide to the National Strategic Plan, final report. Grand Cayman: Vision 2008 Secretariat, 1999.

Waddell, Rev. Hope Masterton. *Twenty-Nine Years in the West Indies and Central Africa: A Review of Missionary Work and Adventure, 1829–1858*. 2nd ed. London: Frank Cass, 1970.

Wallace, Elisabeth. *The British Caribbean: From the Decline of Colonialism to the End of Federation*. Toronto: University of Toronto Press, 1977.

Ware, John D., and Robert R. Rea. *George Gauld: Surveyor and Cartographer of the Gulf Coast*. Gainesville: University of Florida Press, 1982.

Watson, J. Steven. *The Reign of George III, 1760–1815*. Oxford: Clarendon Press, 1960.

Watts, David. *The West Indies: Patterns of Development, Culture, and Environmental Change since 1492*. Cambridge: Cambridge University Press, 1987.

Webb, Jackie Bodden. *On the Island of Grand Cayman*. [Grand Cayman]: n.p., 1981.

Webster, Bonnie-Lee E.. *Beyond the Iron Shore*. Grand Cayman: n.p., 1991.

West India Atlas. London: Sayer and Bennett, 1775.

Williams, C.R. "Thomas Modyford, Planter-Governor of Barbados and Jamaica, 1620–1679." Ph.D. diss., University of Kentucky, 1979.

Williams, Neville. *A History of the Cayman Islands*. George Town: Government of the Cayman Islands, 1970; George Town: CINA, 1992, 1995, 1998, 2001.

Wilson, Peter J. *Crab Antics: The Social Anthropology of English-Speaking Negro Societies in the Caribbean*. New Haven: Yale University Press, 1973.

Woodbury, George. *The Great Days of Piracy in the West Indies*. London: Paul Elek, 1954.

Woodward, Mary E. *The Lighthouse*. George Town: The Ecclesiastical Corporation, 1997.

Woodward, Ralph Lee, Jr. *Central America: A Nation Divided*. 2nd ed. Oxford: Oxford University Press, 1985.

———. "Central America, 1812–1879." In *Cambridge History of Latin America*, vol. 3. Cambridge: Cambridge University Press, 1985.

Young, Thomas. *Narrative of a Residence on the Mosquito Shore*. London: Smith, Elder and Co., 1842.

List of Illustrations and Acknowledgements

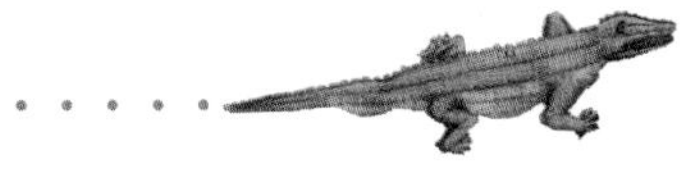

The selection and layout of illustrations was undertaken by a team consisting of Robert Harris (designer), Roger Craig, Philip Pedley, Claudette Upton, and Ian Randle.

The Cayman Islands Government (CIG) and the Cayman Islands National Archive (CINA) gratefully acknowledge the following institutions for their assistance in preparing this publication and for permission to reproduce items from their collections.

Archivo General de Simancas, Spain
Biblioteca Estense di Modena, Italy
British Library
Cayman Brac Museum
Cayman Islands
Cayman National National Museum
Cayman Free Press Cultural Foundation
Civil Aviation Authority, CIG
College of Arms, London
Department of Lands and Survey, CIG
Edinburgh University Library (New College Library)
Free Library of Philadelphia, Rare Book Department
Government Information Services, CIG
Jamaica Archives
John Carter Brown Library at Brown University
Hispanic Society of America, New York
Institute of Jamaica
Metropolitan Museum of Art, New York
Ministry of Defense Hydrographic Office, Taunton, UK (MODHO)
Mosquito Research and Control Unit, CIG (MRCU)
Museum National d'Histoire Naturelle, Paris (MNHN)

National Maritime Museum, London
National Library of Jamaica
National Library of Scotland
National Portrait Gallery, London
National Trust for the Cayman Islands
Newport Museum and Library, Wales
Northwester Company
Pierpont Morgan Library, New York
Public Record Office, UK (PRO)
Tourism Attractions Board, CIG

In addition to individual photograph credits given below, the Cayman Islands National Archive would like to recognise and thank the donors of the following collections, images from which have been used in this publication:

Gemmel Alexander
John Brock
Kathleen Bodden-Harris
Paul Comissong
John Croft
Arthur Ebanks
S. O. Ebanks
Ewart Ebanks
Dennis Foster
Benson Greenall
Everett Humphrey
John Jenkinson
Alex Johnson
Doris Wood Levy
Jeanne Masters
Sybil McLaughlin
George Nelson
Ed Oliver
Reginald Parsons
Denny Ranson
George Roy
George Tucker
Jack Andresen
Marcia Bodden-Bush
Floyd Bush
Lucinda Cruickshank
Edwin Doran
Audrey Ebanks
Ertis Ebanks
Annie V. Foster
Doris Fulford
Helen Hirst Gamble
L.E. Hines
Paul Hurlston
Aarona Kohlman
Bernard Lewis
John Mackenzie
Olive Miller
George Nowak
Colin Panton
Oswell Rankine
Jack Rose
Ivor O. Smith
Marion Walker

COVER, FRONTISPIECE AND RUNNING HEAD

Watercolour of a cayman by the French naturalist Jean Théodore Descourtilz, 1824 Museum National d'Histoire Naturelle, MSS 549. Cop Bibliothèque centrale MNHN, Paris.

COVER AND ENDPAPERS

"General Map" by Baptista Boazio, 1589. Included in *The Famouse West Indian Voyadge made by the Englishe Fleet of 23 Ships and Barkes . . .,* 1589, Rare Book Department, Free Library of Philadelphia.

CHAPTER 1

p. 2. "Lisle des Cayamans" (The Island of the Caymans). The Pierpont Morgan Library, New York, MA 3900, fols. 93–4.

p. 3 Details of cayman and turtle. The Pierpont Morgan Library, New York, MA 3900, fol. 53.

p. 4 The *Nova May* under construction, 1949. CINA (Doran collection).

p. 5 Catboats, 1950. CINA (Smith collection).

p. 6 Aerial view of George Town, 2001. CINA (Mackenzie collection). Plate between chapters 1 & 2: The schooner *Banks*, ca. 1928. CINA (Kohlman collection).

CHAPTER 2

p. 12 Cayman Brac from the northeast, 1949. CINA (Doran collection).

p. 13 Columbus's fourth voyage. CINA (map prepared by Roger Craig). The exact route past the Sister Islands is not known, but it is quite possible – even probable – that the two ships sailed between Little Cayman and Cayman Brac. This route would match Ferdinand Columbus's statement that the islands were "low" and "full of turtles", as both islands appear low from the channel (from which Cayman Brac's Bluff is not visible), while the eastern end of Little Cayman and the western end of Cayman Brac provide attractive locations for turtles to come ashore.

p. 13 Detail of a painting by Sebastiano del Piombo (Sebastiano Luciani.) Portrait of a Man, Said to be Christopher Columbus (born about 1446, died 1506), 1519. Oil on canvas (106.7 x 88.3cm); The Metropolitan Museum of Art, Gift of J. Pierpont Morgan, 1900 (00.18.2). Photograph © 1979 The Metropolitan Museum of Art.

p. 14 Detail from the Cantino Planisphere of 1502 (Biblioteca Estense di Modena); detail from world map by Vesconte de Maggiolo, 1511 (John Carter Brown Library at Brown University).

p. 15 Details of world maps by Juan Vespucci, 1526 (courtesy of the Hispanic Society of America, New York) and Pierre Desceliers, 1545 (The Pierpont Morgan Library, New York, MS M.506, fols. 1v–2).

p. 16 Detail from Cosmographie Universelle by Guillaume Le Testu, 1556. Reproduced with permission from Kenneth Nebenzahl, *Atlas of Columbus and the Great Discoveries* (Rand McNally & Company, 1990), p. 117. (A bona fide attempt was made to obtain a copy of this item and permission to use it from Ministère de la Défense Service de l'Armée de Terre, Vincennes, France.)

p. 16 Sir Francis Drake. CINA collections.

pp. 17–20 General Map and details of cayman and turtle from related maps by Baptista Boazio, 1589, included in *The Famouse West Indian Voyadge made by the Englishe Fleet of 23 Ships and Barkes . . .*, 1589, Rare Book Department, Free Library of Philadelphia.

p. 20 Turtle bones, harpoon head, and pottery. Cayman Islands National Museum collections. Photo: Mark Leach.

p. 21 Description of turtle, ca. 1662. PRO: CO 324/1 fol. 149r.

p. 22 Port Royal and Kingston Harbours in the 1700s. CINA, from Edward Long, *The History of Jamaica* (London: printed for T. Lowndes, 1774),

vol. II, plate 10, facing p. 139. The original image from the copperplate engraving was reversed and has been corrected.

p. 23 Spanish Commission of War. PRO: CO 138/1, fol. 46.

p. 24 Modyford's declaration of war against the Spanish. PRO: CO 138/1, fol. 47.

p. 25 Rivero Pardal's challenge. PRO: CO 138/1, fol. 49.

p. 26 Henry Morgan. Detail from a painting in the Newport Museum and Library.

p. 28 A "boucan" or "bucan". The British Library.

Plate between chapters 2 & 3: Surveying the land. Photo ca. 1928. CINA (Kohlman collection).

CHAPTER 3

p. 34 Campbell-Middleton land grant. Jamaica Archives: 1B/11/1/ 20, Liber Patents 20, fols. 151–2.

p. 34 Aerial view of the airport, industrial park, and Red Bay, 1999. Department of Lands and Survey, CIG.

p. 36 Samuel Spofforth land grant. Jamaica Archives: 1B/11/1/ 22, Liber Patents 22, fols. 47–8.

p. 36 Aerial view of northern West Bay, 1999. Department of Lands and Survey, CIG.

p. 38 Murray Crymble land grant. Jamaica Archives: 1B/11/1/ 22, Liber Patents 22, fols. 46–7.

p. 38 Aerial view of land between George Town and West Bay, 1999. Department of Lands and Survey, CIG.

p. 40 William Foster land grant. Jamaica Archives: 1B/11/1/ 22, Liber Patents 22, fol. 46.

p. 40 Aerial view of George Town–South Sound, 1999. Department of Lands and Survey, CIG.

p. 41 Mary Bodden land grant. Jamaica Archives: 1B/11/1/ 22, Liber Patents 22, fols. 59–60.

p. 41 Aerial view of Newlands, 1999. Department of Lands and Survey, CIG.

p. 45 Sketch of Port Royal, ca. 1830. © National Maritime Museum, London: LOG/N/S23; D7660.

p. 45 First known Caymanian marriages. Registrar General's Department, Jamaica. Port Royal Copy Register, vol. 1, fol. 2.

p. 46 First known Caymanian baptisms. Registrar General's Department, Jamaica. Port Royal Copy Register, vol. 1, fols. 116ff.

p. 46 First known death notice of a Cayman settler. British Library. *The Gentleman's Magazine and Historical Chronicle*, vol. LIX, July 1789, pp. 670–1.

p. 47 Sketch of Savanna-la-Mar, ca. 1830s. © National Maritime Museum, London: LOG/N/S23; D8031.

p. 48 Robert Hodgson's sketch-map. Archivo General de Simancas: Mapas, Planes y Dibujos, xi–165 (1783).

p. 50 Record of mahogany export 1744. PRO: CO 142/15, fol. 73v.

p. 51 Mortar. CINA (Humphrey collection).

p. 52 Description of Grand Cayman from HMS *Alarm,* 1764. MODHO: Miscellaneous Papers, vol. 2, fols. 42A–43. This and other items in chapters 3, 6, and 7 from the MODHO are © Crown Copyright. Published

by permission of the Controller of Her Majesty's Stationery Office and the UK Hydrographic Office.
p. 53 Description of Grand Cayman from HMS *Camilla*, 1787. MODHO: Miscellaneous Papers, vol. 42, fols. 558–61.
pp. 54–55 First survey of Grand Cayman, by George Gauld. Reproduced from the version published jointly by MODHO and CINA, 1994.
p. 56 *Susan and Kitty*, built in 1783. PRO: CO 142/27, fol. 46v.
p. 57 First census of Grand Cayman, by Edward Corbet. National Library of Jamaica, Nugent Papers, MS 72.
p. 58 Route of the convoy under HMS *Convert*. CINA (map prepared by Roger Craig).
p. 58 Admiral Sir John Lawford. Reproduced, courtesy of the National Portrait Gallery, from *One Hundred Silhouette Portraits from the Collection of Francis Wellesley* (Oxford University Press, 1912).
p. 59 Aerial view of the East End coast, ca. 1990. Photo: Dennis Denton.
p. 60 Cannon recovered from HMS *Convert*. Peggy Leshikar-Denton.
Plate between chapters 3 & 4: Anchor off East End, ca. 1992. Photo: Mike Guderian.

CHAPTER 4

p. 64 Slaves logging in Grand Cayman, 1730s. CINA (Chris Mann collection).
p. 66 Shipping register showing export of cotton and turtle, 1804. PRO: CO 142/21, fol. 135r.
p. 67 Shipping register showing import of slaves, 1804. PRO: CO 142/21, fol. 155r.
p. 69 Pedro St. James. CINA, from G.S.S. Hirst, *Notes on the History of the Cayman Islands* (Kingston: P.A. Benjamin Manf. Co., 1910).
p. 71 Slave dwellings. CINA (Chris Mann collection).
pp. 74–76 Public Recorder's records: Rachel Ebanks purchases, frees, and marries George Bodden, 15 April 1816. CINA: Public Recorder's Records, vol. 1, fols. 25–8.
p. 80 Sam Sharpe. Photo: Robert Harris. Interpretive sign in northern Jamaica. Photo: Claudette Upton.
p. 81 William Wilberforce. CINA, from Robert Wilberforce and Samuel Wilberforce, *The Life of William Wilberforce* (London: John Murray, 1838), vol. 4, frontispiece.
p. 83 Governor Sligo addressing slaveowners, 2 May 1835. CINA (Chris Mann collection).
p. 84 Captain Pack reading the Emancipation Proclamation. Painting by Chris Mann. Brian Kieran Collection. Reproduced with permission.
p. 85 The Emancipation Proclamation. PRO: CO137/198, fol. 318v.
Plate between chapters 4 & 5: Custos James Goodchild Coe. CINA collections.

CHAPTER 5

p. 90 Sir George Nugent. CINA, from Frank Cundall, ed., *Lady Nugent's Journal* (London: Adam and Charles Black, 1907), published by the Institute of Jamaica and used with permission.

p. 91 Fort George. CINA collections.
p. 93 The trial of Long Celia. CINA (Chris Mann collection).
pp. 94–95 Creation of the first elected legislature, December 1831. PRO: CO 137/367, fol. 342.
p. 97 Meeting at Pedro St. James, December 1831. CINA (Chris Mann collection).
p. 100 Private Hunter brought to Magistrate Thompson's house. CINA (Chris Mann collection).
p. 104 Emancipation Proclamation being read in Little Cayman. CINA (Chris Mann collection).
p. 106 Ex-slaves riding to church. CINA (Chris Mann collection).
p. 110 Two ex-slaves dancing. Sketch by Chris Mann. Brian Kieran Collection. Reproduced with permission.
pp.113–14 Map of British islands in the West Indies in the 1830s and detail of Grand Cayman. CINA, from *The British Islands in the West Indies*, published under the Society for the Diffusion of Useful Knowledge, [n.d., ca. 1835].
p. 116 Andrew Malcolm teaching in Bodden Town. CINA (Chris Mann collection).
p. 117 The "slave wall" in Bodden Town. CINA collections. Photo: J. Kimlon Woods.
p. 118 Elderly Caymanians who had been born into slavery. CINA, from G.S.S. Hirst, *Notes on the History of the Cayman Islands* (Kingston: P.A. Benjamin Manf Co., 1910).
Plate between chapters 5 & 6: Catherine Susanna Connolly (née Bodden) of East End. CINA (Levy collection).

CHAPTER 6

p. 124 Route of the steamship HMS *Shannon*, 1863. © National Maritime Museum, London, LOG/N/S/31; D8033.
p. 125 Sketch of Cayman Brac, 1820. MODHO: Miscellaneous Papers, vol. 41, fol. 567.
p. 126 First known survey of the Sister Islands, 1831. MODHO: H 56, shelf 737.
p. 127 Sketches of the Cayman Islands, ca. 1833. MODHO: Album 8I, West Indies, vol. II, fol. CE.
p. 128 Migrations of Caymanians, 1830s to 1860s. CINA (map prepared by Roger Craig).
p. 131 Bonacca as seen from Half Moon Cay, 1842. CINA, from Thomas Young, *Narrative of a Residence on the Mosquito Shore* (London: Smith, Elder and Co., 1842), frontispiece.
p. 132 French Harbour, Roatán. CINA collections.
p. 133 Evangelist's Meeting House, French Harbour. CINA collections.
p. 135 Map of the Swan Islands. CINA collections (Nelson collection, Accession 237).
p. 136 Harvesting coconuts, Swan Islands. CINA collections. (Nelson collection, Accession 237).

p. 137 Mr. and Mrs. Tom Ebanks. CINA collections (Nelson collection, Accession 237).
p. 138 Loggerhead turtle eggs arranged by size. CINA collections (Nelson collection, Accession 237).
p. 138 Loggerhead turtle eggs hanging up to dry. CINA collections (Nelson collection, Accession 237).
p. 139 Old Providence Island, Colombia. Photo: Martin Keeley.
p. 140 Old Providence Island. Photo: Martin Keeley.
p. 141 Robert Woodville gravestone. Photo: Heather McLaughlin.
p. 142 Gravestone of Grace Azelda Ebanks. CINA (Bush collection).
Plate between chapters 6 & 7: Resilience and self-reliance. Photo ca. 1928. CINA (Kohlman collection).

CHAPTER 7

p. 146 Shipwreck off East End, 1845. CINA (Ann Gaylor collection).
p. 150 The first seal of the Cayman Islands. PRO: CO 137/392, fol. 558v.
p. 152 Land registration form, 1850. CINA, from *Laws of the Cayman Islands* (Kingston: Government Printing Establishment, 1889), p. 11.
p. 153 Sir John Peter Grant. National Library of Jamaica.
pp. 155–56 George Town and South West Sound from HMS *Eclipse*, 1874. MODHO: Album 8I, West Indies, vol. II, fol. CE.
pp. 158–59 First chart of all three Cayman Islands, 1882. Reproduced from the version published jointly by MODHO and CINA, 1996.
p. 163 First published report about the Cayman Islands, 1887. Jamaica: Government Printing Establishment, Kingston, 1887.
p. 167 Custos Edmund Parsons. CINA collections.
p. 168 Remnants of phosphate mining. CINA (Alexander collection).
p. 169 First publication by a Caymanian. William T. Eden and E. Noel McLaughlin, *The Island of Grand Cayman at the Jamaica Exhibition* (Kingston: DeOrdova & Co., 1891).
Plate between chapters 7 & 8: Caymanian merchants advertise their wares. CINA, from G.S.S. Hirst, *Notes on the History of the Cayman Islands* (Kingston: P.A. Benjamin Manf Co., 1910).

CHAPTER 8

p. 174 George Town Harbour, 1906. CINA, from Vaquero, *Life and Adventure in the West Indies* (London: John Bale, Sons & Danielsson, Ltd., 1914).
p. 176 Cayman Islands postage stamps. Tourism Attractions Board, CIG.
p. 177 Catboats on Little Cayman, 1938. CINA (Lewis collection).
p. 178 Court House at Stake Bay, ca. 1910. CINA (Gamble collection).
p. 182 Commissioner Hirst with daughters, ca. 1910. CINA (Gamble collection).
p. 184 Bodden Town road, ca. 1910. CINA, from G.S.S. Hirst, *Notes on the History of the Cayman Islands* (Kingston: P.A. Benjamin Manf. Co., 1910).
p. 185 Early legislators. CINA, from *A Souvenir of June 22, 1911* (George Town, Grand Cayman, 1911), p. 11.
p. 187 Government House, 1948. PRO: INF 10/100.

Plate between chapters 8 & 9: Advertisement for the Government Savings Bank. CINA (Annie Foster collection).

CHAPTER 9

p. 193 Seven ladies from Grand Cayman, 1906. CINA, from Vaquero, *Life and Adventure in the West Indies* (London: Bale & Danielsson, Ltd., 1914).
p. 196 The doctor's house and pony, 1906. CINA, from Vaquero, *Life and Adventure in the West Indies* (London: Bale & Danielsson, Ltd., 1914).
p. 197 South Sound scene, 1906. CINA: from Vaquero, *Life and Adventure in the West Indies* (London: Bale & Danielsson, Ltd., 1914).
p. 199 *Rainbow* unloading turtle, 1906. CINA, from Vaquero, *Life and Adventure in the West Indies* (London: Bale & Danielsson, Ltd., 1914).
p. 200 Shipbuilding in Grand Cayman, 1906. (CINA: from Vaquero, *Life and Adventure in the West Indies* (London: Bale & Danielsson, Ltd., 1914).
p. 201 House, family, and provisions in Grand Cayman. Cayman Free Press collections. Photo: Joseph Steinmetz, 1950.
Plate between chapters 9 & 10: Caboose. Photo ca. 1970. CINA (Oliver collection).

CHAPTER 10

p. 206 Farmer, 1938. CINA (Lewis collection).
p. 207 Working a provision ground, ca. 1930. CINA (Kohlman collection).
p. 207 Farmer's hut, 1949. CINA (Doran collection).
p. 208 Wompers. CINA (Andresen collection).
p. 208 Plaiting silver thatch. CINA collections.
p. 209 Twisting strand for ropemaking, 1948. PRO: INF 10/96.
p. 209 Laying rope, 1938. CINA (Alexander collection).
p. 210 Thatching a roof, 1938. CINA (Lewis collection). Grinding sugar cane, ca. 1930. CINA (Kohlman collection). Wompers. CINA (Andresen collection).
p. 211 Transporting bananas, ca. 1930. CINA (Kohlman collection).
p. 211 Dugout canoes. CINA (Nowak collection).
p. 212 Captain Rayal Bodden, ca. 1930. CINA (Kohlman collection).
p. 212 George Town boatyard, 1917. PRO: CO 137/724; included with despatch from Commissioner A.C. Robinson, 28 May 1917.
p. 213 Launching of the *F.A Marie,* 1917. PRO: CO 137/724; included with despatch from Commissioner A.C. Robinson, 28 May 1917.
p. 213 Catboat, 1949. CINA (Doran collection).
p. 217 Using a waterglass, 1938. CINA (Lewis collection).
p. 218 Hawksbill nets, Little Cayman, 1938. CINA (Lewis collection).
p. 219 Turtle crawl on the Miskito Banks. PRO: CO 137/644; included with confidential despatch, 13 April 1905.
p. 220 Crew aboard the *Banks,* ca. 1938. CINA (Kohlman collection).
p. 221 Turtlers at the Miskito Cays, 1939. Photo: David Douglas Duncan.
p. 222 Description of Caymanians turtling, ca. 1840. CINA, from Thomas Young, *Narrative of a Residence on the Mosquito Shore* (London: Smith, Elder and Co., 1842), p. 17.

p. 223 Hawksbill shell. Cayman Free Press collections.
Plate between chapters 10 & 11: "Strawrope Industry Pledge". CINA (Central Registry file 138/42).

CHAPTER 11

p. 227 Rev. James Elmslie, ca. 1863. CINA (collection 11). Reproduced courtesy of Edinburgh University Library, New College Library.
p. 229 Rev. William Whitecross. CINA (collection 11). Reproduced courtesy of Edinburgh University Library, New College Library.
p. 230 Rev. John Smith. CINA (collection 11). Reproduced courtesy of the National Library of Scotland.
p. 230 George Town Presbyterian Church. CINA collections.
p. 231 Rev. John Edmond Martin. CINA (collection 11). Reproduced courtesy of Edinburgh University Library, New College Library.
p. 231 Rev. Thomas Redpath. CINA (Levy collection).
p. 232 Rev. William Pouchie. CINA (Masters collection).
p. 232 West Bay Presbyterian Church elders, early 1900s. CINA (Arthur Ebanks collection).
p. 233 North Side Presbyterian Church, ca. 1970. CINA (Oliver collection).
p. 233 Presbyterian Mission Council, Jamaica, 1930s. CINA (collection 11). Reproduced courtesy of the National Library of Scotland.
p. 234 Marriage of Bentley Ross and Leila McTaggart, 1915. CINA (Bodden-Bush collection).
p. 234 Presbyterian Church at Prospect, ca. 1915. CINA (Bodden-Bush collection).
p. 235 Little Cayman Baptist Church, 1938. CINA (Lewis collection).
p. 236 Graves in Grand Cayman. CINA (Ann Gaylor collection).
p. 239 F.S. McTaggart with family, ca. 1900. CINA (Bodden-Bush collection).
p. 240 F.S. McTaggart's school register. CINA collections: MSD 154.
p. 241 Smiley Conolly's school, early 1900s. CINA collections.
p. 243 Creek schoolhouse, 1938. CINA (Lewis collection).
p. 244 Miss Izzy's schoolhouse, ca. 1955. CINA (Walker collection).
p. 248 George Town school, 1938. CINA (Lewis collection).
Plate between chapters 11 & 12: A youngster eyes a distant schooner. CINA (Roy collection).

CHAPTER 12

p. 253 The *Rubens*. CINA (Lewis collection).
p. 255 Advertisement for the *Noca*. CINA collections: MSD 343.
p. 256 Aarona Booker Kohlman on the Isle of Pines. CINA (Kohlman collection).
p. 257 Isle of Pines. CINA (Kohlman collection).
p. 261 Turtle canning factory. PRO: CO 137/724; included with despatch from Commissioner A.C. Robinson, 28 May 1917.
p. 262 Going to the Vestry. CINA (Fulford collection).
p. 263 Commissioner H.H. Hutchings, ca.1928. CINA (Kohlman collection).
p. 264 George Town Town Hall, 1938. CINA (Lewis collection).

p. 264 Two kinds of transport in the 1920s. CINA (Kohlman collection.)
p. 265 *Cimboco*, 1938. CINA (Lewis collection).
p. 266 Launching of the *Lady Slater*, 1934. CINA (Bodden-Harris collection).
p. 271 The path of the 1932 hurricane. CINA (map prepared by Roger Craig).
p. 272 Fleeing the storm surge. CINA (Nancy Kirkaldy collection).
p. 272 Spot Bay, 1994. CINA (collection 46). Photo: Wallace Platts.
p. 273 Commissioner E.A. Weston. CINA (S. Ebanks collection).
p. 274 Aston Rutty and family. CINA (Lewis collection).
p. 275 R.B. Leitch home. Cayman Brac Museum collections.
Plate between chapters 12 & 13: Boyd Hydes. Photo ca. 1985. CINA (Nowak collection).

CHAPTER 13

p. 281 Commissioner A. W. Cardinall. CINA (Fulford collection).
p. 282 George Town scout troop, ca. 1930s. Cayman Free Press collections.
p. 282 An annual regatta. CINA (Parsons collection).
p. 283 Regatta programme. CINA (CINL Accession 2301).
p. 284 Sharking, 1930s. CINA (Kohlman collection).
p. 285 1929 Ford on Cayman Brac. CINA (Lewis collection).
p. 286 Opening of the wireless station. CINA collections.
p. 288 West Bay Town Hall, late 1930s. CINA (Bodden-Bush collection).
p. 289 1938 Oxford expedition: homemade still for recovering waste alcohol. CINA (Lewis collection).
p. 289 Oxford scientific expedition—Sam Ebanks, Gerald Thompson, and John Howard. CINA (Lewis collection).
p. 291 Address to Caymanian volunteers joining the TRNVR, 1941. CINA collections: MSD 343.
p. 292 TRNVR volunteer Ewart Ebanks. CINA (E. Ebanks collection).
p. 293 Cayman Home Guard, ca. 1943. CINA (Audrey Ebanks collection).
p. 294 Home Guard lookout, 1948. PRO: INF 10/100.
p. 295 U.S. Navy base, ca. 1942. CINA (Roy collection).
p. 296 U.S. Navy personnel, ca. 1942. CINA (Roy collection).
p. 296 Three members of the Cayman Home Guard. CINA (Audrey Ebanks collection).
p. 297 PBM Mariner in North Sound. CINA (Tucker collection).
p. 298 Marriage of Lillian Bodden and Jack Howard, 1942. CINA (Roy collection).
p. 299 Arnold A. "Cappy" Foster at his boatyard. CINA (Jenkinson collection).
p. 299 Boats under construction at Cayman Boats Ltd; Cappy Foster and Errol Flynn. CINA (Jenkinson collection).
p. 300 Daniel K. Ludwig. From a booklet published by Concordia Publications, [n.d.] ca. 1980s..
p. 301 Government demobilisation notice, 1945. CINA: Government Notice No. 66/45.
Plate between chapters 13 & 14: Christmas beef. Photo ca. 1960s. CINA (Andresen collection).

CHAPTER 14

p. 307 Alexander Bustamante. CINA collections.
p. 308 Elected Vestrymen, 1944. CINA: Government Notice No. 85/44.
p. 309 Cayman representatives at the second conference on the British West Indies Federation. CINA collections.
p. 310 Sir Kenneth Blackburne. CINA (S.O. Ebanks collection).
p. 311 Annie Huldah Bodden, ca. 1970s. CINA collections.
p. 312 Women's petition, 1948. CINA: Central Registry file 202/48.
p. 313 Sybil McLaughlin, ca. 1960s. CINA (S. McLaughlin collection).
p. 314 Administrator Jack Rose and CO officials at the Lancaster conference, 1961. CINA (Rose collection).
p. 320 Meeting of the new Executive Council, 23 November 1976. CINA (*Annual Report 1976*, p. 8).
p. 322 Mabry Kirkconnell. CINA collections.
p. 323 Legislative Assembly, 1970s. CINA (Miller collection).
p. 324 Senior civil servants with Governor Thomas Russell, in front of the new Government Administration Building, 1976. CINA collections.
p. 324 Opening of the Grand Court at the new Courts Building, 1974. CINA (Humphrey collection).
p. 325 Government Administration Building, Cayman Brac, ca. 1960. CINA (Brock collection).
p. 326 Grand Cayman police force, ca. 1940s. CINA (Panton collection).
p. 327 Hell Post Office, 1973. CINA (Humphrey collection).
Plate between chapters 14 & 15: Mr. Tomlinson, a member of the legal profession from Jamaica, ca. 1930. CINA (Kohlman collection).

CHAPTER 15

p. 332 Galleon Beach Hotel, ca. 1956. CINA (Greenall collection).
p. 333 The *Santa Maria*, ca. 1950. Cayman Free Press collections. Photo: Joseph Steinmetz.
p. 334 Wing Commander Owen Roberts. Courtesy Civil Aviation Authority.
p. 334 First landing at Owen Roberts Field. CINA (Miller collection).
p. 335 Cattle being unloaded from a LACSA plane, ca. 1960s. CINA (Hines collection).
p. 336 Opening of Edward Bodden Airfield, Little Cayman, 1962. CINA (D. Foster collection).
p. 337 James Manoah Bodden. CINA, from *The Man Who Changed the Face of Cayman* (CINL Accession No. 631).
p. 337 Cayman Brac Airways, 1960s. CINA (Cruickshank collection).
p. 339 Benson Greenall and staff at Galleon Beach Hotel, ca. 1955. CINA (Greenall collection).
p. 340 Ruston electrical generator, ca. 1960s. CINA (Bodden-Bush collection).
p. 343 MRCU fogger. *Northwester,* April 1975. Used by permission of Desmond Seales, MBE, publisher.
p. 344 Dr. Marco Giglioli. *Northwester,* April 1975. Used by permission of Desmond Seales, MBE, publisher.

p. 344 MRCU spray plane, 1970s. MRCU, CIG.
p. 345 Aerial view of dykes and canals, 1975. CINA (*Annual Report 1975*, p. 41).
p. 347 Galleon Beach Hotel, 1956. CINA (Greenall collection).
p. 348 Buccaneer's Inn, Cayman Brac, 1960s. CINA collections, from a brochure designed by Design/Print, Miami, n.d. [mid-1960s].
p. 349 The first Holiday Inn, 1973. CINA (Ranson collection).
p. 350 Advertising poster for fishing trips with Capt. Ertis Ebanks, ca. 1960s. CINA (Ertis Ebanks collection).
p. 351 The *Stella Polaris* off George Town, ca 1960. CINA (Comissong collection).
p. 351 Cruise-ship passengers on Harbour Drive. CINA: Mackenzie collection.
p. 352 The first Royal Bank building, 1965. CINA (Cruickshank collection).
p. 354 Sir Vassell Johnson being knighted by H.M. The Queen. Courtesy of Government Information Service.
p. 356 Cayman National Bank building. CINA collections. Photo: J. Kimlon Woods.
p. 357 Cable & Wireless, George Town. CINA collections. Photo: Mark Leach.
Plate between chapters 15 & 16: Leah Bush sweeping the sand yard, ca. 1960s. CINA (Croft collection).

CHAPTER 16

p. 364 Road to East End, 1949. CINA (Doran collection).
p. 365 Opening of Comart Ltd., 1968. CINA (Humphrey collection).
p. 369 Immigration Department. CINA collections. Photo: J. Kimlon Woods.
p. 370 Cayman family, ca. 1960. CINA (Johnson collection).
p. 372 Northward Prison. CINA collections. Photo: Mark Leach.
p. 373 Cuban refugee vessels, 1994. CINA (Rankine collection).
p. 374 District Administrator Oswell Rankine with Cuban boats, 1994. CINA (Rankine collection).
Plate between chapters 16 & 17: Pausing to chat, ca. 1980s. CINA (Nowak collection).

CHAPTER 17

p. 378 Steering Committee of the NCSS. CINA (*Annual Report, 1974*, facing p. 45).
p. 379 Lions and Leos on Cayman Brac. Photo: Catherine Chesnard.
p. 380 George Town Hospital, 1950s. CINA collections.
p. 382 Faith Hospital, Cayman Brac, 1970s. *Northwester*, June 1973. Used by permission of Desmond Seales, MBE, publisher.
p. 384 Spot Bay school, 1938. CINA (Lewis collection).
p. 386 Rev. George Hicks receiving the MBE. CINA (Bodden-Bush collection).
p. 387 Triple C School, 1964. CINA (Humphrey collection).
pp. 387–88 Cayman High School, 1949, and Rev. John Gray and CHS staff, ca. 1950. CINA, from *The Prep School Story* (CINL Accession No. 699).
p. 389 Cayman Brac High School, 2002. Photo: Martin Keeley.

p. 390 Community College, 2002. CINA collections. Photo: J. Kimlon Woods.
p. 392 North Side United Church, ca. 1970. CINA (Masters collection).
p. 395 Church of God, Holiness, Watering Place, 2002. Photo: Martin Keeley.
p. 396 Cayman Gospel Press, ca. 1950s. CINA (Johnson collection).
p. 397 *The Caymanian*, 1908, and *The Tradewinds*, 1964. CINA collections.
p. 398 Radio Cayman, ca. 1977. CINA (Bodden-Bush collection).
p. 398 The Islander Theatre, George Town. CINA (Johnson collection).
Plate between chapters 17 & 18: Heroes Square, 2003. CINA (Humphrey collection).

CHAPTER 18

p. 402 George Town Port at night. CINA (Mackenzie collection).
p. 403 Central Mangrove Wetlands. Department of Lands and Survey, CIG.
p. 403 John McLean and H.M. Queen Elizabeth II. Courtesy of Government Information Service.
p. 404 Mariculture Ltd., 1960s. CINA (Johnson collection).
p. 406 Official coat of arms. College of Arms, London.
p. 407 Remembrance Day, Stake Bay. Cayman Free Press. Photo: Nicky Watson.
p. 407 Ship-to-ship oil transfer off Little Cayman. *Nor'wester,* May 1982. Used by permission of Desmond Seales, MBE, publisher.
p. 409 HMS *Zest*, 1967. CINA (Cruickshank collection).
p. 409 Queen's Birthday parade. CINA (Hurlston collection).
p. 410 Pirates Week programme. The Northwester Company, 1977.
p. 412 Pedro St. James, National Historic Site. CINA collections. Photo: Mark Leach.
p. 413 Truman Bodden Sports Centre. CINA collections. Photo: Mark Leach.
p. 414 *Homage to Cayos Miskitos I.* CINA collections. Photo: Roger Craig.
p. 415 *Peace Be Still.* Henry and Marcia Muttoo collection. Reproduced with permission. Photo: Roger Craig.
p. 418 Pirates Week, 1977. CINA collections. Reproduced with permission.
Plate after chapter 18: Celebration fireworks over Hog Sty Bay. Photo: Justin Uzzell, October 1999.

BACK COVER

The national symbols of the Cayman Islands
Banana orchid. Photo: Fred Burton.
Cayman Parrot. Photo: Fred Burton.
Silver thatch palm. Photo: Mark Leach.

Index

Page numbers set in italic type refer to illustrations or captions to illustrations.

A

Adriaensz, Pieter (Admiral), 17
Adventists. *See* Seventh-Day Adventist Church
Agricultural Show, 183, 184
AIDS, 383
aircraft, World War Two. *See* flying boats
airfields, 332
  Cayman Brac, 335–6
  Grand Cayman, 334–5
  land ownership, conflicts over, 339
  Little Cayman, 336
air transportation, 332–9
  to Sister Islands, 335–6
alcohol
  import and re-export of, during Prohibition, 266–8
  laws respecting, 96, 98, 440n. 15
Anchorage Centre, 349
Anglican Church
  division into two bodies, 393–4
  in the colonies, 113
  influence of, during apprenticeship, 82
apprenticeship. *See* emancipation
Arch, Heber, Sr. (shipwright), 266, 281
Arch, Loxley (builder), 274
archaeology, Amerindian, 11–12
arts, creative, 413–16
Ary, "Governor", 24, 25
Asquith, Lord (constitutional expert), 319–20
Assembly of Magistrates (*later* Justices) and Vestry
  agreement to pay Commissioner's salary, 170
  comments on, by Commissioners, 473n. 3
  formation of, 3, 98–9
  meetings of, during Hirst years, 184–5
  reorganisation of, planned by Hirst, 186
  satisfaction of, with Jamaican inaction, 154
Atkins, Rev. James (Wesleyan missionary), 118–19
Atlantis (cruise ship), 283

B

Bahamas
  independence, effect on financial industry, 356–7
  rum-running during Prohibition, 266–7
Baillie, Rev. Andrew (Presbyterian missionary), 234–5
Baldpate. *See* United States: Navy base, in George Town
Banker, Ray (artist), 416
banking. *See* financial industry
Banks, 9, 220
Banks, Guy (District Administrator), 274
baptism, in eighteenth century, 45–7
Baptist Church, 234, 395
  education in Sister Islands, contribution to, 243
  mission to Sister Islands, success of, 236–7
Barba (*later* Scott, Ben), 129
Barclays Bank, 352, 479n. 54
Barefoot Man. *See* Novak, George
barking, 208
Barkly, Sir Henry (Governor of Jamaica), 148
Barnett, Curtis (poet), 414–15
Barron, Rev. Charles (Baptist pastor), 237
  education in Sister Islands, observations on, 243
Basdeo, Joy (executive director, Vision 2008), 417
Bass, Isac and Sarah, 45
Battersby, Benjamin (investor), 42–4, 64
Battersby v. Foster, 42–4
Bawden, Isaac. *See* Bodden, Isaac
Bay Islands
  British colonial policy and, 135–6
  British surrender of, to Honduras, 124, 131
  Caymanian families in, 132
  census of 1858, 134
  Crown Colony status, 137–40
    loss of, 139–40
    reaction to, in United States, 138
    success of, 137–8
  disadvantages of, 131

migration from, to Cayman Islands, 140
migration to, by Caymanians, 131–4
opportunities in, for Caymanians, 120
racial issues in, 133–4
religion, in colony, 138
trade, 135, 449n. 29
work patterns, 135
Belmont Dry Dock (Jamaica), 298
Bergstrom, Eric (director, Department of Tourism), 348, 349
Bird, Rev. Mark (Wesleyan missionary), 119
Blackburne, Kenneth (Governor of Jamaica), 309
self-government debate, resolution of, 316–17
West Indies Federation, proposals for Cayman's role in, 314–15
women suffrage, granting of, 313
Blackman, Rev. John (Presbyterian minister), 232, 267
Black River: trade route with Cayman and Jamaica, 49
Blake, Sir Henry (Governor of Jamaica), 453n. 33
Cayman Brac, private school in, 242
visits to Cayman Islands, 169–70
Bloody Bay
first settlement in Sister Islands, 127
marked on first map of Little Cayman, 126
Boase, Capt. Joseph (*Iphigenia*), 215–16
Boatswain's Bay: population, in 1802 census, 56
Bodden, Alice V. (librarian), 288
Bodden, Amy: Grand Cayman Benevolent Society for Women, 183
Bodden, Annie Huldah (legislator), 311
Bodden, Eleanor Grant: memories of '32 Storm, 273, 276
Bodden, George (freedman), 428n. 16, 438n. 5
marriage to Rachel Ebanks, 74
Bodden, George Edward (slaveowner), 72
Bodden [Bawden], Isaac, 428n. 18
baptism of sons, 45–6
first recorded inhabitant of Grand Cayman, 35
marriage to Sarah Lamar, 45
Bodden, James (Magistrate), 70, 91
Bodden, James Manoah (National Hero, MLA), *320*, 337–8
Pirates Week, 410
Tourism, Aviation and Trade, Minister of, 349
Bodden, John (overseer), 42–4
Bodden, John, Sr.: number of slaves owned by, 68
Bodden, Joseph (Magistrate)
doubts about abilities, 91
number of slaves owned by, 68
Bodden, Lilian (daughter of Rayal), 297
Bodden, Mary (land grantee), 42. *See also* land grants
Bodden, Mary (slaveowner), 78
Bodden, Rayal (shipwright), *212*, 265
minesweepers, commissions for, 292
public buildings built by, 287
Bodden, Capt. Theo (leader, Volunteer Foggers), 344
Bodden, Truman (MLA), *320*, 417
Bodden, Waide (Magistrate), 96–7
Bodden, William, "Governor" (Senior Magistrate), 3, 46, 428n. 18
government under, ineffectiveness of, 91
judicial system, evolution of, 92, 93
marriage to Mary Eden, 47
number of slaves owned by, 68
obeah trial of slave Primis, 439n. 10
salvor, for Wreck of the Ten Sail, 60
shipowner, 70, 434n. 10
Bodden, William (Spotts): number of slaves owned by, 68
Bodden, William James (slaveowner), 107–8
Bodden [Bawden], William Price (Chief Magistrate)
baptism of, 45–6
death notice of, 46
first recorded Caymanian captain, 51
Bodden, Will T. (publisher), 396
Bodden Town
Anglican services in, 114–15
emancipation, reaction to, 102–3, 105–6, 108, 110, 442n. 31
first description of, 51
first "place of worship", 112
heart of Caymanian Slave Society, 79
land use debates, 403
legislative district, 98
literacy level, in 1911, 196
marriage rate, in 1911 census, 193
militia contingent at, 90
population (1773, 1802), 55
post office established in, 176
Presbyterian congregation at, 229
school, Fyfe's report on, 242
telephone service in, 265, 355
Town Hall, construction of, 288
wreck of *Iphigenia*, 215–16
Bonacca (Guanaja). See Bay Islands
Booth American Line, 298
Borden, Lt. Harold (killed in action), 471n. 29
Botanic Park. See Queen Elizabeth II Botanic Park
Boy Scouts, 281
Brac Reef Beach Resort, 350
Brandon, Joy (poet and playwright), 414–15, 487n. 28
British Merchant Service, 290
British West India Airways (BWIA), 335
British West India Regiment, 81
conflicts with local inhabitants, 82, 99–102
contingent, in World War One, 260
withdrawal of, 104
British West Indies Federation. See West Indies Federation
buccaneers, 20, 28
Buccaneers Inn, 348
Bush, Annie (nurse), 436n. 32
Bush, Gladwyn K. (Miss Lassie) (artist), 416
Bustamante, William Alexander (first Chief Minister of Jamaica), 289, 306–7, 335

C

Cable & Wireless, Ltd.
cricket, sponsorship of, 413
radio stations, early, 286–7
telecommunications, modern, 355
caboose, *203*
cadastral survey, 341–3
Camayagua, torpedoing of, 293
Campbell, Daniel (land grantee), 37–9, 43, 427n. 12
Campbell, Mary (land grantee), 37–9, 43
canoes, 211
Cardinall, Allen Wolsey (Commissioner), 5
accomplishments of, 279–88
Assembly, thoughts on, 280
Aston Rutty, relationship with, 280–81
background of, 279
loyalty to British Empire, fostering of, 289–90
Annual Report of 1935, 288–9
tourism, promotion of, 283–4, 347
Caribbean International Airlines, 334
Carib Guano Company, 166–7
CARIFTA Games, 413
Carr, Archie (turtle expert), 404, 405
Carswell, Joseph E. (Holiness missionary), 238
Carter, Richard: charges against, by former slaves, 108–9
Cartwright, William (Chief Magistrate), 428n. 16, 433n. 1, 438n. 5
cash economy: growth of, 208
catboat, 178
invention of, 211
racing, 412, 487n. 21
Catholic Church, 394–5, 484n. 38
CATN/TV-30 (Cayman Adventist Television Network), 398
Cayfest, 413
cayman (caimán, crocodile), 2, 11, 12, 15, 16, 17
etymology of, 422n. 7
Cayman (yacht), 17, 20
Cayman Airways, 337–9
Cayman Boats Limited, 298
Cayman Brac
air service to, 335–6, 338
Barclays Bank branch on, 352, 479n. 54
boatbuilding on, 129
churches on, 395
early lighthouse on, 183
education and churches, need for, 162
emancipation, announcement of, 103
first settlers on, 127, 446nn. 6–10, 447nn. 12–14
hotel development on, 348, 350
observations on, by Governor Norman, 162, 235
phosphate industry on, 167
place names on first map of, 126
race relations on, 447n. 15
radio (wireless) station on, 286
roads, first drivable, 287
ropemaking, 208
schoolteachers, 130, 235, 242, 243–4
Storm of '32, 271–6
tanning operation on, 285
telephone service on, 265, 355
Cayman Brac Airways, 336
Cayman Brac High School, 388, 389, 408
Cayman Brac: Land of my Birth (Dixon), 244
Cayman Compass, 396
Cayman Disease, 380
Cayman Drama Society, 414
Cayman Energy Ltd., 408
Cayman High School, 386
Caymanian (monthly), 188, 396, 397
Caymanian Compass, 396–7, 403, 484n. 44
Caymanian Weekly, 396
Cayman Island Airways, 333
Cayman Islands Corporation, 334, 337
Cayman Islands Health Services Complex, 383
Cayman Islands High School (*later* John Gray High School), 387–8
Cayman Islands Law School, 328, 389
Cayman Islands Motor Boat Company, 265
Cayman Islands National Archive, 410, 412
Cayman Islands National Museum, 410, 412, 415
Cayman Islands Yacht and Sailing Club (CIYSC), 281
Cayman National Cultural Foundation, 410, 413, 414, 415, 416
Cayman National Theatre Company, 414
Cayman Net News, 397
Cayman Singers, 413
Cayman Stock Exchange, 360
Cayman Storage Disease, 381
Cayman Times, 396
Cayman Turtle Farm, 405–6
CCT (Cayman Christian Television), 398
Central Planning Authority, 349, 350, 403
Chamber of Commerce, 283
Chief Minister, post of
excluded, from 1992 amendments, 322
proposed, under Federation, 314–15
children: duties of, 207–8
Christian, Elizabeth Sarah (widow), 126, 446n. 9
Christian, Robert (HMS *Active*): early description of George Town [Hogsties], 51
Christian Democratic Party (CDP). *See under* political parties
Christianity, basis of society, 233, 392, 417
churches, 227–39, 391–5. *See also specific denominations*
diversification of, 395
need for, in Sister Islands, 162
Church of England. See Anglican Church
Church of God, 238, 395
contribution to secondary education, 385
Gospel of the Kingdom, 396
Cimboco, 265–6, 273, 293
CITES (Convention on International Trade in Endangered Species), 405
CITN (Cayman International Television Network), 398
Civil Aviation Authority, 337
civil service: transformation of, postwar, 323–8
Clarke, Henry (owner of George Bodden), 74
Clarke, Robert (partner of "Governor" Bodden), 60

Clayton-Bulwer Treaty, 138
coat of arms, 406, 485n. 8
coconut industry, 176–9
Coe, James, Jr. (Chief Magistrate)
  conflict with Rev. Elmslie, 229
  judicial system, evolution of, 92
Coe, James, Sr. (Magistrate, Custos), 72
  judicial system, evolution of, 92, 93
  obeah trial of slave Primis, 439n. 10
  petition requesting slave registration and owner compensation, 80–81
Coe, William (Holiness minister), 238
colonial development funds
  grant for navigational beacons, 287
  grants and loans for George Town airfield, 334
Columbus, Christopher, 1, 11, 12–14
Columbus, Ferdinand, 13
Commonwealth Games, 413
Community College of the Cayman Islands, 389, 390
Connolly, Erskine (Magistrate): wreck of *Juga*, 216–17
Connolly, Smiley (teacher), *241*
Connolly, William S. (anti-racism crusader), 468n. 32
Connor, Ercel (teacher), 386
Conolly, Warren (MLA)
  NDP, formation of, 315, 316
  official history of Cayman, 409
  tourism, promoter of, 348, 349
conservation, of marine resources, 402
constable, island, 99
constitution, 310
  amendments to, 1962, 318
  Asquith report, 319–20
  changes to, consideration of (1966–9), 319
  draft revision, 1992, 322
  review of, by Smith and Wallace, 322
  revised, 1972, 320–22
Cook-Bodden, E. (women's activist), 311
Cooper, Joseph, and family (Bay Islands settlers), 132, 448n. 21
Coral Caymanian Hotel, 348
Corbet, Edward, 86, 191
  Cayman Islands, report on, 49, 60, 90–91, 93
  church in Bodden Town, report on, 112
  number of slaves, in 1802 census, 68
  Sister Islands, report on, 125
Corn Islands
  Caymanian settlements on, 141
  population of, in 1830s, 450n. 46
cotton
  export of, and import of slaves, 52–3, 67
  industry, 434n. 8
    revival of, Sanguinetti's hope for, 174
    slaves essential to, 63
  plantations, in Grand Cayman, 49, 52, 54, 66, 68
  production, annual, 67
  production, decline in, 69–70, 435n. 16
courts. *See* judicial system
Crawl Bay: marked on first map of Little Cayman, 126
credit system, 198
Creek: Baptist chapel and schoolroom at, 236–7, 243
Crewe Road: builders of, 457n. 31
cricket, revival of, 413
Cromwell, Oliver, 20, 35, 424n. 17
cruise ships, 283, 351–2, 479n. 53
Crymble, Murray (land grantee), 39–40
CTS (Cayman Television Service), 398
Cuba. *See also* Isle of Pines
  ban on foreign fishing, 154–5, 156, 179
  radio (wireless) station in George Town, construction of, 285–6
  refugees from, in Cayman, 373–4
Cumberland, wreck of, 57
currency, Caymanian, 358

D

Darling, Charles (Governor of Jamaica), 148–9
Dealy (settler on Cayman Brac), 103, 446n. 5
death notice of Caymanian, first, 46
Defoe, Daniel (pseud. Capt. Charles Johnson): *General History of the Pyrates*, 28–9
dengue fever, prevention of, 344–5, 381, 478n. 36
Denham, Sir Edward (Governor of Jamaica), 286
dental health, 263, 381–2
dependency status
  advantages of, to Cayman, 150
  formal declaration of, 5, 90, 145, 150–51
development, commercial. See land use
Dickson, Rev. R.N. (Presbyterian minister): anti-alcohol crusade, 267–8
Dignity Team. *See under* political parties
District Heritage Days, 411
Dixon, Hiram: *Cayman Brac: Land of my Birth*, 244
Dobson, Col. B.P. (early expatriate resident), 281
Dolphijn, 17, 424n. 16
Donald, Alan (Commissioner), 309, 313
Doran, Edwin Beale (cultural geographer), 194
Downside Up (McField), 414
Drake, Sir Francis, 2, 16, 423n. 12
drama, tradition of, 414
Drayton, John (Chief Magistrate)
  ally of Stipendiary Magistrate Thompson, 99
  emancipation, assessing results of, 107–12
  judicial system, evolution of, 92
  letter to Governor Belmore (1831), 96–7
  Long Celia, penalty imposed on, 93
  marriage of Rachel Ebanks and George Bodden, 74
  number of slaves owned by, 68
  petition requesting slave registration and owner compensation, 80–81
duppies, 234
Dutch mariners: knowledge of Cayman, 16–20

E

East End
Adventist "station" in, 238
earliest settlement in Cayman, 35
kindness to shipwrecked family, 147
marriage rate, in 1911 census, 193
population, estimated (1773), 55
population, in 1802 census, 56
post office established in, 176
quadrille, survival of, 413
road to, from Bodden Town, 287
ropemaking, 208
school, Fyfe's report on, 242
telephone service in, 355
Town Hall, construction of, 288
wreck of *Juga*, 216–17
Wreck of the Ten Sail, 57–60
Eastman, W.W. (Adventist elder), 237
Ebanks, Allie (artist), 416
Ebanks, Benson (MLA, chairman, NCVO), 379
Ebanks, Capt. Ertis (charter captain), *350*
Ebanks, Ewart (TRNVR volunteer), 292
Ebanks, Grace Azelda, 142
Ebanks, Henry and Augustus (free coloured slaveowners), 68
Ebanks, H.O. "Bertie" (government health officer), 343
Ebanks, Lee A.: description of overseas education, 245
Ebanks, Madeline and Myrtle (owners of Tea Shoppe), 297
Ebanks, Rachel: marriage to George Bodden, 74
Eden, Thomas K.: owner of Long Celia, 92
Eden, William (Chief Magistrate), 51, 430n. 31
Cuban ban on fishing, protest against, 154–5
emancipation, assessing results of, 108
house at Great Pedro (see Pedro St. James)
lease of property to "principal inhabitants", 96
number of slaves owned by, 68
phosphate assay, 166
pleas to Jamaica for assistance, 148, 155–6
Sister Islands, report on (1854), 130
Swan Islands, connection to, 141
thatch roofing, comments on, 208
turtling schooner, Cuban seizure of, 154
Eden, William T. (chief turtle trader), 181
education
Anglican contribution to, 115
Cayman Brac, first schoolteacher on, 130
churches, influence on, 239, 377, 390–91, 443n. 53
comprehensive system, introduction of, 388
compulsory
extensions of age range, 388
Hirst's desire for, 186, 246
introduced, in 1920, 247–50, 263
Sanguinetti's desire for, 174, 245
Education Acts. See laws
Education Development Plan 1995–1999, 391
external examinations, 386–8, 390
Mico schools in Grand Cayman, 116–17
National Curriculum, 391
need for, in Sister Islands, 162
overseas, 244
private, demand for, 390–91
public, development of, 245–50, 386–9
pupil-teacher system, 249–50
Schools Inspectorate, 391
secondary, 250, 385–6
Sister Islands, in, 242–4, 388
tertiary, opportunities for, 245, 389
underfunding of, 384–5
Education, Department of, 414
egging, 285
Elmslie, Rev. James (Presbyterian missionary), 149
Sister Islands, preaching at, 130
Cayman mission, 228–31
school in George Town, 239
Elmslie Memorial Church, 287, 297, 393, 394
emancipation
apprenticeship, 80–85, 101–2
compensation paid to slaveowners, 71, 78–9, 80–81, 111–12
land ownership, conflicts over, 152
migrations after, 124–5, 254
relations between former masters and former slaves, 103–8
results of, assessing, 107–12
results of, economic, in British Colonies, 123
social conditions following, 3–4, 82–6, 89, 109–12
Emancipation Act, 71, 80
Emancipation Proclamation, 82–5
employment, postwar, 298–300, 301
Environment, Department of, 344, 402
Environmental Research Unit (of MRCU; *later* Department of Environment), 402
Environmental Zones, 402–3
Esteban, Horacio (artist), 416
Evans, John (pirate), 28–9
Executive Air Services, 336
Executive Council
creation of, 310
responsibilities of, 321, 349
expatriates
age distribution among, 366–7
dependence on, 7, 323, 368, 384
judicial system, in, 328
differences between, 364
relations with Caymanians, 320
Eyre, Edward (Governor of Jamaica), 150, 151

F

Faith Hospital, 382–3, 408
farming, 205–7
Farrington, Thomas A. (first government candidate at Mico Normal College), 466n. 57
Farrington, Willie (Assemblyman), 307, 314, 316, 318
Festival of Arts, 413
Financial Action Task Force, 359
financial industry, 352–60

advantages of Cayman, for bankers and investors, 331, 355–60
growth of, 355, 357, 360
First Cayman Bank, 359
flying boats, 295, 297, 332–4
Foot, Hugh (Governor of Jamaica), 309, 311, 335
Ford, James (coat of arms designer), 406
Fort George. *See* forts
forts: condition of, in 1802, 90
Foster, Arnold (Cappy), 298, 299
Foster, Capt. Ashlan (*Cimboco*), 273
Foster, Nolan (Sister Islands MLA), 317
Foster, Robert W. (radio operator), 286
Foster, Stephen Taylor (Brac settler), 126, 446n. 7
Foster, William (land grantee), 39, 41–2, 427n. 12. See also land grants
Battersby-Foster case, 42–4
purchase of slaves by, 64
speculations about, by Hirst, 126
Frenchmans Point: marked on first map of Cayman Brac, 126
Friendly Society, 289
Fyfe, Sir Laurence
Caymanian response to report of, 165–6
education in Cayman, report on, 240–42
general condition of Islands, report on, 164
Islands' administration, examination of, 160, 163–4

G

Galleon Beach Hotel, 347
Garifuna (Black Caribs), 131, 134, 137
Gauld, George (Royal Navy hydrographer)
clergyman, people's desire for, 112
description of Grand Cayman, 53–4
map, 35, 50, 55
"Old Isaac", description of, 35, 45
population estimate (1773), 54–5, 65
General History of the Pyrates (Johnson), 28–9
geological prehistory, 421n. 1
George Hicks High School, 390
George Town [Hogsties]
Adventist "station" in, 238
Anglican services in, 114–15
cruise ships, effect on, 351
description of, by Rev. Hope Waddell, 147
early lighthouse in, 183
first description of, 51
legislative district, 98
literacy level, in 1911, 196
marriage rate, in 1911 census, 193
"metropolitan effect", 366
militia contingent at, 90
phosphate industry, 167
population (1773, 1802), 55
public park, first, 184
schools, early, 115–17
telephone service in, 265, 355
turtle canning factory, 261
West Indian market town (1834), 79
George Town Hospital (*later* Cayman Islands Health Services Complex), 382–3
Gerrard, Andrew (Commissioner), 309
women suffrage, opinion on, 311
Gerrard-Smith International Airport, 335–6
Giglioli, George (entomologist), 343
Giglioli, Marco E.C. (director, MRCU), 344
conservation, concern with, 402
Glover, Nathaniel, 35, 112
appointment as Magistrate, 97
charges against, by former slave, 109
emancipation, assessing results of, 108
slavery in Cayman, comments on, 79–80, 433n. 1
Goldfield, 281–2
Gore (Governor of Cayman Islands), 374
Gospel of the Kingdom, 396
Government Savings Bank
advertisement for, 189
establishment of, 183
growth of, 301
limitations of, 352
Governor of the Cayman Islands: responsibilities of, 321, 328
Grand Cayman Benevolent Society for Women, 183
Grand Cayman Phosphate Company, 167
Grand Old House, 296–7
Grant, Sir John Peter (Governor of Jamaica)
Cuban ban on foreign fishing, 155
Morant Bay rebellion, changes resulting from, 153
Gray, Rev. John (Presbyterian minister), 386
Great Britain. See United Kingdom
Great Depression, 6, 249, 253, 259, 270, 288
Green, Rev. John (Wesleyan missionary), 119–20
Greenall, Benson (hotel developer), 339, 347, 348
Grey, Sir William (Governor of Jamaica): indifference to Cayman, 155–6
Gun Bay: site of early lighthouse, 183

H

half-model, 212
Hall, Rev. F. (Adventist evangelist), 237
Handbook of the Cayman Islands (Hirst), 173, 188, 198
Sister Islands, 129–30
vessels listed in, 200
Harquail Theatre, 414
Hawkins, John (sixteenth-century trader), 423n. 11
health care
congenital defects, 380–81
immunisation, 157, 383
Medical Officer, difficulty of attracting, 175
medical services, expansion of, 382–4
medical survey of Cayman Islands, 261–3
report on health conditions, 164–5
Heroes Square, 399
Hewitt, Henry (teacher), 242
Hicks, Rev. George, 297, 386
Hinds, Dorothy (slaveowner), 78
Hirst, George S.S. (Commissioner), 5, 182–8, 412

Boy Scouts, 281
census of 1911, 173, 198
death of, 187, 457n. 40
education system, improving, 186, 246
Foster clan, speculation about founder of, 126
government savings bank, establishment of, 183
Handbook of the Cayman Islands, 129, 173, 188, 198, 200
national debt, paid off under, 175
newspaper, support for, 396
Notes on the History of the Cayman Islands, 173, 188, 198
police force, establishment of, 182
postal service, internal, establishment of, 182
roadbuilding, 184
shortcomings of, personal, 184–7
stamps, overprints of, 176
turtling dispute, settlement of, 181
Hislops' ice cream parlor, 297
Hixon, Hiram W. (oil prospector), 268–70
HMS *Blossom*: first survey of Sister Islands, 125–6
HMS *Convert*. See Wreck of the Ten Sail
HMS *Dragon*, 273–4
HMS *Forte*, 82
HMS *Serpent*, 82, 83
HMS *Sparrowhawk*, 160
Hodgson, Robert, Jr. (Superintendent of the Miskito Coast), 49, 430n. 26
Hogsties. *See* George Town
Holiday Inn, 349
Holiness Movement, 231, 238–9, 395
Home Guard, 290, 293–4
hookworm
eradication of, 381
prevalence of, 262
hospitals
establishment of, 183, 287, 382
growth of, 1970–2000, 382–3
Hotel Association, 348
house styles, on cotton plantations, 69
housing, quality of, 195–8
Howard, Jack (husband of Lilian Bodden), 297
Hull, Capt. John (HMS *Camilla*): description of Grand Cayman (1787), 52
Hulme (Stipendiary Magistrate), 81, 82, 99
Hunter, Charles A. (Supervisory Teacher), 386
Hunter, Robert (Governor of Jamaica), 29–30
Hurlston, Capt. John (turtler), 222
Hurlston, Paul (mariner), 300
hurricanes
1837, 115
1846, 148, 228
1876, 155–6, 231
1877 (Miskito Banks), 155–6, 224
1914, 224
1915, 178–9, 260, 261
1917, 260, 261
1932, 6, 253 (*see also* Storm of '32)
1941 (Miskito Banks), 224
Husvik, 273
Hutchings, Hugh Houston (Commissioner), 5, 263, 288, 468n. 29
alcohol import and re-export, during Prohibition, support for, 266–8
public education, support for, 247
steamship service, support for, 265
U.S. immigration restrictions, concern about, 270
Hutchinson, Capt. Samuel (*Hopewell*), 24–5
Hydes, Bendel (artist), 415
Hydes, Boyd (musician), 277
Hydes, Watkin Jackson (founder of Jacksonville), 257
Hydrick, John Lee: medical survey, 261–3
hygiene, ignorance of, 263

I

immigration, pressures of, 364, 372–4
Immigration Department: contribution to tourism, 349
imports. *See* trade
independence, demand for, in British colonies, 302, 305
effect on Anglican Church, 393
Inn Theatre, 414
In Our Own Write, 414
integration, racial
education, in, 115–17
neighbourhoods, attitudes toward, 194
intermarriage
of close relatives, 45–7
congenital defects resulting from, 380–81
inevitability of, 45
in Sister Islands, 127
racial (*see also* miscegenation)
attitudes toward, 194
International College of the Cayman Islands, 389, 414
Island Air, 336, 338
Isle of Pines, 141, 257–8
isolation
benefits of, for public health, 165, 263
poverty and, 123
radio communication, lack of, 188
self-sufficiency and, 124, 145
steamship service, lack of, 123–4, 157, 457n. 41

J

Jackmauh, Fr. Francis (Catholic priest), 394–5
Jackson, Capt. Nelson (*Carmena*), 272–3
Jackson, Capt. William (privateer), 20
Jackson's Point: marked on first map of Little Cayman, 126
Jacobsen, Capt. Christian (*Juga*), 216–17
jail, in Grand Cayman: establishment of, 183
Jamaica
British conquest of, 20–21
Caymanian relationship with, 81, 102, 148–51
after Jamaican independence, 318
Anglican mission, 113–14
break with, 7, 305–6
coat of arms, symbolised on, 406
dependence on, for legal system, 44, 45–7, 91, 93
fear of domination by, 316
Fyfe recommendations, Caymanian response to, 165–6

indifference to Cayman, 154, 155
pleas to, for assistance, 148, 155–6
political, 306, 307–9, 310, 314–15
Cayman Islands as sovereign extensions of, 21, 26
independence of, 7, 302, 306, 315
opportunities in, for Caymanians, 254
transition of, from maritime base to plantation colony, 22
West Indies Federation, 306–9, 315
Jamaica Air Transport Ltd., 333
Jamaica Church Union Commission, 392
Jamaica Exhibition of March 1891, 168–9
Jehovah's Witnesses, 395
Jennett, Capt. Ebenezer (*Mary Ellen*), 178
Jennings, Richard (surveyor), 39
Jervis, Capt. Daniel (boat-builder), 211–12, 460n. 11
John Gray High School, 390, 414
Johnson, Capt. Charles. See Defoe, Daniel
Johnson, Vassel G. (*later* Sir Vassel), *320*, 353–5
Johnston, William (schoolteacher), 130, 235, 242
Jones, Commissioner, 292–3
Jonkanoo, 463n. 17
judicial system. *See also* laws
beginnings of, 91–2, 96
courts, unprofessional conduct of, 163–4, 170
court structure, expansion of, 324–5
need for, recognized, 93
reform of, recommendations by Fyfe, 165–6

K

Keatinge, Richard (pseud. Vaquero): *Life and Adventure in the West Indies*, 175, 454n. 6
credit system, comments on, 198
housing in 1906, description of, 196–7
Keegan, William (archaeologist), 12
King, William (privateer), 16, 423n. 13
King George V, 286, 287
King George VI, 287
Kirkconnell, Capt. Charles (Sister Islands MLA), 243, *320*, 322
Kirkconnell, Capt. Eldon (businessman), 316, 318
Kirkconnell, Capt. Mabry (Sister Islands MLA, Speaker), 322
Kirkconnell, William (carpenter), 128, 259
Kirkconnell Community Care Centre, 383, 482n. 12
Kirkconnell family, 243, 259, 485n. 10
Kohlman, Aarona Booker: *Under Tin Roofs*, 264

L

labour, organised: absence of, 289
LACSA, 335
Lady Slater, 266
Lago Oil and Transport Company, 298
Lamar, Sarah, 35
baptism of sons, 45–6
marriage to Isaac Bodden, 45
Lambert, Helen: bequest to hospital, 287
Land Development Control Board, 341
land grants, 33, 37
Bodden (1742), 41, 42, 427n. 6
Campbell-Middleton (1735), 34, 37
Crymble (1741), 38, 39–40
evidence in, of prior settlements, 38
Foster (1741), 39–42, 40, 427n. 12
Spofforth (1741), 36, 39
land ownership
conflicts over, 152, 269, 339
questions about, in regard to oil leases, 269
traditional methods of acquiring, 151–2, 153
land registration. *See also* land ownership
compulsory, 340
lack of, complaints about, 339–40
Land Registration Act, 152–3, 341, 452n. 16
Lands and Survey Department, 342–3
land use
development controls, debates over, 403
environmental concerns, 401–3
Lawford, Capt. John (HMS *Convert*), 57–60
laws
alcohol, import and re-export of, 267
alcohol, sale of, 96, 98, 440n. 15
animal sanctuaries, 402
banking, 353, 355, 357, 359
business, regulation of, 341, 477n. 22
civil courts, regulation of, 98
currency, 358
education, 246–7, 388
hotel development, concessions for, 283, 347, 349
immigration, 341, 369–72, 477n. 22, 481nn. 13, 16
jail and parsonage, construction of, 98
land registration, 151, 341, 452n. 16
land use, 477n. 19
legislature, establishment and regulation of, 151, 441n. 20
livestock, roaming, 96, 98
local laws, passage and administration of, 151
marine conservation, 402
militia, regulation of, 98, 441n. 19
mosquito research and control, 344
National Trust, formation of, 402
oil exploration, 269
police force, raising of, 151
public revenue, raising of, 151
roads, clearing of, 98, 439n. 13
Sister Islands, extension of jurisdiction to, 151
submission of laws to Jamaica for approval (1863), 151
taxes, collection of, 151
threatened and endangered species, protection of, 402
tourism, 349
transported slaves, import of, 96
women's rights, 313, 475n. 16
wrecking and salvage, 216

Lawson-Hemming, Sir Augustus William (Governor of Jamaica), 170
Lazzari, J.C., 243, 285
Lazzari, Wardwill (agent for Ocean Leather Corp. of New York), 285
Lazzari family tanning operation, 285
legal system
robustness of, 328
separation of powers, 325–6
Legislative Assembly
creation of, 310
term of office, 322
legislature. *See* Assembly of Magistrates and Vestry; Legislative Assembly
lighthouses
automatic beacons, 287
oil-fuelled beacons, 183
Lighthouse School, 381, 482n. 5
Lions Club: sight conservation programme, 383, 482n. 11
Lipscomb, Christopher (Anglican bishop of Jamaica), 112
Cayman, intentions toward, 114
pastoral motivation of, 113
liquor. *See* alcohol
literacy rate, 385, 482n. 15. See also under specific districts
Little Cayman
air service to, 336, 338
attack on, by Spanish, 23–5
Baptist chapel and schoolroom at, 236–7, 243
Baptist Church at, 395
Captain Ary, 33
emancipation, reaction to, 103
first settlers on, 127
inhabited in 1670, 33, 426n. 1
observations on, by Governor Norman, 161–2
phosphate industry on, 167
place names on first map of, 126
private school on, 243
ropemaking, 208
Storm of '32, 272, 273
Little Pedro
emancipation, reaction to, 102–3
militia contingent at, 90
population, in 1802 census, 56
Loch Katrine, 273
logging. *See also* mahogany
settled slave community and, 64
slaves essential to, 63
Long, Athelstan C.E. (Administrator/Governor), 321, 340–42
Long, Edward (Jamaican planter-historian), 431n. 37
Long Celia, 92–3
Ludwig, Daniel K., 298–300
Lynch, Sir Thomas (Governor of Jamaica), 22, 27, 425n. 34

M

McCoy, Harris (mariner), 300
McDermott, Miss: teacher at girls' private school, 241
McDermott, Thomas (teacher; *later* pseud. Tom Redcam): school at West Bay, Fyfe's report on, 241–2
McField, Frank (playwright, MLA), 414
McLaughlin, Capt. C.P. (*Fernwood*), 273
McLaughlin, Capt. Gilbert (Adventist elder), 237–8
McLaughlin, Sybil (National Hero, first Speaker), 311, 321
McMillan, Rev. H.L. (Presbyterian minister), 241, 288
McTaggart, Frederick S. (teacher), 240–41
McTaggart, Roy (dentist), 265, 352
NDP, support for, 316, 317, 318
West Indies Federation, 314
McTaggart, Timothy (merchant), 261
mahogany, 42, 43
Battersby-Foster case, 42–4
decline of, in Grand Cayman, 49
logging, on Miskito Coast, 48–9
trade, in eighteenth century, 48
value of, 42, 428n. 14
malaria, 343, 344, 381, 467n. 25, 478nn. 29, 36
Malcolm, Andrew (Mico teacher): desire for racially integrated education, 115–17
Maloney, John (writer): "The Islands Time Forgot", 300
Manley, Norman (Premier of Jamaica), 307, 309, 315
maps
early, 14–19
Gauld map of Grand Cayman (1773), 35, 50, 54–5
Owen maps of Sister Islands (1831), 125–6, 160
Royal Navy chart of Cayman Islands (1882), 158–9, 160
Mariculture Ltd., 404–5
Maritime War (1778–83), 48, 49
marriage
among slaves, 73–5, 76
in eighteenth century, 45–7, 428n. 16
rate, in 1911 census, 192–3
Martin, Rev. John E. (Presbyterian missionary), 230, 232
Mateo (*later* Ritch, Thomas Mathias), 129
Matley, C.A.: survey of Cayman geology, 269
Meany, Msgr. John (Catholic priest), 395
Mearns, Rev. John (Wesleyan missionary), 119–20
medical care. *See* health care
Membership system, 317, 318
nominated Members, 318, 321
abolition of, majority desire for, 319
responsibilities of, 321
Merren, Edlin (dentist), 381
Merren, E. Ducan (businessman, MLA), 309–10
Cayman Island Airways, director of, 333
CDP, founding of, 316
comments on, by Governor Foot, 473n. 4
delegate to Federation conferences, 314
women suffrage, opinion on, 313
Merren, Henry O. (merchant), 309
Michell, Capt. R.C.: Bay Islands Caymanian settlement, report on, 132–3
Mico Charity, 3, 115–17, 148
Middle School (*later* George Hicks High School), 388–9
Middleton, John (land grantee), 37–9, 43, 428n. 15

migration, Caymanian, 4, 254
  Bay Islands, 131–4, 140, 254
  Canal Zone, 254
    American bases in, 290
  Corn Islands, 141, 254
  Gulf Coast states, 254–5
  Isle of Pines, 255
  Miskito Coast, 120, 140
  Nicaragua, 254
  San Andrés and Old Providence, 141
  Sister Islands and outlying areas of Grand Cayman, 124–5
  United States, 259
militia: state of, in 1802, 90
ministerial system, 319, 322
Minot, James, Jr.: slave registration and census, 71, 78, 81, 126
miscegenation, 75, 194, 436n. 32
Miskito Banks (Miskito Cays): turtle fishery, 155, 156–7, 179–81, 218, 222–3
Miskito Coast
  British protection of, 48–9, 139
  British settlements on, 434n. 5
  British surrender of protectorate over, 141
  British surrender of settlements on, 49
  Caymanian migration to, 120, 140
  migrants from, 49, 52, 65–6
missionaries, 3
  Adventist, 237–8
  Anglican, 114–17
  Baptist, 235–7
  Holiness, 238–9
  Presbyterian, 130
  Wesleyan, 118–19
Miss Lassie. *See* Bush, Gladwyn K.
Mittag, Heinz (Cayman Turtle Farm Inc.), 405
Modyford, Sir Thomas (Governor of Jamaica), 22, 23, 26, 425n. 33
Monetary Authority, 359
Morant Bay rebellion, 151, 153
Morgan, Sir Henry (pirate), 22, 425n. 33
  attack on Panama, 26
  Cayman Islands used by, 23
  war against Spanish, 23–7
Mormon Church, 395
Morton, Samuel: number of slaves owned by, 68
mosquitoes
  campaign against, 343–6
  description of, by Governor Sligo, 82
  problem for Andrew Malcolm, 115
  report on, by International Health Board of New York, 262
  tourism, hindrance to, 331
motor vehicles: import of, 264
Mountain, 403
MRCU (Mosquito Research and Control Unit), 344–6, 402
Muddy Foots, 25
Mulgrave, Lord (Governor of Jamaica), 81
Musgrave, Sir Anthony (Governor of Jamaica): indifference to Cayman, 155–7
Musgrave, Anthony, Jr.: report to acting Governor Newton, 157, 160
music, 413–14
Myers, Fred (publisher), 396
My Markings: The Art of Gladwyn K. Bush, 416

N

National Bulk Carriers, 298–300
National Democratic Party (NDP). *See under* political parties
National Children's Festival of the Arts, 413, 414
National Choir, 413
National Gallery, 410, 413, 415
national song, 406
national symbols, 406, back cover
National Team. *See under* political parties
National Trust for the Cayman Islands, 402–3, 412
Native Sons, 416
Natural Resources Laboratory, 344
Naylor, Irwin (Mariculture Ltd.), 404
NCVO (National Council of Voluntary Organisations), 379
Newland, Thomas (surveyor), 42
newspaper, daily: lack of, 319
newspapers, 396–7
Newstar, 372, 484n. 44
Niven, Rev. William (Presbyterian missionary), 227, 228
Norman, Sir Henry (Governor of Jamaica), 453n. 33
  observations on Cayman Islands, 160–3, 242
North East Bay: private school at, 243
North Side
  Adventist "station" in, 238
  land use debates, 403
  marriage rate, in 1911 census, 193
  population, in 1802 census, 56
  road from Frank Sound, 287
  ropemaking, 208
  Town Hall, construction of, 288
Northward Prison, 327–8, 374
Nor'wester, 397, 484n. 44
Notes on the History of the Cayman Islands (Hirst), 173, 188, 198
Novak, George "Barefoot Man" (singer), 414
Nugent, George (Governor of Jamaica), 90, 91–2, 93
Nunoca, 266, 273

O

obeah, 233–4
  trials, 439n. 10
occupations, 56, 205
  barking, 208
  egging, 285
  farming, 205–7
  ropemaking, 208–9
  shark fishing, 284–5
  shipbuilding, 210–14
  in Sister Islands, 130, 160
  tabulated, in 1891 and 1911 censuses, 198–202
  tanning, 285
  turtling, 217–24
  women, in labour force, 199, 201–2
  wrecking, 56, 215–17
O'Connor-Connolly, Julianna (Sister Islands MLA, Speaker), 322
oil exploration, 268–70
Old Providence Island (Providencia)
  migration to, by Caymanians, 141
  Spanish recapture of (1641), 20
Oliver, Ed, 415
Olympic Games, 413

Our Voice, 414
Overton, George N. (Chief Medical Officer), 261–3, 274, 275–6
Owen, John (Governor of the Cayman Islands), 324, 411, 417
Owen, Richard (Royal Navy surveyor), 125–6
 Owen Island named after, 160
Owen Roberts International Airport (*originally* Owen Roberts Field), 332, 335, 336, 347
Owens, Rev. Hay (Baptist missionary), 236
Oxford expedition, 289

P

Pack, Capt. Anthony (HMS *Serpent*)
 departure of, 104
 Emancipation Proclamation, announcing, 82, 102–3
 report to Governor Sligo, 104
Page, William, 446n. 5
 owner of *Speedwell*, 70
 Long Celia, penalty imposed on, 93
 record of, in Minot census, 126
 slaveowner at Little Cayman, 103
Pageant Beach Hotel, 348
Palm Heights (*later* Hyatt Regency Hotel), 350
Panton, A.C. (acting Commissioner), 302
Panton, Ernest (Assemblyman), 307
Panton, James C. (Magistrate, teacher)
 teacher, Prospect and Bodden Town, 240
 wreck of *Iphigenia*, 215–16
Panton, Ormond (MLA), 300, 309–10, 317, 473n. 5
 delegate to Federation conferences, 314
 loss of power, 318
 NDP, formation of, 315, 316
Parker, King, Jr. (aviator), 333–4
Parsons, Chloe (free coloured slaveowner), 68
Parsons, Ebin John: conflicts with black soldiers, 99–101
Parsons, Edmund (Custos), 166, 173
 Jamaica Exhibition of March 1891, 168–9
 occupations, in 1891 census, 198
 phosphate industry, involvement in, 166–7
 postal service, establishment of, 167–8
Parsons, Edmund S., 265, 281
Parsons, Gwendolyn (Postmistress), 176
Parsons, James (Vestryman, free coloured slaveowner): conflicts with black soldiers, 99–101
Parsons, Samuel (Vestryman)
 Bay Islands, connection to, 141
 conflicts with black soldiers, 99–101
 emancipation, assessing results of, 107
 Swan Islands, regarded as British by, 142
Parsons, William (free coloured slaveowner)
 number of slaves owned by, 68
 owner of *Pelican* and *Smash Pipes*, 70
patriotism, Caymanian, 410
Peace Memorial, 264, 287
Pedley, Arthurlyn (née Ebanks) (playwright), 487n. 26
Pedro St. James ("Pedro Castle"), 51, 69
 lease of, for animal pound, court-house, and jail, 96
 meeting at, to form first legislature, 98
 restoration of, 411–12
"Petra Plantation", 296
Phelan, Richard (Clerk of the Court, Magistrate), 112
 conflicts with black soldiers, 99–101
 emancipation, assessing results of, 109
phosphate industry
 expansion of, Sanguinetti's hopes for, 174
 Grand Cayman and Swan Islands, 164
 Sister Islands, 167
pirates
 after 1730, 30
 Evans, John, 29
 General History of the Pyrates (Johnson), 28–9
 misconceptions about, 27–8
 treasure, 29, 30
 Walker, Neal, 29
Pirates Week, 410–11
planning controls, 340–41
police force
 establishment of, 182
 growth of, 327
political parties
 absence of, 305, 306, 319
 Christian Democratic Party (CDP), 316–19
 election of 1962, 318–19
 in Jamaica, 306
 National Democratic Party (NDP), 315–19
 National Team, 321
  draft constitution, shelving of, 322
 Unity and Dignity teams, 320
population, 60. *See also under specific districts*
 decline in, 1911–21, 258
  emigration, effects on, 258–9
 estimated, in 1858, 149
 health of, overall, in 2000, 384
 increase in, 1960–99, 363
  immigration, effects on, 363–4, 372–4
 rate of increase, 1802–1911, 191, 258
  birth and death rates, 192
 Sister Islands, 1833–1900, 131–2, 149, 160
 Sister Islands, 1960–99, 365
 slave, 68
 statistics, 1943–99, 365–6
Port Authority: contribution to tourism, 349
Port Royal, Jamaica, 22, 45
postal service
 establishment of, 167–8
 expansion of, under Sanguinetti, 175
 internal, on Grand Cayman, 175, 176, 182, 264
 unpredictability of, in 1919, 215
Pouchie, Rev. William (Presbyterian minister), 232
poverty, 372–3
Powell, Miss Izzy (teacher), *244*
Powery, Sam (NDP activist), 316
Presbyterian Church
 ecumenical union, discussion of, 392

secondary school, establishment of, 386
success, reasons for, 232–4
Proctor, George R. (botanist), 403
Prohibition, 266–8
Proser, William (sawyer), 43, 44
Prospect
emancipation, reaction to, 102–3
heart of Caymanian Slave Society, 79
legislative district, 98
marriage rate, in 1911 census, 193
militia contingent at, 90
population, in 1802 census, 56
Wesleyan chapel in, 119
prosperity, relative to other Caribbean islands, 301
Public Recorder, 92, 339
pupil-teacher system, 249–50
Puritans, English, 424n. 17

Q

quadrille, revival of, 413
Queen Elizabeth, 327, *354*, 409
Queen Elizabeth II Botanic Park, 403, 484n. 2

R

race relations, in Cayman Brac, 447n. 15
racial distribution, in 1911 census, 195
radio broadcasting service
development of, 397
lack of, 319
radio stations, 397
radio (wireless) communication
establishment of, 285–7
lack of, 188
Radley Gourzong and his Happy Boys, 413
Ratzlaff, Nina (teacher), 385
Re Cayman Islands Public Service Co. Ltd., 325–6
Redcam, Tom. See McDermott, Thomas
Red Carpet Airlines, 336
Redpath, Rev. Thomas (Presbyterian missionary), 230, 231, 466n. 57
The Great Crocodile, 442n. 31
refugees, Cuban, 373–4
regatta, annual, 281–2, 412
Remembrance Day, 290, 407, 409
Rivero Pardal, Manuel (privateer)
attack on Little Cayman, 23–5, 33, 426n. 1
archaeological evidence of, 425n. 27
challenge to Henry Morgan, 25–6
Rivers, Rachael: number of slaves owned by, 68
Roatán. See Bay Islands
Roberts, Owen "Bobby" (aviator), 334
Robinson, Arnold Dixon "Sonny-Boy" (singer), 258
Robinson, Arthur (Commissioner)
economy, attempts to improve, 261
education, report on (1914), 247
ropemaking. See thatch rope
Rose, "Dr." (pharmacist, political activist), 312–13
Rose, Jack (Commissioner/Administrator), 309
self-government, position on, 315, 316, 318
land registration, position on, 340
Rose, Richard H.: *Utilla: Past and Present*, 132
Ross, John (Mico teacher), 117
Ross-Shier, Leila (née McTaggart) (author, national song), *234, 239,* 406
Roy, George R. (commander, U.S. Navy base Baldpate), 294
Royal Bank of Canada, 352
Royal Cayman Islands Police Service. *See* police force
Royal Navy: Remark Books, 50–2
rum-running. *See* Prohibition
Russell, Thomas (Governor of the Cayman Islands), *320, 324*
Rutty, Aston (Collector), 272, 274, 280–1
Rutty, Burns: CDP, founding of, 316
Rutty, Rev. H.W. (Baptist missionary), 236
Rutty, H.W. (Collector of Customs)
education overseas, for Cayman Brackers, 243
occupations of Sister Islanders, 130
settlement of Cayman Brac, early accounts of, 126, 129
Ryan, Capt. James (*Melpomene*), 273
Ryan, Moody H., 127
Ryan, Sarah (née Foster), 128
Ryan, William Stephen (Senior Magistrate), 130
Ryan, William Wallace (Brac settler), 127
marriage to Sarah Foster, 128

S

San Andrés Island
migration to, by Caymanians, 141
population of, in 1830s, 450n. 46
Spanish recapture of (1641), 20
Sanguinetti, Frederick Shedden (Commissioner), 170
annual reports on Cayman, 173
coat of arms, 485n. 8
compulsory education, possibility of, 174, 245
expansion of economy, hopes for, 173–4
Sister Islands, visits to, 176–7
turtling dispute, 179–81
Saunders, Samuel Sydney (teacher, district constable), 243–4
schooners, Cayman-built
in Jamaica-Cayman trade, 1808–18, 70, 214, 434n. 10
launching, 214
in Sister Islands, 130, 177
Star, Cuban seizure of, 154
Schroeder, Robert (Mariculture Ltd.), 404
Scott, A.J. (Governor of the Cayman Islands), 411
Scott, Elgin (prisoner of war), 290
scuba diving, 348
Sea Grape Bay: marked on first map of Little Cayman, 126

Seales, Desmond, 397
Seaview Lodge, 347
Secondary Modern School, 387, 388
self-government, internal
- commitment to, by NDP, 315–16
- general election (1962), focus of, 318
- provision for, in 1992 draft constitution, 322
- support for, by CDP, 316
- West Indies Federation, proposed under, 314–15

settlement, permanent, 11
- British, on Miskito Coast, 49
- earliest, 35, 39
- Grand Cayman, 2, 33
  - advantages of, over Sister Islands, 35
- indicators of, 33
- Sister Islands, 4, 124–30
  - early accounts of, 126–9
  - oral traditions, 127

settlement, seasonal, 27–28
settlers, early, 2
- Grand Cayman, in, 35–42
- Miskito Coast, from, 49, 52, 65–6
- Sister Islands, in, 127–9

Seven Mile Beach
- cost of land on, in 1950, 300–1
- development of, 350
- first hotels on, 339, 347, 349

Seven Years' War, 50
Seventh-Day Adventist Church, 231, 237–8, 395
shark fishing, 284–5, 301, 470n. 13
Sharpe, Sam (Jamaican slave), 80, 97
Sharpe, Rev. Thomas (Magistrate), 81, 82, 99, 112, 438n. 41
- departure of, 115
- resident Anglican clergyman, 1831–4, 114
- return of, in 1837, 115

shipbuilding
- main industry, 164, 210–14, 301
- praised, by Governor Darling, 149
- process of, 212–14, 460n. 15
- promise of, after emancipation, 111
- Sister Islands, in, 129–30, 177, 214
- skills required for, 212
- woods used for, 213

ship registration, 357
shipwrecks, 56
- *Balboa*, 271, 273
- *Carmena*, 272–3
- *Cumberland*, 57
- *Fernwood*, 273
- *Iphigenia*, 215–16
- *Juga*, 216–17
- *Majestic*, 224
- *Melpomene*, 273
- *Prince Frederick*, 243
- Wreck of the Ten Sail, 57–60

silver thatch palm (*Coccothrinax proctorii*), 208
Sister Islands. *See also* Cayman Brac; Little Cayman
- Baptist Church in, 234, 243, 23–7, 407
- boatbuilding in, 130, 177, 407
  - unique reputation for, 214
- coat of arms, symbolised on, 406
- coconut industry in, 176, 177–9
- constitutional change, position on, 319–20
- Cuban refugees in, 373–4
- description of, earliest, 17
- discovery of, 12, 13
- District Administration, 408
- economy of, 407, 408
- education, beginnings of, 242–4
- Executive Council, voice on, 320, 322
- first survey of, 125–6
- Grand Cayman, relations with, 406–7
- loyalty to Britain, 407–8
- marriage rates, in 1911 census, 193
- migration to, from Grand Cayman, 120
- mosquito control efforts in, 345
- "notable persons" listed in Handbook, 130
- observations on, in 1882, 160
- opportunities in, 130
- permanent settlement of, 4, 124–30
- population of, 1833–1900, 131–2, 149, 160
- population of, 1884, reported by Rev. Sobey, 235
- prosperity of (1907), 177
- separation from Grand Cayman, threat of, 317, 407
- shark fishing, 284–5
- ship-to-ship oil transfer, 408
- survey of, by Royal Navy (1882), 160
- tourism development in, 348
- turtling in, 160, 178, 407
- West Indies Federation, views on, 309

Slader, C.H. Yorke (acting Commissioner): first separate Annual Report, 182
Slave Court, 92
- Long Celia, trial of, 92–3
- obeah trials, 439n. 10

slavery, 3
- African cultural traditions, 72, 437n. 37, 463n. 17
- bequest of slaves by owner, 78, 436n. 33
- comments on, by Nathaniel Glover, 79–80
- compared with other West Indian islands, 63, 64, 65
- Cuban, 255–6
- earliest slaves, arrival of, 433n. 1
- end of, 80–6, 89, 102–3
- family patterns, 65, 74, 76–7
- import of slaves to Grand Cayman, 52–3, 67
- living conditions, 69
- manumission, cost of, 76
- marriage among slaves, 73–5, 76
- price of slaves, 71, 78
- slave naming patterns, 72–3
- slave ownership
  - distribution of, 77–8
  - free coloured persons, by, 68, 74–6
  - sign of rank, 78
- slave population
  - Corbet's report, 60, 68
  - demographic health of, 72
  - Gauld's estimate of (1773), 65
  - geographical distribution of (1834), 79
  - Minot census of (1834), 71–4
  - on other West Indian islands, 435n. 20
  - proportions of males and females in, 73

rate of increase, early nineteenth century, 70–1
underworked, after decline of cotton plantations, 92
slave rebellions in West Indies, 80, 89, 92, 97
slave registration, 71, 80–81, 126
wrongful, of Sambos, 89–90, 438n. 2
Slave Society, 60, 63. *See also* slavery
Bahamas, compared with, 64
cotton boom, during, 68–9
definition, 433n. 2
Jamaica, compared with, 63, 64, 65
Miskito Coast, compared with, 65
Sligo, Lord (Governor of Jamaica), 81
decision to free apprentices, 82–6, 102
description of Grand Cayman, 81–2
visit in 1834, 99
Sloane, Hans (writer), 65
sloops, Caymanian, 210
Small, Laurence (Anglican catechist), 394
Smith, Sir Frederick (constitutional commissioner), 322
Smith, James (HMS *Ferret*): first description of Bodden Town, 51
Smith, Rev. John (Presbyterian missionary), 230, 231, 234–5
Smith, Peter (Governor of the Cayman Islands), 418, 486n. 15
Smith, Veronica: memories of '32 Storm, 274–5
Sobey, Rev. Joshua Heath (Baptist minister), 235, 243, 453n. 37, 463n. 25
social services, 377–80
Social Services Department, 377–9
Society for Propagation of the Gospel (SPG), 113
Sonny-Boy. *See* Robinson, Arnold Dixon
Soto, Bob, 348, 478n. 43
Southern Cross Club, 348
South West Sound
emancipation, reaction to, 102–3
legislative district, 98
militia contingent at, 90
population, in 1802 census, 56
slave distribution, 79
Spofforth, Samuel (land grantee), 39. *See also* land grants
owner of trading vessel *Experiment*, 50, 427n. 10
sponge fishing, 470n. 13
sports, competitive, 412–13
Spotts (Spot's Bay)
emancipation, reaction to, 102–3
militia contingent at, 90
population, estimated (1773), 55
population, in 1802 census, 56
St. Alban's Anglican (Church of England) Church, 394
St. George's Anglican (Episcopal) Church, 115, 394
St. Ignatius, Church of, 394
St. Ignatius School, 395
St. Mary's Anglican (Church of England) Church, Cayman Brac, 394
Stake Bay
Baptist chapel and schoolroom at, 236–7, 243
first settlement on Cayman Brac, 127
marked on first map of Cayman Brac, 126
private schools at, 242–3
second Caymanian post office, opened in, 175
stamps, postage
overprints, 176, 455nn. 8–10
sale of, revenue from, 175–6, 263, 288, 467n. 20, 470n. 21
Star: seizure of, at Cienfuegos, 154
status, Caymanian, 370–1, 372
steamship service
Jamaica-to-Tampa, cancellation of, 261
lack of, to Cayman, 123–4, 157, 175, 188
effect of, on courts, 170
regular subsidised service, possibility of, 265
Stewart, Sylvia (Bodden Town student), 290
Storm of '32, 270–76
Stubbs, Edward (Governor of Jamaica), 268
suffrage
qualifications for, 322
universal adult, 310
women, 306, 310–13, 474n. 11, 475n. 16
Sunrise Training Centre, 482n. 5
surnames, Caymanian, 426n. 3, 427n. 4
Swaby (Anglican Bishop of Jamaica), 394
Swan Islands
phosphate industry on, 141, 164
population of, in 1830s, 450n. 46
regarded as British, 141–2
U.S. weather station on, 285–6
Sykes, Rev. Nicholas J. (Anglican priest), 394
The Dependency Question: A Study of Church and State in the Cayman Islands, 444n. 58

T

Tatum [Tatham], Benjamin: marriage to Rebecca Boden, 46
Tatum, Isaac: sharkskin market, comments on, 285
Tatum [Tatham], James
marriage to Mary Boden, 46
number of slaves owned by, 68
Tatum [Tatham], John
marriage to Rebecca Boden, 46
number of slaves owned by, 68
taxation
collection of taxes, 164
direct
resistance to, 174
revenue from, 176
low levels of, 174
telecommunications, modern, 355
telephone service, 265
television, 398
Ten Years' War, 154–5
Terror, 211
thatch rope, 208
coat of arms, presence on, 406
economic importance of, 209–10, 301
ropemaking, process of, 208–9
"Strawrope Industry Pledge", 225
theatre, 414
Thompson, Elizabeth Mary (slaveowner), 75

Thompson, Robert (Stipendiary Magistrate), 82
concerns about social conditions, 105–7
conflicts between black soldiers and local inhabitants, 99–101
departure of, 104
post-emancipation social upheaval, 103–12
relations between masters and apprentices, 101–2
responsibilities during apprenticeship, 99
Thompson, Thomas
bequest of slaves to children, 78, 436n. 33
number of slaves owned by, 68
owner of *Favourite*, 70
Thrift, Rev. Joseph (Baptist missionary), 236
Tiara Beach Resort, 350
Tibbetts, Darwin (mariner), 300
Tibbetts, Capt. Keith
'32 Storm, comments on, 270
Caymanian losses during World War Two, comments on, 291–2
self-government debate, Sister Islands petition, 317
service, World War Two, 290
Tibbetts, Linton, 485n. 10
Time Longer Dan Rope (McField), 414
Todd Insecticidal Fog Applicator, 343–4
tourism
attractions of Cayman for, 331, 454n. 52
increase in, after mosquitoes controlled, 346
promotion of, 283–4, 346–9
stayover vs. cruise-ship, 479n. 53
Tourism, Department of, 349
Tourist Board, 348
trade, 214–15
cotton, decline of, 69–70
cotton exports, 67
imports and exports
after 1804, 70
in 1764, 50–51
in 1780s, 52–3
mahogany, logwood, and fustic, 48, 52
shipping registers
early 1740s, 50
for 1802–4, 66–7
slave imports, 67
Tradewinds, 396, *397*
Trans-Island Airways, 336
Treaty of Madrid, 26, 27, 409
Treaty of Utrecht, 27
Treaty of Versailles, 49
Trinidad Royal Naval Volunteer Reserve (TRNVR), 290–1, 297, 302
Triple C School, 385–6
truck system, 288, 462n. 31. *See also* credit system
Truman Bodden National Sports Complex, 412–13
Trusty, Elizabeth Jane (freedwoman), 75–6
turtle
canning factory, 261
early records of, in Cayman Islands, 13, 16, 17, 21
eggs, *138*
green, 2, 160, 217
hunting, description of, 218–21
coat of arms, presence on, 406
hawksbill, 160, 178, 217
hunting, description of, 218
location of, in 1787, 52
stocks, depletion of, 404
Turtle Farm. *See* Cayman Turtle Farm
turtling
"the [Miskito] Banks", life at, 222–3
crew, 220–21
decline of, 223, 281, 403
description of, in Sister Islands, 160, 178
dispute, with Nicaragua, 179–81, 403–4, 456n. 24
disruption of, in Cuban waters, 154, 155–6, 179
main industry, 52, 164, 301
promise of, after emancipation, 111
risks of, 223–4
sales, direct, to turtle agents, 220, 462n. 30
Twigg, George: report on Caymanian health conditions, 164–5
typhoid, 467n. 25

U

Under Tin Roofs (Kohlman), 264
United Church in Jamaica and the Cayman Islands, 392–3, 395
United Fruit Company, 298
United Kingdom
Caymanian loyalty to, 260, 289–90, 305, 316, 407, 409–10
White Paper (2000), 486n. 15
United States
Britain, relations with, in Caribbean, 138–40
Caymanian ties to, 259
Cuban policy, effect of, on Cayman, 373–4
Endangered Species Act, effect of, on marketing of turtle products, 405
immigration restrictions, tightening of, 270
Navy base, in George Town, 7, 292–8, 472n. 42
visa waiver concession, 300
Unity Team. *See under* political parties
Utila. See Bay Islands
Utilla: Past and Present (Rose), 132

V

Vaquero. *See* Keatinge, Richard
Vision 2008, 7, 417–18
visual arts, 415–16
Visual Arts Society, 415, 416
voluntary organizations, 379–80
Volunteer Foggers unit, 344
voting. *See* suffrage

W

Waddell, Rev. Hope Masterton (Presbyterian missionary)
advocacy for mission to Cayman Islands, 227
description of Cayman, 146–7
Walker, Capt. Neal (pirate), 29–30
Wallace, Walter (constitutional commissioner), 322
Ware, Capt. (wrecker), 29–30
Watering Place: home of first black settlers in Cayman Brac, 129

Watler, Conwell (owner of *Goldfield*), 281
Watler, Ena (legislative candidate), 313
Watler, James (shipowner), 70, 76
Watler, Robert (Magistrate): letter to Governor Belmore (1831), 96–7
Watler [Walter], Stephen: marriage to Sarah Bodden [Bawden], 46
Watler, Waide, Jr.
  marriage to Elizabeth Hughes, 47
  number of slaves owned by, 68
  owner of *Eliza*, 70
Watler [Walter], Waide, Sr.
  marriage to Rachel Bodden [Bawden], 46
  number of slaves owned by, 68
Watler, W.C. (Senior Magistrate), 267
Webster, George (Rhodes scholar), 245
Webster, James S. (businessman), 254
Webster, William Bodden (Senior Magistrate), 157, 161
  resignation of, 166
  tension among Magistrates, source of, 163
  wreck of *Iphigenia*, 215–16, 461n. 23
Wesleyan Missionary Society, 118–20, 227
West Bay
  first Holiness church in Cayman, 238
  first Wesleyan chapel in Cayman, 119
  legislative district, 98
  literacy level, in 1911, 196
  marriage rate, in 1911 census, 193
  phosphate industry, 167
  population, in 1802 census, 56
  post-emancipation social conditions, 105
  road to, from George Town, construction of, 184
  ropemaking, 208
  slave distribution, 79
  telephone service in, 265, 355
  Town Hall, construction of, 288
West India Regiment. *See* British West India Regiment
West Indies Commission, 289
West Indies Federation, 7, 302, 30
  collapse of, 315
  role of Cayman in, 307, 314–15
Weston, Ernest (Commissioner), 273, 274, 279, 280
Whitecross, Rev. William (Presbyterian missionary), 149, 229–31
Wilberforce, William (British M.P.), 81
Wilson, Rev. David (Anglican missionary), 114–15
wireless. *See* radio (wireless) communication
Witt, Rev. Stephen (Baptist missionary), 236
women, status of, 306
  political rights, 310–13
  women's petition (1948), 311
  women's petition (1957), 313
Wood, Evelyn (first woman elected to legislature), 311, 316
Wood, John (Magistrate), 148
Wood, John Jarrett (first Caymanian teacher), 117, 228, 239
Wood, Joseph (migrant from Miskito Coast), 65
Woodville, Robert, 141
World War One, 6, 254
  Britain, Caymanian support for, 260
  hardships of, in Cayman Islands, 260–3
World War Two, 7, 249, 253, 288
  in Cayman, 290–98
  losses in, Caymanian, 471n. 33
Wreck of the Ten Sail, 57–60, 432n. 47
wrecking, 56, 111
  description of, by Rev. Hope Waddell, 146–7
  disruption of, in Cuban waters, 154
  final years of, 215–17
  reputation of Caymanians, 147, 431n. 40
Wyke-Cruz Treaty, 139

Y

yellow fever, 343, 344, 345, 381, 478n. 29